THE YEARS OF
MacArthur

Volume I

1880–1941

THE YEARS OF
MacArthur

Volume I

☆ ☆

1880–1941

D. CLAYTON JAMES

*Illustrated with Photographs
and Maps*

HOUGHTON MIFFLIN COMPANY

Boston

SECOND PRINTING   C

COPYRIGHT © 1970 BY D. CLAYTON JAMES

LIBRARY OF CONGRESS
CATALOG CARD NUMBER: 76-108685

Passages from *Reminiscences,* by Douglas MacArthur,
© 1964 Time Inc., are reproduced by permission.

PRINTED IN THE UNITED STATES OF AMERICA

To

Newell Woodruff Bankston

and Emma Dorris Bankston

Foreword

THIS IS THE FIRST volume of a two-volume biography of General of the Army Douglas MacArthur. No character in modern American military history, even Patton, has been the subject of as much adulation and condemnation as MacArthur. In the twenty or more biographies and quasi-biographies of him which have appeared, there has been virtually no middle ground; he has been extravagantly praised or severely censured. Many of these writings have been marred by excessive insertions of conservative or liberal convictions held by the authors. Some who have written about MacArthur were too intimately associated with him to be able to achieve objectivity, while others wrote about a legendary or stereotyped figure, seldom concerning themselves with historical facts and documentation. With the exception of a few works, these writings have been unworthy of their subject. MacArthur's significant roles in national and international affairs, both military and nonmilitary — from World War I through the "Great Debate" of 1951 — mark him as one of the important leaders of this century. This study is an attempt to present a reasonably comprehensive, balanced, and honest life-and-times biography of the general. Because the man and his professional environment affected each other in vital ways, this is also, in some respects, a study of the development of the modern American Army.

My attraction to MacArthur originated with my interest in the occupation of Japan, 1945–51. From my studies I concluded that the uniqueness and significance of the "American period" in postwar Japan have been largely neglected by professional historians, and at first I intended only to write a scholarly monograph on the occupation. But gradually I became more and more fascinated with the "proconsul" himself. In deciding to undertake a biography of him, I did so with the conviction that a century hence MacArthur will be most appreciated for his role as an administrator, rather than as a warrior. Since my two volumes will appear separately, the reader will have to wait until the second volume to examine my case for the years 1945–50 as the most important period of his life, during which he made his chief contributions to history.

Even in dealing with his less controversial career up to the declaration of war in 1941, which is the scope of this volume, I have found it difficult to be objective. Indeed, I have no doubt that my efforts at "honest" appraisals will appear to some readers as quite biased judgments. In interviewing for this volume and the later one, I have found few persons of adult age in 1941–51 who are neutral on the subject of MacArthur. Perhaps, like Reconstruction, MacArthur is a subject about which true objectivity cannot be achieved. Likewise, no biographer will ever know all about a character as complex as this general. There are aspects of his personality and behavior which neither I nor any other writer will ever comprehend fully or explain satisfactorily. This is true because of not only his complexity but also the extent and nature of his personal papers, which are disappointingly few and unrevealing. I admit that MacArthur, like a great fire, fascinates me, but I am hopeful that some readers will find this biography to be neither adulatory nor contemptuous. If it contributes toward a fairer, franker understanding of MacArthur's place in history, this study will have satisfied my aim.

My obligations in this project are many, but the individual whose insights helped me most to understand the pre-1942 MacArthur was the late General of the Army Dwight D. Eisenhower. Since he worked longer and more closely with MacArthur before the war with Japan than any other surviving colleague, I especially appreciate the generous amount of time he gave me in 1967 in discussing his former superior of the 1930's. Other officers who contributed to this work by granting me interviews and/or providing information by correspondence were General Harold K. Johnson, General J. Lawton Collins, Major General Charles A. Willoughby, the late Major General Courtney Whitney, Major General Richard J. Marshall, Major General Spencer B. Akin, Brigadier General Bonner Fellers, Colonel Arnold D. Amoroso, and Colonel Edgar W. Schroeder. Major General Kenneth G. Wickham, the adjutant general of the Army, was most cooperative, as was also Colonel H. A. Schmidt, chief of the historical services division of the Office of the Chief of Military History, Department of the Army Headquarters. W. O. Spencer, a member of the Olympic team of 1928, also provided helpful information.

My special thanks are extended to Philip P. Brower, the able director of the MacArthur Memorial Bureau of Archives; his interest and help have been invaluable. Of great assistance, too, were the competent staffs of the Modern Military Records Division and Old Military Records Division of the National Archives, particularly Thomas E. Hohmann and John E. Taylor of the former office. Splendid cooperation was obtained from various persons in the Office of the Chief of Military His-

tory; Dr. Stetson Conn, Miss Hannah Zeidlik, and Detmar
Finke were especially helpful. Others who assisted me in lo-
cating and using materials of their institutions were E. P.
Droste, president of Texas Military Institute; Art Lentz, director of the United States Olympic House; Joseph M. O'Donnell,
chief, and Kenneth W. Ropp of the archival staff of the United
States Military Academy; Dr. Elizabeth B. Drewry, director of
the Franklin D. Roosevelt Library; Dr. Forrest C. Pogue, director of the George C. Marshall Research Center; Dwight M.
Miller, senior archivist of the Herbert Hoover Presidential
Library; Mrs. Nancy C. Prewitt, assistant director of the West-
ern Historical Manuscript Collection, University of Missouri
Library; Jack D. Haley, assistant curator of the Western His-
tory Collections, University of Oklahoma Library; Thomas E.
Powers, assistant curator of the Michigan Historical Collections,
University of Michigan Library; Miss Judith A. Schiff, head of
the Historical Manuscripts and University Archives Depart-
ment of the Yale University Library; the excellent staff of the
Manuscripts Division of the Library of Congress; George R.
Lewis, director, Miss Margarete Peebles, acquisitions head,
Miss Willie D. Halsell, special collections head, and John M.
Carter, assistant director, of the Mitchell Memorial Library,
Mississippi State University. Professors whose assistance is grate-
fully acknowledged are Harold S. Snellgrove, Glover Moore,
Roy V. Scott, and James R. Chatham of Mississippi State Uni-
versity, and Dennis S. Nordin of Chicago State College.

Grants from the National Endowment for the Humanities
and the Graduate School of Mississippi State University and a
generous advance from Houghton Mifflin Company enabled
me to complete this volume. The personal interest and professional guidance of Craig Wylie, Philip Rich, and Mrs. Ruth K.
Hapgood of Houghton Mifflin have been valuable. I am also
grateful for the help of my student assistants, William R. Anderson and Miss Nancy Lee Young. As always in my research and

writing ventures, I am deeply indebted to my dedicated "secretarial" staff — Erlene, Sherrie, Ned, Judy, and Allie James — for encouragement, all sorts of advice, and various forms of material aid.

Mississippi State University   D. CLAYTON JAMES
August, 1969

Contents

Part I. In the Shadow of His Father

Part IV. Chief of Staff

Part V. Philippine Military Adviser

Illustrations

MacArthur as Philippine military adviser, probably spring, 1940. *MacArthur Memorial Bureau of Archives*

With Sir Robert Brooke-Popham, British air chief marshal, in Manila, October, 1941. *United Press International*

Arthur MacArthur, IV, about the time of the Japanese invasion, December, 1941. *Wide World Photos, Inc.*

Maps

THE YEARS OF
MacArthur

Volume I

1880–1941

Prologue: 1937

MANILA, SEPTEMBER 16, 1937. The Military Adviser's office
bore the trappings of a formal drawing room of the late nineteenth century. Inlaid bookcases and cabinets of dark native
woods lined the walls. The shelves were crowded with volumes
whose titles ranged over many fields of learning; a large number of the books were dated before 1900. Here and there lay
mementos of the early years of the American occupation of the
archipelago. In prominent display were framed pictures of the
officer's wife, parents, and brother. The furniture in the spacious room included a long sofa, several well-padded chairs, a
screen decorated with a Chinese brush-stroke painting, military and national flags on stands, and a large Chippendale desk.
A ceiling fan droned monotonously, stirring the hot air of the
upstairs room. The office windows offered the panorama of bustling street activities and the calm, blue expanse of Manila
Bay. At the desk Major General Douglas MacArthur was com-
posing a letter to General Malin Craig, the Army chief of staff.
The letter was to accompany MacArthur's application for retirement from active service in the United States Army.

General MacArthur, who had been military adviser to the Commonwealth government for the previous two years, informed Craig that he had been "seriously considering retiring" from the Army "for a number of years." A veteran of nearly four decades of active duty, MacArthur explained: "I have already contributed everything constructive I am able to offer the service . . . I find the thought repugnant of resuming a subordinate command in routine service after having been the military head of the Army for so long a time." His retirement would give "acceleration to the promotion of junior officers which is so sadly needed in our service . . . I am sure it would be the practically unanimous thought of the Army that I should make way for other and worthy officers."

"My Philippine work is practically accomplished," MacArthur continued, "and I am very anxious indeed to return to my ancestral home in Milwaukee, Wisconsin, and resume the tradition there of my father and grandfather. There are many cultural matters that all my life I have been anxious to explore . . . I cannot tell you with what pleasurable anticipation I contemplate their pursuit." Another reason for retiring was that "the doctors tell me that I have worked too hard . . . They have been advising me for some time that it would be dangerous to continue active service." He added: "I would, of course, be as available for war service on the retired list as I would be on the active list. I am convinced, however, that the United States will not become involved in war in my day. The magnificent leadership of President Roosevelt practically assures against such a calamity." [1]

While the fury of the new Sino-Japanese war mounted that autumn, the War Department and the President duly approved MacArthur's application for retirement, effective December 31, 1937. Roosevelt sent a cablegram to MacArthur in which he praised his service record as "a brilliant chapter in American history," offered his "best wishes for a well-earned rest," and invited MacArthur to visit him "as soon as you get back" to the States.[2]

As a later president would also learn, the general proved to be a difficult man to retire. In the fourteen years after his letter to Craig, MacArthur was often at or near the center of the stage of history, dazzling or irritating persons high and low with his command performances in the Pacific war, the occupation of Japan, and the conflict in Korea. The MacArthur whose feats are recounted to school children today is the brilliant and controversial figure of 1941–1951.

But, unlike many of the commanders of World War II, MacArthur did not suddenly "emerge full blown from the sea" when America entered that struggle. As he reminded Craig in 1937, "I have been a General Officer on the active list nearly twenty years — longer indeed, I believe, than any other officer in the history of the Army since the Civil War period."[3] MacArthur's achievements as a combat officer in the First World War, a progressive superintendent at West Point, and an outstanding chief of staff were widely hailed in military circles. His reputation as a provocative individualist was also well-established by the mid-1930's. Although he was well-known early in his career, no one then or later managed to capture the full measure of the man in print. Just as post-1945 writers have evaluated him largely in terms of extreme adulation or hostility, so historians, journalists, and others of the earlier period rarely overcame their strong feelings about him.

Douglas MacArthur was one of the most complex characters of modern times, and many of the key traits which he exhibited during the stormy years of 1941–1951 were manifested during his earlier career. The previously quoted letter to Craig suggests some of the contradictions in his nature and career. As chief of staff, MacArthur could be tough-minded and imperious; but his tenderness toward his aged mother was sincere and moving, and even when he was military head of the Army, he was remarkably dependent upon her presence and judgment. Long popular in the service for his zealous crusade to get a just and fair promotion system, MacArthur was partly responsible for retarding the advancement of some of the Army's most capable officers, including George C. Marshall and Dwight D. Eisenhower. Like his father and grandfather, MacArthur spoke often and proudly of his Scottish ancestry; but he developed a phobia toward Europe in general and Great Britain in particular. He was acknowledged as one of the Army's most perceptive and experienced authorities on the Far East; but he badly misjudged the military potentiality of Japan and the Philippines. He was vehemently anti-New Deal and critical of Roosevelt; but he reached the zenith of his pre-1941 career during the New Deal and gained from Roosevelt the appointments which led to his later and greater fame.

In order to fathom the complicated, fascinating personality of Douglas MacArthur, it is necessary to begin with the family heritage which, as he claimed in the memoirs penned in his dying days, profoundly influenced him. That heritage was personified mainly in the characters and careers of three Mac-Arthurs who set an ambitious pace for him — Arthur, I, his grandfather; Arthur, II, his father; and Arthur, III, his brother.

PART I

In the Shadow of His Father

CHAPTER I

The MacArthur Heritage

1. The Judge

STRANGERS IN A NEW LAND, the young boy and his widowed mother arrived in Chicopee Falls, Massachusetts, in 1825. Arthur MacArthur and Sarah, his mother, had come from Glasgow, Scotland, where the lad had been born ten years earlier. Fifty miles northwest of Glasgow in the hills of Argyllshire lay Loch Awe, near which was the *duthus,* or ancestral home, of the MacArthurs, a clan renowned for its fierce bravery in Robert the Bruce's army long before. The early years of Arthur are shrouded in obscurity, but, like most immigrants, he must have found his adjustment to the New World lonely and bewildering. Forever removed from the familiar sights and sounds of his birthplace, he faced the struggle for existence without the security of a father.[1]

Arthur's new home, however, offered some consolations. Situated near the confluence of the Chicopee and Connecticut rivers, Chicopee Falls was in the heart of one of New England's most fertile and scenic valleys. The hamlet was located several miles north of Springfield, the seat of Hampden County and a thriving commercial center. Between 1790 and 1820 Springfield's population had nearly trebled, numbering 3914 persons in the latter year. Like the MacArthurs, many of the area's residents were new arrivals from Europe and harbored similar feelings of insecurity, excitement, and hope.[2]

Mrs. MacArthur remarried, and provision was made for Arthur, upon reaching young manhood, to attend Wesleyan College, a small Methodist school at Middletown, Connecticut. Later Arthur moved to New York City to study law and was admitted to the Massachusetts bar in 1840. Soon after starting his law practice in Springfield he gained appointments as public administrator of Hampden County and judge advocate of the Western Military District of Massachusetts. In the two decades since his sailing from Glasgow he had made his adjustment; the insecure Scottish lad was now a promising American attorney.

The Springfield years were marked not only by professional success but also by romance. In 1844 Arthur married Aurelia Belcher, daughter of Benjamin Belcher, a small manufacturer of Chicopee Falls and a descendant of the colonial governor Jonathan Belcher. In June of the next year Aurelia gave birth to a son, named for his father, and four years later the family forsook comfortable New England to establish a home in a far-off town named Milwaukee.[3]

MacArthur must have had some important connections in Wisconsin, or else secured them soon after his arrival, for two years after moving he was elected city attorney. In this capacity he enjoyed close relations with leading city and state figures, including Governor Nelson Dewey and his secretary of state, William A. Barstow. In 1853, five years after Wisconsin achieved statehood, Barstow was elected governor. Despite opposition charges of fraudulence in the Barstow administration's handling of school lands, mental institutions, and state printing, MacArthur agreed to accept the Democratic candidacy for lieutenant governor when Barstow ran for re-election in 1855.

In that contest the Republicans offered Coles Bashford for governor. Barstow and MacArthur were elected in spite of charges of corruption against the former and the unpopularity of the Democratic support of the Kansas-Nebraska Act in a state of nonslaveholders. On January 7, 1856, the day that Barstow and MacArthur were inaugurated, the state supreme court, pressured by outraged Republicans, announced that it would examine charges of voting irregularities. When the court found that votes from nonexisting precincts had been counted in Barstow's favor, he resigned, and MacArthur served as governor from March 21 until March 26 when the court certified Bashford as the victor in the gubernatorial election. The Democrats did not contest the judges' verdict. Barstow's secretary observed: "So highly had the passions of men been wrought up by the political contest in which we were emersed [*sic*] that it was at one time here dangerously near a collision . . . It was well, perhaps, that the Kansas and Nebraska excitement directed the minds of those compromising political parties elsewhere." Governor Bashford and several of his lieutenants were later disgraced by the exposure of bribes which they had accepted in the interests of the LaCrosse and Milwaukee Railroad. An authority on the state's past nominates the period 1854–58 as "the most unsavory in Wisconsin's political history." [4]

Amazingly, the Barstow taint did not handicap MacArthur's career. In 1857 he was elected a judge of the state's second judicial circuit and was re-elected six years later. After the Civil War President Johnson selected him to head the American delegation to Napoleon III's magnificent Paris Exposition. In 1870 President Grant appointed MacArthur as an associate justice of the supreme court of the District of Columbia, a position he held until retirement with full pay in 1887. He was one of four justices on this court, which had functioned since 1863 as the District's highest judicial body, supplanting

the earlier civil court, district court, and criminal court. Two
years after joining the District court, MacArthur, whose wife
had died in 1864, married Mrs. Mary Hopkins, the widow of
Benjamin F. Hopkins, who had served as Governor Bashford's
secretary and later as United States representative from Wisconsin.

From the time he moved to the national capital until his
death in 1896, Judge MacArthur was very active in civic, cultural, and educational affairs. Socially, he moved in the highest
circles. For many years he served as president of the city's
humane society and also headed the united charities organization of the District. He had a lively interest in history and
belles-lettres and was often invited to lecture to Washington
clubs on topics in those fields. Between 1875 and 1892 he wrote
ten books, including five volumes on law, two on English history, two on education, and one on linguistics.[5]

One of Judge MacArthur's principal interests was the ill-fated National University. A great institution of higher education sponsored by the federal government had been discussed
ever since the nation's birth. Although strongly endorsed by
George Washington, John Quincy Adams, and a host of distinguished men for a century, the proposal had been thwarted
by entanglements over constitutional issues, financial support,
administrative control, and other problems. Educator John W.
Hoyt revived the movement after the Civil War and enlisted
the support of many educators, politicians, and businessmen.
A law school was opened in Washington in the late 1870's as
the harbinger of a full program for the National University,
but the law school was moribund by the mid-1890's and the
other colleges of the proposed university were never organized.
When Judge MacArthur, a regent of the law school, delivered
the commencement address to the ninety-three law graduates
in June, 1882, he was optimistic about the program, which
"has been marked by some progress and important work in
the line of legal education . . . Our professors, I will say with-

out presumption, will compare with any body of teachers in practical experience and special competency." He envisioned future expansion which would culminate in a great institution "devoted to the highest scientific instruction, and the broadest mental and moral culture." He noted that "the press which was formerly so indifferent now shows itself fully alive to this great need of American scholarship." On the eve of his death he was still working zealously with Hoyt and other devotees to make the dream of a national university into a reality.[6]

Douglas MacArthur, who was sixteen years old when his grandfather died, remembered him as "a large handsome man, of genial disposition and possessed of untiring energy. He was noted for his dry wit and I could listen to his anecdotes for hours." The judge introduced his grandson to poker and, as Douglas recalled, tried to impress upon him the dictums "Never talk more than is necessary" and "Nothing is sure in this life." [7] Douglas never developed either laconicism or wittiness, but the boy was undoubtedly impressed by the versatile achievements and the prestigious position of his grandfather in Washington society. It is significant that the main contacts between the two were in 1889–93 when the boy was passing the age of discretion and the judge was a successful and highly respected member of the Washington gentility. The grandfather who impressed young Douglas entertained senators, college presidents, eminent jurists, and business tycoons. His charitable interests were the epitome of *noblesse oblige*. The family heritage which he largely created and passed on by example to Douglas was one of nobility: A MacArthur is a man of superior mind and talents, a potential master of sundry fields; a MacArthur commands the respect of important personages at the highest levels of government and society; a MacArthur, by virtue of his family's high rank in the Scottish aristocracy of blood and the American aristocracy of success and wealth, is obligated to conduct himself with honor, gallantry, and magnanimity.

2. The General

Arthur, II, son of the judge and father of Douglas, came to Milwaukee in 1849 when he was four and the town was about fifteen years old. By the time of the MacArthurs' arrival, however, Milwaukee boasted a population of 20,000; it would increase to 71,440 by 1860. The town was a mecca for immigrants, especially Germans, who constituted nearly 40 per cent of the residents. Besides being the state capital, Milwaukee was already a robust Midwestern commercial center and port with thriving banks, breweries, and rail and dock facilities. By the 1850's Milwaukee had shed its frontier garb and showed some signs of urban sophistication, but there were still exciting attractions for a boy: sailing vessels on Lake Michigan, railroad hands loading grain and flour for distant markets, occasional fur trappers from the Canadian woods and the Rockies, and — the special delight of the young — frequent and deep snows during the long winters.[8]

While his father was advancing his fortunes in the legal and political circles of Wisconsin, Arthur, II, attended public school in Milwaukee; became an ardent reader, especially of military and historical works; skirmished with Frank, his brother who was born in 1853; and cultivated a number of boyhood friendships which lasted throughout his life. One of his closest companions was young James G. Flanders, who would become a prominent lawyer-politician and Progressive leader of Wisconsin.[9]

When the Civil War began, Arthur wanted to join but was detoured by Judge MacArthur to a private military school for a year. In May, 1862, the judge yielded and wrote President Lincoln about a possible appointment to the United States Military Academy. "This is not a light or sudden impression with him," Judge MacArthur told the President, "for he has been dwelling upon it or the Navy for the last two years, so that it has become the fixed bent of his inclinations." Senator James R. Doolittle took young Arthur to visit Lincoln, but the President informed them that there would be no presidential vacancies until the plebe class of 1863. Impatient and headstrong, Arthur, II, volunteered his services to Major Elisha C. Hibbard, commander of the 24th Wisconsin Infantry, a volunteer regiment being formed in Milwaukee that summer. On August 4, 1862, seventeen-year-old Arthur was commissioned a first lieutenant of volunteers and assigned the position of regimental adjutant.[10]

In early autumn the 24th Wisconsin was sent to Kentucky as part of Brigadier General Philip A. Sheridan's division in the Army of the Ohio. Searching for water in a region parched by a severe drought, a Confederate army commanded by General Braxton Bragg launched a surprise assault on October 8 against part of the Army of the Ohio which was camped at a water hole on Chaplin Fork of the Salt River, near the village of Perryville. While some Federal units retreated in confusion, Sheridan's division held firm in the center of the Union line and even managed to counterattack. Afterward Sheridan cited MacArthur for gallantry under fire and awarded him a brevet captaincy. Neither army could count the battle as a clear-cut victory, but the Confederates soon abandoned Kentucky. The Army of the Ohio, including the 24th Wisconsin, then marched into Tennessee and occupied Nashville without encountering serious resistance.[11]

MacArthur's next combat experience was in the fierce battle of Stone's River, near Murfreesboro, Tennessee, which began on the last day of 1862 and raged for four days. Bragg centered his attack on the right flank of the Army of the Cumberland, as the Army of the Ohio was now called. Major General Alexander M. McCook's corps, which included the 24th Wisconsin, bore the brunt of the assault. The regiment suffered nearly 40 per cent casualties, including almost all of its officers. The right flank of the Federals was bent back at right angles for a while, but held until Bragg's attack faltered. The battle ended in another draw, but again Bragg withdrew southward. Major Hibbard, who was wounded on the first day, praised MacArthur's gallantry in his report and predicted that he could have an outstanding career if he stayed in the military service. Another officer of the 24th Wisconsin commented that, when Hibbard fell during the Confederates' main charge, MacArthur "at once grasped the situation, and being the only mounted officer in sight, for the moment assumed command, and by his ringing orders and perfect coolness checking the impending panic, restored confidence, rallied and held the regiment in line." [12]

The action for which MacArthur ultimately received the Medal of Honor occurred on November 25, 1863, at Missionary Ridge near Chattanooga. In September Bragg's Confederates defeated the Army of the Cumberland at Chickamauga, drove the Federals into Chattanooga, and besieged the city. Finally Major General Ulysses S. Grant arrived with reinforcements and broke the siege. On November 23–24 Grant launched counterattacks intended to drive the Confederates from the heights south and east of Chattanooga. A Federal assault secured Lookout Mountain, but Major General William T. Sherman's attack against Missionary Ridge was repulsed. Believing that it might take several days to dislodge the strong positions on the ridge, Grant gave the Army of the Cumberland the limited objective of carrying the rifle pits at the foot of Missionary Ridge on November 25. The Union soldiers, including the 24th Wisconsin in the center, not only captured the Confederate positions at the foot but, on sudden impulse and without orders, charged up the steep, rocky face of the ridge. The dramatic and unexpected assault panicked Bragg's troops and routed them from their entrenchments on the crest.

In the wild charge up the ridge MacArthur was in the van-guard, seizing the regimental flag when the color bearer was hit and planting it on the crest. Major Carl von Baumbach, then commanding the 24th Wisconsin, stated later: "What flag was first, is perhaps not susceptible of demonstration; but . . . I am satisfied that no standard crested the ridge sooner than that of the 24th Wisconsin." In recommending MacArthur for the Medal of Honor, the regimental commander said, "I think it no disparagement to others to declare that he was most distinguished in action on a field where many in the regiment displayed conspicuous gallantry, worthy of the highest praise." [13]

Two months later MacArthur was promoted to major and given command of the 24th Wisconsin, a position he held until the war's end. After participating in an operation which cleared the Confederates from the Knoxville area, the 24th Wisconsin returned to Chattanooga in May, 1864, in time to join Sherman's 100,000-man army for the advance to Atlanta. MacArthur valiantly led his troops in thirteen battles en route to Atlanta from May to September. In a vain and costly assault against a Confederate force entrenched on Kennesaw Mountain on June 27, Major MacArthur suffered wounds in the chest and right wrist, but he was back in combat a week later.[14]

During the Atlanta campaign MacArthur exhibited rare skill in executing the reconnaissance in force. His reconnaissance on the eve of the battle of Kennesaw Mountain was "brilliantly handled" and "furnished an exception to the general rule of severe losses on special reconnaissance," according to Colonel A. L. Wagner in his *Service of Security and Information,* a standard textbook for officer examinations for decades after the war. Captain T. E. Balding, who accompanied MacArthur on a reconnaissance in force just before the battle of Peach Tree Creek, reported that for a time "the regiment was standing squarely between the opposing armies, and the enemy was advancing impetuously. It was a critical situation, and one well calculated to test the fortitude of the most determined." But MacArthur remarkably extricated his troops, said Balding: "The retrograde movement was under perfect control, was made deliberately in good formation, and without the loss of a single straggler, although at the moment we passed into our own works firing had been commenced on each side of us." [15]

While his main force began the "march to the sea" in the autumn, Sherman sent a smaller force, including MacArthur's regiment, to pursue and destroy a Confederate army which was headed northwest toward the Federal supply lines in Tennessee. On November 30 the two armies met in a bloody clash at Franklin, south of Nashville. The issue was in doubt for several hours when the Union lines were broken, but after two days of heavy fighting the Confederates were routed. MacArthur's brigade commander wrote Secretary of War Edwin M. Stanton that the counterattack led by the 24th Wisconsin restored the Union position and may have turned the tide of battle. MacArthur, the Secretary was told, "bore himself heroically" and "with a most fearless spirit." Later in the action, however, MacArthur was shot in the leg and through the breast.[16]

The wounds suffered at Franklin ended his combat service. For "gallant and meritorious services in the battle of Franklin, Tenn., and in the Atlanta campaign," he was promoted to brevet colonel in March, 1865, and to the permanent volunteer rank of lieutenant colonel in May. He was mustered out of the service at Milwaukee in June, by which time he had recuperated from his wounds.[17] Like thousands of youths who served through the war and survived its horrors, twenty-year-old MacArthur was now a man among men. Unlike most of the youthful veterans, he had also proven to be a gifted leader.

Undecided about a career, MacArthur studied law under his father for several months. Probably influenced by his regimental colleagues in Milwaukee who extolled him as a hero and

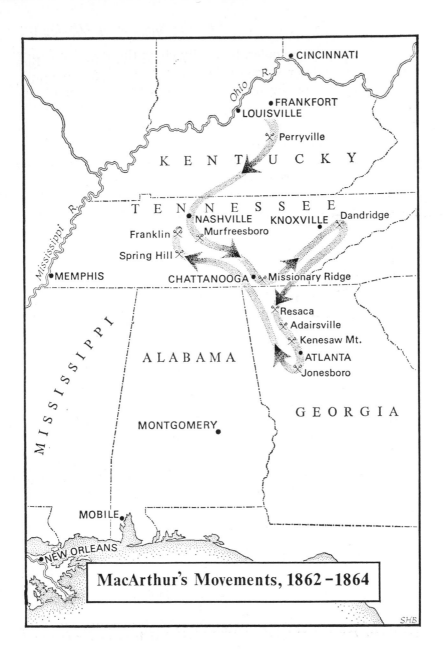

CINCINNATI

FRANKFORT
LOUISVILLE

Perryville

Ohio R.

K E N T U C K Y

T E N N E S S E E

Mississippi R.

NASHVILLE   KNOXVILLE   Dandridge

Franklin   Murfreesboro

Spring Hill

MEMPHIS   CHATTANOOGA · Missionary Ridge

Resaca
Adairsville
Kenesaw Mt.
ATLANTA
Jonesboro

A L A B A M A

M I S S I S S I P P I

G E O R G I A

MONTGOMERY

MOBILE

NEW ORLEANS

MacArthur's Movements, 1862−1864

SHB

an outstanding commander, he finally chose the Regular Army for a career. Officer strength, however, was being drastically reduced by an economy-minded Congress, so that, despite endorsements from senators and generals, he was able to get only a second lieutenant's commission. By the next July, however, he was a captain, serving with the 36th Infantry in New York City. The pace of his advancement was illusory, though, for twenty-three years would pass before his next promotion.[18]

During the two decades following the Civil War the Army's main units constituted a frontier police force, guarding settlers, travelers, miners, and rail hands from marauding Indians. Absorbed in its far-flung, isolated operations in the West, the Army lost contact with the mainstream of American life not only physically but also politically and intellectually. Popular and congressional reactions to military matters ranged from indifference to open hostility, with so-called "business pacificism" dominating public attitudes. The era marked an ebb in Army influence so extreme that it has been called the "dark ages" of American military history. Army appropriations, measured in billions of dollars during the Civil War, fell to $35 million in 1871 and $29 million in 1880. The infantry was reduced to twenty-five regiments, and the Army's aggregate strength seldom exceeded 25,000. New equipment was difficult to obtain, and development of new weapons was virtually at a standstill. Salaries were at pitiful levels, and promotions were rare, even in the cavalry, which gained most of the glory in the Indian wars. Isolation and rejection, nevertheless, permitted the Army to concentrate on internal reforms and creation of a high degree of professionalism in its small officer corps — the only positive aspects of the epoch from the War Department's viewpoint. From the officers serving on the frontier would come the outstanding leaders of the Spanish-American War, the Philippine Insurrection, and World War I. But for many years after Appomattox these men, including Captain

MacArthur, served in obscure, forsaken posts in the Rockies and the Great Plains with little hope of professional advancement or recognition.[19]

In the fall of 1866 the 36th Infantry was sent to Fort Kearney, situated on the Platte River in the Nebraska Territory. There the unit's assignment was to protect emigrants traveling along the Oregon Trail and crews constructing the Union Pacific Railroad. As the rail line was extended from the Great Plains into the Rockies, the regiment was transferred farther westward to continue protection of the construction gangs. By the next summer MacArthur and the company he commanded were stationed at Fort Sanders, Wyoming Territory. Nearby was Laramie, a small but significant town which lay on the routes of wagon trails, stage express lines, and the Union Pacific. To the north was the Sweetwater mining district, which was booming with 10,000 prospectors who needed protection from each other as much as from the Shoshoni, Crow, and Sioux. In May, 1868, MacArthur's outfit was sent to Fort Bridger in the mountainous southwest corner of the Wyoming Territory. The fort was a major Army supply depot and an important point on the key overland routes for stage, wagon, and train. MacArthur was stationed there when the Union Pacific and Central Pacific lines joined near the Salt Lake, a short distance westward. Because of another reduction in military funds, the 36th Infantry was consolidated with the 7th Infantry shortly afterward. MacArthur, who was far down on the regiment's list of captains, was left unassigned. He obtained a summer leave, which he enjoyed with his father in Milwaukee, and then spent the next year on recruiting duty in New York City. The Army had been involved in several bloody Indian wars since he had come to the West, but there had been no large-scale engagements in the Platte region where he had served.[20]

In the summer of 1870 MacArthur appealed to General Sheridan, commanding general of the Army, to have him trans-

ferred to the cavalry. Instead, orders were issued in September
assigning him to the 13th Infantry, then stationed at Fort
Rawlins, near the base of the Wasatch Mountains in the Utah
Territory. The post was only two months old when he arrived,
and the garrison lived in tents. The winter of 1870–71 must
have been the coldest MacArthur ever endured; blizzards were
dreaded even at forts with sturdy permanent quarters, which
Rawlins never had. His next station was little better — Camp
Stambaugh, on the edge of the Sweetwater mining district.
The troops' main job was to protect the miners from the Shoshoni, whose reservation adjoined the district, but more time
was probably spent in preventing wild, irresponsible miners
from provoking an Indian war. In the fall of 1873 MacArthur
and his company were sent to nearby Fort Fred Steele where
they remained a year. Again, as during his previous tour of
duty on the frontier, Indian battles raged in the Rockies and
on the Plains, but none of significance in MacArthur's vicinity.
Because of the hit-and-run tactics of the Indians, the cavalry
grabbed whatever honors were to be had; swift pursuit, impossible for infantry, was essential to engage the braves. Finally,
in October, 1874, the 13th Infantry was relieved from frontier
duty and transferred to Louisiana, with MacArthur's company
going to Jackson Barracks, New Orleans. Aware that his
chances of advancement, meager at the best, were largely dependent upon distinction in combat against the Indians, Mac-
Arthur was undoubtedly chagrined that after eight years spent
mostly at frontier posts, he had not earned a single campaign
badge.[21]

   The commander of the 13th Infantry through the 1870's was
Colonel Philippe Régis de Trobriand, one of the most colorful,
talented officers in the Army. A Frenchman of wealth and nobility, Trobriand fled with the émigrés during the French
Revolution but later returned and served as an officer in Napoleon's campaigns. After the battle of Waterloo he won dis-

tinction as a French cabinet official, literary journalist, novelist, artist, and cosmopolite. He married an American lady of high social rank, became an American citizen, and served ably as a Union general in the Civil War. He remained in the Army after the war and commanded an infantry regiment in the Dakotas until 1869 when he was assigned to the 13th Infantry. His journal of the years 1867–69 was later published and won acclaim for its superb portrayal of Army life on the frontier. The popular, dashing Trobriand was probably one of the few attractions MacArthur found in regimental life. Along with the other officers of the 13th Infantry, MacArthur must have been impressed by the regimental commander, who was the epitome of the Renaissance ideal of the versatile gentleman. Indeed, in view of the versatile talents and interests which MacArthur later displayed, he may have taken Trobriand as his model.[22]

The regiment anticipated Louisiana as a more attractive station than the frontier. But the troops' duties in buttressing the Radical Republican regime in the state proved distasteful and sometimes dangerous. Since 1872 carpetbagger William P. Kellogg had been maintained in the governor's chair mainly through President Grant's brazen use of soldiers against the opposing conservatives. At Coushatta, New Orleans, and elsewhere across the state in 1874 there was rioting and some killing, precipitated by deepening hostility between the Kellogg and anti-Kellogg forces. The unpopular duties of the 13th Infantry included cordoning the state capitol to prevent the seating of legislators whose elections were not recognized by the Kellogg-controlled election board. An authority on the era states, with some hyperbole, that the Kellogg administration marked "a reign of irresponsible lawlessness unequalled in the history of civilized peoples." By the end of military occupation in Louisiana, following the Compromise of 1877, the Army seemed to many persons, Northern as well as Southern, to be the brutal arm of corrupt regimes in Washington and New

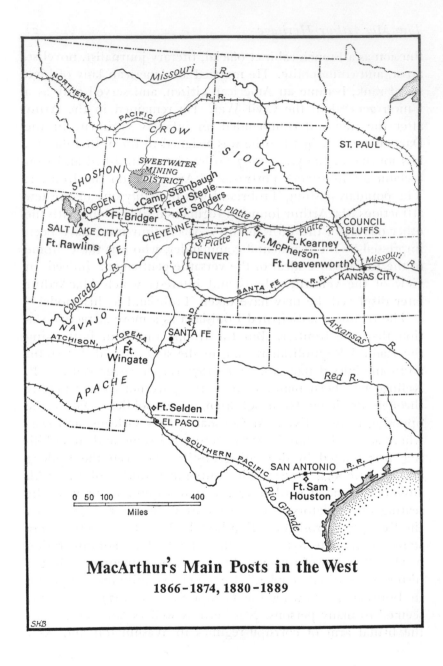

MacArthur's Main Posts in the West

1866–1874, 1880–1889

SHB

Orleans.[23] Captain MacArthur, who had found action, glory, and praise in the Civil War, must have been a disillusioned officer by that time. Never had the Army been so unpopular, and never had his professional future looked so unpromising.

The single bright spot in the period was his marriage to Mary Pinkney Hardy, a twenty-two-year-old belle from Virginia whom he met at a Mardi Gras ball in New Orleans in the winter of 1874–75. Strong-willed and vivacious, Mary, or "Pinky," came from a family steeped in Southern traditions. Her father, Thomas A. Hardy, was a well-to-do planter and commission merchant of Norfolk; four of her brothers were Confederate veterans. When the family mansion, "Riveredge," was taken over by the Union Army during the Civil War, the Hardys moved to North Carolina and later to Baltimore, at last returning to "Riveredge" in the postwar period. While in Baltimore, Mary, though Episcopalian, attended Mount de Sales Academy, a Catholic girls' school, where she won high academic honors. She was visiting in New Orleans when she met Captain MacArthur and fell victim to "love at first sight." After a courtship by correspondence through the spring, MacArthur obtained a three-month leave, journeyed to the Hardy home on the banks of the Elizabeth River in Virginia, and married her in May, 1875. Several of her brothers reputedly absented themselves from the wedding in protest against her union with a Yankee officer. Apparently none of the MacArthurs ever became close to the Hardys, but Mary was not ostracized by her family. In fact, she returned home for the birth of her first two children: Arthur, III, born at "Riveredge" on June 1, 1876, and Malcolm, born on October 17, 1878, at New Britain, Connecticut, where the Hardys were vacationing.[24]

The new Mrs. MacArthur's first taste of Army life was in Washington, D.C., where she became acquainted with the elder MacArthurs while her husband served on examining and retiring boards for nearly a year. Captain MacArthur returned

to Louisiana in late 1876 as commander of Company K of the
13th Infantry. By then, ebbing morale and high desertion
rates loomed as the officers' chief worries, as in other units.
The only excitement came in mid-1877 when the regiment was
sent to the mining area around Wilkesbarre and Scranton,
Pennsylvania, during an outbreak of labor violence. But the
Secretary of War later stated that the units "sent to quell these
disturbances met with little resistance, and were able to execute all their orders without firing a gun and without bloodshed." [25] The operation was unpopular and inglorious, just as
had been nearly all of MacArthur's assignments since he left the
battlefield at Franklin thirteen years earlier.

With the Army in the South again withdrawn into its forts
and camps, the late 1870's were quiet times for Captain and
Mrs. MacArthur and Company K, the main bustle accompanying their frequent moves to various posts in Louisiana and
Arkansas. The highlight of the MacArthurs' last year in this
region was the birth of their third son. Mary is said to have
intended to go to "Riveredge" for the delivery, but he arrived
sooner than expected: Douglas MacArthur was born on January 26, 1880, at the 13th Infantry post at Little Rock in a two-
story towered building which had recently been converted from
an arsenal into quarters for married officers.[26]

That summer the regiment was sent to New Mexico, with
Company K assigned to Fort Wingate in the northwest corner
of the territory. To the north lay the Navaho reservation, to
the south the Zuni Mountains, and to the east about 100 miles
Albuquerque, the nearest town of any size. The company's task
was three-fold: to keep the Navaho on their reservation and
guard them from the hostile Apache to the southwest; to protect travelers on the nearby Kansas and Stockton Express route;
and to guard the crews building the Atchison, Topeka and
Santa Fe Railroad, now working near Fort Wingate. Far to
the south, along the border, Geronimo and a band of Apache

were on the warpath, but the chief concern of the Army in northern New Mexico was the numerous desperadoes who prowled the overland routes and raided isolated settlements. Except for three weeks at Fort Dodge, Kansas, as judge advocate of a general court-martial, Captain MacArthur remained at Wingate until early 1884. The soldiers' morale was never lower. The average strength of the 13th Infantry was about 440; with 248 desertions in 1881–82, its ranks were severely depleted, and replacements were slow in arriving. Facilities for families were bare at Wingate, and life for Army wives was rugged.

While the family was at Norfolk in April, 1883, during one of the captain's rare leaves, tragedy struck when five-year-old Malcolm died of measles. To avoid returning to Wingate, MacArthur tried, through General Grant, to get an appointment as military attaché in China, but was rejected. Grant supported his application, but predicted its ultimate disapproval because "there is a sort of morbid sensitiveness on the part of Congress and the press generally against trusting soldiers anywhere except in front of the cannon or musket." The MacArthurs dejectedly returned to New Mexico. The discouraging years at Wingate were climaxed by a 300-mile journey by wagon and foot in February, 1884, when Company K was transferred to Fort Selden near the Mexican border.

The new station lay about a mile east of the Rio Grande and twenty miles west of the bleak San Andres Mountains in the arid southern region of the New Mexico Territory. Sixty miles downriver was El Paso, the closest sizable community. The troops' job was to guard the area against depredations by the vicious, clever Geronimo and his raiders moving north out of Chihuahua, the border province of Mexico. Between the fort and the border ran the new Southern Pacific line and a stage express route which had earlier been the main route of the Butterfield Overland Express.

In early 1885 Geronimo and a small band of Chiricahua
Apache broke out of the Arizona reservation, precipitating the
last Apache war and striking terror in settlers and travelers in
the Southwest. Geronimo headed for northern Mexico, however, and most of his depredations were against Mexicans. The
Chiricahua traveled lightly and quickly, sometimes covering
1200 miles in one month. Experts at ambush, they struck savagely and could be 100 miles away within a day. As usual, the
Army's tactics had to be based on pursuit; again the honors
went to the cavalry, while the infantry was left to guard forts,
settlements, and express stations. In August, 1886, Geronimo
surrendered, with most of the credit going to Major General
Nelson A. Miles, overall commander of the 5000-man Army
operation, and Captain Henry W. Lawton, whose cavalry unit
accepted the chieftain's capitulation in northern Mexico. No
major engagements took place near Fort Selden, and Geronimo
was never in the vicinity. But campaign badges were awarded
to officers and men of all units engaged in defensive as well as
offensive operations in the Arizona–New Mexico border area.
It was thus that Captain MacArthur received his first campaign
badge since joining the Regular Army.[27]

MacArthur, who was commandant of Fort Selden as well as
of his company, had missed the combat but had performed his
duties well during the emergency, namely, maintaining the post
in excellent military order and keeping his troops in combat
readiness. When the departmental inspector from Fort Leavenworth visited Fort Selden in the fall of 1885, he reported: "The
military bearing and appearance of the troops were very
fine . . . Captain MacArthur impresses me as an officer of
more than ordinary ability, and very zealous in the performance
of duty. The company and post show evidence of intelligent,
judicious, and masterly supervision." [28] Disappointed at missing
the action against Geronimo, MacArthur reconciled himself
to the fact that the inspector's laudatory report would receive

scant attention at Fort Leavenworth. But not all such reports
are buried, particularly if the reader has a special interest in
the subject.

With the termination of Apache hostilities in the Southwest,
the ten companies of the 13th Infantry were dispersed to posts
over a wide area, ranging from Fort Crawford, Colorado, to
Little Rock. Regimental headquarters was established at Fort
Supply in the Indian Territory (later Oklahoma). The prize
assignment went to MacArthur and Company K, who were sent
to Fort Leavenworth, Kansas, to participate in the instructional
program of the Infantry and Cavalry School, now five years old.
The move was a welcome change for Mary since Leavenworth's
quarters were luxurious compared to the adobe structures of
the forts in New Mexico. Also the boys could receive formal
schooling for the first time. The assignment was most significant for Captain MacArthur, who absorbed much from his
experience on the staff of the advanced school for infantry
officers. The school commandant was Major General Alexander M. McCook, who had been impressed by MacArthur's
"great coolness and presence of mind" at Stone's River where
the 24th Wisconsin was a vital unit in McCook's corps. The
commandant had also noted MacArthur's leadership ability as
post and company commander in New Mexico. At Leavenworth, MacArthur seized his opportunity and performed well
in the instructional and administrative assignments which Mc-
Cook gave him. When Brigadier General J. C. Kelton, the
adjutant general of the Army, confidentially inquired about
the captain as a prospect for a job in his Washington office,
McCook replied that "Captain MacArthur is beyond question
the most distinguished Captain in the Army of the United
States for gallantry and good conduct" — quite an assertion
since MacArthur then was not even the highest ranking captain in his own regiment. But McCook strongly recommended
him: "He is a student; is master of his profession; has legal

ability which fits him for the position; is unexceptional in
habit; temperate in all things, yet modest with all [*sic*]." Learning of the possible appointment, Judge MacArthur rallied his
influential friends to write recommendations for his son. The
judge wrote the Secretary of War that it was a "gross injustice"
that Captain MacArthur "has been jumped over sixty times by
junior officers and persons taken from civil life." On July 1,
1889, MacArthur received not only his long-awaited promotion
to major but also orders to report to Washington where he was
to be assistant adjutant general.[29] The years of sacrifice and
oblivion were done, thanks to the fortunate reunion with a
former superior who had not forgotten the bold young adjutant
of the 24th Wisconsin.

The year 1889 was a turning point both in MacArthur's career and in the nation's history. Two months before his departure for Washington, his comrades of the 13th Infantry
stationed in the Indian Territory were rushed to the Oklahoma
District to preserve order during one of the last great land
rushes in American history. At the signal of guns fired by
land-office agents, 100,000 waiting "boomers" rushed into the
district to stake off nearly two million acres of former Indian
lands. The federal census superintendent concluded in his report the next year: "Up to and including 1880, the country had
a frontier of settlement, but at present . . . there can hardly
be said to be a frontier line." [30] The closing of the frontier
ended a romantic era in the development of the nation. But
MacArthur and the other Army men who had spent long years
at lonely frontier posts would not have cared to relive the
epoch.

The next four years in Washington were happy ones for the
new major and his family. Mary and her two sons enjoyed their
first extended opportunity to be with Judge and Mrs. MacArthur. With his many contacts in Washington's high society, the
judge must have introduced his son and his family to numerous

important political and military figures. Arthur, III, received an appointment to the United States Naval Academy, while his father obtained a law degree from the brief-lived school which was intended to be the first division of the National University. Major MacArthur also was finally awarded the Congressional Medal of Honor for his action twenty-seven years earlier at Missionary Ridge. Moreover, General Kelton was highly pleased with the major's work as assistant adjutant general. Several years after MacArthur finished this tour of duty, Kelton wrote to him:

> I wish to tell you that I regard your assignment to duty in The Adjutant General's Office at the time you were, a most fortunate circumstance for the office and the Army. Every duty assigned to you you have performed thoroughly and conscientiously. Every recommendation you have made has been consistent and without color of prejudice or favor, but solely for the good of the Army. The conspicuous part you took in framing the Act approved October 1, 1890, and the General Order elucidating it, in respect to examinations and promotions of officers, — an Act which must be regarded now and for all times as the most important impetus the Army could have received for its emancipation from mental and physical stagnation, opening to it the way to military enlightenment — cannot be too much extolled. It places you at the head of the military reformers of the Department, where I look for you always to be found.[31]

Work in the adjutant general's office probably was not especially challenging to MacArthur, except for his role in drafting the above-mentioned measure to require merit examinations for promotions below the rank of colonel. The department's principal functions included recording and communicating War Department orders, instructions, and regulations; preparing and distributing commissions and military decorations; compiling registers and directories of personnel; consolidating general returns from posts and commands; publishing and distributing manuals and miscellaneous documents; and preserving the historical records of the military establishment. Though associated with an office mainly concerned with records-keeping, MacArthur at last found himself in the mainstream of military administration. The position of Kelton himself as adjutant general was most powerful, ranking above that of the commanding general of the Army in many matters. MacArthur, indeed, was not yet an officer of much influence, even in departmental affairs: The adjutant general's office at that time consisted of Kelton and sixteen assistant adjutant generals, all of whom were senior to MacArthur at the time of his appointment. But, sitting in his office in the War Department, Major MacArthur could better comprehend how far, far away was Fort Wingate.[32]

In late 1893, while continuing in the capacity of assistant adjutant general, MacArthur was transferred to the headquarters of the Department of Texas at Fort Sam Houston, San Antonio. There his efficiency won the praise of Brigadier Generals Frank Wheaton and Z. R. Bliss, the successive departmental commanders under whom MacArthur served. In May, 1896, he was promoted to lieutenant colonel. While their father was at the large Texas post, Douglas attended the West Texas Military Academy and Arthur, III, the Naval Academy. In October, 1897, with both sons graduated from their schools, Lieutenant Colonel MacArthur was assigned to the headquarters of the Department of the Dakotas in St. Paul, while continuing in the position of assistant adjutant general of the Army. He was working there in April, 1898, when war broke out between the United States and Spain.[33]

Soon awarded a brigadier generalship of volunteers, MacArthur was sent to Camp Thomas at Chickamauga, Georgia, where the III Corps was assembling and training for an invasion of Cuba. There, as adjutant general and subsequently chief of staff of the corps, MacArthur got more than a glimpse of the nightmare of confusion which attended the mobilization for the "splendid little war" against Spain. Camp Thomas had facilities for a maximum of 20,000 men, but somehow over 76,000 trainees were lodged there. The Regular Army, whose strength was less than 30,000 at the outbreak of hostilities, had the tasks of housing, feeding, equipping, training, and transporting 125,000 volunteers in the first weeks of war and double that number later. The chaos extended from shortages of summer uniforms and ammunition to noxious food at camp messes and typhoid fever raging virtually unchecked through the tents. When MacArthur moved with the corps to the embarkation center at Tampa, conditions were, if possible, even worse.[34]

Most officers believed that the main action would occur in Cuba and that the Philippine fighting ended with the Navy's quick triumph in Manila Bay on May 1. But the Cuban expedition departed in June without MacArthur, who had been transferred to a camp near San Francisco. There he was given command of the 1st Brigade, 1st Division, scheduled for Philippine duty. On August 4, a month after hostilities ceased in Cuba, MacArthur and his 4800-man brigade disembarked at Cavite, south of Manila. With him was Major General Wesley Merritt, who assumed overall command of the troops, numbering 11,000, which were preparing to move against Manila. In far-off Milwaukee, meanwhile, Mrs. MacArthur and Douglas read the war news avidly and rejoiced that Douglas had passed the entrance examination for West Point. Somewhere on the high seas Ensign MacArthur, having participated in the naval battle off Santiago, was en route to join naval operations in the Philippines.

Hopelessly surrounded by Merritt's soldiers and Emilio Aguinaldo's Filipino insurgents, the Spanish commander at Manila negotiated an agreement with Merritt and Commodore George Dewey whereby, in order to save face for the Spanish and prevent the insurgents from taking the city, the Spanish

troops would offer a brief show of token resistance and then
would surrender to the Americans. The farcical "battle" of
Manila, it was agreed, would take place on the morning of August 13, 1898.

The agreement worked smoothly for a time, with the Spanish abandoning their shoreline positions as Brigadier General
Francis V. Greene's 2nd Brigade neared them. But suddenly
at the Singalong crossroad, south of Manila and near Pasay,
MacArthur's 1st Brigade ran into heavy fire from a Spanish
unit which had not received word of the show-of-force understanding. First Lieutenant Peyton C. March led a brave but
unsuccessful charge against the Spanish position, for which Mac-
Arthur later recommended him for the Medal of Honor. That
afternoon the Spanish, finally getting the word, abandoned the
strong point. The commander at Manila surrendered the city
shortly thereafter. In his report Merritt extolled the "outstanding" role played by the 1st Brigade in the "capture" of the city
and MacArthur's display of "much gallantry and excellent judgment" during the skirmish at Singalong, the only significant
action of the operation. He also appointed MacArthur provost
marshal general of the Army in the Philippines and military
governor of Manila.[35]

With the signing of the Treaty of Paris on December 10,
Aguinaldo began laying plans for war against the Americans,
who he thought had come to bring independence to the archipelago and instead had supplanted the Spanish overlords. In a
surprise attack on the outskirts of Manila on February 4, 1899,
Aguinaldo launched his war, which ultimately would be far
bloodier and less popular for the Americans than the brief conflict with Spain.

The insurgents' initial attack was repulsed by troops under
the command of MacArthur, now a major general of volunteers
and commanding the 2nd Division. That spring MacArthur
was placed in charge of the Department of Northern Luzon

and was the field commander in a dozen costly but victorious battles against the rebels. By May he had driven Aguinaldo's forces from the lower half of the Central Luzon Plain. Malolos and San Fernando, where Aguinaldo had maintained successive military and governmental headquarters of his so-called Philippine Republic, were captured by MacArthur's troops. By the time he reached San Fernando, however, MacArthur found that nearly a fourth of his men were disabled by diseases, mainly amoebic dysentery. Moreover, American deaths in combat from February to May, 1899, had exceeded the aggregate battle fatalities of United States forces in the Spanish-American War. With serious depletions also because volunteer enlistments were expiring, MacArthur was compelled to halt the offensive until reinforcements came.

In September, 1899, Major General Elwell S. Otis, now in overall command of Philippine operations, plotted a pincer movement designed to trap Aguinaldo's main army. MacArthur was to continue up the Central Luzon Plain toward Aguinaldo's new headquarters at Tarlac, while Major General Henry W. Lawton, the captor of Geronimo thirteen years earlier, was to proceed along the edge of the mountains on MacArthur's right flank. Brigadier General Lloyd Wheaton would lead an amphibious operation which would land at Lingayen Gulf and move inland to link up with the forces pushing northward, thereby enveloping the insurgent army. In early November MacArthur captured Tarlac, and later that month his forces and those of Wheaton joined near Lingayen Gulf. Aguinaldo himself escaped the trap, but many of his subordinates were captured. With the American troops now numbering over 50,000, the rebels avoided large-scale battles after the fall of 1899, resorting to guerilla warfare instead.[36]

On November 23 MacArthur, who was with his troops near Tarlac, reported to Otis in Manila that "the so-called Filipino republic is destroyed . . . The army itself as an organization

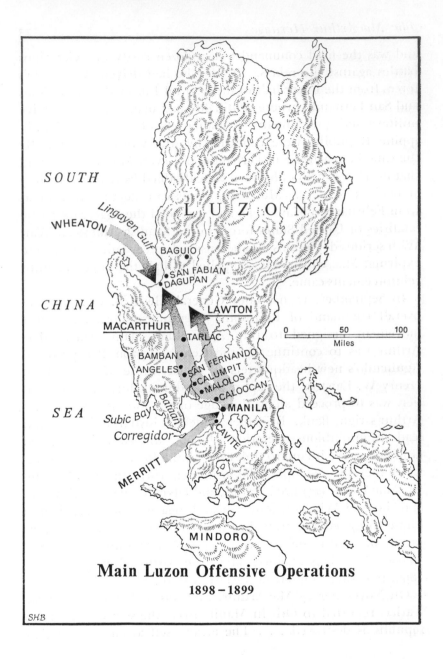

Main Luzon Offensive Operations

1898–1899

has disappeared." Since "men who now try to continue the strife by individual action become simply leaders of banditti," MacArthur suggested that Otis should issue a proclamation "offering complete amnesty to all who surrender within a stated time." He proposed that each rebel who gives up his rifle should be paid thirty pesos. But, said MacArthur, Otis should emphasize that "after the date fixed the killing of American soldiers will be regarded as murder." Never prone to accept advice from his field commanders, Otis rejected MacArthur's proposal.[37]

Though a favorite with President McKinley, Otis was often criticized by his subordinates in Luzon and by his superiors in the War Department for his inefficiency, indecision, and refusal to budge from his office in Manila. On one occasion, after receiving an ambiguous order from Otis, MacArthur became so enraged that he threw his hat on the ground and shouted: "Otis is a locomotive bottom side up, with the wheels revolving at full speed!" Because of Lawton's volatile remarks about Otis in the presence of correspondents, however, MacArthur's friction with the commander got less public attention. On May 6, 1900, Otis was finally relieved of command, with MacArthur succeeding to his position and also given the title of military governor of the Philippines.[38]

Unlike his predecessor, MacArthur was widely respected by his men as a pugnacious leader, and the pursuit of the rebels was relentless, although often futile, in the ensuing months. A number of officers involved in the Luzon operations would play key roles in military affairs in the future. Nearly all of them deeply admired General MacArthur and were indebted to him for promotions, citations, medals, and opportunities to prove their skill in leadership. They included young Peyton March, who served as MacArthur's aide and would be chief of staff during the First World War; William Mitchell, a signal officer who would gain fame and infamy with the air service; Charles

P. Summerall, a lieutenant who distinguished himself with the field artillery on Luzon and in the 1920's rose to chief of staff; Enoch H. Crowder, MacArthur's secretary and legal adviser and later the Army's judge advocate general; Frederick Funston, a daring little officer who captured Aguinaldo in March, 1901, and thirteen years later commanded the Veracruz expedition; J. Franklin Bell, who succeeded to Lawton's command (after an insurgent's bullet ended Lawton's life in late 1899) and within six years was military head of the Army; and John J. Pershing, whose leadership qualities displayed during the insurrection, especially in pacifying the Moros, soon gained him a promotion from captain directly to brigadier general.

MacArthur's achievements as military governor were limited not only because he held the office for only fourteen months but also because much of his attention still was directed toward supervising operations against the guerillas, who continued to ambush and raid with ferocity. Shortly after Otis' departure, he issued an amnesty proclamation similar to the one he had proposed to Otis. By the end of 1900, however, it was obvious that MacArthur's policy was a failure since very few Filipinos cooperated with his amnesty provisions. In December he issued another proclamation, calling for "precise observance of the laws of war," with severe punishments for civilians who aided the guerillas. By then MacArthur was convinced that the enemy was not merely small bands of rebels but the hostile population of the islands, who must be kept under firm military rule for the foreseeable future. Yet he did try to govern humanely, introducing, among other things, a rudimentary system of elementary education; a revision of the harsh Spanish civil code, including the introduction of *habeas corpus;* and the establishment of a commission to draft the first American tariff system for the islands. Most of his plans, which were largely in the preliminary stages of study, were absorbed into the work of the Philippine Commission, which arrived in June, 1900, and was headed by William Howard Taft. MacArthur, who did not believe that the Philippines were ready for civil rule yet, firmly opposed the sending of the Taft group, whose instructions from President Roosevelt were to effect the transition from military to civil government.[39]

When Taft's vessel anchored at Manila, MacArthur remained in his office and sent Colonel Enoch H. Crowder to receive the commissioners. Taft later recalled that when he went ashore the Army's reception "somewhat exceeded the coldness of the populace." The elephantine Taft said that, though the day was unusually hot and he was sweating profusely, his perspiration suddenly stopped when he shook the frigid hand of Mac-Arthur at the latter's office. Taft maintained that he tried to assure MacArthur, who now held the rank of brigadier general in the regulars, that he would continue as military commander, to which MacArthur reputedly answered: "That would be all right if I had not been exercising so much more power before you came." The basic difference between the two men was soon evident when Taft expounded his view that the "little brown brothers" should be pacified more rapidly and should be given a voice in their government as quickly as possible. MacArthur, who almost daily received reports of deaths of his troops in guerilla ambushes, was convinced that a decade of military rule was necessary. The disgusted military governor cabled the War Department in July, 1900, as plans were being rushed to send a force to relieve the Peking legations besieged by the Boxers: "As paramount situation has for time being developed in China, request permission to proceed thereto in person to command field operations until crisis has passed." Instead, Secretary of War Elihu Root chose Major General Adna R. Chaffee to head the relief expedition and, against MacArthur's protests, reinforced Chaffee's command with units from Luzon. Confronted by Taft's commission on the one hand and by the unrelenting guerillas on the other, MacArthur must have felt as trapped as the foreign legations in Peking.

In the following months Taft bombarded Root's office with

reports of his difficulties with MacArthur, who was accused of being jealous of the prerogatives of the civil commission and of obstructing its work in petty ways. In early 1901 Root made up his mind that the best road to effective administration and pacification of the islands would be to end the military regime. On February 27, shortly after approving MacArthur's promotion to the permanent rank of major general, Root confidentially notified Chaffee, who was still in China, that he would succeed MacArthur as military head in the Philippines that summer. He emphasized, however, that Chaffee would be subordinate to Taft, the civil governor, in matters of common interest. With MacArthur obviously in mind, Root said: "An officer who has exercised both civil and military power, and who is called upon to surrender a portion of his power to another cannot, unless he is free from the ordinary characteristics of human nature, altogether divorce himself from the habit of exercising civil power and the tendency to look with disfavor upon what seems to be a curtailing of his authority." Root added: "You will be free from any such predisposition, and will take your position purely as a soldier to discharge difficult and delicate but well-defined duties." On June 21, 1901, Mac-Arthur was informed by the War Department of the change, to take place on July 4. On the latter day in an inaugural ceremony at Malacañan Palace in Manila, Taft was sworn in as the civil governor, with MacArthur and Chaffee standing beside him. Shortly afterward MacArthur packed his bags and boarded a ship for the States where he would assume command of the Department of the Colorado.[40]

Under the emergency conditions existing during his brief term as military governor, General MacArthur had performed his difficult dual role creditably. The fault underlying the Mac-Arthur-Taft friction lay more with the War Department than with the two men in the islands. The relationship between the powers and functions of the commission and those of the military governor were never clarified by Root. In monetary matters, for example, appropriations for the Philippines were controlled by the commission, whereas MacArthur retained executive power until July 4, 1901. Indeed, Root attempted to rectify the mistake in the lucid orders he gave to Chaffee, but it was unfortunately too late as far as MacArthur's reputation in official Washington was concerned. Taft was one of President Roosevelt's closest friends and would soon be Secretary of War.

By 1902 there were so many stories of Army scandals and atrocities perpetrated in the Philippines that the Senate launched an investigation. MacArthur's name, of course, was frequently mentioned in the hearings, and he was called to testify on several occasions. But the Senate investigation showed that, though some officers and men had been cruel and sadistical in their treatment of the Filipinos, MacArthur himself had been firm but just in his relations with the natives and had even developed a friendship with the captured Aguinaldo. Taft admitted that MacArthur was "strongly in favor of cultivating the good will of the Filipinos, and a neglect of military officers to take such a course meets with no favor from him. He is strongly in favor of punishing military officers and men who have been guilty of cruelty to the natives." As for the Army's behavior in the islands in 1900–01, Taft claimed with some exaggeration that "there never was a war conducted, whether against inferior races or not, in which there were more compassion and more restraint and more generosity."

Shortly after arriving in Manila in 1900, Taft had written to Root that MacArthur seemed to be "a very courtly, kindly man; lacking somewhat in a sense of humor; rather fond of generalizations on the psychological condition of the people; politely incredulous, and politely lacking in any great consideration for the view of anyone, as to the real situation, who is a civilian and who has been here only a comparatively short time and firmly convinced of the necessity for maintaining military etiquette in civil matters and civil government." Dr. H. E. Stafford, an Army surgeon and active Mason in Luzon,

1899–1901, recalled that MacArthur showed great benevolence in allowing Filipino civic and fraternal groups, even secret societies, to continue their meetings simply on the pledge of their leaders that they would not be used as "centers of insurrection." Lieutenant March said that MacArthur earnestly endeavored to acquaint himself with the past and present ways of the islanders and "had a standing order with Kelly, the bookseller of Hongkong, to send to him every book in stock published on Far Eastern matters, particularly those devoted to colonial administration." [41]

The feud with Taft was the beginning of the end for MacArthur's career. While serving at various times in the next several years as commander of the departments of the Colorado, the Lakes, and the East, MacArthur became increasingly vociferous in his denunciations of the War Department and the White House on sundry matters. He was critical of Root's military reform plans, which included the creation of a general staff modeled after that of the German army. The selections of chiefs of staff under the new plan irritated him since they had served under him and still were outranked by him. In 1904 he objected vehemently to the recruiting of German-Americans in the Army and National Guard; he also predicted that a war with Germany was imminent. In March of that year Roosevelt told Taft, who was then Secretary of War and would retain that post until 1908: "Recently I had to rebuke MacArthur for speaking ill of the Germans. I would like a statement about this matter. Our army and navy officers must not comment about foreign powers in a way that will cause trouble." The origin of MacArthur's bias against all things German is not known, but may have dated back to his childhood days in Milwaukee, which was predominantly German-American. Later, while commanding the Division of the Pacific with headquarters at San Francisco, MacArthur became embroiled in a heated controversy with some local businessmen when he tried to pressure the city fathers to close the saloons bordering the Presidio. The protestors wrote Taft that MacArthur "is taking upon himself the duties of administering in municipal affairs." [42]

When the Russo-Japanese War exploded in early 1904, eight American officers were promptly sent to the Manchurian front as observers. Chafing at the bit at his headquarters in San Francisco, MacArthur requested that he also be assigned as a military observer. He finally secured the appointment, but arrived in Manchuria in mid-March, 1905, just after the major fighting had ended with the Japanese triumph at Mukden. When the Portsmouth peace conference was convened in August, MacArthur was sent to Tokyo as military attaché to the American legation.

With the approval of Taft, he began planning a grand tour of East and South Asian military posts, and in November, 1905, he departed on this rather enigmatic "reconnaissance." He was accompanied by his wife, who had been in Tokyo for eight months, and by Douglas, who had arrived in Japan in October as his aide-de-camp. By late February, 1906, the MacArthurs, traveling by ship and train, had visited dozens of military posts in South China, Malaya, Burma, India, and Ceylon. That spring they moved on to Siam, French Indo-China, and North China, observing military facilities and operations and attending state functions. In August, 1906, they returned to the United States, whereupon General MacArthur resumed his post at San Francisco as commander of the Division of the Pacific and Douglas entered the Engineer School at Washington Barracks, D.C. The general did not submit a full report on his Asian observations, which lends further mystery to Taft's motivation in sending him. Coincidentally, there was a change in chief of staff while MacArthur was in Asia, the honor going to Major General J. Franklin Bell, who had gained his brigadier generalship while serving under MacArthur.[43]

In September, 1906, MacArthur was promoted to lieutenant

general, but, though now the highest ranking officer, was not elevated to chief of staff then or later. In early 1907 the War Department informed him that the administrative units called divisions were being abolished; he was offered command of the Eastern department. He refused, stating that it would mean a humiliating reduction in authority for him. He proposed that the War Department either accept his retirement or assign him to some "special duty" which would not be an affront to his honor. "The sooner the depressing condition is terminated," he wrote Taft, "the better it will be for all the interests involved." Shortly he received orders "to proceed to Milwaukee, there to perform such duties as may hereafter be assigned," but no further duties were given to him. On June 2, 1909, three months after Taft's inauguration as President, he retired quietly from the Army. Shorn of the powers and honors traditionally accorded the sole holder of the lieutenant generalship, Mac-Arthur departed a deeply hurt and chagrined man. In his eyes, the proper way to have climaxed his forty-seven years of devoted, distinguished service would have been in the chair of the chief of staff. Isolated from nearly all contacts with the Regular Army after 1907 and suffering from a serious case of hyperacidity of the stomach, MacArthur became increasingly absorbed in the activities of the Military Order of the Loyal Legion of the United States, a group of old veterans, mainly of the Civil War, who still remembered the "boy colonel" of the 24th Wisconsin and elected him as the organization's national president.[44]

While addressing a reunion of the 24th Wisconsin veterans in Milwaukee on September 5, 1912, said to have been the hottest day of the year in that city, General MacArthur was suddenly and fatally stricken by an apoplectic attack. A young medical intern, serving as a waiter at the banquet, pronounced him dead on the platform. Charles King, a retired officer and close friend of the general, said of the funeral: "Mrs. Mac-

Arthur told me, as I already had heard from his lips, that the general desired *not* to be dressed in his uniform, and added that he had explicitly told her he wished his funeral to be simple as it could be made and *utterly* devoid of military display." Except for his two sons, the only active military officer present at the funeral was a solitary colonel from a nearby fort. At the general's behest, his remains were interred in a cemetery in Milwaukee rather than in Arlington National Cemetery.[45]

The Military Order of the Loyal Legion prepared and printed a eulogy praising his military record and extolling "his fervent patriotism, his unshaken loyalty, his silent and soldierly acceptance of conditions little looked for in view of his great services and exalted rank." The general left an estate of $10,000, most of which he undoubtedly inherited from his father. For some reason, his widow was granted a pension of merely $1200 a year, whereas the widows of all other lieutenant generals were receiving $2500. James Flanders, a Milwaukee attorney and lifetime friend of MacArthur, led a long but successful fight to get Mrs. MacArthur's pension raised to that figure.[46]

In view of the unusually close relationship between father and son, Douglas MacArthur's comment on his father's death is not surprising: "My whole world changed that night. Never have I been able to heal the wound in my heart." Douglas deeply admired him not only as his parent but also as his ideal of the military leader. General MacArthur, in turn, bore himself as an officer just as Judge MacArthur might have done, had he donned an Army uniform instead of a judge's robe. The general displayed traits of versatility and nobility similar to those of his father. He excelled as a combat leader and as an administrator, demonstrating professional excellence, fierce ambition, and superior intelligence in both roles. Like the judge, he had a keen sense of magnanimity as well as of justice. Just as his father became an aristocrat of the bench, General MacArthur became an aristocrat of the military elite — always dig-

nified, usually formal, and never guilty of the common officers'
vices of excessive cursing, drinking, gambling, and promiscuity.

But the general's contributions to the heritage bequeathed
to Douglas also included two liabilities: his disdain and contempt for civilian officials who interfered in what he considered
to be his domain, and, a corollary, his own outspokenness on
matters beyond his jurisdiction. The neglect of Washington to
utilize fully the services of its highest-ranking general in his last
years of active duty must have had a lasting impact on Douglas.
Nor could he forget the lonely figure representing the Army
at his father's funeral. But General MacArthur's most significant legacy to his son was the talented gathering of young officers who served under him in the Philippines when his career
was at its zenith. Then he was widely respected in military
circles, especially by the Marches and Pershings whose abilities
he recognized and whose careers he abetted. As will be seen
later, these officers did not forget this when General Mac-
Arthur's son served under them in future years. Talented as
he was, Douglas would enjoy a meteoric rise due in no small
measure to the special interest of officers who were beholden
to his father.

3. *The Captain*

Arthur, III, who was three and a third years older than
Douglas, made certain that he would never be stranded at a
lonely fort in an arid land. Perhaps that never-to-be-forgotten
journey from Fort Wingate to Fort Selden convinced him that
as an adult he wanted no part of the interminably marching
Army. So the first-born of General MacArthur chose a naval
career. He entered Annapolis at the age of sixteen as surely
one of the youngest midshipmen at the Naval Academy. Others
attending the Academy during his years there included future

novelist Winston Churchill and such admirals-to-be as William
D. Leahy, Thomas C. Hart, and William H. Standley. Graduating with high honors in 1896, Arthur was commissioned an
ensign and was soon serving the first of many tours of sea duty.

Ensign MacArthur was aboard the gunboat *Vixen* in the battle off Santiago in July, 1898, when the Spanish fleet in Cuban
waters was annihilated. He later participated in naval operations during the Philippine Insurrection and the Boxer Rebellion. His career was not handicapped when he married the
daughter of Rear Admiral Bowman McCalla in 1901. The next
year he took command of the *Grampus*, a newly commissioned
submarine and the first to be built on the Pacific coast. He
was soon given command of a division of submarines and, according to his brother, "was one of the original developers of
underwater tactics and strategy." In 1906 Arthur, now a lieutenant, returned to the Naval Academy as aide to the superintendent and faculty secretary. Another young lieutenant on
the staff at the time was the gunnery instructor, Ernest J. King,
who would be chief of naval operations in World War II. By
1909, when his father retired, Arthur, III, was a lieutenant
commander serving aboard the battleship *Louisiana*. Two years
later he was given command of the *McCall*, a new destroyer.
In 1912 he was transferred to the General Board of the Navy,
the equivalent of the Army's General Staff. (The superintendent of the State, War, and Navy Building, where his office was
located, was Captain Douglas MacArthur.)

Promoted to commander in 1915, well ahead of most of
of his Academy classmates, MacArthur returned to sea duty as
captain of the *San Francisco*, a mine sweeper. When war came
in 1917, he was commanding the armored cruiser *South Dakota*
with the Pacific fleet. He was transferred soon to the Atlantic
and given command of the light cruiser *Chattanooga*, which was
on convoy duty. For distinguished work in protecting transports from prowling German U-boats in 1918, he was awarded

the Navy Cross and the Distinguished Service Medal, as well as promotion to captain. After the war he commanded the important San Diego Naval Training Station for two years and then went back to sea on the *Henderson,* which was on duty with the Naval Transportation Service. In the spring of 1923 Captain MacArthur returned to Washington to serve on boards of examination for promotion and retirement of naval officers. He was working in the Navy Department when he suddenly suffered an attack of appendicitis and died on December 2, 1923.[47]

During his thirty-one years of naval service, including nineteen spent at sea, Captain MacArthur had won wide recognition, according to a contemporary, as an able, energetic, and popular officer. To the MacArthurs, Arthur's career was convincing proof once again that a MacArthur possessed superior intellectual and leadership abilities and could master any field of his choosing. Outside the family, such would be dismissed as myth-weaving, but the MacArthurs believed it. Even the critic must admit that if Captain MacArthur's promising career had continued according to its already established pattern, he would have been a strong contender for chief of naval operations in the 1930's. In fact, he might have won distinction in World War II comparable to that which several of his Academy classmates attained who were his juniors in rank at the time of his death.

Of the three men who contributed to the MacArthur heritage, the influence of Arthur, III, on Douglas was the least, but it was by no means insignificant. No discerning parent would discount the impact on a young man of a successful older brother. The important factor, then, which Arthur contributed to the molding of his brother was the competitive stimulus; he was the pace setter for Douglas.

Despite the fact that most of Arthur's years in the Navy were spent far away from Douglas, the two brothers were close in their mutual feelings. Arthur named one of his sons for Douglas, and, interestingly, that son became the most prominent of his five offspring, attaining the positions of ambassador to Japan, Belgium, and Austria. In his memoirs Douglas commented: "I loved my brother dearly and his premature death left a gap in my life which has never been filled." [48]

The most enigmatic affinity within the family was between Douglas and his mother, a relationship which was strong until her death in 1935. The story of her life and of her dynamic impact on her son properly belongs with the story of Douglas' rise to chief of staff of the Army. The three Arthurs created the MacArthur heritage, both its myths and its realities. But it was Mary who preserved and nourished the heritage. It was she who somehow instilled in Douglas an almost mystical bond of unity with the family past and a burning desire to carry on and surpass the achievements of his predecessors. Indeed, few families in American history have produced more capable leaders in three successive generations than the MacArthurs.

CHAPTER II

Visions of Glory

1. Boyhood on the Frontier

NEW MEXICO was a wild frontier territory when the Mac-
Arthurs arrived there in the summer of 1880. The climate and
terrain were inimical to human habitation. The motley settlers were engaged in a war of survival against the hostile environment and against each other. A few scattered companies
of soldiers, a handful of civilian lawmen, and some hastily
formed vigilante committees constituted the only semblance of
law and order in the isolated region.

"It is a self evident truth," the Las Vegas *Gazette* reported in
November, 1880, "that New Mexico has been for years the asy-
lum of desperadoes. Mingled with as good people as are to be
found anywhere on the continent is the scum of society from
all states. We jostle against murderers, bank robbers, forgers,
and other fugitives from justice in the post office and on the
platform at the depot." The most talked-about desperado of
that time was William Bonney, alias "Billy the Kid," who had
terrorized northern and eastern New Mexico for several years.
Captured in late 1880, Bonney escaped from jail and was killed
at Fort Sumner, which was east of Fort Wingate in northern

New Mexico. The demise of Billy the Kid, however, brought no surcease to violence in the territory.[1]

For seven years prior to the MacArthurs' arrival, marauding bands of Apache had menaced travelers and residents of the region. After the killing of Victorio in 1880, the mantle of Apache leadership fell to Geronimo, a crafty, vicious Chiricahua who was determined to resist all efforts by whites to restrict his people to a reservation. Fear and insecurity gripped settlers as his Apache struck along the border in the ensuing months. Despite the presence of eleven forts in New Mexico and Arizona, Geronimo moved with boldness and impunity. Since Apache prisoners were often sent to Fort Wingate, MacArthur was expected to keep his troops in a state of readiness in case Geronimo tried to rescue the captives.[2]

Meanwhile the territorial officials, led by Governor Lewis Wallace, sat helplessly in their offices in Santa Fe. Handicapped in law enforcement by inadequate funds, poor communications, and a scattered populace, they could only hope that the rail and telegraph lines then being built across the territory would help the lawmen and soldiers in curbing outlawery. Besides, the governor's mind was often centered not on New Mexico's plight, but on a small land in the Near East. In mid-1880, about the time the MacArthurs moved to Fort Wingate, Wallace sent a manuscript which he had just completed to a publisher in New York. It was entitled *Ben Hur*.[3]

In the eyes of the MacArthurs' three young sons, life at Fort Wingate was packed with adventure. Stories and rumors of notorious outlaws circulated often in the little world within the walls of the fort. Indians, whether sullen Chiricahua prisoners or peaceful Navaho sheepherders, were a daily sight. Nearby ran the newly constructed line of the Atchison, Topeka, and Santa Fe Railroad, the sole contact with the civilized world. The mornings were filled with the cadenced sounds of barking sergeants and marching soldiers in close order drill. The crack-

ling of Krag rifles and the booming of field guns on practice
ranges were everyday noises as familiar to the ears of Douglas
as were factory whistles to young boys in the industrial district
of distant Pittsburgh. All of life seemed regulated by the crisp,
sometimes harsh, notes of bugles. Occasionally the boys' sleep
was punctuated by the violent scuffling of drunken soldiers
somewhere out in the dark. A troop of cavalrymen would in-
frequently stop at the fort, to the envy of the foot soldiers and
the delight of the children. With their tales of battles against
the Apache, the colorful cavalrymen upon their well-groomed
horses seemed to the boys like modern-day knights, surely the
most dashing of all troops. For young and old at Wingate, the
highlight of the year was the fourth of July when parades, shoot-
ing contests, sack races, and other competitions marked the joyous celebration from early morning until late in the evening.

The terrain around Fort Wingate was the most majestic and
beautiful a boy could imagine. Located nearly on the Continental Divide, the tiny fort was surrounded by mountains, some
rising to 11,000 feet. Nearby ran the cold, clear headwaters of
Rio Puerco, where the boys often went to wade and play while
the soldiers were drawing water for the fort's supply. There
were few toys and only a handful of playmates for the Mac-
Arthur boys, but the soldiers, lonely themselves, treated the
children of the post with special attention and affection. There
was also the blessing, from the children's viewpoint, of no
formal school. Education was a matter of tutoring by the mothers and probably was conducted in an irregular manner.[4]

For Mary MacArthur, the years at Fort Wingate, when her
sons were young and she was a novice among the Army wives,
were the most difficult of her life. With only a few women at
the post and perhaps none of them possessing the aristocratic
upbringing she had experienced, Mary must have enjoyed little
female companionship or social life. The cramped quarters offered little privacy, and few were the luxuries that women love

and find so necessary to their morale. The primitive adobe buildings, the worn pieces of furniture, the patched dresses, the dust from the drill ground which crept into every nook of the quarters — such depressing sights must have made her feel that she was trapped at the far edge of nowhere. Of the wives of his officers, Colonel Trobriand observed: "The ones whom I admire as much, at least as I pity, are these young women who brave all these mishaps — and for them I could even say suffering — with courage and even an heroic gaiety." Mary, who seldom showed her disappointment, was the type which Trobriand had in mind when he commented: "If they complain, it is with a rather resigned manner that clearly indicated that they foresaw all this and do not regret that they have exposed themselves to it. But most of the time, they have the good spirit to be the first to laugh at their misfortunes and prefer the funny side of things to the tragic." Mary's sternest test was the loss of Malcolm in the spring of 1883. Douglas recalled that his brother's death was "a terrible blow to my mother, but it seemed only to increase her devotion to Arthur and myself. This tie was to become one of the dominant factors of my life." She also nursed Douglas through attacks of diphtheria, measles, scarlet fever, and mumps during his childhood years. Despite the difficult adjustments and her heartache, Mary became an inspiring leader among the women of the post. A lady who remembered her during the hard years in New Mexico compared Mary to "a young falcon," with "her swift poise and the imperious way she held her head." Mary's eyes were "keen and soft at the same time," and "in my picture of her there is a lot of white muslin dress swishing around and a blaze of white New Mexican sunlight, and in the midst of it this slender, vital creature that I have never forgotten." [5]

The education and future of her two remaining sons must have been much on Mary's mind as she returned from Norfolk after Malcolm's burial. She may have considered sending the boys to school in Virginia, but her husband's salary precluded any plans to pay tuition fees, much less to maintain households in separate locations. Trobriand claimed that even a colonel with a wife and two children at a frontier post was compelled, because of his meager pay and the rough living conditions, to exist in a state of poverty, "in which not even appearances can be kept up." But Arthur was now eight years old and had never attended formal schooling, and Douglas would soon be of school age. On the long trip back to Wingate, Mary must have wondered what kind of future her sons faced when her husband could not hope even for a colonelcy until he neared retirement.[6]

When Captain MacArthur received orders in February, 1884, to move to Fort Selden on the Rio Grande, Mary must have shuddered at the news. She would be required to take her young sons on a 300-mile trek by foot and wagon during the blizzard season and at the height of Geronimo's depredations in the Southwest. Douglas recalled that he "trudged" beside Sergeant Peter Ripley "at the head of the column," though it is hard to imagine a four-year-old maintaining that position very long on the march. The route to Selden was down the banks of Rio Puerco to its confluence with the Rio Grande, a few miles south of Albuquerque, a journey of about 100 miles on the first leg. There the troops and wagons turned directly south, following the east side of the Rio Grande another 100 miles to Fort Craig, a landmark which had figured prominently in the Navaho and Apache campaigns of the 1850's and 1860's. Across the river the battle of Valverde had been fought in 1862, one of the first engagements of the Civil War in the Southwest. The final and most gruelling stretch of the journey was the last 100 miles, from Craig to Selden. Few houses were seen since the frontier movement had not yet penetrated the lower Rio Grande in New Mexico. The heat and aridity grew worse the farther south they moved. To their left almost the entire way from Fort Craig lay a huge alkali flat called White Sands. After a month of

marching the MacArthurs and Company K finally reached Fort
Selden. Tired and dirty, the adults were at least grateful that
they had encountered no hostile Indians. But the trip had been
high adventure for young Douglas. It and the death of Malcolm
were the only experiences of his first four years which he recalled in his memoirs.[7]

The journey had been an arduous one for the women, and
what they found at the end of the trail was not encouraging.
Except for being hotter and dustier, Fort Selden's adobe structures differed little from what they had left. Located on a knoll
overlooking the Rio Grande, the fort had been abandoned for
several years. With Geronimo on the warpath again, Major
General Nelson Miles, the department commander, had ordered its reactivation, but the War Department decided against
making it into a permanent post. Indeed, a few years after the
MacArthurs left Selden, it was abandoned again.

The major change from Wingate to Selden was the greater
degree of tension and anxiety at the latter, especially after May,
1885, when Geronimo and his Chiricahua again escaped from
the reservation in Arizona and resumed their raiding. Although
none of the Indian skirmishes occurred near Selden, there was
much more troop activity, with various cavalry units moving in
and out for provisioning. For the boys the increased troop
movements and talk of Geronimo were adventurous. Life at
Fort Selden, Douglas later commented, was "vivid and exciting
for me." From his point of view, it must have been disappointing when news came in the late summer of 1886 that Geronimo
had surrendered.[8]

It was at Selden, according to Douglas, that his mother, "with
some help from my father," began tutoring him in "the simple
rudiments" of education. Partly because of a lack of books and
partly because of her own strong convictions, Mary put the
stress on moral principles, particularly on developing "a sense
of obligation." "We were to do what was right," Douglas said,

"no matter what the personal sacrifice might be. Our country was always to come first. Two things we must never do: Never lie, never tattle."

It was during these years, too, that Douglas learned to ride a horse and shoot a rifle, achieving considerable skill in both. He and his brother must have led many gallant charges against imaginary Geronimos hiding in the sagebrush around the fort. Accompanying them in battle was Douglas' buddy, William Hughes, the son of an officer of Company K. "We were inseparable comrades then," Douglas said of the boy who in 1918 would serve beside him in the 42nd Division on the fields of Lorraine. Innocently expressing the secret desire of their father, the MacArthur boys envisioned themselves as dashing cavalry officers. Though they did not encounter any live Apaches in their skirmishes, the youngsters did reach a zenith of excitement one day when they met a camel, one of the survivors of the herd which Secretary of War Jefferson Davis had introduced as an experiment in supplying garrisons of the Southwest in the 1850's. With such experiences and adventures, the boys must have been puzzled when they overheard their parents yearning for orders to move to posts in the East.[9]

The transfer to Fort Leavenworth in the early autumn of 1886 meant a joyous return to civilization for the adults, but a departure from paradise for the children. As the train rolled toward Kansas and the beginning of a new future for the Mac-Arthurs, other children were busy in their own distantly separated worlds, unaware that someday their paths would intersect those of each other and of Douglas. A newborn male child named Chiang K'ai-shek played in his cradle in a poor farm house in Chekiang province in eastern China, while in a home in Japan another baby, Hideki Tojo, was learning to walk. Outside a mansion at Hyde Park, New York, four-year-old Franklin D. Roosevelt, bedecked in long blond curls and a dress, played on the shaded lawn. George C. Marshall, Jr., eleven months younger than Douglas, was learning to fish in Coal Lick Run, the creek behind his home in Uniontown, Pennsylvania. In a leaky hut east of the Black Sea, Josef Djugashvili, seven years of age, watched his peasant father mending shoes; someday the boy would be better known as Josef Stalin. Meanwhile Herbert C. Hoover, a youth who had been born on a small farm in Iowa in 1874, was now an orphan living with his uncle and picking potato bugs to earn his keep.[10]

2. Signs of Promise

At Fort Leavenworth, Douglas saw historical landmarks and heard stories of the fort's vital role in the development of the West. Built in 1827 on the banks of the Missouri near the starting points of the Sante Fe and Oregon trails, Leavenworth had served as a base for military escorts along those trails, as well as for the exploratory expeditions of Colonels Henry Dodge and Stephen Kearney. Indian treaty councils had met at the fort, which housed the Upper Missouri Indian agency for many years. During the so-called "Kansas War" between free-soil and pro-slavery forces in the turbulent fifties, Leavenworth had served for a time as the seat of the territorial government. The fort had functioned as a major training center and ordnance arsenal during the Mexican War and the Civil War. By 1886 it housed the headquarters of the Department of the Missouri, commanded by Brigadier General Wesley Merritt. It was also the location of one of the nation's largest military prisons and of the Army's principal advanced school for officers, the Infantry and Cavalry School. Thus from a small, temporary fort on the fringe of the frontier the MacArthurs had been transplanted to an installation which for over a half century had served as the hub of military operations west of the Mississippi River. Despite his initial disappointment over the move, Douglas experienced, in his words, "a never-ending thrill" watching the drills and parades of "the cavalry on their splendid mounts, the artillery with their long-barreled guns and caissons, and the infantry with its blaze of glittering bayonets." The color, excitement, and romance of the military life had cast a spell on the youngest MacArthur which would last his entire life.[11]

In his report to the War Department in 1888 General McCook, the commandant of the Infantry and Cavalry School, complained that housing for married officers at Leavenworth had deteriorated badly and should be brought up to the standards of forts in the East. He said that the quarters for his married officers were "very uncomfortable; but little privacy for them and almost without conveniences for health; no modern improvements in their apartments." But Captain and Mrs. MacArthur, with the adobe hovels of New Mexico fresh in their minds, had no complaints about the typical apartment which they were assigned in a large two-story frame house on officers' row.

Douglas, however, soon found a major grievance at Leavenworth, namely, the post school. By his own admission, he was "a poor student" during the three years of schooling which he endured there. His explanation was that "the freedom and lure of the West was [*sic*] still in my blood." He begged to go along when his father was temporarily assigned to Oklahoma during the land rush, but Captain MacArthur, pointing to his report card, rejected his son's scheme to escape classes. Added to his woes was the fact that his mother kept his brown hair in long curls and dressed him in skirts until he was about eight years old.[12]

When the MacArthurs moved to Washington, D.C., in July, 1889, young Douglas' unhappiness increased. With his father holding a desk job in the War Department and the family living in a residential area on Rhode Island Avenue, Douglas was completely separated from the soldiers' way of life for the first time. "Washington was different from anything I had ever known," he commented. "It was my first glimpse at that whirlpool of glitter and pomp, of politics and diplomacy, of statesmanship and intrigue. I found it no substitute for the color and excitement of the frontier West."

At the Force Public School on Massachusetts Avenue, Douglas reluctantly completed his schooling through the eighth grade in the next four years. He confessed that he was "only an average student," which was at least better than the poor rating he gave himself at the Leavenworth school. The annoyances of his life now included also a pair of glasses, which a physician in Washington prescribed to "strengthen his eyes," and the formal attire of tie and plaid tweed suit, which his mother made him wear to school every day. How wonderful life had been at Selden where he could go without shirt or shoes, ride his pony for hours, and shoot at rabbits in the sagebrush.[13]

During the years in Washington, Douglas must have heard his father, and Judge MacArthur, and the latter's influential friends discussing Populism, the rising political phenomenon in the Midwest. In the presidential election of 1892 the Populist candidate carried Kansas and three other Western states, and the new party was girding for a major nation-wide effort in the next presidential contest. On the surface the Populists seemed to be anti-militaristic and anti-imperialistic, but, as crises in Chile, Venezuela, and Cuba would reveal in the 1890's, they could be ballyhooed into espousing righteous wars for humanity, while at the same time opposing wars of conquest. Jingoism and Populism rose concurrently during that decade. Moreover, the Populists argued that the nation's troubles, augmented by a financial panic in 1893, were largely rooted in conspiracies born in decadent Europe, the leader of which was England, the center of the gold power. It would be farfetched to maintain that the thinking of a grade-school boy was influenced by the Populist ideology, but the coincidence between such Populist notions and some of the adult beliefs of Douglas is amazing.[14]

When his father received orders in the fall of 1893 to join the headquarters of the Department of Texas at Fort Sam Houston, Douglas was overjoyed at the prospect of residing at a military post again. Located just north of the Alamo at San Antonio, the fort was one of the country's largest, with two cavalry regiments, two infantry regiments, an artillery regiment, and a number of headquarters and auxiliary units stationed there. According to General Wheaton, the departmental commander, the Mexican border had for some time been "the scene of turbulence and disorder" because of revolutionists and outlaws who crossed back and forth along the Rio Grande in violation of neutrality and customs laws. Patrolling the river banks and chasing bandits along the border constituted the main combat-like activity of the Army in the early 1890's, and the command post was at Fort Sam Houston.[15]

Douglas' absorption in the busy activities at the fort was soon eclipsed, however, by his unexpected fascination with another institution. Two weeks before the MacArthurs moved to the fort, the Right Reverend J. S. Johnston, an Episcopal bishop, founded the West Texas Military Academy (later Texas Military Institute) on Government Hill, overlooking the city and adjoining the military reservation. The first church-operated school for boys in Texas, the academy offered, besides a small primary department, six "forms," or years of education roughly equivalent to the seventh through the twelfth grades. Johnston obtained the services of an officer at the fort to teach military science and required the students to wear "a braided uniform and cap of cadet grey." "In a military school," Johnston stated, "a boy most readily acquires the habits of neatness, attention and obedience. Besides the charm which exists in a military atmosphere, which tends to make one upright in principles and morals, as well as in bearing, there is, in a corps of young men where rank and promotion depend upon merit, a healthful incentive to excel found nowhere else." [16]

Shortly after the school year began in October, Major MacArthur entered Douglas in the academy's fourth form, or ninth grade, as a day student. Besides paying the tuition fee of $15.00 per twelve-week term and $13.50 for a cadet uniform, the major was required to provide Douglas with a Bible, prayer book, hymnal, six napkins, and a napkin ring. The campus at first was not very charming, with its solitary frame building and the grounds which, according to an early graduate, were "part grass and part dirt, in good weather, all mud in rainy weather." For the day students the school day began at 8:25 A.M. and ended at 5:55 P.M., which included classes, chapel services, military drills, and athletics. Most of the cadets were from San Antonio and the immediate vicinity, and some, like Douglas, were sons of officers at nearby Fort Sam Houston. As seems to be typical of academies for boys, the school had its share of miscreants who were enrolled apparently because neither their parents nor other schools could handle them. One graduate boasted that the corps of cadets consisted of "some of the meanest boys this side of hell." Nevertheless, under the competent leadership of its rector, the Reverend Allen L. Burleson, the academy grew rapidly in size and in its standard of excellence. During its first year West Texas Military Academy had forty-nine students, ten faculty members, and one structure. By the time Douglas graduated in 1897, the institution had grown to 115 cadets, sixteen teachers, and five buildings, and a number of colleges were accepting its graduates without entrance examinations.

The maturation of Douglas as a student and young man occurred at a rapid pace also during those four years. Exactly what his chief inspiration was — the military atmosphere, the able teachers, or the stage of young manhood which he had reached — is conjectural. But it was at this school that Douglas first showed signs of promise, and it was this period which he

later called "the happiest years of my life." "There came a
desire to know," he explained, "a seeking for the reason why, a
search for the truth. Abstruse mathematics began to appear as
a challenge to analysis, dull Latin and Greek seemed a gateway
to the moving words of the leaders of the past . . . My studies
enveloped me."

In his first year at the academy Douglas maintained an average of 96.3 of a possible 100 points and 95.15 the next year. A
classmate claimed that MacArthur "was doing Conic Sections
when the rest of us were struggling with Elementary Algebra."
At the commencement exercises at the end of his third year his
average of 97.65 earned him a citation for "superior excellence"
in scholarship; he was also awarded a medal for the highest average in mathematics. C. A. Dravo, a fellow cadet, said of Douglas:
"His ability to analyze a problem and arrive at a sound conclusion are just out of this world." At the graduating ceremony
on June 8, 1897, Douglas was awarded the coveted gold medal
for "the highest standing in scholarship and deportment," his
final year's average being 97.33. At that commencement he also
won medals in Latin, mathematics, and competitive speaking.
Rector Burleson considered him "the most promising student
that I have ever had in an experience of over ten years in schools
both North and South." [17]

Although his academic record was brilliant from the start at
West Texas, Douglas did not become active in extracurricular
activities for some time. Perhaps it was simply because, as a day
student, he was not as well known as the boarding students.
During his first two years he played on no athletic teams, held no
positions in the military organization, and was elected to no
student offices, except secretary of the literary society. Willard
Simpson, a classmate, remembered him as a "very modest" but
likable boy who did not assert his brilliance when in the company of other cadets. When Charles H. Quinn, a cadet and later
head of an engineering firm in California, became discouraged

during a final examination and at the end threw his paper into the waste basket, MacArthur retrieved the test, signed Quinn's name to it, and placed it on the teacher's desk. Quinn passed the examination, which was essential for his entrance into Purdue University the next fall, and thanked MacArthur decades later for saving his career. Slowly the cadets began to like and appreciate the wiry, handsome fellow who was outdistancing them in the classroom.

Suddenly in the third year Douglas' acceptance came, accelerated probably by the skill he displayed in varsity sports. That year he was a substitute on the football team, won the school's tennis championship, and played shortstop on the baseball team, which won seven out of eight games. In his last year he was the quarterback of the football team and guided it to an undefeated, unscored-on season. That spring, while continuing as shortstop, he was selected as manager of the baseball team, which also was unbeaten. MacArthur's forte was bunting; in one game he executed a bunt which allowed a runner to advance from first to third — a rare feat in the sport. In the military organization of the school he was promoted to first sergeant of his company and was selected for the Crack Squad, an elite drill unit of ten cadets which staged exhibitions at the city armory and at other schools. As his proud parents sat at the commencement exercises in June, 1897, while their son, the valedictorian, recited J. J. Roche's "The Fight of the Privateer *Gen. Armstrong*," their thoughts may have drifted back a few years to a young boy who despised tweeds, glasses, and school. Now that inexplicable spark which generates ambition and drive was burning deep inside him. Looking back on his experience at West Texas six decades later, Douglas put it simply, "This is where I started." [18]

Spiritually and socially the years in San Antonio were likewise ones of growth and change for him. On April 1, 1894, he was confirmed at St. Paul's Memorial Church, the ivy-covered stone Episcopal edifice near the academy where the cadets assembled

for chapel services daily. He noted that his spiritual awakening
occurred about the time that his interest in scholarship quickened: "Biblical lessons began to open the spiritual portals of a
growing faith." Socially, his development took the form of his
first dates, some of which were with girls of St. Mary's Hall, the
Episcopal female academy of the city. One young lady who
caught his attention was Amy Gillette, whom he came to visit
on "a many-gaited dun horse," according to her young cousin
who peeped at them. Another was Elizabeth Houston, remembered by a friend of Douglas as "one of the most popular and
beautiful girls of that day" in San Antonio. MacArthur and
Miss Houston led the grand march at the charity ball in 1897,
the outstanding event of the social season in the city. These
early romances were short-lived, however, since Cadet Mac-
Arthur was bent on West Point, not marriage. Interestingly,
both Amy and Elizabeth became spinsters, though Douglas can
hardly be blamed.[19]

In the spring of 1896 Douglas applied for an appointment at
large to enter the United States Military Academy in June, 1897,
upon his graduation from West Texas Military Academy. Judge
MacArthur, who would be dead in a few months, and Colonel
MacArthur persuaded a score of distinguished men to recommend Douglas. The letters in his behalf, which were addressed
to President Cleveland, included ones from four governors,
three senators, two representatives, two generals, and two bish-
ops. Except for a few like clergymen Johnston and Burleson,
the referees did not know Douglas well, if at all, and therefore
spent their words largely in praise of his father. A typical letter
ended: "This at least is a case that meets the Rule of Precedent
by which you have several times told me you would be governed
in such matters, that is, 'The deserving son of an Army officer,' and I beg to assure you, Mr. President, the father is as
deserving as the son." The son, however, did not get one of the
four presidential appointments.[20]

While his fellow graduates of the academy at San Antonio took jobs or entered college, Douglas — restless and anxious to launch his career — moved with his mother to a well-to-do hotel in Milwaukee, the Plankinton House, in October, 1897. His father, who had been transferred to the headquarters of the Department of the Dakotas at St. Paul, spent the weekends with his family in Milwaukee, 330 miles southeast of the Minnesota capital. The MacArthurs probably decided upon this living arrangement for two reasons, both in the interest of securing Douglas' entry into West Point. First, it would enable Douglas to establish residency in the congressional district of Representative Theabold Otjen, a friend of Judge MacArthur. Second, Douglas, who had developed a slight spinal curvature, could be placed under the care of Dr. Franz Pfister, a widely known specialist in Milwaukee.

For the next year and a half Douglas studied to prepare himself for the competitive examination in May, 1898, which would determine the appointee to the Military Academy from the fourth congressional district of Wisconsin. Besides reading profusely on his own, he entered classes at West Side High School for refresher courses in history, mathematics, English, and other subjects likely to be covered on the examination. He also received special tutoring from the popular principal, "Mac" McLanagan, and from Miss Gertrude Hull, a young, vivacious instructor of history at West Side who had just graduated from the University of Michigan. Both tutors took a keen interest in Douglas' determined effort to qualify for West Point. Miss Hull, said one of her pupils, "was an exceptional teacher, well versed in her subject, with the rather unusual talent of communicating her enthusiasm for this study to her pupils." On the day that the Treaty of Paris was announced, ending the Spanish-American War, McLanagan, playing a fife, led a victory parade of his students down the streets of Milwaukee. Liking his teachers and devoted to his studies, Douglas, according to one of the West

Side students, "was always there when we came in for class." "Every school day," Douglas said, "I trudged there and back, the two miles from the hotel to the school. I never worked harder in my life." [21]

Frank C. McCutcheon, the young assistant desk clerk at the Plankinton House, became a close friend of Douglas. The two would talk for hours about their future plans, with Douglas still convinced that his own career lay with the cavalry. When the war with Spain erupted and Douglas' father went to the Philippines, the boys, both tempted to volunteer for the action, avidly followed the movements of the armies and debated strategy. Mrs. MacArthur also became fond of Frank and, when her husband left St. Paul, gave him one of the colonel's fine silk hats, which, said McCutcheon, "makes a hat connection between the two families." Later a prominent businessman in Milwaukee and a lifelong friend of Douglas, McCutcheon recalled an incident at the Plankinton House one night when a fire broke out in a wall at one end of the structure. Douglas and his mother lived in that section of the hotel and barely escaped down the rear fire escape. When the fire was extinguished, apparently without serious damage, McCutcheon was amused at the sight of the MacArthurs — "a smutty faced boy and his equally smutty faced mother."

Among the close friends of the MacArthurs in Milwaukee was the Mitchell family. Alexander Mitchell and Judge MacArthur were staunch friends for four decades. When the judge was starting his career in Milwaukee before the Civil War, Alexander was a leading banker and railroad executive there, later serving in Congress. Their sons, John L. Mitchell and Douglas' father, served together in the 24th Wisconsin, their friendship continuing when John later became a banker and a United States senator. John, in fact, wrote a letter to the President recommending Douglas for West Point. While living in Milwaukee, Douglas dated one of John Mitchell's daughters and, smitten by love for the first time, dedicated his earliest known poem to her: "Fair Western girl with life awhirl / Of love and fancy free, / 'Tis thee I love / All things above / Why wilt thou not love me?" While on leave after the Cuban campaign of 1898, William Mitchell, John's son and later famed leader in the field of military aviation, became acquainted with Douglas, mainly at parties honoring William, considered a local hero. Contrary to a host of published statements, however, William and Douglas did not grow up together, and their early acquaintance was mainly because of the deeper ties between their fathers and grandfathers. William had not resided in Milwaukee since 1889 when he departed to attend school in Racine and later in Washington, D.C. Upon the termination of his leave in 1898 he was assigned to General MacArthur's command on Luzon where he participated in operations against the Filipino insurgents.[22]

After the inauguration of McKinley, Douglas had again tried to secure an appointment at large to the Military Academy, while at the same time continuing his preparation for the competitive examination for a congressional appointment. As late as February, 1898, referees' letters were sent to McKinley in his behalf. Like the earlier ones, however, most praised his father rather than Douglas. Senator Redfield Proctor of Vermont, for example, concluded: "All that I can say is, that I know of no officer who better deserves the privilege of having his son educated at West Point than MacArthur." Again a presidential appointment was not forthcoming.

On the morning of the long-awaited examination Mrs. MacArthur accompanied her son to the city hall. Nervous and nauseated, Douglas had been unable to sleep the previous night. His mother tried to reassure him: "Doug, you'll win if you don't lose your nerve. You must believe in yourself, my son, or no one else will believe in you. Be self-confident, self-reliant, and even if you don't make it, you will know you have done your best. Now, go to it." His mother's counsel and the long months of studying paid off. When the results of the examination were announced in June, 1898, MacArthur received the congressional appointment, having scored 93.3 on the test, sixteen points ahead of the next competitor. He later commented, "It was a lesson I never forgot. Preparedness is the key to success and victory." [23]

CHAPTER III

Monastery on the Hudson

1. The First Hurdle

SPORTING a light-colored fedora and accompanied by his mother, MacArthur stepped off the coach of the West Shore Railroad on a warm afternoon in early June, 1899, and cast his eyes for the first time on the buildings of the United States Military Academy. At a distance the granite structures of Tudor and Greco-Roman lines atop the west bank of the Hudson River seemed like a scene from a painting of medieval castles overlooking the Rhine. The rugged granite cliffs, the verdancy of the thickly wooded hills, and the broad sweep of the Hudson left an impression of isolated, majestic beauty. Riding in a horse-drawn coach up the steep incline from the railway station, the young man was probably impressed by the cold, grim appearance of the towered structures. Like other cadets before him, MacArthur may have compared the facilities to those of a penitentiary. Glimpsing the austere interiors of the buildings, especially the barracks, he may have thought of a strange monastery hidden from the beaten paths and existing as a world unto itself.

"The cadet who entered the West Point barracks the first day the institution opened its doors, nearly 100 years ago, found himself surrounded by almost as many comforts and conveniences as the cadet who entered last June," the academy's board of visitors commented caustically in a report the next year. Also in decrepit condition was Craney's Hotel, which was located on the northern edge of the West Point Plain and would be Mrs. MacArthur's residence until her husband's return in mid-1901. "It is, perhaps, because of the relation between cleanliness and godliness," the board of visitors said, "that so many ungodly remarks are provoked by even a temporary sojourn in this hotel." [1]

Traditionally the most difficult phase of the cadet's life was his first summer camp, before the first-year classes began in September. Through July and August, MacArthur and the other plebes, or fourth classmen, lived in "Beast Barracks" under the tutelage of the upperclassmen and were subjected to a rugged program of indoctrination and preliminary training. It was during these weeks that hazing was always at its worst. The practice, which involved sundry diabolical means of humiliating the newcomers and ridding them of conceit, arose mainly after 1865 as a substitute for amusements, which were direly lacking. By the time of MacArthur's arrival, hazing was widely, if secretly, espoused by upperclassmen, professors, and alumni as an essential step in orienting the plebes to the school's system of discipline and obedience. In its early stages the practice had consisted merely of innocent pranks, but by 1899 it encompassed vicious exercises which occasionally resulted in serious injury and even death. If the plebe refused the hazing, he was "called out" to fight with bare fists against a skilled pugilist of the upper classes until one fighter, almost always the younger cadet, was knocked unconscious. MacArthur was a good boxer, but was not impressive in size, standing five feet, eleven inches, and weighing 133 pounds that summer. He and most other plebes chose hazing, though on one occasion he did act as second for a poor plebe who preferred to fight.

During their first summer camp MacArthur and Ulysses S. Grant, III, were the plebes marked for special attention by the hazers. Word had quickly circulated that they were "mother's boys" since their mothers both resided at Craney's — indeed, an unusual phenomenon at West Point. Assuming that cadets descended from famous persons were bound to be conceited and obnoxious, the upperclassmen cruelly tormented the two youths, yet without slighting the other plebes. The preferred target was MacArthur since his father, leading the forces in the Philippines, was often in the headlines that summer. "We always prepared a warm reception for the sons of well-known men," said Robert E. Wood, a first classman and later head of Sears, Roebuck, and Company, and "the well-known man in this instance was General Arthur MacArthur." An additional strike against Douglas was his looks — "the handsomest young man I have ever seen," remarked Cadet Hugh S. Johnson, later chief of the National Recovery Administration.[2]

Among the lighter forms of hazing to which he was subjected, MacArthur was required to "make funny speeches," recite his father's military record, "take a turtle and go through the formations of parade" with the turtle "representing a battalion," and hang by his toes and fingers from a cot until he dropped in exhaustion to the floor. One night, however, he was taken by some upperclassmen into a darkened tent and required to perform 250 "spread eagles" and 200 "wooden willys," the ground around him deliberately strewn with bits of broken glass. "Eagling" meant "standing on his toes with his arms extended, dropping down to a sitting posture, rising part way, waving his arms like wings, again depressing his body to a sitting posture, rising in like manner." "Wooden willying" involved "taking the regulation gun and drawing it up to the position of 'fire,' then dropping it to the position of 'ready,'" and, as in the case of "eagling," repeating the exercise until the hazers tired of the amusement. MacArthur, however, fell unconscious before satisfying his tormentors. When he awakened, he suffered severe convulsions, with his arms and legs jerking uncontrollably. Plebe Frederick H. Cunningham, his roommate, said that Mac-Arthur "finally asked me to throw a blanket under them [his feet] in order that the company officers could not hear his feet striking the floor." On another occasion, when he had recuperated, some upperclassmen gave him a "sweat bath," wherein they made him dress in full uniform, don a raincoat, wrap blankets tightly around himself, and sit through a hot night inside a small closed tent. To the surprise of the older cadets, MacArthur took the hazing and other rigors of summer camp with "fortitude and dignity," according to Wood, who added: "I recall that all members of the First Class watched him for any signs of weakness, but he emerged from camp with flying colors. He showed himself a true soldier." [3]

Although hazing was privately condoned by many members of the staff, there was a regulation of the academy forbidding the practice, the penalty being dismissal. The rule also contained a curious provision whereby the victim was considered "equally guilty with the hazing party." When the superintendent heard of the severe hazing that summer, which was worse than usual, he launched an investigation. MacArthur was summoned to testify and name his tormentors. The fear of dismissal, together with his mother's admonition that "the world will judge largely of mother by you," convinced him that "come what may, I would be no tattletale." He refused to give the names to the superintendent.

When Cadet Oscar L. Booz died after being repeatedly and savagely hazed by members of MacArthur's class the next year, investigations of hazing at the academy were undertaken by a military court of inquiry at Governors Island, New York, and later by a special committee of the United States House of Representatives. MacArthur was questioned at both hearings about the actions of hazers whose names had been obtained from cadets testifying earlier. The rule implicating the recipient of hazing had been stricken from the academy regulations by then, but MacArthur still dreaded appearing before the examiners. Suffering from nausea, the embarrassing sickness which hit him during moments of crisis, he reluctantly divulged the details of his own hazing as a plebe under the sharp questioning of the court of officers. In a longer, more grueling experience before the congressional committee, he told what he knew of hazing and hazers at the academy, the congressmen already having most of the facts and all of the names. MacArthur made it clear that he was adamantly opposed to hazing, but felt that hazing during his plebe year had been exaggerated. He stated that the hazing to which he was subjected was rather ordinary and that he would not have suffered convulsions if he had not already been exhausted from the seventeen-hour work day in summer camp. Noticing the pallid look of Cadet MacArthur, who again felt a desire to vomit, one congressman quipped, "You do not look very robust now." The cadet hastily explained that he was not suffering ill effects from hazing. MacArthur and the other cadets called before the committee were finally allowed to return to their studies, and some of the guilty cadets were dismissed from the academy. In March, 1901, Congress passed a law forbidding acts against plebes which were "of a harassing, tyrannical, abusive, shameful, insulting or humiliating nature, or that may endanger the physical well-being of such candidate or cadet." For the remainder of MacArthur's time at West Point and for a number of years afterward, severe hazing was not a major problem on the Plain.[4]

2. *The Academic Regimen*

When classes began in September, 1899, Plebe MacArthur was fortunate to share a room in the central barracks' tower with Arthur P. S. Hyde, a first classman who had been sergeant and adjutant at "Beast Barracks" and later in life would become an Episcopal minister. "During camp," said Hyde, "I had occasion to watch MacArthur's activities rather closely and had been impressed with his attention to duty and his manifest determination to make good as a cadet." When Hyde invited him to share his quarters, MacArthur, to the amusement of the upperclassman, "asked for time to run over to the hotel to talk to his mother about my invitation. In half an hour he was back with word that he would be glad to accept."

Being in a first classman's room meant that MacArthur enjoyed the privilege of keeping the lights on until 11:00 P.M., an hour later than cadets below the first class were allowed. He studied until the last minute "every night," Hyde claimed, and "often was up an hour before reveille." MacArthur was "one of the hardest working men I have ever known," his roommate commented, and "his every energy was directed to the attainment of . . . number one in his class." Hyde said that MacArthur "often" talked of his father "with affection and pride" and felt deeply obligated to become "a worthy successor" of the general.[5]

MacArthur had not attended many classes before he became aware of the staff's dedication to the institution's traditional ways and refusal to consider changes in the content or method of instruction. Perpetuated by an elderly faculty, several of whom had served in the Civil War, and by intensely loyal alumni, the academy's conservatism was at its apex when MacArthur entered. Once a leader in some disciplines, particularly engineering, West Point had gradually secluded itself from the changing currents of higher education. Its instructional methods, with emphasis on memorization and "frontboard recitations," had been discarded by the more progressive schools, such as the University of Chicago and Johns Hopkins University, where the stress was now on novel methods and creative ideas. Most colleges prided themselves on the diversity of schools from which their professors came, but at West Point inbreeding was nourished as a bulwark against disturbing the status quo. One concerned graduate of 1862 lamented at the turn of the century that in the intervening four decades he had sadly watched "West Point fall from the level of a university to that of a post school at a garrison."

Some reform-minded persons claimed that West Point was indifferent toward advances in weapons, tactics, and strategy and was not actually preparing its graduates to be military officers. Lieutenant John J. Pershing, who served on the teaching staff in 1897–98, tried to update the instruction in tactics but incurred "stony hostility" from his superiors and finally "got the message — avoid original ideas and above all do not interrupt the even flow of lethargy." Referring to the academy's five decades following the Civil War, a noted authority on its history says: "West Point, which before the Civil War had been ahead of the army in its thought and methods was after that conflict providing instruction that was increasingly irrelevant to the needs of the army." The general consensus of many critics was that the school was deficient both as a military institute and a college of higher learning. Although a new building program was inaugurated toward the end of MacArthur's cadetship, there were few signs that West Point would adapt to new techniques in education or warfare.[6]

Traditionalism was apparent in the curriculum which MacArthur encountered. In contrast with the trend toward electives in the civilian schools, the academy stayed rigidly with its program of required courses from the plebe year to graduation. Except for the addition of four courses (most recently Spanish, in view of the Philippine acquisition), the curriculum was the same as that established by Superintendent Sylvanus Thayer nearly a century previous. The time and attention given to various disciplines was indicated by the number of "merits," or points, they were accorded on the general merit roll, which decided the cadet's class standing and eligibility for commission in the several arms of the Army. Mathematics, valued at 400 merits, dominated the curriculum, being more than the combined merits of the last four subjects. Natural and experimental philosophy was worth 300 merits, as was also civil and military engineering. Next came the physical sciences of chemistry, physics, mineralogy, and geology, together valued at 225 merits. The remaining subjects ranked as follows: French, 150; ordnance and gunnery, 150; history, 100; Spanish, 85; drill regulations, 75; English, 50; and practical military engineering, 45. On the general merit roll another 400 merits were allotted for the nonacademic categories of conduct, soldierly deportment and discipline, and military efficiency. Demerits were charged for disciplinary offenses, not classroom deficiencies. Answering the critics who charged that the program was ill designed to prepare an officer to lead cavalry, infantry, or artillery, the defenders of the system maintained that the academy's principal task was to develop character and wholehearted devotion to duty, honor, and country. Its secondary function was to provide the cadet with a sound foundation in the disciplines upon which his future technical training and experience would be based.[7]

The method of teaching varied little from discipline to discipline. The cadets were expected to memorize the daily assignment, and most of the time in class was spent in monotonous recitation by rote, either orally or on the blackboard. The instructor, whose main function was to grade the cadets' performances, rarely lectured or explained the material. In a typical instance, a cadet asked a question about the content of the lesson, whereupon the instructor responded, "I'm not here to answer questions, but to mark you." Grades were assigned on the basis of the students' preparation and proper presentation of the daily assignment, with little opportunity or stimulus for provocative discussions, conflicting ideas, or experimentation. MacArthur, who enjoyed analysis and inquiry, nevertheless bent with the system, aware that a lowly cadet could not change it. His high marks were based mainly on his thorough preparation and ability to retain the material, though had there existed an effective measure of intelligence, he probably would have scored well.[8]

If not distinguished or progressive, the faculty was capable within its limits. Superintendent Albert L. Mills was a brevet colonel with a permanent rank of captain of cavalry, though in 1904 he would be suddenly elevated to brigadier general. Mills lost an eye fighting in Cuba in 1898, but was awarded the Medal of Honor for his gallantry in action there. Regarded as the father of the school's modern building program, he unfortunately limited his energy in reconstruction to plans for the physical plant and was quite conservative on academic matters. Colonel Peter S. Michie, a veteran of McClellan's campaigns in Virginia and the owner of an impressive long, black beard, wrote several learned works. A sensitive man of deep religious convictions, he had a penchant for expounding his beliefs on spiritual matters in his classes in natural and experimental philosophy, none of the students daring to disagree. The head of the department of modern languages was Colonel Edward E. Wood, who had enlisted in the Civil War at fifteen, rising to regimental adjutant before the end of the conflict. Though competent in French grammar, the tobacco-chewing Wood omitted conversational French from his courses since he could not speak the language himself. Lieutenant Colonel Otto T. Hein, commandant of cadets and head of the department of tactics, had recently come from a tour of duty as military attaché in Vienna. Having learned much about the German Army, he gradually altered West Point's instruction in tactics, which had been based on the wars of the early nineteenth century, and also began introducing the cadets to Gatling guns, attack formations, and many other contingencies of actual service in combat. Two members of the staff later became superintendents of the academy, though neither they nor their terms at the helm were distinguished: Colonel Samuel E. Tillman, professor of chemistry, mineralogy, and geology since 1880, and Captain Fred W. Sladen, an assistant instructor of tactics. Two of the more capable instructors were Captain Joseph E. Kuhn, future head of the Army War College, and Captain Johnson Hagood, who rose to prominence with the A.E.F. services of supply in World War I.

MacArthur was an excellent student in most of his classes and undoubtedly enjoyed good relations with his professors, with one notable exception. The only known clash between him and a professor probably occurred toward the end of his second year. As the academic term neared its closing in May, 1901, it was generally known that MacArthur would rank first in his class, as he had the previous year. But when the list of cadets required to take the final examination in mathematics was announced, MacArthur was shocked to learn that he was not exempt. It was customary to excuse students from the final examination if they maintained a certain high average, and MacArthur knew his average was the highest in the class. Enraged, he ran to the residence of Lieutenant Colonel Wright P. Edgerton, the head of the department. Edgerton calmly informed him that, in order to be exempt, a cadet, besides maintaining the stipulated average, must take two thirds of the quizzes in the course. MacArthur, who had been hospitalized that spring with a minor illness, lacked one quiz in meeting this requirement. He boldly insisted that Edgerton should have told him of this additional requisite and allowed him to make up the quiz. Edgerton, who had come to the academy only eight months before MacArthur and may have lacked the assurance of the older, established professors, patiently tolerated the cadet's effrontery. Finally MacArthur proclaimed that he would not be present at the examination. Edgerton made no response, so the exasperated cadet saluted and stormed back to his barracks. George W. Cocheu, his roommate at the time, asked, "What are you going to do?" "If my name is not off that list before 9:00 in the morning," MacArthur exclaimed, "I'll resign!" At 8:50 A.M. the next day, ten minutes before the examination began, an orderly came to MacArthur's room with a message from Edgerton excusing him from the examination. Possibly echoing MacArthur, Cocheu concluded from the experience that MacArthur believed it was his duty to obey an order, "no matter how disagreeable," but "to be turned out unjustly" affronted his "personal honor." [9] The incident is significant in revealing not only the amazing tolerance of the professor but also the first known manifestation of MacArthur's acute sensitivity when his pride and honor seemed to be at stake. Perhaps it was well that the schedule did not require him to take any more courses in mathematics.

Like his academic record at San Antonio, MacArthur's work in the section rooms at West Point was outstanding from plebe year onward. He ranked first in his class for three of his four years, dropping from the top (to fourth) only in his third, or second-class, year. He earned 2424.12 merits of a possible 2470.00, or 98.14 per cent, for the four-year program. In the standings on the general merit roll of the ninety-four-man class which graduated in 1903, there was a greater difference between MacArthur's total of merits and that of Charles T. Leeds, who finished second, than between Leeds' total and that of the cadet in fifth place. Grant, who offered MacArthur his keenest competition for first place in their plebe year, had fallen from the list of "distinguished cadets" (the top five) by the time of graduation. Harold C. Fiske, who held the first position in MacArthur's class in their third year, graduated in third position. MacArthur led his class in mathematics, English, drill regulations, history, ordnance and gunnery, law, and military

efficiency. In English, history, and law he earned 100 per cent
of the possible merits. His weakest showings were in practical
military engineering and in drawing, ranking thirty-seventh
and twenty-fourth, respectively. His position of twenty-seventh
in demerits was "earned" by committing such infractions as
"long hair at inspection," "slow obeying call to quarters,"
"trifling with drawn sabre," "absent from room at inspection,"
and "swinging arms excessively while marching." None of the
citations against him on the "skin sheets" were for major violations, though without Edgerton's mercy he might have finished
very poorly in demerits. As for his overall record, some have
claimed that his was the academy's best in twenty-five years,
while others said it was the highest since that of Robert E. Lee
(98.33 per cent) of the class of 1829. A fair comparison of
cadets' records from different classes over long spans of time is
impossible because the content of the curriculum and the system of grading changed. It can be safely claimed, nevertheless,
that MacArthur's score on the general merit roll was one of
the highest in the history of the academy.[10]

3. *Outside the Classroom*

In the military organization of the corps of cadets MacArthur
progressed steadily upward in rank. He served as a corporal in
Company B in his second year and first sergeant of Company
A the next year. During his final year on the Plain he held
the positions of captain of Company A and first captain of the
corps of cadets, the latter being the highest military honor a
cadet could receive. "He was the First Captain in fact as well
as in name," said Cocheu, who pointed to an incident in the
spring of 1903 when the waiters in the mess hall suddenly quit
just before the noon meal one day, probably striking for higher
wages. Colonel Charles G. Treat, who had recently succeeded

Hein as commandant of cadets, appealed to the noisy, annoyed cadets at mealtime to "put up with the situation" until the waiters returned or new ones were hired. Cocheu, who was present during the "chaos" that noon, stated: "When the Colonel had finished making his appeal, MacArthur, the First Captain, got up to speak. He did not *ask* the Corps to do anything. He *told* them, in plain words, just what they would do. And they did it." Wood recalled that three years earlier, when he was a first classman and MacArthur a plebe, many of the older cadets had "recognized intuitively that MacArthur was born to be a real leader of men." [11]

In the realm of sports Cadet MacArthur was not outstanding, but did gain the distinction of scoring a run in the first varsity baseball game against the midshipmen of the United States Naval Academy. The contest was played at Annapolis on an overcast day in May, 1901, and was won by the Army team, 4–3. Besides scoring what may have been the winning run (the accounts vary), left-fielder MacArthur stole a base, but got no hits and caught no flies. He won his varsity letter and played on the team again in the spring of 1902, gaining recognition as a dependable fielder but a light hitter. Weighing about 135 pounds, he wisely did not try out for the football team, but was one of its most ardent fans and served as its manager in the fall of 1902. A varsity basketball team was organized during his last year, with its star being Joseph W. Stilwell, commander in Burma during the future war against Japan. MacArthur probably became an enthusiastic supporter of the physical fitness program — one of the first in American institutions of higher education — which Lieutenant Herman J. Koehler, instructor in the department of tactics and former national champion in gymnastics, introduced at the academy. Like Koehler, MacArthur believed that all cadets should develop adequate fitness and skill to be able to enjoy some form of athletics, even if only a few could play at the varsity level.

After MacArthur's departure from the Plain, President Theodore Roosevelt, a zealous advocate of physical fitness, ordered that all classes participate in Koehler's program of exercise, the fourth class being the only required participants formerly.[12]

Other than on the athletic field, West Point offered little in the way of organized recreation and amusements, and cadets were seldom permitted to step beyond the gates. They had to obtain special passes to go to Craney's Hotel on the edge of the Plain and got such permission only to visit their parents. The only student organizations were the Y.M.C.A. and the Dialectical Society. The latter sponsored the Hundredth Night, a festive evening of songs, jokes, and skits which marked the point when there were 100 days left before graduation for the first class and elevation for the other classes. Only one furlough was given, during the summer after the third year; no Christmas leaves were granted. "West Point was like a monastery," Wood observed, "separated as it was from the outside world. Cadets could only leave the reservation when they went on horseback, and then they were on their honor not to dismount or halt." Under close supervision the corps of cadets was permitted to attend its football team's out-of-town games when held at New York, Annapolis, or Philadelphia, and sometimes the corps marched in parades in various cities of the Northeast. On one occasion during MacArthur's third-class year, Colonel Mills, a cavalryman, allowed the cadets to attend, en masse and under careful chaperoning, a major horseshow in New York. Somehow MacArthur, Charles F. Severson, his roommate at the time, and "Dotty" Laurson, a first classman, managed to slip away. MacArthur said that the three "swaggered into Rector's on Broadway, shook hands with 'Diamond Jim' Brady, and called for nine martinis . . . And then we swanked out to a burlesque show. We loved it!" Such escapades were rare, however, since the penalty could be suspension or dismissal.[13]

When the heavy schedule of sections, drills, and studying permitted, the academy did sponsor a few dances each year, most of the girls coming from New York and the fashionable female schools of the region. On those rare occasions MacArthur, who was manager of one of the hops, fully enjoyed the "excitement and gay hours with beautiful ladies." Once an officer caught him "publicly kissing a girl" on Flirtation Walk, grinned at the embarrassed cadet, offered his congratulations, and walked away. MacArthur remembered it as an "awful moment," needlessly fearing that the officer would report him. He was later credited with engagements to eight girls during his days as a cadet, which he denied in an often-repeated retort: "I do not remember being so heavily engaged by the enemy." Cocheu, his roommate during their final two and a half years, said that MacArthur did not discuss his dates with him. Nevertheless, a record remains of one young lady's impression of Cadet MacArthur. For a program dance one Saturday night in February, 1903, Miss Bess B. Follansbee of Brooklyn accepted a blind date with him, which was arranged by a mutual friend, Cadet James Mars. It began snowing heavily as she left New York by boat that afternoon, and the grounds at West Point were buried beneath a fresh blanket of snow by the time she arrived. After the dance she returned to her room at Craney's Hotel and wrote in her diary: "I liked him [MacArthur] immensely and thought him a splendid dancer. He is tall, slim, dark with a very bright, pleasant manner." The next afternoon MacArthur and several other cadets visited their dates of the previous evening at Craney's, the hotel being off limits except for the purpose of visiting parents and then only by written permission. Bess later recorded in her diary: "We sat in the hall of the Hotel, where there was an old-fashioned iron stove burning, and talked until Mrs. MacArthur (Douglas' mother) announced that an officer was just arriving at the Hotel, to make a call, and the cadets had better hide. Immediately they put on their overcoats and hid downstairs . . . Fortunately the call of the officer was brief and our callers soon returned from their hiding places."

Mrs. MacArthur served as the cadets' reliable lookout on a number of occasions. Cocheu remembered an incident when he and Douglas were "visiting in the hotel's back parlor" with some young ladies. Mrs. MacArthur rushed in with news that the superintendent was approaching. "The only way out," according to Cocheu, "was through the cellar, so it was there that we ran, and we escaped, undetected, by crawling through the coal shute." In many instances Mrs. MacArthur provided Douglas and his friends with "fruit and other delicacies." It is no wonder that his mother, whose presence made her and her son subject to ridicule at first, was eventually regarded with strong affection by many cadets. After all, she played an important role in the young Casanovas' stolen hours at the hotel.[14]

Cadet MacArthur may have been involved in some shenanigans, but, contrary to legend, he was not regarded by his fellows as one of the leading pranksters. For many years after his graduation he was credited with the best-known trick of that era of West Point — hoisting the reveille gun to the tower of one of the academic buildings. Recently, however, it has been proven that this notable exploit was performed by some plebes during MacArthur's second-class year. Cocheu regarded Charles F. Thompson of the class of 1904, later a major general, as one of the most notorious pranksters: "Nothing happened to that class while cadets, or even after, that he was not mixed up in." Hugh Johnson, who finished fifty-third in MacArthur's class, also was a prominent mischief-maker, who "rebelled at the rules, hated to study, looked sloppy and was generally a most likable fellow." When the corps went to Washington to participate in the inaugural parade for McKinley in January, 1901, MacArthur was assigned to a room in the Ebbett House with Johnson and some other cadets. While MacArthur was out of the room on the evening before the parade, Johnson

staged a wild battle scene from *Macbeth,* during which he drew
his sword and pinioned MacArthur's shako, or dress hat, to the
door. There it hung when MacArthur returned, his reaction
being unrecorded.[15]

The principal event in the life of West Point during the
years 1899–1903 was the centennial celebration, held during
the week of graduation in June, 1902. The days were filled with
reviews, speeches, and athletic competitions, as well as parties
and dances, the events coming to a climax on graduation day
when President Roosevelt awarded the diplomas. The guests
that week included high-ranking dignitaries from Washington
and several foreign countries and also veterans of all American
wars of the previous sixty years. The speakers paid tribute to
the heroism and leadership of the institution's graduates, especially of the last four years when West Pointers played key
roles in the combat against the Spanish and later the Filipinos,
with sixteen graduates losing their lives. President Roosevelt,
after reviewing the corps, presented the Medal of Honor to
Calvin P. Titus, a plebe who had earned the award for his
gallantry as an infantryman while fighting against the Boxers at
Peking in 1900. Lieutenant General John M. Schofield, a hero
of the Civil War and former Secretary of War, reminded the
cadets in one of the major addresses that "the Corps of Cadets
has always been a real American aristocracy — an aristocracy
of character." Another high moment of the centennial was
the unveiling of a plaque commemorating the milestone. In
part, the inscription read: "Let us all pledge ourselves to our
country that the best efforts of our lives shall be to make the
record of the second century even more memorable than that
of the first." [16]

Major General MacArthur obtained a leave from his duties
at San Francisco to attend his son's graduation at West Point
on June 11, 1903. As he watched the impressive ceremonies and
listened to Secretary of War Elihu Root warn the graduating

cadets to prepare for the war which was "bound to come" in
their time, General MacArthur may have drifted in thought
back to the spring of 1861 when he, too, dreamed of attending
the elite "school for future generals." At the present age of
Douglas, twenty-three, he had been an infantry captain, the
rank he was to hold for over two decades. Now his son was
graduating first in his class, with a commission as second lieutenant in the corps of engineers, currently considered to be the
most desirable branch of the Army. On the other hand, Douglas, who confided to his roommate that "next to his family, he
loved West Point," was solemnly aware that from henceforth
he must strive to be worthy of two proud heritages — that of
the MacArthurs and the illustrious record of the "Long Gray
Line." Douglas' devotion to the academy was deep, and his
loyalty would be steadfast the rest of his life. At an emotion-
packed ceremony on the Plain fifty-nine years later, he would
tell the young cadets assembled in his honor: "In the evening
of my memory, always I come back to West Point. Always there
echoes and re-echoes in my ears — Duty — Honor — Country
. . . When I cross the river my last conscious thoughts will
be of the Corps — and the Corps — and the Corps." [17]

CHAPTER IV

Travels and Tribulations
of a Young Engineer

1. Adventures in Asia

THE YEAR 1903 found Americans singing "Sweet Adeline," reading *Rebecca of Sunnybrook Farm,* and watching the pioneer motion picture, "The Great Train Robbery." They talked excitedly about the strange-looking machine which flew over the sand dunes at Kitty Hawk, the great strike which paralyzed the anthracite coal mines, the muckrakers' exposés of the machinations of John D. Rockefeller and other robber barons, and the swirl of reforms introduced by the Progressives, the latest crusaders for political, economic, and social justice. John Philip Sousa's new march, "The Stars and Stripes Forever," caught the aura of chauvinism which made the nation's experiment in empire seem a glorious enhancement of American prestige. With the old qualms against imperialism now quieted, the people reveled in the vigorous leadership of President Roosevelt, who that year could boast of the seizure of Panama from Colombia, the protectorate forced upon Cuba, the pacification of Puerto Rico, and the continuing consolidation of American control over the Philippines. So absorbed were they in the happenings at home and in their new imperial realm, few Americans noticed the headlines proclaiming Germany's plans for a Berlin-to-Baghdad railway or Japan's demand that Russia evacuate Manchuria.

The American Army in 1903 faced managerial and technological changes which would soon propel it along the road toward modernization. Early that year Congress approved a bill creating the General Staff, a body which would ultimately lead the way toward eliminating much of the War Department's disharmony and inefficiency and would produce the first long-range plans for mobilization and war. Another measure, the Dick Act, provided for making the cumbersome, politics-ridden National Guard a more effective reserve component. The Regular Army's authorized strength was set by Congress at a record peacetime ceiling of 100,000 men, a small figure compared to that of the major European armies, but four times the size of the United States Army a decade earlier. Furthermore, the service schools were reorganized, and some new ones established, including the Army War College, which opened its doors in November, 1903. In weapons, the Army was beginning to update its arsenal. The Springfield Model 1903 was adopted as the standard rifle for infantrymen, which it would remain for three decades. The field artillery now had a new three-inch gun which employed smokeless powder, optical sights, and recoilless mechanism; it would prove at least as good as the French 75-mm. gun of World War I. There were a few automatic machine guns, designed by John M. Browning, but the deadly effectiveness of the weapon was not then appreciated. Nor were the ramifications of the new internal combustion engine fully comprehended as sounding the eventual death knell of conventional cavalry and horse-drawn transportation. Although the Wright brothers' heavier-than-air craft was successful, an Army-subsidized experiment that same year by Samuel P. Langley ended with his airplane crashing into the

Potomac; military tests of aircraft were subsequently post-poned for five years. Thus at the time that MacArthur entered the Regular Army as a second lieutenant, the military establish-ment was on the threshold of a new era, but the full implica-tions of the recent developments were dimly seen in 1903. Moreover, many Americans, including some influential military men, were affected by the Rooseveltian contagion of conceiving of warfare in the romantic, histrionic terms of the Spanish-American War. For them, war was a matter which concerned professional soldiers and, on a temporary basis, some citizen-soldiers; but it did not involve the masses, weapons of mass destruction being unthinkable and armies of huge proportions unnecessary.[1]

MacArthur's first two months as a lieutenant were spent on furlough with his parents at Fort Mason, San Francisco. There his father, the commander of the Division of the Pacific, was busily preparing his critique of the War Department's plan for organizing the General Staff, a copy having been sent to him for comment. The general, who must have discussed the docu-ment at length with his son, returned it with a scathing denun-ciation of nearly every section. His main criticisms revolved about the nature of the office of chief of staff, and he felt strongly that the position should go to the highest-ranking of-ficer: "There is probably no principle of military ethics more firmly established than the proposition that rank is absolutely essential to give proper effect to authority in all military trans-actions." Douglas also had an opportunity to sit as observer at a meeting in his father's office when a number of important political, business, and military leaders, including George C. Pardee, governor of California, and Edward H. Harriman, rail tycoon, were discussing plans to expand the state's international trade. Douglas recalled that the germinal idea for an artificial harbor at Los Angeles came from his father, though authorities on California's history have not since given him this credit.

Besides meeting some influential persons, Douglas also encountered and captured an escaped prisoner from the guardhouse at Fort Mason. All in all, it was, as Douglas phrased it, "a pleasant summer." [2]

At the end of his furlough MacArthur joined the 3rd Engineer Battalion, which was preparing to embark for the Philippines. The unit arrived at Manila in late October, 1903, after three weeks at sea. All of the engineers probably hoped for assignment in Manila because of the city's cosmopolitan atmosphere and sundry attractions. Also, since diehard bands of guerillas still roamed the outlying provinces, it was the safest place for Americans. After three days in the city, however, MacArthur was assigned as assistant to Captain Thomas H. Jackson, chief engineering officer of the Department of the Visayas, and was sent to Iloilo, a primitive port on the southern coast of Panay, over 300 miles south of Manila. There he took charge of completing a wharf, retaining wall, and earthen fill at the landing at Camp Jossman. His assignment was typical for the battalion's junior officers, who were sent to various parts of the archipelago searching for suitable sites for military installations, surveying the chosen locales, and preparing landings and facilities for incoming garrisons. After completing the task at Iloilo in two weeks, MacArthur was sent to survey military reservations at Tacloban, Leyte, in November and December; at Calbayog, Samar, in January, 1904; and at Cebu, Cebu, in February. He also served on a board of inquiry which investigated the sinking of an Army transport off Polompon, Leyte. Brigadier General Theodore J. Wint, commanding the Visayas when MacArthur came, and his successor, Brigadier General Charles H. Carter, both rated MacArthur "excellent" in all categories of their efficiency reports on him, Carter adding that he "appears to be an active, capable officer who needs only experience to fit him for any military work."

Lieutenant MacArthur was off to a good start, but the experience in the Visayas included one incident which almost cost him his life. In early November, 1903, he accompanied a party of engineering troops to Guimaras, an island off the harbor of Iloilo, where they were to cut timber for pilings. Walking along a narrow trail in the jungle some distance from the chopping detail, MacArthur was ambushed by a pair of guerillas or bandits, one of their shots ripping through the top of his campaign hat. Quickly returning their fire with his pistol, he killed both of the Filipinos. What were his feelings as he looked down on the corpses of the first humans he killed? Unfortunately nothing is known, but, like most soldiers at their first killing, he must have felt revulsion and shock. In his individual service report for the year, he wrote: "Participated in no battles, engagements, or actions." In his memoirs he recalled only his expertness with the pistol and a sergeant's reaction that "the rest of the Loo'tenant's life is pure velvut." [3] Perhaps later he contemplated the irony of his baptism of fire, which had come quickly and unexpectedly and not against professionals of a powerful enemy but against peasants of a nation which his country was trying to pacify and to which he later became deeply devoted.

In March, 1904, MacArthur was transferred to Manila as disbursing officer of his battalion and assistant to Major Charles D. Townsend, chief engineering officer in the Philippines. A month later he was promoted to first lieutenant. Much of his work now was confined to a desk, but he did oversee surveys of military reservations at Caloocan and Mariveles, the latter lying at the tip of Bataan peninsula across the bay from Manila. He was "charmed" by the city and enjoyed the social life and amusements with the American officers stationed there and at nearby Fort William McKinley. He and Lieutenant William H. Rose, a close friend of West Point days, often attended performances at the opera house. Rose remembered an occasion when the two lieutenants listened to "the little Tamanti, as

gorgeous in person as in voice," who got a "hysterical demonstration by the audience." Captain James G. Harbord, head of
the Philippine constabulary and in 1918 chief of staff of the
A.E.F., invited MacArthur to dinner one evening at the Army
and Navy Club where he met two recent law-school graduates,
Manuel L. Quezon and Sergio Osmeña, both destined to be
president of their nation. Perhaps MacArthur's most exciting
moment at Manila came when he narrowly escaped death or
serious injury during a typhoon, which struck suddenly while
he was on the road to McKinley. His tour of duty in the islands
was cut short when he contracted malaria and "dhobe itch"
during the survey on Bataan. In October, 1904, he sailed for
San Francisco, his record embellished with Townsend's ratings
of excellence, but his body wracked by disease.[4]

The next few months were spent "reading engineering literature and studying office methods and records" as assistant to
Colonel Thomas H. Handbury in the district office of engineers
at San Francisco. The colonel found MacArthur to be "a very
promising young officer with good judgment and ability and
so far as known to me of good personal habits." Gradually he
was given more responsibilities in the office and in the field.
Colonel William H. Heuer, Handbury's successor, considered
him "exceptionally bright" and "very attentive to his duties"
and gave him "full charge of the fortification works in San
Francisco harbor." In May, 1905, however, MacArthur suffered a relapse of malaria, was hospitalized for two weeks, and
was bothered by a painful eye infection when he returned to
work. "Owing to trouble with his eyes," MacArthur said that
he "would like to have outside work" and obtained a transfer
to the California Debris Commission, stated Major William W.
Harts, his superior on the new assignment. The commission
was a federal agency set up to regulate hydraulic mining in the
Sacramento and San Joaquin valleys where unrestricted mining
of gold had resulted in "enormous quantities of debris being

washed down into the rivers," obstructing navigation. Harts gave him the task of serving as "foreman or overseer" of excavations at Dagueree Point. "Lieutenant MacArthur seemed to be pleased with this opportunity, but a few days later stated that his departure for so long a time from San Francisco would be impossible owing to his father's absence and the necessity he was under of tending to some of his father's affairs," said Harts, who then gave him the job of "inspecting hydraulic mines," which involved only brief absences from the city. Less enthusiastic about him than Handbury and Heuer were, Harts said that MacArthur was "usually prompt in complying with orders," but he could not predict "with what enthusiasm he would carry out work assigned to him if there was no objection in the way." Nevertheless, in July, 1905, Heuer elevated MacArthur to the position of acting chief engineer of the Division of the Pacific, a responsibility rarely, if ever, given to a lieutenant.[5]

A month after the signing of the Treaty of Portsmouth, which formally terminated the Russo-Japanese War, MacArthur received orders to report to his father, who was military attaché in Japan, as his aide-de-camp. Captain Paul W. West had been the general's aide for over a year, and the reason for the change is not clear. In a letter written on September 19 to Major William D. Beach of the General Staff, West stated: "I am to return home and Douglas MacArthur to accompany the General on the China-India trip. The General had an interview with William Taft, when he was in Yokohama two days ago, and it was arranged that as soon as he reached Washington the General is to cable him and request that I return to the States and to get Douglas here." Farther on in the letter is this enigmatic sentence: "The General's relatives and mine are of the best, but for reasons which I will explain when I see you it is absolutely necessary that Douglas take my place, and I want to do all I can to arrange it so."

Douglas arrived at the Oriental Palace Hotel in Yokohama,

where his parents were residing, on October 29, 1905, and three days later the MacArthurs departed on the "reconnaissance mission" to various Asian countries. After touring Japanese military bases at Kyoto, Kobe, and Nagasaki, they sailed to Singapore, with brief stops en route at Shanghai and Hongkong. The general and his aide inspected British garrisons at Singapore and at several stations to the north on the Malayan peninsula, then on November 30 departed for Java. As was true throughout the Asian tour, Mrs. MacArthur staunchly accompanied her two men on all of their travels. On the Dutch island, where they remained three weeks, the MacArthurs traveled 1200 miles by train and carriage to visit twelve military bases, from Jakarta on the west end to Surabaya on the east end of Java. General MacArthur commented that because of "tropical heat and irregular connections" their progress was "slower than I expected," and by the time of their return to Singapore they were nearly a month behind their schedule. Christmas was spent in Singapore, and the next day they departed by ship for Rangoon. Two weeks were spent touring British stations in Burma, the three going by river boat up the Irrawaddy to Mandalay and on to Bhamo on the border of China. Returning to Rangoon, they boarded a vessel bound for Calcutta where they arrived on January 14, 1906.[6]

Nearly eight weeks were spent in India. From Calcutta the MacArthurs journeyed northward to the "roof of the world," the Himalayas, where they visited the frontier post at Darjeeling. Then they crossed the Indo-Gangetic Plain by rail, stopping at nine British military installations. By mid-February they were in the mountains of northwestern India, inspecting the posts around Peshawar and the fabled Khyber Pass. Turning southward, they visited Quetta and Karachi, sailed to Bombay, and traveled through southern India via Hyderabad, Bangalore, Madras, and Tuticorin. After a brief visit in Colombo, Ceylon, they returned to Singapore in the middle of March, 1906, having traveled — according to the vouchers which Douglas completed — 19,949 miles. General MacArthur was high in his praise of the "warm professional hospitality" which they received in India: "In order to expedite my observations, all the Generals concerned practically put their commands under emergency orders." Looking back years later, Douglas recalled that at the time he was impressed chiefly by the plight of the underprivileged masses of India.

The first non-colonial army the MacArthurs visited was that of Siam in early April, 1906. With no colonial overlords to make arrangements, Prince Krom Varoprakar, the minister for foreign affairs, handled their reception, treating the MacArthurs like visiting royalty. The American minister at Bangkok, Hamilton King, said that the general "was given audience by His Majesty the day following his arrival and dined at the Royal Palace a week later," all the Siamese ministers in the meantime showing him "great respect" and rendering him "every assistance in their power." King observed that "outside the reception given His Royal Highness Prince Heinrich of Prussia and Prince Waldemar of Denmark on their visit to Siam some years ago, no man has been accorded such a royal and generous welcome as was the General since I have been in this country." Since Lieutenant MacArthur was son as well as aide to the general, he was invited to the various festivities, including the dinner given by King Chulalongkorn (whose father was made famous in Margaret Langdon's *Anna and the King of Siam*). Douglas demonstrated his alertness by quickly replacing a fuse when the lights went out at the royal banquet. The king, said Douglas, "was so delighted he proposed to decorate me there and then," but the offer was declined.[7]

After a brief visit at the French military headquarters at Saigon, the MacArthurs went to Canton and Wuchow in southern China where they received "cordial assistance" from the Chinese authorities. General MacArthur remarked, "I was especially interested in a military academy and a garrison at Canton, in the first of which there are some 250 cadets and a corps of 17 Japanese instructors; and in the latter about 2000 fairly good looking modern-type soldiers, quartered in really good, clean, sanitary barracks." In May they moved on for a week's stay at the large German base at Tsingtao, a port on the Shantung peninsula which had been grabbed from the Chinese in 1897. From there the MacArthurs journeyed to Peking via Tientsin, passing areas where American and other Western troops had died during the Boxer Rebellion in 1900. Traveling southward from Peking by rail, they finished their tour of Asian military stations by inspecting Chinese units stationed in the lower Yangtze Valley, from Hankow to Shanghai.

Returning to Japan in late June, 1906, the MacArthurs spent the next three weeks in the Tokyo-Yokohama area where they conversed with some of the Japanese field commanders in the recent victorious war against Russia, including Generals Oyama, Nogi, and Kuroki. Douglas was impressed by them as leaders of "iron character and unshakeable purpose" and found the Japanese soldiers to be men of "boldness and courage." Like his father, he was made aware of Japan's emergence as a major military power. General MacArthur prepared a paper for the War Department on what he considered to be "the problem of the Pacific," stressing the rapidly rising strength of Japan and the need for better defenses in the Philippines "in order to prevent its strategic position from becoming a liability rather than an asset to the United States." Thoroughly convinced of Japan's current and potential might, the MacArthurs sailed from Yokohama for San Francisco on July 17. Looking back on their eight months in East and South Asia, Douglas stated that "the experience was without doubt the most important factor of preparation in my entire life . . . It was crystal clear to me that the future and, indeed, the very existence of America, were irrevocably entwined with Asia and its island outposts." [8]

2. *The Brink of Oblivion*

Arriving in San Francisco in early August, Douglas lacked new orders, so he continued for the next five weeks as aide to his father, who resumed his duties at Fort Mason as commanding officer of the Division of the Pacific. In September, Lieutenant MacArthur received orders to report at Camp Tacoma, Washington, to participate in maneuvers there, at the conclusion of which he was to join the 2nd Battalion, engineers, at Washington Barracks, D.C. (now Fort MacNair) and also was to enroll in the Engineer School of Application at that post.

Founded at Willets Point shortly after the Civil War, the Engineer School was moved to the national capital in 1901, with the Army War College being constructed next to it soon thereafter. Lieutenant MacArthur was one of eleven student-officers enrolled in the school for the session of 1906–07. Major E. Eveleth Winslow was commandant of the school and also taught military engineering, the faculty including only two other professors, one in civil engineering and another in electrical and mechanical engineering. Besides his studies and classes, MacArthur, like the other students, also had duties with the 2nd Battalion, whose principal responsibility was operating the engineer depot at Washington Barracks, one of three such repositories of engineering equipage which the Army maintained.[9]

Appointment to the advanced school for engineering officers was an opportunity highly prized by ambitious junior officers. MacArthur was especially fortunate since he was selected for the school a year before the other members of his class at West Point who had been "distinguished cadets" and had entered the corps of engineers. But he showed little interest in the school after his first month. Winslow later reported to Brigadier General Alexander MacKenzie, the chief of engineers:

I am sorry to have to report that during this time [session of 1906–07] Lieutenant MacArthur seemed to take but little interest in his course at the School and that the character of the work done by him was generally not equal to that of most of the other student officers and barely exceeded the minimum which would have been permitted. Toward the latter part of his course at the School he was sent out in charge of a survey party composed mostly of civilians, and owing to his ignoring or misunderstanding the instructions given him, the results were quite unsatisfactory. Indeed, throughout the time Lieutenant MacArthur was under my observation, he displayed, on the whole, but little professional zeal and his work was far inferior to that which his West Point record shows him to be capable of.[10]

On the contrary, Major Chester Harding, who was commandant of the school up to December 1, 1906, said that MacArthur's work was "excellent" and he was "zealous in his profession." Perhaps the explanation for his academic negligence under Harding's successor lies in the additional assignment he was given on December 4 as "an aide to assist at the White House functions." The request for his service was made personally by President Roosevelt, possibly as a tribute or even a palliative to General MacArthur, who had been recently promoted to lieutenant general but was not appointed chief of staff. Lieutenant MacArthur served at the White House under Colonel Charles Bromwell, the senior military aide to the President. Most of the aides' duties were of a social nature and required their attendance at dinners and receptions at the White House, which consumed many of Douglas' evenings. Moreover, the winter of 1906–07 was one of tension in Japanese-American relations, precipitated by the San Francisco school board's decree segregating Japanese students. Douglas said that the President "was greatly interested in my views on the Far East and talked with me long and often." An indication of Douglas' interests at the time is revealed in his memoirs where he devotes one sentence to the Engineer School and four paragraphs to Roosevelt and Joseph Cannon, the dictatorial speaker of the House of Representatives — the two men who fascinated him most of the many leaders he met at the White House functions. As the young lieutenant's absorption in this dazzling world grew, his concern about his engineering studies declined accordingly.

Since the student-officers entered the Engineer School with different degrees of training at garrison schools, ranging from two years' experience to none, the commandant established the content and length of the program "as if all the officers had completed both years of the garrison school work, the portion of the garrison school course which had not already been pursued by some of the officers to be continued by them at a later period either at the Engineer School or elsewhere." Douglas was required to stay for the summer session of 1907, after which he still had to complete some work in garrison school on his next tour of duty, in Wisconsin. He finally graduated in absentia from the Engineer School on February 28, 1908.[11]

His assignment to the district office of engineers in Milwaukee in August, 1907, should have pleased him since General and Mrs. MacArthur were residing on Marshall Street in that city. Douglas was to serve as assistant to Major William V. Judson, commander of the district and a graduate of West Point in 1888. Judson had served with the Russian army as observer in 1904–05 and was captured by the Japanese in the battle of Mukden. His horse, incidentally, was given by the Japanese commander to General MacArthur, who arrived several days after the fall of the city. Judson's engineers in Wisconsin were mainly engaged in deepening channels and constructing piers at the harbors of Manitowoc, Two Rivers, and Sheboygan to make them usable by commercial vessels on Lake Michigan. As his first task, MacArthur was told to study the plans and specifications on these projects, which were in Judson's office. "Whenever in his studies he had familiarized himself with work at a particular place or of a particular character," Judson said, "I would order him to visit and study such work on the ground. I took him about with me or sent him wherever it seemed to his professional advantage to observe anything of special interest." Judson also assisted MacArthur in completing the requirements for his diploma from the Engineer School by examining and passing him on the garrison-school subjects. Moreover, Judson stated, "I spent many hours in conversation with Lieutenant MacArthur on engineering subjects. I gave him the best I had of knowledge in such matters, so far as I had time and opportunity." [12]

But MacArthur turned his superior against him by insisting on special privileges so that he could be with his parents more often, Judson claimed. The major, who came to view his assistant as "lacking a zeal to learn," reported to the War Department:

> During the first three months Lieutenant MacArthur was on duty with me I was of the opinion that he exhibited less interest in and put less time upon the drafting room, the plans and specifications for work and the works themselves than seemed consistent with my instructions, and I spoke to him several times about it. I observed that he was absent from the office during office hours more than I thought proper, and I spoke to him about this also. By the end of three months I concluded that the best way to secure his interest in the work and his proper qualification for the duties that would come to him in the future was to give him practical charge of the most interesting and one of the largest pieces of work I had, to-wit, the reconstruction of the Manitowoc Harbor. He remonstrated and argued verbally and at length against assignment to this duty, which would take him away from Milwaukee for a considerable portion of time. He said that he wished to be undisturbed for about eight months while he got ready for and passed his examination in the subjects of the garrison school course.[13]

MacArthur reluctantly went to Manitowoc on November 23,

staying on the job until the week before Christmas when winter conditions forced curtailment of work on the harbor. From then until the next April he was in Milwaukee, performing minimal chores in Judson's office and, said the major, expressing "by word and manner his dissatisfaction at going to Manitowoc" when the ice melted; studying for the garrison-school examinations, which Judson warned him must not interfere with his regular duties; and visiting with his father and mother, the former being without assignment for some time and undoubtedly disgruntled. When a vacancy among instructors in engineering at West Point occurred in February, Lieutenant MacArthur was nominated for the post by both Colonel Gustav J. Fiebeger, head of the department, and General MacKenzie, chief of engineers. But Superintendent Hugh L. Scott, later to be chief of staff, rejected MacArthur for reasons unknown and reprimanded Fiebeger for promoting MacArthur's candidacy through the chief of engineers. On April 6 MacArthur returned without enthusiasm to the project at Manitowoc. Five days later he received orders, signed by General Bell, the chief of staff and his father's old friend, relieving him of his present duty and directing him to report to the 3rd Engineer Battalion at Fort Leavenworth.[14]

On July 1, 1908, while MacArthur was happily occupied with his first command of troops, Company K, Major Judson submitted to the War Department his efficiency report on him for the fiscal year 1907–08. Judson's comments were highly critical of him in every category except "general bearing and military appearance." Major General Fred C. Ainsworth, the adjutant general, returned the report to Judson upon the recommendation of Brigadier General William L. Marshall, the new chief of engineers. Judson was told to submit a detailed statement in support of his accusations concerning MacArthur's attitude and conduct. Judson did so promptly, relating the account of the lieutenant's behavior and concluding: "I am of the opinion that Lieutenant MacArthur, while on duty under my immediate orders, did not conduct himself in a way to meet commendation, and that his duties were not performed in a satisfactory manner." As a sort of postscript, he added: "Lieutenant MacArthur possesses excellent ability and has it within his power to become an officer who will do great credit to his corps and to the public service. If my certificate compels me to report upon him adversely, I hope the effect upon Lieutenant MacArthur will be for his good." Copies of the efficiency report and Judson's supplementary statement were sent by General Marshall to MacArthur and to his former commanding officers for comment. Of his previous superiors, all gave him excellent recommendations except Winslow, who was as critical as Judson, and Harts, who recalled the special consideration MacArthur obtained while under him.

MacArthur's rebuttal of Judson's charges was based on his professed ignorance of having incurred his superior's displeasure; his knowledge of the projects and plans, which he challenged Judson or anyone to test him upon by oral or written examination; and his claim that Judson's "serious charge is not supported by specifications of any kind whatever," though MacArthur had a copy of the supplementary statement by the major. He concluded: "I feel keenly the ineradicable blemish Major Judson has seen fit to place upon my Military record, as I am confirmed in the belief that nothing occurred when I was on duty in his office to deserve such drastic action." MacArthur sent his rebuttal directly to the chief of engineers, ignoring the proper channeling, which in this case would have been to Judson for the first indorsement. Marshall promptly returned it to MacArthur with a reprimand and told him to send it through Judson. The major forwarded MacArthur's statement without further comment, though he held it several weeks. On August 5 Marshall wrote MacArthur that, having read the lieutenant's response, he believed that his self-defense "is of itself justification of Major Judson's statement, in view of Mr. MacArthur's evident inclination to avoid work assigned to him elsewhere. The Chief of Engineers expects of all officers under his command promptness and alacrity in obeying orders, and faithful performance of duties assigned them." [15] The matter was apparently closed with Marshall's sharp admonition, but now MacArthur was truly a marked man, far more so than in the days when he was a plebe. With his unsatisfactory performances during the past two tours of duty, he must redeem himself at Leavenworth or face oblivion as a junior officer.

3. Recovery and Surprise

By 1908 Fort Leavenworth was the heart of the Army's advanced educational program. The service schools located there included the School of the Line (formerly the Infantry and Cavalry School), the General Staff School, the Signal School, the Field Engineer School, and the Field Service and Correspondence School for Medical Officers. Many of the junior officers then associated with the service schools as students or instructors would be future leaders of the Army. Captains John McAuley Palmer, LeRoy Eltinge, George Van Horn Moseley, William Mitchell, and James W. McAndrew, as well as Lieutenants George C. Marshall, Walter Krueger, and Robert L. Eichelberger were among the young men who would achieve renown with the A.E.F. in France, and some of them in World War II. Since MacArthur's duties at first were with the training of troops and the operation of the engineer depot, he probably did not enjoy close associations with any of these men until he was assigned later as an instructor in the Field Engineer School.[16]

Company K was, said MacArthur, "the lowest-rated of the twenty-one companies at the post" when he took command.

Acutely aware that he must make good on this assignment, MacArthur worked hard to build up his men's morale and skills. The soldiers of Company K found themselves hiking twenty-five miles a day, developing expertness in demolitions and pontoon bridge building, and improving their abilities in riding and marksmanship. When the company was declared the post's best at the general inspection, MacArthur was justifiably elated: "I could not have been happier if they had made me a general." The company's celebration at setting an Army-wide record for speed in building a pontoon bridge over a stipulated distance was dampened, however, by the loss of one of the enlisted men who drowned accidentally during one of the exercises. Thirty-five years later Henry Mikkelsen, who had been in MacArthur's company at Leavenworth, reminded his former commander: "You were very proud of your Co. 'K.' . . . Of your Mounted Section with Sgt. Moeller and his little black dog 'Vilhelm.' Of your long legged Kentucky mare . . . That small command thought as highly of their 1st Lt. in command as we all at home now think of the General." Little did MacArthur's men in 1908 realize that the company's renascence also marked the start of a revived career for their commanding officer. Colonel Thomas H. Rees, the battalion commander, wrote in his efficiency report on MacArthur in June, 1908, that he was "a most excellent and efficient officer." Major Clement A. F. Flagler, who succeeded Rees that September and would be MacArthur's divisional commander in the Rhineland in 1918–19, gave him ratings of "excellent" in all categories in his efficiency reports for the next two years.[17]

In the autumn of 1908 MacArthur capitalized on another chance to recoup his career. When the commandant of the Mounted Service School at nearby Fort Riley asked Flagler for an instructor to teach pioneering and explosives in a special short course, MacArthur got the assignment. Since the course was a new one at Riley, he had to develop it from the beginning and had only a short time to do so. After the termination of the concentrated ten-day course in October, marking Mac-Arthur's debut as an instructor, he received a letter from the commandant of the school at Riley, Brigadier General Thomas R. Kerr, commending his work as "eminently satisfactory." "The results reflected credit," Kerr remarked, "on your energy, ability and good judgment . . . It is my intention to again apply at the proper time [in 1909] for your detail in charge of this work." MacArthur came back to Fort Riley to teach the course for the next three years. In the meantime he became so engrossed in the field of demolitions that he wrote a manual on the subject, which won the praise of the chief of engineers. Next he was invited to introduce a course in "practical and theoretical demolitions" at the Leavenworth schools. Before long he had built up a reputation as an authority on pioneering and explosives, which, the chief of engineers remarked to Flagler, "Lieutenant MacArthur has well earned." Another officer who probably noticed MacArthur's work was Major Peyton C. March, commander of a regiment of field artillery at Riley and in 1918–21 military head of the Army.[18]

In the meantime Mrs. MacArthur, residing in Milwaukee, had been thinking about the Army's treatment of her husband and her son; she decided to assist the latter without his knowledge. "I would like to see my son filling a place promising more of a future than the Army does," she wrote to Edward H. Harriman in April, 1909. "At Ambassador Griscom's in Tokio some three years ago, I had the good fortune to be seated next to you at luncheon. The amiable manner in which you then listened to my talk, in behalf of a possible future for my son Douglas MacArthur outside the Army, encourages me now, to address you in that connection." She hoped that Harriman could find a place for him "in connection with some of your vast enterprises," chief of which at the time was the Union Pacific Railroad. "I do not know that I could persuade him to surrender his military career," she admitted, "but I do feel that I owe it to maternal solicitude to make every possible effort in behalf of what I conceive to be his future welfare."

Harriman was in Europe, but his secretary sent Mrs. MacArthur's letter to officials of the Union Pacific, who instigated a check on Lieutenant MacArthur. Charles H. Bates, an attorney for the railroad in Washington, queried some officers in the War Department and learned:

> This Officer's record at the War Department for efficiency and conduct is most excellent. I understand there has been only one question as to his service at any time and that was due to a disinclination on his part to accept a detail of service which he considered not to accord fully with his dignity after being Military Aide to the President. This, however, has not impaired his standing whatever with the War Department, but only brought about an insistence on his performing the duty assigned him, and since then the experience is believed to have proven greatly for his good.

D. C. Buell, an official of the Union Pacific's traffic division, went to Fort Leavenworth and talked with some of MacArthur's associates. Buell reported that the lieutenant was "very much of a gentleman . . . well liked by his men and fellow officers . . . evidently a good executive and so far as I could judge, a man of good habits." He also talked to MacArthur about joining the Union Pacific, but "Lieutenant MacArthur knew nothing whatever of any plans to get him into railroad service. Was much surprised and a little annoyed to think that we had been put to the trouble of coming down here." Buell concluded: "It is evidently a case where the mother wants to get her son out of the army, and not where the son is figuring on getting out himself, and you can say that Lieut. MacArthur, according to his own statement, is not desirous of making a change to any position that he feels we would be justified in offering him." Besides, MacArthur felt that at the age of twenty-nine he was too old "to start in almost at the bottom and work up again." [19] After Buell's report, the Union Pacific officials and Harriman dropped the matter.

Mrs. MacArthur's well-meaning "maternal solicitude" may also have been at the root of her son's earlier difficulties with Major Harts in San Francisco as well as with Judson. She had been separated from Douglas, so that daily visits were not possible, for the equivalent of only two of the ten years since he entered West Point. Most of his efforts to obtain special privileges were probably because of her demands upon his time, which, in turn, were related to her frequent illness after their return from Asia. So far she had proven to be a mixed blessing to his career, ambitiously driving him to succeed and giving him the love which he needed, but also interfering with his duties and trying his loyalty to his chosen profession.

Lieutenant MacArthur's gamble to stay with the Army began to pay off soon. In the fall of 1909 he was appointed adjutant of his battalion and became engineer officer of Fort Leavenworth the next summer. At various times during his four years at Leavenworth he also held for short periods the positions of quartermaster, commissary, and disbursing officer of the 3rd Battalion, besides serving on boards of officers to arrange military tournaments and to propose "certain changes in the ponton equipage." In recommending him for promotion, Flagler stated that he was "an exceptionally excellent officer in every respect," while Lieutenant Colonel Joseph E. Kuhn, who succeeded Flagler as battalion commander in mid-1910 and had taught MacArthur at West Point, commented: "I believe he has a thorough appreciation of his responsibilities as an officer. He has good control of troops. He has a marked capacity for commanding." In February, 1911, MacArthur was promoted to captain and later that year was appointed head of the department of military engineering of the Field Engineer School. Both Major Meriwether L. Walker and Colonel Daniel Coruman, director of the Field Engineer School and overall commandant of the Army Service Schools respectively, considered him an excellent instructor and officer.

In the spring and summer of 1911, MacArthur served with the so-called "Maneuver Division" during its training exercises near San Antonio. There were no regular divisions in the Army, and the maneuvers brought together 11,000 troops, the largest concentration since the Philippine Insurrection. Besides providing valuable training at the large-unit level, the maneuvers afforded the Army a chance to make a show of force along the Mexican border. South of the Rio Grande, the Mexican Revolution was gathering momentum, with Porfirio Diaz, the long-time dictator, being forced to resign in May. The Maneuver Division was commanded by Major General Charles H. Carter, MacArthur's former superior in the Visayas, who before the exercises in Texas were finished probably wished he was back in the Philippines. Almost every operation of the Maneuver Division ended in a hodgepodge of confusion, mainly because the traditional American system of dispersing troops in small, scattered posts afforded them no preparation for working together at brigade and divisional levels. Major General Leonard Wood, who succeeded Bell as chief of staff in 1910, said that the maneuvers in Texas "demonstrated conclusively our helplessness to meet with trained troops any sudden emergency." MacArthur's only recorded recollections of the episode were of the receptions he encountered when he revisited his old haunts at West Texas Military Academy and Fort Sam Houston. At the former, the cadets "burst out into mockery and raillery" at the new style of hat he wore; recent regulations required it to be "peaked into a nondescript sort of pyramid." Pausing in front of his old home at the fort one evening, MacArthur, absorbed in memories, was approaching the front porch when a young lady came to the door and, assuming he was drunk, threatened to call the police. MacArthur hastily retreated, promising himself that he would "never try to regain the past" again.

Returning to Leavenworth in August, 1911, he was immediately detached for a brief tour as instructor of the Michigan National Guard at its encampment. That fall he resumed his work as adjutant of the battalion and professor of military engineering at Leavenworth. The only noteworthy event of the season was a fracture of his left hand, which, the medical record said, was "accidentally incurred while wrestling in quarters." The injury curtailed his participation on the engineers' baseball and polo teams, which he had enjoyed for the past two years.

During January and February, 1912, he was in the Panama Canal Zone on another detached-duty assignment. The canal was within two years of completion, and the Army was now busy planning permanent defenses there. MacArthur was one of a number of engineer officers from various posts who were sent that year to Panama to observe and advise on the new fortifications, as well as to study the brilliant engineering feat of the canal itself. While on the isthmus, he spent much of his idle time with Captain Robert Wood and his wife in their home at Culebra. Wood, who was with a cavalry unit on regular duty there, had met MacArthur when they were cadets on the Plain. Now their acquaintance deepened into a friendship of lifetime duration. "From that time on," Wood said, "though I remained on the Isthmus I followed his career in the Army with a special interest." When, upon completion of his assignment in Panama, Captain MacArthur journeyed back to Leavenworth, he found his battalion getting ready to depart for the Philippines. His own orders, however, called for him to remain on the faculty of the Field Engineer School.[20]

After the sudden death of their father on September 5, 1912, Douglas and his brother, who had just completed a tour of duty at sea, stayed in Milwaukee for a while to care for their

mother and to wind up their father's affairs. But when the
two brothers reported back to their stations, Mrs. MacArthur's
health deteriorated rapidly (the nature of her illness being un-
disclosed). In early October, Douglas asked Brigadier General
William H. Bixby, the chief of engineers, to assign him as
commanding officer at the district headquarters of the corps of
engineers in Milwaukee. The post was vacant at the time, but
had always been filled by an officer of the rank of major or
higher. MacArthur said that his request for the transfer to
Milwaukee was made "at the expense of outraging many of
my own instincts," but "so fearful am I of fatality in this
matter." His mother, he explained, had been "seriously ill"
for two years, and her condition had become "alarming" after
the general's death. Receiving a negative reply from the chief
of engineers, he submitted his request again on October 19,
adding: "I mentioned Milwaukee originally as all conditions
seemed to fit in perfectly, but as the Chief of Engineers has
other views in regard thereto, I would respectfully state that
any other city of such size as would furnish the needed requi-
sites would now be equally acceptable." He suggested that
"Washington, on account of its proximity to Johns Hopkins
Hospital, would offer more of advantage for Mrs. MacArthur
than any other possible station." Pending final action on his
plea, MacArthur moved his mother to Fort Leavenworth, but
soon found "the quarters to which my rank entitles me totally
inadequate for the housing of an invalid." An entry by an
Army physician in Captain MacArthur's own medical history
for October 29–November 10, 1912, reads: "Insomnia, cause
undetermined."

Although unknown to him at the time, action was under way
on his case at the War Department. Secretary of War Henry
L. Stimson received a memorandum on MacArthur's situation
from General Wood, the chief of staff, who had known the
MacArthurs since their days together at Fort Wingate. Stim-

son, undoubtedly influenced by Wood, sent a note to the adjutant general, Ainsworth: "In view of the distinguished service of General Arthur MacArthur, the Secretary of War would be pleased if an arrangement could be effected by which the request contained in the accompanying memorandum could be granted." In early December, Captain MacArthur received his orders, the assignment surprising him. He was to report to General Wood in the War Department where he would serve in the office of the chief of staff. Though not designated a member of the General Staff, MacArthur would have a grand opportunity to work immediately under Wood in the Army's center of high command.[21] The ironical workings of fate, which had brought him opprobrium for his past requests for special consideration, now, as a result of another such request, bestowed upon him the chance to prove himself in the presence of the military head of the Army.

CHAPTER V

Important Friendships

1. Wood Is Impressed

WHEN CAPTAIN MACARTHUR began his new assignment as assistant in the office of the chief of staff in late 1912, the War Department was recuperating from one of its ugliest episodes of internal strife. Since its creation nine years earlier, the General Staff had incurred increasing hostility and jealousy from the chiefs of the departmental bureaus. They feared that if the General Staff was allowed leeway, it would produce centralization of authority in the department and diminution of the near autonomy of the bureaus. Misunderstandings between the officers of the bureaus and the General Staff were abetted by the lack of any lucid and formalized delineation of the nature and scope of the General Staff's planning and coordinating functions. A number of important members of Congress feared that the General Staff, like the Prussian one, "might grow into a tyrannical and arbitrary power." Adjutant General Ainsworth, the leader of the department's bureaucratic faction, carefully nourished his friendship with these politicians, ever reminding them of the dangers of militarism.

Backed by Secretary of War Stimson, Chief of Staff Wood

brought the struggle to a climax in early 1912 by charging Ainsworth with insubordination and obstructionism. The Wood-Ainsworth showdown had been building for some time and had many facets, including personal ambition for power as well as differences over minor issues like muster rolls, recruiting, and terms of enlistment. The crucial underlying issues at stake, however, were the validity of the chief of staff's claim to be military head of the Army and the General Staff's assertion to be the central, supreme planning body of the military establishment. At the zenith of the clash Wood correctly observed that "the Army's worst enemies are within itself," but incorrectly classified Ainsworth's supporters as "stupid fools." Rather than face a court-martial which Stimson and Wood were preparing with diabolical delight — the immediate issue being an offensive memorandum sent by Ainsworth to Wood — the adjutant general retired from the Army in February, 1912. But the retreat of the politically influential Ainsworth did not leave a clear field for the General Staff in controlling policy making and administration in the War Department. For years afterward there were sharp reverberations in Congress and within the department, which pointed clearly to a persisting distrust of the General Staff and its chief by many politicians and officers. The battle surely established the primacy of the chief of staff as the dominant officer of the Army, but Wood's victory was costly for the General Staff, which Congress kept small and carefully restricted until war was declared in 1917. Moreover, so many persons' feelings had been injured in the fray that the General Staff and the bureaus found it difficult, if not awkward, to work together.[1] MacArthur came into the office of the chief of staff without, of course, any taint from the bitter fight, but it was not long before he was labeled as one of "Wood's boys." Had he joined Wood a year earlier and had Ainsworth triumphed instead, MacArthur's career might well have been retarded by the association. But, with the chief of staff now unmistakably the supreme figure in the military hierarchy, the affinity with Wood worked to MacArthur's advantage.

Possibly it had been Wood's intention to appoint MacArthur to a post on the General Staff from the start, but in December, 1912, Congress, influenced by the pro-Ainsworth faction, reduced the size of the General Staff from forty-five to thirty-six officers. So Wood, who was allowed four commissioned assistants in his office, carried MacArthur on his personal staff until April, 1913. At the time that Captain MacArthur joined him, Wood was busy on plans for summer camps where college students, paying their own way, could receive military training. Obsessed with the idea of preparedness based on a strong citizen-army reserve, he was also planning toward a similar camp at Plattsburg, New York, for business and professional men. MacArthur probably found himself working at times with the Army League, an organization which Wood had helped to found in order to enlist popular support for a larger Army. MacArthur was fascinated by the versatile, hard-driving, ambitious chief of staff, who had started as a physician, joined the cavalry and won the Medal of Honor during the last Apache war, served as colonel of the Rough Riders in Cuba and as military governor of that island, and later as commander in the Philippines in the aftermath of the insurrection. Though President Taft was "lukewarm" toward him and Stimson got "a little sick" of his egotism and heroics, Wood was sincerely determined to make the Army into an effective force.

"But what attracted me most," MacArthur said, "was working as Wood's assistant in his indefatigable crusade for military preparedness. The work was long and confining, and left me little time for relaxation, but it was rewarding." The chief of staff also assigned to MacArthur "for study and report" a problem concerning certain disputed lands in the Panama Canal Zone which the Republic of Panama claimed. At one stage on this project MacArthur optimistically told Stimson, who had likewise wrestled with it, "I would like, if possible, to bury the Panama contention for all time." But the question of the zone's exact boundaries was not settled by the captain or anyone else for many years. Wood, nevertheless, was highly impressed with the work of MacArthur, and when the captain left his office in April, the chief of staff wrote him a personal commendation noting "the very able and efficient manner" in which he had performed his duties. Their mutual admiration would continue until Wood's death in 1927.[2]

From April through September, MacArthur served as superintendent of the State, War, and Navy Building. Colonel Edward Burr, the acting chief of engineers and his superior, found him to be "an able, capable, reliable, and self reliant officer, with a deep interest in his duties." MacArthur's concern for the assignment as a kind of exalted custodian may have been quickened by the fact that his brother, who was then on the General Board of the Navy, occupied one of the offices in the building. On September 25, 1913, Captain MacArthur was appointed to the General Staff, an expected opening probably being the reason Wood retained him in Washington on the brief-lived assignment as superintendent. Perhaps recalling the unhappy consequences of his earlier "overtime" duty at the White House, MacArthur turned down an invitation from President Wilson a few weeks later to serve as presidential aide. Moreover, he undoubtedly was aware of Wood's strong Republican ties and may have felt that such a dual role would have been indiscreet.

Although crises in Mexico and Bosnia would lead to hostilities of far-reaching consequences for the United States in the next half year, the War Department in the fall and winter of 1913 was a scene of tranquillity. Except for some mementos of previous wars in showcases in the halls, there were few signs to indicate the nature of the department's business. Officers and even guards wore civilian attire, and documents marked "urgent" were seldom seen. The General Staff was small, its members congenial, and its chores not particularly burdensome. Wood continued to campaign vociferously for preparedness, but without tangible results. The General Staff's projects consisted of studies on routine matters, such as drill regulations, military instruction in the colleges, and provision of reserve matériel. Despite its placidity, the staff included a group of talented officers, whose abilities would be challenged and proven in World War I and afterward, for example, Majors William Lassiter and William D. Connor and Captains Frank R. McCoy and William Mitchell, all of whom were closely associated with MacArthur in the staff's various projects. Three of the members whom MacArthur got to know especially well were Colonel William A. Mann, later commander of the Rainbow Division; Major Robert A. Brown, whom MacArthur succeeded as a brigade commander in World War I; and Captain George Van Horn Moseley, a strongly opinionated cavalry officer whose path would cross MacArthur's many times in the future.

The General Staff's organization at that time was simple, consisting of four divisions — mobile army, coast artillery, militia, and war college. MacArthur was assigned to the mobile army division, which was concerned mainly with investigating and reporting "upon all questions affecting the efficiency of the Army and its state of preparation for military operations." The war college division was responsible for war plans, the militia bureau for reserve and National Guard matters, and the coast artillery division for harbor defense problems. MacArthur's duties consisted largely of routine studies and reports on sundry topics including one entitled "Educational Systems in the American Army," which the federal commissioner of education liked so well he included it in his annual report in 1914. Wood thought highly of his performances, stating in his efficiency report that year: "Captain MacArthur is a highly intelligent and very efficient officer. He has discharged all duties assigned him with promptness and ability." Indeed, some close to Wood felt that MacArthur was the chief of staff's favorite among the younger officers.

For the MacArthurs, the days in Washington passed happily and peacefully. With brother Arthur, his wife, and their children also living in the city, it was the first opportunity Douglas had to get to know Mary and her offspring, who numbered four by 1914. Douglas lived with his mother on 16th Street in a fashionable neighborhood of northwest Washington. The general's estate had not been considerable, but his widow, whose health improved steadily, purchased a new Cadillac touring automobile and employed a Negro chauffeur to drive her in the afternoons and Douglas and his dates in the evenings. Clarence Thomas, the chauffeur, later recalled to Douglas those days when "I use to take you out to Lincoln Park North East to a young ladys house you were going to see an then Drive you an the lady all around the Potomac Park an the Monument grounds an back to Lincoln Park an wait an take you home." Captain MacArthur, who looked strikingly handsome and trim at 140 pounds and five feet, eleven inches, in height, was a desirable prospect to the young ladies of Washington society, but he continued to be more interested in professional advancement than in marriage.[3]

2. Mission to Veracruz

In 1911 Mexico's dictator of a quarter century was overthrown, and it seemed that under the enlightened leadership of Francisco Madero, the new president, the nation was moving toward democracy. But less than a month before Wilson's inauguration in Washington, Madero was assassinated, and

Victoriano Huerta, a cruel, reactionary general, took over in Mexico City. President Wilson showed his displeasure at what he considered a setback for the Mexican people by refusing recognition to the new regime and embargoing shipments of arms to Huerta. The United States Navy began patrolling the waters off Mexico to prevent supplies from reaching Huerta. On April 9, 1914, some sailors from the U.S.S. *Dolphin* went ashore at Tampico, but were arrested by Mexican troops. Despite their prompt release and an apology from the local commander, Wilson backed the Navy's ridiculous demand for a twenty-one-gun salute to the American flag. Huerta retorted that he would permit it only if the Navy rendered an equivalent salute to the Mexican standard. Wilson, now bent upon ousting Huerta, refused to allow the return honors. On the morning of April 20 the American President met with his top civilian and military leaders to lay plans for possible military action, and that afternoon he asked Congress for authorization to use the armed forces to obtain redress. Brigadier General Frederick Funston was sent to Galveston to prepare the 5th Brigade of the 2nd Infantry Division for an imminent movement against Huerta's forces.

The next day, April 21, news reached Washington that a German ship bearing a large cargo of arms and ammunition for Huerta was headed for Veracruz, Mexico's main port. Without waiting for Congress' approval, Wilson ordered the Navy to send sailors and marines ashore to occupy the city. At a cost of over 500 casualties on both sides, Veracruz was secured, and on April 30 Funston's brigade, numbering 7000 men, relieved the naval forces occupying the city. In the United States there was widespread approval of Wilson's "punishment" of Huerta, but officials in the War Department and many Republican congressmen were disappointed that the American troops were not ordered to march against Mexico City. For the next few weeks the two nations were perilously close to war. But Wilson, who was sincerely anxious to avert war and had predicted that the landing at Veracruz would be unopposed, now was willing to bide time until the Mexican people rose and ousted Huerta, as he was sure they would do. Funston was told to keep a close check on his troops, confining them to the immediate vicinity of the city and refraining from any hostile action against the Huertistas.[4]

On April 22 Secretary of War Lindley M. Garrison designated Wood "to command a possible expeditionary force" to advance to Mexico City if war came. Major General William W. Wotherspoon assumed the post of chief of staff of the Army that day, while Wood immediately began laying plans for his field organization, even selecting his headquarters staff the first day. MacArthur, who was recuperating from a case of acute tonsillitis, was one of the first chosen to Wood's staff. On the 23rd, however, Wood decided to send him in advance to Veracruz as a special intelligence agent with instructions, in Wood's words, "to obtain through reconnaissance and other means consistent with the existing situation, all possible information which would be of value in connection with possible operations." Wood secured passage for MacArthur on the battleship *Nebraska,* which was sailing shortly from New York.

When he arrived at Veracruz on May 1, 1914, Captain MacArthur went to General Funston, now in command of all American forces in the city, and explained his mission, during which he would be under direct orders of the War Department and would be working independently of Funston's command. Contact would be maintained secretly through Captain William C. Ball, Funston's aide. In addition to thousands of anti-Huerta and anti-American rebels roaming the nearby countryside, Huerta had about 11,000 Mexican regulars in the cordon around Veracruz. Funston could face a quick disaster and the United States a major war if Huerta learned that the War Department was seriously contemplating an advance upon the Mexican capital, hence the secrecy of MacArthur's intelligence-gathering mission. Funston wrote in his diary on May 3: "Trouble is, we, not being permitted to scout beyond outposts, cannot discover a concentration made close thereto. If a disaster should result from this condition, I must not be held responsible." As Ball explained regarding MacArthur's relations with Funston's headquarters, "It was imperative that the information that had been obtained should be kept as secret as possible" since "this information became practically the basis for our future plans."

By the morning of May 6 an atmosphere of tense expectancy pervaded the gatherings of officers of the 5th Brigade, according to Captain Constant Cordier of the 4th Infantry Regiment: "It was believed by everyone that the First Field Army [Wood's command] was to be ordered to Vera Cruz immediately, and that the Brigade here was to be at once thrown forward to seize Jalapa as an advance base." The main problem, Cordier said, was that "with practically no wheel transportation, and with the rainy season on, it would have been well-nigh impossible to reach Jalapa without using the railroad for our advance. We had ample cars but no engines." Cordier learned from a drunken Mexican railway engineer that there were a number of locomotives at Alvarado, a town located about forty miles southeast of Veracruz. Having known MacArthur in Washington and being aware of his mission, Cordier discussed with him the "advisability" of a reconnaissance to Alvarado. "But as I was serving with troops," he said, "and inasmuch as the orders of the Commanding General proscribed any member of the re-enforced brigade from going beyond the lines, I was unable to accompany MacArthur, who, nevertheless, made the trip practically as we had planned it." [5]

After sobering up the Mexican engineer and bribing him, MacArthur persuaded him to lead the way to the locomotives. For $150 in gold, the captain also obtained the services of two other Mexicans who agreed to transport them by handcar along the Alvarado line. Nine miles south of the city the Alvarado Railroad ran through the village of Tejar, which was the location of the pumping station for Veracruz' water supply and the farthest outpost held by the Americans. The only exchanges of shots between the sides had occurred there, and it was known that the Mexican regulars held a sector of the track just south of Tejar. So MacArthur decided to detour around this troubled area and reach the Alvarado line via another railway which intersected it four miles beyond Tejar.

Setting out at dusk with the weather "squally and overcast," MacArthur and the engineer made their way unobserved to the rail intersection where the other Mexicans met them and transported them by handcar to Alvarado, which they reached shortly after one on the morning of May 7. Five engines were found there, two of them being switch engines, but the others, MacArthur reported, "were just what we needed — fine big road pullers in excellent condition except for a few minor parts which were missing." So far the reconnaissance had gone smoothly, but on the return trip MacArthur, who carried only a 38-cal. revolver and had disarmed the three Mexicans for fear of treachery, was engaged in hostile actions with several different bands of rebels. He vividly recounted the experiences in his later report to Wood:

> At Salinas, while moving around the town with one of my men . . . we were halted by five armed men. They were on foot and wore no uniforms . . . We started to run for it and they opened fire and followed us. We outdistanced all but two and in order to preserve our own lives I was obliged to fire upon them. Both went down . . .
>
> At Piedra, under somewhat similar circumstances and in a driving mist, we ran flush into about fifteen mounted men of the same general type. We were among them before I realized it and were immediately the center of a melee. I was knocked down by the rush of horsemen and had three bullet holes

through my clothes, but escaped unscathed. My man was shot in the shoulder but not seriously injured. At least four of the enemy were brought down and the rest fled. After bandaging up my wounded man we proceeded north with all speed possible.

Near Laguna we were again encountered and fired upon by three mounted men who kept up a running fight with the hand-car. I did not return this fire. All but one of these men were distanced, but this one man, unusually well mounted, overhauled and passed the car. He sent one bullet through my shirt and two others that hit the car within six inches of me, and I then felt obliged to bring him down. His horse fell across the front of the car and on the track, and we were obliged to remove the carcass before proceeding.[6]

MacArthur returned safely within the American lines about dawn, thankful that "owing to the darkness I was not recognized as an American soldier and in consequence no alarm was ever felt for the engines" by the Mexicans. Cordier told Wood: "Knowing the outlying conditions as well as I do it is a mystery to me that any of the party escaped. When I saw MacArthur he still displayed signs of the tremendous nervous strain that he had been under." Unknown to MacArthur, Private Samuel Parks of the 28th Infantry had stolen two horses and deserted into the Mexican lines that same night. When Funston learned a few days later that the Mexicans had executed Parks, he strengthened the sentry lines of the perimeter around Veracruz to prevent other Americans from venturing beyond the outposts. MacArthur told Ball about his trip, but, possibly because of his commander's reaction to the Parks episode, Ball did not inform Funston of the Alvarado reconnaissance. Funston stated later: "Until after the return of the expeditionary force from Vera Cruz [in November], and the entire severance of my connection therewith, I had not the slightest information regarding the reconnaissance made by Captain MacArthur."

Cordier, convinced that MacArthur "is the type that will never open his mouth with regard to himself," wrote Wood about the reconnaissance and suggested that the former chief of staff nominate MacArthur for the Congressional Medal of Honor: "The Navy Department, in recognizing its Vera Cruz heroes gave eleven Medals of Honor and over a hundred lesser awards, but I do not believe there would be a man of those hundred or more who would not, on the relative merits of the case, yield the palm to MacArthur, for heroism displayed, for dangers braved, and for difficulties overcome." Cordier did not tell MacArthur of this letter, written on May 19, until sometime in the middle of the summer. As for the data which MacArthur obtained on his mission, there proved to be no need for him to report to Funston since the occupation soon settled into a quiet routine of administering municipal affairs, collecting customs revenues, and introducing public health and judicial reforms. MacArthur's reconnaissance, which resulted in the deaths of perhaps seven Mexicans, was the only hostile action involving fatalities during the entire seven-month period of the Army's occupation. Luckily for MacArthur and for the two nations already at the brink of war, no knowledge of his mission to Veracruz or of his daring, if reckless, reconnaissance to Alvarado reached Huerta.[7]

MacArthur wrote Wood on May 7 briefly mentioning the Alvarado affair but dwelling more on the occupation in general. He was also careful to remind his former superior of his continued devotion to him: "General Funston is handling things well and there is room for little criticism, but I miss the inspiration, my dear General, of your own clear-cut, decisive methods. I hope sincerely that affairs will shape themselves so that you will shortly take the field for the campaign which, if death does not call you, can have but one ending — the White House." On May 18 MacArthur was transferred to Funston's staff as assistant engineer officer, with headquarters

at the Terminal Hotel near the waterfront. His duties were
in connection with the operation of the engineer depot, which
was established on the 19th to store and issue equipage of the
company of engineers stationed in the city. The engineers'
main tasks were constructing water and sewage lines, maintaining several short-line railroads operating between the city
and the outpost lines, and stockpiling rail ties and fittings,
shipped from Panama, in anticipation of a move toward Mexico
City.

After a few weeks in Veracruz, MacArthur undoubtedly
agreed with the American correspondent's opinion that "there
are only two vivid things about Vera Cruz — the smells and
the colors." At a distance, from the deck of a vessel, the
ancient port appeared placid and beautiful — the massive walls
of the fortress of San Juan de Ulua guarding the entrance to
the harbor, the long waterfront with its gray granite blocks
covered with white gulls, the brightly colored commercial and
governmental buildings, and the surrounding hills with rugged
mountains visible in the far background. On closer look, however, the *zopilotes,* or vultures, seemed to be everywhere in
the garbage-strewn streets — perching on window sills, picking
through the refuse of the market places, and boldly obstructing
the traffic of carts and wagons. An American Red Cross
worker discovered chickens roosting above the stove in the
kitchen of a prominent hotel whose menu listed the house's
specialty as "chicken cooked in its own moist." About half of
the city's business houses were cantinas, which sold beverages
fiery enough to shock Funston's strongest drinkers. Many of
the other commercial establishments, as well as the saloons,
catered to man's sexual desires, the prostitutes' numbers rival-
ing those of the garbage-hunting pariah dogs and *zopilotes.*

During his fourteen weeks in the port MacArthur probably
had considerable leisure to enjoy some of the finer aspects of
life there, such as the justly famous seafood menus at the fine

hotels and the dazzling white beaches. There were also noisy places of public amusement where Mexicans and Americans mingled and forgot their animosities while wagering on the exciting action in the cock pits or the bull ring. Of course, all such enjoyments were predicated on the ability to ignore the filth, vultures, flies, mosquitoes, and temperatures over 100 degrees. MacArthur also enjoyed reunions with a number of his old classmates from West Point and must have been surprised to meet his childhood playmate, William Hughes, who was serving as a captain with the 7th Infantry.[8]

Acting on orders from Chief of Staff Wotherspoon, MacArthur left Veracruz on August 20 to return to his duties on the General Staff in Washington. Wood, now at Governors Island commanding the Department of the East, wrote him after his return mentioning Cordier's correspondence and requesting a detailed report on the Alvarado episode, which MacArthur sent him on September 30. In the last week of November, shortly after Major General Hugh L. Scott succeeded Wotherspoon as chief of staff, Wood recommended to the War Department that MacArthur be awarded the Medal of Honor. Basing the nomination on the reports by MacArthur and Cordier, Wood concluded that the reconnaissance was made "on his own initiative" and "at the risk of his life" and "indicates an amount of enterprise and courage worthy of high commendation." [9] Wood's letter and the reports of MacArthur and Cordier were referred by the adjutant general to Funston for comment. On January 13, 1915, Funston replied:

As the reconnaissance was made on the theory that Captain MacArthur was not a member of my command at the time, and as I had no knowledge of it until many months later, I am at a loss to know how I can properly make official recommendation on the subject. As a matter of personal opinion I should say that the risks voluntarily taken and the dangers encountered were of a most exceptional nature, and that the

awarding of the Medal of Honor would be entirely appropriate
and justifiable.

I do not consider this the occasion to enter into a discussion
of the advisability of this enterprise having been undertaken
without the knowledge of the commanding general on the
ground, who from the first was acting under definite, confidential instructions from the Secretary of War, and who understood
thoroughly that without specific instructions nothing was to be
done that might lead to a resumption of hostilities. However,
it must be presumed that Captain MacArthur was acting in
good faith, and any error of judgment he may have made in
undertaking his hazardous expedition should not, in my opinion, cause him to lose the appropriate reward.[10]

The next week Scott, who enjoyed reliving his own exploits
against the Indians on the frontier, appointed a board of officers from the General Staff to consider the case. The officers
chosen — all recent appointees to the General Staff — were
Colonel Charles G. Treat, who had been commandant of
cadets during MacArthur's final two years at West Point, Lieutenant Colonel William H. Johnston, and Major P. D. Lochridge. Treat, the senior member, served as chairman. Before
the board's first meeting on February 2, Captain Ball submitted an unsolicited testimonial in which he enthusiastically
proclaimed MacArthur's action to be "one of the most dangerous and difficult feats in army annals." Ball tactlessly continued: "This officer clearly earned a Medal of Honor. I believe a grave injustice will be done if such action is not taken."

The board restricted itself to the documents of the case and
called no one to testify. The matter was complicated by the
fact that regulations required the oral or written testimony
of at least two eyewitnesses to the action. But the board
magnanimously waived this requisite as "impracticable" and
accepted MacArthur's report as "an accurate and truthful
statement of the affair." Yet the majority report, signed by
Treat and Johnston on February 9, recommended against the
award on the following grounds, perhaps unique:

Captain MacArthur's "distinguished gallantry in action" consisted in making the reconnaissance at the risk of his life. But the board questions "the advisability of this enterprise having been undertaken without the knowledge of the commanding general on the ground." . . . To bestow the award recommended might encourage any other staff officer, under similar conditions, to ignore the local commander, possibly interfering with the latter's plans with reference to the enemy.

Lochridge filed a minority report stating that he also opposed the award, but on different grounds: "Captain MacArthur's report of these combats shows nothing unusual in combat, nothing 'extraordinary' and such 'as clearly to distinguish him for gallantry and intrepidity above his comrades.' " Moreover, said Lochridge, the only firsthand report was that of MacArthur: "I fully believe the report, but it does not fulfill the requirement of 'incontestable proof.' " [11]

Even with the board's negative reports, the War Department did not close the case for another two months, probably because of the influence of Wood. General Crowder, the judge advocate general, was brought into the affair when Garrison asked for his interpretation as to whether MacArthur's performance constituted gallantry "in action," some doubt having arisen since no state of war existed and Mexican regulars were not involved. In fact, an armistice between Mexican and American forces was concluded just prior to MacArthur's mission, though he was not aware of it. Crowder responded that "any one of the three combats in which Captain MacArthur was engaged in Mexico on the night of May 6–7, 1914, constituted an 'action' within the meaning of that word in the Act of April 23, 1904, conferring authority to present medals of honor." On February 23 Wood, Wotherspoon, and Scott submitted their efficiency reports on MacArthur, all highly praising his work during the past year, but saying little of relevance to the case at hand. On March 2 Colonel Eugene F. Ladd, the adjutant general, wrote Wood: "I am directed by the Secretary of War to inform you that the Department has approved the adverse recommendation of the Board of Officers convened to report upon the award of the Medal of Honor to Captain MacArthur for the services in question." Apparently Funston's statement, which was the focus of the board's majority report, was the key to the department's final decision.

On the other hand, MacArthur's brazen response to the board's judgment may also have affected the ultimate outcome. Mistakenly concluding that the board's verdict of February 9 was the end of the matter, MacArthur, thoroughly "incensed" over the officers' "rigid narrowmindedness and lack of imagination," wrote a "straightforward" memorandum to Scott on the 12th protesting the decision. Even Frazier Hunt, a correspondent who greatly admired MacArthur, admitted that "to many in the army inner circles his protest seemed rash and impertinent." Those who so considered his memorandum probably included the three men responsible for the final endorsements on the board's judgment — Scott, Brigadier General Tasker H. Bliss, assistant chief of staff, and Henry Breckenridge, assistant secretary of war.

Perhaps there was something "courageous and commendable" about Captain MacArthur's protest, as Hunt claimed some officers interpreted it.[12] But it seems highly doubtful that anyone, except his most uncritical friends, could have viewed his response as anything short of presumptuous and arrogant. More important, a pattern of behavior was becoming increasingly evident in him which would brand him in the eyes of many officers as a pleader for special consideration and a sensitive, self-righteous protestor against any infringements upon what he felt were his prerogatives. In his defense, however, it may be noted that disgust and impatience with the slow-moving, seniority-minded men who too often handled matters of promotion and recognition in the War Department were exhibited by other ambitious, talented officers. Moreover, it does seem that the Distinguished Service Cross could have been awarded as a consolation, particularly in view of the profusion of medals which the Navy bestowed for its two days of action at Veracruz. As it was, the proceedings of MacArthur's case represented a reprimand, not a tribute, and if the board's reasoning was extended, the bestowal of any medal for his Alvarado reconnaissance might "encourage" others to "ignore" the plans of the local commander.

3. Drifting toward the Abyss

"I had a feeling that the end of things had come . . . I stopped in my tracks, dazed and horror-stricken," said David F. Houston, Wilson's Secretary of Agriculture, when he heard the news that Europe had plunged into war in the summer of 1914. Wood's preparedness campaign took on new life in the ensuing months, with the emphasis now on the need for a massive citizen-army which only conscription could produce. Despite the marshaling of widespread popular support by Wood, Stimson, Theodore Roosevelt, and other devotees of preparedness, Wilson maintained at first an aloofness to the agitation, dismissing it as "good mental exercise." Colonel Edward M. House, his trusted adviser, observed that the President believed that "if the Allies were not able to defeat Germany alone, they could scarcely do so with the help of the United States because it would take too long for us to get in a state of preparedness." Under pressure from the administration, Garrison was compelled to reject a proposal from the General Staff that a plan of conscription be prepared for future use. When Wilson read in the Baltimore *Sun* that the General Staff was working on a war plan which was based on hostilities between Germany and the United States, he directed the Secretary of War to launch "an immediate investigation, and if it proved true, to relieve at once every officer of the General Staff and order him out of Washington," claimed General Bliss, the acting chief of staff at the time in Scott's absence. Once Bliss explained to Wilson that preparation of theoretical war plans had been a primary function of the war college division since 1903, the President dropped the matter. But, Bliss noted, "Mr. Breckenridge directed me to caution the War College to 'camouflage' its work. It resulted in practically no further *official* studies." In February, 1916, Garrison, who could be quite antagonistic and headstrong, resigned after a clash with the House's military affairs committee, which opposed his plan for virtually scrapping the National Guard in favor of a 500,000-man "Continental Army," or ready federal reserve, to back up the regulars. Republicans, alert to the presidential election only seven months away, joyfully seized upon Garrison's departure as indicative of the President's indifference to national defense.[13]

Such criticism, however, was obsolete well before Garrison's resignation because the President had been quietly but steadily shifting his position on preparedness since the sinking of the *Lusitania*. In fact, in December, 1915, the administration sent to Congress a comprehensive bill on national defense which the General Staff had prepared. While Congress haggled over the measure, Wilson came out openly for preparedness, making numerous speeches in favor of the cause. In March he selected Newton D. Baker, a reform-minded ex-mayor of Cleveland and recent convert to preparedness, as Secretary of War. Two days after Baker took his oath of office, "Pancho" Villa's rebels raided Columbus, New Mexico, setting off a new crisis in relations with Mexico and garnering new support in Congress for a stronger military establishment. While Brigadier General John J. Pershing led a force of 5000 American troops into northern Mexico in pursuit of Villa, Congress proceeded to approve, and the President to sign into law, the National Defense Act of June, 1916 — the most comprehensive legislation on military affairs the nation had known. The measure provided, among other things, for a gradual increase of the Regular Army, whose strength was then 108,000, to 175,000 men in peacetime and 286,000 in wartime; a 400,000-man National Guard, which would be under much tighter federal supervision; reorganization of the administration of the military establishment; and authorization for planning toward economic mobilization. Contrary to the act's generally progressive features and thanks to Ainsworth's persisting influence, it also contained a section on the General Staff which, though providing for a gradual overall increase, had the immediate effect of reducing the staff's size with regard to members on duty in Washington. That section also contained a vague clause which could have limited the General Staff's authority to nonadministrative matters only, but Baker quickly nullified the statement's effect by cleverly interpreting it so as to leave the General Staff's authority unimpaired. Two weeks after he signed the measure, Wilson called the bulk of the National Guard into federal service, principally to gird the defenses of the southern border, which were stripped of regulars when Pershing's punitive expedition was assembled.[14]

MacArthur, who was promoted to major on December 11, 1915, had worked on the drafting of the national defense legislation. In the spring of 1916 Scott appointed him and Major Palmer E. Pierce as a committee of the General Staff to study motor transportation. The efforts to supply Pershing's troops in Mexico clearly showed the superiority of motor vehicles over mule wagons, both of which were used by the expedition. But MacArthur and Pierce soon found that a host of problems were associated with effective utilization of motor trucks, such as the lack of dependable engines, spare parts, mechanics, and factories capable of mass production. The two majors worked closely with a similar committee of the Navy's General Board and with leading civilians in the field of transportation. At a joint meeting in July, 1916, for example, they met with ranking naval authorities, leaders from Detroit's automotive industries, the president of the American Automobile Association, and the heads of the United States Chamber of Commerce and the Society of Automobile Engineers. Also vitally concerned with military-civilian cooperation in planning toward economic mobilization was the enthusiastic, likable assistant secretary of the Navy, Franklin D. Roosevelt, with whom MacArthur sometimes worked in the spring of 1917.

MacArthur's sundry assignments on the General Staff also included occasional duty as host and guide for visiting dignitaries of the armed services of other nations. This was probably one of his most pleasant chores, and his poise and personality made him unusually well suited for this type of assignment. Even the Navy Department requested his services in 1915 when Admiral Dewa, a distinguished Japanese naval leader, visited the United States. Scott agreed to allow MacArthur "to accompany him on such visits as he may make to points of interest in this vicinity, and remain with him until he has completed his visit to West Point, New York." There was no question that MacArthur could be most charming when he so wished, and one of those who came to like and admire him after earlier adverse impressions was Scott himself. In early 1916 Scott commented in his efficiency report: "Major MacArthur is a very well appearing, high-minded, conscientious and unusually efficient officer, well fitted for positions requiring diplomacy and high-grade intelligence." [15]

Shortly after Baker became Secretary of War in the spring of 1916, he had MacArthur assigned to his office as military assistant in charge of the newly created bureau of information. The major's job was largely that of press censor, and, according to MacArthur, he "became the liaison link with the newspaper men who covered the War Department." He has since been regarded as the Army's first public relations officer. Specifically, his major tasks involved the preparation of press releases and the granting of press interviews relating to the operations of Pershing's punitive expedition, the implementation of the National Defense Act of 1916, and official views of the War Department on military legislation before Congress. Colonel R. Ernest Dupuy, a leader in public relations in the Army later, maintained that MacArthur's efforts "went far to condition the nation and the Congress for acceptance of the seemingly impossible: a draft act. Make no mistake; it was the then Major Douglas MacArthur, Class of 1903, who sold to the American people the Selective Service Act that was passed on May 18, 1917." In promoting the measure, MacArthur worked closely with the men who drafted the measure and perfected the system of registration, namely, General Crowder, the judge advocate general and onetime assistant to General Arthur MacArthur on Luzon, and Lieutenant Colonel Hugh Johnson, who was on Crowder's staff and was, it will be recalled, a friend of MacArthur during their days at West Point.

With the position of press censor a new one and the duties as yet ill defined, MacArthur soon found himself working strenuously into the evening hours. William M. Ingraham, the acting Secretary of War in October, 1916, had to tell the adjutant general that MacArthur's annual fitness test in horseback riding, still required of officers then, would have to be postponed: "Owing to the necessity of Major MacArthur's practically continuous presence at the War Department on his duties as Censor, it will be impracticable for him at present to absent himself for three days." [16] On April 4, 1917, two days after Wilson's dramatic appearance before Congress asking for a declaration of war and on the day the Senate concurred in the President's request, twenty-nine correspondents covering the national capital for newspapers and syndicated news services presented a letter to Baker. It was a tribute to MacArthur

personally signed by all of them, a group which included some
of the most hard-crusted, cynical men in the reporting business,
as well as some of the most distinguished. One of the signatories who became a lifetime admirer of MacArthur was
Stephen I. Early, who would someday be Franklin D. Roosevelt's presidential secretary. The letter read, in part:

> . . . We of the 4th Estate wish to express to you, and through
> you, to Major Douglas MacArthur, our appreciation of the way
> he has dealt with us for all these months in his trying position
> as military censor.
>
> We feel no doubt of what the future holds for Major Mac-
> Arthur. Rank and honors will come to him if merit can bring
> them to any man; but we now wish to say our thanks to him
> for the unfailing kindness, patience and wise counsel we have
> received from him in the difficult days that are past.
>
> Our needs have compelled us to tax that patience at all hours
> of the day and night. We have never failed to receive courteous
> treatment from him. Although the censorship imposed was but
> a voluntary obligation upon the press, it has been kept faith-
> fully, and we feel that it has been largely because of the fair,
> wise and liberal way in which Major MacArthur exercised his
> functions that this was possible. He has put his own personality
> into his task.
>
> No man can ever know to what extent the cordial relations
> the major has maintained with the press may have influenced
> national thought on military matters. It is unquestionable that
> his hours given to our conferences have not been wasted. They
> have borne fruit in what we in turn have written and if wise
> decisions are reached eventually as to the military policy of
> the country, we cannot but feel that the major has helped us
> to shape the public mind.[17]

In the next year when the press would complain bitterly and
loudly about the War Department's handling, or mishandling,
of wartime censorship, Baker would probably wish that Mac-
Arthur was still beside him. MacArthur's finesse in this job
endeared him to Baker with important consequences for the
major's future.

When war was declared against Germany, there were just twenty officers on the General Staff in Washington, of whom only eleven could be freed from other duties for "the study of military problems, the preparation of plans for the national defense, and the utilization of the military forces in time of war," Scott lamented. The Army War College, headed by Brigadier General Joseph Kuhn, who had instructed Mac-Arthur at West Point, bore the responsibility of formulating a basic war plan. Unfortunately the administration and Congress continued to restrict the War Department in funds and planning until after the declaration of war. Scott complained in February, 1917, "The President does not want us to do anything which will give Germany the idea that we are getting ready for war, so we are not allowed to ask for any money or to get ready in a serious way, until the soft pedal is taken off." When Pershing arrived in the War Department on May 10, he found that "the General Staff had apparently done little more, even after war was declared, than to consider the immediate question of organizing and sending abroad one combat division and 50,000 special troops, as requested by the Allies." He stated bluntly, "To find such a lack of foresight on the part of the General Staff was not calculated to inspire confidence in its ability to do its part efficiently in the crisis that confronted us." Elevated to major general and given command of the then nonexistent American Expeditionary Forces, Pershing hurried off to Paris to set up his headquarters and prepare for the coming of his troops, whose numbers would be disappointing for many long months. Meanwhile in Washington both Congress and the General Staff were casting off their inertia, and the latter body was at last authorized to expand to meet its growing responsibilities. By June the General Staff had been increased to forty-seven officers, but by November, 1918, it would comprise nearly 1000.[18]

In the early summer of 1917 MacArthur's chief concern was how to secure an assignment with the troops going to France.

His solution came in an unexpected way. When a study recommending an ultimate strength of 500,000, all regulars, for
the war was sent to him for endorsement, MacArthur said that
he wrote on it that he "completely disagreed with its conclusions," but did not elaborate since he felt his views on the
issue would not receive "the slightest attention." Scott approved the study, but Baker, like MacArthur, favored "the use
of unlimited force and the employment of the National Guard
to its full capacity." Baker sent for MacArthur, and the two
of them conferred with President Wilson. According to Mac-
Arthur, Wilson concluded the discussion on the use of the
National Guard with the remarks: "I am in general accord
with your ideas. Baker, put them into effect. And thank you,
Major, for your frankness."

Baker and the War Department then faced the problem of
selecting the first National Guard divisions for overseas assignment. "If we sent the New York National Guard first," Baker
said, "we might have encountered two kinds of comment: first,
from the people of New York who might have said why send
our boys first; or, we might have had comment from other
states charging that we were preferring New York and giving
it first chance." As Baker well knew, "public psychology was
still an uncertain and mystifying factor," and National Guard
affairs were so interwoven with politics and public opinion that
the wrong move might affect the War Department's sensitive
relations with both Congress and the people. "I disclosed my
puzzle to Major MacArthur, who was attached to my office at
the time," Baker said. MacArthur "suggested the possibility
of our being able to form a division out of the surplus units
from many states, the major part of whose National Guard
organizations were in multi-state divisions." Brigadier General William A. Mann, chief of the War Department's militia
bureau, concurred with the major and pointed out some states
from which units could be drawn to form a composite division.

According to Baker, "Major MacArthur, who was standing alongside, said, 'Fine, that will stretch over the whole country like a rainbow.' The Division thus got its name."

On August 1, 1917, Baker directed that the 42nd "Rainbow" Division be formed as a composite National Guard division. Four days later he signed MacArthur's commission as a full colonel in the National Army, as the new force of citizen-soldiers would be called. Before doing so, he gave MacArthur the choice of his colonelcy in the engineers or in the infantry. Despite an objection from Colonel William M. Black, the chief of engineers, who argued in vain that he "could not properly accept such a commission," MacArthur chose the infantry. He said, in recollection, that at the time "I could think only of the old 24th Wisconsin Infantry." [19] Perhaps the romance and thrill of his father's tales of the Civil War swept through him again as when he was a child. Or he may have shrewdly reasoned that whereas in peacetime the most rapid promotions were in the corps of engineers, in wartime the quickest advancements were enjoyed by officers of the line. Whatever his motivation, little did he or any American officer then realize the inglorious experiences and hideous slaughter toward which they were inexorably moving.

PART II

Emergence of
the Hero Image

CHAPTER VI

From Long Island

to Lorraine

1. Birth Pangs

THE "RAINBOW" CHARACTER of the 42nd Division precluded its rapid, orderly formation. Some units from New York and New Jersey arrived in the third week of August at Camp Albert L. Mills, the division's training center near Mineola, Long Island, but systematic training of the entire division did not get under way until mid-September. Mann and MacArthur had hoped that it could be the second complete American division to embark for France (the 1st Division having left in June), but the complex problems of concentrating, equipping, and training the Rainbow's variegated units, from twenty-six states, proved formidable and time-consuming. As it turned out, New England's 26th Division, as well as some units of the 2nd Division of regulars, preceded the 42nd to France.

The Rainbow Division was organized into three brigades, two infantry and one field artillery, in addition to divisional and auxiliary units and various trains. The 83rd Infantry Brigade, commanded by Brigadier General Michael J. Lenihan, included the 165th and 166th regiments. Brigadier General

Robert A. Brown commanded the 84th Infantry Brigade, its regiments being the 167th and 168th. The 67th Field Artillery Brigade was led by Brigadier General Charles P. Summerall and included the 149th, 150th, and 151st regiments. The division's maximum authorized strength was 991 officers and 27,114 enlisted men, about the same as the other A.E.F. divisions. During the ensuing year the 42nd's actual strength would seldom exceed 26,000 officers and men, yet, even so, it was over twice the size of a British, French, or German division. Its main armament consisted of 16,200 rifles, 260 machine guns, forty-eight 75-mm. guns, twenty-four 155-mm. howitzers, and twelve six-inch trench mortars, though seldom would the division enjoy its full quota of these weapons.

As in other A.E.F. units, the officer corps comprised all types — the strong and the weak, the able and the incompetent. For the most part, the senior officers were graduates of West Point and proved to be capable leaders, though several of them were later transferred to positions of greater responsibility outside the division. On the other hand, at least two key officers during the days at Camp Mills would be sent home from France as ineffective or incompetent. A number of junior officers would be found wanting when tested under fire. Nevertheless, from the group of officers assembled at Camp Mills that summer would come, in future years, two chiefs of staff of the Army, six high-ranking generals of World War II, a Secretary of the Army, a Secretary of the Air Force, two large-city mayors, two governors, a United States senator, a federal judge, an ambassador, and a chairman of a federal commission.

MacArthur knew a number of the 42nd's officers from previous tours of duty and may have had a hand in the selection of such old friends as Major William Hughes, Colonel William Kelly, Major Grayson Murphy, Major Samuel Gleaves, and Colonel Robert Wood — the last four being cadet companions of his at West Point. Mann and Brown had served with him on the General Staff, and Lenihan had been commanding officer at Fort Leavenworth during the first years of Mac-Arthur's tour there. In his role as chief of staff of the division, MacArthur soon became well acquainted with all of the senior officers and many of the junior officers also.[1]

Camp Mills, which was named for the superintendent of West Point during MacArthur's cadetship, was located on the western end of Long Island between Mineola and Garden City, about twenty miles from New York City. It was intended to be merely a temporary camp to provide basic training prior to the troops' embarkation for France where their training would be completed. The 500-acre site was flat, but the lay of the land posed no serious drainage problems; part of the cantonment had once been the Mineola fairgrounds. The soldiers lived in tents during their stay of less than two months at Mills, though construction of barracks and other wooden facilities was under way before their departure overseas. In fact, by the time the 41st Division began to assemble at the camp in November, the facilities were reasonably adequate. The tent cantonment and primitive camp hospital surely would have presented serious problems had there been an early onset of winter or an epidemic, but the 42nd was spared such difficulties. Sick men requiring extensive hospital attention were transferred to the Nassau County hospital at Mineola, which could care for twenty-five patients at a time, or to the larger hospitals in Brooklyn. The 167th Infantry arrived in camp in early September with seven cases of measles, which soon grew to 114; but the regiment was strictly quarantined, the stricken men were quickly hospitalized outside the camp, and the epidemic scare subsided.

MacArthur found much of his time consumed in wrestling with problems of supply and equipment shortages, which handicapped the training program and made life miserable for the men. The lists of shortages were long even after the divi-

sion had been encamped six weeks, the needed items ranging
from underwear, woolen clothing, and shelter halves to pistols,
wagons, and engineering equipage. A major detriment to
health and morale, according to a divisional report, was "the
marked overcrowding of tents and poor ventilation, twelve men
having been quartered in many tents" which were intended to
house only half that number.[2]

Captain John B. Coulter, an aide to Mann and many years
later a general under MacArthur in Korea, recalled that "the
stay at Camp Mills was one of feverish preparation, from the
Division Commander to the rawest recruit, for the arduous
duties ahead. While working tirelessly to whip the Division
into shape, General Mann gave constant thought to the welfare and comfort of the personnel . . . and frequently visited
the unit camps to observe and chat with his men." MacArthur
observed that "the division worked day and night . . . There
were no leaves, passes were limited, officers and men fared
alike." The days were long for everyone, many of the soldiers
being in poor physical condition at the start and knowing little
about military ways despite their membership in the National
Guard. The mornings were spent on close and extended-order
drills, physical exercising, and bayonet practice, while the afternoons were devoted to instruction in schools of the soldier
and the company, care of weapons, target practice, sentinel
duties, and a host of other subjects basic to the combat soldier's
training. Specialized instruction was given to men assigned to
artillery, engineer, signal, machine gun, sanitation, ammunition, field hospital, and ambulance units.

Frequently Pershing sent messages back to the War Department regarding particular aspects of training and qualification
for the troops which he wanted in the A.E.F., his judgments
being based on his observation of French and British units in
the front lines. Sometimes copies of his remarks were sent to
Camp Mills and the fifteen other cantonments around the

nation where they were posted or circulated among the officers. On October 6, for example, MacArthur sent to all of his unit commanders copies of a cablegram from Pershing which stated: "Long experience [with] conditions in France confirms my opinion [that it is] highly important infantry soldiers should be excellent shots . . . Therefore strongly renew my previous recommendations that all troops be given [the] complete course [in] rifle practice prescribed [in] our firing manual before leaving [the] United States. Specialty of trench warfare instructions at home should not be allowed to interfere with rifle practice nor with intensive preliminary training in our schools of soldiers, companies and battalions." In another message Pershing noted: "My observation of British and French armies and most exacting arduous service conditions at the front fully convinces [me] that only officers in full mental and physical vigor should be sent here." Despite his admonitions, however, the 42nd and the rest of the divisions in training in the United States would arrive in France with an alarming number of inadequately trained men and physically and mentally unfit officers, largely because of the brief time between concentration and embarkation, which did not permit thorough training of soldiers and careful selection of leaders.[3] The haste and confusion of America's last-minute mobilization would soon exact a terrible toll of her sons on the fields of France.

On September 30 Secretary of War Baker, Major General Tasker H. Bliss, the new chief of staff of the Army, and several other high-ranking officers reviewed the division at Camp Mills. The troops elicited "a most favorable comment from all" as they went through "intensive drilling in School of the Soldier and School of the Company in both close and extended order, sighting and aiming exercises, estimating distances and instruction in semaphore and wig-wag." The division showed ineptitude, however, during its parade past the review stands, with one regiment almost colliding with another, soldiers executing hand salutes when an "eyes right" order was given, and officers improperly attired. Afterward MacArthur sent a circular to all commanding officers analyzing the irregularities and reminding them of "the vital necessity of suppressing all desires, however natural and commendable it may be, of favoring his organization by any movement or action in conflict with arrangements prescribed for the operation of the division," referring to the embarrassing near-collision. Baker and Bliss returned on October 7 for the next divisional review, at which time the 168th Infantry, commanded by Colonel E. R. Bennett, followed the wrong road to the parade grounds, got lost, and finally showed up after the review was well under way. General Brown, commander of the 84th Brigade, was reprimanded by Mann, and Brown, in turn, chided Bennett, emphasizing that he "must realize that a similar delay in action might be attended by the most fatal results." [4]   Although the 42nd's faults were probably no worse than those of the other divisions which they reviewed, Baker and Bliss must have lamented the fact that the desperate Allied situation compelled them to send such units to France before their training was farther advanced.

At 3:00 P.M. on October 18 the division's headquarters staff, 83rd and 84th Infantry Brigades, 67th Field Artillery Brigade, and several auxiliary units began boarding trains to Brooklyn, inaugurating the complicated process of embarkation. At the Brooklyn waterfront they were transferred to ferryboats, which took them across the harbor to Hoboken where six transports were waiting. The short journey from the cantonment to the port of embarkation was not without its aggravations. Three of the thirteen trains were late, the last not arriving at Camp Mills until after midnight. At the Brooklyn pier one of the ferries did not make an appearance until nearly dawn the next day, over twelve hours behind schedule. The 117th Engineer Regiment was delayed in boarding its train because of the soldiers' "confusion and disregard to orders as to cohesion and silence" and also "due to the endeavor of several ladies to give the troops milk, pies, and other foods." The conclusion of headquarters was that the movement to the ships was accomplished with reasonable orderliness, "considering the more or less undisciplined condition of the troops and the inexperience of the officers." On the recommendation of the divisional surgeon, 501 enlisted men of these units were left behind to be discharged as physically unfit.

The transports left Hoboken on October 19, escorted by the cruiser *Seattle* and two destroyers. MacArthur sailed on the *Covington,* a Hamburg-American liner seized at the start of the war, but its re-outfitting was not finished in time for the voyage, its decks and rooms being in considerable disarray and "none too clean." The seas were rough for the first four days out, and on the fifth day the *President Grant,* which was carrying over 5000 soldiers, mainly of the 168th Infantry, developed engine trouble and turned back to Hoboken. These troops, along with some other units of the division left behind at Mills, sailed in three separate convoys from New York and Montreal between October 27 and November 23, thus arriving in France up to six weeks after the original contingent.

Before the first embarkation Mann had received a letter from James Carlin, an ex-officer of the United States Coast Survey, in which he prophesied the sinking of the transports carrying the Rainbow troops. Carlin claimed that in a dream he saw several acres of ocean off the Irish coast covered with blood and debris: "This was the scene where the entire division from Camp Mills would be sunk by the Enemy's submarines — that is to say — if unfortunately they were to sail without taking the serious notice called for in dealing with the warning given by *The Almighty.*" The divine warning, as it turned out, was related to Carlin's efforts to sell the government some sort of "anti-submarine device" which he had invented and maintained was "the correct antidote to the submarine scourge."

Forty miles from the port of St. Nazaire at the mouth of the Loire River, the *Covington* ran aground, about the same time that "an apparently authentic report" came in that a German U-boat was prowling eighteen miles away. During those anxious hours Mann and MacArthur may have wished for Carlin's device, whatever it was. Seven patrol boats were sent out from St. Nazaire to protect the hapless transport, while the rest of the convoy continued to port. But the submarine moved on, apparently unaware of the inviting prey. When the *Covington* finally arrived at St. Nazaire on November 1, there were no berths left at the docks; so the ship lay anchored in the harbor for three days, the officers frantically endeavoring to maintain discipline and morale. MacArthur's first glimpse of France was through "a misty, drizzling rain," which persisted throughout the week he spent at St. Nazaire. On her trip back to America the *Covington* was sunk by a German U-boat, undoubtedly proving to Mr. Carlin that Washington should have accepted his invention.[5]

2. *Valley Forge in France*

By the time of the 42nd Division's landing in France, the Allied military situation was grim. Since July the British had suffered 400,000 casualties in gaining five miles in front of Passchendaele; in November their great tank-led offensive at Cambrai was stopped, and the savage German counterattack recouped most of the lost ground. The French suffered heavily in their attempted offensives in the Aisne and Champagne regions, which failed disastrously; mutinies had occurred that summer and fall in sixteen French corps. The Italians in the autumn of 1917 suffered their worst setback of the war, being routed at Caporetto and at a cost of nearly 300,000 casualties.

On the high seas Germany's submarine strength now stood at 134, its zenith, and over 8,000,000 tons of Allied shipping had been sunk by November. That month also a steadily swelling stream of German troop trains was carrying divisions from the Russian to the Western front since the Bolshevists, successful in their *coup d'état,* were negotiating an armistice with the Central Powers. When the year 1917 opened, the Allies had three soldiers to every two of the enemy, but by autumn the numerical balance had been reversed.

Another half year would pass before the trickle of American reinforcements became a torrent and gave the numerical edge to the Allies again. Four American divisions were in France by early December, 1917, but only the 1st Division had completed its training. According to Pershing's schedule, the 26th Division would be ready to enter the front-line trenches on May 1, 1918, the 42nd Division on May 15, and the 2nd Division on June 1. Baker gave Pershing "a free hand" regarding the amalgamation of his units with British and French divisions, but, despite vigorous Allied protests, the A.E.F. commander steadfastly refused to commit his men to battle until their training program was completed and then only as a distinct American force with its own front. He did agree, however, to employ British and French advisers in their training and to assign the A.E.F. divisions to Allied corps in quiet sectors for their advanced training in trench warfare.[6]

On November 7 the elements of the Rainbow Division at St. Nazaire started toward their new stations — the 67th Field Artillery Brigade to Camp Coëtquidan on Breton peninsula and the rest to Vaucouleurs in Lorraine. Mann, who was within a year of retirement and suffered from poor health, became virtually inactive as the troops at Vaucouleurs began a stepped-up training program amid almost daily rains. MacArthur, the chief of staff, became *de facto* commander of the division. Pershing visited the 42nd's headquarters soon after its arrival at Vaucouleurs, and a few days later he cabled the War Department that Mann must be relieved: "Division commanders who are in any way unable to stand continuous work actually in the trenches under conditions found on the Western front are useless here . . . Their physical infirmities disqualify them to stand the cold, the discomfort, the continuous strain, and the nerve-racking bombardments." On December 19 Major General Charles T. Menoher, a classmate of Pershing at West Point and an experienced officer of the field artillery, assumed the helm of the 42nd Division. Menoher and MacArthur respected and liked each other from the start, with MacArthur characterizing his new superior as "an able officer, an efficient administrator, of genial disposition and unimpeachable character." [7]

The loss of Mann was surely no handicap to the division, but other actions of the A.E.F. headquarters at Chaumont did hamper its program seriously and almost led to its dissolution as a combat division. In the final days at Camp Mills the division had been amply supplied with new equipment, clothing, and other supplies, but a large portion of these items were immediately taken over by Chaumont to fill deficiencies in the 1st and 26th divisions, which would likely be prepared for combat before the 42nd. Despite protests from Mann, Menoher, and MacArthur, thirty-three of the division's best officers, including Summerall, were transferred to Chaumont or to the other divisions. Herbert Corey, a reporter with the A.E.F., learned of the Rainbow's losses to other units, including 50,000 pairs of shoes, and tried to get an article on the division's plight to newspapers in the States, but the story was censored at Pershing's headquarters. MacArthur, thoroughly aroused over the rape of his division, not only supplied Corey with the data but also traveled to Chaumont to protest some of the transfers of officers — actions which were resented by some members of the Chaumont staff.

On November 20 Colonel Fox Conner, Pershing's G-3 (operations and training officer), recommended that "steps be taken to place these divisions [1st, 2nd, and 26th] at full strength and also that all absent units now in France join their divisions. The 42nd Division (*replacement division*) is partially available for the above purposes." For some time Pershing and his general staff had planned to utilize the 42nd's troops as replacements, not as a separate combat division. Soon after Conner's proposal, MacArthur somehow learned of the plan to decimate his division. Mann, who was still commander at the time, had many influential political friends through his many years of work with the National Guard and as the militia chief of the War Department. He and MacArthur, who probably contacted his friend Baker, bombarded Washington with cablegrams to various powerful individuals. Soon the War Department, in turn, was deluged with calls and letters from important persons demanding that the Rainbow be kept together as a combat division. MacArthur went to Chaumont to see Brigadier General James G. Harbord, Pershing's chief of staff and a friend of MacArthur since their days together in Manila in 1904. "I asked him to come and see the division," said MacArthur, "and judge himself on the merits of the situation whether such a splendid unit should be relegated to a replacement status." [8] Harbord went to Vaucouleurs and later, on November 25, submitted the following memorandum to Pershing:

> Certainly every consideration dictates that some division be used as a replacement division without delay. The following is submitted as some reasons for and against in the case of the 42nd Division:

FOR	AGAINST
Has an inactive division commander.	The division commander is an inactive man but an active politician.
Comes from 25 different states.	
Not yet embarked on training here as a division.	Has perhaps more ésprit than any other division.

Its artillery not yet assigned its matériel.	Has figured more in the press and has more friends to resent the matter.
It is the only division with personnel complete to go to different units.	The 69th New York, protégés of "The Friendly Sons of St. Patrick," are a regiment [165th] of one of its brigades. It comes from a part of New York City hostile to the President and liable to be more so if offended.
	Its training has been on saner lines than any other division likely to come — no trench or bomb nonsense, straight soldier-making.
	It is the first division to arrive complete.
	I much fear that if you used it for replacement without notice to the War Department that you would be reversed; on the other hand if you ask the War Department that you will not be permitted to do it.[9]

Regarding his appeal to Harbord, MacArthur admitted, "My action was probably not in strict accord with normal procedure and it created resentment against me among certain members of Pershing's staff." But his fight was successful, and the 42nd was saved. Pershing decided that the fifth division to arrive, which was the 41st, would serve at supply depots in the rear, while the 32nd Division, which arrived in early 1918 prepared to fight, learned that it was to be the replacement reservoir for the other divisions.[10] Obviously the 32nd and 41st divisions did not have the influential friends which the 42nd possessed.

After a month of intensive training at Vaucouleurs, the Rainbow Division was transferred to a training area between Lafauche and Rimaucourt, which were located just north of Chaumont. By that time the division was complete except for the field artillery brigade, which was still training in Brittany. On the day after Christmas the divisional units in the Lafauche-Rimaucourt area departed for still another training area at Rolampont, which was situated on the Langres Plateau south of Chaumont. Both moves in December were made on short notice and by forced marches, the troops averaging fifty-five kilometers (thirty-four miles) per day. The three-day march to Rolampont was undertaken in "a blinding snowstorm," according to Captain Walter B. Wolf of the divisional headquarters staff, who considered the experience "one of the most trying and arduous tasks with which the division was ever confronted. From this march the spirit of the division was born." The temperature was below freezing, the roads were nearly impassable, and many of the men marched without underwear or overcoats, so muddled was the A.E.F.'s supply situation. By the last day the path the soldiers had tramped was marked by splotches of blood on the snow since many men wore shoes and boots which should have been replaced weeks earlier. As the division passed through Chaumont, the A.E.F. inspector general and some of his officers noted defects in the marching columns and sent a detailed list to MacArthur when he got to Rolampont. Menoher, though sympathetic with the men's condition, was also aware of the importance of "sound march discipline" and ordered the division to undertake practice marches by regiments every afternoon for the first week after their arrival at Rolampont. A private, his feet wrapped in burlap and his pack soggy with snow, snarled, "Valley Forge — hell! There ain't no such animal."

At Lafauche, Rimaucourt, and Rolampont officers of the French Army were attached to the 42nd Division as instructors in trench warfare. On the eve of their arrival MacArthur told the Rainbow's officers: "Though it is to be borne in mind that our methods are to be distinctly our own, it would be manifestly unwise not to be guided by their long practical and recent experience in actual trench warfare." He added: "Any criticism which may be made by them will be taken as it is meant, in the spirit of friendly and helpful constructive advice . . . No pains will be spared to establish and maintain cordial and harmonious personal and official relations with them." Unlike several American divisions which drew French advisers who were disdainful of the Yanks' abilities as fighting men, the Rainbow's contingent of French officers were polite and constructive in their criticisms of the American novices. Other than some misunderstandings due to language difficulties, no problems arose. In fact, the French officers associated with the 42nd in the next seven months, first in advisory and later in liaison capacities, seemed, from Menoher and MacArthur's view, to think more highly of the Rainbow's performances than did Pershing and his Chaumont staff.[11]

At Rolampont especially, the division's training program was guided largely by the French mission. The stress was on training of skirmishers, combat formations of platoons and companies, duties of sentries and patrols, and practice with grenades. Rapid assemblies were sometimes difficult, with the troops billeted in houses and haylofts for several miles around Rolampont. The moist cold of France's worst winter in decades was partially alleviated by "an influx of stoves such as that region of France had never known," commented an American. MacArthur and other senior officers were billeted in châteaux where possible, but, according to one report, "officers in chateaux, where great rooms were heated by a small grate, suffered more than the men who were in barracks." MacArthur's only comment on the matter in his memoirs was that "the billets were crowded, miserable affairs."

The climax of the division's training program came on February 11–13, 1918, with the visit of an inspection team from

Pershing's headquarters to determine whether the division was ready to enter the trenches in a quiet sector. The visitors included Major General Andrew W. Brewster, inspector general of the A.E.F., and seven other high-ranking officers from Pershing's "miniature War Department" at Chaumont. Various kinds of drills and field exercises were conducted at company level and above. In their report to Pershing the inspectors had one complimentary remark: "The discipline of this organization, as evidenced by attention to saluting and neatness of personal appearance, is very good." But the rest of the report was bitingly critical. The simulated attacks by the infantry regiments were poorly conducted. In the case of the 166th Infantry, "neither the regimental nor the battalion commander seemed to understand the purpose of a formation in depth and how to produce such." The machine gun, engineer, sanitary, and signal units "showed little training." Two of the four commanders of infantry regiments, Colonels E. R. Bennett and Benson W. Hough, were considered of questionable ability: "It is doubtful if these officers will in any reasonable time be able to instruct their commands, both by reason of a lack of proper fundamental military education, and in Colonel Bennett's case, probably also because of a lack of personal initiative and aggressiveness." The inspectors recommended that "if these officers do not promptly manifest adequate capacity for instructing and training their commands upon return to the training area, they should be replaced by carefully selected regular officers." Bennett was subsequently replaced by Colonel Matthew A. Tinley, but Hough's later performances satisfied Chaumont.

On February 13, the day that the inspection was completed, Pershing ordered the 42nd Division to move to the Lunéville sector of southern Lorraine for a month's training at the front with the French VII Corps. Of course, he had not yet received the inspectors' report, but even if he had, he probably would have issued the order, so intense were the pressures on him from the States and from Allied leaders to get the A.E.F. into action before the next German offensive, expected in the spring. In the following months Pershing would reluctantly assign many divisions to the lines before he felt their training was adequate. The news of the move to Lunéville was received jubilantly by the soldiers of the 42nd, but their officers, who knew the opinion of Brewster's group, must have soberly wondered if one more month was sufficient to get the division ready for combat.[12]

3. *A Quiet Sector No Longer*

The 42nd Division entrained for Lunéville on February 16; it was joined by the 67th Field Artillery Brigade shortly. The sector lay fourteen miles up the Meurthe River from the city of Nancy and on the western edge of the Plain of Lorraine between the Moselle Plateau and the Vosges Mountains. The plain, actually a low plateau, was characterized by vast expanses of spruce forest, sandstone ridges, and dark ravines strikingly similar to the terrain of the Argonne Forest of Champagne. The sands and gravels washed down from the Vosges Mountains, which began twenty miles to the east, left little land in that part of the Meurthe Valley suitable for crops. Livestock raising was common, however, and afforded the troops of both sides with ample quantities of meat. Marshy, peaty areas along the river produced an abundance of willows and rushes, which were used by the many basket weavers of Lunéville and neighboring towns. Large clay deposits near Lunéville provided raw material for crockery and ceramics manufactures, the chief local industry. Occasionally the town's inhabitants were subjected to bombardments by enemy artillery or airplanes, but most of the damage in that area had been wreaked by French and

German armies battling in the first year of the war. Since then, both sides had used the sector mainly as a place of rehabilitation for divisions worn by the slaughters of the Somme, Aisne, and other active fronts to the northwest. While only nine miles east of Lunéville the front-line trenches of the French VII Corps ran in jagged lines through the Parroy Forest, the region's beauty and relative calmness produced the illusion of an Eden which both armies had tacitly agreed to despoil no more.[13]

The Rainbow's soldiers were distributed over the entire sixteen-mile front of the sector, from Lunéville past St. Clément to Baccarat. As far as administration, supply, and discipline were concerned, the division was part of Major General Hunter Liggett's I Corps, A.E.F., but for combat and training purposes it was under General Georges de Bazelaire of the French VII Corps, with each of the 42nd's regiments assigned to one of the French divisions holding the sector. Each American battalion served one week at a time on the front line, then spent the next week on the second line of defense and the third week in reserve, the process of rotation continuing thus as long as the 42nd was in the sector. Acute shortages of some types of equipment still existed, as evidenced, for example, by Menoher's order that troops of a battalion leaving the front line were to yield their pistols to the men of the relieving battalion.

MacArthur organized the divisional general staff into three sections in February, corresponding roughly to Chaumont's divisions of G-1, G-2, and G-3. Heading his G-1, or personnel and administration, section was Lieutenant Colonel Frank H. Lawton, with Major Noble B. Judah in charge of G-2, or intelligence, and Lieutenant Colonel William N. Hughes, Jr., over G-3, or training and operations. During the Lorraine tour MacArthur inexplicably left vacant the post of G-4, or supply chief, preferring to handle it himself or with Lawton's help. Captain Wolf, MacArthur's aide, said of the 42nd's chief of staff: "MacArthur worked very early in the morning on his field plans. Alone, he made notes on a card, and by the time we met for a staff discussion he had the plans all worked out. He asked for our opinions but, more often than not, we all concurred with his. His plans invariably covered the optimum situation as well as the minimum. He was meticulous in organization and consummate in planning."

In earlier years MacArthur had often drawn favorable comments on his sharp appearance, but during the Lunéville tour and afterward he adopted an attire which was smart-looking, but far from conventional. Removing the metal band from the inside of his cap, he gave his headdress a distinctively casual, even jaunty, appearance. He was seldom seen during the cold season without his heavy muffler and bright turtleneck sweater; a riding crop and shining puttees also became MacArthur trademarks. The nicknames began to sprout — "The Dude," "The Stick," "Beau Brummell of the A.E.F." — but he seemed oblivious to all snickering and side remarks. The fact that he perspired very little, together with his unusual dress and great concern for neatness, made him appear like a dandy from the council tables in Paris. Actually MacArthur visited the front-line trenches more often than most, perhaps all, other divisional chiefs of staff in the A.E.F.[14]

Much of the time in the Lunéville sector was spent in routine chores of training and becoming adjusted to the dreary life in trenches. Visiting the 42nd as a war correspondent, Irving S. Cobb, the humorist-novelist, found soldiers at advanced outposts moving about in the open, except between 2:00 and 4:00 P.M. An officer explained to Cobb: "The officer in command of the German battery just over the hill from where you were to-day probably has instructions to shoot so many rounds a day into us. So in order to simplify the matter he, being a true German, starts at two and quits at four, when he has used up his supply of ammunition for the day."

It was not long, however, before the Yanks felt the urge to cross No Man's Land, especially after their French comrades' raid on February 26. That afternoon elements of the French VII Corps launched a surprise attack against German forward posts near Réchicourt, which lay across the Meurthe River from Lunéville. Menoher and MacArthur got Bazelaire's permission to allow them and their brigade commanders to observe the start of the raid from a ridge which overlooked the area of operations. According to Menoher, MacArthur and Captain Thomas T. Handy, an aide to Menoher who would someday be a four-star general, "got completely lost from us. I saw them as they were taking a sneak around the point of a hill but said nothing, and we did not see them again until next morning." The raid was highly successful, netting over 600 German prisoners. Delighted to be on the scene, MacArthur reported that "the fight was savage and merciless." Apparently MacArthur assisted in the capture of several enemy soldiers. "When we returned with our prisoners those veteran Frenchmen crowded around me," he said, "shaking my hand, slapping me on the back and offering me cognac and absinthe." Bazelaire decorated him with the Croix de Guerre — the first such award to a member of the A.E.F. — while Menoher recommended him for the Silver Star, which he subsequently received. Menoher told correspondents that "Colonel MacArthur is one of the ablest officers in the United States Army and also one of the most popular." [15]

After the Réchicourt raid the Rainbow officers and men began to clamor for a raid of their own. While plans for an American raid were being mapped, the Germans surprised the 168th Infantry with a savage raid near Badonviller, east of Baccarat. The attack was repulsed, but one American platoon was "almost completely destroyed," according to Pershing, who visited the regiment the next day. On March 7, three days after the Badonviller incident, German artillery destroyed a 165th Infantry post in the Rouge Bouquet section of the Parroy Forest, the losses including nineteen Americans killed in one dugout. Chaplain Francis P. Duffy of the 165th Infantry conducted the funeral service at the collapsed dugout, the tomb of the regiment's first men slain in battle. Corporal Joyce Kilmer, the famed poet, composed a eulogy commemorating the tragedy, and Duffy read it during the service. It began:

> In the woods they call Rouge-Bouquet
> There is a new-made grave today,
> Built by never a spade nor pick,
> Yet covered with earth ten meters thick.
>   There lie many fighting men,
>   Dead in their youthful prime,
>   Never to laugh or live again
>   Or taste of the summer time;
> For death came flying through the air
> And stopped his flight at the dugout stair,
>   Touched his prey —
>   And left them there —
>   Clay to clay.
> He hid their bodies stealthily
> In the soil of the land they sought to free,
>   And fled away.[16]

The 42nd Division retaliated on March 9 with three raids; MacArthur joined a company of the 168th Infantry which attacked German trenches in the Salient du Feys. He showed up before the assault wearing his turtleneck sweater and muffler, carrying his riding crop, and refusing to accept a helmet or pistol. One soldier commented, "I couldn't figure what a fellow dressed like that could be doin' out there. When I found out who he was, you could have knocked me over with a feather." Much to the disappointment of most of the participating units of the 42nd, the 67th Field Artillery had laid down such a devastating barrage that the Germans had evacuated most of the forward trenches before the Americans attacked. In the Salient du Feys, however, the 168th Infantry ran into a hornet's nest of machine guns. That MacArthur was not along just "for the show" was attested by Menoher's later evaluation of his role: "On this occasion, in the face of the determined and violent resistance of an alert enemy, he lent actual advice on the spot to the unit commanders and by his supervision of the operations not only guaranteed its success, but left with the entire division the knowledge of the constant attention of their leaders to their problems in action, and the sense of security which his wise and courageous leadership there impressed on the engaged companies." For his part in the action at Salient du Feys, MacArthur received the Distinguished Service Cross, the citation noting that "his coolness and conspicuous courage aided materially" in the success of the operation.[17]

Two days later the Germans countered with a poison-gas bombardment, using 75-mm. and 105-mm. shells filled with deadly palite. MacArthur, who inconsistently set forth stringent regulations regarding the wearing of gas masks but seldom carried one himself, was still in the front-line trenches and was gassed. By the time the news reached the States, the story had been somewhat garbled, the War Department telling Mrs. MacArthur that he had been wounded in combat but giving no details and the newspapers reporting that he had been "severely wounded." His mother, then living with Arthur's family at Santa Barbara, immediately sent a cablegram to Pershing inquiring about her son's condition. The A.E.F. commander knew nothing of the episode and inquired through divisional headquarters for the details. It was found that MacArthur had been "slightly gassed" on the 11th while "in action," but had recuperated within a week and had requested that his condition not be reported on the list of casualties. Pershing cabled Mrs. MacArthur this information, to which she responded: "Only God alone knows how great the comfort your reassuring message was to me, and I thank you right from the core of my heart for your prompt and gracious reply." She continued: "I pray God may bless you — and keep you safe — in this awful crisis our country is now passing through. We know your courage and ability — and realize you are the right man — in the right place." MacArthur later received the Purple Heart for this gassing, but suffered no permanent aftereffect.[18]

His recovery was rapid enough to enable him to accompany Secretary of War Baker on a brief tour of the Rainbow's position on March 19. Although Pershing tried to discourage him from venturing near the front lines, Baker, who spent several weeks with the A.E.F., insisted on visiting the forward trenches as well as the training areas in the rear. While he was touring the forward positions of the 166th Infantry, a unit from his home state of Ohio, a German 105-mm. shell exploded about twenty-five yards from his automobile. "That was a shell, wasn't it?" he asked his hosts, who yelled "Yes!" while frantically trying to get him out of the area. "Then I may say I've been under fire, mayn't I?" Baker happily quipped while continuing to stop and chat with the boys from Ohio. Before the distinguished visitor left the 42nd's sector, MacArthur gave Baker the helmet of a Bavarian officer whom he had "captured single handed in a trench raid." Upon his return to the United States, Baker sent the helmet to Mrs. MacArthur, telling reporters that he "decided not to keep it himself, because it had a greater value to the mother of the Colonel." On another occasion Baker told a group of correspondents that MacArthur, whom the press was already calling the "D'Artagnan of the A.E.F.," was "the greatest fighting front-line general" in Pershing's army — an opinion which the Chaumont folk undoubtedly would have preferred that Baker keep to himself.

Lieutenant Colonel Hugh A. Drum, a member of Pershing's general staff who was assigned to the 42nd's headquarters during the Lunéville tour, found MacArthur to be "a bright young chap — full of life and go. He will settle down soon and make his name." Of the division's tour of duty in Lunéville sector, Drum observed that "the troops had an excellent experience and received good training," but there was "failure on the part of the officers to look for and sometimes to correct errors of tactics and discipline. The principle of teaching constant observation for errors and correction of faults has not been developed sufficiently in this division." He noted, however, that the division "made a very favorable impression on the French and performed its work with excellent spirit and aggressiveness." His remarks on the divisional headquarters staff are interesting: "While the office and technical work of the staff is excellent, there is little outside work; that is, the staff does not mingle nor work in person with the troops in any great extent." MacArthur apparently employed a double standard with his subordinates, keeping them busy with paper work while he himself felt free to visit the trenches or join raids. The fact that the divisional general staff was "well organized," as Drum admitted, undoubtedly made possible MacArthur's ventures into No Man's Land.[19]

4. Holding the Line at Baccarat

Just before daybreak on March 21 some 4000 German guns began a barrage on the Picardy front which, observed an eminent authority on the war, "heralded the breaking of a storm which, in grandeur of scale, of awe, and of destruction, surpassed any other in the World War." Within a few days enemy forces had gouged a hole forty miles wide and nearly forty miles deep in the British lines before Amiens. The breakthrough produced a crisis for the Allies comparable only to the Boches' Marne offensive of 1914. German strength on the Western front had increased alarmingly — over 30 per cent — between November, 1917, and March, 1918. Moreover, the

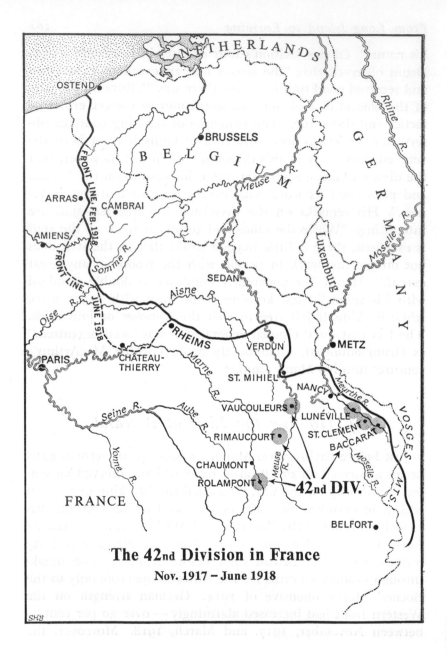

OSTEND

NETHERLANDS

BRUSSELS

BELGIUM

GERMANY

Rhine R.

Moselle R.

Luxemburg

Meuse R.

ARRAS

CAMBRAI

AMIENS

Somme R.

FRONT LINE FEB. 1918

FRONT LINE JUNE 1918

SEDAN

Aisne R.

Oise R.

RHEIMS

VERDUN

METZ

PARIS

CHÂTEAU-THIERRY

Marne R.

ST. MIHIEL

NANCY

Meurthe R.

VOSGES MTS.

Seine R.

Aube R.

VAUCOULEURS

LUNÉVILLE

RIMAUCOURT

ST. CLEMENT

BACCARAT

Yonne R.

CHAUMONT

Meuse R.

Moselle R.

ROLAMPONT

42nd DIV.

FRANCE

BELFORT

The 42nd Division in France
Nov. 1917 – June 1918

SHB

number of German divisions rose from 195 on March 21 to 207 by May 30, the addition coming from further transfers from the Russian front. On the other hand, the number of Allied divisions in France at the end of May stood at 174, the same figure as when the Germans' spring offensive began.

A week after the enemy assault started in Picardy, Pershing, who had repeatedly refused to commit his men before their training was done, gallantly compromised his convictions and placed the A.E.F.'s four divisions at the disposal of Marshal Ferdinand Foch, the recently appointed commander-in-chief of the Allied armies. "There is no question at this moment except fighting," Pershing told Foch. The 1st Division was soon committed to battle near Cantigny on the British front, but the other American divisions were sent to so-called "quiet" sectors to relieve veteran French divisions for large-scale fighting elsewhere. About the time that the great German drive began, the 42nd Division, pursuant to orders of the previous week, withdrew from the Lunéville lines and concentrated in the rear at Gerbéviller, preparatory to returning to Rolampont for further training. On March 28, however, Pershing canceled these orders and, on the advice of the French high command, sent the division to the Baccarat sector to relieve three French divisions, which, in turn, were dispatched to help stem the enemy tide north of Paris.[20]

Lying sixteen miles up the Meurthe Valley from Lunéville and twelve miles from the edge of the Vosges Mountains, Baccarat was a quaintly pretty town of 15,000 inhabitants, the main local industry being glassware manufactures. As in most French towns, the parish church was the tallest, most elegant edifice, but its "elegance is just now slightly marred by two clean shell-shots, one through its square tower and the other through the octagonal spire," observed Chaplain Duffy. Between the church and the river lay blocks of charred ruins, with only the chimneys still standing. One Rainbow soldier, looking at the devastation, remarked: "In case of bombardment, I know the safest place to get. Sit right upon top of a chimney and let them shoot away." Menoher and MacArthur set up divisional headquarters at Baccarat, the front lines extending through the heavily wooded terrain seven miles to the northeast. The division was not unfamiliar with the area since some units had been posted there during the previous month before the French command split the Baccarat subsector from the Lunéville sector.

The 42nd Division became the first American division to take over an entire sector on its own, and it held the Baccarat sector three months — longer than any other American division occupied a sector alone. Menoher commented, "I look upon this as perhaps the most interesting of the Division's service — it was the training we needed for the work that was to come after." Both Menoher and his aggressive-minded chief of staff were concerned with instilling an "offensive spirit" in their soldiers. "The first thing I did in this connection," Menoher said, "was to announce as a policy that when we got into the sector we would take over No Man's Land. We did take it over and kept it. It took us six weeks to do this, but after we once got it we kept it." MacArthur stated, "For eighty-two days the division was in almost constant combat." The division suffered over 2000 casualties from February to June, most of them incurred during the Baccarat tour. General Pierre Georges Duport, commanding the French VI Corps to which the division was attached, cited the 42nd for its "offensive ardor, the sense for the utilization and the organization of terrain for the liaison of the arms, the spirit of method, the discipline shown by all its officers and men." Duport was especially complimentary of the division's "distinguished commander" and "his staff so brilliantly directed by Colonel MacArthur." Menoher noted, however, that not all Frenchmen were pleased with the Rainbow's aggressiveness, namely, the French inhabitants of the sector. "There was a kind of understanding," he explained, "that we were not to fire on certain villages . . . I had given orders that for every shot the Germans fired we should fire at least two back. The result was that instead of firing an average of a few hundred a day we got up in the thousands and one day thirty thousand — that meant a good deal of 'boom-boom,' as the French say." Soon, Menoher said, he was pestered by civilian protestors: "They said the fool Americans were drawing the German fire and they did not like it." [21] In view of the number of glass factories in the area, their concern was at least understandable.

One American officer said of the 42nd's activity in its "private" sector: "Raids became almost as popular as going for the mail to a country post office. Everybody must have part in one, and when a raid carried through to the second German line without finding any Germans there was severe disappointment." During the first two weeks of June the division carried out ninety raids and "extended patrols" into or beyond No Man's Land.[22] Father Duffy, who became senior chaplain of the division, wrote in his diary on May 21:

> Our Chief of Staff chafes at his own task of directing instead of fighting, and he has pushed himself into raids and forays in which, some older heads think, he had no business to be. His admirers say that his personal boldness has a very valuable result in helping to give confidence to the men. Colonel [Frank R.] McCoy and Major [William J.] Donovan are strong on this point. Donovan says it would be a blamed good thing for the army if some General got himself shot in the front line. General Menoher and General Lenihan approve in secret of these madnesses; but all five of them are wild Celts, whose opinion no sane man like myself would uphold.[23]

By early summer the 42nd Division was, in Menoher's opinion, "a complete, compact, cohesive, single unit which ran like a well oiled machine . . . The Division was privileged to plume itself more or less on its excellent staff work," which was spearheaded by MacArthur, "a most brilliant officer." The soldiers were beginning to perform like veterans; raids were conducted with precision and savage effectiveness; German attacks were countered with fierce resistance and seldom caught the Rainbow troops by surprise. An indication of the division's growing efficiency was the fact that only sixty-two casualties were suffered in May in eleven German gas bombardments, involving yperite and palite gases. The amount of poison gas the enemy was hurling into the division's positions was far greater than during the Lunéville period, but the 42nd's losses therefrom were much lighter. At Lunéville many Americans at first had viewed box respirators and gas masks nonchalantly, but after heavy losses from gassing that first month, they quickly learned the value of anti-gas equipment. Indeed, during the Baccarat tour the Germans suffered more from gas than did the Yanks. On April 17, for instance, the 67th Field Artillery drenched the enemy's trenches in the Bois des Chiens with 1650 poison-gas projectiles in one morning's bombardment. The men of the Rainbow were still capable of tragic mistakes, as when a patrol was surprised and decimated by Germans on April 18 and when the 150th Field Artillery fired on the 42nd's advanced positions on May 14. But by June, Menoher and MacArthur could be cautiously optimistic; their division seemed to be gradually but surely shaping into a first-class combat unit.

Because of the dashing ways and heroics of officers like MacArthur and Donovan, the latter ultimately garnering more medals than any other 42nd officer, Menoher has been overlooked as the principal leader of the division. In fact, biographers of MacArthur suggest that the chief of staff of the 42nd really led the division during Menoher's commandership as he had under Mann's titular command. Actually Menoher was at all times in unquestioned command, while at the same time he maintained an amazingly harmonious relationship with his ambitious, high-strung chief of staff. The proof of Menoher's ability is evident not only in his leadership of the 42nd but also in the capable manner in which he served later as a corps commander and, after the war, as head of the air service. Duffy characterized Menoher well: "If he were out of uniform he would impress one as a successful business man — one of the kind that can carry responsibility, give orders affecting large affairs with calmness and certainty, and still find time to be human. He is entirely devoid of posing, of vanity, or of jealousy. His only desire is to see results." [24]

Reflecting on the accomplishments of the 42nd Division during its four months in Lorraine, Colonel Henry J. Reilly, commander of the 149th Field Artillery, reached a three-fold conclusion. First, the experience in the Lunéville and Baccarat sectors gave the Rainbow's soldiers "combat skill and confidence." Second, the division's takeover of the Baccarat line relieved three battle-trained French divisions to "fill a crucial gap in the lines to the north." Third, and "of greatest importance," he maintained, "the Rainbow in the course of its tour of duty in Lorraine demonstrated to the French, the British, and to the American high command that American citizen soldiers could take their place beside the best troops the war had produced and equal their best performance." Though Reilly, the division's official historian later, may have exaggerated his third point, he was correct in adding that the 42nd's performance, along with the records of the 1st, 2nd, and 26th divisions, "gave the Allies the confidence to use American divisions in the fateful days which were to follow."

In late May the German high command, initially intending to create merely a diversion to lure Allied reserves from the Flanders front, gave orders for an offensive against the French forces in the Aisne-Marne region, north and northeast of Paris. The diversionary thrust was a startling success, carrying the

Germans to Château-Thierry and forming a menacing salient pointed directly at Paris, which lay only fifty miles farther down the Marne. Pershing decided it was time to commit the 2nd, 26th, and 42nd divisions in the effort to save Paris and Rheims, the 1st Division already being engaged on the British front. By June, Pershing had over 510,000 combat troops in France, including eighteen full divisions, but only the original four could be considered ready for large-scale fighting. On June 16 he sent orders to Menoher to be prepared in the next week to march his division to Charmes and other nearby railheads in the rear of the Baccarat front. There the 42nd would entrain for the Champagne region east of Rheims to be assigned to General Henri Gouraud's Fourth Army, while command of the Baccarat sector would be formally relinquished on June 21 to the relieving American 77th and French 61st divisions.[25]

The busiest day in loading the 42nd's troops and thousands of tons of personal gear, caissons, tents, and other equipment was June 21. Since early that morning MacArthur and his aide, Captain Walter Wolf, had been at the loading ramps in the rail yard at Charmes. That afternoon Pershing and some of his Chaumont staff paid a surprise visit. The A.E.F. commander had just come from inspecting the weary troops and battle-scarred wagons as they neared Charmes. A tall, handsome man whose features were accentuated by his piercing eyes, square jaw, and neatly cropped mustache, Pershing was already widely known in the A.E.F. as a leader of great ability but a severe disciplinarian whose displeasure could be scathing. As he strode toward MacArthur on the loading ramp, Pershing suddenly barked out when still a dozen feet away: "This division is a disgrace. The men are poorly disciplined and they are not properly trained. The whole outfit is just about the worst I have seen." Dozens of officers and enlisted men were on the ramp and could clearly hear every word of Pershing's searing rebuke. "MacArthur," he said loudly, "I'm going to hold you personally responsible for getting discipline and order into this division. I'm going to hold you personally responsible for correcting measures with the officers at fault. I won't stand for this. It's a disgrace." All that the shocked MacArthur could stammer out was "Yes, sir!" before Pershing abruptly turned and walked off. MacArthur's face was flushed; without a word to Wolf or anyone, he left the ramp and walked into the town. Wolf followed and joined him as he sat for a long time on a bench in the town square. MacArthur finally began to talk, trying to fathom Pershing's motivation. At the time it would have been little comfort to MacArthur had he known that he had just been initiated into a growing fraternity of officers who were the targets of the perfectionist-minded Pershing's wrath. In the following days inspectors from Chaumont often dropped in on the 42nd unannounced to find faults, MacArthur finally ordering one such visitor to leave the division area or "he would personally shoot the troublemaker if he found him there again!" It is unlikely that Pershing or his headquarters staff needled or gibed the 42nd more than other divisions, but the Charmes incident marked the germination of MacArthur's notion that the "Pershing faction" was against him.[26]

Nevertheless, five days after Pershing's visit, MacArthur received his commission as a brigadier general. Either brooding or simply too busy, he procrastinated until July 11 before sending his acceptance to Pershing. Unknown to him, his mother, then staying at the Brighton Hotel in Washington, had written Pershing on June 12:

My dear General Pershing:
I am taking the liberty of writing you a little heart-to-heart letter emboldened by the thought of old friendship for you and yours, and the knowledge of my late husband's great admiration for you.
First allow me to assure you that my son, Colonel Douglas

MacArthur, knows absolutely nothing whatsoever of this letter and its purport to you.

I understand there will be made, in the near future, approximately 100 new appointments to General Officers and that all appointments for the Expeditionary Forces in France will of course be made upon your recommendations. I am most anxious that my son should be fortunate enough to receive one of these appointments, as he is a most capable officer and a hard working man.

I take it for granted that in a general way you are familiar with Colonel MacArthur's record — that he stood first in his class upon graduation at West Point, and held this position in the class for four consecutive years at the Academy; that he has always shown preference for duty of a strictly military character, or duty that would bring him in touch with the troops; that since serving in France he has had the "Croix de Guerre" and also your own "Distinguished Service Cross" bestowed upon him, and I have recently been told that his Division Commander has officially recommended that he be made a General Officer.

I know the Secretary of War and his family quite intimately, and the Secretary is very deeply attached to Colonel MacArthur and knows him well, as he served for two years as his Military Secretary at the same time that he was the War Department's Censor, both positions which he asked to be relieved in order to go to France.

I am told by the best authority that if my son's name is on your list for a recommendation to a Brigadier General that he will get the promotion. As much as my heart and ambition is involved in this advancement, neither my son or I would care to have a Star without your approval and recommendation, as we both feel so loyal to you and the cause you are defending.

During April three officers Colonel MacArthur's juniors in the National Army were selected to be Brigadier Generals including a classmate of his (General Hugh S. Johnson), who has served for several years in the Judge Advocate General's Office under General Crowder. General Johnson is a fine, capable officer, but he graduated far below my son in the class of 1903 and is nearly a year younger in years. Several other officers, junior in years, and many junior in the National Army, to my son, have been promoted to Brigadier Generals since we entered this war, and I feel that my son should not be left out on the score of age as he will be thirty-nine January next.

I am free to confess to you that my hope and ambition in life is to live long enough to see this son made a General Officer, and I feel I am placing my entire life, as it were, in your hands for consideration, and I trust you can see your way clear, dear General Pershing, to give him the recommendation necessary to advance him to the grade of Brigadier General.

With best wishes for yourself, I remain with great esteem,

Very cordially yours,

MARY P. MACARTHUR

Unfortunately Mrs. MacArthur's handwritten letter bears no marking of the date of receipt by Pershing. Since even troop transports and other high-priority vessels seldom made the trans-Atlantic voyage in less than twelve days, the letter undoubtedly reached Pershing after the incident at Charmes. On June 29 she wrote him again after reading in the newspapers of her son's promotion, along with forty-three others, to brigadier general: "I am sending in return, a heart full, pressed down, and overflowing with grateful thanks and appreciation . . . You will *not* find our Boy wanting!" On July 11, the date of his acceptance, MacArthur addressed a handwritten note to Pershing, which said in part: "The warm admiration and affection that both my Father and Mother have always expressed for you, and their confidence in the greatness of your future, have only served to make my own service in your command during the fruition of their prediction the more agreeable." He closed with a comment reminiscent of his flattering wish for Wood in 1914: "May you go on and up to the mighty destiny a grateful country owes you."

Despite his reputation as a grim, cold-hearted martinet, Pershing also could exude graciousness and charm. The day after receiving MacArthur's letter, he cabled Mrs. MacArthur: "With reference to your son, I am pleased to extend my sincere congratulations upon his advancement to the grade of Brigadier General. With very best wishes for your continued good health, believe me as always, Cordially yours, John J. Pershing." The *New York Times,* quoting a press release from Baker's office regarding MacArthur's promotion, said that he "is by many of his seniors considered the most brilliant young officer in the army." It is true that at the time of his promotion MacArthur was the youngest brigadier general in the A.E.F. (a record soon broken by two other A.E.F. officers), but if the whole story could be known, it is likely that his advancement was instigated by Baker and reluctantly approved by Pershing. The commander of the A.E.F. was a dedicated professional soldier who was not yet convinced that the acclaimed Rainbow Division and its highly touted chief of staff deserved their reputations on the basis of service in a comparatively inactive sector. The German staff, however, was planning the first test of the mettle of the 42nd Division, and the challenge would be soon in coming.[27]

CHAPTER VII

Turning the Tide
in Champagne

1. The Last German Offensive

TIME BECAME A PARAMOUNT FACTOR in the deliberations of the German high command in June, 1918. The drive down the Marne Valley toward Paris was thwarted that month by the savage counterattacks of the 2nd and 3rd divisions, A.E.F., at Belleau Wood and Château-Thierry. Since early spring one blow after another had been hurled against the Allied forces on the Western front, but none had brought the vital decision which the Boche desperately desired. Aware that huge numbers of fresh American troops were landing in France each week, the total passing the million mark by July, the German strategy-makers bent their efforts toward gaining a major breakthrough before the Yankee reinforcement became insurmountable. General Erich von Ludendorff, the German chief of staff, conceived an all-out offensive through the British positions in Flanders as his decisive, climactic drama to end the war. As a preliminary diversion, he plotted a two-pronged drive on either side of Rheims — one toward Châlons-sur-Marne and the other in the direction of Epernay. Even the diversionary offensive was planned on a grand scale. If successful, the attackers would converge south of Rheims, surrounding that key city, separating the defenders of Verdun from those of Paris, and greatly improving rail communications within the Marne salient. Three armies, comprising forty-seven divisions, would be committed to the Champagne-Marne attack, with many of the infantry and artillery units scheduled for transfer to the Flanders front five days later, so quickly did the Germans expect to reach Châlons and Epernay.

Since the last week of June the 42nd Division had been in the vicinity of Châlons-sur-Marne in reserve of General Henri Gouraud's Fourth Army. On July 5 the division was given the responsibility of defending the so-called second position, or rear line of defense, in the Espérance and Souain sectors, twenty-five miles east of Rheims. The first and intermediate positions in these sectors were held by the French 13th and 170th divisions. Five battalions of the 42nd were assigned to the intermediate position, which ran several kilometers north of the towns of St. Hilaire-sur-Suippes, Souain, and Perthes-les-Hurlus.

The plan of defense used in the Champagne-Marne operation was originated by General Henri Philippe Pétain, Gouraud's superior. The first, or forward-most, position would be held by the barest minimum of defenders. Much of the enemy's pre-assault barrage was expected to fall on this line. When the German infantry neared the first position, the troops at those outposts would signal the forces on the intermediate position by means of rockets and flares and then evacuate the forward line. Thereupon the American and French artillery would bombard the advancing Germans, who would be beyond the assistance of most of their own artillery by the time they reached the intermediate position, which was the most heavily defended line. The second position, which was actually the third, would constitute the rear line of defense. Though this plan of elastic defense in depth was as old as the battle of Cannae where Hannibal used it effectively, its most telling application would be in the impending Champagne-Marne defensive.[1]

The Espérance and Souain sectors lay in the forest-splotched, rolling chalk plain of Champagne. Running in a northerly direction across the western end of the 42nd's positions was the narrow Suippes River. The most heavily forested area along the first and intermediate positions was the Spandau Woods, located northeast of Souain. A sunken Roman road, still a distinctive landmark, bisected the highway between Souain and Châlons-sur-Marne, midway between the intermediate and rear positions. Unlike the beautiful country of Lorraine where the 42nd had been stationed, the Champagne Plain justified historian Jules Michelet's description of it as "a melancholy sea of stubble spreading over a plain of plaster." A popular saying among the local peasants was that the land was so poor that "an acre of land, when it had a hare on it, was worth just two francs." Hunting, sheep raising, and pine lumbering were the chief vocations on the plain. The pervious chalk, however, did offer its advantages, affording drier trenches and smoother roads than in Lorraine. The chalk plain was not unlike that of the battlefield of the Somme, though the Champagne Plain had not been subjected to as much devastation as the plain on the British front. Most of the high ground in the Champagne-Marne area lay to the north of the Allied positions, the Germans holding the forested elevations from Notre Dame des Champs Ridge northwest of Souain to Souain Butte to the northeast. Gouraud anticipated that an enemy offensive in that region would probably follow the lines of least topographic resistance, namely, up the Suippes Valley toward St. Hilaire and along the Sommepy-Souain road.

Expertly overseeing the preparation of the defenses were Generals Gouraud, André Pretelat, the Fourth Army's chief of staff, and Pierre Naulin, commander of the French XXI Corps, to which the 42nd Division was attached. Gouraud was almost a legendary figure in French military circles, having won glory in the Algerian campaigns before 1914 and against the Turks at Gallipoli in 1915–16. MacArthur was fascinated by him: "With one arm gone, and half a leg missing, with his red beard glittering in the sunlight, the jaunty rake of his cocked hat and the oratorical brilliance of his resonant voice, his impact was overwhelming." Looking back years later, MacArthur said of Gouraud: "I have known all of the modern French commanders, and many were great measured by any standards, but he was the greatest of them all." In turn, the French general was profuse in his praise of MacArthur, as Lieutenant Colonel S. L. H. Slocum testified in a letter to the adjutant general in Washington just after the war: "Recently while visiting the French Front and the Army of Occupation, I met General Gouraud, French Army, at luncheon in Strasbourg. After the luncheon General Gouraud came up to me and asked me if I knew General Douglas MacArthur of the American Army. I stated I did know him. He then remarked: 'I consider General MacArthur to be one of the finest and bravest officers I have ever served with.'" MacArthur said of their relationship: "The more I saw of him the more I liked him. It became a mutual friendship that lasted until his death many years later." [2]

From late June onward Gouraud was convinced that the Germans were going to launch a major offensive in the area around Rheims, though neither the generals at Chaumont or Rainbow headquarters agreed with him for a while. Nevertheless, on July 7 Gouraud sent the following dramatic message to the XXI Corps:

We may be attacked at any moment.
You all know that a defensive battle was never engaged under more favorable conditions. We are awake and on our guard. We are powerfully reinforced with infantry and artillery. You will fight on a terrain that you have transformed by your work and your perseverance into a redoubtable fortress. This invincible fortress and all its passages are well guarded.

The bombardment will be terrible. You will stand it without weakness. The assault will be fierce, in a cloud of smoke, dust and gas. But your positions and your armament are formidable.

In your breasts beat the brave and strong hearts of free men. None shall look to the rear; none shall yield a step. Each shall have but one thought: to kill, to kill, until they have had their fill.

Therefore your General says to you: You will break this assault and it will be a happy day.[3]

On the afternoon of July 14 Gouraud hosted the generals and colonels of the 42nd Division at an early dinner. Everyone was braced for the German assault, which was expected shortly. "During July 13 and 14 the Germans were especially careless about concealing the movements of their troops," Menoher commented, "either doing this for the effect that large reserve movements might have on us, or that they considered concealment unnecessary and were going through anyway." Not long after the officers had left Gouraud's dinner, twenty-seven German prisoners were brought in by a French patrol. A quick but thorough interrogation of them revealed that the enemy artillery barrage was scheduled to begin at midnight, with the infantry assault to follow four hours later.

At 11:30 P.M. the French artillery and the guns of Brigadier General George G. Gatley's 67th Field Artillery opened fire on the soldiers massing for the attack. The intense bombardment caused such severe casualties in some Boche units that they had to be replaced before the assault began. Shortly after midnight the German barrage started, concentrating mainly on the first position, which was thinly manned. "It is estimated that on both sides 5500 guns were in action," Menoher said, "and it was probably as heavy as any firing of artillery during the war. The noise was so great that no one could make himself heard, all orders had to be written." Father Duffy remarked, "The whole sky seemed to be torn apart with sound."[4]

As planned, the few soldiers left on the first position gave

warning of the German advance four hours later. These heroic
men included some troops of the Rainbow Division, nearly all
of whom lost their lives during the shelling or when the enemy
masses overran their outposts. The German advance was swift,
of course, through the first position; delighted Boche officers in
the front lines sent back reports that "the shock of the initial
onslaught had been irresistible." For the first hour or so of the
German assault, some French commanders "showed a little
nervousness as to the ability of the American soldiers" to withstand the enemy, an American officer noted, "but as soon as the
reports began to come in, their confidence was restored." The
headquarters of the 42nd was near Vadenay Farm, several miles
to the rear, but MacArthur was with the troops on the intermediate, or main, line when the waves of German infantry hit.
"When they met the dikes of our real line," he said, "they were
exhausted, unco-ordinated, and scattered, incapable of going
further without being reorganized and reinforced." Between
the first and intermediate positions the Allied artillery barrage
"descended like an avalanche" on the advancing enemy, as Mac-
Arthur described it. Private Charles MacArthur, a future play-
wright and no kin to the divisional chief of staff, jotted in his
diary: "A boiling bank of dirty smoke hides the flower of the
Prussian Guard. In back, ammunition trains race across the
fields at a dead gallop, the drivers beating their horses with
steel helmets . . . The guns are so hot now that they have to
be swabbed after every shot." Time after time that day the Germans attacked the intermediate position, only to be thrown
back repeatedly with horrendous losses. The most savage fighting on the 15th took place north of Souain on the east side of
the road to Sommepy where the Boche made two slight penetra-
tions in the line of the 167th Infantry, but were dislodged
shortly in a bloody counterattack. About 750 American soldiers
died during the first twenty-four hours of the battle, but the
42nd Division and the two French divisions held firm on the

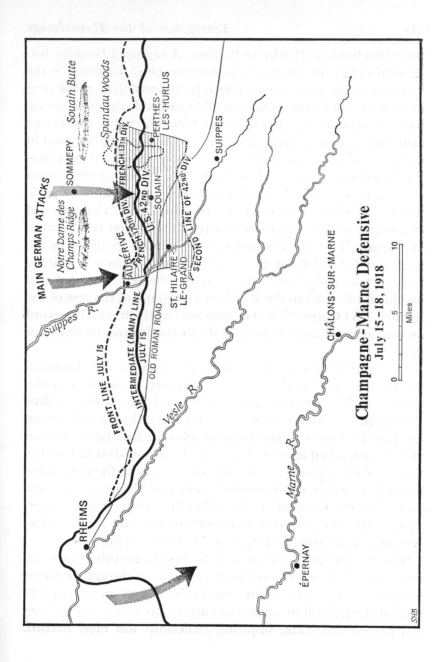

Champagne-Marne Defensive

July 15–18, 1918

MAIN GERMAN ATTACKS

Notre Dame des Champs Ridge

Souain Butte

Spandau Woods

SOMMEPY

PERTHES-LES-HURLUS

FRENCH 13TH DIV.

U.S. 42ND DIV.

FRENCH 170TH DIV.

SOUAIN

LINE OF 42ND DIV.

SUIPPES

Suippes R.

AUBÉRIVE

FRENCH 170TH DIV.

SECOND

ST. HILAIRE-LE-GRAND

FRONT LINE JULY 15

INTERMEDIATE (MAIN) LINE JULY 15

OLD ROMAN ROAD

Vesle R.

CHÂLONS-SUR-MARNE

RHEIMS

Marne R.

ÉPERNAY

0   5   10

Miles

SHB

main line from St. Hilaire to Perthes. A captured German battle plan called for the Boche infantry to be in Châlons by the morning of the 16th, but despite repeated assaults for the next three days, the Germans were unable to break through the intermediate position. "There was no flinching on the part of our men," an American officer observed. "Wounded artillerymen in their gas masks continued serving their guns; infantrymen, knocked down and bruised by shells, picked up their rifles again and continued firing." MacArthur noted with justifiable pride that the division's conduct was "inspiring" and "characterized by a degree of determination worthy of the highest traditions of our Army. This was due not only to natural qualities in the men, but behind them there was something more, a driving force of powerful effect." As the smoke cleared, Gouraud sent his congratulations to the Rainbow Division and the rest of the staunch XXI Corps: "The German has clearly broken his sword on our lines. Whatever he may do in the future, he shall not pass." [5]

Meanwhile the French Fifth Army, to which the American 3rd Division was attached, had not prepared its defenses as adequately or wisely as Gouraud's forces, and several enemy divisions managed to get across the Marne southwest of Rheims. By July 18, however, the German advance had been checked and never reached its goal, Epernay. After four days of fury the Germans' Champagne-Marne offensive was dead; the great drive through Flanders was postponed, and the Marne salient now seemed to the Germans to be a liability rather than an asset. "The German's last great attack of the war had failed," MacArthur commented, "and Paris could breathe again."

The fighting near Souain was the first large-scale combat in which MacArthur had ever been engaged. Although he might have had good excuses, as divisional chief of staff, to remain well behind the main line, he was usually found where the fighting was fiercest and calm, inspiring leadership was most needed.

Staff planning, its spadework well prepared by him in advance, did not seem to suffer when he was absent from headquarters during the fighting. Menoher later remarked, "MacArthur is the bloodiest fighting man in this army. I'm afraid we're going to lose him sometime, for there's no risk of battle that any soldier is called upon to take that he is not liable to look up and see MacArthur at his side." On Menoher's recommendation he was awarded his second Silver Star. At Châlons several evenings after the victory he joined some fellow officers who were celebrating at a bar, enjoying the traditional drinking and carousing of post-battle relief. Sensitive to the horrible carnage he had just witnessed, MacArthur found that he could not enjoy the raucous festivities: "I found something missing. It may have been the vision of those writhing bodies hanging from the barbed wire or the stench of dead flesh still in my nostrils. Perhaps I was just getting old; somehow, I had forgotten how to play." [6] Soldiering did not seem romantic any more.

2. *The Ourcq and Beyond*

After the collapse of the German offensive, Foch wasted no time launching a counteroffensive, designed to wipe out the Marne salient. Three French armies, with nine American divisions included, were to attack simultaneously the western, southern, and eastern faces of the salient. The most critical operation was that in the Soissons area, which was launched on July 18 and within two days had succeeded in cutting the enemy's main communications within the salient. Confronted with the possibility of its divisions to the south being trapped, the German command decided to evacuate the salient by progressive withdrawals to defensive lines on the Ourcq and Vesle rivers. By the evening of the 21st the Boche, while offering fierce rearguard resistance, had withdrawn from the Marne and the immediate vicinity of Château-Thierry. General Liggett, whose I Corps was attached to the French Sixth Army at the southern tip of the salient, became highly annoyed with the failures of the commander of the 26th Division, which was supposed to be the main attacking force north of Château-Thierry. On July 25 the commander of the I Corps, in disgust, relieved the 26th Division and assigned its sector to the Rainbow Division, which had been rushed from the Souain-Châlons area. The relief took place eight miles northeast of Château-Thierry in the Fère Forest, just east of the town of Beauvardes; a steady rain was falling, turning the few roads in the region into quagmires. In the next two days the 42nd was ordered to relieve also a brigade of the 28th Division and two French divisions, which had been operating on the flanks of the 26th Division. Hardly recuperated from their first major ordeal of combat, the Champagne-Marne operation, the Rainbow troops now found themselves responsible for the entire front of the I Corps — a line running from Beauvardes completely across the rugged terrain of the Fère Forest.[7]

The troops of the 42nd had moved only a short distance northward when one of the brigades, the 84th, was stopped by the withering fire of a cluster of machine-gun nests hidden in and around the half dozen stone-walled buildings of Croix Rouge Farm, located in a large clearing in the middle of the Fère Forest. The stronghold was ideally situated to cover the main road running north through the forest to Villers-sur-Fère and the Ourcq River. Until late in the afternoon of July 26 the Americans' advance was stymied by the Germans at Croix Rouge Farm, the infantry being unable to approach the bastion because of the open fields surrounding it. Then some soldiers discovered a ditch, hidden by straggly bushes and running from the edge of the forest to the entrance to the farm compound. Toward dusk two platoons crept along the ditch, caught the German gunners off guard, and seized the farm after a period of ruthless hand-to-hand fighting. Corporal Sidney E. Manning, in charge of an automatic rifle squad, was wounded early in the attack, but continued to lead his squad, himself killing several Germans in individual combat. When his superiors in the platoon fell dead or wounded, he took command and skillfully and bravely led the soldiers in repulsing a determined Boche effort to retake the farm. Thanks to Manning and the men of those two platoons, Croix Rouge Farm was permanently secured, and the momentum of the advance was regained. Several hours after the fighting ended at the farm, Manning died, nine wounds being found in his body. He was posthumously awarded the Congressional Medal of Honor, the first such honor for a member of the 42nd Division.[8] There would be many more valorous sacrifices in the division's immediate future and, unfortunately, more fortified farms like Croix Rouge.

Unknown to the advancing Americans, the main enemy forces had withdrawn to the Ourcq during the night of July 26–27, leaving behind, however, some well-placed machine-gun nests to slow their pursuers. One such obstacle was encountered at Croix Blanche Farm, which the 42nd finally secured after several costly charges. Breaking out onto the wide apron of open fields which swept down toward the Ourcq, the Rainbow's two infantry brigades were able to move forward more rapidly, the impression being that the Boche were in full retreat. On the afternoon of the 27th the New Yorkers of the 165th Infantry occupied Villers-sur-Fère, a town located just south of the Ourcq. As the division neared the river, it was subjected to heavy shelling from artillery pieces located on the high ground beyond the Ourcq. Corporal Elmer W. Sherwood wrote in his diary: "We are encountering every sort of German gas . . . One thing which saves us from being gassed is the warning the gas shells make when they burst . . . The approaching sound reminds one of the meowing of a cat, developing into a scream as it approaches." Moving across the open ground, the Ameri-

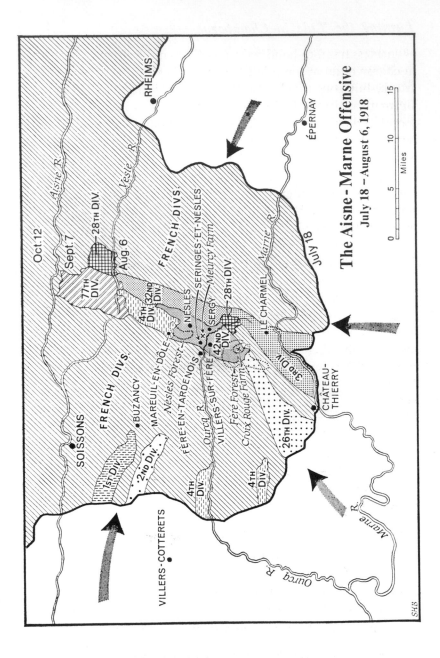

The Aisne-Marne Offensive
July 18 – August 6, 1918

Miles
0   5   10   15

RHEIMS

ÉPERNAY

Oct.12

Sept.7

Aug.6

28TH DIV.

77TH DIV.

Aisne R.

Vesle R.

FRENCH DIVS.

SERINGES-ET-NESLES

Meurcy Farm

SERGY

NESLES

4TH DIV. 32ND DIV.

28TH DIV.

42ND DIV.

LE CHARMEL

Marne R.

July 18

3RD DIV.

CHÂTEAU-THIERRY

26TH DIV.

FRENCH DIVS.

SOISSONS

BUZANCY

MAREUIL-EN-DÔLE

Nesles Forest

FÈRE-EN-TARDENOIS

Ourcq R.

VILLERS-SUR-FÈRE

Fère Forest

Croix Rouge Farm

1ST DIV.

2ND DIV.

4TH DIV.

4TH DIV.

VILLERS-COTTERETS

Ourcq R.

Marne R.

SHB

cans were also easy targets for bombing and strafing German aircraft; inexplicably no Allied airplanes were sent against them.
Sergeant Frank Gardella, however, offered effective individual
opposition when two enemy aircraft strafed his outfit. According to one account, he "coolly sighted his gun and riddled the
upper plane, causing it to collapse and fall in flames. In falling
it struck the lower plane and brought it to the earth also."

Though swollen somewhat by the recent rains, the Ourcq was
only about fifteen yards wide and three feet deep, presenting no
difficulty in crossing. Immediately to the north of the stream
were several patches of woods between which ran the main
road from Sergy westward to Fère-en-Tardenois. Beyond the
road the ground sloped steeply 200 feet or more upward to
create the Ourcq Heights, atop which the Germans waited in
well-prepared positions. The principal enemy fortifications
along the three-mile stretch of high ground facing the oncoming
42nd were centered about the towns of Seringes-et-Nesles and
Sergy, respectively at the western and eastern ends of the divisional front, and in a thick-walled farm complex between
these towns known as Meurcy Farm. From the upper slopes
and crest of the heights the Germans enjoyed excellent fields of
fire. Because of the rapidity of the Boche withdrawal from the
Fère Forest, the French and American commanders were uncertain whether the enemy would make a stand at the Ourcq.
Near midnight of July 27 Menoher received orders from the
headquarters of the French Sixth Army directing his division
to cross the Ourcq before dawn, seize the heights, and, if the
enemy did not make a stand, continue the pursuit northward
to the Vesle River. MacArthur, on behalf of Menoher, responded that the 42nd infantry had outdistanced most of their
supply trains and artillery support, but, nevertheless, the division would carry out the attack that night.[9]

An hour before sunrise on July 28 the 42nd Division, with
the 83rd Brigade on the left and the 84th on the right, stormed

across the Ourcq, quickly seized the road to Sergy, and started ascending the heights. The 84th Brigade's progress was impressive at first, the troops capturing Hill 212 and fighting their way into Sergy. But the defenders, reinforced now by the crack 4th Prussian Guard Division, counterattacked and retook the town. By nightfall Sergy had changed hands seven times, but the Boche were in control at the end of the day's fighting. To the west the 83rd Brigade also got off to a good start, only to be forced back down the slopes before sunset. The soldiers of that brigade advanced all the way to a ridge east of Meurcy Farm before a German counterattack compelled them to withdraw toward the river. That day the American 28th Division and the French 62nd Division, on the Rainbow's right and left flanks respectively, met similar fates, crossing the Ourcq but failing to take the high ground beyond, which was the day's objective for all three divisions. That evening MacArthur must have been irked when he read a new order from the Sixth Army calling for the 42nd to renew the attack the next morning and break through to the Vesle. In the typical confusion of battle the French headquarters apparently had not received word that the Germans were no longer withdrawing. It was a sleepless night for MacArthur, who moved from one command post to another hurriedly arranging preparations for the new attacks.

Reinforced by two battalions of the fresh but inexperienced 4th Division, the troops of the Rainbow started moving up the slopes again on the morning of July 29, with the enemy machine-gun fire seemingly more devastating than the previous day. According to MacArthur, who earned his third Silver Star for his bravery under fire during the action that day: "Bitterly, brutally, the action seesawed back and forth. A point would be taken, and then would come a sudden fire from some unsuspected direction and the deadly counterattack . . . There was neither rest nor mercy." Sergy was taken and lost four times before late afternoon when the 84th Brigade permanently secured the battered town. To the left the 83rd took the Colas Woods, in front of Meurcy Farm, and drove the Germans out of Seringes-et-Nesles, killing the stubborn defenders to a man in the latter action. A German general, commenting on the actions at Sergy and Seringes, exclaimed that "the Americans appeared inexhaustible." Part of the reason for the day's success was the effective support given by the division's artillery, now reinforced by the 4th Division's field artillery brigade. The next day the 83rd Brigade, paying a frightful toll in lives, finally captured strongly held Meurcy Farm; some of its units advanced as far as the southern edge of the Nesles Forest, north of Seringes. Despite a two-hour artillery barrage preparatory to its attack, however, the 84th Brigade was unable to progress beyond the northern outskirts of Sergy. By late afternoon the Americans' forward movement was checked all along the divisional front because of mounting German resistance, abetted by a newly arrived Bavarian division of veterans. Moreover, the 42nd's right flank was now dangerously exposed because of the failure of the 28th Division to push forward during the previous three days.[10]

At the height of the fighting on the 31st, with neither brigade making much progress, Menoher notified Liggett that Brigadier General Robert Brown was "no longer fit to command a Brigade in combat" and must be relieved as commander of the 84th. He requested authority to assign MacArthur as acting commander of the brigade, which the I Corps leader approved. Both Menoher and Liggett had a high regard for MacArthur's leadership ability and knew that he was anxious for a command of his own. The officers and men of the 84th were already well acquainted with MacArthur as a most unusual divisional chief of staff — daring, indeed, reckless, in exposing himself to enemy fire as he moved from post to post along the front lines. MacArthur's performance as chief of staff would later bring him the Distinguished Service Medal and, more precious to him, a gold cigarette box from his former staff bearing the words, "The bravest of the brave." Until August 6, when an order came through making official his appointment as acting brigade commander, MacArthur continued to carry the title of chief of staff, but actually was in the field leading the 84th. Lieutenant Colonel William Hughes' selection as acting chief of staff, soon to be made permanent, was, no doubt, the work of his childhood friend, MacArthur.[11]

With little progress made on the morning of July 31, the 42nd got orders to attack at four-thirty that afternoon in concert with the 32nd Division, which had just relieved the 28th Division on the Rainbow's right. A brigade of the 4th Division was attached to the 42nd as divisional reserve. The 83rd Brigade was able to move into the Brulé Woods, just north of Meurcy Farm, but was hurled back elsewhere along its front. MacArthur's brigade tried again and again to advance north of Sergy, but was thwarted by intense enemy fire and the failure of the 32nd Division to move forward on its flank. That evening another rankling order came from Sixth Army directing the 42nd to attack in force before the next dawn, break through the German lines, and — not surprising to Menoher by this time — pursue the enemy to the Vesle.

In the pre-dawn darkness on August 1 MacArthur's exhausted troops renewed the attack north of Sergy. This time a battalion of the 168th Infantry succeeded in capturing the high ground from which enemy machine-gunners had been so effectively raking the American ranks. Again, however, the 32nd Division did not keep pace, exposing the right flank of MacArthur's brigade, so he reluctantly ordered his advanced forces to pull back to the edge of Sergy. A regiment of the 4th Division, serving with the 84th Brigade, suffered heavy losses in a vain effort to advance west of the town. As for the 83rd Brigade, it also made no appreciable progress on August 1. That afternoon an order came from Liggett's headquarters declaring that the Rainbow Division would be relieved by the 4th Division on the night of August 2–3. The news must have been a keen disappointment to MacArthur, who, like the other dedicated officers and men of the Rainbow, wanted desperately to reach the corps' original objective, the Vesle.[12]

A German deserter picked up by a French unit east of the 32nd Division on July 31 disclosed that his division and others were withdrawing northward that day. But no lessening of enemy resistance was noticed along the 42nd's front for some time. At 3:30 A.M., August 2, MacArthur, having heard "the rumbling of many vehicles on the move" along the German line opposite his brigade, took an aide and ventured into No Man's Land above Sergy. Except for occasional sniper fire and sporadic shell bursts, he found the area near the German lines disturbed only by "the moans and cries of wounded men," apparently forsaken by their retreating comrades. MacArthur estimated that he passed at least 2000 enemy corpses; stopping at some, he counted insignias of "six of the best German divisions." Once, in the light of a flare, he saw with alarm a German machine gun close by, pointed directly at him. When the crew did not fire, he crawled to the gun and discovered "they were dead, all dead — the lieutenant with shrapnel through his heart, the sergeant with his belly blown into his back, the corporal with his spine where his head should have been." About daybreak MacArthur and his aide made their way back into the American lines with the momentous news that the German front line was abandoned. Hurrying to divisional headquarters at Beauvardes, where he found Menoher and Liggett in conference, he told them of the withdrawal. As the generals hastily set about mapping plans for the pursuit, MacArthur, who had not slept for ninety-six hours, settled into a chair and fell into a deep slumber. Liggett looked at him sympathetically and said, "Well, I'll be damned! Menoher, you better cite him." MacArthur, awakening a short time later, learned that the division was already moving forward and he was to be the recipient of another Silver Star, his fourth.[13]

Whereas for five days the 42nd's progress had been measured

in yards, on August 2 the division raced northward four miles in close pursuit of the Germans. MacArthur's brigade, operating largely over open ground, was able to outdistance the 83rd Brigade, which was moving through the Nesles Forest. While the 167th Infantry took the town of Nesles and pushed on another mile, the 117th Engineers, acting as infantry, passed through the 168th Infantry, hardest hit of the 42nd's regiments, and reached the northern edge of the Voizelle Woods, only five miles from the Vesle. To the west the 83rd Brigade pushed through and beyond the Nesles Forest, its farthest units temporarily occupying the town of Mareuil-en-Dôle, between the forest and the Vesle. The French 62nd and American 32nd divisions on the Rainbow's flanks made similar long strides that day as the Boche fled toward the Vesle.[14]

In a field message to Menoher, marked 12:10 P.M., August 2, MacArthur revealed the frantic nature of the chase and his own intense, enthusiastic involvement:

> Have personally assumed command of the line. Have broken the enemy's resistance on the right. Immediately threw forward my left and broke his front. Am advancing my whole line with utmost speed. The enemy is immediately in front but am maneuvering my battalions so that he can not get set in position. If he has not already a prepared position of defense in the Foret de Nesles, I intend to throw him into the Vesle. I am using small patrols acting with great speed and continually flanking him so that he can not form a line of resistance. I am handling the columns myself, and my losses are extraordinarily light. Am transmitting by later message instructions with reference to 4th Division. Have thrown my artillery across the Ourc [*sic*], both lights and heavies. Am strengthening and making additional bridges across Ourc. Have ordered forward all field trains.[15]

MacArthur did not get the chance to drive the enemy into the Vesle, for that night the 4th Division, as scheduled, began relieving the 42nd, the change being completed by early morning of August 3. MacArthur's brigade, fatigued by nine straight days of combat, turned over its sector to the 8th Brigade and began the wearisome march back to the Fère Forest where the 42nd was to remain in corps reserve. Father Duffy, who had faithfully stayed with the front-line troops throughout the Ourcq battle, observed: "Back came our decimated battalions along the way they had already traveled. They marched in wearied silence until they came to the slopes around Meurcy Farm. Then from end to end of the line came the sound of dry, suppressed sobs. They were marching among the bodies of their unburied dead." Accustomed to seeing French civilians fleeing southward to escape the Germans, Corporal Sherwood, a Rainbow artilleryman, wrote in his diary: "The most impressive sight along the way is the returning of the refugees . . . I saw an old woman just returned home searching through the pile of debris for something she, no doubt, had hidden in haste when she was driven away by the advance of the enemy . . . Their dauntless spirit compels these children and older folk to return to their homes almost before the smoke of battle has cleared away." [16]

The division's losses were appallingly apparent when the men reassembled in the Fère Forest. Some regiments looked like battalions, and some battalions were reduced to company size. Since July 25 the 42nd's casualties in dead, wounded, and missing had numbered nearly 6500 officers and men. The 84th Brigade, whose authorized strength was 8454 officers and men, had entered the Aisne-Marne offensive with only 5155. Of these, 566 had been killed, 2123 were wounded, and 146 were missing. One of those who died in combat west of Sergy was a young sergeant whose personality, bravery, and ability to write poems had made him a popular and respected comrade in the 165th Infantry. His name was Joyce Kilmer.[17]

For a week the division continued in the forest in corps reserve, ever on the alert for possible recall to action in the fighting now raging along the Vesle. "Living conditions were bad," commented one Rainbow soldier, who found that his regiment had lost most of its gear during the battle and did not even have sufficient tents to protect the men from the rains, which came almost daily. Another tired veteran declared that the reserve area was "on the verge of becoming a pesthole," with "the country full of ruined villages, dead, unburied bodies — Boche and American — and thousands of dead horses. The men were dirty; baths were next to impossible . . . Sickness broke out." On August 4 Menoher wrote Liggett requesting that the division "be withdrawn to a rest area in order to recuperate, reconstitute, re-equip and amalgamate the replacements it is to receive." Reminding the corps commander that the Rainbow had sustained casualties of nearly 9000 in three weeks, Menoher stated that during that period "the division had only two nights' rest to alerts, fighting and advancing." He emphasized that "the loss and deterioration of animals and of organization and personal equipment has been in proportion to the casualties sustained in men," all of which "have left their mark on the division." Without at least a month's rest, he warned, "the division will deteriorate to a marked extent." Liggett responded that the request was "a reasonable one" and would be granted "if matters become stabilized in the near future." For the time being, the best he could give the 42nd was a visit by entertainer Elsie Janis. "Into the middle of this filthy backyard of war with its sickening smells and sights and its unkempt, lousy men there bounded on a fine afternoon one Elsie Janis — fluffy, beautiful, piquant," said a Rainbow soldier, adding: "An aeroplane came whirring overhead while Elsie Janis sang 'Oh, You Dirty Germans!' It came so low that you could see the black maltese cross on the lower wings. But nobody minded." [18]

Along the Vesle the Germans held staunchly until late August when their position became untenable after an Allied break-through north of Soissons. Although the American 1st, 2nd, and 32nd divisions, which fought along the western face of the Marne salient, have received the most attention from authorities on the campaign, the 42nd could be justly proud of its role in wiping out the salient. As Menoher reported on August 2, "In eight days of battle, the 42nd Division has forced the passage of the Ourcq, taken prisoners from six enemy divisions, met, routed, decimated a crack division of the Prussian Guard, a Bavarian division and one other division, and driven back the enemy's line for sixteen kilometers." A post-battle analysis prepared later by divisional headquarters noted, however, that the 42nd's effectiveness in the Aisne-Marne offensive would have been measurably increased if it had been supported by tanks and aircraft. The report also stressed that "the supply problem in a rapid advance of this character is serious and should be carefully organized in advance. With American troops, the matter of water supply is a most important one, and considerable sickness has resulted from the use of infected or impure water." Of interest in view of Menoher's postwar position as head of the Army's air service was the emphasis placed on the potential role of air power: "The fact that the enemy had practically complete control of the air not only prevented our troops from receiving adequate information but enabled the enemy to adopt a very aggressive attitude in the way of firing on our troops with machine guns and bombs." [19]

Besides the American medals he received, MacArthur was awarded a second Croix de Guerre and was made a Commander of France's Legion of Honor. His reputation as a gifted leader in battle was established firmly, and he now commanded an infantry brigade which, though depleted by heavy losses, was regarded by friend and foe as a first-class attack force. As he discovered in the weeks after the Ourcq fighting, however, his position as commander of the 84th Brigade was somewhat tenuous for a while. Toward the end of July, General Peyton C. March, the Army's chief of staff in Washington, had decided to call MacArthur back to the States to command and train an infantry brigade of the recently organized 11th Division, which was assembling at Camp Meade, Maryland. The *New York Times* on August 3 reported that "it was officially learned today" that MacArthur had been ordered to return to lead the new brigade. Exactly when the order reached MacArthur is not known, but it probably arrived toward the end of the division's stay in the Fère Forest. Correspondent Frazier Hunt, who was in France and knew MacArthur well, said that when Menoher received it, he "registered his violent protest. Captain Wolf hurried to Chaumont with the plea that MacArthur could not be spared." On August 7 MacArthur sent a telegram to Chaumont requesting that his assignment as 84th commander "be made permanent"; he did not mention the recall order, which probably had not yet reached him. On the 11th the adjutant general of the A.E.F. notified Menoher: "Retain Brigadier General Douglas MacArthur on duty with your division and in command of Brigade pending further instructions." On August 18 orders were issued giving him permanent command of the 84th, the orders from Washington having been voided.

Regardless of what MacArthur partisans may conjecture, no evidence was found that Pershing or his staff at Chaumont initiated the move to have MacArthur sent back to America. Indeed, by that critical stage in the war Pershing must have been thankful to have officers of his caliber in the field. If the whole truth could be known, the idea may have germinated in the mind of MacArthur's good friend, Secretary Baker, who probably knew that MacArthur desired a combat command and would prove able in such a role. However it came about, it was most fortunate for MacArthur and the 84th Brigade that he was allowed to retain the command. For him, it was a position which he deserved and wanted; moreover, he was well

aware that combat command was the surest ladder upward to
a successful military career. For the brigade, he was, according
to Menoher, "the source of the greatest possible inspiration";
his men "are devoted to him." [20] Perhaps in no other role during his long career would MacArthur fit so naturally and derive
such deep satisfaction.

CHAPTER VIII

The Easiest and

Hardest Battles

1. Prelude to St. Mihiel

THE WEARY SOLDIERS of the Rainbow Division received only a week's rest, near La Ferté-sous-Jouarre, after leaving the Fère Forest in mid-August. When the division was sent to the Bourmont training area, northeast of Chaumont, for twelve days of intensive drilling in offensive tactics and formations, grumbling was widespread among both officers and men. "The new Brigade Commander, General MacArthur, who then as always showed a lively interest in his troops' welfare," said First Lieutenant John H. Taber of the 168th Infantry, "took matters in his own hands, and on his own responsibility decided to grant forty-eight hour passes to Paris, ten per cent of the officers and men to go at one time . . . The brigade rubbed its eyes in disbelief — it was too good to be true." On the morning of August 22 the first contingent to receive the passes, a group of 200 happy men of the 168th, set off by train for the French capital and two glorious days of wine and women. At Langres, however, the group was ordered to return to its station at Bourmont. "The worst had happened," Taber related. "General Mac-

Arthur had exceeded his authority, it appeared, in granting passes beyond the limits of brigade area." While waiting at Langres for another train which would carry them back to the training area, the doughboys spotted an empty train, rushed aboard, and were about to get it started when a military police detachment thwarted their bold plan. "What would have happened had they actually set out on an uncharted trip to the capital of France," Taber commented, "is problematical — it leaves much to the imagination." The disappointed soldiers returned to the encampment at Bourmont, the incident soon being overshadowed by the exciting news that they would participate in the first independent American operation — the St. Mihiel offensive.

For the next two weeks MacArthur and the other Rainbow officers were busily occupied training replacements, re-equipping units, and conducting attack maneuvers. The several thousand replacements which the 42nd received during this period were, according to Taber, "cannon fodder, if there ever was any." One company commander reported a typical instance of receiving forty-three replacements of whom "one man had had but one week of training; four had had two weeks; twenty, three weeks; six, four weeks; and the rest anywhere between one and three months." On August 28 the 42nd was sent to a training area near Neufchâteau and a week later to one near Colombey-les-Belles — each move bringing it closer to the St. Mihiel salient. Early on the morning of September 9 the troops marched into the Reine Forest, just south of the front. "Rain was still falling," observed a soldier of the 167th Infantry, "and the darkness was impenetrable. No lights could be employed and the tired troops plunged blindly from the muddy road into the thick forest, cast aside their heavy, water-soaked burdens, pitched shelter-tents, and wrapped themselves in wet blankets to enjoy a rest which tired soldiers alone can appreciate."

During the night of September 10–11 the division quietly

moved into the front-line trenches from Seicheprey to Flires, along the southern face of the salient. By then four French and eight A.E.F. divisions were in line along the salient, ready to participate in the first offensive of the newly created American First Army. On September 7 Pershing had visited several of the divisions, including the 42nd, and "found much enthusiasm regarding the coming offensive." On the other hand, a Rainbow lieutenant concluded on the eve of the big operation that "an attack under the existing circumstances would certainly be a failure unless the High Command used submarines for tanks, ducks for carrier-pigeons, and alligators for soldiers." [1]

The American First Army had been organized in the second week of August, ending a long and bitter struggle between Pershing and the other Allied military chiefs. With its creation, however, the Allied leaders professed great expectations, some secretly hoping that its early failure would bring its dissolution and the assignment of its divisions to British and French armies. Georges Clemenceau, the French premier and a frequent critic of the A.E.F., expressed his confidence in a message to Pershing: "History awaits you. You will not fail it." Pershing was undoubtedly too busy to ponder the hypocrisy of the premier's words. Yet the American commander-in-chief was so dependent upon the French and British, especially the former, to provide his new army with artillery, tanks, aircraft, transportation, and supporting troops for the operation that he agreed to let Pétain retain supreme command over the American forces. Perhaps surprising to the Chaumont staff, Pétain discreetly refrained from exercising this authority to an annoying extent and gave Pershing the matériel and personnel he needed for the offensive. Besides almost 100,000 French troops, Pershing obtained for the St. Mihiel action over 3000 pieces of field artillery of French manufacture; about 270 French tanks, nearly half of which were manned by French crews; and approximately 1400 airplanes, which, though under the command of Colonel William Mitchell of the A.E.F.'s air service, included 600 French aircraft and several British squadrons.

The St. Mihiel salient, 200 miles in area and sixteen miles in depth, was the largest German wedge still embedded in the long Western front, which extended from the English Channel to the Swiss border. For nearly four years the Boche had held it in spite of repeated French attempts to eliminate the salient. The defenders of Verdun in the great battle of 1916 and afterward had "fought half-choked and always in danger of being suddenly strangled" because of the salient, according to a distinguished authority on the war. The salient interrupted the Allied rail lines from Paris to Nancy and from Verdun to Nancy and Toul. From the high ground of the Meuse Plateau, which ran through the western part of the salient, the Germans could cover with artillery any Allied thrust near the western bank of the Meuse. Moreover, the Boche defenses in the salient protected the routes to the strategic rail center of Metz and the rich coal and iron fields in the Briey-Longwy region, which had been used by the Germans for four years. Since Foch was already planning a major offensive toward Sedan, to move between the Meuse River and the Argonne Forest, the reduction of the salient was imperative. The awarding of that assignment to the American First Army delighted Pershing, who had hoped for that task ever since the first American units were sent into the French trenches along the salient for their initial training "under fire" in the spring of 1918. He believed that the St. Mihiel operation not only would provide the first test for his independent field army but also, if successful, would menace the security of the entire German position on the Western front. The St. Mihiel salient may well have been the most sensitive and vulnerable point along the Boche line in September, 1918.[2]

Whereas the western portion of the salient was marked by a plateau running from the town of St. Mihiel northward along the Meuse, the broad, level Woëvre Plain stretched through the eastern half of the salient. From the western heights, especially the hills at Montsec and Loupmont, the Germans could easily observe and shell any Allied movements across the Woëvre. During periods of heavy rainfall, the clay soil of the plain held the rain on the surface, turning the Woëvre into a huge slough where neither soldiers nor horses could get firm footings. Shallow, stagnant bodies of water, dignified by being called lakes, dotted the plain, and numerous streams, most with low flood levels, crisscrossed the Woëvre. "For a hostile army to maneuver on the clay plain," observed Major Douglas W. Johnson, later a physiographer at Columbia University, "is of itself a difficult task, especially when the surface is soft with winter rains. To force a path across it in the face of a determined enemy skilfully utilizing rivers, lakes, and forests as defense barriers is a task of more serious proportions." [3] The 42nd Division faced such a challenge: the division's projected path of advance was across the Woëvre, and, as the troops well knew, the rains had already begun.

Until late August, Foch had been agreeable to Pershing's plan to include the capture of Metz in the objectives of the St. Mihiel offensive. But Sir Douglas Haig, the British commanding general, persuaded Foch to limit the A.E.F. to the reduction of the salient, the bulk of the American forces to be shifted then to the general advance west of the Meuse, which was planned for late September. Pershing received word of the delimited operation on August 30 and, after objecting to Foch and Pétain, finally yielded. The new plan of attack, issued during the first week of September, called for Major General Joseph T. Dickman's IV Corps, which held the center of the line along the southern face of the salient and comprised the 1st, 42nd, and 89th divisions, to carry out the main attack, striking northward toward Haumont generally and bisecting the salient. The 26th Division would advance from the western face and meet the 1st Division near the town of Vigneulles in the center of the salient. The American I Corps, to the right of the IV Corps, would move across the narrow eastern end of the salient, and the French II Colonial Corps was to advance on either side of the town of St. Mihiel, covering the flanks of the 26th and 1st divisions. MacArthur's 84th Brigade would occupy the right portion of the 42nd's sector, and its first day's objective would be a map line on the Woëvre Plain a mile northeast of Pannes — a goal of over five miles for the first day. On the second day the brigade was expected to move forward another four miles, reaching the eastern edge of Grande Souche Woods, less than a mile from Haumont. It was, indeed, a bold plan — even for Dickman, who, as commander of the 3rd Division earlier, had displayed audacity and strong-mindedness, and MacArthur, who had unbounding confidence in his brigade.[4]

In the three weeks prior to the St. Mihiel attack, Pershing, on Pétain's suggestion, had developed and carried out a deceptive maneuver later called the Belfort ruse. Major General Omar Bundy and a corps staff were sent to Belfort in southern Lorraine with orders to prepare for an offensive in that area. Bundy and his officers were not told that it was a trick and energetically went about the preparations. The sudden increase in air and ground activities on that front led the Boche to send three divisions to buttress their defenses there. Though not drawn from the St. Mihiel front, these troops did decrease the reserve which would be available for the defense of the salient. MacArthur, whose command post in the Jury Woods behind the 84th Brigade's front line was mercilessly shelled for hours just before the St. Mihiel offensive was launched, probably would not have had a very high opinion of the effectiveness of the Belfort ruse, had he known of it.

Another kind of ruse was under way along the front of the salient on the night of September 11. Sergeant William L. Langer, a member of a gas regiment and later a renowned historian, said that when he arrived at the front early that evening, "the trenches were a hopeless labyrinth, full of mud and water, and, as I found to my surprise, practically empty." All around him Langer could see "countless batteries" of field artillery, "apparently in position and yet silent as a group of sphinxes." By midnight, however, the American trenches were filled with soldiers, tensely waiting with bayonets drawn, and promptly at 1:00 A.M. the "sphinxes" spoke: nearly 3000 guns opened fire, inaugurating the St. Mihiel offensive.[5]

2. *A Splendid Triumph*

"A man-made aurora borealis shot out of the wall of darkness . . . There were darts of flame in the foreground from nearby batteries, while the leaping, continuous flashes ran on clear to Pont-à-Mousson. All the world, inclosed under canopy of night, was aflame." So Major Frederick Palmer, a press-relations officer from Chaumont, described the St. Mihiel bombardment. Sergeant Langer compared the sound of the shelling "to what one hears beneath a wooden bridge when a heavy vehicle passes overhead. The low grumbling of the echoes, punctuated by the loud reports of new shots and the sudden flashes that set off the landscape in a weird light, all this makes a unique impression on the human mind." As spectacular as the barrage was, the artillery's hits on German rail lines, battery emplacements, command posts, and other targets within the salient were disappointingly few, as a later study of the area showed. Fortunately the ineffective preparatory barrage mattered little because the Germans in the salient, vastly outnumbered, had earlier received orders to evacuate and were in process of withdrawing when the shelling began. Some brief periods of heavy fighting would ensue during the operation, but largely against scattered Boche units which were tardy in moving northward or were left behind temporarily to delay the Americans' advance.[6]

At 5:00 A.M., September 12, over 600,000 American and French infantrymen began moving into the salient from the south and west. The Sonnard Woods, which MacArthur feared might conceal masses of well-entrenched Germans, lay immediately ahead of the 84th Brigade. To no one's surprise, MacArthur accompanied the first assault troops to climb out of the 84th's trenches. On the right of the brigade's line was the 168th Infantry, commanded by Colonel Matthew A. Tinley, and to the left Colonel William P. Screws' 167th Infantry. The progress of both regiments exceeded MacArthur's expectations; they passed the first day's objective early that afternoon. A squadron of Major George S. Patton's tanks were supposed to support the 84th's attack, but, stated MacArthur, they "soon bogged down in the heavy mud." Stubborn resistance was encountered at first by the 168th Infantry in the Sonnard Woods, but the regiment soon broke through and closely pursued the retreating Germans. Likewise, after an initial slowdown at the western edge of the Sonnard Woods, the 167th Infantry outflanked and overcame the enemy positions, thereafter moving rapidly through the towns of Essey and Pannes. At Essey the Germans had departed so hastily that MacArthur, arriving soon after its capture, saw there "a German officer's horse saddled and equipped standing in a barn, a battery of guns complete in every detail, and the entire instrumentation and music of a regimental band." He said that the Rainbow soldiers "had great difficulty" in persuading the town's residents, "mostly old men, women, and children," to come out of their hiding places. "They did not know that the United States soldiers were in the war," he stated, "and it was necessary for us to explain to them that we were Americans." Corporal Sherwood, who was with a 75-mm. battery to the rear of the advancing Rainbow infantry, soon began to see "prisoners in droves of from ten to a hundred with a doughboy in the rear prodding the laggards with a bayonet whenever necessary." As a group of Boche prisoners passed carrying their wounded comrades, Sherwood noticed "a sedate looking officer wearing white gloves," who "had to bow his back to the work just as his men did. It seemed to do these enemy enlisted men good to see their officers thus reduced to their own plane." By nightfall the 84th Brigade had progressed well beyond Pannes into a region of the Woëvre which, according to the battle plan, was not expected to be reached until the next afternoon.[7]

The 84th had, indeed, enjoyed great success on the first day of action, but MacArthur, who won his fifth Silver Star for his gallant leadership during that advance, was too extravagant about his brigade's achievements when he recalled in his memoirs: "We turned in 10,000 prisoners and, although my brigade had pierced further than any other unit, and had been the spear point of the American advance, it suffered fewer casualties than any other." Actually about 1000 prisoners were taken by the entire 42nd Division on September 12, about half of which were captured by MacArthur's brigade. The whole First Army's "bag" of prisoners did not exceed 15,000 for the first week of the operation. The 84th Brigade's losses in killed and wounded for September 12–16 (the first day's figures are not given separately in the divisional statistics) were 528, whereas the 83rd Brigade lost only 317 killed and wounded. The 83rd Brigade, moreover, had not only kept pace on MacArthur's left but patrols of the 165th Infantry had reached the northern edge of Béney Woods, considerably farther north than the 84th Brigade's advanced troops. The 1st and 89th divisions, on either flank of the Rainbow, had also enjoyed rapid advances and were past their first day's objectives. Surely the most sensational advance of the first twenty-four hours of the offensive was that of the 26th Division, which had been disappointing in its previous action above Château-Thierry. The New Englanders of the 26th thrust nearly ten miles into the salient from the west and during the night of September 12–13 seized Vigneulles.[8]

The general advance was resumed at daybreak on the 13th, with the Rainbow Division driving hard toward the Germans' next major line of defense, the Michel Stellung, which was part of the vaunted Hindenburg Line. The town of St. Benoît fell to MacArthur's brigade late that morning, the infantry pushing on through the Grande Souche Woods to the north. "I am sorry to say we just missed capturing," said MacArthur, "the Headquarters of the 19th German Army Corps in the St. Benoît Chateau. Amongst many other evidences of their hasty departure we found a fully set dining room table, and a prepared meal." A patrol of the 167th Infantry reached the outskirts of Haumont before withdrawing under heavy fire from the Michel Stellung fortifications. The 83rd Brigade, led by Brigadier General Michael J. Lenihan, also encountered light opposition on the second day and advanced through the Vignotte Woods, capturing the village of Hassavant. By 4:30 P.M. the 42nd Division had reached the final objective of the St. Mihiel operation. Before nightfall the other American and French divisions had also reached the last objectives set by First Army headquarters. In less than forty-eight hours the St. Mihiel salient had disappeared. An officer of the veteran German 10th Division, captured by Rainbow soldiers that day, admitted that "the morale of his division is now considerably lower than in the spring" and "the Americans are excellent soldiers." This was hardly news to the exuberant men of the Rainbow Division.

At the southern tip of the former salient on September 13, Baker, Pershing, and Pétain entered the town of St. Mihiel, walking across a rickety bridge over the Meuse to be enthusiastically cheered by the emancipated residents. According to one witness, "Children after having been prisoners indoors for four years by German orders, ran up and down the streets, shouting and waving tricolors that had been hastily dug out of hiding-places, wildly enjoying their first freedom in the sunshine since September, 1914." Meanwhile, far to the north, communiqués from the front were carried to General Paul von

Hindenburg, the Boche commander-in-chief. His consternation was evident in the message he sent to General Max von Gall-witz, who commanded the group of armies opposite the American First Army: "The severe defeat of Composite Army C on September 12 has rendered the situation of the Group of Armies critical . . . There is now nothing left for us to do but offer stubborn defense. I can only hope that the Group of Armies employing the forces which I am allotting to it will hold the position" along the Michel Stellung.[9]

On September 14–16 the 42nd Division consolidated its position, which ran along an irregular line from Boutonneau Lake, near Hassavant, to the western edge of Charey Woods, bordering the 89th Division's sector. No major engagements occurred, but patrol action was lively. On the night of September 13–14 MacArthur, accompanied by his adjutant, Wolf, sneaked through the enemy lines east of Haumont and "reconnoitered in the direction of Mars-la-Tour," a town seven miles northeast of Haumont and ten miles west of Metz. From a high hill he could see, with binoculars, the rail and road traffic in and around Metz, the Germans apparently using lights without much fear of attack. "As I had suspected," he said, "Metz was practically defenseless for the moment. Its combat garrison had been temporarily withdrawn to support other sectors of action." From this reconnaissance and evidence he obtained from German prisoners, MacArthur concluded that "here was an unparalleled opportunity to break the Hindenburg Line at its pivotal point." He enthusiastically recommended to Hughes that the 84th Brigade be permitted to attack Metz immediately. But the divisional chief of staff replied that "the orders were definite and came from the highest authority, so there was nothing to do but halt where we were." Appeals to corps and army headquarters were likewise rejected. MacArthur continued to believe until his death that "had we seized this unexpected opportunity we would have saved thousands of American lives lost in the dim recesses of the Argonne Forest. It was an example of the inflexibility in the pursuit of previously conceived ideas that is, unfortunately, too frequent in modern warfare." [10] Many years later he told Brigadier General Henry J. Reilly, who in September, 1918, was a colonel commanding an artillery regiment of the division, that he was still convinced that the 42nd should have attacked Metz: "I could only come to one conclusion: it was no time to stop!" [11]

The idea of seizing Metz, not a new one to Pershing and many other American generals, seemed to gain new momentum for a while after MacArthur's agitation. Reilly said that the officers and soldiers on the line before Haumont often speculated: "Why did we stop? Why didn't we keep going to Metz at least?" Corporal Sherwood wrote in his diary in late September: "Our fellows are impatient and want to advance. 'On to Metz' is the shibboleth of the Rainbow." Menoher, who backed Hughes at the time, concluded years later that "in this case, at least, the limited objective, with no automatic means provided for advancing beyond such objectives, was a mistake, and was the direct means of causing the loss of a golden opportunity such as seldom comes." In postwar remarks both Pershing and Dickman argued that it was a mistake not to continue to Metz. "Without a doubt," said Pershing, "an immediate continuation of the advance would have carried us well beyond the Hindenburg Line and possibly into Metz." Dickman maintained that "the failure to push north from St. Mihiel with our overwhelming numbers will always be regarded by me as a strategical blunder for which Marshal Foch and his staff are responsible." He added, echoing MacArthur: "It is a glaring example of the fallacy of the policy of limited objectives." Colonel George C. Marshall, operations officer of the First Army, favored continuing to Metz, but yielded to Pershing and Drum, who at the time knew of Foch's disapproval and "thought they should let well enough alone." Foch, Pétain,

and Haig were looking toward the great offensive planned for
late September, in which all of the Allied armies on the Western front would strike toward the Mézières-Sedan region, the
A.E.F. scheduled to move through the Meuse-Argonne area.
Continuation of the St. Mihiel offensive would be tangential,
diverting badly needed forces from the main operations. Besides, Foch already had plans for an offensive to start from
southern Lorraine, which would begin November 14 and pass
through the Metz region eventually. Von Gallwitz, the German commander in that area, later commented on the possibility of an American seizure of Metz in mid-September: "In
order to capture this position a further . . . operation on a
very large scale would have been required."

Historians and other authorities on the war have disagreed
over the years as to the wisdom of terminating the St. Mihiel
operation short of Metz. Sir Basil H. Liddell Hart, probably
the leading authority on the strategy and tactics of World War
I, emphasizes the problem of logistics, which seems to be the
crux of the issue. He admits that "it would have demanded
a penetration deeper and quicker than any achieved by the
Allies on the western front. With an untried army this was
surely a remote hope." Yet he adds that "the St. Mihiel salient
offered the chance of attempting the yet untried method of
dual penetration under almost ideal conditions. If two powerful attacks had broken through the flanks of the salient, — and
better still, beyond them to the right and left, — the defenders
in the centre would have dissolved into chaos and been securely
'caged.' " But he concludes that "the main factor would not
have been defenses or defenders, but supplies. The road blocks
and transport difficulties actually experienced in the limited
advance do not encourage an optimistic answer." Indeed, the
traffic jams and logistical confusion in the salient had been
acute during the advance and persisted for many days afterward. Perhaps unknown to MacArthur, his friend Hughes

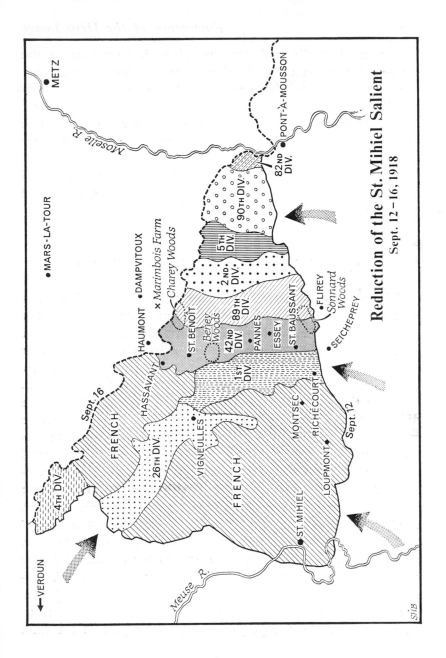

Reduction of the St. Mihiel Salient
Sept. 12 – 16, 1918

boldly and heatedly told Pershing himself, on a visit by the
commander to the 42nd's headquarters on September 14, that
the division "has not been receiving the supplies of all kinds
which are necessary" just to assure that the men "are adequately
fed and their clothing and shoes kept in good condition." The
question of Metz was soon a theoretical one that September
anyway, because, as MacArthur stated, the Germans "brought
up thousands of troops from Strasbourg and other sectors, and
within a week the whole Allied army could not have stormed
Metz." [12]

3. Holding the Essey-Pannes Sector

Following the termination of the St. Mihiel offensive, Mac-
Arthur's brigade took over the divisional front, designated the
Essey-Pannes sector, while the 83rd Brigade went into reserve.
The 84th Brigade held the three-mile front until September
27 when it was relieved by the 83rd and, in turn, withdrew
to a reserve position in the southern part of the former salient.
Holding the sector was no passive affair: though the Boche
did not try to retake the area, patrol skirmishes, large-scale
raids, and bombardments by aircraft and artillery were frequent occurrences. Major George Patton, who would command
an army against the Germans in the next world war, commented on a conversation he had with MacArthur at Essey:
"We stood and talked but neither was much interested in what
the other said as we could not get our minds off the shells."
    Part of MacArthur's time during the last half of September,
aside from his duties as brigade and sector commander, was
occupied in the preparation of a plan for a new A.E.F. personnel system. Brigadier General Robert C. Davis, the adjutant
general at Chaumont, came to MacArthur's headquarters to
work with him on the project. MacArthur praised the final

plan as "one of the most practical and comprehensive personnel systems that could be desired." Incorporating the "best features of the British and American systems with centralized control," it included, stated MacArthur, "a personnel center to be established with coordination branch, transfer center, trade test, artificer's depot and supervision personnel adjutants." Why Davis chose MacArthur for this task is not known, but it does point up the Chaumont staff's increasing recognition of his abilities in administrative and field leadership.[13]

For a while after the capture of the St. Mihiel salient, MacArthur lived in grand style. For his headquarters he selected a magnificent old château at St. Benoît. MacArthur adamantly refused to move his command post from the château despite some narrow escapes, including a shell burst which almost hit the room in which he was sleeping. On September 23, however, German prisoners revealed that "a big gun" was being moved up to fire on the château. MacArthur decided it was time to move his headquarters and did so that day. On the 24th, 280-mm. projectiles began crashing into the château with devastating accuracy. "The next day all that remained of the ancient and proud Château de St. Benoît," remarked Sergeant William H. Amerine of the 167th Infantry, "was a smoldering heap of stone and a jagged mass of walls with smoke-blackened, gaping window spaces. Its pink and blue draperies, and furniture similarly upholstered; its music room; its old tapestries hanging in its stone hallway — all were gone." Amerine quipped: "It was the most impressive example of property destruction that the Alabamians [the 167th] had ever seen."

An oft-repeated but probably apocryphal story relates that during MacArthur's stay at St. Benoît he was seated at dinner with his staff one day when a German shell landed nearby, killing an orderly. All of the officers at the table, except MacArthur, dived for cover. MacArthur reputedly said in an unperturbed voice: "All of Germany cannot fabricate a shell that

will kill MacArthur! Sit down again, gentlemen, with me."
This tale is particularly hard to believe in view of his ready
flight from the château when he felt that its destruction was
imminent. Moreover, as Corporal Sherwood observed, "A
great majority of the men in the Rainbow Division are fatal-
ists . . . Possibly this idea that there is a certain time for each
one of us to die and no circumstances can alter the fact is more
prevalent among volunteer outfits. At any rate it is an excellent
reason not to fear death." Surely, MacArthur did at times
expose himself recklessly, but he did not, as some of his critics
have maintained, consider himself a man of destiny invulnera-
ble to enemy fire.[14]

The prisoners who disclosed the impending destruction of
the château had been captured in one of a series of highly
successful raids which the 84th Brigade conducted between September 16 and 26. On the 16th a raid on Marimbois Farm, a
Boche stronghold south of the town of Dampvitoux, resulted
in five Germans captured, thirty killed, and many more
wounded, the Americans suffering but two wounded. Four
nights later the Germans retaliated with a raid of their own,
but it was repulsed with heavy losses to the enemy. On the
night of September 21–22 elements of the 167th Infantry raided
Haumont, while troops of the 168th Infantry hit Marimbois
Farm again. Over two score Germans were killed, and twenty-
five prisoners taken in these two raids. MacArthur encouraged
and helped plan the raids, which he considered to be excellent
morale stimulants for his men. As for the effect on the enemy,
Lieutenant Taber reported that "the blood curdling yells of
the Americans as they rushed in to attack gave the Boche
strange ideas." He quoted from a letter found on a German
prisoner: "Indians of the Sioux tribe were identified in one of
the last attacks . . . We are expecting the Americans to come
over every day."

Orders from Pershing's headquarters announced that on the

night of September 25–26 and the following day, as the massive Meuse-Argonne offensive was launched, the 42nd Division and other divisions holding the front northeast of St. Mihiel were "to support the attack of the First Army west of the Meuse by joining in the artillery bombardment and by making deep raids at the hour of attack." As his diversionary effort, MacArthur planned an elaborate double raid involving a large portion of both of his infantry regiments, again aimed at Marimbois Farm and Haumont. The preparatory artillery barrage "was so accurate and so overwhelming," MacArthur claimed, "that both German garrisons were practically annihilated." Official divisional reports, however, stated that the American troops "met with strong resistance," especially "heavy machine gun fire." The raids were successful, but their diversionary influence is moot. MacArthur accompanied the raiders and won his sixth Silver Star.[15]

The Rainbow was relieved by the 89th Division on the night of September 30–October 1. The 42nd would enjoy no rest, though, since it had orders to move to the Meuse-Argonne region. The troops, at least thankful that they would not have to march there, were loaded aboard trucks and transported to the reserve area of the American V Corps in Montfaucon Woods, about nine miles east of Sommerance. The trucks were driven by volunteers from Annam, commented Sergeant Amerine, "the same kind of little people who had hauled the regiment to the Chateau-Thierry [Aisne-Marne] battle . . . They still talked in their sing-song way, and gave the soldiers a lot of amusement."

The light chatter quieted, however, when the soldiers debarked in the Montfaucon Woods, scene of recent desperate fighting in the Meuse-Argonne offensive. Captain R. M. Cheseldine of the 166th Infantry found it to be a depressing, desolate abode: "Literally every inch of the ground had been torn by shells. Craters fifteen feet deep and as wide across, yawned on all sides. All around was a dreary waste of woods, once thick with stately trees and luxuriant undergrowth, but now a mere graveyard of broken limbs and splintered stumps." Chaplain Duffy said that even for officers "there were very few dugouts, all of them small and most of them dirty and wet." To make matters worse, the weather had turned so cold, said Sherwood, "we had to stamp our feet to keep from freezing." MacArthur's dugout in the "soaked and crowded woods" was, indeed, a far cry from the splendid château at St. Benoît. Viewing the destruction about them, he and his men probably sensed that the fighting in the days ahead would be much more ferocious than that of the "quick and satisfying success in the St. Mihiel salient.[16]

4. *"Give Me Châtillon"*

The first phase of the Meuse-Argonne offensive started on September 26, with 200,000 Americans (eventually a million would participate) moving out along a twenty-four-mile front. Only five Boche divisions faced the initial assault, but they were entrenched in some of the best defensive positions on the Western front. Moreover, most of the Yankee troops were untried in battle, the bulk of the veterans being still stationed in the St. Mihiel region; and the hastily drafted plan of battle was seriously wanting in anticipating transportation and control problems. Soon the advance was measured in yards; by the third day the offensive momentum had disappeared in a welter of command and logistical confusion. Several units could not be located, supplies were not reaching the front, the terrain was more difficult than expected, enemy resistance was intense, and American losses were frightfully high, particularly in view of the small gains. When the massive offensive had not achieved by the fourth day the objectives expected to be reached on the

first day, Pershing called for a pause in order to get his bewildered forces in order again. When the attack was resumed
on October 4, the progress was again disappointing, though
after another week of heavy fighting the Germans were finally
dislodged from the Argonne Forest. By then the weather had
become bitterly cold, and, to add to the First Army's woes,
an influenza epidemic had broken out, with 16,000 soldiers
stricken already.

It was a time of intense strain for Pershing, who was scath-
ingly denounced by some French and British generals whose
forces were progressing well in the general advance in early
October. Pershing bore the heavy responsibilities of commanding the entire A.E.F. as well as taking charge personally of
the First Army in the Meuse-Argonne operation. Finally facing the reality that his burdens were too great, he relinquished
command of the First Army to Liggett, one of his fattest but
ablest generals. On the same day, October 12, he also created
the Second Army, to be formed from the divisions stationed
east of Liggett's and to be commanded by Major General
Robert L. Bullard. Several new corps commanders were appointed, including Summerall, the dynamic, hard-driving leader
of the 1st Division and former commander of the 42nd's field
artillery brigade. Fortunately for the Rainbow, Summerall was
named to head the V Corps, of which the division was now a
part. "He was always prepared, always anxious to do, always
on the right spot," Bullard said of Summerall, adding: "His
sense of justice was as great as his sense of loyalty, honour, and
duty. He let no man who merited it go unrecognized or un-
rewarded." Before the Meuse-Argonne campaign was over,
MacArthur would be very grateful for this trait of his corps
commander.[17]

On the night of October 11–12 the 42nd Division relieved
the 1st Division on a line running from the town of Sommerance eastward through the northern edge of the Romagne

Woods. In the next thirty-six hours the Rainbow's front was expanded as its units relieved troops of the 82nd and 32nd divisions, on its left and right flanks. By the night of October 13–14 the 42nd's front line stretched from a point west of Sommerance, bordering the 82nd's sector, to a point in the Gesnes Woods, three miles to the east, where it joined the sector of the 32nd Division. The 84th Brigade held the right side of the divisional front and was situated in heavily wooded hill country; on the other hand, the 83rd was located on open ground to the west where terrain would not hinder its advance. Ahead of MacArthur's men were Hill 288 and Châtillon Hill, two of the key positions of the strongly fortified Kriemhilde Stellung, as that portion of the Hindenburg Line was called. Lieutenant Taber said of his regiment's position: "The terrain was as forbidding as any the 168th had ever seen. Thick woods, tangled underbrush, scarred trees, gaping shell holes, deep ravines, and lofty ridges united to make a country already desolate and difficult still more forbidding." He continued, "Dead bodies, some of them in a bad state of decomposition, littered the woods and slopes." Taber and his men must have been sobered by the thought that shortly they must charge those formidable hills where previous efforts by other divisions had failed and at terrible costs.[18]

MacArthur set up his brigade headquarters at a farm east of Exermont, two miles behind the front lines and within easy range of German artillery, which was most active. On the night of October 11–12 he went to the dugout-headquarters of Lieutenant Colonel Walter E. Bare, acting commander of the 167th Infantry. The Germans shelled the valley heavily with mustard and tear gas while he and Bare talked. "I remember well that both the General and I consumed so much of the gas," said Bare, "that neither of us could hardly see or talk on account of the effect of the fumes." On a reconnaissance the next day MacArthur, who still foolishly refused to carry a gas mask, was caught in a lethal yperite gas barrage and barely escaped. He was violently ill when he returned to his command post; Major Wolf "feared that the war was over for him." But MacArthur was determined to lead the impending attacks against the vaunted hill positions and refused to be hospitalized. He later said of himself that he "was wounded, but not incapacitated, and was able to continue functioning." His condition was serious enough, however, to earn him a second Purple Heart.[19]

MacArthur admitted that he had "many misgivings" when he learned from his reconnaissance that his men "would have to cross open country absolutely dominated by the German fire from around the base of and on the Côte de Châtillon." When Menoher asked him whether his brigade could take Châtillon, MacArthur said that "I told him as long as we were speaking in the strictest confidence that I was not certain." On the night of October 13–14, the eve of the attack, Summerall, looking "tired and worn," visited MacArthur's headquarters. While drinking a cup of coffee, he turned abruptly to MacArthur and in a desperate tone demanded, "Give me Châtillon, or a list of five thousand casualties." Startled out of his uncertainty for the moment, MacArthur responded, "If this Brigade does not capture Châtillon you can publish a casualty list of the entire Brigade with the Brigade Commander's name at the top." According to MacArthur, "Tears sprang into General Summerall's eyes. He was evidently so moved he could say nothing. He looked at me for a few seconds and then left without a word."[20]

"October 14th," reported Lieutenant Taber, "dawned dark, misty, and forbidding. It had rained all night, and the men, still wearing summer underclothing, with but one blanket apiece and no overcoats, rose stiffly from their beds in the mud." All night Gatley's artillery had been pounding known enemy positions on the hills ahead. At 8:00 A.M., with the field artillery providing a rolling barrage, the 42nd's infantry rushed forward all along the divisional front. Lenihan's 83rd Brigade progressed about a mile above Sommerance over easy ground and against light enemy fire. But his troops fell back when they encountered "very severe gun fire from the front and both flanks" as they approached the Germans' entrenched positions and lines of barbed wire south of St. Georges and Landres-et-St. Georges. Menoher and Summerall were disappointed to get a message from Lenihan that his men had dug in for the night over a mile south of the enemy-held towns, their first objective. As expected, MacArthur's brigade "met stubborn resistance almost immediately." Thanks mainly to the fierce determination of Major Lloyd Ross' battalion, the crest of Hill 288 was seized. "Of about 2,000 Germans defending the hill," Corporal Sherwood stated, "not one escaped. A hundred of them were taken prisoner. The rest had been slain." Repeated assaults against Châtillon Hill were tried that day by units of both of MacArthur's regiments, but by nightfall they could claim only a tenuous foothold on the southern slopes. When Private Michael A. Donaldson's company was forced back down the hill, he returned, on his own volition and under intense fire, six times to rescue that many wounded comrades who had been left behind. He later received the Medal of Honor, and a number of his fellow soldiers earned medals for bravery in action that terrible day. American losses were extremely heavy, and, unlike the 83rd Brigade, MacArthur's forces had no roads on which motorized ambulances could move their casualties quickly to the rear. "Their wounded," commented Colonel J. Monroe Johnson of the 117th Engineers, "had to be transported to Exermont by handlitters and by mule ambulances." And, despite all the gallant sacrifices of that day, the 84th's objective, Châtillon Hill, was still firmly held by the Germans.[21]

At the height of the fighting on the afternoon of the 14th,

MacArthur sent the following message to Menoher, revealing his desperation and frustration over the failure of the division on his right flank:

> The following situation on my front at 2 PM. The 32nd Div. has not progressed a foot and the enemy still holds Hill 286. All along my right as I go forward I have to establish a line of defense against heavy German fire, artillery, machine gun, and infantry . . . I am therefore, due to my exposed right flank, covering an actual front of about four kilometers. Along the Cote de Chatillon, the enemy's position is reported by the 167th Infantry to be of great strength . . . It is impossible, in my opinion, to take this position without a careful artillery preparation. My axis of attack, due to my exposed flank, is now northeast, and, if I advance, my line will be divergent from that of the 83rd Brigade.[22]

Artilleryman Sherwood wrote in his diary on the next day: "For the first time since we have been on the line in this drive the fog cleared away today and a great rainbow emerged from the clouds. Our men regard this as an omen of good luck, and shout to each other encouragements and orders to press on." But, as hard as the men of the 84th tried, they could advance on October 15 only to a point midway between Hill 288 and Châtillon Hill. Some of this ground was yielded late in the afternoon when the Germans launched a vicious counterattack. To the west, Lenihan's brigade reached the line of barbed wire south of St. Georges and then was driven back, its front line by nightfall being the same as that of the previous evening. The 15th was, indeed, a bloody and disappointing day for the Rainbow Division.

That night Summerall stormed into Lenihan's headquarters and demanded to know why the 83rd had not advanced. Dissatisfied with the brigade commander's response, he relieved Lenihan and placed Colonel Henry Reilly, an artilleryman, in charge of the infantry brigade. Several lesser officers of the

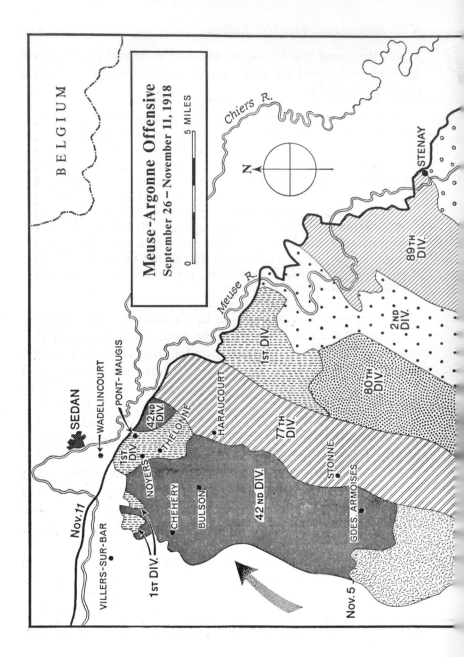

Meuse-Argonne Offensive
September 26 – November 11, 1918

5 MILES

N

BELGIUM

Chiers R.

STENAY

89TH DIV.

Meuse R.

2ND DIV.

1ST DIV.

80TH DIV.

SEDAN

WADELINCOURT

PONT-MAUGIS

42ND DIV.

THÉLONNE

HARAUCOURT

77TH DIV.

1ST DIV.

NOYERS

CHÉHÉRY

BULSON

42ND DIV.

STONNE

GDES. ARMOISES

Nov.11

VILLERS-SUR-BAR

1ST DIV.

Nov.5

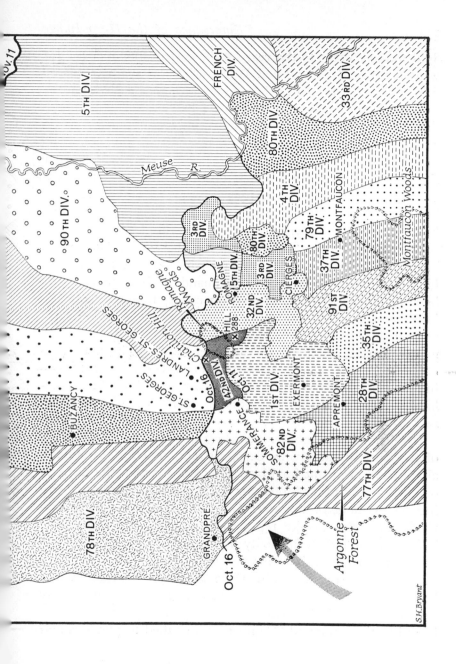

83rd were also sent to the rear by the corps commander. "He wanted results," commented Duffy, who was sympathetic toward Lenihan, "no matter how many men were killed, and he went away more dissatisfied than he had come." Summerall then telephoned MacArthur, who was in a conference with his regimental and battalion commanders, and told him, according to Bare, that "the Côte de Châtillon was the key to the entire situation and that he wanted it taken by 6:00 P.M. the next evening." Whether in sincerity or in an effort to avert Lenihan's fate, MacArthur gave Summerall the same response that had worked previously, telling him that the 84th would take the hill by that time "or report a casualty list of 6,000 dead. That will include me." Summerall shed no tears this time, but he did leave MacArthur in command of his brigade. Upon hanging up the receiver, MacArthur calmly resumed his meeting, the group finally agreeing to try to sneak Ross' battalion around the hill to attack the Germans from the rear, with a massive frontal assault to follow immediately. The plan, proposed by Bare, was enthusiastically adopted, and after dismissing the officers. MacArthur lay down for a few hours' rest, perhaps with some second thoughts about his promise to Summerall.[23]

October 16 was another heartbreaking day for the soldiers of the 83rd Brigade, who, despite strenuous efforts, were unable to advance. But for MacArthur and his men the day was one they would never forget, for it marked the brigade's crowning achievement of the war: Châtillon Hill was finally captured and held, despite repeated enemy efforts to retake it. The honor was shared equally by the 167th's Alabamians and the 168th's Iowans. The brigade also overran Tuilerie Farm at the base of the hill, which the Boche had turned into a hornet's nest of machine guns. Commenting on the bloody but glorious day, MacArthur said, "Officers fell and sergeants leaped to the command. Companies dwindled to platoons and

corporals took over. At the end, Major Ross had only 300
men and 6 officers left out of 1,450 men and 25 officers. That
is the way the Côte-de-Châtillon fell." The heroes were many,
foremost being Private Thomas C. Neibaur, whose exploits,
while shot in both legs, earned him the Medal of Honor. With
deadly automatic rifle fire he thwarted a wave of counterattack-
ing Germans at the crest of the hill and, despite his wounds,
managed to bring in eleven prisoners he had captured single-
handedly. Corporal Joseph E. Pruett, another Rainbow infantryman, was awarded the Distinguished Service Cross for attacking a machine-gun nest alone and capturing sixty-eight German soldiers who were hiding in a nearby dugout. Summerall,
highly pleased with the brigade and its commander, recommended MacArthur for the Medal of Honor and promotion to
major general. MacArthur received neither, but the awards
board at Chaumont did authorize a second Distinguished Service Cross (Oak Leaf Cluster) for him. The citation noted that
in the battles for the hills he "personally led his men" and
"displayed indomitable resolution and great courage in rallying broken lines and reforming attacks, thereby making victory
possible. On a field where courage was the rule, his courage
was the dominant factor." [24]

Referring to the capture of the Romagne Heights, which
included Hill 288 and Châtillon Hill, Pershing remarked later:
"The importance of these operations can hardly be overesti-
mated. The capture of the Romagne Heights . . . was a decisive blow. We now . . . flanked his [the enemy's] line on
the Aisne and on the Heights of the Meuse." Colonel Reilly
pointed out three important consequences: The Americans had
penetrated the Kriemhilde Stellung; the right flank of the
troops moving against Landres-St. Georges was now protected;
and the 42nd's artillerymen could bombard the entire valley
of the Rau de St. Georges, a strategic area previously out of
range of the American guns. MacArthur viewed the victory

as "the approach to final victory": "We broke through a prepared German line of defense of such importance to them, that their retreat to the other side of the Meuse River was already forecast because of the advantageous position given to the American Army for the attack of November 1st." Still chafing over Lenihan's performance, Summerall drafted a citation praising the 42nd Division, in which he extolled the services of the 84th Brigade and the field artillery, but conspicuously omitted any mention of the 83rd Brigade. Of the 84th, he said that it "has manifested the highest soldierly qualities and has rendered service of the greatest value during the present operations." Its assaults were performed "with a dash, courage and fighting spirit worthy of the best traditions of the American Army." [25]

For the next two weeks the 42nd Division remained in the front line consolidating its position and organizing the line for defense, no further advance being attempted. Reminiscent of the sad moments after the Ourcq battle, the officers and men were not as fully aware of the division's heavy casualties, this time totaling about 4000 killed and wounded, until the units reassembled in the reserve area. Since the Rainbow was initially included in the force scheduled to renew the offensive on November 1, Menoher was deeply concerned about his men's ability to fight again so soon. The division's shortages below authorized strength in late October included over 100 officers and over 7100 enlisted men. At a meeting in MacArthur's headquarters at Neuve Forge Farm, near Exermont, Menoher asked his brigade commanders if their units were prepared to resume the offensive. MacArthur, after a "brilliant" impromptu speech for which, Reilly quipped, there was regretfully "no stenographer present to take it down and preserve it," concluded that his brigade was "fully capable of playing its part in such an advance." In his turn, Reilly responded less dramatically that the 83rd Brigade was eager to go on the offensive again. Nevertheless, in the days just before the new attack, Pershing decided to relieve the battered, under-strength 42nd; the 2nd Division replaced it on the night of October 30–31. The Rainbow's units then moved into I Corps reserve near Sommerance, the men undoubtedly more grateful than their commanders for the reprieve.[26]

Despite Crown Prince Wilhelm's order of October 19 that "on all army fronts a decisive stand will be made," there were signs, obvious to both sides, that the end was near. Gallwitz reported on the 30th that many soldiers of the 18th Landwehr Division "refused to go into the line." Soon there were reports of mutinies in other Boche divisions. One German colonel noted on October 31 a new insidious influence which was affect-ing his men: "Some of the troops employed in the east up to the present, were exposed too long to the demoralizing influ-ence of the Russian revolution and Bolshevistic propaganda. With their ideas they are poisoning the minds of the soldiers of the army on the Western front which so far had remained firm." News also came of mutinies in the Kaiser's navy and of mounting revolutionary violence in German cities. Luden-dorff, who since summer had been convinced that his nation's cause was lost, resigned under pressure during the last week of October. The allies of Germany were crumbling fast, Bul-garia capitulating on September 30, Turkey on October 30, and Austria-Hungary four days later.

Meanwhile the soldiers of the 42nd drearily kept themselves in readiness for their next call to front-line duty. As they drilled near Sommerance, they could see the dark outline of Châtillon Hill to the east. Often their thoughts went back to that awful period when they had looked up at Châtillon with fear as beloved comrades fell on every side. Now an individual could walk to the top of the hill in a matter of minutes, where only two weeks earlier it took three nightmarish days for 8000 soldiers to force their way to the crest. The Rainbow's sur-

vivors probably realized, too, like the veteran in F. Scott Fitzgerald's *Tender Is the Night,* that they had witnessed an "empire walking very slowly backward a few inches a day, leaving
the dead like a million bloody rugs." [27]

CHAPTER IX

The Long Road to Hoboken

1. Scramble for Sedan

WHEN THE MEUSE-ARGONNE OFFENSIVE was renewed on November 1, the Yanks broke through the German defenses with unexpected speed. The operation quickly developed into a wild pursuit of the Boche toward Sedan and Stenay, near the Belgian border. More troublesome than enemy resistance was the problem of keeping supply and ammunition trains in the immediate rear of the fast-moving American infantrymen. "The weather continued miserable," Langer remarked, "and above Sommauthe the roads were unspeakably muddy, until finally it was barely possible for traffic to make any headway." Unlike the attack of September 26, this time the ranks were leavened with St. Mihiel and Marne veterans, commanders were not bound by restrictive orders on objectives, and, despite the rains, the offensive momentum was continued relentlessly, keeping the Boche off balance and unable to form a line of defense south of the Meuse.[1]

As the front line moved forward, the 42nd and other divisions in reserve marched northward, too — ready to relieve the units to the fore at a few hours' notice. On the night of November

4–5 the Rainbow Division relieved the exhausted troops of the 78th Division, the change in the line occurring just south of Grandes Armoises and about twelve miles below Sedan. The pace of the advance was not slackened; on the 5th and 6th Menoher's division advanced to within three miles of the Meuse, with MacArthur's brigade moving up the ridges and hills northeast of Bulson. "Due to the bad condition of the roads, the exhausted condition of our horses and the fact that we are heavies (big guns)," Sherwood griped, "it seems likely that we are not going to get to go up unless the enemy puts up a bigger fight and stops our infantry long enough for us to catch up." Menoher may have been somewhat dubious of realizing the divisional objective soon when Dickman ordered him on the 5th "to advance and capture the bridgehead at Sedan," but by the afternoon of the 6th the possibility seemed very real of entering Sedan within twenty-four hours. Liggett noted that the 42nd's advance had been "remarkable" and had "prevented the enemy from reorganizing," a strong German defense line on the banks of the Meuse now appearing as the only obstacle that could keep the Rainbow from winning one of the most coveted prizes of the war.[2]

The battle formation of the 42nd Division as it advanced toward the Meuse was the same that Menoher had employed in the Souain, Ourcq, St. Mihiel, and Romagne Heights operations. The 84th Brigade held the right portion of the divisional front, and the 83rd Brigade the left. Four infantry battalions were in the advance, one each from the 166th, 165th, 167th, and 168th regiments in that order from left to right, the rest of the infantry battalions echeloned behind the front ones. Major Cooper D. Winn's 151st Machine Gun Battalion supported Screws' 167th Infantry and Tinley's 168th, while the 149th Machine Gun Battalion moved with Reilly's brigade. One company of Johnson's 117th Engineer Battalion was assigned to each infantry brigade, the rest of the engineers being held in divisional reserve, along with most of the 150th Machine Gun Battalion. Gatley's field artillery brigade, consisting of three regiments, was endeavoring to keep up and provide its usual effective support. Though morale was at a peak, the division was seriously understrength, lacking over 120 officers and nearly 7500 enlisted men. The operation had become such "a mad chase," as Sherwood called it, that replacements could not locate or catch the units they were supposed to join. Fortunately, as it turned out, they would not be needed.[3]

Nevertheless, MacArthur anticipated increasing resistance as the division approached Sedan and so notified Menoher on the evening of November 6:

> At 7:10 this evening I had the heights dominating the Meuse. My line runs parallel to the river from Thelonne to a point south of Angecourt. I had hoped to cross at Pont Maugis, turn north and attack Sedan from the south, thus opening a passage for the 83rd Brigade. The bridges at Pont Maugis, both foot and railway, were blown up this afternoon in the very face of my scouts, and no crossings remain in front of my sector . . . I have learned that the enemy is preparing to defend the line of the Meuse at all costs.[4]

"Signs on the highway now said 'Nach Sedan,'" observed Captain Cheseldine, "and in some mysterious way the men learned that it might mean something to reach Sedan ahead of other outfits. This acted as a spur and jaded spirits were stimulated as if dope had been administered." Liggett commented, "The phrase 'take Sedan' became a sort of fetish, on account of the historical significance of the place, I suppose. But the appeal had an especial meaning for the French on our left, where the IX French Army Corps formed the right of the Fourth French Army." He explained that these French troops "naturally wanted to go back there" because it was their corps which the Germans drove out of Sedan in 1914. Furthermore, no Frenchman could forget that it was at Sedan in 1870 that

Napoleon III was forced to surrender to the Prussians. Yet Liggett emphasized that actually the military value of the city itself was negligible: "The heights commanding Sedan and the Meuse Valley, and especially the great railroad line, were really all that mattered to us, and these we reached by the night of November 6–7." [5]

Pershing undoubtedly realized that the heights were strategically more significant than the city, but he desperately wanted his soldiers to be the first in Sedan, perhaps, as one authority suggests, "to demonstrate in this way the superiority of his army to that of the French." On the afternoon of November 5 he sent Brigadier General Fox Conner, his operations officer at Chaumont, to First Army headquarters at Souilly with verbal orders to press vigorously the advance on Sedan. Colonel George Marshall, in the absence of Liggett and Drum, wrote down the message as dictated by Conner. When Drum arrived, after Conner had left, he added a last sentence to the message.[6] The now-famous communication, which was relayed to the I and V Corps commanders by telephone, read as follows:

> Memorandum for Commanding Generals, I Corps, V Corps
> 1. General Pershing desires that the honor of entering Sedan should fall to the American First Army. He has every confidence that the troops of the I Corps, assisted on their right by the V Corps, will enable him to realize this desire.
> 2. In transmitting the foregoing message, your attention is invited to favorable opportunity now existing for pressing our advance through the night. Boundaries will not be considered binding.[7]

Drum, who was chief of staff of the First Army, signed it "by command of Lieut. General Liggett," who was in the field at the time and, amazingly, did not learn about the message until November 7.

Drum later maintained that he had been informed that "the

question of boundaries between the Fourth French Army and the First American Army had been arranged" between Pershing and the French commander. Pershing, in turn, asserted that he had "suggested to General Maistre that the prescribed boundary line between our First and the French Fourth Army might be ignored in case we should outrun the French, to which he offered no objection, but on the contrary warmly approved." Ensuing developments indicate that Pershing must have misinterpreted the French general, and the commander of the I Corps misunderstood Drum's statement about disregarding boundaries. Pershing's message, MacArthur declared, "precipitated what narrowly missed being one of the great tragedies of American history." [8]

Summerall received the communication about 7:00 P.M. on the 5th, mulled over it during the night, and went to the headquarters of the 1st Division early the next afternoon. There he ordered Brigadier General Frank Parker, who commanded the 1st, Summerall's old division, "to march immediately on Sedan with mission to cooperate and capture that town," said Parker. The division, whose left flank was over seven miles southeast of Sedan, would have to cut across the sectors of the American 77th and 42nd divisions of Dickman's I Corps and the French 40th Division, at least the way Summerall and Parker plotted it. Parker sent a messenger to inform Dickman that the 1st Division would advance in five columns across the boundaries of the I Corps en route to Sedan.[9]

Meanwhile, Dickman had contacted Menoher, and at 9:00 P.M. on the 6th the latter issued an order to his brigade commanders: "Orders from the I Corps are most positive and explicit that the pursuit be kept up day and night without halting; and that Sedan must be reached and taken tonight, even if the last man and officer drops in his tracks." According to Reilly, "General MacArthur carefully studied what this meant. He took into consideration the position of his brigade already on the heights above the Meuse, with most of the enemy to his front already across the river; and the condition of the intervening ground." MacArthur thereupon requested and obtained permission to postpone his attack until daylight since such an assault "over unfamiliar and rough ground gave greater promise of success than one made at night." Reilly's 83rd Brigade, on the other hand, resumed its advance toward Sedan about 2:00 A.M.[10]

By midnight of November 6–7 all five of Parker's columns had set forth on forced marches. One battalion of the 16th Infantry struck out for Pont-Maugis on the Meuse, crossing the fronts of the 77th Division and MacArthur's brigade. Two other battalions of that regiment moved toward Thélonne and Noyers, operating about a mile south of the first column. The plan called for these two columns to merge at Wadelincourt, a town across the Meuse from Sedan. The third column, consisting of the 18th Infantry (less one battalion) marched into the rear of the 84th Brigade near Bulson. The 28th Infantry, the fourth column, headed toward Chéhéry along the eastern banks of the Bar River in the rear of Reilly's brigade, and the 26th Infantry, Parker's fifth column, brazenly crossed into the sector of the French 40th Division and advanced toward Omicourt.[11]

During the night Reilly's surprised men began reporting the presence of Parker's troops in their midst, congesting road traffic, crossing the 83rd's fields of fire with reckless abandon, and generally creating pandemonium. As MacArthur's men prepared to move out at dawn, similar reports began to reach him at his headquarters in Bulson. Soon a colonel of the 1st Division came into town with a column of his troops. He showed the 84th Brigade commander the orders from Parker to capture Sedan. MacArthur stated that he told the officer that the 1st Division should be withdrawn at once since its movement "was very dangerous and might be disastrous." The colonel responded that he could not halt the advance and did not know where Parker was, but would confer with the 1st Division commander as soon as he located him.

After sending warnings to his commanders of the presence of the 1st Division and the danger of attacks of friendly forces against each other, MacArthur said that he "proceeded within the front of the brigade in order to prevent personally any of these occurrences." While on his way with Wolf to Tinley's command post, MacArthur was intercepted by a 16th Infantry patrol near Beau-Ménil Farm, northeast of Bulson. The 84th Brigade commander, as he told it to Menoher, "was brought in at the point of a pistol," the patrol thinking that he was a Boche officer, possibly because of his floppy hat and flowing scarf. The mistake was cleared up quickly and MacArthur was released amid a profusion of apologies. News of the incident provided guffaws in the ranks, but astonishment and wrath at army and corps headquarters. Liggett commented, "MacArthur had taken his 'capture' as something of a joke, but not I Corps headquarters. I had been furious myself, but I recovered my temper in soothing the indignation of General Dickman and his staff." The various versions of the "capture," as reported by Wolf, MacArthur, Menoher, Liggett, Dickman, and Parker, differ in details, but agree on the nonchalant manner in which Mac-Arthur reacted to the affair — rather surprising in view of his sensitivity to the slightest affront in earlier days.[12]

Meanwhile the confusion and intermingling of units mounted, and early in the afternoon Menoher notified Dickman: "Situation here as between 1st and 42nd Divs. intolerable." Parker had set up headquarters at Chéhéry and told Reilly that "he was going ahead without regard to the 42nd Division." Menoher asserted that "troops of the 1st Div. were intermingled with our troops on the firing line, and their trains and personnel were complicating our operations in such a way as to make the situation impossible." Dickman, in turn, reported to Liggett that Parker's movement has "cluttered up our already congested and blocked roads, contributed nothing whatsoever to the military side of the question, but on the contrary has raised questions of bitterness between divisions which are deplorable, do not add to efficiency and will be hard to overcome." Before Dickman informed him, however, Liggett had learned of the 1st Division's action from another quarter — an enraged French commander whose sector had been entered by American units. The confusion in the western part of the I Corps area had resulted in troops of both the 1st and 42nd divisions obstructing the advance of the French 40th Division. The French warned Liggett to get these troops out of the sector, especially since they were in an area scheduled to receive an artillery barrage. Menoher later admitted that "our troops had some under artillery fire from the French" before their withdrawal from the west side of the Bar River could be effected, some of Parker's soldiers also coming under French fire.[13]

When Liggett learned of the order Drum had issued in his name, he immediately sent orders to evacuate the 1st Division from the I Corps sector, told Drum to get full reports from all commanders involved in the episode, and set out to consult personally with the corps and divisional commanders. "This was the only occasion in the war," said Liggett, "when I lost my temper completely." He explained, "I had been holding this fine division [the 1st] back to be used when we crossed the Meuse, when we might have needed them very badly . . . Moreover, the movement had thrown the I Corps front and the adjoining French front into such confusion that had the enemy chosen to counter attack in force at the moment, a catastrophe might have resulted." Luckily, the Germans to their front had no knowledge of the Americans' blundering; besides, the Boche were barely able to prepare a new line of defense along the north bank of the Meuse, much less mount a counteroffensive.

After Dickman had hospitably supplied them with rations, the troops of the 1st Division began their withdrawal from his corps sector on the night of the 7th, about the same time that the German armistice commission crossed the French lines to the west, headed for Compiègne. At the request (or demand) of the French, Pershing belatedly acceded to their wish to enter Sedan first. The 83rd Brigade was pulled back into reserve the next day, and the French 40th Division shifted eastward into its place, taking over the left flank of MacArthur's brigade and commanding the most direct route into Sedan. The coveted city, though, was not captured by either French or American forces during the three days which remained before the armistice. On November 7 and 8 patrols of the 42nd Division entered Torcy and Wadelincourt, just across the river from Sedan, but they were forced back by intense enemy fire. Without the disruption occasioned by the 1st Division's bizarre movement, the Rainbow Division might have entered Sedan before the night of the 7th, but it is doubtful that Menoher's units, without tremendous reinforcements, could have seized and held the city. For the soldiers of the 42nd the matter became an hypothetical, if lively, topic after the night of November 9–10, for it was then that they were relieved by the 77th Division and marched to V Corps reserve near Buzancy, leaving the front lines for the last time.[14]

"Perhaps no one, more than I," Parker wrote to Major General James G. Harbord in 1935, "knows the truth of the march on Sedan of the 1st Division. Certainly no one has suffered more than I as a result thereof." Parker became a scapegoat in later years, most of his tours of duty being "assignments in oblivion," but he seems to have been the only one who suffered in any way as a result of the shameful episode in front of Sedan. Whatever the truth about the responsibility for the incident, it was skillfully suppressed. "Under normal conditions," claimed Pershing, "the action of the officer or officers responsible for this movement of the 1st Division directly across the zones of action of two other divisions could not have been overlooked, but the splendid record of that unit and the approach of the end of hostilities suggested leniency." Although Liggett required his commanders to render reports on the affair in what looked like the prelude to court-martial proceedings, nothing transpired then or later in the way of official punitive action. Indeed, Pershing could well suggest leniency since he was the chief culprit in the farce, which was unworthy of him or his excellent army. His vain desire for the city and his calloused disregard of French feelings set the burlesque in motion. On the other hand, Drum must bear some of the guilt: he presumed too much in adding his sentence on disregarding boundaries, besides wording it ambiguously. Both Drum and Marshall were at fault in not informing the First Army commander as quickly as possible; surely Liggett, no inconspicuous figure in physique or prestige, could have been located in a matter of hours rather than days. Summerall might plead that he misunderstood the order, but, in view of his widely known personal feud with Dickman, his behavior in the Sedan affair seems to have been motivated largely by jealousy and "glory hunting." Likewise, Dickman let his personal feelings toward his fellow corps commander show when he accelerated the advance on Sedan while knowing of the 1st Division's actions. As for Parker, he also must bear the taint of seeking glory for himself and his organization. Moreover, his attitude toward officers of the 42nd who tried to reason with him while he was in their sector was despicable and irresponsible. Both he and Summerall saw in Pershing's order only what they wished to see; the order, though wanting in clarity in places, was lucid on the assisting role of the V Corps.[15] MacArthur must have been relieved, perhaps amused, to find himself in the swirl of a controversy wherein he was innocent and others were guilty of placing personal feelings and ambitions ahead of the Army's interests and welfare. He also probably developed a keener appreciation of the extremely effective maneuvering of the close-knit "Pershing clique" — the small circle of officer-friends who would be influential in high-command affairs for many years to come. Had MacArthur and Menoher been offenders in the incident, their futures would undoubtedly have been much darker than those of the officers who actually were responsible for the foolish race for Sedan.

2. *On to the Rhine*

"Tonight for the first time since 1914," wrote Sherwood on the evening of the armistice, "lights are seen along the front in every direction. Last night not even a cigarette could be lighted for fear of directing an air raid or bombardment. We have just found an enemy signal dump containing many rockets and flares, and the skies are ablaze in celebration." Despite their generals' remonstrances to be prepared for a renewal of the fighting, Allied soldiers enjoyed such impromptu festivities all along the front from the Belgian coast to the Vosges Mountains. Like other unit commanders, MacArthur was required to pass on to his officers a solemn reminder from Pershing: "The fact must be emphasized in no uncertain manner that the present state of affairs is an armistice and NOT A PEACE, and that there must be no relaxation of vigilance on the part of your command. Advantage will be taken of the occasion to rehabilitate equipment, push training and prepare troops for further operations at any instant demanded by the situation." [16]

The officers and men of the Rainbow Division were proud of their record in the great war and were happy to tell correspondents and other visitors that theirs was the best division in the A.E.F. In a statement to the press shortly after the armistice, MacArthur, just as officers of other veteran outfits were doing, bragged about the 42nd's exploits, telling his listeners that the division had taken prisoners from twenty-six German divisions and nineteen independent enemy units and was in combat for 180 of the 224 days it was at the front. "The remainder of the time," he explained, "it spent moving from front to front or waiting in reserve close to the front." Actually official statistics show that the Rainbow was in the front lines 162 days, the 1st and 26th divisions serving there considerably longer. Other figures reveal that the 42nd's ranking among the twenty-nine A.E.F. divisions was thus: third in distance advanced (55 kilometers), eighth in enemy prisoners captured (1317), sixth in enemy artillery pieces seized (25), fourth in enemy machine guns taken (470), seventh in Medals of Honor (5), and sixth in Distinguished Service Crosses (271). The Rainbow's involvement in fierce fighting is evident from its total casualties of 14,683, with only the 1st Division (22,320) and the 3rd Division (15,401) suffering more losses in killed and wounded — and none of these three units was known for wasting human lives. Nevertheless, despite the fondness of Army statisticians for compiling tables of figures purportedly comparing the divisions' performances in categories such as those mentioned, statistics, of course, do not tell the entire story and can be misleading. For instance, large numbers of prisoners were taken usually during the pursuit phase of an operation and not during the assault stage, the 42nd's role often being in the latter. Among the best gauges of the combat quality of the A.E.F. outfits are captured German intelligence reports, and in those documents the Rainbow Division was repeatedly rated among the three or four American divisions which the Boche considered on par with the elite shock divisions of the French and British.[17]

MacArthur's personal record in France had brought him fame as one of the few generals who actually accompanied his troops into battle. His seven Silver Stars, the last awarded for

his gallantry in action on the Meuse Heights, may have been a
record for A.E.F. officers, surely for generals. In addition, it will
be recalled, he won the Distinguished Service Cross twice, the
Distinguished Service Medal, two Purple Hearts, and a number
of French awards. He and Donovan emerged as the best known
officer-heroes of the division. MacArthur was again recommended for promotion to major general, but on the day after
the armistice March informed Pershing that the War Department would not authorize any more promotions of general officers for the duration, thus ending the spate of quick promotions occasioned by the emergency.

MacArthur finally gained command of his beloved division,
but his appointment resulted from some interesting, if enigmatic, behind-the-scenes moves. When the division was relieved
after the fighting on the Romagne Heights, the word circulated
that Menoher, a highly regarded divisional leader, was being
seriously considered for a corps command. Shortly an officer
from Chaumont made a mysterious visit to 42nd Division headquarters and inquired of various officers their opinions of Mac-
Arthur. The visit could have been ordered by Pershing or his
adjutant general because MacArthur was being considered for
command of the 42nd. But MacArthur saw the visitor in a
different light and was convinced that he was there because
"without my knowledge, criticism of the fact that I failed to
follow certain regulations prescribed for our troops, that I
wore no helmet, that I carried no gas mask, that I went un-
armed, that I always had a riding crop in my hand, that I
declined to command from the rear, were reported to G.H.Q."
Whatever the mission of the interviewer, the chief of the
A.E.F.'s personnel bureau announced on October 25 that Major General Charles D. Rhodes, commander of the 82nd Division's field artillery brigade, "has been temporarily attached to
the 42nd Division, with a view to his later assignment to command that Division" when Menoher took charge of the VI

Corps. Three days later orders were issued for the new assignments of Menoher and Rhodes, and Liggett was told that
"when operations permit, direct Maj. Gen. Menoher to proceed
to join his new Corps." [18]

On November 2, with Menoher still in command of the
42nd and preparing to direct it in the advance toward Sedan,
Liggett sent the following message to Pershing: "It is requested
that Brig. Gen. Douglas MacArthur be assigned to command
the 42nd Div. upon the departure of Maj. Gen. Menoher. Gen.
MacArthur has been identified with the division from its organization and is thoroughly competent to take over the command." Liggett's request was denied, and on November 10,
when Menoher took command of the VI Corps, Rhodes became
commander of the 42nd Division, some of the divisional orders
that day being issued by the latter general. But before the day
was over, orders from Chaumont arrived authorizing MacArthur to succeed Rhodes as commander of the Rainbow. The
suddenness of Rhodes' relief remains an enigma, but he was
soon appointed to the Permanent Interallied Armistice Commission. In his memoirs MacArthur attributes his advancement
to Pershing, who allegedly called the 84th Brigade commander
"the greatest leader of troops we have." But this explanation
is suspect on two grounds: the unlikely use by Pershing of
such a superlative about MacArthur (or anyone else), and the
prior selection of Rhodes for the job. If Pershing thought so
highly of MacArthur, why did he not choose him instead of
Rhodes in the first place? Though Liggett supported Mac-
Arthur for the position, the First Army commander considered
Rhodes to be "a thoroughly efficient officer." Why then, once
the choice of Rhodes had been made, was MacArthur rushed
in to relieve him before Rhodes had even a day to prove himself as a divisional commander? If Liggett's influence was a
paramount factor, why did not MacArthur give some of the
credit to him? On November 10 Menoher sent a laudatory

letter to Pershing about MacArthur, praising him as "a very brilliant and gifted officer who has . . . filled each day with a loyal and intelligent application to duty such as is, among officers in the field and in actual contact with battle, without parallel in our army." But it is unlikely that Menoher was influential in the matter since his deep admiration of MacArthur was already well known at Chaumont. Besides, his letter undoubtedly reached Pershing after MacArthur had assumed command of the 42nd, the omission of the subject in the contents suggesting that the matter was settled by the time of writing.[19]

Although there is, admittedly, no way to prove it, an interesting theory might be developed that the divisional command was given to MacArthur in order to keep him quiet after the Sedan affair. After all, he was known to be sensitive and outspoken, was a close friend of Baker and March, and could provide the stimulus for a full-scale investigation by the War Department of the farce of November 5–7. Such a theory might explain why, instead of protesting heatedly about his "capture" and lost opportunity in the days following, he atypically let the blunders and the whole Sedan matter drop as quickly and nonchalantly as did Pershing. Of course, such conspiring was unworthy of Pershing and his clique, but, after all, so was the race for Sedan. Also, such a theory discounts the contradictory personality of MacArthur, who in the past had displayed little consistency in his outbursts of righteous indignation, sometimes becoming angry over trivial matters and at other times remaining quiet and calm.

MacArthur retained command of the division until November 22 when he was replaced by Major General Clement A. F. Flagler at a time when most divisional commanders of brigadier rank were being returned to brigade commands. Five days earlier Brigadier General Frank M. Caldwell had been assigned to head the 84th Brigade, with Reilly continuing as commander of the 83rd Brigade. On the 19th MacArthur had received orders to take over the 83rd Brigade when he relinquished the divisional command a few days hence. That same day he notified Chaumont that he was giving the 83rd to Caldwell and he would resume command of the 84th on November 22: "The 84th Brigade is General MacArthur's old brigade which he has commanded for many months in active operations. The mutual transfer of both brigade commanders is in accordance with the desires and wishes of both brigade commanders, and I have accordingly directed it as for the best interests of the service." MacArthur's reference to himself in the third person in the telegram, which he signed, probably evoked some chuckles at Chaumont, but his changes were confirmed.

The same week that MacArthur went back to the 84th Brigade, Parker was demoted from division to brigade command, as befell other brigadier generals. It was the beginning of a sickening period for Regular Army officers who were systematically returned to lower ranks and lesser positions of responsibility and prestige. It would be many years before most of the A.E.F.'s career officers advanced up the ladder again to the rank and authority they had attained during the war. To be returned to his permanent rank of the spring of 1917 would mean reversion to major for MacArthur, but, like the others who became general officers during the emergency, he expected the discouraging news to come soon. One of the consolations of being in the occupation army was that he could probably expect a reprieve until his return to America and the division's demobilization.[20]

MacArthur did not have an opportunity to command the division in combat since, it will be remembered, the 42nd withdrew into corps reserve near Buzancy on the night of November 9–10. From then until November 20 the division shifted stations frequently in the complicated movement of aligning various units for the march to the Rhine where an American occupation zone was to be established. MacArthur's chief responsibilities during his twelve days as divisional commander involved training several thousand replacements, re-equipping of units and individuals, and instructing officers and men in the duties they would perform in the occupation. He also led the division on the first leg of the long march, relinquishing the divisional command to Flagler on the 22nd at Arlon, Belgium, just before the division crossed the western border of Luxemburg.[21]

The armistice provided for Allied occupation of German territory west of the Rhine, with bridgeheads of thirty kilometers in radius at Cologne, Coblenz, and Mayence. The American zone would include the Coblenz bridgehead and a 2800-square-mile rectangular area from the Rhine north of Coblenz westward to Luxemburg, the southern boundary being the Moselle River, with the French and British occupying the regions to the south and north, respectively. Pershing created the Third Army, with Dickman in command, to be the American occupation force; nine veteran divisions were assigned to the occupation. Six days after the armistice was signed, Belgian, British, American, and French armies of occupation crossed the truce line simultaneously and started marching slowly toward their designated zones in Germany, allowing the evacuating Boche troops plenty of time to keep ahead on their journey homeward. The 42nd Division constituted part of the Third Army's reserve in the movement and stayed about three days' march behind the advanced units. Wolf, who continued as MacArthur's adjutant when he reverted to brigade commander, said that the march to the Rhineland was "difficult for both men and animals, covering as it did a distance of approximately 250 kilometers [c. 155 miles] over the shortest route, the first half of which was under favorable weather conditions over fairly good roads, and the latter half in Germany through abominably wet and raw weather and over heavy roads that were badly torn up by the great German exodus over them." [22]

The crossing of the border into Germany occurred on December 1, with everyone in the march anxious about the reception they would get. The most noticeable contrast with the war-ravaged countryside of northern France was, as Hughes reported, the German territory's "excellent condition, with carefully cultivated fields and prosperous villages." As for the inhabitants, Duffy observed: "The greatest surprise of our first week in Germany was the attitude of the people towards us . . . Farmers in the fields would go out of the way to put us on the right road; . . . the women lent their utensils and often helped soldiers with their cooking, even offering stuff from their small stores when the hungry men arrived ahead of their kitchens." One discordant note in divisional reports was that even in the Rhineland "officers and soldiers of the retreating armies have shown general lack of consideration for the population of the territory through which this division has passed. Petty thievery and seizure of desirable articles by enemy troops has been frequent." General Fox Conner, who was Pershing's chief of operations, verified that the general impression was that "the arrival of our troops was watched with unfeigned interest by the inhabitants and without any manifestation of hostility." [23]

The American troops who trudged into the German villages west of the Rhine were undoubtedly an unimpressive-looking horde — weary from over two weeks of marching, rain-soaked and muddy, and depressed by thoughts of thousands of other Yankee soldiers boarding ships at Brest for homeward voyages. As on previous marches, a periodical irritant was the appearance of neatly dressed officers from the inspector general's office, casting critical looks at the long lines of foot soldiers and ever writing in their black notebooks. Shortly after such visits Flagler and other divisional leaders could expect communications citing the faults found by the inspectors. One typical message stated that the inspectors had found in some of Flagler's ranks "formations were not well observed, men marching without helmets in many instances, and with lack of uniformity in others, and in some instances with overcoats unbuttoned. There was lack of uniformity in head dress. While a majority wore caps, a few were wearing helmets." After helping to defeat one of history's greatest armies, the soldiers of the Rainbow were obviously not too receptive to such carping, but regulations had to be obeyed, and the officers watched more carefully for miscreants with buttons unbuttoned. The inspectors reported that MacArthur's brigade looked "very good and the march discipline excellent," discreetly omitting any mention of the commander's unconventional attire.[24]

In mid-December the Rainbow Division finally arrived in the sector which it would occupy for the next four months — the Kreis of Ahrweiler, a district bordering the Rhine north of Coblenz and in the northeast corner of the American zone. Divisional headquarters was established at the town of Ahrweiler in the center of the divisional sector, while MacArthur set up his headquarters at a château in Sinzig, a village near the Rhine and several miles south of Remagen. MacArthur described Sinzig as "a beautiful spot filled with the lore and romance of centuries." Sergeant Raymond S. Tompkins, a Rainbow soldier, said that he and his comrades looked like "a band of men who were almost ragamuffins" when they entered the region, but they soon "went from ragamuffinism to a state of baronial opulence" as they set up quarters in the numerous spacious residences of the Ahrweiler district. "Ruined castles that seemed as old as the hills themselves," observed Tompkins, "etched ragged-edged blotches against the sky-line. Nearer at hand were modern chateaus — rich-looking summer houses surrounded by professionally-tended gardens. On the inlaid and marble floors of these the men of the Rainbow dumped their duffle-bags, packs and blanket-rolls and made themselves at home." Not all of Flagler's soldiers were so fortunate, but generally the division's quarters were by far the best yet. Moreover, the terraced hillsides of the deep, narrow valleys of the region were covered with vineyards, from which were produced in the villages' wine presses some of the most delicious fermented juices found in Europe.[25] To MacArthur, residing in a luxurious château, the scene must have brought back memories of those brief moments of splendor at the St. Benoît château, but this time there would be no bursting shells to disturb his slumber.

3. Life in the Ahrweiler District

On November 15 Marshal Foch, in his capacity as Allied commander-in-chief, issued to the generals commanding the armies of occupation a general statement of policies and procedures which would be followed in the administration of the Rhineland. Under him, the Permanent Interallied Armistice Commission would handle matters relating to the enforcement of the armistice and particularly the occupation. Eventually fourteen other commissions were established under this one to deal with such problems as transportation, communications, municipal affairs, food production, and coal distribution in the Rhineland. Though many French leaders were bent on vengeance toward the Boche, Foch earnestly tried to assure that the occupation would "disturb existing conditions as little as possible when compatible with the best interest of the general public" in the German territory west of the Rhine. Whether the zone was held by British, Belgian, French, or American forces, its administration was essentially an interallied concern, and there was considerable similarity in the way the various zones were administered. At the local level, however, commanders were allowed a degree of autonomy, and it was there

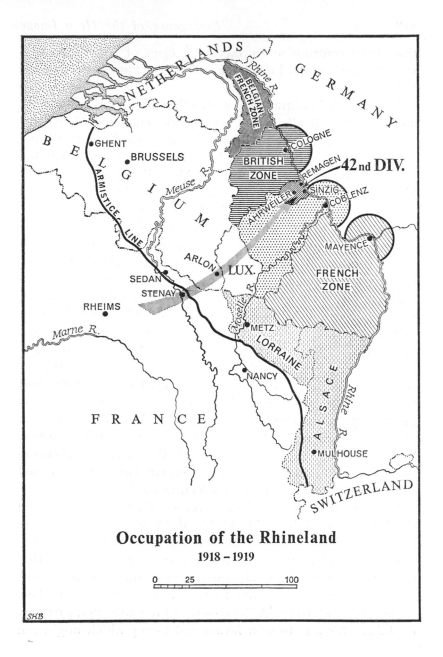

Occupation of the Rhineland
1918–1919

0   25   100

that sharp contrasts arose, especially cases of Americans who were too lenient and French officers whose controls were overly strict.

At Flagler's headquarters, as in other divisional commands, an office of civil affairs was set up and consisted of five departments to supervise and control public works and utilities, fiscal affairs, sanitation and public health, schools and charitable institutions, and legal affairs in the Ahrweiler district. Gregory Mason, an American correspondent, visited the various Allied zones and concluded that "Marshall Foch's police rules are strict but not harsh. They are aimed to protect the people of the occupied zones, and they are softened everywhere as soon as the conduct of the natives justifies such relaxation." Controls over telephone, telegraphic, and postal communications, for example, were lessened considerably after the first month of the occupation. But, asserted Mason, "There has been no softening of the regulations in regard to the press and public meetings . . . the sole exception being in the case of the German churches, which are allowed to hold services as usual." Although the occupation was administered with "dignity and firmness" generally, Mason discovered in some areas, especially in the American zone, that "so light is the heel of the conqueror on their necks that some Germans do not believe that the Allies are conquerors at all. Their theory is that when the revolution came in Germany the German Government called in the Allies as trustees to care for its interests." [26]

On the eve of the armistice Premier Clemenceau told the British prime minister, David Lloyd George, that "Germany will break up and Bolshevism become rampant." During the winter of 1918–19 there was much fear among the Allies that the revolutionary upheavals convulsing Germany would result in the Bolsheviks' accession to power in Berlin. The Ebert regime, with which the Allies concluded the armistice, shrewdly exploited this fear to gain favors and mercy which might not

otherwise have been meted to it; Foch, for example, even allowed German constabulary troops to use French machine guns
to suppress Bolshevist uprisings. The Spartacus League, or
German Communist party, grew rapidly in numbers in the
Rhineland, but the strikes and violence which the Spartacists
fomented during the winter and spring occurred mainly in urban areas east of the Rhine. A 42nd Division intelligence
report in January, for example, noted that "in the cities and
the more congested manufacturing districts there is much labor
trouble and a good deal of voluntary unemployment." But in
the Ahrweiler district, which comprised small towns and
farms, "the people hereabouts have a very lively sense of the
favors which may be obtained from the U.S. . . . They are
obliging, courteous, and increasingly often they try to enter into
friendly relations with our men. If they feel resentment against
the American Army, as they probably do, the feeling is skillfully masked." In March, 1919, the Bolshevist agitation reached
a zenith in Berlin, with over 3000 persons killed in furious
street battles between radical workers and Lüttwitz soldiers, but
in the Ahrweiler district the month passed rather quietly.[27]

At times, Foch seemed more understanding toward the
Rhinelanders than toward Pershing and the American Third
Army. On December 8 the French marshal decided to assign a
French division to occupy about half of the Coblenz bridgehead, against Pershing's heated protests. Ultimately Foch reduced the Third Army's frontage on the Rhine by nearly 40
per cent until the American troops, constituting a third of the
Allied occupation strength, held only a twelfth of the Rhine
frontage. Puzzled, Dickman commented, "The reasons for this
change are not known; perhaps it was pique at our refusal to
have Colonial Troops in the Third Army." A new flurry of
controversy between the French and Americans developed
when the French liaison mission at Dickman's headquarters
filed a formal protest charging that "the position of the French

officers and soldiers on duty with the Third Army was becoming intolerable; that there were no restrictions on the German people, who received better treatment from the Americans
than from their own Prussian officers." In the spring the
French commander at Mayenz helped organize a brief-lived,
independent Rhenish republic, but the move was severely condemned by both American and British authorities, who saw
it as another vindictive maneuver against Germany. The grand
alliance which had bound American and French armies on
the battlefields disintegrated quickly during the occupation.[28]

Pershing and Dickman prescribed a rigid training program
for the Third Army, starting December 20. "Despite the damp
and inclement weather," Wolf stated, "the division drilled and
maneuvered for a period of at least five hours a day . . . Later
the rigors of this schedule were, simultaneously with the breaking up of winter, ameliorated." The relaxation of the program
was not quite as simple as Wolf described it. Most soldiers
found it difficult to maintain maximum efficiency on the drill
ground or the target range when the emergency seemed to be
past. Men who had shot live enemy soldiers could not be motivated easily to trudge through the mud now to a target range
and fire practice rounds at straw-filled targets. The reports
filed by inspectors of the Third Army provide an index to the
alarming decline in morale and efficiency. MacArthur, who
took great pride in the spirit and discipline of his brigade,
found that even his soldiers were affected. On January 10, for
instance, Colonel Walter C. Short, Dickman's G-5 and later
the commanding general at Pearl Harbor when the Japanese
struck, inspected the infantry regiments of the 84th Brigade
and found that "the 167th Infantry was not doing the required
five hours' work per day in instruction," and part of the 168th
"has apparently been working with very little supervision from
the regimental commander." Before long, Flagler was compelled to issue memorandums repeatedly warning his officers
about "the very slovenly manner" of saluting and obeying or-

ders observed in their outfits. The situation in the 42nd Division was, nevertheless, not as serious as in some divisions where living quarters and messes were intolerable. In one such division the men refused to fall into formation when Pershing arrived for a review and actually jeered him when he tried to address them. Raymond B. Fosdick, who headed the War Department's commission on training camps, visited the Third Army in January and reported: "The situation over here is, I believe, little short of desperate . . . The feeling of bitterness among the troops is growing." [29]

In mid-February the Army's high command in Europe belatedly responded to the crisis and instituted the changes recommended by Fosdick, which included "the improvement of billets, the extension of leaves, the encouragement of athletics and entertainment . . . and a stimulation of the activities of the non-military societies, such as the Y.M.C.A., the K. of C. and the Red Cross." Probably most effective was the vast athletic program which was instituted; the competition between units was lively, and the champions in various sports could look forward to the Interallied Games, held near Paris at Pershing Stadium, which was built by American engineer troops. In addition, an extensive system of education was set up and received an enthusiastic response from the men of the A.E.F. At most stations, courses were organized in various subjects taught in American secondary and trade schools, with competent instructors secured through a special educational commission of the War Department. At Beaune, France, an A.E.F. university was established, and over 9000 officers and men enrolled in its courses in business, agriculture, medicine, education, engineering, and arts and sciences. Yet the key problem remained unsolved, as Fosdick wisely realized: "The thing uppermost in the minds of the troops is the desire to return home. This question dwarfs all others and has apparently become in some parts of the Army almost a mania." [30]

The reduction of the training schedule afforded the soldiers the opportunity for much sight-seeing and illegal fraternizing. Sergeant William H. Amerine, of the 167th Infantry, recalled that the Americans "roamed about over the surrounding hills, along the beautiful valleys, and made trips by train and by auto or motor-truck into the surrounding country, and visited the cities along the Rhine. Ancient castles received the attention of many of them." The soldiers enjoyed excursions on "the great Rhine steamers," said Amerine, and as winter came, "ice formed in the back waters of the Rhine and the men enjoyed skating." He added: "The German girls were there to help out the best they could in the face of the anti-fraternization orders. Some day when you ask a 'doughboy' where he learned to skate on ice, he will tell you and let you know, perhaps, the name of the 'fraulein' who taught him." MacArthur commented: "The division thoroughly enjoyed those days of rest and relaxation. The warm hospitality of the population, their well-ordered way of life, their thrift and geniality forged a feeling of mutual respect and esteem."

The lessening of military chores also meant more time for the pranks and shenanigans in which soldiers excel. Perhaps the best known incident of mischief-making during the occupation, as far as the 42nd was concerned, was the so-called "egg affair." Eggs were a rare treat for the troops on duty in the Rhineland, and when an entire carload of eggs arrived at the rail station at Sinzig, intended for distribution to all units of the Rainbow Division, the Alabamians of the 167th Infantry, declared Reilly, "took immediate possession of the whole carload and lived happily on eggs for some time thereafter." Colonel Screws, the regiment's commander, explained that his men seized the eggs because another regiment had earlier stolen a carload of tobacco which the citizens of Alabama had sent for the 167th. "Of course, we Alabamians being the 'he-men' we are," Screws remarked, "we would sooner 'chaw' on tobacco than eggs, but we had the eggs and we didn't have the tobacco."

MacArthur chose to ignore the incident, possibly for the reason Screws offered: "I sent a few around to the other Colonels and Generals to keep them from starting something." [31]

During his four months in the Rhineland, MacArthur was plagued by disappointments and poor health. The futile effort to secure a promotion for him was renewed by Flagler in January, possibly because of a temporary lifting of the ban on advancing general officers. Flagler wrote Pershing: "MacArthur has twice served under my command before the War and I know him to be an excellent officer, and further his recent service in the Army of Occupation has convinced me of the recommendations previously made for his promotion." He went on to quote the recommendations by Menoher in September and October that, because of "his outstanding qualities of mind, resourcefulness and leadership," MacArthur should be elevated to major general and given a division of his own. Not only was Flagler's proposal turned down, but also when Flagler vacated the divisional command in late March, the position went to Gatley. At least approval was obtained for MacArthur's application to enter the advanced school of artillery studies at Treves, southwest of Coblenz. But on February 13, just before the start of the term at Treves for which MacArthur had applied, Flagler had to wire Dickman: "Brig. Gen. MacArthur is recovering from an attack of diphtheria . . . Request order be revoked as he is unable to comply therewith." This illness was his second serious one at Sinzig. Before Christmas, MacArthur said, "I fell desperately ill with a throat infection — too much gas during the campaign — but the brigade surgeon and good luck pulled me through." [32]

His illnesses may have curtailed some of his sight-seeing, but MacArthur was still able to charm visitors who came to his château. Joseph C. Chase, an artist commissioned by the Army to paint portraits of certain prominent A.E.F. officers and enlisted heroes, came to Sinzig and painted the 84th Brigade commander. "He is a thorough-going, brainy young man," the artist observed, "distinctly of the city type, a good talker and a good listener, perfectly 'daffy' about the 42nd Division, and, of course, positive the 42nd Division won the Great War." Captivated by his subject, Chase continued: "He is quick in his movements, physical and mental, and is subject to changing moods; he knits his brows or laughs heartily with equal facility, and often during the same sentence." [33] Another visitor who discovered MacArthur's magnetism was the famous journalist William Allen White, who was invited to lunch at the general's beautiful mansion overlooking the Rhine. MacArthur had "the grace and charm of a stage hero," White found:

> . . . I had never before met so vivid, so captivating, so magnetic a man. He was all that Barrymore and John Drew hoped to be. And how he could talk! He was a West Pointer, son of the old General, General Fred Funston's friend, and was widely read. He stood six feet, had a clean-shaven face, a clean-cut mouth, nose, and chin, lots of brown hair, good eyes with a "come hither" in them that must have played the devil with the girls, and yet he was as "he" as Chapman's bull in the Estes Park meadow. His staff adored him, his men worshipped him, and he seemed to be entirely without vanity. He was lounging in his room, not well (an ulcer in his throat), and he wore a ragged brown sweater and civilian pants — nothing more. He was greatly against the order prohibiting fraternization. He said the order only hurt the boys. He told of going out for a Christmas visit to the troops. In one little town of a thousand people, the boys had rigged up a Christmas tree in the town hall. They had decorated it beautifully and were solemnly having a stag dance, while outside looking in at the windows were two hundred girls. The General danced around with a sergeant to show his good will, and went on to the next town.
>
> He felt that the common people of Germany had had war crammed so far down into their bellies that it had gone into their legs, and they were done with it and all who advocated it. He said the German women were all voters and were study-

ing politics in a thorough-going scientific manner. He said the women of his household were solemnly going into their duties as voters, and that they all despised the Kaiser. He knew; no man with his eyes and face was going to be fooled on the woman vote. He said — and we found it to be true when we got to Cologne — that the German army was practically demobilized in the last few weeks and that there was no attempt to reorganize it except on a volunteer basis . . . He thought Baker and Wood would be the presidential nominees, and he was greatly interested in the radical movement in America. We visited with him for two hours.[34]

MacArthur's men received their share of attention and praise when Pershing led a grand review of the 42nd Division on a plain near Remagen on March 16, three weeks before the men were to move to French ports for the shipment home. Pershing "looked every soldier in the face" as he strode down the lines, and, said Dickman, the A.E.F. commander "spoke pleasantly to all bearing on the right sleeve the gold chevron indicating a wound in battle." He delivered a farewell address, as well as pinning medals on a number of soldiers, including the Distinguished Service Medal on MacArthur, for which he had been cited in the autumn. In his speech Pershing reminded the men of the Rainbow that membership in the A.E.F. had afforded them the privilege of representing their nation in a great cause. "The result," he declared, "has been a broadening of vision to each individual man. The result has been a strengthening of character to each individual man. It has given him something to be proud of, something to carry home with him that he didn't have when he came over." The men appeared to listen solemnly and intently, but Father Duffy probably typified the men's interests when, in his journal, he dismissed Pershing's visit with a few words and went on at length about the events of the next day — St. Patrick's Day — when "we celebrated . . . in the best approved manner with religion, games and feasting." Later the soldiers of the 42nd Division, in an unusual plebiscite, voted against participating in any welcoming parades "at a distance from their homes" when they returned to America and expressed "their desire to promptly return to their homes." They were simply weary of all things military — of pomp and ceremony, as well as battle and glory. And there were too many memories — of mud and filth, of screaming sounds and blinding flashes, of agony and death.[35]

Between April 1 and 5 the various units of the 42nd entrained for the port of Brest, a few going to St. Nazaire. With ten divisions departing in March and April, the confusion and congestion at the ports prevented quick departures. After watching the chaotic embarking situation for what must have seemed to him an interminable period, MacArthur dispatched a telegram from Brest to Davis, the A.E.F. adjutant general, on April 14: "Rumor here that request is to be made for my detail as member of machine gun board in France. Am intensely desirous of returning to U.S. with my brigade, half of which has already sailed and remainder booked to leave within thirty-six hours. My mother's health is critical and I fear consequences my failure to return as scheduled. Appreciate greatly your help." The divisional and 84th Brigade headquarters staffs, including MacArthur, sailed from Brest on April 18, along with about 12,000 Rainbow soldiers. The voyage was made on the *Leviathan,* a converted German liner which was the largest and fastest of the American transports.

Not all of the A.E.F. were so fortunate, a force of a few thousand troops under Brigadier General Henry T. Allen remaining on occupation duty until early 1923. In view of their previous experiences on the battlefields of France, the weather was fitting for both MacArthur's departure and Allen's: it was raining.[36]

PART III

Troubled Interlude

CHAPTER X

Father of the
New West Point

1. A Season of Reaction

AMERICANS WERE TIRED of parading doughboys by the time
MacArthur returned from Europe. When he and a shipload
of his soldiers arrived aboard the *Leviathan* at a New York
pier on April 25, 1919, he expected a "howling mob to proclaim us monarchs of all we surveyed." Instead, a young boy
met them at the foot of the gangplank and asked who they
were. "We are the famous 42nd," MacArthur proudly answered. The mighty fell quickly when the lad next inquired
if they had been in France. "Amid a silence that hurt — with
no one, not even the children, to see us," lamented Mac-
Arthur, "we marched off the dock, to be scattered to the four
winds — a sad, gloomy end of the Rainbow." [1]

Reporting for duty in the War Department, MacArthur was
soon aware that the nation's mood had changed markedly
since his departure for France nineteen months earlier. The
cherry blossoms along the Potomac Tidal Basin were as profuse and colorful in the spring of 1919 as ever, but the newspapers left on the benches beneath the cherry bowers bespoke

ugliness: demobilized soldiers without jobs, striking workers
with bloodied shirts, and citizens gripped by the Great Red
Scare.

On April 28, the day after MacArthur returned to Washington, a bomb was discovered in the mail of the Seattle mayor,
a crusader against labor radicalism. The next day a package
addressed to the chairman of the Senate immigration committee exploded in the hands of the servant who opened it.
On the following day bombs were uncovered in thirty-six
packages in the New York City post office, all addressed to
high-ranking federal officials. Battles between policemen and
marchers erupted during May Day parades in several cities. A
record number of wage earners were involved in strikes across
the land, with the number of strikes and incidents of labor
violence increasing weekly. Nourished by the intolerance and
nativism which was rampant during the war years, many people feared a Bolshevik revolution and struck out blindly
against alleged radicals. With his own home shattered by a
bomb, Attorney General A. Mitchell Palmer laid plans to jail
or deport all Bolshevists. The actual number of Bolshevists
in America was small, however, and the hysteria would gradually subside in the years ahead as the economy revived after
severe postwar dislocations.[2] But truth has a small voice when
fire bells are clanging, and they were ringing loudly in 1919.

The War Department, like the rest of official Washington,
viewed the spreading labor agitation with alarm. From July,
1918, through October, 1919, the Army dispatched troops on
sixteen occasions to help in suppressing riots, most of which
the leaders in the War Department considered to be Communist-inspired. General Wood, the former chief of staff and
a contender for the Republican presidential nomination in
the coming convention, personally led 900 soldiers in curbing
an Omaha riot, and he commanded 1500 troops used against
rioting steel workers in Gary, Indiana. Probably expressing
the sentiment of many of his fellow officers, Wood wanted to

see all Bolshevists deported "in ships of stone with sails of lead, with the wrath of God for a breeze and with hell for their first port." [3]

Wrenched by fears of radicalism, economic depression, and renewed entanglement in Europe's distresses, the American people yearned for conditions of tranquillity, innocence, and isolation. A pervading sense of revulsion against war accentuated this desire. Many persons talked of the need for a return to "normal" conditions, and few heeded the occasional reformers and liberals who dared to speak. The people were weary of ideals and crusades. They would soon spew from their mouths the lofty words of President Wilson and would unashamedly retreat from domestic reforms and international responsibilities.

Into this chaotic, reactionary atmosphere strode MacArthur, a heralded combat leader, but one imbued with liberal, reform ideas for his profession. When he reported to Chief of Staff March, MacArthur was promptly told that he was to assume the superintendency at West Point in June. Caught by surprise, he objected: "I am not an educator. I am a field soldier. Besides there are so many of my old professors there. I can't do it." His protest was abruptly dismissed by March's retort: "Yes . . . you can do it."

The thirty-nine-year-old brigadier general would be the youngest superintendent of the United States Military Academy since Sylvanus Thayer, who held the position just after the War of 1812. Although several members of the faculty in 1919 had been MacArthur's professors when he was a cadet, March warned him that his problems on the Plain would comprise more than the diplomacy necessary to handle former mentors. "West Point is forty years behind the times," March stated bluntly, adding that during and since the World War the institution had been "in a state of disorder and confusion." The chief of staff's instructions to MacArthur were succinct: "Revitalize and revamp the Academy." [4]

While temporarily assigned to the General Staff in Wash-

ington for the next six weeks, pending his move to West
Point, MacArthur worked feverishly to acquaint himself with
the academy's problems. Poring over West Point files in the
War Department and cornering colleagues familiar with the
situation on the Hudson, he learned why March was so critical.
For seven months the chief of staff had been trying to get
seventy-two-year-old Superintendent Samuel Tillman and his
faculty to broaden and modernize the curriculum, but March
had flailed in vain against these uncritical traditionalists. In
step with most of the nation, they desired to return to the
tranquil past. MacArthur also learned that, as of the summer
of 1919, the academy's program would be three years, which
meant that he must both revitalize and compress the prewar
four-year plan. Moreover, Congress was preparing to launch
an investigation of cadet hazing, which was at an all-time peak
of viciousness and had recently resulted in the death of a
plebe. But the congressmen's interest in the school did not
extend to generous appropriations, as hearings and actions on
the budget in 1919 clearly showed. Sensitive to many constituents' reactions against military matters in general, some
politicians on Capitol Hill publicly questioned the worth of
the academy.

During the war years March himself had contributed to poor
morale and organizational confusion at West Point by endorsing a reduction of the school's four-year program to one year.
"This will permit us," he explained at the time, "to graduate
from West Point annually over 1,000 officers instead of the 200
that we are now getting from this elaborate and expensive
plant." Justifying the action by the acute shortage of officers, the War Department allowed five classes to graduate in
1917–18. Only the fourth classmen were left on the Plain by
the time the guns ceased firing in France, and they were
promised graduation by the next June. The august institution
had descended to the level of just another officers' training
school.

The problem was compounded when the War Department decreed in late November, 1918, that a new, fourth class was to be admitted that winter. These plebes were required to wear privates' uniforms in order to distinguish them from the fourth classmen already enrolled, who wore the traditional gray outfits. Furthermore, the class of 1921, which had graduated prior to the armistice with only sixteen months of work at the academy, was ordered back to West Point for another half year of training. Already possessing commissions, they wore officers' uniforms, but underwent the regular disciplines of classes and drills with the other cadets. When the three-year program was announced in May, 1919, the "grays" and the "privates" were embittered because they had anticipated graduating in one year. Over 100 cadets resigned, and many of the remainder were melancholic and churlish. Old Tillman and his staff vainly tried to cope with the critical disciplinary and morale problems. Major Jacob L. Devers, a tactical officer on the academy's staff and a distinguished corps commander in World War II, affirmed that MacArthur "inherited an old institution with a great heritage of success and tradition, but now reduced to a pitiable state as a result of action of the War Department." [5]

Despite his initial protest over the assignment, MacArthur really welcomed the opportunity to take the reins at West Point. Although most of its alumni felt a strong attachment to the school, MacArthur's loyalty and affection for his alma mater were unusually deep and seemed to grow with the years. Besides, the superintendency was one of the most prestigious jobs in the Army. MacArthur's holding of the position was probably a paramount factor in his promotion to the permanent rank of brigadier general in January, 1920, when most regular officers with brevet generalships had already been reduced to their permanent ranks of prewar days. This enabled him to pull well ahead of other officers of his age and experience, most of whom did not attain brigadier general again until the Second World War. But foremost in MacArthur's mind at the time was a burning desire to reform West Point on the basis of his experiences in the war and the Rhine occupation. He had developed a conception of the type of officer that he felt the Army desperately needed, and he was eager to implement his theory at the elite military school.

On the battlefields of Lorraine and Champagne, MacArthur had witnessed West Pointers in action all around him. Thirty-four of the thirty-eight corps and division commanders of the A.E.F. were graduates of the academy, and above the corps command level in Pershing's army the West Pointers had a virtual monopoly. There were numerous young alumni, too, who commanded regiments, battalions, and companies in the fighting in France. Most West Point men had performed with distinction and intrepidity under the stresses of combat, but MacArthur concluded that too many of them had come from the cloistered confines on the Hudson inadequately prepared to cope with volunteers and draftees straight from civilian life. The citizen-soldiers of the National Guard and National Army divisions constituted the vast majority of American troops in the war, and they represented the highest physical and educational standards of any soldiers the United States had ever sent into battle. But too often, he believed, they were handled like the scurvy soldiers of professional armies of old, "which frequently required the most rigid methods of training, the severest forms of discipline, to weld them into a flexible weapon for use on the battlefield." The new type of soldiers needed officers who could command obedience based on loyalty, respect, and understanding, "rather than be forced by fear of consequence of failure." The West Point graduate of the future, as MacArthur envisioned him, must be of "a type possessing all of the cardinal military virtues as of yore, but possessing an intimate understanding of his fellows, a comprehensive grasp of world and national affairs, and a liberalization of conception which amounts to a change in his psychology of command."

MacArthur's concept of the new officer stemmed not only from combat situations in France but also from adverse experiences of the Third Army. American officers in the Rhineland, it will be remembered, encountered serious difficulties with surly, sometimes rebellious troops who felt that they should have been sent home when the war ended. According to MacArthur, some West Pointers in the occupation showed little knowledge of any fields beyond the military, yet the administration of the Rhineland required them to deal with political, economic, social, and psychological problems. In molding the new kind of military leader at West Point, MacArthur aimed "to introduce a new atmosphere of liberalization in doing away with provincialism, a substitute of subjective for objective discipline, a progressive increase of cadet responsibility tending to develop initiative and force of character rather than automatic performance of stereotyped functions, to broaden the curriculum so as to be abreast of the best modern thought on education, to bring West Point into a new and closer relationship with the Army at large." [6]

The accomplishment of these goals depended upon the support of the academic board (faculty), corps of cadets, alumni, War Department, and Congress. Each of these groups, in its turn and in its own way, would enjoy a season of reaction during the three-year superintendency of MacArthur. The times were not propitious for a liberal-minded reformer, as the new superintendent would soon learn.

2. *The Anguish of Change*

Moving into the superintendent's house with his mother, who was in her sixty-seventh year and still sickly, MacArthur took formal command at the United States Military Academy on June 12, 1919. Earl Blaik, then a cadet and later a famous football coach there, recalled: "There was no ceremony, not even a review of the Corps, when MacArthur took command. We soon learned he was not one to soiree the Corps with unnecessary pomp and ceremony." But the new superintendent was hard at work from the first day, quietly meeting with small groups of faculty members and cadet officers to lay down his reform plans. The news of his proposed changes spread quickly through the corps, and, according to Blaik, "the air was charged with renewed vitality." [7]

For certain professors less amenable to change than cadets, the three years would be most upsetting. Major Robert M. Danford, the new commandant of cadets in 1919 and a friend of MacArthur since their days together as cadets on the Plain, noted that from the start there was "a feeling of resentment" and "a real but polite hostility" toward the superintendent on the part of perhaps six professors. The leader of the faculty opposition to MacArthur's reforms was Colonel Gustav J. Fiebeger, head of the department of civil and military engineering. He had come to the school as a cadet in 1875 and was appointed to its faculty in 1896; he would retire, as it turned out, a month before MacArthur left in 1922. Another conservative leader was Colonel Cornelius W. Willcox, head of the department of modern languages. He was a native of Switzerland and entered the institution as a cadet about the time of MacArthur's birth, later returning as a member of the academic board. Colonel Charles P. Echols, in charge of the mathematics department, had been an associate professor when Cadet MacArthur clashed with Colonel Edgerton, then the head of mathematics. Another of the old guard was Colonel Frederick P. Reynolds, professor of military hygiene and a graduate of the University of Pennsylvania medical school in 1890. Younger than these men but tending to side with them were Colonels Clifton C. Carter in natural and experimental philosophy and Wirt Robinson in chemistry, mineralogy, and geology. Major Charles Hines, acting professor of ordnance and gunnery, was thirty-one years old and probably had little voice in faculty sessions. The only major professor who consistently backed MacArthur and his changes was Colonel Lucius H. Holt, head of the department of English and history and the faculty's only Ph.D. (a Yale graduate). Commandant Danford, Major William A. Ganoe, MacArthur's adjutant, and Captain Louis E. Hibbs, aide to the superintendent, were intensely loyal to MacArthur and enthusiastically endorsed his proposals.[8]

The academic board consisted of the superintendent, the cadet commandant, and the heads of the departments of instruction. Each board member had one vote, with the adjutant serving as a non-voting secretary. The board's powers were sweeping in such matters as the curriculum, textbook selections, instructional methods, examinations, and admission and graduation of cadets. MacArthur, Danford, and Ganoe were new members of the board and lacked knowledge of the inner workings of academy affairs. Possessing tenure and, in most cases, long experience as academy professors, the department heads viewed superintendents as passing phenomena. A superintendent might stay for several years, but they remained at West Point for decades. The professors felt that they were the ones most responsible for preserving the hallowed traditions and standards of the institution. They were not favorably impressed by a reform-minded superintendent who wanted to turn the system upside down and then depart in a few years, leaving them with the shambles. Most important, the professors had the voting power to prevent significant changes to which they were opposed. The consequence during the years 1919–22 was a collision between an ambitious superintendent and a faculty which Ganoe described as "powerful and deeply

entrenched." Storm King Mountain, rising majestically to the
north of the Plain, seemed aptly named during those tem-
pestuous years.

The ensuing friction and misunderstanding were by no
means the fault solely of the conservative professors. Bringing
to his new job some preconceived biases born during his cadet
days, MacArthur set forth his proposals to the professors in
what seemed to them to be ultimatums. They were not accustomed to transient superintendents making peremptory demands or acting first and consulting them afterward. When
they reacted negatively to his plans, Superintendent Mac-
Arthur, apparently oblivious to the impact of his high-pressured
approach on the staid academic board, commented to Ganoe:
"The professors are so secure, they have become set and smug.
They deliver the same schedule year after year with the blessed
unction that they have reached the zenith in education."
Hibbs said that the superintendent sometimes seemed to antagonize the teachers deliberately. During a period of tension
between the faculty and MacArthur over setting qualifications
for instructors, for instance, Hibbs was preparing to announce
a meeting of the academic board and asked MacArthur if it
should be set for 11:00 A.M., the usual time for faculty sessions.
" 'No!' General MacArthur replied. 'Call the meeting at
4:30 P.M. I want them to come here hungry — and I'll keep
them here that way till I get what I want.' " [9] In a sense, Mac-
Arthur's relations with the academic board were similar to
Wilson's with the Senate in 1919: so zealous was his dedication
to his mission, neither man saw that the opposition was provoked by his methods as well as his ends.

As seems to be a rather typical human reaction when an
individual is placed in a position of authority over older, more
experienced persons, MacArthur assumed an aura of seriousness and majestic aloofness which impressed some as simply a
superiority complex. Colonel Wilbur S. Nye, then a cadet, re-

called: "Neither I nor the vast majority of my class saw the general, except when he was walking across Diagonal Walk, apparently lost in thought, his nose in the air, gazing at distant horizons." General Mitchell's sister, who had known Mac-Arthur since their youth in Milwaukee, had lunch with him at West Point and was surprised at his demeanor, "for he was now quite serious and reserved, no longer gay and full of fun." Some professors saw him as an arrogant individualist who was "a law unto himself." [10]

On the other hand, Ganoe maintained that MacArthur's attitudes and behavior were those of an aristocratic gentleman: "To him the word 'gentleman' held a religious meaning. It was sacredly higher than any title, station or act of Congress." Thus, according to this interpretation, MacArthur was easy to meet but difficult to get close to, as the gentleman should be. Hibbs observed that MacArthur "had implicit faith" in the ability of his immediate staff, but "he was one of the loneliest men I have ever known" and "missed the companionship of men below his rank." If true, his aloofness could be partially explained as a manifestation of loneliness. Danford maintained that MacArthur's "was a gifted leadership, a leadership that kept you at a respectful distance, yet at the same time took you in as an esteemed member of his team, and very quickly had you working harder than you had ever worked before in your life, just because of the loyalty, admiration and respect in which you held him." Sergeant Marty Maher, longtime athletic trainer at the academy, found MacArthur to be very cordial toward the enlisted men on duty at West Point; they "could always count on him for a square deal." Apparently the impression of Superintendent MacArthur tended to be favorable or unfavorable corresponding to the particular person's closeness to him, and unfortunately few professors if any were allowed by him to enter that intimate circle of friends.[11]

During his first half year in the superintendency MacArthur also created adverse impressions upon traditionalists by his unconventional attire. As he had done in France, he took the wire brace out of his hat so that it sat on his head in a most cocky and slouched manner. Like a Prussian staff officer, he was seldom seen without his riding crop. When the brisk autumn air swept across the Plain, out walked MacArthur in a smart short overcoat, a style expressly forbidden by the War Department. This practice quickly disappeared, however, when Inspector General Eli A. Helmick visited the academy wearing an overcoat which nearly touched the parade ground. Later MacArthur also saw fit to wear orthodox hats. In themselves, of course, such eccentricities in dress were of minor concern, but some officers felt that the superintendent's cavalier attitude toward such regulations set a poor example for the cadets.[12]

Commandant Danford could remember only one occasion when the animosity between MacArthur and the conservative professors was openly exhibited at a faculty meeting. An elderly professor interrupted the superintendent repeatedly with critical and arrogant remarks which "bordered on the insubordinate." According to Danford, "MacArthur took it patiently for as long as he could, then suddenly he froze with indignation. 'Sit down, Sir,' commanded the Superintendent. 'I'm talking.'" Danford considered the chastisement "a wholesome lesson" for the faculty, but it is unlikely that the professors so interpreted the incident.[13]

An early and lasting dispute developed when MacArthur told the members of the academic board that more stress must be placed on the social sciences. In line with his aim to produce officers who understood human motivations and were knowledgeable about national and foreign affairs, he urged the introduction of courses in political science, economics, sociology, and psychology; enlargement of the offerings in English and history; and creation of a department of economics, government, and history. Professor Holt had been crusading for these changes since 1911, but most of the faculty believed that greater attention should be given to improving and extending the courses in military and technical subjects. After all, they argued, the academy has a highly specialized function and was never intended to compete with civilian universities. The academic board grudgingly gave MacArthur a few tidbits, but nothing more. The classroom hours in English and history were increased somewhat, and a combined course in economics and American government was introduced.

Other curriculum changes, which MacArthur obtained with less opposition, included dropping courses in geology and mineralogy and using that time to extend the offering in electricity and to introduce instruction in internal combustion engines, radio communications, and aerodynamics. Spanish, which had been discontinued during the World War, was added again; the only other offering in modern languages was French. Instruction was added also in the use of the slide rule, precision measurements, graphical methods, optics, and applied mechanics. In revamping the curriculum, moreover, MacArthur brought over ninety civilian leaders in higher education to West Point at various times to appraise the current program and advise him on constructive changes.[14]

The severest criticism of the West Point system came from an educator who had served earlier on the academy's board of visitors, the annual inspection team of distinguished educators and political leaders. Dr. Charles W. Eliot, president emeritus of Harvard, gave an address at Boston in the spring of 1920 which was widely publicized because of his scathing analysis of the faults of the West Point system. Eliot castigated the "completely prescribed curriculum" of the school, the "ill-prepared material" which the academy accepted as plebes; the inbreeding of the faculty, particularly the use of recent graduates with no teaching experience as instructors; and the inability of West Pointers during World War I "to adapt to new methods in the fields of supply and procurement, because of their stifled training." A member of the General Staff in Washington offered a public rebuttal of Eliot's speech, but MacArthur stayed out of the controversy over the charges. Nevertheless, the superintendent's efforts at the academy clearly manifested his agreement with most of Eliot's criticisms.[15]

MacArthur did not attempt to inaugurate an elective system, but he did make a sound start toward broadening and modernizing the curriculum. Entrance requirements were considerably stiffened. Moreover, new instructors were required to spend the first year of their appointment studying at civilian universities in the disciplines which they would teach at the academy. Also, extensive changes in training were made in the tactical department to update the cadets' education in supply, procurement, and modern ordnance. Devers said that Danford, too, "recognized the rigidity of the training program and supplemented and complemented the new Superintendent's recommendations for increased flexibility." [16]

Probably few of the professors would have admitted it, but a factor in what partial success MacArthur achieved in the academic area was his decree that each professor must spend one month each year visiting civilian institutions of higher learning. His order was resented most by the four non-degree career officers on the academic board. By June, 1921, however, nine of the professors had visited twenty-four colleges and universities, mostly in the Midwest and East. The visitation program was not a total success, but Devers was impressed by the professors' changed attitudes: "When the new orders had been carried out, and the fresh breezes had carried off some of the old, stagnant air, the individuals involved in the changes began to see the wisdom and validity of the demands of the young Superintendent." Ganoe found that "the young members expressed enthusiasm for the experience on their return, but the older members continued to protest that the practice was valueless." [17]

Contrary to the fears of some professors, MacArthur did not crusade for the hiring of professors from civilian schools or even of non-academy officers. True, more non-academy instructors were employed than before in such areas as gymnastics and languages, but in the one case where he had a chance to make an appointment at the professorial level, he followed the custom of selecting a West Point man. When the professorship of law was vacated in the summer of 1919, General Crowder, the judge advocate general, submitted to MacArthur for his consideration the names of a number of qualified officers. The superintendent chose Major George V. Strong, whom he had known when they were fellow cadets. "All other conditions being equal," MacArthur wrote Crowder, "I think it advantageous to have a graduate of the Academy detailed as Professor of Law rather than a non-graduate." [18] There was one holy niche at West Point wherein even MacArthur dared not to tread.

One of his characteristics which some professors found shocking was his periodical visiting in classes. In an unprecedented action for a superintendent, MacArthur would suddenly appear in a classroom, take a seat in the rear, and start making notes. Afterward he would visit the particular professor or instructor in his office and offer suggestions on ways to improve his teaching methods. His presence and counsel were obviously abhorred by some teachers, but he was able to persuade several men to introduce new methods. He induced Holt, for example, to place more emphasis on training in oratory and debate and to require cadets in history and government sections to study two newspapers daily and discuss current events in class. In military art and history the superintendent obtained a much-needed substitution of the analysis of World

War operations in place of the study of Civil War campaigns.

MacArthur was never satisfied with the daily recitation method of education, which was used by all of the departments. Most colleges had long ago abandoned the recitation as an ineffective instructional method. In his first year Mac-Arthur announced that the "front-board recitation" was not to be considered as mandatory "in subjects which do not lend themselves readily to it." Hoping to get the cadets out of "the habit of just going along by rote," he encouraged instructors to allow less time for routine reciting and more time for lectures, class discussions, laboratory work in the physical sciences, and oral drills in foreign languages. The faculty, accustomed to serving largely as graders of cadets' performances on rote exercises, called his proposal "a dangerous innovation" which would upset "the thoroughness of study and recitation." While some teachers stopped marking cadets long enough to answer their questions and some scientific laboratories were set up, generally MacArthur was not very successful in altering the time-honored system of "front-board recitation." [19]

In order to make the academy's program more attractive and to introduce persons and views from the world beyond the Plain, MacArthur made West Point for three years a mecca for visiting scholars, political leaders, and military experts. Difficult to reach geographically and deliberately isolated from contact with the outside world for over a century, West Point suddenly found its gates opened and its cadets exposed to distinguished visitors. Besides the usual visits by officials of the War Department, MacArthur was successful in bringing to the Plain such figures as the King of the Belgians, the Prince of Wales, Marshal Foch, President Harding, and the head of Mexico's Chapultepec Military Academy, as well as a host of guest lecturers from colleges. One of the most significant addresses, which brought a standing ovation from the corps and some discomfort to the War Department, was delivered by the assistant chief of the Army's air service, Brigadier General William Mitchell. On January 20, 1920, Mitchell spoke for an hour and a half before the spellbound cadets, relating exciting stories of the air war over France and predicting a marvelous future for air power. Two weeks later during a House hearing in Washington he threw down the gauntlet to the Navy for the first time, stating that his bombers could sink the most powerful ships of the line.[20] Perhaps unwittingly, the superintendent had exposed his cadets to the inauguration of one of the most controversial crusades in the nation's military history.

Despite the criticism by old-line professors and alumni that he was a liberal innovator, MacArthur was actually as concerned about preserving the spirit of the old West Point as he was interested in modernizing the school's curriculum and methods. He preciously guarded the principles of the West Point motto — "Duty, Honor, Country" — while simultaneously trying to cast out obsolete techniques and practices. In order to impress upon the corps that academic work alone did not make the West Pointer, he insisted that character and loyalty be counted in the merit standings of the classes. Cadets were to be evaluated by company tactical officers and fellow cadets on these virtues as manifested in their bearing and performance in athletics, choir, and other extracurricular activities, as well as in the classroom and on the drill field. In the class standings military efficiency and conduct, the category which showed the cadet's measurement as a whole person rather than merely as a student, was assigned 250 merits. This rating placed military efficiency and conduct ahead of thirteen academic subjects in the graduating merit roll. Military engineering, for example, counted 150 merits, and tactics only twenty-five merits. Furthermore, on MacArthur's suggestion, Danford introduced a course on military leadership in the tactical department; therein the anatomy of successful leadership was analyzed, and class discussion was encouraged. Though constituting more innovations for the academy, such moves were conservative in that they re-emphasized the old virtues of West Point and contradicted a current trend in higher education of ranking students on academic work only.[21]

"The highest standards of honor were to be demanded," MacArthur proclaimed, "as the only solid foundation for a military career — a code of individual conduct which would maintain the reputation and well-being of the whole — a personal responsibility to his mates, to his community, and above all to his country." Implementing his belief with action, he appointed a group of cadets, selected for their integrity, to constitute an honor committee. An honor system had functioned unofficially at the school since its early days, but largely on a vigilante basis. Now MacArthur created a cadet body empowered with authority to investigate and recommend to the academic board on matters of cadet honor. The committee was also charged with drawing up a code of ethics for the corps. The resulting honor code, which became a model for those of other educational institutions, obligated each cadet to forswear acts of dishonesty, such as cheating and lying, and to report to the committee any breach of the code which he committed or witnessed. Thereafter instructors and proctors were not expected to remain constantly on guard over cadets during examinations. No longer were tactical officers to challenge, without solid evidence, a cadet's excuse for missing a drill or an assignment. Many faculty members entered upon the experiment with trepidation, but the honor committee and the code worked well and became proud, lasting possessions of West Point. MacArthur had gambled, so some thought, but he was confident and correct in his premise that the corps, as a group and as individuals, would proudly protect its honor system.[22]

The honor code, however, did not cover hazing, one of the

most notorious practices on the Plain and one which was still privately endorsed by many alumni. As formally defined for the corps in 1910, hazing was "any unauthorized assumption of authority by one cadet over another cadet whereby the latter shall or may suffer or be exposed to suffer any cruelty, indignity, humiliation, hardship, or oppression, or the deprivation or abridgement of any right, privilege, or advantage to which he shall be legally entitled." In the past cadet hazing had assumed many forms — as innocent as requiring a plebe to polish an upperclassman's boots and as dangerous as forcing a newcomer to swim across the Hudson in dead winter. Recalling the severe hazing which he underwent as a cadet, MacArthur was determined to eradicate the cancerous practice. Other superintendents had tried, but the midnight push-ups, spread eagles, and other exercises to which plebes were subjected continued year after year. Each third class felt bound to make life hellish for the fourth class, especially during the plebes' first summer. The penalty for hazing was suspension or dismissal, depending upon the severity of the offense, but the number of cadets thus penalized had been negligible over the years.

MacArthur approached the persisting problem of hazing through the tactical department, which was headed by Danford, a stern but respected officer. Danford was instructed to set up a committee of first classmen to study the problem and "related fourth class customs." Captain Charles F. Thompson, a tactical officer, and Chaplain Clayton E. Wheat were to act as advisers to the committee. A pamphlet codifying upperclassmen's relations with plebes was ultimately prepared by the committee and approved by a majority vote of the first class at a meeting in the gymnasium. Blaik noted, however, that "bitter feelings arose as the presentation of changes to the Class was vigorously resisted by the traditionalists — supported as they were by some officer sentiment." But the action was a major step in curtailing hazing, and there were no serious incidents of hazing during the rest of MacArthur's superintendency. After the Second World War, Thompson, who was a general officer by then, looked back on the action of the committee of first classmen as "the most important single accomplishment of the Corps" in its history. There were, of course, other factors involved in the demise of the practice of hazing, such as the frank, open discussion of hazing allowed by Danford's tactical officers in the course on leadership. Another deterrent can be traced to Danford's decision, backed by the superintendent, to use tactical officers to command the plebes' barracks during their first weeks of orientation. This eliminated much of the summer hazing, which had centered about the so-called "Beast Barracks," previously run by upperclassmen.[23]

The procedure in handling delinquent cases was expedited by a plan developed by Danford. The old practice of "skin lists" was abolished, whereby in former times tactical officers charged cadets with demerits and the accused cadets were required to respond with written explanations on prescribed forms. Instead, Danford now set up a company orderly room in each barracks where a tactical officer met personally with the offending cadet and decided the case promptly, as officers in the Regular Army customarily handled enlisted delinquents at the company level.

The administration's offensive against hazing and even the ouster of the "skin lists" brought grumblings and remonstrations from the alumni, but the old guard's loudest outcries were heard when MacArthur began to relax discipline and allow privileges to the cadets which were unthinkable in West Point's previous history. Convinced that cadets should be treated as responsible men and permitted more freedom, MacArthur shocked the traditionalists by allowing first classmen to take six-hour weekend leaves off the reservation, set up a

first classmen's club in Church Hall, and enjoy limited frater-
nization with post officers, including visiting their homes and
playing cards together. The three upper classes were allowed
to elect class officers for the first time, and upperclassmen were
permitted to start a cadet newspaper, *The Brag* (forerunner
of *The Pointer*, the present-day publication). In another tra-
dition-shattering move, the superintendent issued to each cadet
a cash allowance monthly ($5.00) to spend as he pleased. Also
for the first time the corps accompanied the football team to
games beyond New York City. Professors and alumni protested, but MacArthur was adamant about the disciplinary
changes. He believed that the privileges "would serve both as
a relaxation from the rigid grind of study and training, and
as a means of keeping touch with life outside the walls of the
institution." The cadet, he maintained, had been too long
"cloistered almost to a monastic extent," and then, upon graduating, was "thrust out into the world a man in age, but as
experienced as a high school boy."

Offsetting the extension of privileges and bringing howls
from cadets, staff, and alumni was MacArthur's decision to
abolish the traditional summer camp at Fort Clinton, just east
of Trophy Point. For many decades the cadets and officers had
looked forward to the gay weeks at Fort Clinton, which consisted of "hops, band concerts, the pranks of guard duty, and
only a minimum of military training." Condemning the
summer camp as "a ludicrous caricature of life in the field,"
MacArthur ordered the cadets to report for summer training
at Camp Dix, New Jersey. Instead of carefree gaieties, there
they encountered tough sergeants of the Regular Army who
handled them like basic trainees, taught them to use modern
weapons, and exposed them to realistic field exercises. At the
end of the exhausting training at Camp Dix, MacArthur required the cadets, laden with full packs, to march all the way
back to West Point. Blaik observed, however, that the greatest

disappointment over the termination of the Fort Clinton encampments was felt by the academy's officers and their wives, who missed the social whirl: "The resentment by the permanent staff was so great that shortly after MacArthur's departure, the first change made was the re-establishment of summer camp." Fort Clinton was not to be abolished permanently until after World War II.

Superintendent MacArthur's experiences in the World War and the Rhine occupation, which prompted the above plan to bring the cadets into closer contact with actual Army conditions, contributed also to his introduction of a comprehensive system of intramural athletics at the academy. Recalling the difficulties with troops in poor physical condition on the battlefields, as well as the benefits of athletics during the tour in the Rhineland, MacArthur planned the intramural program "not only to fit future officers physically for the rigors of military service, but also to qualify them as physical directors and instructors for their future commands." Furthermore, he believed that "the training of the athletic field which produces in a superlative degree the attributes of fortitude, self-control, resolution, courage, mental agility, and, of course, physical development, is one completely fundamental to an efficient soldiery." His plan called for every cadet to participate in company competition in at least one of nine intramural sports. The program was received enthusiastically by the cadets, and the contests became so spirited and rough that they were soon nicknamed "intra-murder." Meanwhile a permanent inscription, written by MacArthur, was placed over the gymnasium entrance: "Upon the fields of friendly strife are sown the seeds that, upon other fields, on other days, will bear the fruits of victory." [24]

MacArthur's interest in athletics became unbridled zeal when the varsity football team was practicing or playing. Blaik, then a star on the Army team, commented: "Never a practice period passed that did not see the Supe, carrying a riding crop, jauntily striding onto the practice field." As usual, the corps reached a feverish pitch of excitement as the annual rivalry with the Naval Academy neared, but no one on the Plain lived those moments more anxiously than MacArthur. Sending courtesy tickets to General Pershing for the Army-Navy game to be played at the New York Polo Grounds in November, 1919, MacArthur told his former commander: "The Army will turn out that day a well-rounded team. The line is excellent, the ends good, and the backs fair, with a superb fighting spirit. It will not be a great team, but it will take a great team to beat it." The Army team won no victories over Navy during his superintendency, but MacArthur's program of avidly recruiting and encouraging skilled football players "paid off so well that by the late twenties the Navy was growing weary of Army victories," said Blaik.

The superintendent was keenly interested in the varsity baseball team since he had won his varsity letter in that sport. Blaik, who also played baseball, recalled a practice session when he was having trouble hitting curve balls. He turned for advice to MacArthur, who, as usual, was watching; the superintendent happily offered to show Blaik the proper method. Loosening his collar and removing his Sam Browne belt, the general stepped into the batter's box and swung at several pitches. "It must have been the only time," Blaik commented, "I ever saw him fail to accomplish something he set out to do. When it was my turn to bat again, I not only couldn't hit a curve I couldn't even hit a straight ball." How the flustered superintendent excused himself is not known; perhaps he explained to the players that Cadet MacArthur's forte had been fielding, not batting.[25]

Ironically, MacArthur's first experience with World War veterans demanding more money was in the realm of athletics. In March, 1922, he responded favorably to a request from

Major George Marshall, the chief of staff in World War II but
then an aide to Pershing, to send the West Point track and
field teams to a benefit meet in Washington against the Annapolis teams. According to Marshall, the event was sponsored
by the American Legion, and "the proceeds from this affair are
mainly to be used here for the needy and destitute ex-service
men who daily come to Washington primarily to press their
claims against the United States Veterans Bureau." Marshall
explained that these veterans "are more or less thrown upon
the people of Washington and the District Legion has had the
main task of looking after them as to food, lodging and even
wearing apparel." [26] Ten years later MacArthur would be connected with veterans in Washington again, but under less be-
nevolent circumstances.

Dedication to the Army football team was almost the sole
common denominator between MacArthur and the old-guard
professors and alumni. The changes he brought had been fast,
furious, and far-reaching in the eyes of his critics. But Mac-
Arthur realized that he had failed in the area which most
needed reform, namely, the curriculum. The conservatives at
the academy and in the Regular Army admitted that some
changes in training in weapons and tactics were in order after
the experiences of the World War, but they rejected Mac-
Arthur's theory of the new type of officer which the academy
should produce to lead the citizen-soldiers of the future. They
saw the West Pointer as a technical specialist; MacArthur conceived of him as a versatile leader of men, knowledgeable in
civilian ways and affairs and obtaining the obedience and
loyalty of his troops through understanding and respect, not
through fear and strict regimentation. As MacArthur endeavored to create his ideal officer through the broadening of the
cadets' knowledge of the social sciences, making them more
aware of rights and responsibilities and increasing their contacts with the civilian world, the old guard viewed his moves

as threats to the essential order, discipline, and specialized function of West Point. To many alumni especially, who were alarmed over the radicalism allegedly rampant in the nation, less exposure of the cadets to the outside world, rather than more, seemed in order. Despite their differences, MacArthur maintained, except on rare occasions, the surface appearances of politeness and civility toward his opponents. But both camps stubbornly refused to close the breach that separated them on basic philosophies of the nature and function of the United States Military Academy.[27]

3. *Static from Washington*

By virtue of his position, MacArthur was called upon repeatedly to testify before congressional committees on military affairs and appropriations. Sometimes a senator or representative would call him and expect him to appear before his committee in Washington within twelve hours. Undoubtedly irked by the numerous interruptions, MacArthur duly packed his bags and made the trips to the capital. As recorded in his memoirs, however, his recollection of the congressmen's reception of his budgetary requests was inconsistent. After stating that Congress "was in an economic mood and threatened to strip the school to a skeleton," MacArthur stated a few sentences later in his memoirs that he "always found its members patient, courteous, and efficient. When the true facts had been presented to them, they had always acted with patriotic courage and fearless determination, irrespective of party affiliation." His first description seems more accurate, judging from the congressmen's decisions on West Point and War Department matters. Moreover, when in Washington, he probably did not hide his disappointment at the Republicans' selection of Har-

ding over Wood. Though he could not publicly support the
former chief of staff's candidacy, MacArthur engaged, said
Ganoe, in "continual discussion of the campaign to put Leonard
Wood into the Presidency. He would pace and go over every
move the managers were making, criticizing every detail. The
fact that the candidate was a personal friend made him act
as if he himself were charged with the responsibility of nomination and election." [28] A likely consequence of his avid support of Wood was, after the election, an equally zealous opposition to Harding and his policies, which would not have
escaped the President's followers on the congressional committees.

A measure of vital concern to the Army and to MacArthur
was the National Defense Act adopted in 1920. A compromise
between plans for peacetime conscription and a large professional force, the measure provided for a military establishment
consisting of a regular force of 288,000 enlisted men and
18,000 officers (the latter figure set later) and a relatively large
National Guard and an Organized Reserve. The War Department's proposed strength for the Regular Army had been
nearly double the figure obtained in the act, but generally the
Army was satisfied with the legislation, particularly its provisions for modernizing the tactical and administrative framework of the military establishment. Among other favorable
points, the act provided for the Regular Army to be largely
responsible for training and equipping the National Guard,
Organized Reserve, Reserve Officers Training Corps, and Citizens Military Training Camps. Indeed, never before had the
regulars been so extensively connected with the citizen-soldier
elements. This portion of the act was especially pleasing to
MacArthur, who must have felt that his emphasis on the need
for professional officers who could work well with civilian
trainees was justified.

But Congress quickly crushed the Army's hopes by cutting

the enlisted strength of the regulars to 150,000; in the following years it would be reduced to less than 119,000. Budget
requests by the War Department in 1919 totaled $1,300,-
000,000, but Congress appropriated only $900,000,000. The
next year was worse, the Army getting $392,000,000 after asking
for a billion dollars. National Guard units, which were dependent upon federal funds for drill pay, seldom reached 50
per cent of their authorized strength. Furthermore, many men
in the Organized Reserve, receiving no pay for their drills,
became inactive or were separated from the service. Because
of the niggardliness and complacency of Congress and the
executive branch, the military establishment by 1922 was almost worthless even as a nucleus for mobilization. As might
be expected, MacArthur's hopes for increased funds for West
Point died with the War Department's plans for an adequate
system of national defense.[29]

Nevertheless, Superintendent MacArthur crusaded strenuously on behalf of his institution — in testimony before committees of Congress, in public speeches, and in reports to the
War Department. He pointed out in vain that "the government's expenditures for military needs are a form of national
insurance from which come dividends year by year . . . A
comparatively small outlay by the United States will serve in
the future to lessen the tremendous expense and the loss of
blood for which no money can repay when the unforeseen
tragedy is upon us." He argued that the size of the corps of
cadets should be increased from 1334 to 2500, explaining that
the academy "cannot now supply more than one-third of our
officers even in times of peace." In addition, he called for a
gigantic expansion of the academy's plant and facilities. The
$12 million which he asked for new construction during the
next four years would have been quite a change, particularly
since less than $20 million had been spent on buildings at West
Point during the entire period since 1802. His requests fell

on deaf ears; Congress did not increase the corps or provide the requested funds for construction. Returning from one of his frustrating sessions in Washington, MacArthur let loose his pent-up feelings in a discussion with his trusted friend Danford. The latter said that MacArthur "paced the floor almost angrily, saying that during the war everyone connected with West Point must have been sound asleep. 'Here, while we spent billions on the Army, not a penny of it came to West Point!' " [30]

In the spring of 1920 MacArthur gained his only significant success in the struggles on Capitol Hill: Congress re-established the four-year program at the academy. The inadequacy of the shorter plan was evident even to his die-hard opponents on the faculty, and thus he was able to carry to Washington a four-year proposal which had the endorsement of the entire academic board. His plan was also backed strongly by Pershing and Tillman, the former superintendent, in the congressional hearings. The approved program called for each of the three current classes to graduate one year later than scheduled. But every cadet then enrolled was given the option of staying the additional year or graduating under the three-year plan.[31] Since the congressmen were not disposed to increase the budget along with the lengthened program, the triumph was probably of little consolation to MacArthur.

As long as Baker was Secretary of War and March the chief of staff of the Army, MacArthur was reasonably secure in pushing his claims for the academy before Congress and the War Department. The civilian and military heads of the military establishment were both close friends and strong admirers of the superintendent. As his mother had told Pershing earlier, Baker was "very deeply attached" to her son. March had served as a junior officer under MacArthur's father in the Philippines and had long known his son, too. The chief of staff considered MacArthur an outstanding superintendent who "has been brilliant from the day he graduated at the head of his class at West Point." [32]

With the advent of the Harding administration in the spring of 1921, John W. Weeks, a wealthy Boston broker and not an acquaintance of MacArthur, took over as Secretary of War. More significant, a few months later a general was appointed chief of staff whom MacArthur knew only too well: Pershing. Like March, Pershing had served under MacArthur's father, but, as already related, misunderstandings and sharp exchanges had occasionally marred the relations between Pershing and MacArthur on the fields of France. Nevertheless, as the new chief of staff began his job as the military head of the Army, he and MacArthur exchanged the expected pleasantries. On the day MacArthur read of Pershing's appointment in the newspapers, he wrote him: "I cannot refrain from telling you how complete a sense of relief and of confidence this action gives to the Army . . . I only hope that you will not be hampered by restrictions and will be given complete latitude for the reconstruction work which faces you." In reply, Pershing was equally polite, although his words, in retrospect, may have been barbed in implication: "The success of any army administration must depend upon the cooperation of all those who have the best interests of the service at heart. This cooperation, I am sure, I shall have from you." [33]

As chief of staff, Pershing performed more conventionally and less boldly than when leading America's great army in France. Along with Secretary Weeks and the General Staff, he duly resigned himself to the Army's constitutional role as executor of military policies formulated by civilian leaders. While reminding the executive and legislative branches of the federal government that "our present combat strength will be insufficient to fulfill the functions required by our national defense policy," he and the War Department meekly accepted the separation of civilian and military powers and their subordination to civilian controls. A prominent military historian later commented: "The routine, disciplined obedience of the Army to the President as Commander in Chief and to such of his agents as the Budget Director was itself a handicap to Army programs, barring any save a refractory officer from demanding more funds than were approved by the White House." With the Harding administration and Congress bent upon retrenchment and balancing the budget, the War Department humbly cooperated by reducing its budgetary requests and restricting its programs. In view of the anti-military opinions being voiced in numerous organs of public opinion, the War Department also hesitated to push vigorously its monetary needs in fear of creating charges of militarism and warmongering, which might lead to greater financial cuts.[34] MacArthur's outspokenness in endeavoring to secure more funds for West Point must have irritated Weeks and Pershing. Also, the intense pace of the superintendent's reforms at West Point, as well as the nature of those changes, must have been contrary to their wishes, judging from the type of individual they selected to succeed MacArthur.

Suddenly on November 22, 1921, Pershing notified MacArthur: "It is important, I think, that you should be made aware of the decision of the War Department to make the regulation with reference to foreign service applicable to the entire official personnel of the Army. The roster shows you to be high up for this service, but, in considering your case, it was not thought advisable to make a change during the academic year." He continued: "I am writing now to advise you that at the end of the present school year you will be available for a tour of service beyond the limits of the United States. The selection of your successor will be made shortly in order that he may have time to study his new duties, and be prepared to take over the office immediately after graduation in June, 1922." MacArthur was surprised, apparently thinking that he would be allowed a four-year term as superintendent, though there was no established length for such a tour of duty. Probably reflecting MacArthur's thoughts, a correspondent of the *New York Times* speculated: "Why is Gen. MacArthur being removed from West Point? This is a question asked not only by his friends, but by many other people who have been interested in the improvements he has made in West Point . . . The answer . . . will be seen in the type of officer chosen by this department to succeed him." [35]

At the end of January, 1922, Pershing announced the appointment of Brigadier General Fred W. Sladen, commanding officer at Fort Sheridan, Illinois, as MacArthur's successor at the end of the academic year. MacArthur, in turn, was to be transferred to the Philippine Department. Sladen, who was a graduate of West Point in 1890, had served as a tactical instructor and company commander there when MacArthur was a cadet. He had established a creditable record in the A.E.F., but he was known to be a staunch conservative on Army policies. Discussing the selection with Ganoe, MacArthur correctly predicted: "I fancy it means a reversal of many of the progressive policies which we inaugurated." Sure enough, in the next several years Superintendent Sladen would try to abolish nearly all of the reforms his predecessor had introduced at the academy.[36]

On the day he announced Sladen's appointment, Pershing wrote to MacArthur about another matter. The superintendent had recently visited Washington briefly to testify before the House's military affairs committee on current needs of the academy. Pershing stated in his letter: "I am astonished to hear this as evidently you neither called at this office nor on the Secretary of War during your visit. I think a proper conception of the ordinary military courtesies, to say nothing of Army regulations and customs of the Service, should have indicated to an officer of your experience and rank the propriety

of making known your presence in Washington, the purpose
of your visit, and to have considered with the Department the
matters you proposed to bring to the attention of the Military
Committee." The chief of staff went on to admonish Mac-
Arthur for ignoring Weeks' expressed desire to discuss with
him "some views relating to the Academy and its conduct."

Mystified by the contentious attitude of his superior, Mac-
Arthur answered promptly and tried to explain his actions. He
began by quoting in full an order from the adjutant general
requiring him to report before the congressional committee
within twenty-four hours. He left West Point, MacArthur
stated, "having barely time to make the necessary arrangements
and rail connections," and registered his presence "in The
Adjutant General's book at the earliest practicable time." As
for his appearance before the House committee, he contended
that such testimony by a West Point superintendent "is largely
routine and has never to my knowledge followed any other
course than the present one." He added: "It has never been
customary for the Superintendent to report for immediate instructions to his military superiors when summoned by a committee of Congress. The department has always, as in this year,
returned his estimates with the necessary instructions as to the
policy to be pursued." He reminded Pershing that "in this
particular case it would have been practically impossible to
have reported for such a consultation even had I known it was
desired, on account of the short notice given by the War Department order." At the close of the committee session Colonel James B. Allison, Pershing's aide, informed MacArthur by
telephone that the chief of staff wanted to see him. MacArthur
replied that he was available at Pershing's convenience, but,
according to MacArthur, Allison called back later and "informed me over the telephone that the Chief of Staff had
changed his mind and did not care to see me." In conclusion,
MacArthur offered his apology to Pershing: "I regret exceed-

ingly if this incident may have given any impression of dis-
courtesy to two superior officers whom I hold in the highest
respect and esteem; as shown by the above statement of fact
none was intended." [37] If MacArthur's version is correct, then
either Allison was responsible for the misunderstanding or
Pershing, having decided upon Sladen, was looking for some
trumped-up charges against MacArthur.

About the same time that the above correspondence was under way, rumors began circulating that Pershing was an unsuccessful suitor of Mrs. Louise Cromwell Brooks, a wealthy,
attractive divorcee whose engagement to MacArthur was announced in mid-January, 1922. The Brooks-MacArthur marriage took place a month later, on February 14, at her family's
sumptuous Spanish-style villa at Palm Beach, Florida. Pershing
retaliated, so the story goes, by removing MacArthur from the
headship at West Point and "exiling" him to the Philippines.
This myth has circulated persistently in articles and books for
four decades and has overshadowed the realities of the case.[38]

In the first place, both Pershing and MacArthur were known
for their frankness, and both denied the divorcee was a factor
in the dismissal. When queried about the rumor by reporters
on February 9, 1922, Pershing replied with considerable annoyance: "It's all damn poppycock without the slightest foundation and based on the idlest gossip. If I were married to all
the ladies to whom the gossips have engaged me I would be a
regular Brigham Young. General MacArthur is being ordered
to the Philippines because he stands at the top of the list of
officers due for foreign service." In his memoirs MacArthur
remarked simply: "Late [*sic*] in 1922, being at the top of the
roster of general officers for foreign service, I was relieved as
superintendent." [39]

Several months after her marriage to MacArthur, Louise
stated in a letter to Pershing: "I wrote you a couple of weeks
ago asking you to come up for a Sunday and as I did not hear

from you I know my letter has been lost. I want so much to have you with me and see how I have been able to fix up this shabby old house! . . . I adore it here. I have plenty of room so that you can bring a maid and valet!" It is ridiculous to suggest that she extended this invitation without MacArthur's knowledge or that she intended it to be a reunion with a rejected suitor, much less with a current lover, as some gossip spoke of a continuing affinity. Pershing had met her in Paris in 1917, and they were often seen together socially after his return to Washington. But the extant correspondence between them suggests nothing more than a deep friendship, though it does point to a romantic relationship between Louise and Major John G. Quekemeyer, who was on Pershing's staff — a topic to be dealt with later. Other discrepancies in the "exile" theory are numerous, among them being the fact that Pershing's notice of impending transfer for MacArthur preceded the announcement of the engagement by two months. Moreover, it is hardly likely that the relationship between Pershing and MacArthur would have improved, as it did in succeeding years, if the charge had been true.[40]

In the final analysis, the key to understanding MacArthur's dismissal is less sensational than the vengeance of a jealous lover, but far more significant. As the journalist predicted, the type of officer chosen to replace MacArthur did reveal the War Department's position on his reforms. It seems that MacArthur's place on the foreign-duty list served as a convenient pretext for removing a refractory individualist who created difficulties and embarrassments for the War Department in its relations with Congress, the White House, and the conservative alumni of West Point. The coincidence of the announcements of the engagement and the dismissal, coming the same month, exposed the transfer of MacArthur to glaring publicity — and thus was born the myth which helps to sell books. The truth is that the War Department in the early 1920's was enjoying a season of reaction and had no room in the higher echelons of the military establishment for a liberal reformer. The appointment of Sladen is the real key to the case, for MacArthur was ousted by traditionalism, not by a frustrated suitor.

MacArthur, his bride, and her two children moved out of the superintendent's quarters in late June, 1922, taking his mother to Washington to live with Arthur's family. After a two-month leave MacArthur, Louise, and the children sailed from San Francisco on September 5 for his new assignment in the Philippine Department.[41] Neither in his memoirs nor elsewhere on record did MacArthur ever express feelings of disappointment or bitterness over his transfer. After all, he had a deep affection for the Philippines, and he may well have felt that his effectiveness as superintendent was near its end. Surely, another year or two on the Plain would not have brought the conversion of the recalcitrant old guard.

Sladen and the conservative faction underestimated the durability and vitality of the spirit MacArthur had brought to the academy. As hard as Sladen tried to restore the old West Point, he could not. The windows had been opened, if only a little. Tradition had been challenged, ideas had been introduced, experiments had been tried. After Sladen's reactionary reign the superintendents who followed generally concurred in MacArthur's reforms, and the windows were gradually opened wider. By the eve of the Second World War, West Point was a highly respected pacemaker among the world's elite military academies, and it was producing a type of professional officer well trained to handle citizen-soldiers. A leading authority on the school's history assesses MacArthur's contribution thus: "Slowly his innovations would be restored, his ideas accepted. If Sylvanus Thayer dominated West Point in the nineteenth century, Douglas MacArthur dominated it in the twentieth. The chief difference was that Thayer had sixteen years in which to impose his personality and ideas, while MacArthur had but three." Though a close friend of MacArthur, Ganoe may not have exaggerated when he asserted: "If Sylvanus Thayer was the Father of the Military Academy, then Douglas MacArthur was its savior." [42] Many aspects of MacArthur's long career are still controversial, but in the Long Gray Line there is general agreement that he, more than any other man, led West Point across the threshold into the rapidly changing world of modern military education. Indeed, his pioneering efforts at the United States Military Academy rank as one of his most important contributions to the development of the modern Army.

CHAPTER XI

The Discouraging Years

1. Problems in the Philippines

WHEN MACARTHUR REACHED MANILA in early October, 1922, he soon was aware that profound changes had occurred in the islands since his tour of duty there fourteen years earlier. Aguinaldo and his insurrectionists of old were now peaceful farmers and laborers who, for the most part, admitted grudgingly that the Americans had not proven to be oppressive masters. Governor General Leonard Wood, MacArthur's friend and idol, reported that "peace and order reigned throughout the year in every Province and municipality of the archipelago," with even the formerly fierce Moros of Mindanao "now a peaceful people." Since 1916 the Filipinos had had an elective, bicameral national legislature, and the percentage of qualified voters casting ballots in national elections often exceeded 90 per cent by the early 1920's. Though some predicted that the legislature would become a tool of the Americans, it was displaying an energetic, independent spirit, under the able leadership of Manuel Quezon, leader of the dominant Nacionalista party. Not long before MacArthur's coming, for instance, it had proceeded to license commercial radio stations, wringing some concessions from the military authorities as to restrictions thereon. Quezon had led the first independence mission to Washington in 1919, and, though unsuccessful, he could point to an awakening national consciousness among his people. In fact, Wood, who was more conservative than his predecessor, was sometimes publicly criticized by Filipino politicians and journalists for not being more sympathetic toward the islanders' aspirations for independence.

At the time of MacArthur's arrival Wood was more concerned, he said, with "the ravages of the business depression," which had resulted from "the sudden stoppage of war demands" for Philippine hemp and coconut oil. The consequences since 1919, Wood stated, had been that "unemployment prevailed, credit deflation continued, monetary circulation fell off, bank deposits decreased, imports diminished, while exports increased." The niggardly appropriations which Congress approved for the War Department meant cuts in funds and personnel for the Philippine Department, which further aggravated the economic crisis. In spite of the depressed conditions, MacArthur marveled at "the progress that had been made" since 1904: "New roads, new docks, new buildings were everywhere." It seemed to him that both politically and economically the Philippines' situation had improved remarkably since the insurrection, and the islands' future looked bright.

Assigned to command a somewhat nebulous and newly created administrative unit known as the Military District of Manila, MacArthur found himself with considerable leisure. He proceeded to cultivate friendships and social relations with Quezon and other Filipino leaders, but quickly discovered that many influential Americans of the business and military communities resented his familiarity with the natives. Some were perhaps antagonized by his association with Quezon, whom they regarded as a political antagonist who was not properly obeisant toward the colonial administrators. But most objectors harbored a sense of racial superiority, which was widespread among American and European whites in all Southeast Asian lands. "Attitudes die hard," MacArthur observed of Manila's upper-class whites, "and the old idea of colonial exploitation still had its vigorous supporters." [1]

Governor General Wood, as well as the high-ranking officers of the Philippine Department, was quite anxious about the impact of recent diplomatic developments on the defenses of the islands. In the Five-Power Naval Treaty, signed at the Washington Conference of the previous winter, Japan had consented to the American proposal for a reduction in capital ships and a ten-year holiday in their construction only when the United States and Great Britain had agreed not to erect further fortifications at their outposts in East and Southeast Asia. In the early fall of 1922 Secretary of the Navy Edwin Denby visited Japan and returned with the optimistic report that "[Admiral] Kato and the other big men in Japan are very much in earnest in carrying out the terms of the ten-year treaty . . . All anti-American agitation in Japan has died down." Secretary of War Weeks commented shortly afterward, "It is very important that we give no cause to any of our co-signatories of the Treaty for belief that we are not wholeheartedly carrying it out." The subsequent reductions in the authorized enlisted strength of the Philippine garrison surely could not have been offensive to the Nipponese: in 1920, it was 18,887, in 1921, 15,868, and by 1925, only 12,115, despite a sharp rise in anti-American feeling in Japan after Congress' decision in 1924 to end Japanese immigration to America.[2] Weeks stated the War Department's position to Wood in November, 1922:

> While the Joint Army and Navy Board, in its report of May 17, 1922, expressed the opinion that "as a matter of policy it is, for the present, inadvisable to increase or decrease the military forces," the strength of the Regular Army as now provided

for by law and other practical considerations will not permit of the maintenance of the desired American component of the [Philippine] garrison. It was realized that it would be impossible to maintain a garrison which in itself would be adequate for the defense of the vital areas and that the garrison now authorized must be considered the nucleus for the development of adequate native forces and for special missions.[3]

Nevertheless, that same autumn the Joint Army and Navy Board drafted War Plan Orange to deal with a hypothetical war with Japan in which the enemy would attack without warning, making it impossible to reinforce the Philippines for as long as six months. The mission of the Philippine Department, aided by such native forces as were available, would be to hold Corregidor and Bataan at the mouth of Manila Bay, thereby preventing the Japanese from using that harbor. With the continued slashes in funds by Congress, however, it became increasingly apparent to officers of the Philippine Department that the garrison's strength in personnel and matériel was inadequate to fulfill the Orange mission. The departmental chief of staff so informed the War Department, but the chief of the war plans division perfunctorily responded that, because of the Army's shortage of funds, "the Philippine Department must carry on under the status quo until the time arrives for the establishment of a stable and continuing policy."[4] In 1924 a bill was introduced in Congress calling for the withdrawal of the United States from the Philippines in twenty years. The War Department, which had on file repeated reports from Manila about the weakness of the islands' defenses, vehemently and successfully fought for retention of the archipelago. Colonel E. R. Stone, head of the war plans division at the time the bill was under consideration, stated the War Department's position thus:

All indications are that the race consciousness of the Asiatics is constantly increasing and the superiority of the white people being challenged. China today is in a state of ferment. Withdrawing our strength from that quarter of the globe is leaving our friends of the European nations to bear the white man's burden alone, and would only add strength to the charge of selfish isolation brought against us. Our withdrawal would be encouragement to the Pan-Asiatic movement. From a more local viewpoint, it is believed that mere talk of our withdrawal would start an insurrection in the Philippines, particularly among the Mohammedans, and lead to more serious trouble throughout the Islands.

It is believed that the withdrawal of our troops from the Philippines would, perforce, result in our eventual return there in greater strength and at an immense cost.[5]

Soon after his arrival MacArthur was briefed by Major General William M. Wright, the departmental commander, on the political, economic, and military situation in the islands. Wright had been Pershing's roommate at West Point and served with distinction as a divisional commander in the A.E.F. where he probably first met MacArthur. He was succeeded shortly by Major General George W. Read, a tall, dashing cavalry officer who held the position until about the time of MacArthur's departure in 1925. A graduate of West Point in 1883, Read had known MacArthur when they were stationed at Fort Leavenworth; in the World War he had served ably as a divisional and corps commander with the American forces located on the British front in Picardy. Both Wright and Read were convinced that the Philippine Department was seriously deficient in men and equipment for the mission it had been given, but both had been reminded by the War Department that the Army was spread too thinly at its other strategic stations also.[6]

The principal unit under MacArthur in the Manila district was the 31st Infantry, which was the only entire regiment of American foot soldiers in the Philippines. Many of the men detested duty in the hot, disease-infested islands and complained frequently about the Army's overseas replacement system, which did not allow them to state their preference of assignment. After a visit to the department Major General Eli A. Helmick, the inspector general of the Army, said of the 31st Infantry: "The men appeared to me to be an excellent body of men, but their training was not up to the standard of other organizations in the department." The regimental commander was Colonel Willis Uline, who had fought in the last Sioux war and served under MacArthur's father against the rebels on Luzon until seriously wounded in the head. Helmick found Uline to be an ill man, "who drinks constantly" and "should be forcibly retired," but his removel, on grounds of disability, was not accomplished until 1928.

MacArthur's work in Manila was interrupted in February and March, 1923, when he and his family returned to Washington because of the desperate illness of his mother, suffering from a heart ailment. Thanks to the skillful and ceaseless care of Dr. Howard J. Hutter, an Army doctor who would later become MacArthur's physician and close friend, Mrs. MacArthur passed through the crisis and recuperated. The occasion of their mother's illness marked the last time the MacArthur brothers would see each other; in December, Arthur died suddenly of appendicitis.[7]

MacArthur was given command of the 23rd Brigade of the Philippine Division in June, 1923. The divisional commander was Brigadier General Omar Bundy; MacArthur called him "an old friend of Milwaukee days." A short man, Bundy had a reputation for being overly zealous about small details of administration. Pershing had relieved him as commander of the 2nd Division before the battle of Belleau Wood because "he lacks the grasp." He is best remembered from the World War as the officer who was sent to organize the Belfort operation, without being told that it was a ruse. In the relatively tranquil, unhurried atmosphere of Fort McKinley in the early 1920's, however, Bundy was able to utilize his meticulosity to good advantage in organizing the Philippine Division, which he founded in April, 1922. Commenting on departmental developments during the fiscal year 1921–22, Wright stated: "Economy in funds and manpower has been a predominant feature of the policies of last year, and all measures and policies inaugurated have been tested for both economy and efficiency prior to adoption." The new division, whose main units were the 45th and 57th regiments of Philippine Scouts, would have to operate on the barest expenditures possible, and Bundy was in his element when it came to watching the smallest outlays of funds.[8]

The Philippine Division, consisting of about 7000 troops, held its first maneuvers at Fort Stotsenburg in the Central Luzon Plain during February, 1923, having marched there from Fort McKinley, sixty-six miles to the south. Then and on other occasions of field exercises the Scouts consistently outperformed the American soldiers, particulary in marksmanship wherein the Filipinos seemed to possess innate talent. In the summer of 1923 Read reported to the War Department that "all companies of the 57th Infantry (PS) qualified 100% in rifle and machine gun marksmanship. I believe this is the first regiment in the Army of the United States to make such a remarkable record." MacArthur found that a brigade command in the Philippines involved a greater variety of responsibilities than in France. His brigade and the rest of the division were employed in such varied activities as administering livestock vaccinations during epidemics of anthrax and rinderpest, helping to organize and train an R.O.T.C. unit at the new University of the Philippines, and assisting the Philippine Constabulary in suppressing outbreaks of banditry. When the devastating earthquake hit the Tokyo-Yokohama area on September 1, 1923, the Scouts were instrumental in the ship-loading operations that enabled the Philippine Department to send to the stricken Japanese over 16,000 tons of its subsistence stores, tentage, clothing, and medical supplies within the first week.

Aside from his regular duties as commander of the 23rd Brigade, MacArthur also was placed in charge of the survey and mapping of Bataan peninsula. Despite heavy jungles, mountainous terrain, and a malaria epidemic among the troops of the 14th Engineers, he was able to report forty square miles mapped during the fiscal year 1923–24. The next year the project was placed under the department's chief engineer where, it would seem, it should have been from the start. MacArthur was undoubtedly happy to be relieved of the responsibility — his last engineering project.[9]

Suddenly on the morning of July 7, 1924, officers came rushing into MacArthur's office with the news that mutiny had broken out in the ranks of the Filipinos of the two Scout infantry regiments. Several hundred soldiers of MacArthur's brigade were refusing to form, drill, or obey any orders. Military police were hurriedly called to the scene, and 222 Scouts were taken to the guardhouse, apparently with a minimum of violence involved. News of the incident and the ensuing trials and convictions swept through the islands with the expected responses, the Filipino population sympathizing with the mutineers and the whites excoriating their action and fearing a general insurrection. Read admitted that if there was an uprising, he no longer could trust the Scouts, and of his 12,115-man garrison only 4100 were Americans. No public disorders followed the mutiny, but a departmental report to Washington the next summer stated that "a new and difficult situation confronts this department. A situation [exists] in which Scout soldiers will have to be recruited, whereas in the past, they have applied for enlistment in sufficient numbers so that in many organizations a waiting list was maintained."

In the aftermath of the mutiny, which shook the complacent atmosphere of Fort McKinley, the department made efforts to determine the causes of the Scouts' discontent. Bundy was shortly replaced by MacArthur as divisional commander, the change possibly being made in an effort to placate the Filipino soldiers since MacArthur was known to favor equal status for them with the white troops. As might be expected, Wood was convinced that the mutineers "undoubtedly indirectly received encouragement and stimulation from the public utterances of certain political leaders condemning all who cooperated with and supported the Governor General, the representative of the United States in these islands." Read finally penetrated to the crux of the Scouts' dissatisfaction when he stated, "It is clear that the grievance these men allege as a basis for their mutinous action is discrimination against the Philippine Scout soldier in pay, allowances, and benefits." It was true that Scouts were seriously discriminated against in these areas, as well as many others less tangible. Some efforts were made in the following months to adjust the Filipino soldiers' salaries and allowances more equitably, but the combination of inadequate funds and entrenched prejudice precluded any sweeping changes that would afford the Scout the same benefits and opportunities as the American soldier of equivalent rank and experience. More-over, no Scout commissioned or noncommissioned officers were permitted to be in a position over white troops. The mutiny was forgotten in a few years, but the Army continued to find it necessary to recruit Filipinos to fill Scout units.[10]

In the days following the mutiny MacArthur, though avoiding the role of scapegoat, must have wondered what course his career would take next. In September, 1923, he had been considered for the post of military attaché in London, but the job had gone to a general whom the War Department considered more "eminently qualified." Later he had likewise been nominated and rejected for the position of military attaché in Tokyo.[11] Unknown to him, before Pershing vacated the post of chief of staff in September, 1924, MacArthur had been recommended for promotion — by his mother again:

Confidential

My dear General Pershing:

It was a real joy to see you on Saturday looking still so young and wonderfully handsome!

I think you will *never* grow old. I have felt particularly unhappy since I had my little heart-to-heart chat with you. It is just because I know you to be such a noble, broadminded and just man and friend that I am presuming on long and loyal friendship for you — to open my heart in this appeal for my Boy — and ask if you can't find it convenient to give him his promotion during your régime as Chief of Staff?

He now stands number 7th on the list. He made good on the battlefields in France — And And [*sic*] I have your fine letter to him written in France, telling him that you had recommended him to be a Major General. The mear [*sic*] fact that he is younger in years than other deserving officers should not be sufficient reason for overslaughing him again — And of course you must know that every junior man the Department places above him, becomes an actual punishment to him that will last for a life time. Men of great prominence, as well as men at large — have told me that the whole country would approve his promotion. You are so powerful in all Army matters, that you could give him his promotion by the stroke of your pen! *You* have never failed me yet — and somehow I feel you will not in this request. Your own life is so full to overflowing with joys and happiness — and deserving success — that it may be hard for you to understand the heartaches and bitter disappointments in the lives of others. Won't you be real good and sweet — The "Dear Old Jack" of long ago — and give me some assurance that you will give my Boy his well earned promotion before you leave the Army? I would rather have this promotion from *your* hands — than from any other hands in the world. I *pledge* to keep *absolutely to myself* — in strictest confidence — any hope you may give me in this matter. If I had the power — there is nothing on earth I would not do for *you* to prove my loyalty and admiration for you. God bless you — and crown your valuable life — by taking you to the White House.

Faithfully your friend —
MARY P. MACARTHUR[12]

On September 23, 1924, only ten days after Pershing left the office of chief of staff and Major General John L. Hines took the reins, the newspapers published a War Department release announcing MacArthur's promotion to major general, effective January 17, 1925. The *New York Times'* article stated that "he will be the youngest Maj. Gen. on the active list of the army." The writer remarked that MacArthur "is considered one of the ablest and brightest of the younger officers of the regular army," and "with good health he stands a splendid chance of some day becoming head of the army." [13] How much influence the sentimental, ambitious mother had on Pershing will probably never be known, but, reading the news, she undoubtedly felt that he still had "never failed me yet." MacArthur never commented on his mother's opportunistic maneuvering in his behalf, and it is not certain that he ever knew of it.

2. *"One of the Most Distasteful Orders"*

In the spring of 1925 MacArthur and his family returned to the States, and after an all-too-brief leave in Washington he took command of the IV Corps Area on May 2, with headquarters in Atlanta. He probably expected the job to be a routine one, but the next three months were livelier than anticipated. Shortly after settling in his new office, he received a call from the governor of North Carolina asking for assistance in rescuing a group of miners entombed after an explosion at the Coal Glen mine in the western part of the state. MacArthur rushed troops from Fort Bragg to the scene in time to save the trapped men before their air supply was gone. The governor and the War Department praised "the prompt, vigorous and efficient manner in which assistance was given." In addition to helping in civilian emergencies, MacArthur found that summer was the busiest season for a corps area commander, with thousands of young men of the Reserve Officers Training Corps, Organized Reserves and Citizens Military Training Camps pouring into the area's various forts and camps for brief periods of intensive training. One of MacArthur's chief concerns was the maneuvers to be conducted at Camp McClellan, Alabama, by the 8th Infantry Brigade. He was able to report later that the field exercises "were excellent and very beneficial to both troops and officers. All units of the 8th Infantry Brigade . . . were present for combined training for the first time since the World War."

Toward the end of the busy summer he received orders to report to Baltimore where he was to assume command of the strategically more significant III Corps Area, whose forces were responsible primarily for the defense of the Washington-Chesapeake Bay region. It was a welcome move for the MacArthurs since they could live at Louise's Rainbow Hill estate at Eccleston, near Baltimore, and would be closer to his mother, then living with MacArthur's widow in Washington.[14]

About two months after the transfer to Maryland, MacArthur got what he termed "one of the most distasteful orders I ever received": he was detailed to serve as a judge in the court-martial of Brigadier General William Mitchell, which was scheduled to begin in late October. MacArthur had last seen Mitchell in January, 1924, when the latter, as the assistant chief of the air service, came to the Philippines to inspect its almost non-existent air defenses. Undoubtedly at that time Mitchell discussed with MacArthur his accelerating campaign for a stronger air arm, which he had carried on largely through speeches, articles, and books highly critical of the military establishments's indifference to aviation. He may have told MacArthur about the opposition he had encountered from Menoher, the chief of the air service, 1919–21, and his successor, Major General Mason M. Patrick, as well as most of the brass of the Army and Navy. In September, 1923, he had again, as in 1921, used his bombers in a demonstration to sink obsolete battleships, but, instead of winning accolades and converts, he had been sent on the Pacific inspection tour "to quiet down." En route to the Philippines, he had infuriated Summerall, commanding the Hawaiian Department, by denouncing the lack of attention to air defenses on Oahu. After the Pacific tour Mitchell, instead of cooling off, renewed his aggressive fight for air power; in April, 1925, he was removed as assistant air chief and transferred to the post of corps air officer at San Antonio. There on September 5 he told the press that the recent crash of a Navy dirigible was the result of inexcusable neglect of aviation by naval leaders, at the same time savagely indicting the Army's high command for its callous disregard of the air service's needs and potentiality. The public statement at San Antonio led to his summons to Washington to stand trial on eight charges of violating the Articles of War, especially by "conduct prejudicial to good order and military discipline" and "conduct of a nature to bring discredit upon the military service."

MacArthur was the youngest member of the court which filed into the Emory Building, near the Capitol, on October 28 for the start of the court-martial. The thirteen judges, none of whom had any experience with the air service, expected the trial to be completed in a short time. Unexpectedly, three of the judges were removed when defense challenges revealed their prejudice against Mitchell; they included Summerall, who was president of the court, and Sladen, the superintendent at West Point. Major General Robert L. Howze, a cavalryman who had commanded an infantry division in France, was appointed court president. The best known of the other judges was Major General William S. Graves, who in 1918–20 had commanded the American troops involved in the Siberian expedition against the Russian Bolsheviks. The member who would be most closely connected with MacArthur's later career was Brigadier General Frank R. McCoy, who may have first met MacArthur when they were both in the Philippines in 1903–04. In the World War, McCoy won distinction as a brigade commander and later served on a number of special military and diplomatic missions. In 1930 he would be seriously considered for chief of staff, and in 1945–49 he would serve as chairman of the Far Eastern Commission, the Allies' main policy-making body for the Japanese occupation.

When Mitchell's counsel was allowed to introduce all the testimony and other evidence it could bring together in support of the defendant's view, the trial developed into a highly publicized, but legally irrelevant debate on air power, even getting off on the questions of a separate department of the air corps and unification of the armed services under a department of defense. Some of the testimony was so humorous and much of the questioning so ridiculously apart from the legal issues at stake that discipline began to sag in the courtroom, with judges, spectators, and guards joining in outbursts of laughter. A reporter commented, "As the days passed the snickers blossomed out into guffaws . . . It is expected that stamping will be in order before the trial is over." [15] A high point in the burlesque was the testimony of Congressman Fiorello La Guardia, a wartime pilot under Mitchell, champion of air power, and later mayor of New York. According to the only chronicle of the trial based on the actual court-martial records, the Army's cross-examination of La Guardia went thus:

> "Mr. La Guardia, the newspapers recently . . . quoted you as saying . . . : 'Billy Mitchell isn't being tried by a jury of his peers, but by nine beribboned dogrobbers of the General Staff.' Were you correctly quoted?"
> "I didn't say beribboned."
> The laughter in the courtroom delayed the proceedings for several minutes. Howze broke in: "The court would like to have you explain what was meant by your characterization of this court." . . .

"From my experience as a member of Congress and from my contact with the General Staff, I'm convinced that the training, the background, the experience and the attitude of officers of high rank of the Army are conducive to carrying out the wishes and desires of the General Staff." La Guardia had an after-thought: "I want to say that at that time I didn't know General MacArthur was on this court."

The spectators burst into laughter once more, joined by the judges.[16]

Burke Davis, the only writer to be given access to the court-martial proceedings, maintains that "this was the only moment during the trial when MacArthur drew official attention. He was otherwise uncharacteristically silent for the seven weeks." Davis also claims that MacArthur was "especially inattentive" during the trial: "He and his wife were like newlyweds, ex-changing meaningful glances — Mrs. MacArthur smiling over a bunch of violets which she carried each day; her husband could hardly keep his eyes off her." On December 17 the court found Mitchell guilty as charged on all eight counts and sus-pended him from duty for five years; Mitchell resigned from the Army the next February. The verdict required only a two-thirds majority, and the individual votes were never re-vealed, though later statements by MacArthur and others say that he voted for acquittal. In a letter to Senator Alexander Wiley of Wisconsin in 1945 MacArthur said that his role in the voting was "fully known" to Mitchell, who "never ceased to express his gratitude." In his memoirs MacArthur main-tained, "I did what I could in his behalf and I helped save him from dismissal." La Guardia claimed that after the trial a crum-pled ballot was found in the wastebasket in the judges' ante-room; the piece of paper allegedly was in MacArthur's hand-writing and bore the words "Not Guilty. Douglas MacArthur."

The strange silence of MacArthur during the proceedings may have been "the better part of discretion," for, as the re-porter earlier suggested, the young major general had an excellent chance of becoming chief of staff before long. The verdict was almost a foregone conclusion from the start, and, had it not been for the tangential testimony, a decision would have been reached in a few days. As one of the judges, MacArthur could not have engaged in personal pleading for his friend. Moreover, if he felt his own career might be affected by the episode, he must have carefully considered the sentiments of Summerall. Undoubtedly at the time of the trial, rumors were already circulating that Summerall was in line for chief of staff next, and in 1926 he attained the coveted post. When, as court president, he was dismissed after the defense showed clearly his bias, a correspondent observed that "men who knew him as 'Oliver Cromwell in khaki' said they had never seen him so ruffled." Outside the courtroom Summerall, who was one of MacArthur's key professional connections, told reporters, "Now it's all over. We're enemies, Mitchell and I." MacArthur, who was never accused of lacking shrewdness in his rise to power in military circles, apparently saw his own dilemma in the Mitchell affair and opportunistically circumvented it by remaining silent.

Nearly all commentaries on the trial assert or imply that MacArthur voted for acquittal. Mitchell's remarks are contradictory and suggest that MacArthur never told him. In 1933, for example, Mitchell spoke of "how good a friend of mine he was back there in 1925," whereas two years later he wrote that MacArthur "regrets the part he played in my court-martial. May he be brave enough to say it openly." To the end, MacArthur handled the issue elusively, stating in his memoirs that his critics were wrong in charging that he betrayed his friend, yet a few lines later saying, "That he was wrong in the violence of his language is self-evident." In spite of all the fanfare about the air-power crusade, the court-martial really centered on "the violence of his language," so it would seem that MacArthur voted for conviction, though he may have argued for suspension rather than dismissal. In the final analysis, the only assertion that can be made with certainty about his vote is that it will never be determined for certain.

In hindsight and viewing Mitchell's plight in the context of his own dismissal in 1951, MacArthur said, "It is part of my military philosophy that a senior officer should not be silenced for being at variance with his superiors in rank and with accepted doctrine . . . The individual may be martyred, but his thoughts live on." He also asserted that at the time he "was thoroughly in accord with the concept of the massive power of the air and that its development should be greatly accelerated" and that he had "publicly stated" before the trial his opinion that control of the air was indispensable for ground and naval operations. But generals who were ardent advocates of air power in the 1920's were few and conspicuous, and no accounts of the history of military aviation in this period cite MacArthur as a supporter. Like his friends Menoher and Summerall, he remembered battles in France which were won by infantry and artillery, with perhaps some help from tanks when they would run. Machine guns had affected the course of battles, but not airplanes. The aircraft the Germans employed had sometimes been bothersome pests, and the Allied planes were helpful in reconnaissance. But in 1918 and 1925 there simply were no aircraft yet developed to support Mitchell's dreams of their use in affecting the outcome of battles and wars. Moreover, as will be seen later, MacArthur's relations with the air corps when he was chief of staff do not indicate that he was then very enthusiastic about the airplane as a decisive offensive weapon. Actually his remarks about Mitchell's crusade — such as "That he was right in his thesis is equally true and incontrovertible" — were made in retrospect after four decades of progress by military aviation, which he began to appreciate fully only after the Second World War was underway.[17]

3. *Prosperity and Pacifism*

The years 1925–28, when MacArthur was at Baltimore in command of the III Corps Area, saw millions of Americans intoxicated by the greatest prosperity they had ever known. As the speculative boom accelerated in the latter half of the decade, the ticker-tape machines of the stock exchanges seemed to be man's most indispensable devices. Business success became the measure of character, and Wall Street was the holy place of the frenzied devotees of the religion of business. The heroes of the era were the men with the most sensational records of success — Samuel Insull, Henry Ford, Babe Ruth, Knute Rockne, Richard Byrd, Charles Lindbergh. But it was no time for soldiers; disillusionment with war and its heroes was widespread. Over a dozen pacifist societies with national memberships were active and growing rapidly, each group with its own goals, but most pacifists agreeing on the need to rid civilization of militarism and the "war habit" through disarmament and making war "illegal." Some of the nation's most promising novelists exploited the popularity of antiwar literature, including John Dos Passos, Ernest Hemingway, and William Faulkner. Congress faithfully reflected the people's mood by emasculating the Army, cutting it to 135,000 officers and men and annual appropriations of less than $380 million. In the zany era of flappers and flagpole sitters, wild-sounding jazz and soaring stock values, America merrily made herself more impotent militarily than any other major nation, with even Germany, saddled by peace-treaty restrictions, having a larger army. As he left the office of chief of staff in 1926, Hines lamented, "The Regular Army had undergone reductions until it has now barely 40 per cent of the strength originally contemplated by the national defense act of 1920." A prominent military historian maintains that "the Army during the 1920's and early

1930's may have been less ready to function as a fighting force than at any time in its history . . . As anything more than a small school for soldiers the Army scarcely existed." [18]

The skeletonizing of the nation's defenses became startlingly apparent to MacArthur when, on one of his first inspections of the III Corps Area, he toured the coastal defenses of Chesapeake Bay and discovered serious shortages of personnel and supplies, and antiquated guns. Training schedules were supposed to be prepared the year prior to their use, but MacArthur and other corps area commanders found it impossible to do so because of the uncertainty of funds. The report of the III Corps Area for the fiscal year 1927–28 typified the plight faced by not only MacArthur but also generals of every American command in the States and overseas. The report began with the statement that one military district had been abolished in order to consolidate forces and economize on operating expenditures. "Reduction in personnel of the troops under current allotments renders it impossible to supply demonstration units for National Guard camps," the report continued. "It is also found exceedingly difficult to supply specialists asked for, many demands for summer training camp being impossible of fulfillment." As for housing conditions, it noted that "a deficiency in suitable quarters for officers and enlisted men exists at practically every post in the Corps Area." Motor transportation "is in poor condition," and the World War-style truck used in the corps area "has practically outlived its usefulness. It is questionable if the cost of repair of many of these vehicles is warrantable." It was reported that, in carrying out an economy move ordered by the War Department, "Harbor Defenses of the Potomac have been abandoned, and seacoast guns, carriages, and pertaining equipment at Fort Washington, Maryland, are now being dismantled for shipment to designated Ordnance establishments." In spite of the strategic significance of the Chesapeake region, "Air Corps activities have been devoted almost entirely to the training of the National Guard and Organized Reserves. There are no Regular Army Air Corps units under the jurisdiction of this Corps Area." [19] MacArthur would probably have agreed that an invasion force in 1927 would have an even easier time than did General Robert Ross' British troops in 1814 when they burned Washington.

Among the serious, persisting problems in developing an effective defense force, MacArthur learned, were how to attract and retain soldiers in the Regular Army during the prosperous years before the Great Crash of 1929. Long a firm believer in the morale-boosting efficacy of sports, MacArthur stressed organized athletic competition at the various posts and organized district and corps area championships in a number of sports. Colonel Isaac C. Jenks, his chief of staff, reported to the War Department in 1928 that "the athletic competitions for the past year have been very, very successful, and it is believed that they have had considerable influence on the morale of the command. It is also thought that athletics have had a considerable bearing on the re-enlistments which have increased during the past year from 35% to approximately 50%." The recruitment program of the Regular Army was pushed vigorously by MacArthur and bore impressive results: the III Corps Area's record of recruitment was next to the worst among the corps areas when he took command, but was the Army's best for the period 1925–28.[20]

The C.M.T.C. (Citizens Military Training Camps) program, which Wood had begun in 1915 with the Plattsburg camp, was kept going through the 1920's, but only by considerable promotion by the Army. These camps were operated at regular installations of the Army and involved a month's training during the summer for young men of high school and college ages. The program provided a reservoir of partially trained citizen-soldiers aside from the National Guard and Organized Reserves, which maintained continuing training programs throughout the year.

In his efforts to enlist youths for the five camps in his corps area, MacArthur resorted to all sorts of advertising gimmicks: periodical news bulletins to "CMTC Veterans," "neat CMTC Christmas Greeting Cards," promotional folders in racks in public transportation facilities, colored slides for the use of schools and civic organizations, newspaper articles, and specially commissioned movies of camp highlights which Pathé and International News circulated to motion picture theaters. He was quite pleased when "publicity was given in practically all newspapers in the Corps Area to the endorsement of the Daughters of the American Revolution and their laudable plans for promoting greater interest in the CMTC." His promotional campaign stressed "the advantages to be gained by young working men," he stated, "in the matter of improved health, strength, general physical development and discipline, coordination of effort, increased responsibility and team work, which ultimately redound to the advantage of the employer." [21]

His C.M.T.C. program ran into obstacles, one of the chief of which was reluctance on the part of parents, especially farmers, to release their sons for a month during the summer. "It is to be regretted," MacArthur commented, "that so many sturdy working boys and ambitious High School students are prevented from attending the Camps because of the economic demands of parents, when that month's work or profit means so little when compared to the great material advantages to be gained by a month's valuable training in a CMT Camp." Even less could he appreciate the attitude of some teachers, as he told the adjutant general in 1925:

> An appreciable percentage of school teachers are found to be imbued with pacifist ideas and while not openly hostile to the CMTC, their aloofness and indifference to the movement is a serious handicap, especially in small communities where the teacher exercises such an important influence in the lives of the young. A constant campaign of CMTC propaganda should

be kept in the press throughout the year by means of well prepared articles in educational publications and teachers' magazines and by appropriate addresses delivered by qualified representatives of the Army of the United States at Teachers' Conventions and educational gatherings. Next to the CMT Camp graduate himself, the school teacher can be made the most valuable agent in disseminating favorable information on this important phase of National Defense.[22]

Pacifist activity in the United States was at its zenith in 1927 and may have been a factor in President's Coolidge's invitation to the powers which signed the Washington Naval Treaty to reconvene and consider additional naval limitations, especially on cruisers, destroyers, and submarines. Since the Senate had just rejected American membership in the World Court, the President's move may have been calculated to redeem the Republican image among pacifists, internationalists, and other possible pro-Court voters, as well as to avoid the expenditures which the admirals were urging to keep the Navy a major force on the high seas. The conference met at Geneva that summer, but adjourned without reaching any agreement. Senator William E. Borah, the isolationist spokesman from Idaho, blamed the meeting's failure on the want of an "aroused and sustained public sentiment" and believed that peace-lovers must work harder to stimulate "the driving, compelling power of public opinion." Even before the Geneva conference opened in June, however, many pacifists had become more excited over another development dear to their hearts. That spring James T. Shotwell, a professor at Columbia University and a leader of the movement to abolish war, met with Aristide Briand, the French foreign minister, and proposed a treaty between their two countries outlawing war. Shortly afterward, on April 6, 1927, Briand appealed directly to the American people for such a bilateral treaty, evoking ecstasy among pacifists and coolness from the Coolidge administration, which had been slighted. The next month Lindbergh's nonstop flight to Paris produced such effusions of Franco-American good will that the American government yielded to public opinion and opened negotiations with France looking toward a treaty to ban war. Eventually the talks were broadened to include other powers, and the next summer at Paris fifteen nations became signatories of the Kellogg-Briand Pact, which renounced offensive warfare as "an instrument of national policy." In the following months nearly every nation in the world approved the pact, including Germany, Japan, Italy, and the Soviet Union. The United States Senate consented, though at least one senator, Carter Glass of Virginia, was frank enough to say that he hoped his constituents would not think "that I am simple enough to suppose that it is worth a postage stamp in the direction of accomplishing permanent peace." [23]

Like other dedicated Army leaders who were wrestling with the problem of insuring the nation's defenses with skeletonized forces, MacArthur was deeply concerned by the prevailing pacificism of the late 1920's. Whenever the opportunity arose, he delivered public addresses in which he argued that national unpreparedness was not economical in the long run because it encouraged aggressors and led to costly wars. In the midst of the pacifists' excitement over the coming Geneva meeting and Shotwell's mission to Paris in the spring of 1927, MacArthur was given the chance to express his views at a much-publicized banquet of the Soldiers and Sailors Club of New York City, held at the Ritz-Carlton Hotel in commemoration of the tenth anniversary of America's entry into World War I. Somberly and sincerely, MacArthur addressed the distinguished assembly of prominent civilian and military leaders, most of whom had served in that war:

> With the Red menace in Russia, Poland in disorder, Rumania threatened with secession, France fighting in Morocco, Nicaragua in revolution, Mexico in confusion, and civil war raging in China, it does not seem unlikely that our streets will

again be filled with marching men and our country again have
need of our services.

The provisions of our national defense act should be fully
carried out. Total disarmament is unthinkable. No one takes
seriously the equally illogical plan of disbanding our fire departments to stop fires or disbanding our police departments
to stop crime. Our country insists upon respect for its rights,
and gives due recognition to the rights of all others. But so
long as humanity is governed by motives not in accord with
Christianity, we are in danger of an attack directed by unworthy impulses. We should be prepared against brutal attack. Those who would not protect themselves should, as a
matter of common decency, be willing to furnish the reasonable
protection required by others.

Our nation has shrunk from enforced military service. But
between the two extremes has been evolved the conception of
citizen soldiery. Upon the successful solution of this problem
— the citizen soldier — will depend the very life of our nation.
And when the bloody test comes, some American chief, on the
day of victory, is going to thank God for what this nation is
now building up in its citizen soldiery.[24]

The article on MacArthur's speech was buried on page ten of
the next day's issue of the *New York Times*. On the front page
was the startling news that on the previous day, April 6, Foreign
Minister Briand had boldly addressed an open letter to the
American people proposing the treaty to outlaw war. To most
readers who happened to read the excerpt from MacArthur's
address, his message must have seemed incongruous, for the
world suddenly appeared to be moving toward a bright new
era of international good will. In the wonderland of America
in 1927 there was not time to listen to alarmists, whether they
be generals prophesying war or economists predicting a great
crash on Wall Street.

4. Life with Louise

In addition to watching his beloved Army derided and starved in the twenties, MacArthur also faced disappointment in his marriage, which, like the jazz age itself, came to a bitter end in 1929. It would have taken an unusually strong bond of love to keep Louise's tremendous wealth and high-society interests from complicating her marriage to MacArthur. She was born to luxury, her father being Oliver E. Cromwell, a rich New York attorney and prominent yachtsman who boasted of his family's direct descent from England's Lord Protector. While Louise was young, Cromwell died, and her mother married Edward T. Stotesbury, a partner in J. P. Morgan and Company and a leader in Philadelphia banking whose fortune reputedly exceeded $100 million. Louise's brother, James, later married Doris Duke, the tobacco heiress, and — between business ventures — served for a time as United States ambassador to Canada. In 1908 Louise married Walter Brooks, a well-to-do contractor and socialite of Baltimore. She bore him a son and daughter, but the children apparently did not curb the parents' enjoyment of the gay life of high society. During the World War the Brookses lived in Paris where they belonged to the "international set," whose parties were not dulled by the unpleasantries of wartime. Before long, however, the marriage foundered, and in 1919 Louise divorced Brooks. Variously described as "brilliant," "vivacious," and "beautiful," the wealthy divorcee moved to Washington and for a while served as official hostess for Pershing, whom she had known well in Paris.

Louise's inability, after marrying MacArthur in 1922, to forget a previous suitor may have been a key factor which led to the estrangement from her second husband a few years later. In the period 1919–21 she had been courted by Colonel John G. "Harry" Quekemeyer, a handsome bachelor and aide to Pershing. In the World War Quekemeyer had earned the Distinguished Service Medal and the Purple Heart, having been wounded in the Argonne fighting. In early 1926 he was detailed as commandant of cadets at West Point, but died suddenly on February 28 at the age of forty-one.[25] Louise, who was then living at Rainbow Hill outside Baltimore and had been married to MacArthur for five years, wrote a moving letter of condolence to Pershing a few days after Quekemeyer's death. In it she revealed her deep feelings for Quekemeyer and seemed to regret not having married him.[26]

This letter and certain signs of dissatisfaction during her stay in the Philippines seem to contradict her later assertion that the years 1922–25 were "the happiest of my life." In Manila MacArthur was absorbed in his work and led a rigidly regimented life, particularly after his shift from the district administrative post to troop command. When he had some leisure, he preferred to spend it with Quezon and his other Filipino friends, who were socially unacceptable to the high-society whites, with whom Louise was soon associated; or else he would devote his idle moments to fellowship with his stepchildren, Walter and Louise. Walter later said that all he knew about horsemanship he learned from General MacArthur. Unable to find any interests in common with her husband, Louise became more and more involved in the social activities of the elite, including charitable endeavors. In June, 1924, the newspapers reported that she had been commissioned as a policewoman in Manila and had just made her first arrest. "She sought the appointment," one article explained, "to enable her the better to carry on the work of prevention of cruelty to animals. She took into custody the driver of a caromata, or native conveyance, charging him with abusing his horse." In spite of her whirl of social and civic activities, Louise wrote friends that her life in Manila was "extremely dull" and "she hoped to persuade her husband to resign from the Army." She or Stotesbury apparently tried to interest him in a position with J. P. Morgan and Company, for officials of that firm prepared a dossier on him. When he evidenced no interest in this or other civilian positions, she then tried through military and political friends in Washington to arrange his promotion and transfer to the States, and like his mother, may have had some influence in this regard. After her daughter was stricken by malaria, Louise became more anxious than ever to go back to America.

When they moved to her mansion, Rainbow Hill, at Eccleston, Maryland, in the late summer of 1925, Louise was delighted to resume the social life she had earlier enjoyed in Baltimore. Probably in an effort to save his relationship with her, MacArthur joined the nearby Green Spring Valley Club, an elite fox-hunting society, and participated with Louise and her friends in some hunts and social functions of the club. He also tried to be amiable and interested when her family and friends discussed the Florida real-estate boom and other speculative activities in which they were heavily involved. MacArthur allegedly predicted that the Florida bubble would burst, which it did in 1926. Repeatedly his wife, along with Stotesbury and Cromwell, tempted him to leave the Army and try his hand in the world of business.[27] MacArthur left no clue as to his thoughts on this question of resigning from the service, which was a perennial family issue, at least for Louise — and as long as profits were so dazzling. From what his contemporaries have said of him,[28] MacArthur's motivation in staying with the Army was strikingly similar to that of Sam Damon, a fictional character in Anton Myrer's novel, *Once an Eagle*. An officer in the poverty-stricken Army of the 1920's, Damon also was invited to hang up his uniform and enter the business realm, but, like MacArthur, he mulled it over and decided:

> He could make his way as a businessman . . . [His wife] would be happier, unquestionably, out of the world of the Army . . .

And yet . . . he was afraid of this world. He feared it; not
as an arena where he could not prove himself — he had dis-
pelled that qualm effectively enough — but as a good seaman
must fear a recklessly piloted ship. It was too ungoverned,
too avaricious, too headlong . . .

There was more to it than that, he knew; a lot more. He
had chosen to spend his days in the world of men. *Life* was
what mattered, its slow, priceless pulse, its burning fragility;
his debt lay with those importunate Flanders echoes that had
never really left him. The private could aspire to be a general
because both general and private, at their best, recognized the
dire importance of strategy, fortitude, the value of their im-
periled existence; but when the machinist became the executive he left the world of tangibles and human conjugacy and
entered a shadow world of credits and consols — a world that
seemed to reward nothing so much as irresponsibility and
boundless greed. And when the thunder rolled down upon
them — as he knew it would — how would he feel playing
with paper, striving to outwit his fellows, drinking imported
Scotch evenings and listening to the brittle parade of comedians
on the radio . . . ? [29]

By August, 1927, the marriage had deteriorated to the point
of separation, with Louise moving to New York City. There she
obtained a long-term lease on the entire twenty-sixth floor of a
new, swanky residential hotel, the Beverly, on 50th Street. Surprisingly, MacArthur continued to reside at Rainbow Hill for
nearly a year thereafter. In March, 1928, for instance, Louise
was giving parties at her luxurious residence at the Beverly,
whereas on the 28th of that month MacArthur and a host of
servants were fighting a fire at Rainbow Hill which destroyed
the keeper's house. That summer found MacArthur in Europe,
and the next fall he returned to the Philippines, but Louise
made neither journey. On June 18, 1929, while he was in
Manila, she was granted a divorce in Reno, Nevada, on grounds
of "failure to provide," which, of course, was a ludicrous excuse
in view of her immense wealth. She told reporters, however, as

she left the courtroom, "General MacArthur and I divorced because we were wholly incompatible to each other. I have the greatest respect and admiration for him and we part as friends."

Ahead of Louise lay two more marriages, which also terminated in divorces. In the years after 1929 she made a number of remarks to newsmen about her marriage to MacArthur, some of her comments being sarcastic and others almost regretful. On one occasion in her later years she stated emphatically, but without elaboration, that "it was an interfering mother-in-law who eventually succeeded in disrupting our married life." On the other hand, MacArthur, who never discussed his personal problems with anyone outside his family, remained prudently silent about the whole relationship. A lonely man before he met her, he was now both lonely and deeply hurt, probably missing most the stepchildren to whom he had become endeared. In his sketches which he prepared for biographical directories, including *Who's Who*, MacArthur never mentioned the marriage. In his memoirs, likewise, he did not mention her name, though he did state simply: "In February 1922 I entered into matrimony, but it was not successful, and ended in divorce years later for mutual incompatibility." [30]

Louise truly belonged to the jazz age, and, like a delightful, but tragic, heroine in one of F. Scott Fitzgerald's novels, probably looked back on the roaring twenties as a golden age when cocktail parties were gayest, skirts were shortening, and women were freer than ever before. She seemed to belong naturally to that world where, as one commentator on the era put it, "the saxophones wailed and the gin-flask went its rounds and the dancers made their treadmill circuit with half-closed eyes, and the outside world, so merciless and so insane, was shut away for a restless night." [31] A beautifully sensitive and tender woman in many ways, she could never comprehend that "outside world" to which her husband was already supremely attached when she married him. Forty-two years old when he took the marital vows, MacArthur was entrenched in his ways, and his ways were those of the soldier — discipline, courage, austerity, fortitude, honor, and duty to country — which neither Louise nor her society could appreciate. The woman who became his life mate would have to face realistically the truth which his Army colleagues already knew — that MacArthur was dedicated, mind, heart, and soul, to his duty as a soldier for the country which would always be his first love.

CHAPTER XII

Olympus and Beyond

1. "Swifter, Higher, Stronger"

MACARTHUR'S PROMOTION OF ATHLETICS at West Point and in his corps area commands brought him to the attention of the American Olympic Committee, which consisted of representatives of the nearly 200 governing bodies of various sports included in the Olympic program. When the committee's president, William C. Prout, died suddenly in September, 1927, the committee elected MacArthur to its presidency, the next Olympics being only ten months away. Chief of Staff Summerall, who was a sports enthusiast and felt that favorable publicity might accrue to the Army from MacArthur's participation, gave him permission to accept the post. Since Louise had moved to New York the previous month, the Olympic committee's honor must have provided a much-needed boost to MacArthur's morale. His principal job continued to be the III Corps Area command, which he retained for the next eleven months, but he was often away from his office on Olympic business and was on detached duty during the summer of 1928 when he accompanied the team to Amsterdam for the games

of the Ninth Olympiad. From the time of his election until
the next July, MacArthur's presidency went smoothly, the contentious factions of the American Olympic Committee declaring an uneasy truce, the drives to raise funds overreaching their
goals, and the tryouts producing a group of outstanding athletes.[1]

Trouble arose on July 7, four days before the team was to
leave for Holland, when the selection committee got into a
hassle over whether to allow Charles Paddock to participate,
the track star's amateur status being questioned. Brigadier
General Palmer E. Pierce, once MacArthur's instructor at
West Point, later his colleague on the General Staff, and now
the president of the National Collegiate Athletic Association,
argued that Paddock was not an amateur. Reopening an old
feud, Pierce further maintained that the American Athletic
Union, which had certified Paddock's amateur status, had acted
in a supererogatory manner, since the final authority in the
matter lay with the N.C.A.A. The selection committee could
not reach agreement and turned the case over to MacArthur,
who took the A.A.U.'s word on Paddock because, he said, there
had not "any evidence been submitted to me, which would
warrant my casting doubt upon its conclusions." On July 11,
the day that the S.S. *Roosevelt* sailed from New York with the
Olympians aboard, George Wightman, vice president of the
American Olympic Committee, refused to make the trip and
resigned in protest against Paddock's participation. In a statement to the press MacArthur said he "deeply regretted" Wightman's action, but added that Paddock's critics should have come
up "with something more to substantiate their accusation than
whispered innuendo, hearsay, and comment." When the team
arrived in Amsterdam on the 21st, the International Olympic
Committee took up the case in "stormy secret sessions" and
finally ruled in favor of Paddock. Paddock's performance on
the track was anticlimactic; the young man, who had won a

gold medal in the Olympics of 1924, did not place in the races at Amsterdam.

On July 29 the Olympic Games opened with the traditional parade and ceremonies, the speakers at the rostrum expounding on the Olympic motto of "swifter, higher, stronger" and the assembled athletes' pledge to compete "in the true spirit of sportsmanship, for the glory of sport and the honor of our teams." As seems characteristic of all Olympic occasions, there were times when such lofty ideals were forgotten. Absent from the opening ceremonies, for instance, was the French team, which was embittered because of a misunderstanding the previous day with some Dutch grounds keepers who would not let the French runners practice on the track. Wilhelmina, the Dutch queen and a strict Calvinist, refused to attend the convocation because it was held on Sunday. She did not make an appearance at the games until the last few days, though MacArthur found her amiable at a dinner which she hosted for some of the Olympic officials. Other unexpected occurrences as the games progressed included a protest by the Canadian officials over "unfair treatment of Canadians while U.S. athletes are favored" by the judges in the rowing regatta; the American boxing team's threatened withdrawal after a controversial decision against one of its boxers; the discovery of several American athletes who had stowed away on the *Roosevelt* after failing to make the team; and the embarrassing moments for Germany's champion swimmer, Hilda Schrader, when her shoulder straps broke near the end of a race and, according to a reporter, she "was forced to remain immersed in the water until the covering was adjusted."

Before the games began and between events, MacArthur "stormed and pleaded and cajoled," he said, in order to get peak performances from his athletes. A correspondent observed that MacArthur was serious and determined at the frequent sessions he called with his coaches and managers: "These meet-

ings, with about the same chilling spiritual temperature as a
bank directors' meeting, have already produced good results."
When the events were underway, MacArthur seemed to be
everywhere at once; he lived the glories and disappointments
of the outcomes as intensely as any of the athletes. As the
10,000-meter race was nearing its close finish (won by a Finn),
MacArthur was so carried away by the excitement that he
rushed from the officials' box to the sideline near the ribbon.
On another day, when the University of California's eight-
oared shell was rowing to victory on the Sloten River, Mac-
Arthur had his chauffeur drive him along the bank parallel to
the shell as it raced. On August 9, the day after Jacob W.
Stumpf, the American boxing manager, had said his team
might quit, the *New York Times* reported that MacArthur
"had refused permission to withdraw the U.S. team from competition" and later that day "all four American boxers . . .
fought their way into the quarter-finals . . . 'Americans never
quit,' General MacArthur said." When the track team lost
some races it had been expected to win, MacArthur called a
meeting of the coaches, managers, and athletes in the grand
salon of the *Roosevelt*, the ship serving as American headquarters during the games. According to one account, his performance was virtuoso: " 'We are here to represent the greatest country on earth,' he stormed as he strode up and down,
his voice ranging from a stage whisper to a bellow. 'We did
not come here to lose gracefully. We came here to win . . .
and win decisively.' " Although his fierce determination to
succeed and his high-pressure tactics may have brought some
grumbling, the American team did finish with some inspired
performances. W. O. Spencer, an American in the 3000-meter
steeplechase, observed that there was "widespread admiration
among the athletes for MacArthur's earnest efforts and zeal." [2]
   When Queen Wilhelmina presented the medals on the closing day, August 12, the procession of American recipients was

impressive. The United States gained twenty-four first places, more than the total of the next two nations together, which were Finland and Germany. In unofficial team scoring the United States had 131 points, with Finland garnering sixty-two for second place and Germany next with fifty-nine. The Americans set seventeen Olympic records and seven world records, which was an improvement over the impressive record of the United States team in the Olympics at Paris four years earlier. Amid the celebrations aboard the *Roosevelt* on the return voyage, however, Jack Ryder, one of the coaches, sounded a warning: "We in the United States have swelled heads — the managers, the coaches, the athletes, and the public. We think we are the best, but it has been proved that we are not the best. We are one nation, and there are fifty other nations in the world." Perhaps he had in mind the fact that in team competitions Germany had outscored the United States. Ryder's words proved prophetic because the United States, which had won every modern Olympics, was headed toward its first defeat eight years later at Berlin where the winner would be Nazi Germany.[3]

As the Americans were preparing to depart aboard the *Roosevelt,* two of the stowaways found that this time they could not get past the ship's officer at the gangplank and would be stranded penniless in Holland. The rails were lined with their fellow athletes who sympathized with their plight, but were helpless to assist them. Suddenly MacArthur appeared; with a few indistinct words to the ship's officer, he rushed the boys on board. "You should have heard the cheer that went up for MacArthur," said Russ Saurer, a University of Michigan wrestler who was one of the stowaways. He added, "After the ship was well clear, he [MacArthur] came to us and told us he had managed to wangle jobs for us to pay our way back home. He put us to work scraping paint all the way to New York."

Upon returning to his corps area headquarters at Baltimore, MacArthur received shortly a message from Summerall which stated, in part: "You alone are responsible for cementing the bonds between disorganized and factional organizations, infusing a spirit and resolution and will to win in the contestants, and maintaining before the world the noblest ideals of American citizenship." During the presidency of Avery Brundage, who succeeded MacArthur at the helm of the American Olympic Committee in 1932, the "MacArthur Room" was established at the Olympic House in New York, and as late as the 1950's an effort was made to enlist his leadership in the United States Olympic Association, as it is now called.[4]

Soon after his return from Amsterdam, MacArthur wrote the official report of the American Olympic Committee on the recent games, which was traditionally addressed to the President of the United States. Forgetting for the moment the bitter dregs of his marital failure and his Army's pitiful condition, MacArthur was still drinking deeply of the sweet triumphs of Amsterdam when he penned the report to Coolidge. The extraordinary document marks the first lengthy burst of that "purple prose" for which MacArthur later became well known:

> In undertaking this difficult task, I recall the passage in Plutarch wherein Themistocles, being asked whether he would rather be Achilles or Homer, replied: "Which would you rather be, a conqueror in the Olympic Games or the crier who proclaims who are conquerors?" And indeed to portray adequately the vividness and brilliance of that great spectacle would be worthy even of the pen of Homer himself. No words of mine can even remotely portray such great moments as the resistless onrush of that matchless California eight as it swirled and crashed down the placid waters of the Sloten; that indomitable will for victory which marked the deathless rush of [Ray] Barbuti; that sparkling combination of speed and grace by Elizabeth Robinson which might have rivaled even Artemis herself on the heights of Olympus. I can but record

the bare, blunt facts, trusting that imagination will supply the magic touch to that which can never be forgotten by those who were actually present . . .

Of equal importance with the actual competitive success which was achieved, it is a matter of pride to report that the American team worthily represented the best traditions of American sportsmanship and chivalry. Imperturbable in defeat, modest in victory, its conduct typified fair play, courtesy and courage. In this most intense competition of highly trained teams the American represented rivalry without bitterness, contest without antagonism and the will to win tempered and restrained by a spirit of mutual consideration and generosity. It was worthy in victory; it was supreme in defeat . . .

To the team I voice a real affection. It has made me proud to be an American. I reserve for my last and greatest tribute, the American Sportsman, that inarticulate public who by their contributions made this enterprise possible, who by their plaudits have inspired the team to its successes, and who by their sympathy and understanding have dignified and ennobled the entire adventure . . .

"Athletic America" is a telling phrase. It is talismanic. It suggests health and happiness. It arouses national pride and kindles anew the national spirit. In its fruition it means a more sturdy, a more self-reliant, a more self-helping people. It means, therefore, a firmer foundation for our free institutions and a steadier, more determined hold on the future. Nothing has been more characteristic of the genius of the American people than is their genius for athletics. Nothing is more synonymous of our national success than is our national success in athletics. If I were required to indicate today that element of American life which is most characteristic of our nationality, my finger would unerringly point to our athletic escutcheon.[5]

Coolidge, who in 1924 had left the final game of the World Series with the score tied in the eighth inning because "he had seen enough," was not another fitness-minded Theodore Roosevelt and probably found MacArthur's rhetoric rather puzzling.[6]

2. Back to Manila

It was fortunate for MacArthur that, in the wake of his marital separation, his official responsibilities kept him happily occupied. A few weeks after his return from Amsterdam he received orders to go to Manila where he was to assume command of the Philippine Department. "No assignment," he remarked, "could have pleased me more." Manila he found to be "as bright and lively as ever," and the four officer-friends with whom he shared his "spacious" quarters "formed a gay and lively group," he said, "and were a source of constant pleasure to me." For one of these men, First Lieutenant Thomas J. Davis, it was the beginning of a tour of duty as aide to MacArthur which would last many years and would ripen into one of the general's most treasured friendships.

Another blessing to MacArthur during this period of personal distress was the warm relationship which developed between him and Governor General Henry L. Stimson, the two having first met when the latter was Taft's Secretary of War. "He is cold, aloof, criticized as being snobbish," a correspondent said of Stimson, "but does the most generous and thoughtful things for those around him. He is a strange mixture of conservatism and liberalism, of pacificism and militarism, of gentility and democracy." In 1927 he had been sent by Coolidge as a special envoy to Nicaragua, which was in the throes of civil war, and in a remarkably short time had, with great diplomatic adeptness and tactfulness, brought about a truce. Though he had been in the Philippines only six months before MacArthur came, Stimson had won the support of many influential Filipinos, principally by employing less peremptory and abrupt tactics than his deceased predecessor, General Wood. "He had a broad and tolerant attitude toward the Filipinos," observed MacArthur, "and was regarded by them with respect and esteem." MacArthur found, too, that "he was a preparedness man, and supported my military training program with understanding and vigor. We became fast friends." When Hoover picked Stimson to be his Secretary of State in 1929, MacArthur sent the appointee a congratulatory letter in which he wrote: "No one could have more truly earned such a place and no one will more truly grace it. I hope and believe it is but a stepping stone to that last and highest call of America, the Presidency." (The "White House benediction" had by this time become a MacArthur trademark reserved as a supreme tribute to certain friends in high places.) In concluding, MacArthur told Stimson, "My association with you has been so delightful personally and so inspiring professionally that no matter who may succeed you in Malacanan I shall have a sense of unreplaceable loss." [7]

MacArthur and Quezon, the Nacionalista leader, were already friends, but their relationship deepened perceptibly during the years 1928–30. MacArthur was a frequent guest in Manuel and Aurora Quezon's home where the men "discussed freely the growing threat of Japanese expansion" and the nascent nationalist movements across Southeast Asia. "The stage was being set," said MacArthur, "for a vast political and social upheaval, vitally affecting every land and race in East Asia. By evolution, or by revolution, nationalism was on its way." When Stimson vacated the governor generalship, Quezon suggested MacArthur as his successor since, according to one source, he "found his proposed policies as acceptable as his manners were agreeable." Hoover chose Dwight F. Davis, however; he also was well known to MacArthur since he had been Secretary of War, 1925–29.[8]

In April, 1929, before Davis' selection, the *New York Times*, quoting a dispatch from Manila, stated:

> According to highly reliable information, the latest active candidate for the Governor Generalship is Gen. MacArthur, commanding the Philippine Department of the American Army.

It is asserted that Gen. MacArthur can have the position if
he really wants it. It is certain that he stands high in the
esteem of Manuel Quezon and other political leaders, who are
not adverse to seeing him at the Malacanan Palace.

According to close friends, Gen. MacArthur has his eyes on
the White House for eight or twelve years hence via a successful administration as Governor Gen. for four years and then
four years in a Cabinet post, either as Sec. of State or Sec. of
War.

Close observers here point to the remarkable intimacy of
Gen. MacArthur and Senor Quezon, who often are seen together on terms of close friendship. The friendship was evident
previous to the service of Gen. MacArthur in the Philippines.
It is now asserted that Senor Quezon is backing the MacArthur
candidacy. In recent weeks Senor Quezon and Gen. Mac-
Arthur have spent much time together. Gen. MacArthur would
seem a logical choice if Washington agrees on the selection of
an Army man.[9]

The writer of this dispatch was probably a Filipino journalist
who kept his ear attuned to the gossip of Manila's higher circles. This is the first, but by no means the last, time that Mac-
Arthur would be accused of harboring political ambitions of
grandiose dimensions. No evidence was found, however, that
MacArthur was considered for the governor generalship, nor
that he desired it. That he considered the presidency the ultimate reward for great soldiers as well as statesmen is evident
from his flattering remarks to some of his superiors, but no
comments by him or his close colleagues before World War II
substantiate the charge that he had the White House in mind
for himself. His affection for Stimson, as well as Quezon, was
as genuine as was his dedication to soldiering. Moreover, even
the least astute politician would not have suggested the Philippine governor generalship as a stepping-stone to the presidency.

Several months before MacArthur took command in the
islands, the Joint Army and Navy Board had approved a more
restricted mission for the Philippine Department, probably

with the emaciated military budget in mind. Previously the primary mission of the Army in case of war with Japan was "to defend Manila and Manila Bay in conjunction with the Asiatic [Naval] Detachment by operating on the offensive-defensive against enemy forces in the Luzon area." The new directive stated that the Army's main mission henceforth in case of an Orange war would be "to hold the entrances to Manila Bay in conjunction with the Asiatic Detachment" and "to hold the Manila Bay Area in conjunction with the Asiatic Detachment as long as possible consistent with the successful accomplishment of [the defense of Manila Bay's entrances]." MacArthur was told by the War Department that "every preparation will be made in these fortifications [at the bay's entrances] to withstand a protracted siege, and Corregidor particularly must hold out to the last extremity." At the same time the Joint Board admitted that its estimates in 1928 showed that Japan could have an army of 300,000 in the islands within a month after the start of war, against which the Philippine Department could pit 11,000 regulars and Scouts, 6000 Constabulary troops, and an air force of nine bombers and eleven pursuit planes. Also, the time of arrival of reinforcements from the States could not be accurately predicted. Moreover, the Five-Power Naval Treaty forbade further fortifications in the Philippines. Like the authorities in the War and Navy Departments, MacArthur considered the Philippines to be "a military asset" and felt the Army should be retained and strengthened there. He was the first to admit, though, that his forces were "pitifully inadequate" for the mission assigned. One of the few realists about the Philippine situation at that time was venerable W. Cameron Forbes, one of the early governor generals, who predicted in 1927 that in a war with Japan "I doubt very much if any real effort will be made to defend the Philippine Islands as such. They are indefensible and from a military point of view not worth defending. The main thing is to make any interference with them as costly as possible." [10] Since it did not work out a plan for relieving the Philippine garrison, the Joint Board also was stating, less frankly than Forbes, that the islands were expendable.

Four months before the great stock market crash of October, 1929, compelled the federal government to cut back on its spending in all areas, Hoover directed Summerall to survey and report on possible economies which could be effected in the military establishment "without manifest injury to adequate national defense," which, of course, was already grossly inadequate. The General Staff set to work soliciting from the various corps area and departmental commanders, as well as bureau chiefs, their recommendations on reductions in expenditures. MacArthur replied that he saw no way to cut expenses further in his department, but he did suggest that the American garrison in China be withdrawn since "changed conditions have rendered its presence in China a source of potential military danger," a fierce border war between Chinese and Russian armies then raging along the Manchurian frontier. The General Staff's report in late 1929, with respect to the Philippines, stated that, though the mission was to hold Manila Bay until reinforcements arrived, this task would involve expenditures for aircraft and mobile elements which were prohibitive. All the General Staff could suggest was that an economical alternative would be to organize an army of Filipino citizen-soldiers to augment the regular garrison in time of emergency. "By judicious handling," the report stated, "it is quite possible that the expense of this development could be transferred to the Philippine Government." As it turned out, however, the world-wide depression, whose impact was soon felt in the islands, precluded the Army's plans to raise such a force.[11]

The question of Philippine independence complicated the role of the Army in future planning for defense of the islands, as MacArthur and Quezon must have discussed on many occa-

sions. Quezon and his Filipino colleagues were giving independence some serious second thoughts as the American Congress prepared to take up the Hawes-Cutting Bill, which would
provide for freedom after a commonwealth period. Stimson
recorded in his diary that Quezon visited him one evening in
January, 1929, and told Stimson that "he had been considering
calling a convention of the Nacionalista party and trying to get
them to commit themselves to a proposition of a thirty years'
delay in independence agitation in return for a responsible
government for the Islands during the meanwhile and freedom
from tariff agitation." Soon Quezon's thinking swung the other
way again, but there were many factors that Filipino nationalists
had to consider beyond their desire to have an independent
Philippines. The depression and the consequent fall in prices
— "in some cases to the lowest level of forty years," reported
Governor General Davis — made many Filipinos more conscious than ever of their nation's dependence upon the United
States. "There is no question," Davis maintained, "that the
one thing which saved the Philippine Islands from a major
economic disaster was the free access to the enormous American market . . . The financial, political, and social effects
which would have followed the loss of this market under the
existing circumstances can hardly be estimated." With 72 per
cent of the islands' total export-import trade being with America, Quezon and other responsible Filipino leaders had good
reason to speculate on the consequences if the Philippines lost
this free market. They were aware that in America the groups
lobbying for the islands' independence included some powerful economic interests which wanted tariff protection against
Philippine imports, such as sugar and coconut oil. If the archipelago were to be set free mainly because of such pressures and
with no consideration for the Philippines' economic future, the
islands would surely face disaster in their trade and would be
economically prostrate in a short time. Even with a gradual

rise in prosperity within the free-market context, the Philippine government would find it difficult to finance a national defense program; without the free market of the United States, which would terminate with independence, the economic collapse would make the building of a Filipino army impossible. Thus the islands would become easy prey for Japan, whose entrepreneurs and settlers already dominated the economy of the Davao region of Mindanao.[12]

MacArthur and his intelligence officers were concerned about the rapidly growing Japanese colony at Davao, but Quezon and other Filipino political and business leaders welcomed the prosperity which Japanese ingenuity and energy were bringing to that region. In 1930 Quezon, who was president of the Philippine Senate, wrote a prominent Japanese capitalist: "I wish you would convey to your associates in your company the idea that the Philippine Government is not unsympathetic to Japanese capital . . . You may rest assured that legitimate Japanese investments in the Philippines which are made under our laws will be duly protected and will receive as much sympathetic consideration from our Government and people as if given to Filipino capital itself." Although Quezon was alert to the menace of Japanese expansion into Southeast Asia, especially after 1931, neither MacArthur nor any other American authority was able to convince him that the economic influence the Nipponese had and were extending in the Davao area could become a threat to the Philippines.[13]

A phenomenon of slight consequence during MacArthur's previous tour of duty in the islands, but now causing some consternation among officials, was the Communist movement in Luzon, whose numbers grew as the depression worsened. Davis said of the Philippine Communists in 1930: "Their activities have been primarily centered in Manila, and they make no secret of the fact that they receive instructions and financial aid from the Soviet Government of Russia." He saw little chance of the Reds "securing any large following [among urban workers] for the average laborer is a peaceable individual who realizes that in comparison with his status of some years ago he is now much better situated." But, Davis observed, "Among farm tenants and laborers, the situation is by no means so secure." There was a widespread feeling among the rural people that they were "ground down by usurious interest rates" and "frequently deprived of lands" to which they were entitled. "Among such people," he warned, "the speeches of a professional agitator may find receptive listeners and the situation is one which requires careful watching." MacArthur undoubtedly was kept informed by his G-2 of the activities of Communist agitators, but his public addresses of that period were on other themes, particularly the need for whites and Filipinos to show more tolerance, sympathy, and respect for each other's needs, interests, and ways.[14]

As departmental commander, MacArthur's principal duties were concerned with training, maneuvers, inspections, equipment, and the host of other routine matters that make up the activities of an overseas department during peacetime. He obtained a chemical warfare company for his department, successfully opposed a move to sell the United States–owned oil storage facilities at the port of Manila to private interests, and secured quarters for the 31st Infantry in some unused public buildings in Manila — a distinct improvement over the regiment's former housing at the ramshackle Santa Lucia barracks. As might be expected, MacArthur emphasized organized athletics in his command. The annual department-wide athletic meet, staged at Fort McKinley in December, 1929, was the grandest yet, with four days of competition in track and field events, baseball, volleyball, swimming, boxing, and other sports. His "Philippine Olympics" was climaxed with a vaudeville show and a dance on the last evening in honor of the victors.

As in the past, the major excitements in the department in

1928–30 were the calls for the Army's assistance after natural disasters which periodically struck the islands. In the autumn of 1928 alone, there were three major natural catastrophes: a typhoon took over 500 lives, injured several thousand persons, and destroyed an estimated 25,000 houses; an earthquake, described as "the strongest ever felt" in Cotabato Province, caused widespread destruction; and Mayon Volcano, near Albay, erupted for several weeks, hurling its lava and ashes on crops and homes for miles around it. In these situations and other lesser emergencies, the Philippine Department rushed aid to stricken Filipino families, including food, clothing, tents, and medical supplies, and dispatched troops to maintain law and order in ravaged areas where the undermanned Philippine Constabulary needed help. In a message to MacArthur in late 1928, Stimson cited "the many acts of assistance and kindliness" which the officers and men of the Philippine Department had rendered to the Filipinos: "The Army stood ready, as always, to render first aid to those who were in need." [15]

Except for occasional natural disasters and public disorders, however, MacArthur's days in Manila passed pleasantly and calmly. By the spring of 1930 he must have been wondering where his next tour of duty would be. The usual term of a departmental commander was two years, so he anticipated his transfer orders would come in a few months. In the far-off rooms of the War Department, where officers' careers were made and unmade by the stroke of a pen, serious thought was being given to MacArthur's capabilities for a very special tour of duty.

3. *The Pinnacle*

Early in his administration President Hoover began to show interest in MacArthur. Summerall cabled MacArthur in July,

1929: "The President desires to appoint you as Chief of Engineers . . . He is convinced of your organizing ability and professional qualifications." The Army engineers were then developing a massive flood-control system for the Mississippi Valley where disastrous inundations had recently occurred. MacArthur discussed the opportunity with Colonel Edward A. Brown, his adjutant general and a friend since their days together at West Point. Brown urged him to accept the post, although MacArthur had not been on regular duty with the engineers since 1912 and had transferred to the infantry in 1917. But MacArthur turned down the position and recommended his former instructor at West Point, Brigadier General Lytle Brown, who subsequently was awarded the post. In his memoirs MacArthur said that he realized the chief of engineers should be an officer of "outstanding engineering ability, and that ability must be of such general recognition as to give him the complete confidence of the engineering profession at large. I had neither of these qualifications." His correspondent-friend Frazier Hunt said that MacArthur also was aware that "if he accepted the appointment, he would set a roadblock against his chances of ever being made Chief of Staff." The decision was a shrewd one, for his elevation to chief of engineers would have brought a loud uproar from that most professional of military corps. Ed Brown was "disgusted" at his decision and predicted that he had dug his "professional grave," but MacArthur wisely foresaw that, instead, his career would have been wrecked in the office of chief of engineers.[16]

Washington observers said that the cabinet member who, next to Secretary of the Interior Ray L. Wilbur, was closest to Hoover was Patrick J. Hurley, the suave, politically ambitious Oklahoma oil millionaire who became Secretary of War in late 1929. When the Senate's committee on territories was discussing the issue of Philippine independence the next spring, Hurley wrote its chairman, Senator Hiram Bingham, giving his

inexperienced viewpoint on the question. Well acquainted
with War Department methods, MacArthur knew that the decision on the next chief of staff was imminent since Summerall
was to retire that autumn. On May 22 he sent Hurley an epistle
packed with sycophancy, which was probably obvious to any
reader except the vain, proud Secretary himself:

> I have just read in the local papers your letter to Senator
> Bingham dealing with the Philippine problem, and I cannot
> refrain from expressing to you the unbounded admiration it
> has caused me. It is the most comprehensive and statesman-
> like paper that has ever been presented with reference to this
> complex and perplexing problem. At one stroke it has clari-
> fied issues which have perplexed and embarrassed statesmen for
> the last thirty years. If nothing else had ever been written
> upon the subject, your treatise would be complete and abso-
> lute. It leaves nothing to be said and has brought confidence
> and hope out of the morass of chaos and confusion which has
> existed in the minds of millions of people. It is the most states-
> manlike utterance that has emanated from the American Gov-
> ernment in many decades and renews in the hearts of many of
> us our confirmed faith in American principles and ideals. You
> have done a great and courageous piece of work and I am sure
> that the United States intends even greater things for you in
> the future. Please accept my heartiest congratulations not only
> for yourself personally but the great nation to which we both
> belong.[17]

Hearing nothing on the chief of staff situation, MacArthur
asked the adjutant general of the Army on July 7 to give him
the II Corps Area as his next command. Since his mother then
lived in Washington and his former wife resided in New York,
the headquarters of that corps area, MacArthur's request is in-
triguing, especially some of its phrasing: "I have never before made special application for station, and I earnestly solicit
favorable consideration. The most impelling personal reasons
dictate the request." He also asked to be allowed to make an

inspection trip through China and Japan en route to the States after his transfer from Manila had been authorized. The adjutant general replied that his requests would be considered.[18]

In 1930 MacArthur ranked seventh in seniority among the major generals on the active list, but none of those ahead of him had more than two years left before reaching the age of sixty-four and compulsory retirement. Of the eleven major generals who had at least four years of active duty remaining, the expected length of a chief of staff's term, MacArthur was the youngest at fifty. Pershing's choice was said to have been Fox Conner, who had been his operations chief in the World War and in 1930 was commanding the Hawaiian Department, but Pershing was too occupied in France with his pet project, the American Battle Monuments Commission, to push Conner's candidacy with vigor. William D. Connor, the capable head of the Army War College and later superintendent of West Point, was another strong possibility. Both of these officers, like MacArthur, became major generals in 1925. Of those who had attained that rank since 1925, the most promising were Malin Craig and Frank R. McCoy. All of the eleven eligible generals had distinguished records in the World War, wherein most of them had served at the brigade level like MacArthur, but none approached him in publicity garnered or medals received from their combat experiences. Most of these men had served on the General Staff and had commanded corps areas or overseas departments, but only MacArthur had headed the United States Military Academy and was a familiar name to congressmen. Moreover, none of the other ten had filled a post which attracted national and world attention comparable to MacArthur's Olympic presidency.

According to the Army's hallowed seniority system, MacArthur was the man for the job since he was the senior-ranking major general, his date of appointment preceding those of the other two officers achieving that rank in 1925. But there is a strong likelihood that MacArthur would have been given the nod even if he had been lower on the list of eligible major generals in view of the influential men behind his candidacy and Pershing's preoccupation elsewhere. Chief of Staff Summerall's preference was probably MacArthur since he had worked with him more closely than with the others and was known to admire his abilities as a staff organizer and leader of troops. General March, the chief of staff during World War I, heartily recommended MacArthur to Hoover for the position. Hurley is said to have balked at the suggestion of MacArthur at first, reputedly having remarked that "a man who couldn't hold his women shouldn't be Chief of Staff." But sometime in early summer, 1930, Hurley was converted, probably by Summerall rather than MacArthur's flattering correspondence. The President, it will be recalled, had been so enamored of MacArthur that he wanted him to head an arm to which he no longer belonged and with which he had not been actively associated for eighteen years. Hoover later said of his appointment of MacArthur as chief of staff, "I therefore searched the Army for younger blood, and I finally determined upon General Douglas MacArthur. His brilliant abilities and his sterling character need no exposition from me." Pershing returned from Europe just after the decision had been made. When informed of the choice at a meeting with Hoover and Hurley, he allegedly commented, "Well, Mr. President, he is one of my boys. I have nothing more to say." [19]

In announcing the appointment of the new chief of staff to the press on August 6, Hoover was quoted as saying that MacArthur "is the only one of the Major Generals having a sufficient period to serve in the Army before retirement to serve the full four-year term as Chief of Staff." The next day the *New York Times* listed the other ten major generals who were eligible and "deplored" the President's "blunder" in overlooking them, especially since some had "the same qualifications with MacArthur": "Feeling in the Army will be that the records and qualifications of the ten officers . . . should have received consideration." The War Department immediately issued a corrective statement to the effect that "the President said that General MacArthur was the senior-ranking Major General who could serve the full term." Since he had not actually "jumped" over any eligible general outranking him, the "tempest in a teapot" died quickly. A few days later the *New York Times* admitted that "less than the expected amount of outcry thus far has followed the selection of Douglas MacArthur . . . Perhaps this is because General MacArthur has distinguished himself in many fields, has been twice wounded in action, possesses a personality of rare charm and is popular in the service." The journalist, however, could not resist a final, but poorly aimed jab: "Perhaps also some have remembered that the last beneficiary of 'jumping' was a certain Captain John J. Pershing, who lived to justify what Theodore Roosevelt did for him [in elevating him directly to brigadier general]." Another article in the same issue, on the other hand, described MacArthur as "a dashing, fascinating figure," who "personifies the beau sabreur." The Washington *National Tribune* pointed out the contrast in temperament and appearance between the "stocky," "methodical," and "strict" Summerall and the "rangy," "dashing," and "debonair" MacArthur, adding that, in spite of their differences, each was worthy of the office of chief of staff — "the supreme goal of every military man." [20]

MacArthur's departure from Manila on September 19 was preceded by a number of social events in his honor, climaxed by a grand banquet at the Manila Hotel, which was attended by dignitaries of the white and Filipino communities. Quezon, Manuel Roxas, and other governmental leaders praised his services and devotion to the Filipino people. MacArthur rose and thanked the speakers; according to a reporter, he then made "a more or less extemporaneous address," which contained

"some rhetoric and still more wisdom and sound sense." His
words are significant because they mark one of his earliest
known public expressions of the principles which were most
important in his simple philosophy:

> Leaving the Philippines is severing the threads of connection
> that have linked me with this country for thirty years. During
> that span of time the world has changed more rapidly than in
> any other period, and one of the notable features of that change
> is the shift of the center of interest from the Atlantic to the
> Pacific.
>
> You, in this hall, are engaged in a momentous task. The
> Asiatic continent is at present undergoing an adjustment of its
> Oriental background to an Occidental point of view. How
> can this problem be solved? I cannot give you any norm for
> specific action; but I can offer you broad principles of conduct
> which may help you in its solution.
>
> The first is tolerance. History teaches us that, when two races
> are brought by the working of an inscrutable Providence to
> live together, tolerance, a sympathetic understanding of each
> other's desires, hopes and aspirations, is the inescapable neces-
> sity. It is a quality in the exercise of which both sides find
> honor. It raises to sublimity him who extends it, and him who
> by accepting it, shows his readiness to return it in kind.
>
> The second is balance. Balance is a sense of proportion; a
> due recognition of the relative importance of things. Nothing
> too much. Not an excess of smug virtue, nor of misapplied
> zeal. It is, in a way, a sense of humor — that attainment of
> equanimity which the classics have called the golden mean.
>
> The third is intelligence, or rather intellect — the intellect
> that should govern, rather than emotion. Sentiment is most
> unreliable, and so is emotion. We should endeavor always
> to see the white light of truth through the searching beam of
> intelligence.
>
> The fourth is courage. Courage to maintain one's convic-
> tions; to see a thing through — never giving up when one sets
> his mind on the object of his achievements.[21]

The years ahead of him as military head of the Army would

sorely try his own adherence to these principles. In his memoirs he admitted that, after receiving the news in early August, there was a brief time of hesitation when he "shrank" from "the dreadful ordeal" which he would face as chief of staff. His mother, then in Washington, "sensed what was in my mind," he said, "and cabled me to accept. She said my father would be ashamed if I showed timidity." He returned to the States and, after a short time in San Francisco as IX Corps Area commander, was sworn in as chief of staff on November 21, 1930, assuming at the same time the brevet rank of general. The position was, of course, what he wanted more than anything else, but those who knew him well were not surprised that when he moved into the large red-brick house at Fort Myer which was the traditional residence of the chief of staff, he invited his mother to live with him. Even with all his successes in his spectacular rise and the image of self-confidence which he projected, his mainstay was still his mother, who, to him, was a living symbol of his principles and a constant reminder of the proud family heritage. One of the first tasks to which he set himself in his new, august position was not to order some sweeping reform plan in the military establishment, but to authorize the construction of a sun porch across the second floor of his quarters and the installation of an elevator in the house, both for the convenience of his aging mother.[22]

PART IV

Chief of Staff

CHAPTER XIII

A Matter of Survival

1. Budget Battles

WHEN MACARTHUR CAME TO WASHINGTON in the late autumn of 1930, the Great Depression was entering its second year. Industrial production, bank failures, workers' earnings, unemployment, and other indexes clearly pointed to the ever-worsening condition of the sick economy. For millions of Americans, a dismal, humiliating existence of near starvation was already a reality. Lengthening bread lines and burgeoning shantytowns were apparent in most metropolitan areas, including the national capital. The President, however, continued to proclaim that his limited anti-depression policies would work. He reiterated his belief that, because of the people's "sense of voluntary organization and community service," local welfare and charitable societies would be able to provide adequate care for the unemployed, though the number of jobless citizens was then nearing an unprecedented 8,000,000.

The congressional elections in November, 1930, reflected the public's growing fear of national chaos and disintegrating faith in the leadership of the "Great Engineer." The Republicans lost forty seats in the House of Representatives, but retained a plurality of one for a few more months until several incumbents died, and control passed to the Democrats. In the Senate the two parties were evenly divided after the fall elections, but a coalition of Democrats and Republican insurgents exercised effective control of the upper house. In the next two years the opposition's control of Congress would spell trouble for the administration's measures, particularly the federal budgets, which, in turn, meant difficulty for the Army. It would often seem that the President's congressional foes were more intent upon embarrassing him than combatting the economic crisis. Three weeks before MacArthur ascended to the military headship, Secretary of State Stimson wrote in his diary that he could sense "the ever-present feeling of gloom that pervades everything connected with the Administration." He continued, "I really never knew such unenlivened occasions as our Cabinet meetings . . . I don't remember that there has ever been a joke cracked in a single meeting of the last year and a half, nothing but steady, serious grind . . . How I wish I could cheer up the poor old President." [1]

MacArthur developed a relationship of mutual admiration with the President which was about as close to a friendship as anyone in Washington enjoyed with Hoover, with the exceptions of Wilbur and Hurley. In personality the Hoover-MacArthur relationship seemed to be an attraction of opposites, for the President was a colorless, uninspiring individual who could be cold, even forbidding, in the presence of his few friends. A common denominator between the two men was their liking for Hurley, the debonair Secretary of War whose energy, charm, handsomeness, and social poise made him an excellent "go-between" for the less socially inclined President and chief of staff in their dealings with Congress and the high society of Washington. Both Hoover and MacArthur had exhibited unusual degrees of initiative, self-reliance, efficiency, and intelligence in their rise to the top of their respective vocations, engineering and soldiering. Each respected the other as a first-rate professional in his field; the fact that Hoover was not a politician and had never previously held an elective office probably added to his stature in MacArthur's eyes.

Under the tutelage of Hoover, MacArthur's thinking on political and social theory began to crystallize. The several doctrines of a nonmilitary nature which MacArthur would expound in later decades seem to have stemmed from *American Individualism,* a little book which Hoover wrote in 1922 setting forth his rather simple philosophy. Neither man ever deviated far from the ideas expressed in this work, and after the Second World War Hoover would look upon MacArthur as one of the few leaders still active on the stage of history who truly believed as he did. The "rugged individualism" about which Hoover wrote was neither a complex nor an original concept. The virile, free growth of individualism had made America unique and great, he asserted, and it was the key to solving the inequities of society. To Hoover, the reactionary, caste-ridden individualism of Europe was loathsome, as was also the perverted form in America which consisted of "selfish snatching and hoarding of the common product." In order to avert the failures of degenerate Europe, which knew only to turn to venomous socialism as an alternative, Hoover proposed an idealistic individualism based on equality of opportunity and social responsibility. Equality of opportunity meant that each citizen should be allowed to achieve the position "to which his intelligence, character, ability, and ambition entitle him." The duty of government is to protect the citizen's liberty to rise according to his talents and motivation, prevent his domination by political or economic groups which would thwart his opportunities, and promote cooperation among all citizens, workers and tycoons, to produce a maximum output and a higher standard of living. The individual, in turn, should have a sense of social responsibility and service, which would include caring for the unfortunates and the jobless without corrupting their self-reliance and initiative. As for the Great Depression, Hoover looked askance at proposals for direct federal relief and aggressive federal intervention in the economy as menaces to liberty and individualism. Those who espoused federal interference, such as the socialists, were enemies of the "American system." Ultimately President Hoover, who was not a disciple of the Adam Smith form of *laissez faire*, would resort to governmental action to fight the depression, but he would do so with caution, reluctance, and serious misgivings about the consequences for American society. Even in the last days of his life MacArthur could still become excited over these beliefs which were precious to him and Hoover: "The fundamental and ultimate issue at stake is liberty itself — liberty versus the creeping socialization in every domestic field. Freedom to live under the minimum of restraint! A least common denominator of mediocrity against the proven progress of pioneering individualism! The free enterprise system or the cult of conformity! The result will determine the future of civilization." [2]

Because of his and Hurley's high regard for the President, MacArthur tended to blame Congress or the air-power advocates for the troubles which ensued during the struggles to determine military appropriations. He took over as chief of staff near the middle of the fiscal year 1931, which extended from July 1, 1930, to June 30, 1931. The War Department's budget estimate for fiscal 1932 had been submitted to the Bureau of the Budget several months earlier, and the Hoover administration was preparing to submit the federal budget for fiscal 1932 to the session of Congress convening in December, 1930. The War Department had asked for $351 million for its military activities, which was $11 million less than its previous year's request, most of the cut hitting the Air Corps. The Bureau of the Budget reduced the figure another $8 million, but antagonized Summerall and the General Staff by increasing the Air Corps' portion at the sacrifice of the ground arms and civilian components. Thus the stage was set when MacArthur appeared on the scene for a battle between the Army and Congress, which was expected to shave the military budget farther. Moreover, MacArthur's entry came at a time when the General Staff was more determined than ever that there would be a balanced distribution among the various arms and components of the meager funds which the Army could expect for the duration of the economic crisis.[3] As his subsequent actions would show, MacArthur heartily concurred in the conservative viewpoint which Summerall expressed in his final report as chief of staff:

> The sufficiency of appropriations for military purposes has, of course, to be considered in connection with the general fiscal situation of the country and its needs for other governmental purposes . . . [But] the funds provided have been insufficient for even an approximate realization of the military system contemplated in the national defense act . . .
>
> No element in our military forces is independent of the others but each is affected by the state of development of the others. Our tendency in the apportionment of funds for various purposes has, however, frequently been in the contrary direction. We have in recent years, for example, materially added to the strength of our bombardment aviation, but the first major bombing mission on the outbreak of war would exhaust our entire stock of bombs. With our increase in aviation, there has been no parallel development of the related antiaircraft defense. The state of development of all elements of our forces should be considered simultaneously, and our military policy in respect to the development of our forces, whether in the way of expansion or reduction, should be expressed in general projects extending over a period of years.[4]

For the next five years MacArthur faithfully assumed Summerall's stance of reluctant acquiescence in budget reductions because of the fiscal emergency and dogged resistance to any imbalancing of the distribution of funds in favor of one arm. Mac-

Arthur, however, was more concerned about protecting the personnel of the military establishment — numbers of officers and enlisted men, their pay, allowances, and other benefits — since he feared that any imbalance in appropriations would be in favor of matériel over personnel, not simply one arm over another. His views, which would not change in the next five years, were evident during his first appearance as chief of staff before the House's subcommittee on military appropriations. At its hearings in December, 1930, he told the congressmen that the military budget for fiscal 1932 was reasonable and satisfactory in view of the financial stringency of the times. He felt that it provided for a balanced, if minimum, program of training, operations, and supply and was not marred by the "eccentricities of any individual or group" — an obvious jab at the air-power enthusiasts who wanted more aircraft even if it meant a cutback in manpower. On the other hand, the spokesmen for the Air Corps, Major General James E. Fechet, its chief, and F. Trubee Davison, the assistant secretary of war for air, argued vehemently at the hearings in favor of increased appropriations for research, development, and procurement of more planes, especially bombers. In the spring Congress finally approved the War Department's 1932 budget, the total for military activities being $340 million, or $7 million less than the sum appropriated for the previous year. No arm received funds close to its original asking, but the Air Corps fared better than the others.[5]

A champion of air power and mechanization and MacArthur's chief antagonist during his tour as chief of staff was Representative Ross A. Collins of Mississippi, who was chairman of the important subcommittee on military appropriations. "Ordinarily, he is a quiet-mannered man," a reporter noted, "who speaks softly and with a slow drawl," but he is also "a past master of political satire." Again and again Collins, who had long been an admirer of Mitchell, would challenge MacArthur's statements in congressional hearings, mainly attacking the chief of staff's stubborn refusal to cut back on his active and reserve officer corps in order to provide more funds for modernization of the Army's weapons system, particularly aircraft and tanks. A disciple of Basil H. Liddell Hart, the British military thinker, Collins repeatedly hurled his invectives against what he charged was the General Staff's tradition-bound notions of manpower needs and its blindness to the mechanization which would be essential for victory in the next war. MacArthur asserted, in response, that he and the General Staff were keenly interested in mechanization and modernization and realized their great significance in future warfare, but he inevitably returned to the depressed conditions and fiscal stringency which, he maintained, made it impossible for the Army to do more than develop pilot models of new bombers, tanks, and other costly weapons. Procurement of such matériel on a large-scale basis would mean abolition of the reserve components and further skeletonizing of the Regular Army's personnel, to which he was adamantly opposed. The influential *Army and Navy Journal,* which was edited by John C. O'Laughlin, an admirer of MacArthur who also happened to be aware of the fact that his subscribers were military persons and not machines, denounced Collins and the "little group of willful men" on his subcommittee who were trying to reshape American military policy contrary to the dictates of the hallowed National Defense Act of 1920. If they succeeded, the journal warned, "past and future legislation would be valueless. These men, forming the majority of the subcommittee, will become the real dictators of the Republic." [6]

With the depression deepening each month, Hoover held a meeting of his chief military and political advisers at his Rapidan, Virginia, retreat. The desperate President called upon Hurley and MacArthur to find ways immediately to reduce military spending; he suggested a cutback in personnel by forced retirements and abandonment of semi-active military installations. Later that month, May, 1931, the War Department announced the closing of fifty-three posts, most of which did not have garrisons of company size or larger. Reductions of 15 per cent were required in the headquarters staffs of the nine corps areas, and efforts were made to reduce the enormous amount of paper work demanded by the War Department.

Most far-reaching of the changes inaugurated in the late spring of 1931 was MacArthur's decision to disband Major Adna R. Chaffee's experimental mechanized force, a pioneer armored unit which had been organized three years before at Fort Meade, Maryland. The chief of staff then ordered a complete restudy of mechanization of ground combat, finally concluding that it would be more economical and feasible to allow each arm to develop its armored vehicles separately. The decentralization of the Army's program of mechanization, according to most later authorities, retarded its development of modern tanks and caused the American Army to fall far behind the major European military powers in the development of armored warfare tactics. The Germans, for example, would shortly begin experimenting with independent armored divisions, the fruition of which would be shockingly apparent in September, 1939, as the Nazi Panzers raced across the plains of Poland. Likewise, the Russians purchased two American-made Christie tanks, vehicles of the most advanced tank design in the early 1930's, and developed therefrom the family of tanks which would serve them well in World War II and would outclass any tanks developed by the American Army. In 1931 the United States Army had seven of the Christie tanks, but funds for further experimentation in their design and usage were nonexistent or were siphoned off to meet other needs of the Army. In fairness to MacArthur, however, it must be added that, in view of the virtual strangulation of Army funds through the early 1930's, American tank development could not have progressed far even if it had received more emphasis.[7]

MacArthur found himself fighting an uphill battle again

when hearings before Collins' subcommittee on the fiscal 1933 budget convened in December, 1931. The War Department had asked $331 million for its military activities, and the Bureau of the Budget had cut it $15 million in incorporating the Army's asking in the federal budget presented to the House subcommittee. Hurley cautioned the congressmen that "the pressure of economy which has dominated the military estimates during the past several years has weakened our military establishment to a perceptible extent and has eliminated the possibility of further interior economies. Retrenchment when it cripples the national defense ceases to be economy." As expected, Major General Benjamin F. Foulois, the new chief of the Air Corps, and Assistant Secretary of War Davison argued for more funds for military aviation. They also raised anew before Collins' subcommittee the need for separate departmental status for the Air Corps. Collins seemed to be determined to slash funds for the National Guard, Organized Reserves, R.O.T.C., and C.M.T.C. in order to allot more to mechanization and development of new ground and air weapons. Pressured by powerful National Guard interests in their states, Governor Franklin D. Roosevelt of New York and other governors wrote letters to their congressional delegations protesting against cutting funds of the National Guard. In a move probably intended to embarrass Hoover on the eve of his campaign for reelection, Collins held the Army appropriations bill in his subcommittee until early May, 1932. When the bill was finally introduced on the floor of the House, it came as a shock to the Army and its supporters. The bill provided for $24 million less than the administration's figure, and, causing the most uproar, it included an amendment calling for a reduction in the number of regular officers on active duty from 12,000 to 10,000. Since Collins had not intimated at a cut in officers when MacArthur appeared earlier before his subcommittee, the chief of staff was justifiably upset.[8] In desperation, MacArthur resorted to the political technique of the public letter. On May 9 he gave to reporters a copy of a letter which he was sending to Representative Bertrand D. Snell, minority leader of the House. It set forth the position to which he tenaciously clung throughout his tour as chief of staff:

> In the hearings held by the military subcommittee on appropriations, no indication was given that a reduction of 2,000 officers was contemplated. In consequence, no opportunity has been afforded me to express the opinion of the War Department on such a revolutionary step. As the military adviser of the Government I am, therefore, taking the liberty of presenting to you the views of the General Staff on this important matter, with the hope that you will lay them before the House.
>
> Skilled officers, like all other professional men, are products of continuous and laborious study, training and experience. There is no short cut to the peculiar type of knowledge and ability they must possess. Trained officers constitute the most vitally essential element in modern war, and the only one that under no circumstances can be improvised or extemporized.
>
> An army can live on short rations, it can be insufficiently clothed and housed, it can even be poorly armed and equipped, but in action it is doomed to destruction without the trained and adequate leadership of officers. An efficient and sufficient corps of officers means the difference between victory and defeat.
>
> It is for these reasons and because of the further fact that the success of the American system of (non-conscription) preparedness is peculiarly dependent upon the continued existence of an adequate corps of professional officers, that the War Department views with the utmost concern the proposal in the Army appropriations bill to reduce permanently by more than 16% the number of officers.
>
> Prior to 1920 there existed in the world only two general systems under which military forces were organized and maintained. The basis of one was the conscript; of the other, the professional soldier . . .
>
> The principal element of the American system is two-fold. The first is a small professional force to act as a training cadre

— a covering force in case of need, and a framework upon which mobilization of our full force could be effected. The second essential element is a partially developed organization of citizen soldiers divided into a National Guard and various classifications of reserve and other groupments, backed by a continuous program of limited military training for these elements in time of peace . . .

The Regular Army is the bulwark and basis of the whole structure. It is the instructor, the model and, in emergency, the leader of the whole. The only continuing body in which resides the professional knowledge and technical skill capable of accumulating, organizing, training, and leading to a victory a national army of citizen soldiers is the professional officer corps . . .

. . . In the interest of economy the strength of the professional force was fixed at the minimum considered by Congress in 1920 to be consistent with safety — namely, 18,000 officers and 285,000 enlisted men. Yet during the past decade this strength has been progressively decreased until today it stands at approximately 12,000 officers and 125,000 men.

With a vivid realization of the need for rigid economy in public expenditures, the next War Department budget sacrifices everything in excess of bare necessities. But the Department insists that any retrenchment which destroys or seriously damages a vital element of our already weakened defensive structure is not economy but extravagance of the most expensive kind.

The War Department has frequently reported to Congress that the minimum peace strength of the Regular Army at which it can carry out the missions assigned by the National Defense Act, and make a reasonable preparation for a complete and immediate mobilization in the event a national emergency is declared by Congress, is 14,063 officers and 165,000 enlisted men . . .

Among the armies of the world, the American ranks 16th in strength, although this nation ranks fourth in population and first in wealth. Further reductions would bring us to prostration — a condition not conducive to the promotion of a feeling of security at home nor to enhancing the respect with which our pacific counsels are received abroad.[9]

In spite of MacArthur's efforts, however, the House passed Collins' bill by a margin of 201 to 182, thanks especially to strong support from House Speaker John Nance Garner and Representative Joseph W. Byrns, the chairman of the committee on appropriations who was known as a big-navy advocate. Nevertheless, in the Senate the officer-reduction amendment was defeated, and Collins was unsuccessful in his attempt in the House to override the Senate's veto. The fiscal 1933 military appropriation which was finally approved was only $305 million, the lowest since 1923, but MacArthur was happy because his treasured officer corps had come through unscathed. In a jubilant mood after the House defeated Collins' override move in mid-July, MacArthur sent a telegram to Frederick H. Payne, assistant secretary of war for procurement, who was then in Massachusetts: "Just hogtied a Miss. cracker. House voted our way 75 to 54. Happy times are here again." The anti-Collins *Army and Navy Journal* praised "the gruelling labor involved, the tactful consideration displayed, the careful thought necessary" when "for seven long, dreary months General MacArthur fought the forces of destruction in the Congress." O'Laughlin prophesied, however, that "should the Democrats retain control of the House in the next Congress, Representative Collins doubtless will renew his officer cut demands."

MacArthur was also pleased to see the defeat in that session of several bills which would have established a department of national defense. Some of the measures would also have authorized a separate department of air forces, coordinate with the departments of War and Navy, with all three under the defense department. Proponents claimed that such a system would be conducive to "effecting greater economies" and "would improve the efficiency of the national defense." On the other hand, MacArthur was convinced that the scheme would be "inefficient, uneconomical, and uselessly cumbersome." Voicing the conservatism that had dominated the General Staff since the World War, he concluded, "Governmentally, we have to-day,

Arthur MacArthur, I, Douglas' grandfather.

Captain and Mrs. Arthur MacArthur with their sons Arthur, III, and Douglas (in white), probably at Fort Leavenworth, Kansas, c. 1886.

Right. Douglas at thirteen.

General Arthur MacArthur (Douglas' father) and his staff in the Philippines, 1901.

Left. Cadet MacArthur of West Texas Military Academy, 1896.

Varsity baseball team, West Point, 1901. Douglas MacArthur is seated at the far right.

Lieutenant MacArthur, at ease.
High Point, Virginia, c. 1906.

Demolitions expert, at Fort Leavenworth, c. 1908.

Right. General Mann and Colonel MacArthur supervising the training
of the Rainbow Division, Long Island, 1917.

Officers of the 84th Brigade, Rainbow Division, near Fresnes, France, August, 1918. *From left to right:* Lieutenant Reginald Weller, Captain Walter Wolf, Brigadier General Douglas MacArthur, Lieutenant William Wright, Lieutenant Wilfred Bazinet.

MacArthur in his brigade headquarters at St. Benoît château, St. Mihiel salient, September, 1918.

MacArthur observing the St. Mihiel offensive with French and American officers, between Béney and St. Benoît, France, September, 1918.

On the eve of the armistice, near Sedan, November, 1918.

MacArthur receives the DSM from General Pershing, Remagen, Germany, March, 1919.

Right. General and Mrs. MacArthur arriving from the Philippines, March, 1925.

Mary MacArthur with picture of her son, c. 1925.

Major General MacArthur in 1925.

The Major General addresses CMTC students at Fort Howard, Maryland, c. 1927.

The Chief of Staff with Generals Weygand and Gamelin, Rheims, France,
September, 1931.

MacArthur, Chief of Staff, with Admiral Pratt at a parade in Alexandria, Virginia, February, 1932.

Reviewing stand, Army Day parade, Alexandria, Virginia, April, 1932. *From left to right:* General MacArthur, Mrs. Hurley, Secretary of War Patrick Hurley, President Hoover, Mrs. Hoover, Admiral Sims.

During the eviction of the Bonus Army, July, 1932.

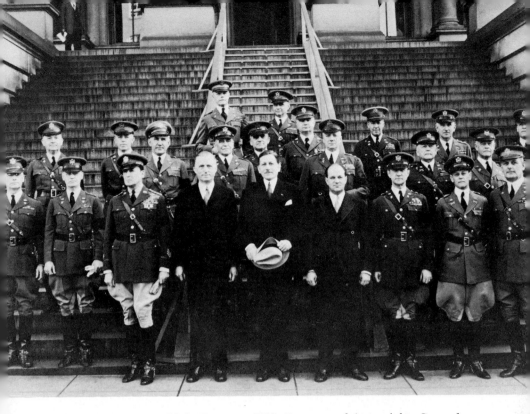

War Department chiefs, January, 1933. *Front row left to right:* Generals Andrew Moses, John DeWitt, Douglas MacArthur, Colonels Frederick Payne, Patrick Hurley, Honorable F. Trubee Davison, Generals George Moseley, Guy Henry, Frederick Coleman. *Second row left to right:* Generals Charles Bridges, Francis Parker, Irving Carr, Blanton Winship, Robert Patterson, Stephen Fuqua, John Preston. *Third row left to right:* Generals Harry Gilchrist, Samuel Hof, George Leach, John Gulick, Colonel Alfred Smith. *Back row left to right:* General Charles Kilbourne, Colonel Julian Yates.

Planning Army maneuvers at Camp Dix and Fort Monmouth, New Jersey, September, 1934. *From left to right:* Generals Andrew Moses, George Simonds, Hugh Drum, MacArthur, Robert Callan, Charles Kilbourne, John Hughes, and Oscar Westover. General Alfred Smith is just out of the picture to the left.

A lighter moment. MacArthur, Secretary of War George Dern, and President Roosevelt in Washington, probably 1934.

MacArthur and his staff arriving in Manila, October, 1935. Major Dwight Eisenhower is seen second from left, in the row behind MacArthur.

Left. Leaving the White House, February, 1935.

MacArthur and Quezon at a banquet at Manila, c. 1936.

Right. MacArthur and his bride, the former Miss Jean Faircloth, leaving the municipal building, New York City, after their marriage, April, 1937.

MacArthur as Philippine military adviser, probably spring, 1940.

With Sir Robert Brooke-Popham, British air chief marshal, in Manila, October, 1941.

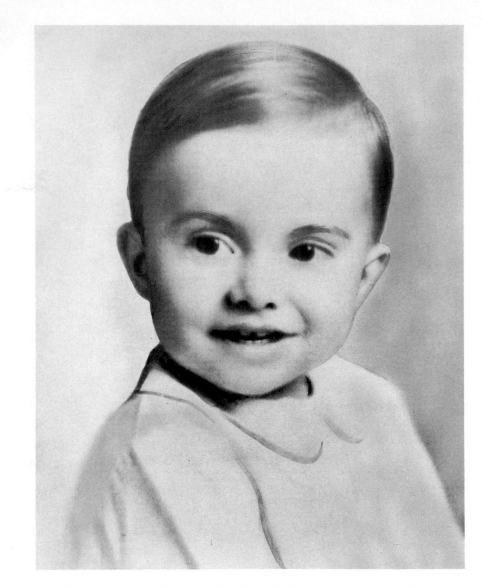

Arthur MacArthur, IV, about the time of the Japanese invasion, December, 1941.

from the standpoint of national strategy and policy, the strongest possible organization for war. It seems almost incomprehensible that this organization, which incidentally has been the envy of soldiers, sailors, and statesmen abroad, should be tampered with in its major elements in favor of a highly speculative experiment." His words were undoubtedly seconded by his predecessors, Summerall, Hines, Pershing, and March, as well as the overwhelming majority of other general officers. It would take another great war to alter the Army's thinking on these matters.[10]

2. *Relief Activities and Organizational Reforms*

The War Department expended more of the taxpayers' money and employed more persons than any other department of the federal government. Therefore it was involved, willingly or not, in combating the Great Depression, and its contributions may have been the most significant federal efforts in that struggle during the Hoover administration. The War Department administered a wide assortment of nonmilitary activities, which included the Inland Waterways Corporation, the main barge line on the Mississippi River and several of its tributaries; the nitrate plants and uncompleted hydroelectric facilities at Muscle Shoals on the Tennessee River; the cable and telegraph systems in Alaska; the Bureau of Insular Affairs, which supervised colonial affairs in Puerto Rico and the Philippines; the canal, railway, and steamship line of Panama; the Dominican customs receivership; over 100 military parks and cemeteries in America and overseas, including eight large A.E.F. cemeteries in France; the Nicaraguan interoceanic canal survey; the national rifle and pistol matches held annually at Camp Perry, Ohio; flood-control projects in the Mississippi and Sacramento valleys; and hundreds of engineering operations to improve harbors and navigable waterways. Among the more minute duties, the War Department was charged with lighting the Statue of Liberty, operating a group of retail stores in Panama, maintaining Mount Vernon, and preserving the American portion of Niagara Falls. Congressmen had long been alert to the "pork barrel" possibilities in appropriating funds for some of the above activities, and, with the pressures of the depression, many Capitol Hill politicians saw work-relief potentialities in the extensive engineering projects particularly. Thus Congress, while reducing military spending, readily increased the War Department's nonmilitary funds in the early 1930's. In fiscal 1932, for instance, the Corps of Engineers was allotted $114 million for its rivers and harbors projects, on which it employed over 40,000 civilians.

Principally through the National Guard, the War Department also engaged in a limited amount of direct relief to depression-stricken areas upon specific requests from state governors. The department sometimes authorized commanders of posts near communities severely hit by unemployment and foreclosures to loan cots, blankets, and tents from post stocks to accredited charitable agencies. Beginning in the winter of 1930–31, the department made available to such societies for purchase at nominal prices Army stocks of salvaged shoes, clothing, and other supplies for local distributions. Of some slight benefit, too, during such desperate times were the pay checks which scores of thousands of civilians received for participation in armory drills, summer camps, and temporary active-duty assignments, as the case might be, as members of the National Guard, Organized Reserves, R.O.T.C., or C.M.T.C. MacArthur reported that over 90,000 youths applied for C.M.T.C. in 1932, but, because of inadequate funds and facilities for the camps, the Army could admit only 37,000. In reference to the War Department's multifarious programs and expenditures for its military and nonmilitary activities, Hurley remarked, "In the last analysis this vast sum, except for insignificant purchases in foreign countries and for personal savings out of pay and salaries, was expended for goods and services furnished by the civil population of the United States . . . The great bulk of the appropriations ultimately went to the wage earner." Lest the public be misled as to the real interests of the Washington generals, columnists Robert S. Allen and Drew Pearson pointed out: "All these and many other things the War Department does with some pride, considerable enthusiasm and a varying degree of efficiency. But none of them does it perform with such wholehearted enthusiasm and such unswerving devotion as it goes about the work of its own self-perpetuation." In a sense, their point was well made, for rarely, if ever, did officials and generals of the War Department become excited over budgetary matters of a nonmilitary nature.[11]

Of course, MacArthur was seldom officially concerned with the department's nonmilitary activities except as they involved national defense and war planning. The chief of staff's authority, as defined in the then current *Army Regulations,* covered "primarily duties pertaining to the command, discipline, training, and recruitment of the Army, military operations, distribution of troops, inspections, armament, fortifications, military education and instruction and kindred matters, but includes also in an advisory capacity such duties connected with fiscal administration and supply as are committed to him by the Secretary of War." His supervisory control extended over all bureaus, arms, agencies, and components of the military establishment, but, in practice, MacArthur did not interfere in some sacrosanct areas, for instance, the activities of the Corps of Engineers. According to a plan drafted by the General Staff shortly after the World War and "revitalized" by MacArthur, the chief of staff also was to become commanding general of all field forces when war occurred, his headquarters to be patterned after Pershing's general headquarters of 1917–18.[12]

One of MacArthur's first undertakings as chief of staff was to
improve the administrative efficiency of the General Staff. Since
the World War, the General Staff had followed the divisional
structure set up by Pershing at Chaumont. An assistant chief
of staff headed each of the five divisions, which were G-1, administration and personnel; G-2, intelligence; G-3, training and
operations; G-4, supply; and the war plans division. "Unfortunately, however," MacArthur commented, "these General
Staff divisions, or some of them, have grown into small bureaus,
entirely too self-contained. The chief of each such division has
generally presented his case to the Chief of Staff either directly
or through the Secretary of the General Staff." Somewhat reminiscent of the autonomy and bickering between bureaus that
existed when Wood took over as chief of staff three decades
earlier, the General Staff's divisions, MacArthur attested, had
"little or no proper meeting of the minds on important subjects.
Uncoordinated action has too often resulted. Here and there
administrative work has been taken over by these divisions in
violation of the law, and to the embarrassment of work of first
importance."

With Hurley's approval, MacArthur corrected the situation
by creating a general council of the General Staff, which would
meet periodically for the purposes of "reviewing and properly
coordinating all major War Department projects, and passing
on matters of current policy." Brigadier General George Van
Horn Moseley, MacArthur's deputy chief of staff and close
friend, would serve as president of the general council, whose
membership would consist of the five assistant chiefs of staff
and the executive officers of the two assistant secretaries of war
(for air and procurement). Other key officials of the War Department, such as the adjutant general and bureau chiefs,
might sit with the general council during discussions relating
to their responsibilities. The body was to be strictly advisory;
its recommendations went to MacArthur, who, if he concurred,

sent them to Hurley. Since the Secretary of War almost invariably agreed with MacArthur's judgments on military matters, the fate of the general council's memorandums was usually decided in the chief of staff's office. There was no uproar comparable to that which Wood provoked with his changes in 1911–12 since, unlike the judge advocate general, inspector general, and other bureau heads, the assistant chiefs of staff served four-year terms and did not become entrenched in their positions. As MacArthur had hoped, the new system resulted in "better work and better feeling throughout the War Department." [13] Indeed, it is difficult to comprehend how the ninety-two officers of the General Staff had functioned that long without such a central coordinating body.

MacArthur's chief contribution in organizational reform during his early years as chief of staff was his four-army plan. The nine corps area commands were the Army's main agencies for normal training activities and also for mobilization in time of war. They were responsible directly to the General Staff and were simply administrative organizations set up along territorial lines, with no network of command linking them horizontally and providing unified tactical functioning. In the summer of 1932 MacArthur brought together the units of the various corps areas in a tactical framework of four armies, which would provide "a logical and definite basis for initial expansion" when mobilization was necessary. The armies' missions would be primarily the defense of the North Atlantic coast and the northeastern frontier of the United States (First Army), the Great Lakes region and the central northern frontier (Second Army), the Gulf of Mexico area and the southern frontier (Third Army), and the Pacific coast (Fourth Army). The army commanders, who would be the senior corps area commanders in the respective army zones, would assume responsibility for the training of tactical units as field forces, which would be concentrated periodically for army-level maneuvers. Routine training and supply duties would be left to the corps area commands. By exercising such tactical and war planning functions, the armies' headquarters would be at all times in a state of instant readiness for assembling their field forces in the event of war. The armies would be interrelated through the A.E.F.-style general head-quarters, mentioned earlier, which would be headed by the chief of staff acting as commander of all field forces. The four-army plan, MacArthur asserted, would eliminate the confusion and delay which occurred in previous emergencies when "the War Department has invariably been compelled to relinquish to one or more virtually independent field commanders its func-tions in the control of operations, while the Department itself has been overwhelmed with matters relating to organization, administration, supply and other features of mobilization."

The four-army organization, of course, did not suddenly come into existence merely by MacArthur's issuance of an order. The undertaking was as complicated, an officer commented, "as rip-ping out and rewiring under a totally new system the entire telephone exchange of New York City." A year later, neverthe-less, MacArthur reported "encouraging progress" and was con-vinced that his plan was "an effective step toward insuring that the intricacies of a major mobilization will not overwhelm at-tempts at prompt tactical employment of troops." The ex-igencies of World War II would compel General George C. Marshall, the chief of staff in 1939–45, to modify MacArthur's system, but, according to the official Army history of the ground forces' organization in that war, "the training functions of the four army commands created in 1932 contained, in germinal form, the primary mission which was centralized in GHQ in July 1940 and in Army Ground Forces after 9 March 1942." The four-army plan was a monumental step toward readying the Army's tactical organization for its gigantic tasks in the global conflict soon to come.[14]

In early 1931 MacArthur and Admiral William V. Pratt, the

new chief of naval operations, tried to settle a ten-year dispute between the two services regarding responsibility for aerial defense of coasts. The controversy had arisen out of the ambiguous wording of a section of the Army appropriations act of 1920, which stated that the Army's air arm was to control all operations from air bases on land, and naval aviation would be confined to fleet operations and "shore stations whose maintenance is necessary for operations connected with the fleet, for construction and experimentation, and for training of personnel." The Navy interpreted this statement loosely and maintained bombers and pursuit planes at its shore stations, even when Army air bases were nearby. As funds became increasingly scarce with the onset of the Great Depression, the superfluity of the two services' duplicate aerial equipment at locales such as Pearl Harbor was criticized by congressmen and journalists. The MacArthur-Pratt agreement provided that "the naval air force will be based on the fleet . . . The army forces will be land-based and employed as an essential element to the army in the performance of its mission to defend the coasts both at home and in our overseas possessions, thus assuring the fleet absolute freedom of action without responsibility for coast defense." The Navy would retain its air stations ashore, but the aircraft there would be mainly training and scout planes, and "except in an emergency, they will not be used in defense of the coast." The *New York Times* optimistically reported that the agreement produced "a clearer evaluation of the fundamental principles involved in the use of the air weapon" and "is being heralded as the beginning of the closest cooperation that has ever existed between the two great branches of our national defense." [15]

By the next spring, however, MacArthur and Pratt were arguing over the types of aircraft which each service should have. One day in April, 1932, MacArthur saw a paper prepared by Pratt in which the admiral stated that the Navy, not the Army, needed torpedo planes. According to Jay Pierrepont Moffat, a close adviser to Stimson who was in the chief of staff's office at the time, MacArthur "read it through hastily while a look of amazement came over his face; he read it again and the storm burst forth." MacArthur charged, said Moffat, that "now, in one fell swoop, Admiral Pratt was proposing to cancel this agreement [of 1931] by allowing to the Navy weapons which he wished to take away from the Army. Torpedo planes were a form of bombing, and if any bombs were allowed either branch of the Service, he must insist upon the right of the Army to have its share." This was not one of MacArthur's most ingenious arguments nor, fortunately for American forces in the future war against Japan, was he successful in keeping the Navy from having torpedo planes. Although MacArthur told a congressional committee the next month that the issue of coastal air defense was "completely and absolutely settled," the question was reopened after Pratt's retirement in the summer of 1933, with no satisfactory solution during MacArthur's remaining years as chief of staff.

The principal importance of the MacArthur-Pratt agreement is that it made the Army primarily responsible for coastal air defense for at least the several years that the understanding lasted, which was long enough to produce a critical re-evaluation of the mission of the Army Air Corps. Since MacArthur was responsible for the definite assignment of coastal defense to the Army's air arm, the representatives of the Air Corps in the War Department reasoned that now they could justifiably press harder for a long-range bomber to fulfill this job. With the chief of staff in little position to oppose such a proposal, Foulois obtained MacArthur's approval to initiate a design competition among aircraft manufacturers for such an airplane. Two years later the Boeing company came forth with the first experimental model of the B-17, and in early 1936 the Army concluded a contract with Boeing for thirteen of these bombers, later versions of which would gain fame as the "Flying Fortresses" of World War II. The official history of the Army Air Forces in that conflict acknowledges that "the story of the Army's long-range bomber has its beginnings in proposals of 1933" for an airplane "intended for a mission of coastal defense," and "to understand those circumstances, it is necessary to turn back two years to the MacArthur-Pratt agreement of 1931." [16] Thus, so far in the story of MacArthur's relations with military aviation, he has vehemently opposed extra funds for the Air Corps, argued for Army torpedo planes, and concurred in the Air Corps' bid for a long-range aircraft which would become its mainstay of heavy bombardment in the Second World War. It is little wonder that Mitchell had difficulty figuring out MacArthur's position at his court-martial.

3. Aggressors on the Rise

"Troubled and confused" was the way MacArthur described Europe after visiting the continent twice during the critical years 1931–32. In May, 1931, four months before his first journey there as chief of staff, Austria's largest bank, the Kreditanstalt, stopped gold payments, precipitating a financial panic which quickly spread to the rest of West and Central Europe. In September, Great Britain, Europe's main creditor nation, went off the gold standard as its economy also plunged toward disaster. While Benito Mussolini's Fascist regime tightened its hold on Italy, the Radical Socialist and United Socialist parties competed for control of the strife-ridden French Chamber. Anti-republican and Communist organizations were growing fast in all of the continental countries. The depression, which was world-wide by that fall, hastened the disintegration of the Weimar Republic, Germany's half-hearted experiment in parliamentary rule. Since 1929, Adolf Hitler's National

Socialist party had risen phenomenally, its representation in the Reichstag soaring from twelve seats in 1929 to 107 in 1930; by the summer of 1932, the Nazi party would hold 230 seats in the German assembly. When MacArthur reached France in mid-September, 1931, it was obvious that the nation's civilian and military leaders, who had been gripped by a security psychosis since the World War, now, more than ever, feared a resurrection of aggressive German militarism.

Near Rheims, MacArthur attended maneuvers staged on the battlefields where he had fought in 1918; the exercises were hailed as the largest that had been held by the French army since that time. Accompanied by Captain Thomas J. Davis, his aide, and Major James B. Ord of the American military attaché's office in Paris, MacArthur carefully observed the operations of the 60,000 troops, which, along with the supporting armored and air units, used the most modern equipment France had developed. A reporter commented that MacArthur "dashed about today in his own high-powered automobile so swiftly that one high-ranking French officer was moved to comment admiringly, 'He seems to be everywhere at once.' " The maneuvers, said an observer, represented "a duel between speed and numbers, force and science": "The Red Army, under General La Capelle, far superior in numbers but badly concentrated, has the task of attacking a Blue Army few in numbers but much better equipped in all modern methods of warfare." The field exercises, together with his conferences with War Minister André Maginot and Chief of Staff Maxime Weygand, were convincing evidence to MacArthur that speed and mobility would be crucial to victory in future battles. But he was not persuaded that an army as skeletonized and financially starved as his own should strive for large-scale mechanization until its funds were sizable enough to avoid further sacrifices of manpower.[17]

Bearing the insignia of Grand Officer of the Legion of Honor which Maginot had presented to him at the end of his visit in France, MacArthur moved on to Belgrade in late September. There he was granted an audience with King Alexander and was the only foreign guest at the maneuvers of the Yugoslavian army, which he found to be an excellent military force, though still supplied in the field by oxcarts. At a lavish party which the Yugoslavian officials staged in his honor, he surprised his hosts by joining in the *kolo,* a folk dance of that nation somewhat similar to an American square dance. In a speech that evening he told the Yugoslavian generals and ministers that "in the great moral principles of right to liberty and peace, the armies of Yugoslavia and America will march parallel in full accord, not disturbing one another since in all fundamental things Yugoslavia and America are in full accord." In Italy a Fascist newspaper stated, under the headline "In a Glass of Wine," that probably the fermented beverages at the Belgrade party "made General MacArthur abandon himself to political oratory."

The next fall he returned to Europe to observe army maneuvers in Austria, Czechoslovakia, Poland, Hungary, Rumania, and Turkey, his itinerary determined, of course, by which nations extended invitations. The attention which he was accorded, in the way of royal audiences, banquets, and ceremonies, was in deference to the nation he represented rather than to the American Army, which was far smaller than the ones he visited. In each of these countries he found military leaders agreed in predicting that the next war would be one of "maneuver and movement" and that conflict would be inevitable if Hitler gained control of Germany. In the second week of October, about the time MacArthur returned to America, aging President Hindenburg granted his first audience to Hitler; five months later the Nazi leader was dictator of Germany.

Three months after Hitler's *coup d'état,* General Werner von Blomberg, the German defense minister, invited Mac-

Arthur to visit his nation's army maneuvers that summer. MacArthur politely declined, citing "the unusual activities affecting our Army this summer in connection with the Civilian Conservation Corps as well as other things." Captain James C. Crockett, with the American military attaché's office in Berlin, said that Blomberg expressed "keen regret" over MacArthur's declination. Crockett added: "It is my impression that the Minister is extremely anxious for the Chief of Staff to visit the German Army as a recognition of that army." [18]

As portentous as the ascension of Hitler was, the Manchurian crisis was of more immediate concern to the American departments of War, Navy, and State during the years 1931–32. When hostilities began between Japanese and Chinese soldiers near Mukden on September 18, 1931, MacArthur was preparing to leave France to visit Yugoslavia. He cut short his European tour, having intended to visit several other nations, and returned to Washington in early October. In the following two months the Japanese army ruthlessly conquered all of South Manchuria. On January 7, 1932, Stimson sent his now-famous notes to Japan and China declaring, in effect, that the United States would not recognize Japan's territorial aggrandizement in Manchuria. With strong backing from Mac-Arthur, Stimson tried to persuade Hoover to impose economic sanctions against Japan and pressure other nations to do so, too, but the President feared that such action would lead to war with Japan and refused.

On January 29 the Japanese attacked Shanghai, in whose international settlement resided a large number of Americans. During the ensuing battle to drive out the Chinese troops, the Nipponese killed thousands of innocent residents of the city, mainly by aerial attacks. The American consul general and the commander of the Asiatic fleet appealed to Hoover to authorize the evacuation of the Americans in the beleaguered port. On February 1 Hoover called a meeting at the White House with his top diplomatic and military officials. Largely because of the fervent suasion of Stimson and MacArthur, the President decided to send the 31st Infantry from the Philippines and a company of Marines to reinforce the tiny American garrison which had been stationed in the international settlement for years. Moreover, Stimson dispatched a strongly worded note of protest to Tokyo against the occupation of Shanghai. For the next several months Japanese-American relations were near the breaking point; but fortunately no clashes occurred between the two nations' troops, and the Japanese withdrew from Shanghai in May.

The reinforcements to Shanghai turned out to be the only action resembling a show of force by the United States during the Manchurian episode. The League of Nation's Lytton Commission (on which Major General Frank R. McCoy represented America ably) went to Manchuria to investigate, and its report in September condemning Japanese aggression was endorsed by the League Assembly, whereupon Japan simply withdrew from the League. Since neither the League nor the United States would venture beyond moral sanctions, many Japanese leaders, especially General Hideki Tojo and his commanders in Manchuria, were convinced that the timorous Western powers could be challenged with impunity. As a prominent diplomatic historian has said, "In a very real sense the Open Door [in China] collapsed, the League fell apart, collective security perished, and World War II began in 1931 on the windswept plains of Manchuria." [19]

4. Pacifism and Disarmament

During the years 1931–32 when tensions were mounting in Europe and blood was already flowing on the fields of Manchuria, the pacifist movements in America seemed to be more vociferous and influential than even during the period preceding the Kellogg-Briand Pact of 1928. As military head of the Army, MacArthur would make a natural target for their barbs, but since he was an outspoken champion of strong preparedness, he provoked the pacifists' wrath and reciprocated in full measure. In May, 1931, *The World Tomorrow*, an influential religious periodical, published the results of a poll conducted by Harry Emerson Fosdick and other leading clergymen in which they surveyed the opinions of 19,372 ministers on questions relating to the churches and clergymen's positions on war and military training. The survey represented about 21 per cent of the ordained clergy in America, but, for some reason, excluded Jewish, Roman Catholic, Southern Baptist, and Southern Methodist ministers or priests. The poll revealed, among other things, that 83 per cent of the respondents opposed military training in high schools and colleges; 80 per cent favored arms reduction, even if it left the United States in a relatively unfavorable defensive position; 62 per cent believed their denominational governing bodies should publicly state their refusal to support any future participation in war by the United States, whether aggressive or defensive in nature; 54 per cent said they would not serve as armed combatants in any kind of war; 34 per cent stated that they could not conscientiously serve on military duty even as chaplains.[20]

Kirby Page, editor of the periodical, invited MacArthur to express his views on the poll. The chief of staff did so with relish in the issue of June 2; copies of his letter were given to newspapermen, who were told that, though the epistle was addressed to pacifist ministers in particular, it was directed to "all those who would refuse to take up arms in defense of their country." He stated his opinion bluntly:

> To exercise privilege without assuming attendant responsibility and obligation is to occupy a position of license, a position apparently sought by men . . . who, in effect, proclaim

their willingness to see this nation perish rather than participate in its defense . . .

That men who wear the cloth of the Church should openly
defend repudiation of the laws of the land . . . seems almost
unbelievable. It will certainly hearten every potential or actual
criminal and malefactor who either has or contemplates breaking some other law . . .

It is my humble belief that the relation which He [Jesus]
came to establish is based upon sacrifice and that men and
women who follow in His train are called by it to the defense
of certain priceless principles, even at the cost of their own
lives.

And I can think of no principles more high and holy than
those for which our national sacrifices have been made in the
past. History teaches us that religion and patriotism have always gone hand in hand, while atheism has invariably been
accompanied by radicalism, communism, bolshevism, and other
enemies of free government . . .

I confidently believe that a red-blooded and virile humanity
which loves peace devotedly, but is willing to die in the defense
of the right, is Christian from center to circumference, and will
continue to be dominant in the future as in the past.[21]

MacArthur's letter, which was reprinted by a number of
newspapers, was a conventional, if frank, statement of the anti-
pacifist position. Nevertheless, it touched off a running controversy in letters to editors which lasted into the middle of
the summer, most of the correspondence being from outraged
pacifists. It was probably an excited extremist of the pacifist
cause who sent an anonymous postcard to the chief of staff in
August containing a threat against his life. Colonel Alfred T.
Smith, intelligence chief of the General Staff, referred the card
to the Federal Bureau of Investigation "for suitable action."
J. Edgar Hoover, the bureau's director, responded that, unfortunately, "there is no statute providing punishment for sending threatening letters through the mail," even if the sender
was identified (which he was not). Nothing further came of

the matter, but MacArthur's feud with pacifists was just beginning.[22]

Pierrepont Moffat, chief of the State Department's division
on West European affairs and Stimson's main adviser on disarmament, wrote in his journal in January, 1932, that pacifist
influence in America was "so strong that something must be
done to make them feel that the administration is in earnest"
about the World Disarmament Conference, which was to con-
vene in Geneva the next month. The fifty-one nation conference soon fell into a state of quibbling, which kept action
paralyzed for five months. Then Hoover suddenly brought the
sessions to life with a proposal that all offensive weapons be
abolished and land forces be reduced by one third. He proposed to abolish submarines, tanks, heavy mobile guns, gas
and bacteriological warfare, and aerial bombardment. At first
enthusiastically received by the delegates, his plan was subsequently buried, and the conference adjourned in July without
reaching any agreement. It was mainly the security-conscious
French and British who killed the Hoover plan, claimed Brigadier General George S. Simonds, military adviser to the American delegation: "Real disarmament would have been better
served had the American Delegation pressed for action on the
Hoover plan . . . The real opposition lay in the hastily organized entente between Great Britain and France, who enticed
our Delegation into private conversations which whittled away
its substance." [23]

In Washington, MacArthur anxiously studied the latest communications from Simonds and the State Department on the
proceedings at Geneva, at first convinced that it was his duty
to the Army to oppose any disarmament plan, particularly since
the idea of arms reduction had been so closely associated with
pacifist agitation in previous years. The conference coincided
with his bitter fight against Collins' faction over the military
budget for fiscal 1933. His intense determination to stop the

efforts of Collins and air-power advocates from raising the Air Corps' appropriations at the expense of Army manpower led him to assume an anomalous position which shocked some of his colleagues and amused pacifists. On April 4 Moffat and Norman Davis, the head of the American delegation at Geneva who was back in Washington briefly, visited MacArthur at his office to discuss the latest developments in the drafting of Hoover's proposal. According to Moffat, the chief of staff

> kept us for nearly three-quarters of an hour developing his theories as to the future of the Army. Briefly he made a few essential points: (1) That aviation was the newest branch of the service and the most expensive. Between 25 and 35 per cent of our Army budget was already devoted to aviation and Trubee Davison [Assistant Secretary of War] was constantly coming back demanding an additional 15 to 20 million dollars each year. (2) Its value as an instrument of war was still undemonstrated. . . . (3) That the whole tendency of war, since the idea of the Prussian staff had become generally accepted, was to regard it as a struggle between whole nations rather than between professional organizations. Effectively to arm all nations or to provide the Army and Navy with weapons that could subdue an entire nation was beyond the economic scope of any power and was more than any other factor driving the world into bankruptcy . . . In his idea, our ultimate aim should be to obtain an agreement on the part of all nations that they would give no government support in any form to aviation. In other words, to give up military and naval aviation in their entirety and not to subsidize directly or indirectly civilian aviation. He admitted that this was too radical a solution but felt it should be the ultimate goal.[24]

For some reason, Moffat did not inform Stimson of MacArthur's startling proposal until June 3. In his journal Moffat wrote of the Secretary of State's reaction:

> . . . This the Secretary refused to believe although we gave him in some detail General MacArthur's reasoning. Mutter-

ing to himself that it was impossible that we quoted him accurately, he seized the telephone receiver and asked the Chief of Staff if he could come around for a few moments. I was a little bit hesitant that General MacArthur might qualify or weaken his statements, but he stuck to his guns firmly and we were treated to the unusual spectacle of the head of the War Department arguing for a decrease in a military arm while the head of the so-called peace department was attempting to prove him wrong . . . When he left the Secretary blew up, said that he [MacArthur] was predominantly concerned with his budget and was not thinking of all the occasions when aviation had been useful.[25]

In March, 1933, after the Geneva Conference had reconvened, Moffat and Davis, the latter again on a brief visit to Washington, discussed disarmament matters with MacArthur. Moffat said of the chief of staff's conversation that day:

> . . . To him disarmament had two purposes: (1) to save on appropriations so that the nations' preparations for national defense would not eat too deeply into their budgets; (2) to make war, when it came, less destructive to private property . . . Aviation, he repeated, was eating up between 25 and 35 per cent of all military budgets and he said that this was only the beginning. More could be done for economy and for civilization by doing away with aviation and secondarily by the abolition of heavy mobile artillery than any other method. However, we must not discard from strength without adequate gain. Our naval aviation was our strongest trump. We should not give it up until we were assured of adequate return.[26]

Neither MacArthur nor hardly anyone else in official Washington sincerely believed that the Geneva Conference would result in any form of disarmament agreement, so he may have reasoned, as Simonds had suggested in a letter from Geneva, that the meeting needed an extreme disarmament proposal, for such "would have brought the opposition to real disarmament out into the open." It may have been MacArthur's influence which led Hoover to include a ban on aerial bombardment in his plan. Nevertheless, Stimson was probably correct that Mac-Arthur's proposal was motivated by his deep concern for the military budget, which, to him, meant mainly funds to house, supply, pay, and train his officers and enlisted men, whose aggregate strength was less than that of the armies of small nations like Greece and Portugal. His behavior during the spring and summer of 1932 was, indeed, strange and sometimes vindictive. In a sense, he seemed to feel that both pacifists and airpower advocates were enemies of Army manpower: the former would do away with it entirely or obstruct its augmentation in time of war; on the other hand, the latter would reduce it to impotence by sapping military funds for unproven, costly machines. MacArthur's crusade for the abolition of military aviation, however, was overshadowed in mid-1932 by his involvement in the eviction of the Bonus Army, which, to many persons, would also seem to be a strange and vindictive performance.

CHAPTER XIV

Prophet Without Honor

1. Unfortunate Coincidence

COMMUNIST LEADERS IN THE UNITED STATES were not slow in realizing that the Great Depression afforded them an excellent opportunity to promote revolution. Whereas the Socialists seemed able to attract only middle-class professionals and intellectuals, the Communists concentrated on organizing jobless low-class workers. Early in 1930 Communist-led hunger demonstrations erupted in Cleveland, Philadelphia, Chicago, Los Angeles, and New York, involving thousands of desperate unemployed persons. The incidents produced some bleeding heads and much publicity for the unemployment crisis, but, to the chagrin of the Reds, no revolution. The House's committee to investigate Communist activities was born out of the violence of that spring. Led by Representative Hamilton Fish of New York, the committee conducted hearings in cities where the Reds were especially active, but the congressmen accomplished little besides adding sensationalism to the growing public anxiety over the spread of Communism. Also in 1930 Father Charles E. Coughlin, a priest who had been conducting little-heeded radio programs in a Michigan city for five years, sud-

denly gained a national reputation with his savage assaults on
Communism and his hard-hitting admonitions to Americans
to awaken to the menace.[1]

That autumn General Moseley, MacArthur's volatile deputy
chief of staff, presented to the General Staff his proposal for
coping with the rising specter of radicalism: "With all the
troubles we have at the present moment in the United States,
why should we allow these aliens, who are now unlawfully
within our gates, to work against us? It seems to me that all
such aliens should be gathered up and either returned to Russia or segregated and held segregated within the United States."
If the Communists could not be deported immediately, Moseley
argued, then the federal government should "gather up the
worst of these offenders and ship them to a selected island in
the Hawaiian group, where they could be held under federal
control while awaiting deportation." He added: "It might also
have a very beneficial effect on the crime wave in America, for
it would be a fine thing if the same procedure could be law-
fully applied in clearing the country of the criminal class." [2]
Nothing came of Moseley's proposal, but his desire to act force-
fully against the Communists was undoubtedly shared by many
of his colleagues on the General Staff, including MacArthur.

The War Department steadfastly and successfully opposed
several congressional measures considered in 1930–31 to organize a special enlisted reserve corps which would utilize jobless men on public works under Army supervision. MacArthur
and Hurley maintained that involvement of the military establishment in work relief or public construction programs to
alleviate unemployment would cripple the Army's defensive
effectiveness. They also feared that the mixing of jobless civilians with Regular Army personnel would undermine the latter's morale and ideological convictions. Besides, federal funds
could be better employed in projects to expand Army housing
and ordnance works, which would, in turn, increase the num-

ber of available jobs, so the War Department officials argued. There is little doubt, nevertheless, that the contagion of radicalism was a primary consideration in their opposition to linking the Army directly with the proposed federal employment projects.[3]

Whereas the national hysteria over Bolshevism after the World War had gradually died during the 1920's, the conservative War Department had continued to nourish its suspicion and fear of Communist subversion of the nation. When Mac-Arthur took over as military head, the reactionary views circulating in the department quickened his own anti-Communist conviction. Moseley was particularly close to MacArthur in the years 1930–33, and the two men continued their friendship by correspondence in later years. Moseley's diatribes of the 1930's would be echoed with striking similarities by MacArthur in his later harangues against Communism, though the latter never condoned the bitter anti-Semitism which was also part of Moseley's nativist ideology. During MacArthur's term as chief of staff, most members of the General Staff probably viewed all outbursts of violence and unrest with red-tinted glasses.

MacArthur's first contact with protesting veterans, it will be recalled, had been the benefit track and field meet in Washington in 1922. There is no indication that in the next seven years he followed closely the course of bonus legislation and veterans' grievances. In 1924 the veterans' lobby had succeeded in influencing Congress to pass, over Coolidge's veto, a measure which provided "adjusted compensation certificates" for World War veterans. The certificates, whose value was based upon the time each man spent in service during the war, would be redeemable in 1945, with the average benefit per veteran at the time of redemption being about $1000. The congressmen, however, did not anticipate the Great Depression, and, with the coming of large-scale unemployment in 1930–31, the veterans began demanding immediate payment of the bonus. Despite the fact that Congress, again overriding a veto by the President, passed a bill permitting payment of half of the bonus, many ex-soldiers were not satisfied and agitated for payment of the balance. In late 1931 Representative Wright Patman of Texas introduced a measure which would authorize payment of the rest of the bonus, by means of the issuance of $2.4 billion in fiat money. Adamantly opposing the bill as abetting inflation and showing favoritism, Hoover influenced the American Legion to reject a resolution at its convention endorsing the measure. By the spring of 1932 the Patman bill, though still in committee, was the subject of heated controversy from country stores to congressional cloakrooms. It was generally felt that the bill would encounter serious opposition in the Senate and, if it passed, would be vetoed by Hoover.[4]

With the floor debates and crucial voting on the Patman bill expected in late spring, many unemployed veterans across the country began to think similar thoughts: they must go to Washington and convince the federal officials of their plight. The motivation differed from man to man, but nearly all had been out of work for many months and had come to view the bonus as a symbol of hope and security, although even full redemption would have brought them little relief. For many, the trip to the national capital would be simply an escape from the everyday reality of starving dependents. When a band of 300 jobless veterans, led by former cannery worker Walter W. Waters, set out from Portland for Washington in early May, their action triggered a spontaneous movement of restless, jobless ex-servicemen to board trucks and boxcars bound for the national capital. The Bonus March was on — the most ambitious venture of the unemployed during the depression years.

Unfortunately for the marchers, their action came in the wake of a series of radical outbursts which had left official Washington gripped with fear and anxiety. In December, 1931, about 1500 out-of-work persons, including a large number of avowed Communists, conducted a brief but portentous hunger march in Washington. A few weeks later a Pittsburgh priest led an army of 12,000 jobless men to the city in an effort to pressure Congress into passing unemployment legislation. On neither occasion did violence occur, and the marchers soon departed without having convinced Congress or the President. But the growing uneasiness of Hoover was evident from the padlocks on the White House gates, the reinforced guard at the presidential mansion, and the infrequency of the President's public appearances. In March, 1932, policemen guarding the entrance to Ford's River Rouge plant at Dearborn, Michigan, panicked and opened fire on a mob of slag-throwing demonstrators. Four were killed in the crowd, and over fifty were wounded. The Communists took control of the funeral procession, exposing the huge crowd of mourners and onlookers to Red banners, portraits of Lenin, and Communist slogans. Though again failing to produce a revolution, the Reds got their desired publicity and further upset the Hoover administration.[5]

Thus when the Bonus Army began to arrive in May, swelling in numbers daily, it seemed to many federal officials that the battle of Armageddon was at hand. Hoover, Hurley, and MacArthur, among others of official Washington, were sure that the march was not an isolated incident, but was closely connected with the previous disturbances. MacArthur believed that through the Bonus March "the Communists hoped to incite revolutionary action." He was certain that "the movement was actually far deeper and more dangerous than an effort to secure funds from a nearly depleted federal treasury . . . Red organizers infiltrated the veteran groups and presently took command from their unwitting leaders." The President and his military leaders saw thousands of Red revolutionaries entrenching themselves within the bounds of the national capital. Others saw only a pitiful horde of ragged veterans exhausted by futility and near starvation.[6]

2. *Where Do We Go from Here?*

"Now I'm not a Red, God damn it, but . . ." the bonus marcher's words trailed off into an indistinct grumble. Novelist John Dos Passos, who chatted with the veterans at their makeshift huts along the Anacostia River south of the Capitol, observed: "That seemed to be in the mind of everybody I talked to around the camps. They weren't Reds, but . . . No, they weren't there for the unemployed generally. Their position as ex-servicemen was special. The bonus was due them and they wanted it now." Dos Passos continued: "Then they'd switch and start talking about a system that allowed such things to get into such shape, damn well needed changing . . . Where do we go from here, boys? Like a hundred million other Americans, the men of the B.E.F. don't know where they're going, but pressed by worry and hunger and humiliation, they're moving." [7]

By the time Waters and his Oregon veterans arrived in Washington in late May, the expedition had more than tripled in numbers, with individuals and groups joining them in nearly every town across the country. A tall, handsome man who spoke eloquently and walked proudly, Waters was a former sergeant in the A.E.F. field artillery and had participated in numerous combat operations in France. Elected as commander of the so-called "Bonus Expeditionary Forces," Waters organized the score or more encampments of bonus marchers along military lines, with formations, bugle calls, and policing assignments by units. He announced that in the Bonus Army there would be "no panhandling, no drinking, no radicalism" and "we are going to stay until the veterans' bill is passed."

As the days became weeks, life in the squalid camps settled into a routine of repairing flimsy dwellings, searching for food, mending clothes, and figuring ways to solve the mounting problems of sanitation. By the end of June the ranks of the B.E.F. had grown to about 22,000.

Most of the bonus marchers acknowledged Waters' leadership, but a band of less than 200 Communists, posing as veterans and camping on the edges of the B.E.F. encampments, took their orders from John T. Pace, a bankrupt Detroit contractor and recent Red convert. Except for exaggerated boasts of the Reds themselves, the testimony of participants and witnesses of the affair overwhelmingly attested to the fact that the Communists' numbers and influence were inconsequential. Generally the bona fide veterans ostracized the Reds and sometimes displayed open belligerency toward them. On several occasions, only quick intervention by the police prevented Pace and his cohorts from being mobbed by B.E.F. members who were enraged by the Red agitators' propagandizing efforts. The *B.E.F. News,* the Bonus Army's weekly newspaper, repeatedly denounced the disruptive and radical activities of Pace's group. Among a force of tired, hungry, and exasperated men as sizable as the B.E.F., there was bound to be some fighting between the marchers. But the evidence indicates that the fisticuffs exploded usually between whites and Negroes, or between veterans and Communists. Outside the billets of the Bonus Army, the marchers displayed surliness in their contacts with the city's residents, but produced no public disorders of consequence.[8]

Actually the large influx of veterans, many with their families, presented a problem of welfare, not of lawlessness, for the authorities of the District of Columbia. The district commissioners turned over the job of controlling the B.E.F. to Police Superintendent Pelham D. Glassford, who had served as a brigadier general in France in 1918 and, in recent months, had tactfully dispersed the other hunger demonstrators who had come to Washington. An intelligent, charming, and aesthetically sensitive man who seemed like neither a general nor a police chief, Glassford believed that the Bonus Army consisted mainly of poverty-stricken veterans who should be treated kindly, but should be encouraged to return home. Riding into the B.E.F. camps daily on his blue motorcycle, he directed his policemen to provide first aid for the veterans and their dependents, secured baseball equipment for them, persuaded the Marine band to serenade them, and procured some bedding and tents for them. He located temporary housing in vacant downtown buildings for some of the ex-soldiers and even handled the finances of the B.E.F. organization for a time, at their request. He also enlisted the aid of the Salvation Army, Volunteers of America, and other charitable groups in caring for the dietary and apparel needs of the bedraggled horde. Glassford opened a commissary for the B.E.F. above a garage, persuaded a local food broker to take charge of it, and obtained large gifts of food for the marchers from various grocers. In addition, he was successful in prompting sundry organizations and wealthy individuals to contribute money for the care of the veterans, besides expending about $1000 of his own funds for B.E.F. supplies. Although he represented the official establishment which the veterans were resisting passively, he gained the admiration and respect of many of the bonus marchers. Waters called him "our friendly enemy." [9]

MacArthur stated in his memoirs that he ordered tents, camp equipment, and rolling kitchens of the Army to be used for the relief of the Bonus Army. He said that they were later withdrawn because of "an outburst in Congress" against such use of military stocks. The Army may have given some assistance in the early days of the episode, but the official records show that MacArthur was opposed to using Army matériel and personnel to assist the veterans by late June, 1932. A congressional proposal to continue and expand the Army's assistance to the marchers was thwarted by the War Department on the grounds that such use of military equipment and soldiers violated "basic principles" of the military establishment and, touching a sensitive area to congressmen, would "require replacement with additional appropriations." Another factor in the Army's resistance to close relations with the B.E.F., according to one officer, was that "initially, the relations between the troops and the marchers were so good as to cause some concern among War Department staff officers who, unlike the officers on duty with the troops, were somewhat doubtful about the reliability of the troops if their services were needed." [10]

MacArthur's first noteworthy confrontation with demonstrators that summer occurred not at Anacostia Flats, but at Pittsburgh. When the president of the University of Pittsburgh announced that the chief of staff would be the speaker at the school's commencement exercises in June, at which time he would also receive an honorary doctorate, the liberal, pacifist element of the student body protested vigorously. At the exercises in the university's stadium on June 8 MacArthur delivered a strongly worded address assailing "pacificism and its bedfellow, Communism." Aroused to a point where he identified all demonstrators against the established order — whether pacifists, leftists, or bonus marchers — as Reds or puppets of Communism, the general made no distinction between these enemies of the state, who were "organizing the forces of unrest and undermining the morals of the working man." Tolerance of radicalism, he warned, would lead America to "dust and ashes," for "day by day this canker eats deeper into the body politic." Several student protestors at the commencement program were arrested and fined, but a county court judge later rescinded the fines and defended the youths' right to freedom of speech. MacArthur returned to Washington more convinced than ever that Communists were behind the unrest in the nation. A spate of anti-MacArthur articles appeared thereafter in liberal periodicals, of which MacArthur remarked: "It was bitter as gall and I knew that something of the gall would always be with me." [11]

On June 10, two days after the incident in Pittsburgh, the chief of staff ordered the nine corps area commanders to provide him with the leaders' names and the numerical strength of any Communist groups which passed through their areas posing as bonus marchers. Only one of the nine reports, that from the Third Corps Area (Baltimore), suggested the probability of trouble in the offing when the marchers reached Washington, and it did not attribute the veterans' hostility to Communist influence. The general tenor of the commanders' replies was that they had no intelligence data which pointed toward a Red-controlled uprising. Major General Malin Craig at San Francisco said that the bonus marchers moving through his corps area were vehemently anti-Communist. Failing to uncover the Communist conspiracy in this way, MacArthur directed the General Staff's intelligence division to investigate the leadership of the marchers who had already arrived in Washington. The G-2 report, submitted on June 12, concluded that only three Communists were among the twenty-six men who seemed to be the key leaders of the Bonus Army. Brigadier General Perry L. Miles, who commanded the 16th Infantry Brigade at Fort Myer, the main infantry unit in the immediate area of the city, reported that "the greater part of the bonus marchers have thus far resisted all attempts of the Communists to gain control of them, but there are a number of well-known Communist leaders here and they are claiming credit for the instigation of the march." [12]

The House of Representatives passed the Patman bill on June 15, but the President emphatically stated that he would veto the bonus measure if it passed in the Senate. Waters and other B.E.F. leaders tried to get an appointment to talk to

Hoover; the White House secretary curtly informed them that he was too busy. Late in the afternoon of June 17 thousands of bonus marchers anxiously waiting on the Capitol lawn were informed that the Senate had just defeated the bonus bill. Belying their desperation and futility, the veterans sang a stanza of "America," fell into formation by platoons, and returned to their grimy dwellings. A few left Washington, but most of the B.E.F. continued their stay. In early July Congress, with some prodding from the nervous President, passed a bill providing transportation funds for the veterans to go back to their homes. The train fares would be deducted from their bonus redemptions in 1945. About 6000 bonus marchers accepted the fares, though some of the recipients did not leave. By the time Congress adjourned in mid-July, however, the B.E.F.'s strength had decreased to about 10,000 die-hards.[13]

Meanwhile, the Army was reinforcing its garrisons in the forts of the capital area. Tanks were lubricated and kept in condition for action; several experimental vehicles from Aberdeen Proving Ground appeared at Fort Myer, ostensibly to show the public the Army's latest mechanized equipment. Special anti-riot training was begun at Fort Myer, with emphasis on preparing the cavalry horses to move against a mob. Generals MacArthur and Miles carefully went over a revised version of the "White Plan," the War Department's plan of operations in case of civil disorder in Washington which required Army forces. In case the bonus marchers became violent, tear gas and possibly "more drastic action" were to be employed against the Reds after "giving an opportunity to the non-Communistic veterans to disperse." The "critical points" to be protected were the White House, Capitol, Treasury Department, and Bureau of Engraving and Printing, the assembly area for the troops being the Ellipse to the rear of the White House.[14]

In the days after the defeat of the bonus bill, patience ran thin and tempers flared within and between the various elements concerned with the bonus affair. Commander Waters became more dictatorial, and the veterans became more indifferent to his imperatives. To a group of dissidents complaining about a new system of regimentation instituted by Waters in late June, the B.E.F. leader shouted: "I'll do what I want whether you like it or not, and those that don't can get the hell out of the B.E.F. I'm going to be hardboiled!" Waters talked about organizing a militant socialist force which he planned to call the "Khaki Shirts." In the future this new army would spearhead the offensive against the "sordid scheme of special privilege" in America. Also in late June the district commissioners began criticizing sharply Glassford's "softness" toward the marchers. Commissioner Herbert B. Crosby, a retired general, demanded that Glassford eject the veterans encamped in some vacant downtown buildings. The police superintendent warned that forcible ouster would surely provoke a riot and therefore refused Crosby. When a newly arrived group of 250 veterans from California proposed on July 12 to set up its camp on the Capitol grounds, it seemed that the moment of violence had arrived. But Glassford tactfully handled the Californians, refusing them their announced campsite but permitting them to parade through the Capitol grounds for several days and evenings. Its tone becoming increasingly belligerent, the *B.E.F. News* chastized the marchers as "yellow cowards" for not demanding their rights. The atmosphere in Washington was growing more and more tense; many city residents who had previously shown sympathy for the marchers now demanded that they pack up and leave. The situation was nearing an explosive stage.[15]

On July 14 Crosby, Glassford, and Admiral H. V. Butler, the Navy Yard commandant, met with MacArthur in the chief of staff's office to review the situation and lay plans to expedite the departure of the B.E.F. According to Glassford, MacArthur

was "highly complimentary" of the way in which the police
had handled the marchers and assured the police superintendent that "the Army would not be used unless directed by the
President." The conferees decided that the veterans parading
on the Capitol grounds would be forbidden to walk on the
plaza in front of the Capitol, a restriction which Glassford
later enforced without incident. Apparently no decision was
reached at the conference on exactly how to compel the Bonus
Army to vacate Washington. The consensus seemed to be
against the use of force since it would precipitate violence.

The next day a group of Communist marchers were turned
back from the Capitol grounds when they tried to demonstrate
and present a petition to Congress, which was nearing adjourn-
ment. On July 16 the district commissioners instructed Glassford to use force, if necessary, to prevent any parading within
several blocks of the White House. The wording of the commissioners' order strongly implied that the Army might have
to supplant Glassford's policemen in enforcing the decree. In
the week following the conference in MacArthur's office, there
was a marked hardening of the heart in official quarters. The
President, the district commissioners, and the War Department
leaders made up their minds sometime during that crucial
week that the marchers had to go. They were now ready to
force the issue, even if it meant bloodshed.[16]

Glassford received an order from the district commissioners
on July 21 to secure the evacuation of the buildings on Pennsylvania Avenue by the end of the next day and of all B.E.F.
encampments before noon on August 4. The pretext for the
first action was that the federal government had contracted for
the structures' immediate demolition to make way for a new
downtown park. Glassford pleaded for more time, again arguing that forcible eviction would bring bloodshed. Moreover,
he maintained, hundreds of marchers were already leaving the
city daily, and time would probably solve the entire problem.

The commissioners reluctantly granted a stay of execution "pending the straightening out of certain legal matters." Glassford then told Waters of the impending action, urging him to get all of the veterans to depart but assuring him that the main B.E.F. base at Anacostia Flats would not be forcibly closed before the stipulated deadline was near. The police superintendent also tried to rush negotiations with Judge William Bartlett, who had tentatively agreed to let the B.E.F. move to his estate near the city. But time ran out for Glassford and the Bonus Army.

Hoover called a hurried conference with MacArthur, Hurley, Attorney General William D. Mitchell, Secretary of the Treasury Ogden L. Mills, and several Treasury underlings on July 27. After the session the district commissioners were notified that demolition of the vacant buildings on Pennsylvania Avenue would begin the next morning. (Only the previous day Hurley had speculated that force would probably be necessary to oust the veterans since the B.E.F. had been so embarrassingly law-abiding.) The Commissioners instructed Glassford to provide protection for the Treasury agents and demolition workers who would go to the disputed structures at 10:00 A.M. the next day. The President had flung down the gauntlet, apparently with solid backing from his cabinet members, generals, and district commissioners.[17]

3. An Ignominious End

The morning of July 28, 1932, seemed like the start of a typically hot summer day in Washington. By 8:00 A.M. hurrying pedestrians and honking taxicabs had resumed their daily battles over rights of way on the broad avenues. An hour later, however, the walks were more congested than usual in the area on Pennsylvania Avenue between Third and Fourth streets. There Glassford and Waters frantically negotiated with each other and with the veterans encamped in the buildings marked for demolition. When the ex-servicemen, 1100 strong, voted to remain in the structure until the government provided other shelter, Glassford's men encircled the old armory where the main body of squatters were located. By the time the Treasury agents and construction workers arrived about 10:40, the police were completing the evacuation of the armory, with much cursing but little physical resistance from the occupants. The police then proceeded methodically to the other buildings nearby. Suddenly a score of Communist marchers appeared on the scene. They set off a brief-lived commotion, rushing the police line and throwing bricks, one of which struck Glassford. The police chief continued in command, arrested a number of the agitators, and ended the disturbance quickly without serious injury to anyone.

Glassford then departed to report to the district commissioners. According to his version, he told the commissioners that the police were in control of the situation, but that no further evictions should be tried that day in view of the excited feelings of the veterans. The commissioners later claimed that Glassford had appealed for federal troops. The misunderstanding possibly arose from Glassford's statement that if the commissioners insisted on continuing the evacuation that day, the Army might be needed. While the police superintendent was on his way back to the tip of the Federal Triangle on Pennsylvania Avenue, the worried commissioners pondered their next move. Sometime in the next hour or so, probably around 1:00 P.M., they dispatched a request to the President for federal troops, stating that it was Glassford's opinion and theirs that "it will be impossible for the Police Department to maintain law and order except by the free use of firearms which will make the situation a dangerous one; it is believed, however, that the presence of Federal troops in some number will obviate the seriousness of the situation and result in far less violence and bloodshed." MacArthur stated that Crosby "communicated with me by telephone before the troops were called out, stating that the Chief of Police reported a very serious situation on Pennsylvania Avenue; that a riotous mob was out of control." According to MacArthur, Crosby told him that Glassford reported that "he had cleared a small area and was holding his line but could make no advance and was entirely unable to evict the mob from the Federal property which they were holding," so the police chief "requested that troops should be held in immediate readiness for action." [18]

As policemen entered one of the partially demolished structures near Fourth and Pennsylvania at 2:15 P.M., a scuffle broke out between policemen and veterans or between veterans and veterans — no one is quite certain of the origin. Bricks began to fly again. A policeman lost his footing on a boardwalk, panicked, and fired into a group of veterans. Before Glassford could get to the scene and restore order, two veterans had been fatally shot, and three policemen injured.[19] Upon receiving the news, Hoover immediately called Hurley and asked for the Army's aid. At 2:55 the Secretary of War sent the following order to MacArthur:

> The President has just informed me that the civil government of the District of Columbia has reported to him that it is unable to maintain law and order in the District.
>
> You will have United States troops proceed immediately to the scene of disorder. Cooperate fully with the District of Columbia police force which is now in charge. Surround the affected area and clear it without delay.
>
> Turn over all prisoners to the civil authorities.
>
> In your orders insist that any women and children who may be in the affected area be accorded every consideration and kindness. Use all humanity consistent with due execution of this order.[20]

Actually Hoover had contacted the War Department shortly after the commissioners had informed him of their conviction that the police would not be adequate to prevent disorder. At 1:40 MacArthur had issued orders to General Miles to assemble his units at the Ellipse. It took over two hours to gather and transport the Army forces to the White House vicinity; the 12th Infantry, for example, was at target practice in the field when the order came to Fort Howard, Maryland, for them to report to Washington. At 4:00 P.M. Miles reported to MacArthur in the latter's office in the State, War, and Navy Building, announcing that the assembled troops were ready to move out against the bonus marchers.

The participating units consisted of the 2nd Squadron, 3rd Cavalry, commanded by Major Alexander D. Surles (with Major George S. Patton, Jr., attached as executive officer); the 3rd Battalion, 12th Infantry, led by Lieutenant Colonel Louis A. Kunzig; the Headquarters Company, Washington, under Captain Alexander R. Bolling; the 1st Platoon, Company B, 1st Tank Regiment, commanded by First Lieutenant Bob Childs (with five tanks); and the 29th Motor Transportation Company, under Captain Raymond Dailey. Joining the operation during the Anacostia phase were the 1st Battalion, 12th Infantry, led by Colonel William W. Taylor, Jr., and a National Guard coast artillery unit commanded by Major General Anton Stephan. The various units were rushed by truck from Forts Myer, Meade, Washington, and Howard — all in the vicinity of the national capital. The total number of Regular Army officers and enlisted men involved in the operation was 793. In addition, the 13th Engineer Regiment and a 34th Infantry battalion were held in reserve at Fort Myer. The brunt of the operation was borne by the units which Kunzig and Surles commanded.[21]

MacArthur informed Miles that he, the chief of staff, would accompany the troops against the bonus marchers, "not with a view of commanding the troops but to be on hand as things progressed, so that he could issue necessary instructions on the ground." Later he told Hurley, "I accompanied the troops in person, anticipating the possibility of such a serious situation arising that necessary decisions might lie beyond the purview of responsibility of any subordinate commander, and with the purpose of obtaining a personal familiarity with every phase of the troops' activities." In his memoirs, MacArthur said that he went with the troops "in accordance with the President's request." Major Dwight Eisenhower, who was on the War Department staff and "fairly close" to MacArthur personally, advised the chief of staff that it seemed "highly inappropriate" for the military head of the Army to be present with the evicting force: "General MacArthur disagreed, saying that it was a question of Federal authority in the District of Columbia, and because of his belief that there was 'incipient revolution in the air,' as he called it, he paid no attention to my dissent."

MacArthur, who had worn a white suit to work that morning, sent an orderly to Fort Myer for his uniform after the decision was made that afternoon to use the troops. The orderly returned with his coat which bore his ribbons and two medals, just as Mrs. MacArthur, not knowing of developments across the Potomac, had selected on other occasions when he was required to attend a formal function on short notice. But even if MacArthur asked specifically for that coat, it was in order for him to be garbed in his chief of staff's uniform once the decision to participate was made — and for the reasons he gave. Few accounts of the events of that day fail to include a barbed comment on the chief of staff's "parade attire." Such criticism is sheer pettiness. MacArthur's ribbons stand out in the photographs of him that day mainly because the officers standing next to him were usually Major Eisenhower or Captain Davis, who had few, if any, ribbons on any of their uniforms at that stage of their careers. The truth is that Mac-

Arthur's presence at the eviction would have provoked a flurry of criticism from many quarters regardless of his apparel.[22]

At 4:30 P.M. MacArthur and Miles led the Army units eastward along Pennsylvania Avenue toward the 3000 bonus marchers assembled in the area between Third and Fourth streets. The waiting veterans, like the huge crowd of spectators gathered along the curbs, seemed spellbound at first by the magnificence and unreality of the approaching procession. The cavalry, sabers drawn, quickly cleared the avenue in front of the disputed buildings. A cordon of infantry pushed forward to the entrances of the structures. Suddenly an officer barked an order; soldiers donned gas masks and rushed indoors, tossing tear gas grenades "by the handful." One witness reported that "the doors and windows belched forth veterans, who were running before their feet touched the ground . . . Black smoke and orange flame rose from the shacks constructed between buildings." Miles commented, "When these fires sprang up so quickly after the arrival of the troops, they were a distinct surprise to me . . . No orders for firing the shacks . . . were given." Within a half hour, the "affected area" was, for the most part, cleared, the veterans retreating southward around the Capitol and continuing along Pennsylvania Avenue. Though its weapons were not fired, a machine gun company was left near the Capitol grounds to deter, mainly by its ominous presence, the swarms of spectators who followed the procession. The first stage of the Army's operation, which was clearing the marchers from the downtown area of Pennsylvania Avenue, had been so precisely and swiftly executed that the veterans did not have time to exhaust their supply of bricks.[23]

"The completeness and finality of the evacuation," said Lieutenant Colonel Kunzig, "inflamed the Bonus Forces as they were forced across Maine and Missouri Avenues. It is believed that lack of leadership at this point prevented the situation from becoming more acute than it was. Growing hate and defiance was evident from the 'boos,' barrage of profanity, the throwing of rocks and the return of tear gas grenades." Kunzig noted that "as the troops proceeded through the area south of Four and One-half Street and Maryland Avenue, occupied by colored people, it was apparent that residents of that area were in sympathy with the Bonus Marchers." At the corner of 11th and M streets, near the Navy Yard, a mob attacked MacArthur's automobile with bricks. The car was badly damaged, but the only occupant, Captain Thomas J. Davis, MacArthur's aide, escaped uninjured. The car was the sole Army vehicle damaged that day. Despite stiffening B.E.F. resistance along the streets southeast of the Capitol, the majority of the veterans had retreated southward across the 11th Street bridge by nightfall. With tears streaming down his cheeks from tear gas, Mac-Arthur remarked to a reporter: "It was a good job, quickly done, with no one injured." Perhaps he had reference to the first stage of the operation. The second phase, from the Capitol to the 11th Street bridge, resulted in the gassing of hundreds of persons, including a baby who died from inhaling the fumes; at least two score persons were injured by bricks, clubs, bayonets, and sabers, including a veteran whose ear was chopped off by a cavalryman.[24]

As the troops neared the 11th Street bridge, Hurley twice sent messengers to tell MacArthur and Miles that the President did not want the Army to pursue the B.E.F. across the Anacostia River. "In neither instance," said Eisenhower, who was with the chief of staff, "did General MacArthur hear these instructions. He said he was too busy and did not want either himself or his staff bothered by people coming down and pretending to bring orders." So far, through the first and second phases of the operation, MacArthur had played the role of interested observer, leaving all field decisions and orders to Miles and his unit commanders.

About dusk, Glassford asked MacArthur if the troops would

be sent into the main B.E.F. billets at Anacostia Flats. The chief of staff responded in the affirmative, but he requested Glassford to go there and inform the veterans and their families that "we would proceed very slowly; that I would stop the command for supper so that full opportunity would be given for everyone to leave without being hurt." MacArthur waited several hours and then ordered the Army to cross the river. His decision may have been prompted by a message he received from Lieutenant Colonel Clement H. Wright, the General Staff secretary. Wright reported that G-2 had information that at Anacostia Flats "all men having firearms were told to use them against the first troops to cross" the bridge.[25] Thus MacArthur may have been convinced that the B.E.F. was regrouping across the river for a counterattack or a "last stand" at the main encampment.

At 11:15 P.M. on July 28 Miles' forces marched across the 11th Street bridge, halting briefly on the south side to allow the veterans one more chance to pack their belongings and depart. "Shortly afterward," Eisenhower stated, "the whole encampment of shacks and huts just ahead began burning." Eisenhower, Miles, and the unit commanders all denied that the troops started the fires. Some officers believed that the veterans acted out of spite, firing the tents which the government had loaned to them. The tent fires spread quickly to the huts and lean-tos, causing a conflagration among the estimated 2100 B.E.F. dwellings on the river flats. Miles reported that "little resistance was met in the camp except on the part of individuals, most of whom were intoxicated." Around midnight 2000 marchers massed along the southern edge of "Camp Marks," as the B.E.F.'s Anacostia encampment was called; but tear gas grenades dispersed them before they could organize and rush the infantry lines. While countless fires lighted the bottomland, the veterans and their families fled in pell-mell fashion into the night. Many residents of the nearby towns of Anacostia, Twining, and Good Hope opened their doors that night to choking, aching bonus marchers. Back at the encampment, meanwhile, mopping-up operations continued. MacArthur turned angrily to an onlooker who yelled, "The American flag means nothing to me after this!" The chief of staff threatened to have him arrested if he spoke again. "The man closed up like a clam," commented a witness. In the flickering light of one hut Major Patton recognized the ragged occupant as the man who had saved his life on a French battlefield in 1918. Elsewhere on the flats, a seven-year-old boy who ran back to his parents' shack to get his pet rabbit was bayoneted in the leg by a soldier. At a White House window stood Hoover commenting to several guests about the crimson glow that was spreading across the sky over Anacostia Flats. The operation's success must have made him forget his earlier instructions against invading Camp Marks, for reporters at the White House were told simply that "the President is pleased." At 2:00 A.M., while Hoover slumbered peacefully, the troops at Camp Marks bivouacked. Coast artillery searchlights swept back and forth across the flats through the rest of the night. Only smoking embers and grotesque hulks of rubble remained where the previous night thousands of poverty-stricken men, women, and children had slept.[26]

As MacArthur prepared to return to the War Department just before 11:00 P.M. on the 28th, Eisenhower cautioned him that correspondents would be waiting. "I suggested it would be the better part of wisdom, if not of valor, to avoid meeting them," Eisenhower said. He urged the chief of staff to let Hurley and the other civilian officials handle the reporters since the dispersal "had not been a military idea really, but a political order." [27] MacArthur again ignored Eisenhower's advice and told the correspondents waiting at the War Department:

. . . That mob down there was a bad-looking mob. It was animated by the essence of revolution. The gentleness, the consideration with which they had been treated had been mistaken for weakness, and they had come to the conclusion, beyond the shadow of a doubt, that they were about to take over in some arbitrary way either the direct control of the Government or else to control it by indirect methods. It is my opinion that had the President not acted today, had he permitted this thing to go on for twenty-four hours more, he would have been faced with a grave situation which would have caused a real battle. Had he let it go on another week, I believe that the institutions of our Government would have been very severely threatened. I think it can be safely said that he had not only reached the end of an extraordinary patience but that he had gone to the very limit of his desire to avoid friction and trouble before he used force. Had he not used it at that time, I believe he would have been very derelict indeed in the judgment in which he was handling the safety of the country. This was the focus of the world today; and had he not acted with the force and vigor that he did, it would have been a very sad day for the country tomorrow.

There were, in my opinion, few veteran soldiers in the group that we cleared out today; few indeed. I am not speaking by figures because I don't know how many there were; but if there was one man in ten in that group today who is a veteran, it would surprise me . . .

I have never seen greater relief on the part of the distressed populace than I saw today. I have released in my day more than one community which had been held in the grip of a foreign enemy . . . . At least a dozen people told me, especially in the Negro section, that a regular system of tribute was being levied on them by this insurrectionist group; a reign of terror was being started which may have led to a system of Caponeism, and I believe later to insurgency and insurrection. The President played it pretty fine in waiting to the last minute; but he didn't have much margin . . .

I have been in many riots, but I think this is the first riot I ever was in or ever saw in which there was no real bloodshed. So far as I know, there is no man on either side who has been seriously injured.[28]

These remarks were destined to sear his reputation for years to come. Eisenhower was correct when he surmised later: "I think

this meeting led to the prevailing impression that General Mac-
Arthur himself had undertaken and directed the move against
the veterans and that he was acting as something more than the
agent of civilian authorities." [29]

At noon on July 29 the troops departed from Anacostia Flats
and returned to downtown Washington to clear out some B.E.F.
stragglers. Major Surles, the cavalry commander, noted that
whereas on the first day his troops were "easily restrained," on
the 29th his men's attitude "was more antagonistic and the men
would undoubtedly have used their permitted weapons more
severely if resistance had been encountered." Over 2500 new
tear gas grenades and candles were flown from Edgewood Arsenal to Bolling Field for the second day's operations. Fortunately there was no serious opposition on the 29th, almost all
marchers having fled from the city. The last pocket of resistance
was cleared about 5:00 P.M. in an area between 12th and 13th
streets in the southwest sector of Washington. James Ford,
Negro candidate for vice president on the Communist ticket,
tried to organize new resistance, but Glassford's police quickly
arrested him and forty-two others at a Red rally. On the evening of July 29 the last Army units returned to their regular
posts; the bonus operation was finished.[30]

4. Bitter Aftertastes

Miles and his staff spent many hours in August analyzing the
operation to figure out how the Army could perform even more
effectively in future civil disorders. It was found that the tear
gas, horses, and sabers were more telling against a mob than
infantry bayonets. No units reported firing bullets, but they
expended over 2000 tear gas grenades and candles. Tests at Fort
Washington, conducted in early August, showed that the type
of gas grenades used against the B.E.F. "ignited soon after its

contact with refuse and caused a large flame"; the type of tear gas candles employed in the operation "failed to emit the white smoke of the tear gas and instead issued a roaring flame." Miles concluded that the first fires, in the shacks along Pennsylvania Avenue, were caused by defective, inflammatory grenades and candles and that the later fires in that area were set by soldiers mistakenly thinking an order to burn the huts had been issued. When the final tally of Army casualties was figured, it was found that only twelve soldiers had been injured, four by bricks and eight by tear gas. In the latter cases, two soldiers were burned by grenades thrown back by marchers, and the other six were injured by defective grenades and candles. The general assessment of the operation by the high command was summed up in MacArthur's words to Kunzig: "The troops were rapidly assembled, promptly moved to the field of disorder, and skillfully employed." In a general order dated August 3, Miles praised his troops for the operation, which was "effected with a promptness, efficiency and expedition that reflected credit on the entire Army." [31]

In the days following the eviction of the Bonus Army, official Washington came forth with its expected justifications. Hoover declared that the federal government had moved "swiftly and firmly" against "overt lawlessness" by "those who would destroy all government." The President said, "It is obvious that, after the departure of the majority of the veterans, subversive influences obtained control of the men remaining in the District." Attorney General Mitchell claimed that "an extraordinary proportion" of the B.E.F consisted of "criminal, communist, and non-veteran elements." Assistant Secretary of War Davison stamped the bonus marchers as "a polyglot mob of tramps and hoodlums, with a generous sprinkling of Communist agitators." Hurley proudly stated, "The duty of restoring law and order was performed with directness, with effectiveness, and with unparalleled humanity and kindness."

The findings of executive and judicial bodies investigating the affair did not generally support the above charges. The Veterans Bureau conducted an extensive check of the Bonus Army's membership and concluded that 94 per cent were bona fide veterans. A federal grand jury which examined criminal charges against various bonus marchers returned indictments against only three, and even these had been wounded in action with the A.E.F. in 1918; the jury report did not mention the presence of Communists. District police records revealed that 350 of the 363 marchers arrested over the previous two months were charged with relatively minor offenses, such as trespassing and drunkenness.[32]

Unlike the Great Red Scare of 1919–20, which gripped nearly an entire nation, the hysteria of mid-1932 was confined largely within the higher echelons of the federal government. The *Washington News* received hundreds of letters about the affair, over 90 per cent of which expressed unfavorable reactions to the administration's handling of the Bonus Army. Correspondents and other eye-witnesses who put their sentiments into print in articles too numerous to cite overwhelmingly agreed that the panic-stricken Hoover administration misjudged the B.E.F. and bungled the eviction. Robert Furman and his wife, who were Associated Press correspondents on the scene from the start to the end of the episode, summarized the lasting impression of most contemporary writers and later historians: "The Communistic threat, which held many close to President Hoover in a vise of fear, was really small, and could not have swept the bonus army into belligerent action. In the main, it was made up of run-of-the-mill, hard-luck Americans, forerunners of the Okies and the Arkies of later years." [33]

Of course, the American Communist party tried to exploit the propagandistic value of the B.E.F.'s eviction to the hilt. A few days after the dispersal of the Bonus Army, a party spokesman bragged: "We agitated for the bonus and led the demonstration . . . We stand ready to go to Washington again and fight for the working men." Pace was sent by the party on a speech-making tour of the country, during which he castigated the ruthless, tyrannical officials and generals in Washington. Both Pace and Benjamin Gitlow, one-time party secretary, later admitted publicly that the American Communist party had instructions from Moscow to infiltrate and gain control of the B.E.F. for the purpose of inciting revolution. Few authorities on the subject question the Red's presence and intent in the affair. But there is also little doubt that the Communists failed in both of their objectives: they neither controlled the B.E.F. nor provoked a revolution. The executive committee of the Comintern, meeting in Moscow in early 1933, adopted a resolution denouncing the American Reds' failure to influence and lead the proletariat during the demonstrations of the previous year.

In mid-August the General Staff G-2 showed MacArthur "a partial list of prominent men throughout the United States marked for assassination by Communists," the information coming from military intelligence sources and probably F.B.I. records also. The list included MacArthur, Henry Ford, Charles G. Dawes, J. P. Morgan, and Representatives Martin Dies and Hamilton Fish, among other prominent names. The intelligence report stated that "they want to 'knock off' Gen. Mac-Arthur because he issued the orders that routed the Red bonus marchers and drove them from Washington." No further action on the matter was uncovered. MacArthur may have had knowledge of this or other reports of Red plots against his life before he gave his fateful press statement on July 28.[34]

In his formal report to the Secretary of War on the operations of July 28–29 MacArthur concluded, "Thus a most disagreeable task was performed in such a way as to leave behind it a minimum of unpleasant aftermath and legitimate resentment." But in the wake of the episode the chief of staff found himself roundly assailed by newspaper and periodical writers, particularly of liberal organs, for his role in the incident. The most valid criticisms were that he was an active leader in the administration's conspiracy to maneuver the B.E.F. into precipitate action that would justify the use of the Army to get a quick eviction; he was misinformed about the nature and intention of the Bonus Army; he had no business assuming any personal role in the action of July 28 and should have refused Hoover's request of his presence in the streets, if, of course, the President gave him that option; he should not have sent the Army into Camp Marks or pre-empted Miles' command at any time during the eviction; and he gave a statement to the press on the night of the 28th which was unnecessary and erroneous. The defense grounds are too weak to try to refute these charges. Once MacArthur was convinced that the affair was a Communist assault against the federal government, he acted with overzealous determination and reckless impulsiveness.

The bitter invectives hurled by his critics in the aftermath included less defensible charges that MacArthur ordered special anti-riot plans and training of Army units in order to force or at least make easier Hoover's decision to employ federal troops; he conducted the eviction brutally and with much bloodshed; and his personal appearance was made in the hope that the American people in their desperation would turn to him as the "savior on the white horse."

There is no evidence to suggest that MacArthur believed that, by ordering anti-riot preparations at Fort Myer, he was influencing executive policy. Had there been no troops especially trained in anti-riot tactics, Hoover would have undoubtedly called upon the troops in the area anyway, and ill-prepared soldiers would surely have provoked more violence than did occur. The American Civil Liberties Union was most active in pressing this charge. When Hoover sent one of the letters he got from the A.C.L.U. to MacArthur, the chief of staff, by then obviously smarting under the mounting criticisms, told the President that "absolutely no instructions have been issued from the War Department at any time during my incumbency of the office of Chief of Staff dealing with any riot troubles or disturbances, and any effort to show any activities along those lines due to the depression are simply fabrications." In this note of August 12 MacArthur also advised the President to ignore the A.C.L.U.: "They have made frequent attacks upon the Army in every possible way. Their basic purpose, of course, is the destruction of all constituted authority. The War Department has long since made it a policy not to answer any of the communications that it receives from such a source." [35] It is not known if the A.C.L.U. learned of MacArthur's response; it would have made superb cannon fodder for the liberals. And like his press statement after the Anacostia eviction, it was so unnecessary. After all, the Army would have been derelict had it not prepared for civil disorder, especially in view of the growing tension after the Senate's rejection of the bonus bill. MacArthur's anti-riot preparedness was prudent, though he acted impulsively during and after the emergency.

As for the charge of brutality, it must be remembered that MacArthur's only active participation in the operation was his order to continue the advance across the Anacostia River. Miles was at all times the commanding officer; but, even so, the Army's handling of the marchers seems rough and harsh only when compared with Glassford's earlier relations with the B.E.F. The police superintendent has emerged as the hero in almost every account of the Bonus March. His leniency up to the time of the Senate vote on the bonus was admirable, but his continuing kindnesses undoubtedly encouraged many marchers to believe that they could stay and become even bolder without facing a judgment day. When the eviction time came, the district police could not command the respect and obedience of the marchers. The two fatal shootings which set off the day's violence were from a police revolver. Indeed, many persons were gassed, including one fatally, and some were injured after the Army took charge and completed the eviction. But when the episode is compared to riots before and since 1932, it is improbable that so large a force of demonstrators has been suppressed with greater swiftness and less bloodshed.

The accusation that MacArthur envisioned himself as the strong leader to whom the desperate nation would turn in the depression crisis was implicit in many caustic appraisals of the affair in the following months. One who harbored fear that MacArthur was politically ambitious was the Democratic presidential candidate, Franklin D. Roosevelt. A few days after the B.E.F. dispersal, Roosevelt and some friends were chatting at his office in Albany. The phone rang; the caller asked for the governor. "God damn it, Frank, don't you know who nominated you? Why do you have Baruch and Young and all those Wall Street blankety blanks up there to see you?" The caller was Huey Long, and the fiery tirade went on for several minutes, with Roosevelt smiling and occasionally trying to interject a soothing remark. When the conversation ended, Roosevelt commented as he replaced the phone on its cradle: "It's all very well for us to laugh over Huey. But actually we have to remember all the time that he really is one of the two most dangerous men in the country." Rexford G. Tugwell, a key member of Roosevelt's "Brain Trust," asked if the other dangerous figure was Father Coughlin. "Oh, no," Roosevelt responded, "the other is Douglas MacArthur." The New York governor explained that "people wanted strong leadership; they were sick of uncertainty, anxious for security, and willing to trade liberty for it." According to Tugwell, Roosevelt said: "What was lacking was the familiar symbolic figure — the man on horseback . . . There was none so well endowed with charm, tradition, and majestic appearance as MacArthur; and the Nazi-minded among American leaders recalled with approval the incident that had seemed to all liberals so reprehensible — that, of course, was 'the battle of Anacostia Flats.' " The governor went on to assure Tugwell and the others present that "this rightist threat was only latent . . . We must tame these fellows and make them useful to us." [36] Tugwell probably quoted him accurately, as some of Roosevelt's remarks and actions later indicated. But nothing in MacArthur's correspondence, addresses, or actions during the remaining years of the Great Depression suggests that he had presidential or dictatorial ambitions. The general's behavior during the bonus affair more nearly resembled that of a nineteenth-century English noble than a twentieth-century totalitarian mass leader. Even later when MacArthur challenged President Roosevelt and his successor on various issues, he did so as the military aristocrat, not as the pretender to the throne. The terms "patrician" and "demagogue" are not synonyms.

There is no question that MacArthur's identification with the dispersal of the Bonus Army was a liability and a sensitive matter to him for years. In 1934 when he filed a libel suit against Robert S. Allen and Drew Pearson of the "Washington Merry-Go-Round," one of MacArthur's seven charges, for each of which he asked $250,000 in damages, was that the two columnists pictured him ousting the B.E.F. in an "unwarranted, unnecessary, arbitrary, harsh and brutal" manner. The case was settled out of court, with the columnists claiming that they paid nothing and gave no apologies or retractions. MacArthur made no comment on the case. In November, 1934, the Columbus (Ohio) *Dispatch* reported that MacArthur "has many enemies" and should not be reappointed as chief of staff: "Although well-liked in the Army, MacArthur is reported to have numerous opponents on Capitol Hill. Most of this opposition is due to the fact that he was in personal charge of the federal troops called out by former President Hoover to evict the bonus army from the capital in 1932." A. P. Lamneck, a Democratic representative from Ohio and one of the leading liberals in the House, strongly opposed MacArthur's continuance as chief of staff on the same grounds. Josephus Daniels, former Secretary of the Navy, wrote Roosevelt in the fall of 1934 that MacArthur's reappointment "would be deeply resented" by the American Legion. At the Legion's national convention in Portland two years earlier, Daniels said that he sensed "the deep feeling of resentment of the whole body toward Pat Hurley and General MacArthur." When Daniels spoke at state Legion conventions in Pennsylvania and North Carolina, he found that "the feeling against the General was very strong." (Roosevelt reappointed MacArthur anyway for reasons which will be explained later.) Eisenhower, who served as MacArthur's assistant for the next seven years, said that MacArthur "had an obsession that a high commander must protect his public image at all costs and must never admit his wrongs." [37] That obsession, unnoticeable in MacArthur's earlier years, may have been born as a result of the B.E.F. experience.

To the end of his life MacArthur was certain that the Bonus March was a Red conspiracy. Quoting statements by Communist leaders in his memoirs, he persisted in identifying the presence of Reds in the Bonus March with Communist domination of the B.E.F. Although the character "General Goober" in Amos Pinchot's farce *General Goober at the Battle of Anacostia* was intended to satirize the President, both Hoover and MacArthur might have profited from reading the playlet. In one scene General Goober, girding himself for battle against the enemy at Anacostia, exclaims to his Negro servant: "My God, man, you don't expect me to fight without a Sam Browne belt? This is war!" The Negro answers: "Dis sure am war. But it ain't de kind ob war you-all kin win with Sam Browne belts nor tank wagons neither. What dis war needs is lunch wagons, an' de ham sandwich division, an' de po'k an' beans brigade. An' de beer wagon. Don's fo'git about dat wagon, suh." [38] Mac-

Arthur's intense dedication to duty, honor, and country were commendable, and he doubtless felt that he was following those principles as he donned his uniform on that July 28th. Perhaps he should have taken a few minutes to read some pages from the delightful tale of Don Quixote and his crusade against the Spanish windmills. But, alas, MacArthur, like Hoover, never was able to laugh at himself.

CHAPTER XV

Those Strange New Dealers

1. A New Deal for the Army

WHEN HOOVER AND HIS PARTY were crushed at the polls in November, 1932, MacArthur must have felt their defeat keenly. Not only did it seem to be a setback for the conservative philosophy of Hoover, which the chief of staff espoused, but also the end of the Republican regime would mean the departure from Washington of some of MacArthur's closest civilian friends, particularly Hoover, Hurley, and Payne. From the speeches of Franklin D. Roosevelt during his campaign, it was difficult to predict his behavior as President or what he meant by the "New Deal" which he planned to introduce. At Pittsburgh in October he had pledged to carry out "the plain precept of our Party, which is to reduce the cost of current Federal Government operations by 25%." MacArthur could anticipate that George H. Dern, the governor of Utah and former mining executive whom Roosevelt had chosen as his Secretary of War, was, like his other cabinet appointees, committed in advance by the President-elect to bring about further economies in his department. On the other hand, perhaps MacArthur could win over the new President to the Army's needs if columnist

Walter Lippmann's analysis in early 1932 was correct: "Franklin D. Roosevelt is a highly impressionable person, without a firm grasp of public affairs and without very strong convictions . . . He is not the dangerous enemy of anything. He is too eager to please . . . He is a pleasant man who, without any important qualifications for the office, would very much like to be President."

For the first time since the World War, General of the Armies Pershing, who was ill, did not lead the presidential inaugural parade on March 4, 1933, yielding the grand marshalcy to MacArthur. As the chief of staff rode his high-spirited stallion at the head of the long procession down Pennsylvania Avenue, his thoughts were probably about what the future months held for him and the Army. His mood may have fitted the sullen sky, cold wind, and occasional rain of that day. Nevertheless, at the round of social festivities in honor of the new Chief Executive, MacArthur "shed benign charm on fellow guests," according to one commentator. Whether that charm would work on Roosevelt remained to be seen.[1]

MacArthur and Roosevelt had known each other since their days in the War and Navy departments on the eve of America's entry into the World War. The chief of staff found that Roosevelt "had greatly changed and matured" since that time. In the days ahead the liberal President and his conservative chief of staff would skirmish many times, but Roosevelt would probably have reciprocated MacArthur's later statement: "Whatever difference arose between us, it never sullied in slightest degree the warmth of my personal friendship for him." Both were well-born gentlemen of their respective realms; both were mightily influenced by their ambitious, strong-willed mothers; and both were characterized by vitality, impatience, dash, bravado, and fierce drive. MacArthur was the more intelligent, forthright, and aggressive of the two, but Roosevelt was the more shrewd, adaptable, and perceptive. Ideologically they were poles apart, MacArthur's antipathy toward the New Deal being pronounced from the start. On matters concerning the armed services the new President would distinctly favor the Navy and sometimes the Army Air Corps. In the long run Tugwell was probably accurate when he remarked of MacArthur and other ambitious persons who sparred with the President: "All were frustrated by the fiercer concentration, the wilier talents, the greater power of the Roosevelt personality. None could compete successfully. He was, as Willkie said, 'the champ.'" Indeed, MacArthur would soon discover that Roosevelt was a master of role-taking, or presenting different faces to different callers; and the chief of staff, like other persons who dealt with him, would never be quite sure which role expressed the President's real self. On the other hand, Roosevelt respected his dedicated chief of staff and found his bedrock patriotism and conservatism refreshingly different from the often vacillating views of his New Dealers. One evening at dinner MacArthur, prompted by "curiosity and perhaps some measure of pique," asked Roosevelt why he frequently sought his opinions on social reforms and other nonmilitary matters of which the chief of staff had no professional knowledge. The President replied, "Douglas, I don't bring these questions up for your advice but for your reactions. To me, you are the symbol of the conscience of the American people." [2]

Roosevelt did not keep MacArthur long in suspense as to his plans for the Army in the New Deal. One of the President's long-cherished dreams was the organization of a force of unemployed young men to undertake projects in reforestation, flood control, soil rehabilitation, development of national park facilities, and other activities aimed at conserving the nation's natural resources. Since Roosevelt was occupied with a host of legislative proposals which would be introduced into Congress during the "Hundred Days" that spring, he left the implementation of his idea of an emergency conservation corps to his sharp-minded, if unkempt and asthmatic, secretary, Louis Mc-Henry Howe. In a few days Howe, working with Tugwell and Secretary of Labor Frances Perkins principally, came up with a draft for such a work force. On March 21 the bill to create the Civilian Conservation Corps was introduced into Congress, and it was passed by voice vote ten days later. The bill left most of the details to the Chief Executive, or rather to Howe, with the exact relations between the several departments to be involved left unspecified. As conceived at first by Howe and his colleagues, the departments of Agriculture, Labor, Interior, and War would assume responsibility over different phases of the C.C.C. program. The Army's function would be to enroll the recruits, put them through a two-week conditioning course, and transport them to the work camps where usually the United States Forest Service would take charge. Roosevelt's stated objective was to have 250,000 C.C.C. workers on the job by July 1.

Reaction to the creation of the Civilian Conservation Corps was generally favorable, but some individuals and organizations were upset because the War Department had a role, if only a small one at first. William Green, president of the American Federation of Labor, charged that the scheme smacked "of fascism, of Hitlerism, of a form of Sovietism" in the use of the Army and the regimentation of labor, while MacArthur insisted that "no military training whatsoever" would be foisted on the C.C.C. program. But the chief of staff, who had been against the Army's participation in any capacity, was uneasy about the possible expansion of the military's role in the C.C.C., particularly in view of the vagueness of the bill's wording and of the President's notions about its scope and duration.[3]

In spite of his reluctance to have the Army engaged in relief work, MacArthur set the General Staff to work on cost estimates and regulations for the reception, organization, transportation, and supply of units of unemployed men as soon as he learned of the administration's proposal. By March 24, a week before the C.C.C. Act was passed, MacArthur presented to Roosevelt and Howe the regulations drafted by the General Staff; they were approved by the President and his secretary. The next day the chief of staff sent secret radio messages to the corps area commanders setting forth the Army's mission in the C.C.C. Thanks to prompt, thorough planning in the War Department, the Army was ready to go when the bill was signed into law. Its plans, however, were based on a temporary involvement with the C.C.C. and a limited function which did not encompass actual administration of the work camps. But by early May delay and confusion had characterized the first month's efforts by the other executive departments in trying to meet the goal set by Roosevelt. A chart prepared by the General Staff on May 3 showed that at the current pace only 115,000 recruits would be in C.C.C. camps by July 1. Robert Fechner, the C.C.C. director and former machinists' union leader, met together with his advisory council and Howe and finally decided to ask the President's authorization to let the War Department take over the mobilization of the C.C.C. They concluded that only the Army had the organization, personnel, and equipment to undertake such a large-scale project in so short a time. Roosevelt was agreeable, and on May 10 Fechner requested the War Department to present a plan to the C.C.C. advisory council for attaining the President's objective by July 1.[4] Colonel Duncan K. Major, MacArthur's acting G-3 and the War Department's representative on the C.C.C. advisory council, described the General Staff's reaction:

> With less than forty hours available from the notice of the Director [Fechner] of his desires until the time for submitting the War Department's plan to meet this task, the three sections of the General Staff assembled data during the daylight hours of the 11th of May and that night a lone officer assembled it in a Memorandum to the Director of Emergency Conservation Work, giving the facts . . . and closing with the recommenda-

tion which a sleepy-eyed girl pounded out on her typewriter at 2:00 A.M., May 12 . . .

It was a momentous day. In a few hours more had been accomplished than in the previous month. A clearcut decision on a definite plan to fulfill a task the complete definition of which was positively ordered electrified the whole effort. The old order had changed. That afternoon all Assistant Chiefs of Staff and Chiefs of Services met in the office of the Deputy Chief of Staff [Drum, who succeeded Moseley in February]. The new mission was given, stirring everyone. Plans and actions for the field were required by the next morning. That night instead of a stray light here and there the War Department's windows were ablaze. The big machine was rolling in a war effort. The Army was under test, but what a grand opportunity the task offered.[5]

On the 12th the War Department's plan was approved by Fechner, his advisory council, and the President. Secretary of War Dern and Chief of Staff MacArthur gave the C.C.C. mobilization their full support and practically brought to a standstill the service schools, training programs, and reserve activities for that summer in order to supply the men, trucks, camp equipment, and other items necessary for the massive mobilization. MacArthur and the General Staff viewed the operation as not only a valuable exercise for the Army comparable in some ways to wartime mobilization but also a means of demonstrating the value of the officer corps to the public and Congress, especially since agitation was again under way on Capitol Hill to reduce the officer strength of the Army.

MacArthur's own contributions in the founding of the C.C.C. were most important at two critical periods. First, it was largely due to his alertness and guidance that the General Staff had a plan of action prepared by the time the bill was passed. Second, in his directives to the corps area commanders in May, as the Army took control of the mobilization, he established the policy that those generals would be permitted as much autonomy and discretion as possible in administering C.C.C. activities in their corps areas. An authority on the C.C.C. maintains, "Perhaps of all factors aiding the success of the Army's role in the CCC, the policy of MacArthur to de-centralize control of actual operation had the greatest import. Besides insuring a low bureaucratic overhead at the top of the organization, de-centralization of responsibility meant expeditious handling of supply bottlenecks and decisive and quick action in relation to all personnel and other administrative problems." [6]

Whereas between April 7 and July 1, 1917 — America's first three months in the World War — the War Department mobilized 181,000 men, the Army during the period May 12–July 1, 1933, mobilized nearly 275,000 C.C.C. recruits in camps in forty-seven states. The huge operation involved over 200 trains and 3600 Army vehicles; the youths were supplied with 1,225,-000 pairs of trousers and 1,700,000 towels, among the hundreds of different items drawn from quartermaster depots; sites were cleared and construction was completed on 1330 work camps. The President's objective was more than fulfilled; by July 1 he was delighted and the War Department justifiably proud of its achievement. Major admitted to Fechner that "the mobilization of the C.C.C. with time as the essential element in the execution of the task has been the most valuable experience the Army has had since the World War." The results, said Major, proved that "the General Staff has justified itself as a planning agency . . . The organization of the U.S. into Corps Area Commands has proved sound . . . The war stocks of equipment of all kinds gave ample testimony of the need to maintain such reserves." Moreover, he emphasized that "it is necessary if the Army is to exert its full power of accomplishment in any emergency that it be given a clearly defined mission, the means and the authority to execute it and be protected from all interference by the Executive." [7] Mindful that congressmen sometimes read annual reports of chiefs of staff, MacArthur in his report for fiscal 1933 said of the C.C.C. mobilization:

> To epitomize the military lessons of the 1933 mobilization, it has given renewed evidence of the value of systematic preparation for emergency, including the maintenance of trained personnel and suitable supplies and the development of plans and policies applicable to a mobilization. Particularly has it served to emphasize again the vital need for a strong corps of professional officers and for an efficient body of commissioned Reserves.[8]

On June 30, with the goal reached, MacArthur sent messages of congratulation to his corps area commanders, in which he declared that the operation "represented the greatest peacetime demand ever made upon the Army and constituted a task of character and proportions equivalent to emergencies of war." The mobilization proved "the superior standard of professional fitness of the Army. Only high morale, a spirit of cooperation, pride of service, and devotion to duty could have accomplished such splendid results." Six weeks later he sent to Roosevelt a photograph of C.C.C. workers attending a worship service at a camp in a redwood forest in northern California. "This photograph," he told Stephen Early, the assistant secretary to the President, "exemplifies to a marked degree one of the President's essential ideals of the entire Civilian Conservation Corps project, the making of better citizens." Early informed MacArthur later that day: "I think it is one of the finest I have ever seen. I gave it to the President, and he was delighted with it. What he liked particularly was the evidence of devotion shown by the boys. He ordered it framed, to be hung in the White House, and asked me to express his appreciation of your thoughtfulness." Although the President left the mechanics of the C.C.C. to Howe and Fechner and the chief of staff likewise left the War Department's problems in the affair mainly to Major, both Roosevelt and MacArthur were jubilant over the mobilization and the subsequent success of the C.C.C. The Army's cooperation and efficiency in carrying out the mobilization improved relations between Roosevelt and MacArthur, which had become tense during congressional deliberations on reducing the officer corps earlier in 1933, as will be discussed later.[9]

In the next two years MacArthur left C.C.C. matters, for the most part, to Major, Fechner, and Howe. In early 1934 MacArthur, who was anxious to get the Army out of the program, began a gradual replacement of regular officers on duty with the C.C.C., substituting officers of the Organized Reserve. When the President decided to include an educational program in the C.C.C., from the elementary to college levels, MacArthur quickly modified a plan presented by the federal commissioner of education to make sure that the War Department would have the final word on "the outlines of instruction, teaching procedure, and the type of teaching materials for use in the camps." Though corps area and camp commanders often interfered with the instruction by forbidding discussion of "dangerous issues" and "radical doctrines," the C.C.C. education service by 1937 had established an impressive record: 35,000 illiterate recruits learned to read and write, 1000 C.C.C. youths received high school diplomas, and thirty-nine got college degrees, largely through courses offered in the camps. In another area, racial discrimination, MacArthur might have been expected to push for harmonious and fair relations for Negroes in the C.C.C., in view of his concern for civil and social equality for the Filipinos. In April, 1934, he did establish a policy of using Negroes as educational advisers, when practicable, in Negro camps, but neither he, Fechner, nor any other authority moved to end the system of separate black and white camps. All in all, the Army's efforts to provide equal opportunities for Negro recruits, who constituted about 10 per cent of the C.C.C. enrollment, were rather halfhearted.[10]

MacArthur's talent for attracting the wrath of pacifists was evidenced in early 1935 when he proposed to the appropriations committee of the House that military training be incorporated in the C.C.C. A year earlier Harry H. Woodring, Payne's successor as assistant secretary of war, had proposed that the C.C.C. "should be expanded and put under the control of the Army" entirely, eliminating the civilian directorship and advisory council. Woodring's statement, appearing in a magazine article, brought him a sharp reprimand from Roosevelt and a flurry of anti-militarist correspondence. Historian Charles A. Beard wrote the President that "it is your bounden duty to yourself and your administration to wash your hands of this fascist doctrine and to remove Woodring within fifteen minutes." Woodring kept his position and weathered the storm, which turned out to be mild compared to the furor MacArthur stirred up with his proposal. The chief of staff remarked to the congressional committee that "nothing would be finer than to take these C.C.C. men who have had six months in camp and give them, perhaps, two months more, in which they would receive military training. We could then enroll them in the enlisted reserve for a certain number of years, with, perhaps, a small stipend — say, a dollar a month." Representative John J. McSwain of South Carolina, chairman of the military affairs committee of the House, introduced a bill incorporating MacArthur's suggestion, but it died in committee after Capitol Hill had been bombarded with heated protests. The Committee on Militarism in Education, whose leaders included philosopher John Dewey and theologian Reinhold Niebuhr, condemned the bill and demanded the "termination of all War Department participation in the C.C.C." Other pacifist groups which cried out against MacArthur's alleged scheme to bring about "the militarization of the C.C.C." included the American League Against War and Fascism, the Anti-War Committee, the Union of Private School Teachers, and the

American Youth Congress, among others. Probably most telling as far as the House committee was concerned was the bitter opposition of Fechner and practically all civilian authorities of the C.C.C.[11]

In September, 1935, as MacArthur was preparing to retire as chief of staff, Fechner wrote him:

> Before leaving Washington I want you to know of my sincere appreciation for the invaluable cooperation and support that you have given me in Emergency Conservation Work. Your personal interest and constant willingness to talk over all problems that have arisen has been of the greatest value to me in this work.
>
> I have repeatedly paid public tribute to the part that the War Department has played in this great undertaking, and I am convinced we could have never made a success of it had it not been for the wholehearted enthusiasm of the Army to do the best possible job in carrying out every part of the program. I know that your sympathetic interest was the main spring in the work that the Army has performed.[12]

MacArthur replied that his connection with the C.C.C. had been "a real inspiration." He told Fechner: "It is the type of human reconstruction that has appealed to me more than I sometimes admit. Your own part in it has been done magnificently, and I think all concerned in this splendid effort have cause for rejoicing in the results that it is producing."[13] Nevertheless, MacArthur probably was still adamantly opposed to the use of the Army in any work relief program. It had been politically expedient for the War Department to cooperate fully in the President's pet project, and the Army's efficiency in handling the C.C.C. had brought the military establishment more favorable publicity than any of its activities since the World War. Both MacArthur and the New Dealers found themselves in anomalous positions regarding the C.C.C. The President and the coterie of liberal advisers around him were indebted to the Army and its conservative generals for the organization and administration of the first and probably the most successful relief program of the New Deal. MacArthur and his military advisers, on the other hand, found in the C.C.C. a lever for prying funds for the Army from the President and Congress. It would be interesting to know what MacArthur had to say to his friend Mr. Hoover about the Army's role in the C.C.C.; perhaps he simply explained that he was obeying the orders of the Commander-in-Chief.

2. *Fighting for Funds*

The final Hoover budget, for fiscal 1934, was a shocking setback to MacArthur. In September, 1932, with the presidential election campaign in full swing, Hoover declared that he wanted the federal budget cut by $500,000,000 for fiscal 1934, the vote-getting lure to taxpayers undoubtedly being a factor in his thinking. The budget presented to Congress that December provided $277,700,000 for military activities, or $43,200,000 less than the War Department requested. The reduction particularly hurt the civilian components, with the C.M.T.C. and R.O.T.C. curtailed severely and the drill schedule of the National Guard cut in half. Collins, of course, was delighted since he had little regard for these components and wanted more of their funds to be shifted to mechanization. "The only way to give adequate military preparedness without putting an overwhelming tax burden on the people," he emphasized, "is to cut down on personnel and put the saving in effective machines." At the hearings of Collins' subcommittee, MacArthur pointed out that the United States Army was seventeenth in strength of personnel among the world's armies, but Collins disputed his figures and chastised the chief of staff for not learning more on his European tours: "The day has passed when a

General Staff can overawe legislators or browbeat the common man by presuming to have inside information or superior knowledge of existing military conditions in other countries." As for the civilian components, MacArthur maintained that they "have made steady progress in attaining proficiency, and thus represent considerable investment in time, effort, and money, and an asset for emergency use that should be jealously guarded." McSwain and other influential congressmen, however, were becoming increasingly disenchanted with Mac-Arthur's arguments for manpower, and, like Collins, they wanted the priority on funds to go to new weapons systems, especially aircraft and tanks. It must have been ominous to the beleaguered chief of staff that in early January, 1933, at the height of the debate over funds for the civilian components, the President invited General Mitchell to the White House for a lengthy private conference on the needs of military aviation.[14]

In March, 1933, Congress passed the Army appropriation bill for fiscal 1934, providing $277,100,000 for military activities — a sum less than that proposed by the Hoover administration. Three weeks later Lewis Douglas, Roosevelt's budget director, decreed that military expenditures for fiscal 1934 must be cut $80,000,000 below the amount appropriated by Congress. Also in March came the Economy Act, which provided for reductions up to 15 per cent in the salaries of federal employees, besides cuts in veterans' pensions. Moreover, that spring the House appropriations committee reported out a bill which stated in one of its provisions: "The President is authorized to place on furlough such officers of the Army, Marine Corps, Public Health Service, Coast Guard, or Coast and Geodetic Survey as he, in his discretion, shall deem desirable." The section of the bill also said that "while on furlough, officers shall receive one half the pay to which they would otherwise have been entitled, but shall not be entitled to any allowance except for travel to their homes." Roosevelt was alleged to favor the furloughing of 3000 to 4000 officers of the Regular Army if the measure passed. These moves to sacrifice the Army in the cause of economy coincided with the Roosevelt administration's use of the Army to mobilize the C.C.C. at a cost of $143,000,000 for the first three months.

Bewildered and angered, MacArthur cornered key leaders on Capitol Hill and persons close to the President in his endeavor to save the Army. The cut of $80,000,000, which he called "a stunning blow to national defense," was subsequently changed by Roosevelt to $51,000,000 less than the sum Congress appropriated for fiscal 1934. MacArthur fought hard in congressional hearings to get the Army's retired list excluded from the Economy Act; he was successful at least in preventing Pershing's pension from being slashed, for which the retired general wrote him a letter of thanks, at the same time praising his efforts on behalf of the Army's budget. The furlough provision, which was part of the Independent Offices Appropriation Bill, was passed by the House, but after the War Department, with MacArthur in the lead, stirred up veterans and civic groups, as well as legislators and editors, to protest against the measure, the Senate rejected the bill.[15]

Sometime during the furor over reducing the costs of the Army, probably in late March, MacArthur went with Dern to appeal personally to the President. Dern pointed out that it would be "a fatal error" to economize further on national defense when Nazi Germany was arming and Japan was already on the road of aggression. "But the President was obdurate," MacArthur said, "and the quiet spoken phrases of Dern were no match for the biting diction of Roosevelt. Under his lashing tongue, the Secretary grew white and silent." MacArthur described the subsequent altercation between himself and Roosevelt:

> I felt it my duty to take up the cudgels. The country's safety was at stake, and I said so bluntly. The President turned the full vials of his sarcasm upon me. He was a scorcher when

aroused. The tension began to boil over. For the third and last time in my life that paralyzing nausea began to creep over me. In my emotional exhaustion I spoke recklessly and said something to the general effect that when we lost the next war, and an American boy, lying in the mud with an enemy bayonet through his belly and an enemy foot on his dying throat, spat out his last curse, I wanted the name not to be MacArthur, but Roosevelt. The President grew livid. "You must not talk that way to the President!" he roared. He was, of course, right, and I knew it almost before the words had left my mouth. I said that I was sorry and apologized. But I felt my Army career was at an end. I told him he had my resignation as Chief of Staff. As I reached the door his voice came with that cool detachment which so reflected his extraordinary self-control, "Don't be foolish, Douglas; you and the budget must get together on this."

Dern had shortly reached my side and I could hear his gleeful tones, "You've saved the Army." But I just vomited on the steps of the White House.[16]

MacArthur recalled that thereafter Roosevelt "was on our side," but the President's behavior that summer surely did not show it. In July officials of the National Guard Association persuaded Roosevelt and Douglas to reinstate the full schedule of armory drills of the National Guard. Several weeks later representatives of the Reserve Officers Association visited the President and got him to allot additional funds for field training of reserve officers. Since the chief of staff had been rejected when he had earlier made similar requests for the civilian components, it seemed to him that the President, deliberately or not, was demeaning the position of the military head of the Army. Also MacArthur was piqued, according to one account, because Roosevelt had demonstrated "that he would be no mere nominal Commander-in-Chief, but would exert the final authority in regard to the peacetime Army." [17]

That summer Harold L. Ickes, the crusty Secretary of the Interior who also headed the Public Works Administration, suggested to Roosevelt that the concentration of the Army in about fifteen large posts and the closing of the nearly 200 others would be a major step in reducing federal expenditures. Without consulting Dern or MacArthur, the President pursued the matter at length in private discussions with Ickes, Douglas, and Hugh S. Johnson, MacArthur's former classmate at West Point and now head of the National Recovery Administration. Ultimately the War Department on its own volition closed some posts which were on a caretaking basis, but it successfully opposed the concentration proposal. In a complicated bit of scheming Ickes tried to tie the closing of Army posts with grants of P.W.A. funds to the War Department for a time. He seemed to get diabolical delight from dangling before Dern and Mac-Arthur prospects for large sums from the P.W.A., up to $300,-000,000, for military construction and mechanization, though the actual obtaining of funds from that agency proved painfully slow and disappointingly small for the Army.[18] Ickes' scornful attitude toward MacArthur and the War Department is evident in his comments about the chief of staff's appearance before the Board of Public Works on July 27, 1933:

> I had asked Chief of Staff MacArthur to come in on some Army projects. He had presented a very large list running into the hundreds of millions, out of which the President allowed him $6 million for coast defenses in the Canal Zone and Hawaii, in addition to $6 million previously allowed for ammunition. MacArthur is the type of man who thinks that when he gets to Heaven, God will step down from the great white throne and bow him into His vacated seat, and it gave me a great kick to have him in and break the news to him. While he was here, though, two or three of the members foolishly asked him some questions which gave him a chance to deliver a lecture on the subject of the necessity for the little old peanut Army posts that we have scattered around the country.[19]

In spite of the personal opinion of curmudgeon Ickes, Daniel W. Bell, who succeeded Douglas as budget director, reported

two years later that "the War Department has been the beneficiary to the extent of many millions of dollars expended from
Public Works Emergency Funds." Bell added: "The Federal
Emergency Relief Administration also provided for the purchase of $1,123,000 of material for the benefit of the War De-
partment out of Civil Works Administration funds. In addition, the War Department had the benefit of work performed
by labor paid for out of funds granted by the Civil Works Administration." By the end of MacArthur's tour of duty as chief
of staff, $100,000,000 in P.W.A. money had been allotted to
the Army, $68,000,000 of which was for construction and the
rest for military purchases mainly of munitions, trucks, armored
vehicles, and aircraft. Since the funds were set up for relief
purposes, Ickes largely determined how they would be used
and usually gave priority to projects employing large numbers
of workers. Though grateful for the extra funds, MacArthur
could not resist remarking: "Could the expenditure of the entire sum have been controlled exclusively by the importance of
the Army's requirements an even greater degree of improvement would have been realized." Even he admitted, however,
that without these relief funds the little progress which the
Army made toward mechanization by 1935 would have been impossible.[20] Yet MacArthur had again found himself in the
anomalous position of working with the New Deal relief program, which he opposed in principle, in order to wring benefits
for his impoverished, understrength Army.

The financial plight of the Army was much on his mind when
he delivered the commencement address at West Point in June,
1933, the thirtieth anniversary of his own graduation. He
solemnly told the assembled cadets what, in similar words, he
had emphasized to the politicians on Capitol Hill: "As the
necessity of national defense is sacrificed in the name of economy, the United States presents a tempting spectacle. It is a
spectacle which may ultimately lead to an alignment of the na-

tions, which may lead to another World War, and that war would find a score of nations ready for the sack of America." Deeply concerned over the Army's situation and the future of the nation, he wrote in his annual report later that summer: "In the obvious state of unrest now prevailing throughout the world, evidences of which are plainly visible even in our own country, an efficient and dependable military establishment, constantly responsible to the will of its Government, constitutes a rock of stability and one of a nation's priceless possessions." He continued: "As much as at any other time in our history, the Army's efficiency should engage the earnest attention of every loyal citizen. It is my conviction that at this moment the Army's strength in personnel and matériel and its readiness for employment are below the danger line." He warned that it was "of the most urgent importance to the United States that this condition be rectified without delay." [21]

But Roosevelt and his budget officials were absorbed in the New Deal domestic programs and failed to grasp "the most urgent importance" of strengthening the Army at that time. For fiscal 1935 the Budget Bureau set the figure for military expenditures at only $285,900,000. In his pleas before the appropriations committees and subcommittees of the House and Senate, MacArthur was legally bound by the injunction of the Budget and Accounting Act of 1921 which stated: "No estimate or request for an appropriation and no request for an increase in an item of such estimate or request . . . shall be submitted to Congress or any committee thereof by any officer or employee of any department or establishment, unless at the request of either House of Congress." In previous hearings MacArthur had comported himself with cautious regard for this law, which left him strictly the agent of the executive branch if the congressmen did not choose to ask for his views on military spending.[22] But before Senator Royal S. Copeland's subcommittee on military appropriations on March 12, 1933,

MacArthur tried in desperation to goad the senators into defying the Budget Bureau:

> Gen. MacArthur: . . . The Army, as you all know, constantly gets less money than it has felt should be consistently appropriated in accordance with the national defense act provisions . . .
> The responsibility for the skeletonization, for the starvation . . . of the Army rests squarely upon those two groups, the budget [bureau] and the Congress . . .
> Sen. Townsend: The way I see it, the responsibility rests largely with the budget. According to your figures, we have only cut the appropriations $7,000,000 in three years from what the budget people recommended. That has been the entire cut by Congress. Is that not true?
> Gen. MacArthur: I certainly think that there is a sharing of responsibility, Senator, but because the budget does not send the figures up here, that does not relieve the Congress of the United States from "raising and maintaining armies." . . . You are not bound by budget figures. The Constitution places the responsibility of this not upon the budget, not upon the War Department, but upon one group alone, and that is the Congress of the United States.
> Sen. Copeland: The Congress may have hidden behind the petticoats of the budget. I will say that.[23]

The chief of staff's efforts were of little avail, for Congress reduced the Budget Bureau's figure, appropriating $280,900,000 for military activities in fiscal 1935. Wearily but determinedly, MacArthur continued to speak and write about the woeful condition of the military establishment. In his annual report prepared in mid-1934 he pointed out that the strength of the Regular Army and National Guard stood "at considerably less than half the strength contemplated by law," that is, the National Defense Act of 1920. The Officers' Reserve Corps was "inadequately supported," and "we have no enlisted Reserve." The matériel of the Army was "inadequate even for limited forces, and, such as they are, comprise principally World War equipment, manifestly obsolescent." He declared that "the preparatory missions devolving upon the Military Establishment in time of peace cannot in some respects be efficiently performed; while the grave responsibilities that would fall to it in emergency would require frantic improvisations and wasteful and possibly ineffective sacrifice of the Nation's manhood and material resources." [24]

Shortly after the writing of this report the Army's budget asking for fiscal 1936 was sent to the Bureau of the Budget. The War Department requested $361,400,000 for military activities — the largest such request since MacArthur had been chief of staff and $55,000,000 more than its asking for the previous fiscal year. Apparently the Army leaders were counting on the alertness of Roosevelt and Congress to the growing international tensions. Hitler had withdrawn Germany from the League of Nations and disarmament talks and was preparing to begin a vast military buildup in open violation of the Versailles Treaty. Mussolini was publicly talking about the seizure of Abyssinia as a possible first step in creating an Italian empire of Roman proportions. In December, 1934, an armed clash between border guards of Abyssinia and Italian Somaliland provided him with the pretext to start preparations for war against the weak African country. On the other side of the globe, Japan, having withdrawn from the League of Nations, continued to disregard with impunity the international treaty structure set up at Washington and Paris in the 1920's. Late in 1934 Japan announced a two-year notice of her withdrawal from the Five-Power Naval Treaty; she immediately inaugurated a large-scale program of naval construction. Meanwhile her officials spoke of a "Japanese Monroe Doctrine," based supposedly on the concept of "Asia for the Asians," but interpreted by some Western observers as Asia for the Japanese. "The world situation," MacArthur observed, "had become too dangerous to allow a weakening of our defense." Surely this time, he and his colleagues in the War Department nervously conjectured, the needs of the Army and national defense would be recognized and met by those who decided the federal budget. A slight improvement of economic conditions in the fall of 1934 also encouraged them to hope that the disheartening trend of shrinking military appropriations since the Panic of 1929 might be reversed in fiscal 1936.[25]

3. Many Critics and a Few Supporters

Since there was no fixed term for the office of chief of staff, MacArthur probably would not have been surprised to find himself ousted when the Democratic administration took over in Washington in the spring of 1933. That September rumors of unknown origin began to circulate that MacArthur was about to be relieved. The *Army and Navy Journal,* which was pro-MacArthur but also reflected the opinion of probably a large majority of Army officers, reported that Dern "tersely and emphatically" denied the rumors about the chief of staff. The journal's editorialist remarked, "The Secretary thoroughly realizes the worth of the General's service; so does the country and especially the grateful Army. Couldn't be better news this week, could there?" When Roosevelt retained MacArthur on into early 1934, it was then popularly assumed that he would be kept in the position until that November since four years was inexplicably but widely regarded as the "term" for the office.

Much was destined to happen before the autumn of 1934 to indicate that MacArthur's chances of reappointment in November were not promising, although the general feeling in the War Department favored his continuance. One factor militating against his reappointment was his alleged mishandling of Colonel George Marshall, a favorite of Pershing, who, in turn, still had considerable influence in Washington. Most recently Marshall had done an outstanding job in troop training at Fort Moultrie, South Carolina, and also had been an efficient leader in C.C.C. administration in that state. After ten years as lieutenant colonel, Marshall finally was promoted to full colonel in September, 1933, but he, Pershing, and others of the former "Chaumont circle" were displeased when he was sent that fall to Chicago as senior instructor with the Illinois National Guard. When General Charles G. Dawes, the former vice-president and a friend of Pershing, heard of Marshall's transfer to Chicago, he roared, "What! He can't do that. Hell, no! Not George Marshall. He's too big a man for this job. In fact he's the best goddamned officer in the U.S. Army." Marshall is said to have appealed directly to the chief of staff to revoke the order, but MacArthur rejected his plea, saying he was the best officer for the Chicago assignment. Marshall's principal biographer states, "A number of his friends shared his feeling that the assignment, by intention or not, put him off the main career road to high command in the Army. It seemed to them an injustice they were determined to correct if possible." But the order stood, and Marshall reluctantly moved to Chicago. Likewise, Pershing's efforts some months later to secure Marshall's promotion to brigadier general also were unsuccessful; it would be a year after MacArthur left Washington before Marshall's next advancement. MacArthur's granting of an office and staff to March to write a book to offset Pershing's memoirs published in 1931 and highly critical of the War Department, together with the Marshall case, created new tensions between MacArthur and Pershing. The latter was hardly expected to support any move to have MacArthur retained as chief of staff.

Actually MacArthur was vitally concerned about the plight of promising officers, like Marshall, whose professional progress had been stalled by the Army's antiquated, unjust promotion system. He had already spent many hours developing a new promotion plan and planned to present it to Congress in the session convening in December, 1934. As for Marshall and the Chicago assignment, MacArthur highly recommended him, and his response to Marshall's request was said to have been "sympathetic." The chief of staff told the commander of the Illinois National Guard Division that Marshall "has no superior among Infantry colonels." In 1935 MacArthur recommended to Dern that Marshall's name be added to the list of officers next in line for promotion to brigadier general, though he had been a colonel less than two years. Pershing wrote Marshall in October that MacArthur "had still intended to make you Chief of Infantry but as no one knows when the vacancy will occur, I told him that you would prefer to be in the line, and so it will be done, at least that is the plan at present." Marshall was initially disappointed over his transfer in 1933, but neither he nor MacArthur appear to have harbored any ill feelings toward each other then or at any time prior to the war with Japan.[26]

Another factor which could have dimmed MacArthur's hope for reappointment was his inadvertent and peripheral involvement in the air mail episode of early 1934. When the office of assistant secretary of war for air had been abolished in mid-1933 upon MacArthur's recommendation as an "economy" move, he had welcomed the expanded authority in Air Corps matters which the change meant for him. But in the next eight months he may have wished Davison was still around to bear the final responsibility for the Air Corps. In January, 1934, a Senate investigating committee headed by Hugo Black of Alabama discovered that, through fraud and without competitive bidding, three large holding companies in the commercial aviation field had garnered all but three of the federal government's twenty-seven air mail contracts, which were let by Hoover's Postmaster General, Walter F. Brown. In anger

and vengeance Roosevelt told James A. Farley, Brown's successor, that the contracts should be canceled at once. Farley sent
two of his assistants to Foulois, the Air Corps chief, to inquire
if the Army's air arm could fly the mails; Foulois affirmed that
his flyers and planes were prepared to undertake the project.
But within a week after the Army planes began carrying the
mails, eight of the aircraft crashed. The Air Corps blamed the
accidents on severe weather and inadequate navigational equipment. Its air mail flights were reduced until weather conditions bettered, and in May, after more wrecks, legislation
was enacted providing for new commercial contracts, this time
through fair competitive bidding. The repercussions of the
affair included heightened animosity by Big Business toward
the Roosevelt administration, criticism of the War Department's negligence of the poorly equipped and trained Air
Corps, and creation of a board headed by Newton Baker to
investigate anew the status, needs, and mission of the Air
Corps. MacArthur was the target of much of the opprobrium
which would otherwise have hit an assistant secretary of war
for air, though Foulois bore the brunt and was shortly relieved
as chief.[27]

It was ultimately determined that MacArthur did not know
about the plan to use the Air Corps until after the decision
had been made and the executive order issued. Strangely, the
chief of staff offered no protest when he learned of it. These
facts came out in March while a Senate subcommittee was
probing into the events of February 9 when Roosevelt ordered
the Air Corps to undertake the carrying of the mails:

> Sen. Reed: And you [Foulois] expressed the opinion to these
> two gentlemen [of the Post Office Department] . . . that the
> Army could do this job?
> Gen. Foulois: I expressed the opinion.
> Sen. Reed: General MacArthur, did you express an opinion on
> that?

Gen. MacArthur: No, sir. I knew nothing about carrying the mails until I was told of it by Mr. Leverts, of the Associated Press. I had not been called into any conference by anyone with reference to that.

Sen. Reed: . . . The Executive Order of the President was made before you knew of it?

Gen. MacArthur: Yes, sir . . .

Sen. Reed: Am I correct in thinking that the Army made no protest after it got this order; it took the order and obeyed it the best it could? . . .

Gen. MacArthur: We received the order, and we have exercised every possible support thereof.

Sen. Townsend: As the Army always does.

Gen. MacArthur: As an army, we always try to do so; yes, sir. That is our position.[28]

Meanwhile that spring the War Department came under attack by the House military affairs committee, which found that "the law directing competitive bidding in airplane purchases . . . had been consistently violated." Since Woodring's main job as assistant secretary of war was procurement of supplies and the supervision of such activities by the various arms and bureaus, he was held responsible for the violations in the opinion of many critics. "A campaign of insinuation and innuendo," in Woodring's words, was begun to force his removal. He tried frantically to shift the blame to Foulois, maintaining that he had made it clear to the Air Corps chief his "insistence on procurement by competitive bidding as against procurement on a negotiated basis." Columnists Pearson and Allen claimed that MacArthur was spearheading a movement to get Woodring out of the department. This charge was cited by the chief of staff in the libel suit which he filed against the columnists in May, but, as noted previously, the case was settled out of court with MacArthur paying the defendants' legal expenses and the columnists yielding no apology or retraction. On the other hand, Woodring said,

"Scurrilous statements and insinuations have been made to the effect that serious conflicts existed between the Secretary of War and myself, and between the Chief of Staff and the General Staff and myself. There is no foundation whatever for such inferences. The most cordial and friendly relations have existed at all times, without a single exception." The truth about Woodring's role in the illegal aircraft deals and MacArthur's alleged effort to oust him was beclouded by a flurry of contradictory statements by accusers and accused. These controversies were eclipsed in June, however, by a new exposé revealing that a colonel, while on duty in the War Department, had accepted handsome fees from private businesses for favors in contracts. Also a House investigating committee brought to light about the same time that the Army's quartermaster general had approved "changes in truck specifications which . . . barred all but the equipment furnished by one motor manufacturing concern." [29] With the perennial budget battle underway, too, the spring of 1934 was an uncomfortable one for MacArthur and the War Department.

These developments coincided with the beginning of the sensational hearings of the Senate's Nye Committee, which was investigating profiteering in the munitions industry, later shifting its attention to the role of munitions makers in influencing American intervention in the World War. MacArthur did not personally testify before the committee, but certain actions of his were brought up antagonistically by Senator Gerald Nye during the hearings that summer. For one thing, the chief of staff "directed" DuPont officials to close some files regarding the firm's dealings with the Army and not to allow Nye's investigators access to them on the grounds that they contained "strategic military information." Also it was reported in the hearings that while MacArthur was in Turkey in 1932 he reputedly "talked up American military equipment to the skies in discussions he had with the Turkish General

Staff." The chief of staff vigorously denied Nye's accusation that he "was pretty much of a salesman" for American armaments manufacturers during his stay in Turkey.

Nye and his followers generally portrayed MacArthur as a warmongering lackey of the munitions tycoons, but at least the chief of staff found the President in agreement with him on the harmful influence of the investigations. MacArthur undoubtedly concurred with the Chief Executive's evaluation of Nye and his supporters: "The trouble is that they belong to the very large and perhaps increasing school of thought which holds that we can and should withdraw wholly within ourselves and cut off all but the most perfunctory relationships with other nations." The President, who was becoming acutely conscious of the menacing world situation, said also of Nye's group: "They imagine that if the civilization of Europe is about to destroy itself through internal strife, it might just as well go ahead and do it and that the United States can stand idly by." [30] Nevertheless, MacArthur knew Roosevelt's role-taking talent well enough to realize that the President's dislike of the Nye Committee was, unfortunately, not tantamount to his endorsement of a major build-up of national defenses.

While Roosevelt and MacArthur were in agreement on the Nye excitement, the President must have been aware of his chief of staff's friendship with certain business magnates who vehemently opposed the administration. Robert Wood, who headed Sears, Roebuck and Company and had been MacArthur's friend since their cadet days, was an important leader of the Committee for the Nation to Rebuild Prices and Purchasing Power, a group of conservative businessmen critical of the New Deal and pushing cheap-money nostrums as the key to economic stability. MacArthur was not actively associated with this organization, but some of his later remarks suggest agreement with certain of its principles. It may have been through Wood that he became acquainted with James H.

Rand, who was head of Remington Rand, a leader of the Committee for the Nation, and two decades later the individual responsible for MacArthur's selection as chairman of the board of Remington Rand. Some of the men influential on the Committee for the Nation also seem to have been sympathetic toward Father Coughlin, the outspoken priest who castigated the New Deal as Communistic and, after the attack on Pearl Harbor in 1941, would demand MacArthur's appointment as supreme commander of all American military forces. No known evidence ties MacArthur in the mid-1930's with either Wood's organization or Coughlin's movement, but Roosevelt knew that his chief of staff was not in accord with his political philosophy. Under normal conditions a President need not be concerned particularly about his chief of staff's political views and reactions to domestic programs, but at this time the Army was engaged on an unprecedented scale in the relief efforts of the administration. Some of Roosevelt's advisers undoubtedly raised the question of how long he could afford to retain a chief of staff who opposed the basic principles of the President's relief programs and many of his other policies. Some probably viewed MacArthur as reactionary in his views, though actually in the thirties he seems to have been simply a Hooverian conservative.[31]

Besides disagreeing with the New Dealers on policies, MacArthur also did not fit into their social life. He had enjoyed some social activities in Washington before 1933, especially in the company of Hurley and his attractive wife, but mutual disaffection with most of the persons Roosevelt brought to the national capital left him socially a "loner" for the next two years. Many of Roosevelt's friends shared Ickes' cruel scorn for the general. "At such social functions as he had to attend," said a correspondent-friend, "he was a lonely figure. No one spoke his language. No one wanted to speak it. At the annual Army-Navy reception at the White House he would arrive just in time to lead the officers in the President's receiving line, pay his respects to the First Lady, for he is the spirit of chivalry, and go back to work." Eisenhower, who worked as his assistant from early 1933 onward for nearly ten years, said that MacArthur "lost himself in his work" and "most of his friends whose companionship he really enjoyed were the officers with whom he worked in the War Department. Except for his mother, General MacArthur's life in Washington was almost entirely centered around the Army, which he loved." There were generals in Washington who mixed in the gay life of the city's high society and developed therefrom connections with persons close to the President who would push their candidacy for the post which MacArthur held. But the only high-ranking person in the circle of Roosevelt whom MacArthur could count on to support his continuation as chief of staff was the unaggressive Secretary of War, and Dern was far from being one of the President's intimate associates. By the end of the summer of 1934 MacArthur, in Eisenhower's words, "felt that his replacement in a few months was a certainty." [32]

From the spring of 1934 through that autumn Roosevelt was freely advised by persons high and low, known and unknown, that he should relieve MacArthur. In March, Josephus Daniels, Roosevelt's former boss in the Navy Department, wrote him that "Secretary Dern asked me what I would do if I were to be Secretary of War. I said: 'Get a new Chief of Staff and a new set up in the Department just as soon as possible. MacArthur is a charming man, but he was put in by your predecessor and thinks he should run the Army." Daniels believed that the loyalty and gratitude of MacArthur and the main officers on the General Staff were still directed to Hoover: "They will have none toward you. I made a serious mistake when I was Secretary by keeping the men named by my predecessor. They thought they were indispensable and had no enthusiasm for what I wanted done. Out of

my bitter experience, I give you this counsel." When a journalist predicted in October that MacArthur would be reappointed, Daniels again pleaded with Roosevelt, emphasizing
the intense feeling against him since the B.E.F. eviction: "The
appointment of MacArthur would be deeply resented . . . My
earnest advice is *'Don't.'* " Representative Kenneth McKellar
of Tennessee, who co-sponsored (with Black) the new air mail
legislation in 1934, pointed out that "no Chief of Staff has
ever been reappointed" and urged F.D.R. not to set such a
precedent. McKellar felt that the selection of Major General
William D. Connor "would be the wisest course." Among
those who wrote opposing MacArthur's continuation were a
number of individuals whose knowledge of the matter is moot,
such as the president of the Teepee Company of Newark, who
felt "strongly" that MacArthur should not be reappointed.[33]

Besides the long and diverse list of critics which MacArthur
had accumulated, there was, according to some reports, "a
larger number of able officers than usual who were qualified
for the position" of chief of staff. One officer in the War
Department commented, "There are probably as many applicants for the job as there are major generals in the army."
In September the *New York Times* reported twelve men were
in contention for the post. Actually only four on the list were
of "eligible age," that is, with at least four years of active duty
left. These major generals were Hugh Drum, MacArthur's
deputy chief of staff, who, according to some officers, was
handicapped by too many years of staff work and too little experience in troop command; George Simonds, commandant of
the Army War College and believed to be MacArthur's choice
as his successor; Stuart Heintzelman, head of the Command
and General Staff School and a friend of Roosevelt since their
days together at Groton, but now in poor health (he died in
1935); and Malin Craig, the IX Corps Area commander who
was highly regarded in Army circles, but had "used his efforts
and influence in persuading all persons and officers he could

to vote for Mr. Hoover and *not* for Mr. Roosevelt," according to one of the President's informants.[34]

Probably of considerable influence on Roosevelt were the views of the leading Democrats on the military affairs committees of the Senate and House. Of those who expressed their opinions on MacArthur's reappointment in extant letters to the President, all were earnestly desirous of retaining him at least through the passage of the military appropriations bill for fiscal 1936. Since some of these men had differed strongly with MacArthur on various Army matters, it is a tribute to their genuine concern for national defense that they recognized his worth to the War Department at that crucial time. For instance, Senator Morris Sheppard, chairman of the Senate military affairs committee, had skirmished with MacArthur at numerous hearings, yet he told Roosevelt that he "very much hoped" that the chief of staff would be retained.[35] Joseph Byrns, the powerful House majority leader, wrote Howe in July:

> I am just getting ready to leave and when I come back in August I want again to talk with the President about General Douglas MacArthur and renew my earnest endorsement of his reappointment as Chief of Staff of the Army. I am so deeply and personally interested in this appointment that I am filing with you this little note so that you may bear it in mind and I also entertain the hope that I will have your assistance.
> It is not necessary for me in this note to you to say anything more concerning General MacArthur and his ability than that I consider him the best fitted man in the country today for this position. He has a deep understanding of our national defense problems; a splendid vision of future military developments; is highly respected and loved by the officer and enlisted personnel of the Army, who have in him the greatest possible confidence.[36]

At Roosevelt's press conferences in October and early November he was repeatedly asked about the chief of staff selection. Each time he either evaded the question or said simply,

"I do not know." Suddenly on November 15 he announced that MacArthur would continue as chief of staff until he made a decision on his successor in about a month.[37] At a press conference called on the morning of December 12, Roosevelt proclaimed his judgment on the matter:

> President: Lots of news today. No. 1, I have sent a letter to the Secretary of War directing that General Douglas MacArthur be retained as Chief of Staff until his successor has been appointed. I am doing this in order to obtain the benefit of General MacArthur's experience in handling War Department legislation in the coming session. I cannot give you any date because I have no more idea than you have when that work upon the Hill will be finished. Of course, obviously, sometime before the end of Congress.
> Question [by a reporter]: That order to keep him on — that is an Order?
> President: Yes.
> Question: We assume from that that General MacArthur will not have an appointment for four years more?
> President: That is right.
> Question: Does this necessitate a new Executive Order?
> President: The other was not an Order, it was a letter to the Secretary of War. The letter says: (Reading)
> "My dear Mr. Secretary:
> I desire you to issue the necessary order to the effect that General Douglas MacArthur will continue as Chief of Staff until his successor has been appointed."
> That is all.[38]

Roosevelt's decision was a shrewd one, for it averted an uproar from the War Department while placating liberals who did not want MacArthur for another full "term" as chief of staff. Shortly after receiving the news, Dern, MacArthur, and Major General James F. McKinley, the adjutant general, "went into a prolonged conference," observed a correspondent at the War Department, "and for the first time in many months the door to General MacArthur's office was closed tightly." The reporter surmised that they were discussing proposals to be taken to Capitol Hill: "A mass of legislation is expected to be laid before Congress by the War Department. Much of this has originated with General MacArthur and in the rest he has cooperated with Secretary Dern." [39] MacArthur knew the President's decision to retain him had been a difficult one, and the chief of staff took it as a mandate to guide, as best as he could, his legislative program for the Army to a successful outcome in the impending session of Congress. There is no indication that MacArthur interpreted his retention as a reward, honor, or even reappointment, though some of his worshipful biographers have represented the President's action as a signal tribute to MacArthur's achievements. An unpredictable President had given him another opportunity to confront an unpredictable Congress with the needs of the Army. He could leave the office of chief of staff with a sense of satisfaction if, in his final battles on Capitol Hill, some victories could be won for the long-deprived military establishment.

CHAPTER XVI

A Few Steps Forward

1. With the Compliments of Congress

MACARTHUR'S TOUR OF DUTY as chief of staff came to a dramatic climax during the session of Congress which convened in December, 1934, and adjourned the next summer. The War Department's military estimate of $361,400,000 for fiscal 1936 provided for increasing enlisted strength from 119,000 to 165,-000 and the number of officers from 12,000 to 14,000. The hoped-for increases would provide the minimum force which the Army's leaders had long considered as necessary to accomplish the military establishment's peacetime missions. Disappointment came early, however, when the Budget Bureau cut the figure to $331,800,000 and deleted the personnel increases. Perhaps realistically aware that enlarging the officer corps was a lost cause for the present, MacArthur pushed hardest to get the enlisted expansion restored. He told Collins' subcommittee on military appropriations that the enlisted cut by the Budget Bureau "is one that I think so fundamental and so basic that its application unbalances the bill from the standpoint of reasonable policy and may jeopardize the prospect of success in the case of major operations." In February, 1935, despite vigorous opposition by Collins' faction and some economy-minded representatives, the House passed an appropriations bill for military activities which was nearly $7,000,000 more than the Budget Bureau's figure. Sensitive to the administration's opposition to a personnel increase, the House voted to give Roosevelt discretionary authority to raise the enlisted strength to 165,000 and made no provision for expansion of the officer corps. Alarmed, MacArthur knew that, though Roosevelt's alertness to world tensions had become keener, he might yield to the counsel of some of his advisers and postpone or even cancel the increase in troops. The chief of staff told the Senate's appropriations committee that the overworked President ought not to have to assume the additional "burden" of deciding this matter; besides, enlisted strength had always been determined by Congress itself. The final appropriations bill, approved in late March, gave the Army nearly $355,500,000 for its military program. Furthermore, Congress authorized the increase to 165,000 enlisted regulars. MacArthur and Dern were jubilant, despite the budget director's decision two months later to withhold $9,000,000, which was not released until early 1936.[1]

In the excitement over the news of the adoption of the largest military budget since the early 1920's, one journalist, apparently forgetting MacArthur's earlier disappointments on Capitol Hill, exclaimed that Congress "voted MacArthur virtually everything he wanted . . . Gen. MacArthur has a way with Congressional committees. He seldom comes away without what he requests." The *New York Times'* explanation of the surprising generosity of Congress was more plausible: "The large increase and the disregard by both chambers of the limits set on budget appropriations in the budget estimates are viewed as being a result, at least in part, of the prevalent war talk." Malin Craig, who would succeed MacArthur that fall, wrote in his first annual report as chief of staff: "In general,

it may be said that the increase in military appropriations for
1936 over those of preceding years marks an epoch in the
period that has elapsed since the end of the World War." [2]
MacArthur remarked with great satisfaction in his final report
that summer:

> For the first time since 1922, the Army enters a new fiscal
> year with a reasonable prospect of developing itself into a de-
> fense establishment commensurate in size and efficiency to the
> country's minimum needs. Obstacles, which for 13 years have
> impeded, if not inhibited, progress toward this goal, have only
> recently been either swept aside by Congress or materially re-
> duced in importance. The present year definitely marks the
> beginning of a long-deferred resumption of military prepara-
> tion on a scale demanded by the most casual regard for the
> Nation's safety and security.[3]

The National Defense Act of 1920 prescribed an enlisted
strength of 280,000, but MacArthur was so pleased to get 165,-
000 that he practically thanked Congress in his annual report:
"The beneficial influence of this act of Congress upon the
future efficiency of our military defenses and the security of
the country is beyond calculation." The enthusiasm of the
chief of staff and other Army leaders, in the opinion of a
scholar on the military establishment's development in this
period, "reflected the fact that military leaders were wedded
to the belief that personnel and manpower were the prime
prerequisites for the military preparedness of the nation, and
that the matériel needs could be met through a modest R & D
[research and development] program in which 'pilot' models
could be produced which would serve as the prototypes to be
turned out by American industry in time of emergency." This
concept would be "repudiated" before America's entry into
World War II.

Nevertheless, in 1935 the increase in enlisted men meant,
said MacArthur, "the filling out of the attenuated skeletons

now attempting to function as tactical units in the Regular Army." The Air Corps and mechanized ground units could be raised to the strengths stipulated in their tables of organization. More efficient training of companies, troops, and batteries would be possible, and large-scale maneuvers could be undertaken to improve their readiness for field service. "The combat effectiveness of the whole Army will be doubled," MacArthur said, "and its ability to carry out a prompt and orderly mobilization will be reasonably assured." Compared to the millions of men under arms already in Europe, the 46,000-man expansion of the United States Army was insignificant, but, like scraps tossed to a starving dog, it looked good to the War Department at that time. MacArthur saw hope in this turn of events that Congress might continue to enlarge the Army. As it turned out, however, enlisted strength would be only 175,000 when the Second World War began.[4]

Congress also cooperated by enlarging the corps of cadets at West Point from 1374 to 1960. This action was particularly pleasing to MacArthur, who was devoted to the academy and believed that the proportion of West Point graduates in the officer corps should never be less than 50 per cent. The officers of the Long Gray Line, he maintained, "have been imbued with the conceptions of duty, integrity, and patriotism which constitute the very basis of West Point training and which these graduates have in turn transplanted into the Army. In a very real sense that institution has thus become the heritage, not merely of those who happen to be its graduates, but of every officer in the service." Less idealistically, the chief of staff welcomed the expansion of the cadet corps also because it "assures, beginning 4 years from now, a gradual expansion of the officer corps on an orderly and efficient basis, assuming that the necessary congressional authorizations will be forthcoming." He now admitted that "no better way suggests itself to begin this necessary enlargement" to 14,000 officers, for which he had been crusading in vain for years. Officer strength would finally reach that level about the time Hitler's army began crossing the Polish border in 1939.

During his last year as chief of staff MacArthur supported the plans which were being laid for a massive construction program on the Plain. It was decided that the new buildings would be designed in the Gothic pattern which was predominant at West Point when MacArthur was a cadet. By 1939 work had been completed on a new barracks, an addition to the gymnasium, an academic building, an engineering-ordnance laboratory, an armory-field house, and additional faculty housing. Major Generals William R. Smith and William D. Connor, the superintendents in the periods 1928–32 and 1932–38, respectively, were able administrators dedicated to the reforms which MacArthur had begun in the early 1920s. They were fortunate during the years 1930–35 to have in the office of chief of staff a general who was one of the most enthusiastic supporters the United States Military Academy ever had.[5]

Some expansion of personnel strength and training activities in the civilian components was also authorized by Congress in the spring of 1935. The National Guard was enlarged from 190,000 to 195,000, and Congress fully restored its training schedule of forty-eight armory drills and two weeks of field service annually, which had been reduced in the previous fiscal year. The Officers' Reserve Corps had formerly been allowed two weeks of active-duty training for each officer once every four years, the limit being 12,000 officers a year so assigned. Now Congress raised the number annually eligible for active duty to 20,000; it also increased the number of reserve officers permitted to attend courses at the Army service schools. In addition, Congress authorized the establishment of new R.O.T.C. units and six weeks of training each summer for R.O.T.C. members, whereas in 1934 only a month had been allowed. The C.M.T.C., whose enrollment had been cut to 14,000 in 1934, was expanded to 30,000. MacArthur had long been a defender of the civilian components and was convinced that the increases for fiscal 1936 were wholly justified: "We cannot too often recall to mind the importance of the missions that will devolve upon the civilian components in the event of war . . . No one part of our military establishment can insure the country's integrity under attack. All are needed."

Next to the increase in enlisted strength, MacArthur considered the new promotion system for officers, passed by Congress in August, the most welcome news from that session on Capitol Hill. Ever since becoming military head, he had worked zealously to develop a promotion plan which would be a combination of the best aspects of merit selection and seniority. But year after year the War Department's proposed bills on promotion had been rejected by one house or the other of Congress. The plan presented to Congress in 1935 represented a compromise between several previous plans and, according to MacArthur, provided "for moderate acceleration of the promotion rate . . . It retains the advantages of seniority promotion but in varying degree provides somewhat faster promotion for every officer below the grade of colonel." One of its principal advantages was to assure that able officers would reach the grade of colonel by the age of fifty. Under the old system an officer normally attained colonel at fifty-nine or sixty, which meant that, even with reasonably rapid promotions by selection thereafter, the most competent officers were major generals on active duty for only a year or two before retirement. MacArthur's own career, of course, was an outstanding exception, largely because of his fortunate breaks in 1917–19 which projected him far ahead of his peers in rank. Roosevelt endorsed the new promotion plan in January, 1935, informing Dern that it "appears desirable from every viewpoint." Sheppard guided it to successful passage in the Senate, and finally in late July, after a near failure, it passed the House.[6] Correspondent George R. Brown of the Washington *Herald* praised MacArthur and Sheppard for their roles, but he gave chief credit to Representative Jack O'Connor for the final success of the bill:

> Brilliant and magnetic General Douglas MacArthur is going out as Chief of Staff in a blaze of splendid glory, the idol of the entire Army. His work in Washington is finished. A year ago the Army was on the rocks, demoralized, discouraged, and out of date. General MacArthur has saved it by putting through Congress the most constructive program for the land defenses since the World War . . .
> Senator Morris Sheppard, of Texas, worked hard for the whole Army program. But in the last analysis, it is to canny Jack O'Connor, of New York City, chairman of the House Rules Committee, that the officers must give the credit for putting their promotion bill through.
> Rep. O'Connor, who has become the ablest Rules chairman since the old Cannon and Dalzell regime, pulled a couple of parliamentary rabbits out of his hat that turned the trick. It was this way. It was the plan of easy-going Uncle Joe Byrns to call the promotion bill up in its turn, under what is called "suspension of the rules." This would have required a two-thirds majority for its passage.
> Rep. O'Connor saw the danger in this. About 10 days ago he quietly reported from his committee a rule giving the bill privileged status, by which it could be passed with but a plain majority vote. The rule provided for two hours of debate. But on the day on which the bill came up, Mr. O'Connor pulled out his second rabbit. He successfully offered from the floor an amendment to the rule reducing the time of debate from 2 hours to one. It developed subsequently that if this had not been done the bill would have lost.
> Unexpected opposition came up. The pacifists were vociferous. Tom Blanton, of Texas, an economy preacher of the Appropriations Committee, with a large following, took the floor against it. If the debate had lasted another hour the bill would have been beaten.

It finally passed by 6 more than two-thirds, but it is conceded that the opposition could have defeated it if Rep. O'Connor had not brought in his rule.[7]

In light of the War Department's bold legislative proposals to this congressional session, it is surprising that MacArthur did not press for new pay schedules for the Army. Except for what he called a "stop-gap compromise" providing slight raises in 1922, the military pay schedules were the same as in 1908. A study in 1929 showed that salaries of federal employees, other than those of the armed services, had risen 25 to 175 per cent since 1908. At the insistence of Hoover and later Roosevelt, MacArthur refrained from crusading for a new pay system; both Presidents believed the matter could wait until the Great Depression had subsided. "It can be adjusted satisfactorily," the chief of staff agreeably concluded, "only when the Government has been relieved of the necessity for solving acute financial and economic problems of a national scope, and opportunity becomes available for exhaustive analysis of every factor of morale, efficiency, and economy." The low pay of soldiers made it hard for him to comprehend Roosevelt's ready agreement to huge outlays of funds for New Deal projects. It irked MacArthur to realize that C.C.C. recruits were paid $30.00 per month, while privates of the Regular Army received only $18.00. Although he showed surprising restraint in the matter of improved pay schedules, he did argue strongly for repeal of the obnoxious Economy Act. Congress revoked the measure in spring, 1935, but the Budget Bureau subsequently ruled that federal officers and employees whose salaries had been cut in 1933 would not be compensated for the lost pay. MacArthur and other Army leaders plunged into the game of behind-the-scenes maneuvering on Capitol Hill, and that summer Congress passed a measure which not only provided for the back pay but also, for the first time, provided a fixed level of allowances for travel, quarters, and subsistence for officers.[8]

In spite of some assistance from the P.W.A. and the increased appropriations for fiscal 1936, the Army's situation in 1935 with regard to mechanization and development and procurement of new weapons was not promising. "In almost every category of munitions [military equipment], the types with which the American Army is supplied," said MacArthur, "were produced during or prior to the World War," except for aircraft. The new 75-mm. gun existed in pilot form only; the field artillery still used obsolescent, worn-out French 75-mm. pieces from World War stocks. "When a worker in the Ordnance Department developed the semiautomatic Garand rifle," asserts a military historian, "the Army was reluctant to give up the modified Model 1903 Springfield, of which large quantities were still on hand." MacArthur appreciated the value of the new rifle, but only 3300 Garands were authorized for 1936, while less than 1500 were already at hand. Only a score or fewer post-1918 tanks were in service in 1935, although seventy-eight new ones were on order and sixty-nine more were authorized for 1936. The aggregate, however, was minute compared to the armored forces of the main European armies. None of the tanks developed between 1919 and 1938 was standardized for regular use by the American Army. Nevertheless, Chaffee was permitted in 1935 to organize at Fort Knox another armored nucleus. Four years later, however, "Chaffee's armored force had developed," says an authority, "into no more than the '7th Cavalry Brigade (Mechanized),' an awkward and feeble conglomeration of light tanks, armored cars, infantry borne in undefended half-tracks, and an artillery composed of 75-mm. mountain howitzers towed by trucks." The new appropriations also provided for moderate increases in the procurement of late models of antiaircraft guns, machine guns, and infantry mortars, but the numbers were woefully inadequate for national defense. MacArthur admitted that the War Department's procurement policy "comprehends the barest requirements of peace-time preparation and depends for war supply upon the production of material after the beginning of an emergency." Four years later significant advances still had not been made in the development and procurement of modern weapons and mechanized equipment, with only 1.2 per cent of the Army budget in 1939 going to research and development. In view of the considerably larger military appropriations of 1936–39, the lack of progress in weapons and mechanization under MacArthur does not appear so atrocious since the Army's status in these areas had not improved appreciably by 1939, despite the worsening international situation during Craig's term.[9]

Neither during MacArthur's tour of duty as chief of staff nor during his successor's was the General Staff abreast of comparable staff groups in Europe in the development of armored doctrine. In the War Department the conception was still nourished of the tank as essentially a support weapon for infantry; therefore stress was placed on the development of speedy light tanks. On the other hand, in Europe the trend was increasingly toward heavier armor and greater fire power in tanks. Development of tank tactics was practically nihil under both MacArthur and Craig.[10] MacArthur, as noted earlier, was firmly convinced that the elements of speed, mobility, and surprise would be essential for victory in the next war. In his final report as chief of staff he pointed this out vividly with an illustration from history:

> Were the accounts of all battles, save only those of Genghis Khan, effaced from the pages of history, and were the facts of his campaigns preserved in descriptive detail, the soldier would still possess a mine of untold wealth from which to extract nuggets of knowledge useful in molding an army for future use. The successes of that amazing leader, beside which the triumphs

of most other commanders in history pale into insignificance, are proof sufficient of his unerring instinct for the fundamental qualifications of an army.

He devised an organization appropriate to conditions then existing; he raised the discipline and the morale of his troops to a level never known in any other army, unless possibly that of Cromwell; he spent every available period of peace to develop subordinate leaders and to produce perfection of training throughout the army, and, finally, he insisted upon speed in action, a speed which by comparison with other forces of his day was almost unbelievable. Though he armed his men with the best equipment of offense and defense that the skill of Asia could produce, he refused to encumber them with loads that would immobilize his army. Over great distances his legions moved so rapidly and secretly as to astound his enemies and practically to paralyze their powers of resistance. He crossed great rivers and mountain ranges, he reduced walled cities in his path and swept onward to destroy nations and pulverize whole civilizations. On the battlefield his troops maneuvered so swiftly and skillfully and struck with such devastating speed that times without number they defeated armies overwhelmingly superior to themselves in numbers.

Regardless of his destructiveness, his cruelty, his savagery, he clearly understood the unvarying necessities of war . . . We cannot violate these laws and still produce and sustain the kind of army that alone can insure the integrity of our country and the permanency of our institutions if ever again we face the grim realities of war.[11]

By his last year as chief of staff, MacArthur was absorbed not only with the necessity for speed in ground operations but also with the need — surprising to his critics — for a strong air force. The fiscal 1936 appropriations act provided $45,000,000 for the Air Corps, an increase of 66 per cent over the previous year. MacArthur supported this increase at the various hearings on Capitol Hill in the winter and spring of 1935. To him, his behavior was not inconsistent, for he had maintained earlier that he was not indifferent to the air arm's needs and

value, but he had felt obligated to place the priority on personnel needs. With the Army's manpower situation improving
to his satisfaction, he now turned to the crusade for aircraft,
as well as tanks and other weapons.

In late 1933 the Drum Board, one of the perennial boards
set up to investigate the plight and grievances of the Air Corps,
recommended the creation of a concentrated tactical air force
of about 1800 planes under a single command for operations.
The idea was reputedly conceived by MacArthur and Drum,
the latter being chairman of the board. The next year the
Baker Board concluded that a separate air force department
would not be feasible or economical, but it did recommend
the establishment of the type of tactical force proposed by
Drum's group. In March, 1935, the General Headquarters Air
Force was organized; Major General Frank M. Andrews was
its commander, with headquarters at Langley Field, Virginia.
Tactical air units of the nine corps areas were concentrated
into three operational wings stationed at fields in California,
Louisiana, and Virginia. Andrews would report directly to
MacArthur, while Major General Oscar Westover, the new Air
Corps chief, would continue to be responsible for procurement, supply, development, and individual training. "Our
General Headquarters Air Force," stated MacArthur that summer, "is fully capable, so far as organization is concerned, of
performing every mission that could be carried out by an air
force organized separately from the Army." Moreover, he
noted, "At the same time it is much more economical. It has
no need for setting up a complete supply and maintenance
system, and is made the recipient of many essential services
which, if independently organized, it would have to provide
for itself." Lieutenant Colonel Henry H. Arnold, future head
of the Army Air Forces in World War II, dramatically demonstrated the rapid striking capability of the G.H.Q. air arm by
leading a group of B-10 bombers from California to Alaska and

back, then immediately flying on to New York and returning to the Pacific coast. MacArthur must have found secret glee in the fact that the effectiveness of the new force stilled the proponents of an independent air arm, at least for a few years. The G.H.Q. air organization provided an improved command structure for tactical operations, though later, when Craig was chief of staff, it proved more efficient for the G.H.Q. air commander to report to the Air Corps chief, not to the chief of staff. Ironically, the plan, which was partly MacArthur's inspiration and had his full support, marked the achievement of virtual autonomy for the Air Corps by the late 1930's and may be considered the first step toward a separate air department, which MacArthur had persistently opposed and thought the plan would obviate.[12]

Buoyed by Congress' splendid cooperation on the fiscal 1936 appropriations, Dern, MacArthur, and the General Staff were already busy on the next year's budget before the budget for 1936 was approved. As was the usual budget-making schedule, the War Department's estimates for fiscal 1937 had to be prepared in the spring and early summer of 1935. They were then turned over to the Budget Bureau, which revised them according to the federal financial condition and the President's dictates. The budget director included the new figures in the administration's budget for 1937, which went to the House appropriations committee in December, 1936. The new asking for military activities was the largest forwarded to the Budget Bureau since that office's creation in 1921: the War Department requested $467,000,000, or over $106,000,000 more than its previous request. MacArthur would leave the office of chief of staff in the autumn of 1935, before the fiscal 1937 budget was introduced into the Capitol Hill arena. Nevertheless, it must have pleased him, as well as his successor, that ultimately, after the Budget Bureau cut the figure to $383,100,000, Congress finally appropriated $388,200,000 for fiscal 1937.

An indication of what MacArthur had in mind for the years ahead can be seen in the list of immediate matériel needs of the Army which he enumerated in his last annual report in mid-1935: procurement of 800 planes a year in order to keep 2500 in service; creation of an enlisted reserve of 150,000 men; a five-year motorization program to provide 18,000 new vehicles; a six-year program of accelerated research and development of new weapons; mechanization of one cavalry brigade, two tank regiments and two tank companies, seven armored car troops, and thirteen scout car platoons; modification of all field artillery pieces for fire flexibility and high-speed towage; stocking of ammunition reserves adequate for at least thirty days of active operations; and procurement of modern mortars, machine guns, antiaircraft guns, searchlights, and signal equipment. Yet the most recent and authoritative history of the United States Army states, "The Army's equipment as well as its manpower and appropriations reached a nadir while Douglas MacArthur was chief of staff." The assertion is true, but in a qualified sense, for it must be remembered that his military headship coincided with the nation's worst depression and the zenith of isolationism and pacifism. MacArthur fought hard for the Army's needs and deserves a large portion of the credit for the upward swing of military appropriations which began in 1935. Certainly his successor's task was made easier because of MacArthur's efforts. Indeed, the start of America's preparedness for the great war toward which the world was rushing was the Army's triumph on Capitol Hill in the spring of 1935.[13]

2. Mobilization Planning

The story of MacArthur's headship of the Army is not complete without an introduction to the War Department's endeavors to plan toward an orderly mobilization of the nation's industries, raw materials, and manpower in the eventuality of war. Under the National Defense Act of 1920 the assistant secretary of war for procurement was charged with industrial mobilization planning. The Planning Branch was established to handle this function under his supervision, while the Army Industrial College prepared theoretical studies and the Army and Navy Munitions Board coordinated procurement and industrial mobilization planning of the two services. During the 1920's, however, the Planning Branch concerned itself almost wholly with procurement, the Army Industrial College was still in its formative stage, and the Munitions Board was virtually dormant. It was not until 1930 that the War Department's first full-scale industrial mobilization plan was finally drafted. Eisenhower, who worked with Payne on this plan, found Chief of Staff Summerall to be "contemptuous" of such activities. When MacArthur became military head in the autumn of 1930, Eisenhower, in his words, "was pleased with General MacArthur's enthusiasm for our planning" and often conferred with him on mobilization planning. "The encouragement and advice of MacArthur," said Eisenhower, "were important in the final formulation of the plan."

The first industrial mobilization plan, completed at the end of 1930, covered a host of topics, such as price controls, priorities, foreign trade, commandeering industrial plants, and special governmental agencies to be created to control the wartime economy. The plan provided for four super agencies to maintain centralized direction over industry, manpower on the home front, selective service, and public relations during mobilization. A presidential advisory council would be set up, comprised of the heads of these agencies, together with the secretaries of the War and Navy departments, the chief of staff, and the chief of naval operations. The main text of the plan dealt largely in generalities about the structure and func-

tion of economic and manpower organization for war. On the
other hand, the appendixes went into considerable detail on
the nature and exact responsibilities of the mobilization agencies and also included a section on legislation needed to implement the plan when a national emergency arose. The plan
made it clear that these central agencies would be under civilian control for the most part and would exist only for the
duration of the emergency.[14]

Meanwhile in 1930 Congress created the War Policies Commission to study "policies to be pursued in the event of war"
and how "to equalize the burdens and to minimize the profits
of war." Headed by Hurley and consisting of eight members
of Congress and six from the Cabinet, the commission conducted hearings for over a year, with principal attention to
control of prices and profits in wartime. MacArthur had the
job of presenting the War Department's hitherto secret industrial mobilization plan, which, in lieu of any comparable
scheme by other governmental departments, became the focus
of the commission's discussions. Although MacArthur could
count on serious interest and constructive criticism from the
Hurley-led commission, the hearings produced some witnesses
who were less than satisfied with the War Department's plan.
Bernard Baruch, who had headed the War Industries Board in
1917–18, argued that in order to achieve wartime stabilization
prices must be frozen at the immediate prewar level. MacArthur defended the War Department's plan, which called for
moderate, gradual controls with emphasis at first on essential
raw materials. Price-freezing, he maintained, would lead to
evasion: "In the end the Government's effort would probably be largely gesture. Attempts at enforcement would likely
create antagonism, and the Government would lose the essential elements of good will. Without complete and unstinting
popular support no nation can hope to fight to victory." Mac-
Arthur's approach to wartime price-fixing was at first similar

to Hoover's method of keeping production and employment levels up during the economic crisis, namely, by depending upon the voluntary cooperation of manufacturers, laborers, farmers, and consumers. The chief of staff "was later to change his mind," Baruch said, "but before the Commission, he and Baker argued against the need for over-all controls, especially over prices. They were willing to rely upon the methods of improvisations and voluntary cooperation which had carried us through World War I. So was the Commission; so was Congress."

In March, 1932, the War Policies Commission issued a majority report, which in effect approved the industrial mobilization plan, but called for revisions every two years by the War Department and subsequent review by congressional groups. The majority report also recommended "a constitutional amendment to be adopted clearly defining the power of Congress to prevent profiteering and to stabilize prices in time of war." Ross Collins, the only member who dissented from the majority report, prepared a minority report in which he vehemently opposed industrial mobilization planning by the military establishment: "I am firmly convinced, whether intended or not, that any war planning as now carried on by the War Department will in the end result in the administration of price fixing laws and the regulation of civilian activities by military and naval officers if the recommendations of the majority members of the commission are finally adopted by Congress." Actually little, if anything, came of the commission's recommendations, except for the preparation of a new industrial mobilization plan and the reactivation of the Army and Navy Munitions Board. Congress did not approve or reject the commission's reports.[15]

In 1933 the War Department produced its second industrial mobilization plan. A fifth super agency for mobilization was added to oversee foreign trade. A war industries administration had been provided in the plan of 1930; the new plan more clearly stipulated its role as the most important of the would-be wartime agencies. The 1933 plan stated that, like the War Industries Board of 1917–18, "the War Industries Administration is the industrial pivot about which war-time control turns. It is the most powerful arm of the President for converting the industries into war uses. It is the meeting point of the war machine and industry." Also the role of the public relations administrator as a censor was spelled out in detail. In addition, the 1933 plan placed more emphasis on integrating price control with other factors of economic planning, such as control of profits, investments, and foreign trade. A price control authority was to be established with authority to set individual prices as well as general price levels. Perhaps revealing the influence of industrial consultants to the War Department, the 1933 plan also stipulated that the war labor administrator was to be "an outstanding industrial leader," rather than "labor's advocate" as described in the 1930 document. Other than these and a few minor changes in agency functions, the 1933 plan was essentially an expansion of the earlier plan, not a major revision. Since the War Policies Commission had not been severely critical of the first plan, the Army's staff planners apparently interpreted its majority report as a mandate to continue working along the same lines.

The Nye Committee in 1934–35, however, did not accept the War Department's scheme for industrial mobilization as readily as did the commission of 1930–32. Nye and his sensation-minded committee subjected the industrial mobilization plan of 1933 to exhaustive analysis, particularly its sections on price controls, public relations, and labor. Prime targets of the committee were the plan's provisions on price controls and censorship. In fact, the senators charged that censorship was implicit in the priorities system since, by withholding priorities in raw materials, transportation, power, and fuel from an offending publisher, the government could deprive him of the essential items for operating his business. The Nye Committee maintained that the appointment of an industrialist to head the war labor administration "prejudiced labor's position from the start." The plan's provision for equal representation of management and labor on the labor administration's advisory council would bring deadlocks, which would leave the labor administrator to make the decisions. The committee also attacked the proposed selective service system, charging that its deferment policy would mean "work-or-fight" orders tantamount to "a draft of labor." In place of the War Department's proposed draft legislation in time of emergency, Nye's group proposed that the government should draft the managers of essential war industries, not their laborers. Woodring later claimed that the plan of 1933 had successfully withstood the onslaughts of the Nye Committee, but there were some changes in the plan of 1936 which surely seem to be responses to some of the committee's criticisms. For instance, the public relations annex was omitted in 1936, the war labor administrator was now simply "an outstanding citizen," more labor representation was provided for, and all mention of selective service was deleted.

In truth, the War Department had been in a vulnerable position on economic mobilization planning from the start. An authority on the subject points out that the War Department was actually formulating industrial mobilization plans "for someone else to carry out in time of war." Moreover, he notes, effective planning was obstructed by "the prevailing climate of public indifference or actual hostility toward measures of any kind which could be described as 'preparation for war.'" When World War II erupted and especially after America's entry, Roosevelt and his advisers hastily set up an organizational framework for economic and manpower mobilization which "bore certain resemblances to the blueprints" of the prewar plans drafted by the War Department. The Office of War Mobilization, for instance, was similar to the super agency conceived in the 1930 and 1933 plans, the war industries administration (called in 1936 the war resources administration). At times in 1939–1942, however, the men responsible for the prewar plans must have wondered if the Roosevelt administration had even seen copies of the War Department's plans. Nevertheless, the thorough theoretical planning of the 1930's made easier the Army's adjustment to its unprecedented involvement in procurement and industrial relations when the great war came.

During all the talk about industrial mobilization one of MacArthur's principal concerns was obtaining congressional consent to place limited "educational orders" with certain manufacturers of munitions. Thereby at least some key firms would be given contracts for limited quantities of new models of military equipment so that, in the event of sudden war, they would have on hand the necessary jigs, dies, and specialized tools to get rapid production underway. But this type of contract was not authorized by Congress until 1938, and only $2,000,000 was allocated at that time. Likewise, MacArthur was anxious to start accumulating stockpiles of critical raw materials, but Congress did not assent to this until 1940.[16]

MacArthur, of course, was less involved than Woodring in problems of procurement and industrial mobilization, but the chief of staff was primarily responsible for planning mobilization of military personnel. In 1933 MacArthur conceived an initial mobilization plan based on neither the then current enlisted strength of 119,000 nor the hoped-for 165,000 troops, but instead on the authorized strength of 280,000 provided in the act of 1920. War plans division leaders protested that the 280,000-man force was unattainable in the foreseeable future, but MacArthur strangely ignored this advice and continued planning in terms of the ideal force. Odd in view of his stress

on the value of the civilian components, the chief of staff did
not include the Organized Reserves in his "initial protective
force"; rather, it would consist only of units of the Regular
Army and National Guard already in existence. "Any World
War would probably be a gradual growth," he asserted, "and
in its initial stages, as would lesser ones, place a premium upon
promptitude and expedition." He believed that the manpower
needed to fill the regular and National Guard units to full
strength could be gained quickly by volunteer enlistments from
"the unused manpower which was stagnating the country, due
to the severe economic depression." He intended to supply
this initial force, which would be the only ground units during
the first two months of war, from stocks of war reserve munitions, which had been produced for the conflict of 1917–18.

When he became Secretary of War in 1936, upon Dern's
death, Woodring set to work on a new protective mobilization
plan because the earlier plan had been "unrealistically" based
upon "supplies which by 1936 had become greatly depleted or
obsolete." Besides the matter of supply procurement, Woodring
found that "the question had arisen in the War Department as
to whether even the rate of personnel procurement contemplated by the original plan could be realized." [17] When he
became chief of staff, Craig was usually complimentary of his
predecessor's work, but he expressed deep anxiety over Mac-
Arthur's optimistic plan for military mobilization:

> The problem I encountered on my entry into office as your
> [the Secretary of War's] principal adviser that caused the great-
> est concern was the lack of realism in military war plans. Of
> necessity, due to grave inadequacies in men and particularly in
> equipment, these plans comprehended many paper units, con-
> jectural supply, and a disregard of the time element which
> forms the main pillar of any planning structure. Military
> planning . . . must be coldly and painstakingly considered in
> the light of intense realism as the basis of all future military

strategy and tactics. What transpires on prospective battlefields is influenced vitally years before in the councils of the Staff and in the legislative halls of Congress . . . Time [is] . . . the keystone of preparation, because it is the only thing that may be irrevocably lost and it is the thing first lost sight of in the seductive false security of peaceful times.[18]

In the first half of the 1930's mobilization planning for procurement, industry, labor, and protective military forces was diligently undertaken by the War Department, but most of the plans were scrapped before the nation plunged into the Second World War. Where had MacArthur and his staff planners failed? Far from being a want of diligent study of mobilization problems, it was because they could not foresee the implications of the mechanical revolution in warfare which had occurred in the previous two decades. They were cognizant of new advances in mechanization, but the Army, for lack of funds, did not have the new weapons in sufficient numbers to engage in large-scale field exercises and thereby develop new tactics. The want of modern tactics and doctrines of warfare, in turn, sorely handicapped staff planners in anticipating mobilization needs. The use of the tank, for example, was still unsettled when MacArthur left the War Department, which meant that the number to be procured for initial mobilization was moot, as well as that weapon's effect on the number of infantry needed for certain types of ground operations. A distinguished military historian says of MacArthur's years as chief of staff:

. . . While it was precisely in these years that the full effects of the mechanical revolution — on the ground, in the air and at sea — were becoming apparent to the more thoughtful staff planners and commanders, there was little or no money with which to translate them into current military policy. A great deal of fairly solid theoretical work had been done, out of which the Second World War armies, navies and air forces were to arise with astonishing speed and effectiveness. But not until the totalitarian dictators — creatures, most of them, of the Great Depression — had arisen to revive war and militarism as instruments of both international and domestic policy, did the democratic peoples begin to convert the new developments of the mechanical revolution in warfare into concrete military planning. And they were to be very slow about it, even so.[19]

He might have added that in America, where the wheels of democracy turn with agonizing slowness, the conversion would be delayed until the eleventh hour.

3. *The Philippine Dilemma*

"Undoubtedly the outstanding development, for good or ill, in the foreign relations of the United States during the remainder of this century, will be that of our relations with the countries on the western side of the Pacific Ocean," Secretary of State Stimson wrote Senator Bingham in early 1932. During the period when MacArthur was chief of staff, there were two momentous developments in the Far East of unusually grave concern to the War Department: the Japanese conquest of Manchuria and the enactment of the Philippine independence legislation. Another war between Japan and China seemed in the offing since the Japanese did not hide their intention of bringing North China into the "Japan-Manchukuo Economic Bloc." Meanwhile the Tydings-McDuffie Act of March, 1934, authorized a commonwealth status for the Philippines until 1946 when complete independence would be granted. The measure, on the insistence of MacArthur and the War Department, provided for the continuance of American military forces and stations in the archipelago during the commonwealth period, with the President of the United States empowered to "call into the service of such armed forces all military forces organized by the Philippine Government" in case of war. Unlike its action on a similar congressional measure of the previous year, the Philippine Legislature approved the Tydings-McDuffie Act and called for a constitutional convention.[20] Despite the misgivings of many American and Filipino leaders about launching the islands on the road toward independence at a time when Japan seemed to be plotting further aggression, the machinery to establish a commonwealth regime was set in motion. What lay at the end of the road — a stable, prosperous, independent republic or chaos and Japanese domination — no one could prophesy with confidence.

Fiery, unpredictable Manuel Quezon and his powerful Nacionalista party had led the successful movement in the Philippines for support of the Tydings-McDuffie Act. The Nacionalistas still dominated the Philippine Legislature and easily won a majority of seats in the constitutional convention. For years Quezon had waxed hot and cold on the issue of immediate independence, but for the present he believed that a transition period was important in order to retain both the free market with the United States and the protective American naval and military forces in the islands. Opinions among Filipinos about independence were mixed. Major General Frank Parker, who now commanded the Philippine Department and, it will be recalled, had led the 1st Division in the Sedan incident of 1918, reported to the War Department in the summer of 1934: "Although the Philippines have just succeeded in achieving the first objective in a long-sought-for and much-talked-about independence, a certain pessimism is the note of the day, instead of an optimism that might have been expected." Parker continued: "Apparently for the first time, many Filipinos are recognizing with genuine alarm, certain inevitable results of independence . . . Sugar, coconut oil, cordage, and immigration quotas are only a few of the sore subjects throughout the archipelago today." The Manila *Philippine Free Press* stated that summer: "The Philippines, on the brink of an independent existence, cannot disregard the forces which are making for a war." *La Vanguardia,* another Manila organ, warned against optimism over the islands' future: "Crushing economic facts and the will-to-power of a great empire which assumes with determination the leadership of Asiatic countries are unfolding the new drama as to what the future holds in this part of the world." [21]

In a confidential report to the War Department on conditions in the Philippines in mid-1934, Parker stressed not the movement toward independence but rather the ominous activities of the growing Japanese population of the archipelago. In the previous decade the immigration of Nipponese to the Philippines, particularly to Mindanao, had risen sharply. The increase had been noticeable when MacArthur was there in 1928–30, but since then, claimed the departmental commander, it had accelerated greatly. Parker found that a suspiciously high percentage of the newcomers in the early 1930's were males of military age, some of whom were known to be reserve officers of the Japanese Army. The general cited numerous examples of obvious intelligence-gathering activities by some of these men. For instance, Mitsui Bussan Kaisha, a large Japanese-owned hemp and copra corporation operating in the southern islands, utilized Japanese reserve officers to drive its trucks. "These officers usually remain in the Philippines for two or three months," said Parker, "and then go back to Japan after accomplishing their missions of familiarizing themselves with different places in the Philippine Archipelago." At the port of Appari in north Luzon, Parker discovered a Japanese photographer whose income from his studio amounted to about sixty pesos monthly, but he spent over 400 pesos a month in boarding and entertaining visiting Japanese from ships which frequented the port. Another Nipponese photographer residing at Appari spent his time "travelling over the northern

Provinces mapping roads and photographing bridges and other points of military interest," reported Parker. When Governor General Frank Murphy toured the Davao area in 1934, he was informed by the provincial governor that "the Japanese control the agriculture and commerce of that province, and that some Filipinos fear that Davao may become a 'second Manchukuo.'" Over 372,000 arable acres of Mindanao were controlled by forty-one Japanese corporations, Parker learned, and much more land was held by Japanese capitalists through "Filipino 'dummy owners.'" The report by the departmental commander was stamped "Noted — Chief of Staff." Apparently MacArthur had it filed since it did not seem to call for any action by the War Department. After all, there was no tangible evidence of Japanese military activities in the islands, and Quezon was convinced that relations between the Philippines and Japan were amiable and lucrative.[22]

War Plan Orange, covering the contingency of a future war between the United States and Japan, underwent no significant revisions while MacArthur was chief of staff. The Philippine Department was still assigned the mission of defending the mouth of Manila Bay until the garrison could be relieved or reinforced about six months after the start of hostilities. After enactment of the Tydings-McDuffie measure, officers in the war plans division, as well as American commanders in the islands, became increasingly convinced that the islands represented an untenable defensive position in case of war with Japan. Over the years no steps had been taken to develop a Filipino defense force; fortifications and military installations in 1934–35 were about the same as they had been fifteen years earlier. In congressional hearings MacArthur had tried to get more funds for the Philippine Department, but it continued to be plagued by inadequate facilities, equipment, and manpower throughout his tour of duty as chief of staff. In mid-1935 the department had only 11,006 officers and men, of which 6437 were Philippine Scouts. Since 1929 the department's strength in regulars and Scouts had been reduced by 243 men, and even the enlarged budget of 1936 brought the total to merely 11,323.[23]

In a study prepared in 1933 by Brigadier General Stanley D. Embick, harbor defense commander on Corregidor, and endorsed by Major General Ewing E. Booth, then commander of the Philippine Department, it was recommended that American military and naval units be withdrawn from the exposed Philippines to a defense line extending from Alaska through Hawaii to Panama. Embick asserted that the islands had become "a military liability of a constantly increasing gravity. To carry out the present Orange Plan — with its provisions for the early dispatch of our fleet to Philippine waters — would be literally an act of madness . . . In the event of an Orange War the best that could be hoped for would be that wise counsels would prevail, that our people would acquiesce in the temporary loss of the Philippines." Embick's recommendation was rejected by the War Department.[24]

In the spring of 1934 when the Tydings-McDuffie Bill was passed, the war plans division raised the question whether the War Department's policy on the defense of the Philippines should be modified. The conclusion, approved by MacArthur and reiterated in various war plans documents until late 1940, was ambiguously stated: "Depending on availability of funds, the War Department desires to keep up the existing strength, both in personnel and matériel, in the Philippines, and in particular to provide adequate protection for the harbor defenses in Manila Bay, but to go to no further expense for permanent improvements unless thereby an ultimate saving will result." The inconsistency between the preparations necessary to implement War Plan Orange and the inadequate provisions for the Philippine Department was resolved neither during MacArthur's term as chief of staff nor during the next two successors' terms. During MacArthur's final year as military head he summoned Embick from the Philippines to lead the war plans division, in which position he continued to argue for a withdrawal from the indefensible Philippine position. No policy change was forthcoming, although nearly everyone in the War Department agreed that the islands would be lost early in a major conflict with Japan. In July, 1934, MacArthur wrote Parker that he was fully aware of the precarious position of the Philippine Department. But, since the Joint Army and Navy Board had recently reiterated its support of War Plan Orange, Parker's duty, in case of Japanese invasion, was still to deny the Nipponese the use of Manila Bay. MacArthur reminded him: "Responsibility for the use of available forces rests solely with you." [25]

That September the commander of the Manila harbor defenses sent an urgent request to the War Department for an adequate supply of ammunition for the pitifully few antiaircraft batteries he had. The reply from Washington was that "due to shortages of war reserve of antiaircraft ammunition in the United States, no increase in the Philippine defense can be made at this time." [26] Similar communications had been sent to the Philippine Department so many times in recent years that officers in Manila probably wondered if Washington chiefs were using a standardized rejection form, merely filling in the type of supplies for which request had been made. In November the war plans division recommended the following action to MacArthur:

> Evacuation of all U.S. troops and of all United States property, except such property as the Philippine Government, after it decides on the eventual form of its national defense, may desire to buy and we may consent to sell, and such other property as may not be worth evacuation, will be effected *during the period of the Commonwealth Government*. This evacuation will begin at as late a date as possible consistent with its completion on the date of final Independence.[27]

The "Not approved" marked on the document at MacArthur's order was simply one more indication of the War Department's unswerving policy that the Army would remain in the Philippines until final independence was accomplished. Shortly MacArthur would be back in Manila where somehow the official position of "no improvements, no reinforcements, no withdrawal" was not as acceptable as in comfortable Washington.

PART V

Philippine
Military Adviser

CHAPTER XVII

A Year of Changes

1. Quezon Gets His General

WHILE THE CONSTITUTIONAL CONVENTION was at work in Manila drafting a constitution for the would-be Philippine Commonwealth, Senate President Quezon journeyed to Washington in the autumn of 1934. His purpose was to discuss with political and military leaders the problem which he considered paramount at the start of his commonwealth, namely, national defense. Quezon had in mind the establishment of an American military mission, which would develop a plan for the defense of the widespread archipelago and guide the development of a Filipino military force through its formative period, perhaps the first six years. Although his stay in Washington was interrupted by a minor operation at Johns Hopkins Hospital, Quezon was able to confer with Dern, MacArthur, and several key senators and representatives. Much to his disappointment, the Philippine leader did not get to talk with Roosevelt, who was then at Warm Springs, Georgia. Quezon, a fervent admirer of the American President, sent him a "warm weather chair" of native craftsmanship, which he had brought from the Philippines. "That delightful chair is out on the porch here at

Warm Springs," Roosevelt responded, "and I take great comfort in lying back in it at just the right angle — with my feet
on about the level of my head." As for Philippine developments and Quezon's mission, the President added, almost as an
afterthought: "I do not need to tell you of my deep continued
interest in the steps that are being taken." [1]

Finding legal grounds for his request for a military mission
in an act of Congress in 1926 which detailed United States
officers as advisers to certain Latin American countries, Quezon
urged the War Department to propose to Congress that the
act be amended to include the Philippines. "Obviously, the
new nation's military policy, both by inclination and compul-
sion," he told Dern, "will be purely defensive, but its defenses
must command respect. No question incident to the establishment of the new government concerns me more than does this
one." Quezon believed that the Philippine Commonwealth
"must have, for a period of at least five or six years, the friendly
counsel and exclusive use of professionally trained military
leaders of wide experience." Dern was agreeable to the proposal and obtained the concurrence of the State and Navy
departments. Then Dern, MacArthur, and Quezon took the
matter to Senator Millard Tydings and Representative John
McDuffie, chairmen of the committees on insular affairs in the
Senate and House. Dern explained to them that the sending
of the Philippine military mission would constitute "aid without assumption of additional authority, an attitude that would
faithfully conform to our disinterested attempt to contribute
toward the development in the Philippine Islands of a status
of complete independence." It was soon common knowledge
that, if the mission was approved, Quezon wanted as its head
his old friend MacArthur. In fact, the chief of staff drafted the
bill which Dern gave the congressmen to consider. Also the
letter which Quezon later signed asking for his services was
composed by MacArthur, at Quezon's request.[2]

Early in his visit to Washington, Quezon pointedly asked MacArthur, "General, do you think that the Philippines, once independent, can defend itself?" MacArthur responded with supreme confidence, "I don't *think* that the Philippines can defend themselves, I *know* they can." The chief of staff went on: "We cannot just turn around and leave you alone. All these many years we have helped you in education, sanitation, road-building, and even in the practice of self-government. But we have done nothing in the way of preparing you to defend yourselves against a foreign foe." [3] It is not known whether he explained to his Filipino friend that, as chief of staff, he had been wholly unable to buttress American military strength and fortifications in the Philippines and that the General Staff's war plans division was in favor of withdrawing American forces altogether. In contrast to MacArthur's optimism about building a defense system in the islands, Dern realistically pointed out to McDuffie in December:

A single decade is none too long a time, even under the most favorable of circumstances, in which to build up from nothing an adequate and completely satisfactory defense for a nation of 14 million people. It is scarcely necessary to dwell upon the magnitude and technical nature of the task. The formulation of basic laws pertaining to recruitment, maintenance and general organization, the development of adequate but economic supply, medical and other technical services, and the establishment of appropriate schools, training centers and other facilities are only a few of the problems that must be successfully solved before a real beginning can be made toward the development of an efficient defense. [4]

During Christmas week, 1934, MacArthur and Dern went to the White House and discussed with Roosevelt the possible detailing of the chief of staff as Philippine military adviser when his tour in Washington was terminated. The President still expected to relieve MacArthur toward the end of the current congressional session, probably in early summer. On December 27 MacArthur wrote Quezon, who was back in Manila, about the conference at the White House: "Both of them were not only in complete sympathy but were enthusiastic. As a consequence I am making definite plans to close my tour as Chief of Staff about June 10th and to leave for the islands immediately thereafter. This would bring me to Manila early in July." In case the inauguration of the Commonwealth was postponed until that fall, as was rumored and later happened, MacArthur left flexible the exact date of his arrival and assumption of the position of military adviser. In closing he assured Quezon: "I am already hard at work drawing up plans and details and by the time I arrive will be able to convince you all that before the close of the ten-year period the Commonwealth, no matter what betides, will be secure from foreign aggression." [5] Thus with boundless confidence in himself and in the Filipino as a soldier, MacArthur eagerly looked forward to the job which many military authorities considered an impossible task from the start.

The appointment of MacArthur as military adviser to the Philippines was eyed with mutual satisfaction by the four key men concerned. With his meteoric advancement in the Army threatened by abrupt, embarrassing termination in 1935, MacArthur faced a dilemma of retiring at fifty-five or accepting a command at corps level or below if he remained in the Army. Prestigious and lucrative, the military advisership seemed to be an ideal solution for him. The probable pay and allowances of the office, together with his Army salary, would place his salaried income above that of either the Philippine president or the American high commissioner. Moreover, he would be serving a people whom he loved deeply and who, for the most part, adored him in return. Quezon obtained a general who was stepping down as military head of the United States Army, recognized as one of its best administrators, and experienced in Philippine affairs. Dern was conscious of the inconsistency in

American policy and practice regarding the defense of the Philippines; the creation of a strong, viable army of Filipinos would remove the onus from the War Department of complete responsibility for the ground defenses of the archipelago. The President, in turn, was satisfied that, if anyone could do the job, his able chief of staff was the best man to undertake the development of a defense system capable of deterring Japanese aggression. Of course, Roosevelt was also relieved that MacArthur, ever regarded by New Dealers as a potential political menace, would be out of the country before the campaigning started for the presidential contest of 1936.

The chief of staff himself talked with and wrote letters to influential senators and representatives urging passage of the military adviser amendment. He did not believe that congressional approval was actually necessary, but felt that "any assistance of this kind would be more effective if supported by the definite approval of Congress." In a letter to McSwain, chairman of the House committee on military affairs, MacArthur argued that "approval of the proposal would be in consonance with the concept of local autonomy, represented in the Commonwealth form of government." Also, "legislative approval would signify to the Filipino people the deep and friendly interest of our Congress in the difficult problems facing the new government." Furthermore, maintained MacArthur, "there would be removed any tendency on the part of the military advisers to adopt a paternalistic attitude or unconsciously to assume any right of dictation, coercion, or unjustified persuasion" — which section of the bill would prevent this was not specified. He continued:

> Another consideration is that a definite law would give positive assurance to the Philippines that this special assistance would be available as long as necessary, even after attainment of independence. Manifestly, the prospect of making a complete change in its military advisers at the expiration of a specific period would impel the new government to turn else-

where initially, so that an unfortunate contingency might be avoided. The possible consequences of such a development furnish a very compelling reason for this amendment. Should the Philippine Government obtain professional assistance from some government whose vital interests might, in the future, run directly counter to our own, the results would certainly be embarrassing, not to say dangerous.[6]

Tydings and McDuffie took the lead in steering the bill to passage in May, and the Philippines was added to the list of countries eligible to receive American military missions. Confident of victory in the presidential election scheduled for the coming summer, Quezon had told the Philippine Legislature in March that he had taken the liberty of asking MacArthur to head the military mission and predicted that the amendment would get quick approval from Congress. When the measure became law on May 14, Quezon and MacArthur, by correspondence, then formalized an agreement they had worked out earlier stating the terms of contract for the position of military adviser. Within the Philippine governmental and military structure, MacArthur would be responsible directly to the Philippine president and would hold the title of field marshal. Among his emoluments, which were in addition to his pay as a major general on the active list of the United States Army, MacArthur would receive from the Commonwealth a salary of 36,000 pesos ($18,000) per year and 30,000 pesos ($15,000) yearly in allowances. A clause was even included to allow for the possibility of MacArthur's appointment as high commissioner; in such case he would temporarily relinquish the post of military adviser, resuming it at the end of his term as high commissioner.[7]

On September 18, 1935, Dern issued Special Orders No. 22:

By direction of the President, General Douglas MacArthur is detailed to assist the Commonwealth of the Philippine Islands in military and naval affairs. He will act as the Military Adviser of the Commonwealth Government in the establishment and development of a system of National Defense. He will confer and advise with the President of the Commonwealth Government under such conditions and arrangements as may be mutually determined. He will in addition carry out such instructions as may be given him by the Secretary of War. He will proceed to and take station at Manila, P.I., in accordance with travel orders to be issued by the Secretary of War. He will stand relieved from duty on the General Staff and as Chief of Staff as of date of December 15, 1935.[8]

Apparently early that summer Roosevelt had agreed to retain MacArthur another half year, but strangely no publicity was associated with his second postponement of the chief of staff's relief. Moreover, no order was found regarding this extension of his tour of duty, which suggests that it was an oral agreement between the President, MacArthur, and Dern. Roosevelt's decision may have been motivated by the postponement of the Commonwealth's inauguration until fall and MacArthur's work on the fiscal 1937 budget prefatory to sending it to the Budget Bureau.

Since MacArthur now knew when he would be departing for the islands, or so he thought, he began selecting the small staff which was allotted to his Philippine mission. For his chief of staff he chose Major Eisenhower, who had been his assistant for two and a half years. Because of his mother's worsening health, he persuaded Major Howard J. Hutter, the MacArthurs' longtime physician and friend, to accompany them to Manila. Captain Davis, the general's aide for a number of years, would also go. According to Eisenhower, MacArthur "lowered the boom on me," and "I was in no position to argue with the Chief of Staff." "Ike" really wanted a troop assignment elsewhere, but MacArthur refused to consider it; Eisenhower then asked him to set a definite terminal date for his duty on the Philippine mission, but MacArthur was vague about how long he expected him to stay. "One privilege he did permit," said Eisenhower, "possibly realizing that a familiar face meant as much to me as to him. He said I could pick one associate from the Regular Army to go along with us." Eisenhower chose Major James B. Ord, a West Point classmate of his who was known for "his quickness of mind and ability as a staff officer," as well as for his mastery of Spanish. MacArthur, it will be recalled, became acquainted with Ord during the French maneuvers in 1931, and in recent months Ord had been detailed to the chief of staff's office. Both he and Eisenhower had assisted MacArthur in the preliminary planning for a Philippine defense system.[9]

At the same time that he was considering problems which would confront him as military adviser, MacArthur was also mulling over the possibility of his appointment as Philippine high commissioner, which would be the top American administrative post in the islands when the governor generalship was abolished with the creation of the Commonwealth. In November, 1934, he telephoned the Bureau of Insular Affairs and asked for data on the "pay, allowances and perquisites of the Office of Governor General of the Philippine Islands." Attached to the bureau's reply (which listed the salary as $18,000 a year) as it is filed in the records of the adjutant general's office is an undated, unsigned note saying: "The President is hereby authorized to appoint DOUGLAS MACARTHUR as U.S. High Commissioner to the Philippine Islands without affecting his status as an officer on the active list of the Army or as adviser on military questions for the Philippine Islands." Apparently MacArthur had been considering the possibility for some months, though with whose encouragement is not known. In early 1935 Brigadier General C. E. Nathorst, a retired officer living near Manila, wrote MacArthur: "There has been a persistent rumor here for some time that you are coming out as High Commissioner." In May, 1935, Quezon informed MacArthur that he was being "seriously considered for the position of High Commissioner to succeed Governor Murphy who will be the first High Commissioner, but only for a short time because he is determined to return soon to the United States." Quezon raised the question: "Will it be more to your interest as well as in that of both the United States and the Philippine Islands that you be the High Commissioner rather than the Military Adviser of the Philippine Government?" Quezon said that he himself did not know which course would be the wisest. When questioned, presumably by Roosevelt, about MacArthur for the post of high commissioner, Quezon had replied that the general was "the best choice they could make" and would be "well received by the Filipino people." Quezon advised MacArthur not to commit himself on the commissionership until he was in Manila for a while and had conferred with him.[10]

In his answer to Quezon on June 1, MacArthur said, "I have received no inkling as to any consideration having been given to my succeeding Governor Murphy as High Commissioner. I do not give much weight to it." Murphy "fills the bill admirably and has the confidence of both Filipinos and Americans," and "every effort should be made to convince him that he should stay in that position indefinitely." MacArthur continued with what must have seemed to Quezon a most sincere and assuring commitment to his role as military adviser:

As for me, I have never given it [the high commissionership] a thought. The great work involved as your Military Adviser seems to me to transcend in ultimate importance anything else that is conceivable. I am prepared to devote the remainder of my life if necessary to securing a proper defense for the Philippine Nation. No question that confronts it in ultimate analysis is of such importance. Some day it will mean the difference between life and death for your people. I believe that many might be found who could fill satisfactorily the office of the

High Commissioner but I do not believe that it is so easy to
find the combination of professional experience and devotion
to a cause which are indispensable to the organizing and establishment of a sound and adequate defense system.

I realize fully the high glamour and potential political possibilities in the office of High Commissioner as compared with
the relative obscurity of a professional military position but in
this instance there is nothing that could tempt me from our
agreement. I do not believe that the matter will be seriously
broached as I cannot conceive, with my intimate knowledge of
what is going on, that it is more than the smoke of camouflage
which is so frequently used when such political questions are
discussed. As the High Commissioner I could at best only give
you the comfort and solace of personal support in your great
task but as the Military Adviser I will forge for you a weapon
which will spell the safety of your nation from brutal aggression
until the end of time. I suppose that few men confronted with
the choice of the two positions would agree with me, but in
potential importance, viewed from the broadest aspect of the
case, I believe the Military Adviser to be of far greater value
than the High Commissioner. If I am approached upon the
matter, which I do not anticipate, I will, as you suggest, not
commit myself until after conferring with you.[11]

MacArthur's temptation came soon, and there is no indication that he discussed the matter with Quezon. At the end of
August the chief of staff received an autographed picture from
Roosevelt and an invitation to dine at his Hyde Park mansion
on September 3. MacArthur accepted, and during the visit,
which apparently involved only the two men, the President offered MacArthur the position of Philippine high commissioner.
There was some question, however, whether there was a statute
requiring military officers to resign from the service before
accepting civilian political appointments. MacArthur returned
to Washington and checked with the judge advocate general.
He discovered that there was such a law, but he did not drop
the matter. Instead, on September 9 he wrote Roosevelt that

he was "somewhat dismayed and nonplussed to find legal prohibitions" barring his continuance in the Army if he accepted the commissionership. He suggested that special congressional legislation would be necessary to make him eligible to hold his rank and the political position. "If you should decide, after consideration of the above factors," MacArthur confided to the President, "to abandon either now or in the future your purpose of making the appointment, great as would be my natural disappointment, I will conform instantly to the revised plan." [12] Perhaps when MacArthur had written Quezon three months earlier that "nothing could tempt me from our agreement," he should have added "except an invitation to be the high commissioner."

On September 19, the day after the order detailing MacArthur as military adviser was issued, Roosevelt informed the chief of staff that he would "take up with the Senate and House people the question of a Joint Resolution and see if it is not possible to put the appointment through and cut the difficulty of Revised Statutes 1222 and 1223," the ones forbidding an officer from accepting a civilian post without resigning his commission in the armed services. "I am inclined to hope," Roosevelt remarked, "that there will be little or no trouble on the Hill." [13]

Meanwhile MacArthur had been gathering ammunition against Murphy to prevent his assumption of the office of high commissioner when the Commonwealth was established that autumn. George A. Malcolm, a justice of the Philippine supreme court, wrote MacArthur in August that he would like the job of legal adviser to the high commissioner if the general was appointed. Malcolm added tactlessly: "At least in a conference with the Governor-General it was agreed that it would be proper to bring the matter to notice in the right quarter." On September 26 MacArthur wrote Roosevelt that Murphy's recent public statements, in which he allegedly insisted on powers and privileges for the high commissioner far beyond those rightly expected, showed clearly that he envisioned himself as the "Super-President of the Commonwealth." MacArthur charged, "The War Department knows of no appointive official in any government having the powers as great as those desired by Governor General Murphy." Learning of the chief of staff's letter, Murphy retorted to the President that MacArthur's charges were allegations "wholly without foundation and unwarranted." This unexpected debacle caught Roosevelt at a time when he was suffering from extreme fatigue and irritability. Referring to his tired condition in late September, the President later admitted to Henry Morgenthau, Jr., the Secretary of the Treasury: "I was so tired that I would have enjoyed seeing you cry or would have gotten pleasure out of sticking pins into people and hurting them." [14] Apparently the Chief Executive chose MacArthur as one of his pin-sticking targets, for about this time the general's name was dropped from consideration for the Philippine high commissionership and subsequently Murphy received the appointment.

Coinciding with the demise of this political possibility for MacArthur was Roosevelt's decision to relieve him as chief of staff ahead of the anticipated date. On July 17 Dern sent a memorandum to the President informing him of his plans to go to Manila for the Commonwealth's inaugural ceremonies and noting that he expected to be back in Washington before mid-December. The Secretary of War further stated:

> . . . It is essential that General MacArthur leave for Manila early in October in order that the new Commonwealth President can have the benefit of his fundamental advice in presenting to his legislature a National Defense Act for enactment. Mr. Quezon has specifically requested that he be permitted to leave at that time as otherwise he would be gravely embarrassed in handling the situation which will confront him. There is no necessity, however, to relieve him as Chief of Staff at that pre-

cise time. It is suggested, therefore, that General MacArthur
be relieved as Chief of Staff on December the 15th by which
time I will recommend to you his successor, probably General
Craig. The advantage of not inducting a new Chief of Staff
until my return is so great as to make me very earnestly recommend this procedure.

. . . The actual set-up is entirely normal, as the War Department plans provide for the Chief of Staff taking the field and
the Deputy Chief of Staff administering the War Department
activities. This is the primary function of the Deputy Chief of
Staff and there could, therefore, be no misunderstanding on the
part of the Deputy with regard to this arrangement.

In order that definite plans can be made, I recommend that
you approve this general arrangement.[15]

The next day Roosevelt responded amiably: "I entirely approve the general arrangement you suggest . . . I see no reason
why you should not tell General MacArthur that the plan
meets with my approval so that he can make his plans accordingly." At his press conferences, however, the President
was evasive or noncommittal about MacArthur's relief. When
a reporter on September 4 probed about the possibility of
Craig succeeding to the position of chief of staff soon, Roosevelt replied tersely, "I have not made up my mind." [16] It will
be remembered that Dern issued the order detailing MacArthur
as Philippine military adviser on September 18, with the date
of his relief as chief of staff to be December 15.

In the meantime that summer and early fall a number of
honors were bestowed upon MacArthur since it was widely
rumored that he was about to leave the office of chief of staff.
Norwich University, for instance, conferred an honorary doctorate on him, and the Reserve Officers Association gave him
a special citation of distinction in recognition of his efforts on
behalf of the civilian components. In a brief ceremony in the
War Department, which caught him by surprise, MacArthur
was awarded an Oak Leaf Cluster to his Distinguished Service

Medal, with Dern citing the chief of staff's "exceptionally meritorious and distinguished services in a position of great responsibility." Woodring sent him a gift and a note which read:
"Nothing can express my regret at your leaving; nor my happiness in my association with you during my stay here . . . I am
happy to call you friend." General Pershing sent him a photograph of himself, beneath which was a handwritten tribute
which began: "I have only praise for General MacArthur as
Chief of Staff. He has fully measured up to that high position."
The Rainbow Veterans honored him by inviting him to be
the keynote speaker at their convention in Washington. Mac-
Arthur used the occasion to give one of his best addresses on
preparedness, reminding his former colleagues of the 42nd
Division that "every nation that would preserve its tranquility,
its riches, its independence, and its self-respect must keep alive
its martial ardor and be at all times prepared to defend itself."
A witness noted, however, that "the Rainbow veterans looked
like men who had never seen a gun or heard a shot. Nobody
seemed to realize how MacArthur felt or really what he was
saying. The yells were loud, but the boys' minds were on
something else."

By September MacArthur's time was largely absorbed in
completing his chores as chief of staff, reappraising the defense
plan which he would take to Quezon, and arranging the many
details involved in moving halfway around the world. His sister-in-law, Mary, agreed to go with MacArthur and his mother
in order to care for the latter, whose health was failing. When
news arrived on September 18 that Quezon, as expected, had
easily won the presidential election, MacArthur cabled him:
"As probably the first one to predict this many, many years ago,
personally it gives me joy and satisfaction." Quezon answered,
"We will need your help very badly and wish to see you here
soon." [17]

With his small entourage of family and staff MacArthur left

the national capital on October 1, headed westward by train for San Francisco. The next day at a train stop in Wyoming he received an unexpected telegram from Woodring, who was acting Secretary of War in Dern's absence. The President had just informed Woodring that he had appointed Craig as chief of staff "effective this date." MacArthur suddenly reverted from four to two stars, his permanent rank being major general. Eisenhower, who was present when he received the shocking news, said that MacArthur burst forth with "an explosive denunciation of politics, bad manners, bad judgment, broken promises, arrogance, unconstitutionality, insensitivity, and the way the world had gone to hell." Regaining his composure, MacArthur sent wires to Roosevelt and Woodring commending the selection of Craig as "not only admirable but timely." He dispatched a telegram of congratulations to Craig stating therein that "the entire Army will look forward with keen anticipation to what cannot fail to be a successful tenure of office." [18] Jim Farley, the Postmaster General and one of Roosevelt's principal confidants, related the following version of the President's decision:

> On November 14, 1935, during a luncheon at the President's desk, I said I had been advised that Secretary of War Dern was surprised by the appointment of General Malin Craig as Chief of Staff of the United States Army. Dern was then visiting Hawaii. I was also surprised since I had supported Major General Hugh Drum.
>
> "Your information is absolutely correct, Jim," Roosevelt laughed. "He didn't know about it. You see General Douglas MacArthur, during his service as Chief of Staff, had been trying to have all his favorites placed in responsible positions. He was arranging it so that he would be succeeded by Major General George S. Simonds.
>
> "Last spring Simonds had four years left to go before retirement and could have served out the term of a Chief of Staff. I had to think fast, so I asked MacArthur to stay until October on the representation that I needed him to assist in the formulation of legislation relative to the War Department.

"MacArthur stayed. When October rolled around Simonds only had three and a half years to serve and that eliminated MacArthur's man. If I had told Dern about it, he might have mentioned it, innocently, to someone in the War Department and pressure might have been brought to bear to force the appointment of Simonds while he still had four years to go. Consequently, I waited; then when Dern and MacArthur left the country, I made the appointment." [19]

If Farley's account is correct, MacArthur would have been justified in wondering how much support the Roosevelt administration would give to his plans to build a Philippine defense system.

2. *Return to Manila*

Sailing from San Francisco on the *President Hoover* in early October, MacArthur suppressed his disgruntled feelings as unexpected developments occurred aboard ship. His mother, now eighty-four years old, became seriously ill shortly after the vessel's departure, necessitating the full attention of her daughter-in-law and much of her devoted son's time. Murphy had invited the MacArthurs to be his guests at dinner on the evening of their arrival in Manila, but MacArthur had to notify him while en route that "due to my mother's illness, neither she nor my sister-in-law will be able to accept your gracious invitation." When the ship stopped at Hongkong in the last week of October, MacArthur, because of her grave condition, cancelled a conference which he had scheduled with the commander of the British Army there. On December 3, about five weeks after their arrival in the Philippines, his mother died of cerebral thrombosis at the Manila Hotel where they lived. She was temporarily interred in a cemetery in Manila, and when MacArthur returned to the United States in early 1937, he had her remains buried beside his father in Arlington National Cemetery (the latter having been moved from Milwaukee in 1926). In his memoirs he commented simply, "Our devoted comradeship of so many years came to an end." But at the time, according to Eisenhower, her death had a "deeply personal effect" on MacArthur and "affected the General's spirit for many months." [20]

Ironically, at the time of his greatest sadness MacArthur found the person who would be the chief joy of the rest of his life. At a cocktail party hosted by the ship's captain in honor of Boston mayor James B. Curley, MacArthur met Miss Jean Marie Faircloth, a petite, vivacious brunette. She was en route to Shanghai to visit some English friends. A native of Murfreesboro, Tennessee, she came from a family which, like the Hardys, was proud of its Old South heritage and the roles of its sons in the Civil War. Thirty-seven and unmarried, Jean Faircloth was captivating in personality; she was poised in movement and cultured in conversation. Interestingly, MacArthur's introduction of her into his memoirs reveals only a single inkling of his initial attraction to her: "She was a rebel . . . and still is." The general and Miss Faircloth were reputedly in love with each other before the *Hoover* reached Shanghai. Abbreviating her visit with the English family there, she moved on to Manila where, though it may not have been her original intention, she established her residence. For the next year and a half she and MacArthur were often seen together, the courtship culminating in their marriage in 1937, a story to be told later.[21] The general's first months in Manila could have been extremely dark and lonely without her. As it was, perhaps never before or again was he torn by so many different emotions — bereavement over his mother, bewilderment and animosity toward Roosevelt, excitement over the challenge of his new job, and love for Jean.

For his home MacArthur chose a large, air-cooled suite atop the new Manila Hotel, overlooking the beautiful bay. Though he enjoyed visiting in the home of Manuel and Aurora Quezon, his social relations were limited by the demands of his new professional tasks. In the days remaining before the inauguration he and his small staff arranged their offices at No. 1 Calle Victoria in Manila's ancient walled sector, completed the final details on the defense plan to be presented to the Commonwealth's legislature, and assisted Quezon in last-minute arrangements for the inauguration. The National Defense Act would be the first measure approved by the Philippine National Assembly after the Commonwealth was begun. Murphy was a little anxious since he had not seen the plan until nearly a month after MacArthur's arrival. "With minor modifications," MacArthur assured him, "it is the same measure that was developed by our General Staff and War College."

On November 15, 1935, the solemn ceremony and gala festivities inaugurating the Philippine Commonwealth took place in Manila. The list of distinguished guests included many Americans, such as Vice President John N. Garner, seventeen United States senators, twenty-six members of the United States House of Representatives, the Secretary of War and several high-ranking officers of the War Department, High Commissioner Murphy and his staff, several Americans who formerly held important posts in the Philippine government, and, of course, MacArthur and his officers. The inaugural ceremony began promptly at 8:15 A.M. in front of the Legislative Building, which faced the old walled city of Manila. The invocation, delivered by the Archbishop of Cebu, was followed by a "memorable address" by Dern, with Murphy thereafter reading a proclamation from Roosevelt certifying the officials' elections and announcing the Commonwealth's establishment. Oaths of office were then administered by the Philippine chief justice to President Quezon, Vice President Osmeña, and the members of the National Assembly. After Quezon's inaugural address a lengthy parade was reviewed by the new president. "The largest mass assembly," said Murphy, "ever to gather in Manila at any one time, estimated by the police at a quarter of a million people, crowded the area around the ceremonial stand to view the inauguration and the parade." That afternoon the National Assembly held its opening session, largely a formality. The evening's festivities began with a colorful fireworks display on the waterfront, followed by a state dinner at Quezon's home in honor of the distinguished American visitors. At 9:30 P.M. began the lavish inaugural ball at the Wallace Field Auditorium, with dancing until the early hours of the morning. MacArthur attended all of the activities, but had no speaking part in any of the programs and ceremonies.[22] If the inauguration was a harbinger, the Commonwealth was off to an auspicious beginning. At least for one glorious day all was joy, all was optimism for the Filipinos. The cost of the celebration could be worried about tomorrow, as well as the many problems which the new regime would face.

Although Murphy reported that the inauguration took place "without any untoward event," behind the scenes the question of honors and precedence of Philippine officials came close to disrupting the harmony of the occasion. The issue, which in retrospect appears trivial, may have been connected with Roosevelt's dissatisfaction with MacArthur that fall and his decisions regarding the posts of chief of staff and high commissioner.

As early as August, 1935, the Bureau of Insular Affairs became concerned over the gun salutes which should be accorded to the Commonwealth president and other high-ranking Philippine officials. Brigadier General Creed F. Cox, the bureau chief, recommended in a memorandum to MacArthur that "the personal salute of the President of the Philippine Commonwealth shall not be that accorded the sovereign head of government." Cox proposed nineteen guns for Quezon rather than twenty-one. Governor General Murphy, who, along with the governors of American states, received nineteen-gun salutes, concurred, thereby possibly precipitating the heated quarrel with

MacArthur which ensued that summer.[23] "I disagree utterly," said MacArthur, who continued to insist on the full twenty-one guns for the Commonwealth's president. While still chief of staff, he cautioned Dern that the issue could become a major one:

> . . . To refuse a sovereign salute to the elective head of this people will create a sense of resentment and insult in the breasts of all Filipinos. Undoubtedly the Philippine Commonwealth will itself prescribe, as is within its sovereign power, the usual salute for its President of twenty-one guns. A strange analogy would, therefore, exist in the Philippines of the United States Federal forces giving the President nineteen guns, and the Philippine forces and other Philippine agencies, as well as visiting Naval forces of other countries, giving him twenty-one guns. I know of nothing which is more calculated to create friction than such a situation.
>
> The salute to the elective head of a people is to that people, and when it is not accorded it offends that people. It is not a personal matter at all. The United States can make no greater mistake, in my opinion, than to attempt to belittle and diminish the social prestige of the sovereign head of this new country.
>
> . . . Such salutes are not dependent upon the size, the wealth, or the power of the nation involved. They are inherent attributes of the sovereignty and dignity of the peoples involved.
>
> By this unnecessary and uncalled for ruling over a trivial matter, a bitter quarrel between two nations will be engendered which will grow out of all proportion to the importance of the matter concerned.[24]

Cox was won over by MacArthur's strong conviction in the matter and his greater experience with the Filipinos. On September 14 the Bureau of Insular Affairs announced that the Philippine president would receive a twenty-one-gun salute and the playing of the Philippine national anthem as ceremonial honors. Roosevelt concurred, thus giving precedence to Quezon over Murphy. After Dern reached Manila and conferred with

American leaders there, however, he began to have second thoughts about the matter. On November 9 he reported to the President that the issue had produced "some discord" and that Murphy felt "very deeply" that twenty-one guns for Quezon "would be incorrect and inadvisable," an opinion shared by "the Vice Governor and all members of the Governor's staff and also by the Chief Military and Naval Officers here except General MacArthur." They maintained that such honors for Quezon "would subordinate the status of the High Commissioner who is the representative of the United States Government in the Philippines, thereby making his position difficult and untenable." They also claimed, said Dern, that precedence for Quezon "would make effective exercise of American sovereignty impracticable." [25]

Roosevelt cabled Dern immediately that, after having given "long consideration" to the matter, he had finally decided that the Philippine president should receive only a nineteen-gun salute, the same as that for the state governors and the high commissioner. The twenty-one-gun salute was to be reserved for the President of the United States, who, in Roosevelt's words, "should be accorded special honors because of his direct supervision and control over foreign affairs." Three days later the President sent Dern a radiogram amplifying his position on the honors for Quezon and Murphy: "Although these two high officials will enjoy equal rank and honors . . . it is proper that the High Commissioner be regarded as the senior official and therefore that as between the two he take precedence over the President of the Commonwealth." When Quezon learned that Roosevelt had reversed his decision, he irately announced that he would not participate in his own inauguration, then only a few days away. Flattery by Murphy and a soothing message from Roosevelt cajoled him, and Quezon finally told Dern to cable the President that "I am perfectly satisfied with his decision in this matter and appreciate his attention giving me his reason therefor." [26] MacArthur did not express in writing his reaction to Roosevelt's decision, but he undoubtedly considered it to be typical of the President's duplicity.

The matter of honors and precedence, beneath the surface of which apparently seethed more ill feeling than is penetrable today, was renewed two months after the inauguration of the Commonwealth. This time the target was MacArthur himself. The National Defense Act, largely conceived by MacArthur and passed by the Philippine National Assembly in December, included a provision that the military adviser would be given the title of field marshal of the Philippine Army. Major General Lucius R. Holbrook, who had recently succeeded Parker as commander of the Philippine Department, raised the question to the War Department whether MacArthur had precedence over him and the commander of the Asiatic Fleet. The rank of field marshal was unknown in the United States Army, but in international military circles it was generally considered to be superior to a department or fleet commander. In April, 1936, the adjutant general of the Army, after consulting with top officials of the War and Navy departments, informed Holbrook that since the Philippine Army "is considered analogous to the National Guard, the Army will render no salutes or honors to officers of the Philippine Army except when actually called into Federal service, nor will officers of the United States Army and Navy on duty with the Philippine Army be entitled to honors or salutes from the United States Army because of and commensurate with increased rank conferred on them by the Philippine Government." [27]

Surely, the matter of ceremonial honors was a minute and vain one, but, as events turned out, it was prophetic of the affinity between MacArthur and Quezon on the one hand and American civilian and military officials on the other hand during the next six years. Only on rare occasions would the Philippine president and his military adviser obtain priority for any of their defense requests, no matter how urgent they seemed in Manila. The Gullivers of Washington would have more important things on their minds than the problems of the leaders with pretentious titles in the far-off Philippine Lilliput.

3. *Birth of the Philippine Army*

The military provisions of the constitution of the Philippine Commonwealth were stated in such brief, general terms that almost any kind of defense system could have been enacted. The plan devised by MacArthur and established under the National Defense Act was closely patterned after the citizen army of Switzerland where a relatively large force of citizen soldiers was partially trained and the professional troops were few. Such an establishment was intended to be defensive only. In the Philippine defense law the first sentences of the section on national defense policy read: "The preservation of the State is the obligation of every citizen. The security of the Philippines and the freedom, independence, and perpetual neutrality of the Philippine Republic shall be guaranteed by the employment of all citizens, without distinction of age or sex, and all resources." All Filipino boys were required by the law to undergo "preparatory military training" in the public schools from ages ten through seventeen, thereafter advancing to the "junior reserve." On their twentieth birthday they were required to register for five and a half months of active duty in the Philippine Army. Afterward they would serve in various stages of ready and inactive reserve status until fifty years old. Even girls were to receive some training in an "auxiliary service" while in the public schools. The act also stipulated that "the national defense organization shall be adapted as closely as possible to the territorial and administrative organization of the Philippines," which would mean, in effect, that the military units would be

scattered through all of the provinces and on dozens of islands
in the archipelago.[28]

Chief of Staff Craig and the General Staff's war plans division
were critical of MacArthur's plan from the time he left for
the islands onward. The wide distribution of training centers,
they feared, might enable "disaffected political leaders" in outlying regions to seize the camps' arms stores and "defy the central government" with rebel bands armed therefrom. Embick
warned in late 1935 that "this danger is not remote. It is more
to be apprehended in the near future than foreign aggression."
Although he had no authority to void the action of the Philippine National Assembly, Craig concurred in the war plans division's conclusion regarding MacArthur's defense plan:

> . . . 2. Such an establishment, or indeed any form of military
> establishment that can be maintained by the Philippine Gov-
> ernment, would be wholly ineffective, in itself, to protect the
> Philippine Islands against Japan. For this there are two major
> causes, both irremediable, viz.:
>
> a. Unlike Switzerland, the Philippines are not a compact
> land unit, but an archipelago. The intervening water areas
> will be controlled in war by the naval forces of the enemy. In
> consequence, the Filipino forces can not be concentrated against
> attack and the various islands can be captured in turn by rela-
> tively small forces of the enemy.
>
> b. Since the Philippines lack the resources to support an
> industry that would avail for munitioning, and are unable to
> support a navy, they would be cut off in war from all foreign
> sources of supply. Hence it would be necessary for them to
> obtain abroad and to continue to maintain during peace, not
> only the initial equipment for their forces but all the muni-
> tions required for the duration of the war. The cost of this for
> a force of any magnitude could not possibly be borne by the
> new Philippine State.
>
> 3. The foregoing objections to a military establishment of
> the character stated are obvious and insurmountable. Such an
> establishment can have little or no value as an end in itself.

Its only value would be that of supplementing military (including naval) measures the United States might be induced to take for the defense of the Philippines. This thought, openly expressed by some, must be in the back of the minds of all informed proponents of such an establishment.

4. A military system created purely and simply for the purpose of maintaining internal order would be infinitely more valuable to the Philippine State than a large expensive national defense force which could neither repel invasion nor cope successfully with internal disorders. The ground work for such a system already exists in the Philippine Constabulary. The Philippine Constabulary has been maintained for many years as a national police force and has carried out the task of maintaining order efficiently and at a reasonable cost. It is organized on a military basis, and but few changes in its organization would be necessary. The funds required to equip and maintain a constabulary force of the necessary size would not be excessive.

5. If the United States does not intend to assume responsibility for the defense of the new Philippine State, it should announce that fact at an early date. A definite pronouncement on the part of our Government that the Philippine State must rely on its own resources and the good faith of nations for the maintenance of its independence might influence Filipino leaders to adopt the type of military force outlined in paragraph four, rather than the type now being considered.[29]

Nevertheless, MacArthur undertook the challenge with optimism, supremely confident that his plan would succeed. As he had requested, the National Assembly appropriated $8,000,-000 for the first year's activities of the Philippine Army. The defense program was expected to entail expenditures of about that same amount each year for the next decade, at the end of which the military establishment was to be fully developed. With this small sum MacArthur expected to operate an 11,000-man force of regular troops, provide five and a half months of training annually for 40,000 citizen soldiers, develop a fleet of fifty torpedo boats, and purchase an air force of 250 planes.

Moreover, the appropriated funds were to be expended also for construction and maintenance of a military academy "built on the lines of West Point," several lesser service schools, and over 120 training camps, besides equipping and supplying of personnel.

In his first formal report to Quezon in late April, 1936, MacArthur declared that "general progress in the development of the army has exceeded original anticipation." He found that "as the people become more conversant with the plan itself and with its modest objectives, spontaneous and effective support is invariably given it." As for costs, he assured Quezon that "directly and indirectly the defense plan makes every possible concession to economy consistent with efficiency. The result is that in the world today there is no other defensive system that provides an equal security at remotely comparable cost to the people maintaining it." He was sure that, when fully developed, his defense system "will present to any potential invader such difficult problems as to give pause even to the most ruthless and powerful." Eisenhower later remarked, however, that this report at the end of the first six months was "far too optimistic. Actually we had barely gotten started, and there was no Philippine Army to speak of. Few of the camps had been built, and the system of registering the Filipinos for training had barely begun functioning." Indeed, the first group of citizen trainees — 20,000 in number — would not report to the camps until early 1937.[30]

MacArthur's purpose in issuing such a glowing report apparently was to boost Filipino morale and support for the defense plan and to convince Washington officials of its worth since he would soon be requesting surplus and obsolete equipment from the War Department. He frankly admitted to Murphy that the Philippine Army "must depend on the United States for cooperation and support, particularly for its source of supply for needed equipment." Quezon and most of his lieutenants shared the military adviser's enthusiasm, though they could see few tangible results yet; the Philippine president's faith in Mac-Arthur at this stage was strong and unquestioning. Copies of the report were sent to numerous political and military leaders, and some of them heartily endorsed it. Admiral O. G. Murfin, commanding the Asiatic Fleet, called it "a splendid document," adding: "You are already going places and are moving along with your plans faster than the most optimistic could have hoped for." Drum, who was in command of the Hawaiian Department, thought MacArthur's defense system was "a happy approach to an ultimate solution." Foulois, now retired, wrote the military adviser: "It is my belief that your plan for a Navy of torpedo boats and subs, an Air Force built around bombers, and every citizen a trained soldier, will go down in history as the first sound plan for *Adequate and Economic National Defense for Defense Purposes Only.*" But Craig and most of the generals in the War Department continued to be skeptical.[31]

The conferring of the title of field marshal on MacArthur was postponed inexplicably until August 24, 1936. In an impressive ceremony at Malacañan Palace that evening Quezon read the commission, and Mrs. Quezon presented the new field marshal with a gold baton. MacArthur, looking very solemn and distinguished, was attired in a specially designed sharkskin uniform consisting of black trousers and a white coat bedecked with braid, stars, and unique lapel designs. He delivered an address which, said one listener, "was a powerful piece of realism" on national defense. J. Weldon Jones, who was on Murphy's staff and would serve later as acting high commissioner, wrote MacArthur the next day: "I wish to express again my congratulations for the honor and compliment paid you last night by President Quezon. This unique experience, this memorable occasion seemed to me to portray the unwritten biographies and unwritten libraries which would adequately present all that time and tide has brought to these shores during the past

37 years." Captain Bonner F. Fellers, who was organizing a reserve officers school at Baguio and would later become one of MacArthur's closest associates, told him: "I shall never forget your speech . . . It is a Sermon on the Mount clothed in grim, present-day reality." From IV Corps Area headquarters in Atlanta, Moseley wrote: "I was delighted to read that the Commonwealth of the Philippine Islands had accorded you further promotion and new honors. There is little further that the Government can do for you now except to make you President of the United States." On the other hand, Eisenhower, the affable, unpretentious chief of staff to MacArthur, found the whole occasion "rather fantastic." He had tried, he later said, "to persuade MacArthur to refuse the title since it was pompous and rather ridiculous to be the field marshal of a virtually nonexisting army." For a long time Eisenhower thought that the notion of the field marshalcy had originated with Quezon, but, "when Quezon came to Washington during the war years, I had a chance to talk to him about it casually one day. I was surprised to learn from him that he had not initiated the idea at all; rather, Quezon said that MacArthur himself came up with the high-sounding title." [32]

There were some snickering, sarcastic remarks in American and Philippine newspapers and periodicals about the ceremony, but by that time a more significant torrent of criticism had built up against the defense system itself. Typical of one wave of criticism emanating from the liberal press in America was Harold E. Fey's article in *The Nation* early that summer. He expressed shock at the conscription system and the size of the defense force MacArthur intended to build: "The policy which General MacArthur has recommended negates the work of thirty-five years during which America has been attempting to teach democratic ideals and techniques to this Asiatic nation." Fey charged that MacArthur was making an "unauthorized move to militarize the Filipino people. It is high time for this

nation to reassert in unmistakable terms that the responsibility
for policy-making on matters of vital national concern belongs,
under our Constitution, to the civilian arm of the government.
The recall of General MacArthur would serve that purpose."
David H. Popper, of the Foreign Policy Association, claimed
that MacArthur was a member of "a covert conspiracy to keep
the United States in the islands" on the pretext that the archipelago was "a strategic asset." [33] MacArthur was probably more
concerned about opposition to his program expressed by Filipino political and journalistic leaders, but in his April report
he tried to discount the seriousness of the dissent in the islands:

To any comprehensive project of this kind some isolated
domestic opposition will always be encountered. In the present
instance individual opponents fall into several classifications.
Some antagonists of the whole movement toward independence
apparently see in the growth of an effective army a blow to
their hopes of maintaining the status quo. These people labor
under a grave misapprehension, for it must be obvious to any
disinterested observer that even should there come about some
change in the political situation, the Philippine Islands could
not hereafter escape the responsibility for providing for their
own local defense. This responsibility is rightfully theirs and
it cannot be discharged except through the development of an
army that will transform the Philippines into a citadel of defensive strength.

Certain enemies of the National Defense Act are secretly, if
not openly, subversive, or at least motivated by a selfish hope
of personal gain through an attempt to make a political issue
out of any effort to produce adequate security. Another group
contends that the Philippine Nation cannot afford to build up
a defense establishment, even while admitting that the approved system is the most economical that could be devised.
The answer to this contention is that self-defense is the first
law of nations, as well as of individuals, and to say that the new
nation cannot defend itself is simply to say that the Philippines
cannot become an independent nation.

Still other opponents of the defense system are simply ig-

norant of the facts and of the lessons of history, while some few
are undoubtedly inspired by idealistic, though impractical motives. This latter class, rightly decrying all war and its deplorable consequences of costs in blood and treasure, foolishly close
their eyes to the degradation and suffering of slavery. Carried
away by fatuous self-deception they hold to the erroneous
belief that weakness is conducive to peace. Happily, however,
only a few individuals are completely blind to the hard fact
that defenselessness always invites, encourages, and practically
assures aggression.

Though the kind of opposition noted has been encountered
from the very beginning of this undertaking, it has not only
been sporadic in nature but most ineffective in result. The
various distortions resorted to by these several classes of individuals have obviously been recognized as invalid by the people at large, as is evidenced by the enthusiastic manner in which
Filipinos of all walks of life have responded to every call the
government has made upon them in carrying into effect the
provisions of the Philippine Defense Plan.[34]

Local voices of dissent continued to mount that summer,
however, and MacArthur became more defensive in his
speeches. When he addressed the Command and General Staff
School at Baguio in August, he told the assembly that the
"scoffers" were largely persons "who know little or nothing of
the facts, but who arrogate to themselves the dogmatic wisdom
of popular slogan and glib generality." He reminded the audience of officers that "there were a multitude of skeptics who
maintained that Fulton's steamboat would not float . . . and
that Marconi was a visionary at best, and possibly a lunatic at
worst." Then, as if he was going to explain subsequently, he
remarked, "Defeatists ask how, within the ten years' military
budget of $80 million, can a sufficient force be equipped includ-
ing an air component and an offshore patrol of torpedo boats."
But, instead of answering, he went on to state axiomatically
that "when the Philippine Defense Plan reaches fruition the
people of these Islands will be in a favorable posture of defen-

sive security." As usual, his rhetoric was impressive and convincing to many, but some persons were still beset by gnawing questions. They included his own right- and left-arm assistants, Eisenhower and Ord. Both were loyal to MacArthur and were working hard to implement his plan, but in private they speculated anxiously on certain questions: Would the Philippine National Assembly be influenced by the growing disaffection and in coming years vote to curtail the defense program? Would the projected expenditures be sufficient to provide the defense system MacArthur envisioned? What would happen if Quezon and MacArthur, both volatile personalities, disagreed on defense policy? Would there be time to build an adequate defense force before the Philippines became involved in a war? "General MacArthur's amazing determination and optimism," said Eisenhower, "made us forget these questions at times, but they kept coming back in our minds." [35]

CHAPTER XVIII

Unexpected Problems

1. An Eventful Year: 1937

THE TRAINING PROGRAM for Filipino conscripts finally got underway in early January, 1937, after a year of intensive preparations by MacArthur and his staff and the newly established
Philippine Army. Satisfied that the first group of 20,000 trainees was in camp and basic training was proceeding properly,
Quezon accepted an invitation from Paul V. McNutt, the former governor of Indiana who had recently been chosen to succeed Murphy, to attend the ceremony in Washington wherein
McNutt would be sworn in as the new high commissioner. In
his letter McNutt had added that Roosevelt wanted to talk to
Quezon. Mapping plans to visit Japan, Mexico, and Europe,
the Philippine president decided to not only confer with officials
in Washington but also investigate other nations' defense establishments, while promoting goodwill for his emerging
nation. The large party which he chose to accompany him included his family, members of the National Assembly, influential commercial leaders of Manila, military officers, and "a number of clerical and personal attendants." MacArthur, Hutter,
and Davis were included, as well as Fellers, the liaison officer

between Quezon's office and the expanding military adviser's establishment. Before the trip would end, both Quezon and MacArthur would furnish reporters with some surprising news stories.

Departing from Manila on January 25 with his entourage aboard an ocean liner, Quezon created complications and embarrassments for American officials nearly everywhere he stopped since he blithely accepted the honors of a head of state, which foreign governments accorded him. At Canton local officials flew the Chinese and Philippine flags, but not the American, during ceremonies honoring him. In Japan he and MacArthur enjoyed an audience with Emperor Hirohito, and the Japanese Navy saluted the Philippine president with twenty-one guns. Joseph C. Grew, the American ambassador in Tokyo, gave a dinner for Quezon and his party. MacArthur told Grew that Quezon "is one of the five great statesmen of the world," which may have seemed plausible if judged by the decorations and ceremonial honors heaped upon Quezon in Japan and other nations on his tour.

Only in Washington was there a distinct want of enthusiasm toward the invading Filipinos; in fact, MacArthur claimed that "Quezon was practically ignored in the United States." The cold reception stemmed, in part, from Quezon's statement to reporters when he arrived in Los Angeles in mid-February that he wanted Philippine independence by the end of 1938. For some reason Quezon and his party went to New York City before descending on Washington. New York officials feted Quezon with parades, banquets, and laudatory speeches, but no invitation from the White House came. After waiting a few days, MacArthur journeyed to Washington to find out why. Roosevelt's secretary said that the President was too busy to see him, then relented and said he could have five minutes. After nearly two hours of heated discussion with Roosevelt, MacArthur finally persuaded him to see Quezon. When the fiery

Filipino came to the White House, he demanded, as expected, that Roosevelt urge Congress to amend the Tydings-McDuffie Act to provide freedom for the islands by December 31, 1938. Roosevelt refused and also rejected Quezon's alternate date of July 4, 1939. On Capitol Hill, however, the Philippine president was more successful in his talks with congressmen. That spring Congress created the Joint Preparatory Committee on Philippine Affairs, whose findings would ultimately result in an amendment to the 1934 act to make the Philippines' economic adjustment to independence easier. But the committee did not recommend freeing the islands before 1946. While Quezon was busy with his entreaties in State Department and congressional offices, MacArthur was making the rounds of the War and Navy departments endeavoring to obtain equipment for his Philippine forces through loans or cheap sales. In the Navy Department he at least got an assurance that the type of torpedo boat he had in mind would be developed, but, said MacArthur, "my request for supplies and equipment went unheeded by the War Department." [1]

After the disappointing reception in Washington, Quezon and his group moved on to Mexico City in April. The main party was housed at Chapultepec Castle, but MacArthur complained of "inadequate accommodations" and, with Davis, his aide, moved to the Hotel Reforma. An American Army intelligence officer in the Mexican capital reported that "General MacArthur, in spite of his efforts to remain in the background, was of considerably more interest to the Mexicans than was President Quezon." The Philippine president's problem of being upstaged was soon solved, however, for MacArthur and Davis shortly returned to the United States. Quezon and the rest of his mission continued on to Europe; it would be August before the Philippine president got back to Manila.

MacArthur had two compelling personal reasons for not accompanying Quezon to Europe. The remains of his mother had arrived for reinterment in Arlington National Cemetery. There in a simple service attended only by MacArthur, Woodring, and a few friends she was buried beside her husband. Pershing sent a floral tribute, and, in thanking him, MacArthur remarked that "nothing could have pleased my Mother more." The other reason for leaving Quezon's mission caught nearly everyone by surprise: on the morning of April 30 MacArthur was married to Jean Faircloth. The civil ceremony was performed by a deputy city clerk in the New York Municipal Building, with Davis and Hutter as witnesses. Miss Faircloth had quietly left Manila by airplane after the *Lurline* had sailed; at Honolulu she had joined the Quezon party aboard ship for the rest of the ocean voyage. While MacArthur had been busy in Washington and Mexico City, she had journeyed to Murfreesboro to make her final preparations for permanently moving to Manila as his wife. As Quezon continued his European tour, MacArthur and his bride returned to Manila. He felt it was imperative for him to be on hand for the final phase of the first training period and the second enrollment of 20,000 trainees, scheduled for July 1. Unlike his bride fifteen years earlier, the second Mrs. MacArthur knew her husband well enough not to expect an extended honeymoon until his soldiering days were done.[2]

Upon his return to the Philippines, MacArthur gained an initial impression that the first training period had "gone exceedingly well." He commented to a journalist, "In every respect the first series of training camps has demonstrated the soundness of the plan . . . The capacity of the Filipino officer and soldier, whether Regular, Reserve or trainee, to overcome difficulties, to absorb fundamentals of the military profession and to sustain a high morale and esprit while doing so, encourages a confidence in the successful outcome to the country's effort to prepare a respectable national defense." But Eisenhower and Ord soon acquainted him with some difficulties besetting the training program. Many of the trainees were not only illiterate but also ignorant of rudimentary sanitation precautions, so military training had to be cut back in order to provide basic language and public health instruction. Moreover, communications on the drill field and elsewhere in the training program had been extremely difficult since a company of trainees might speak a half dozen native dialects, each being unintelligible to the other. Alarming, too, was the fact that there were few officers available who had previous military experience, most coming from the Constabulary, which had been amalgamated with the Philippine Army. In addition, the funds appropriated by the National Assembly for calendar 1937 were exhausted by July, necessitating borrowing against the next year's funds in order to finance the program for the rest of the current year. Equipment of nearly every type — from tents and shoes to rifles and howitzers — was seriously lacking. Three weeks after the second training period began in July, Eisenhower found that "with regard to the cadres the early inspections have been disappointing. In Southern Luzon conditions were found . . . to be very unsatisfactory." He continued, "The constant rains are, of course, partially responsible for this but many other defects were traceable to neglect on the part of cadre officers and in some instances to distinct failures on the part of our Army Headquarters."

Friction had also developed between the military adviser's office and the Philippine Department, which was commanded by Major General Lucius R. Holbrook. A large number of Scout officers had been transferred to the Philippine Army to meet its drastic officer needs, but the War Department was unable to replace them in Holbrook's command. Acting under the authority given him by the congressional act of May, 1935, and his orders of September, 1935, from the War Department, MacArthur had begun in late 1936 to obtain officers and enlisted men from the Philippine Department for his own staff as he was legally empowered to do when he felt the need justified such transfers. By mid-1937 the military adviser's staff comprised over thirty officers and fifteen enlisted men, largely gained at Holbrook's expense. Finally Holbrook was able to get the War Department to require MacArthur to obtain its approval before such shifts of personnel. But the General Staff's G-1 informed Holbrook that the powers which Congress and the War Department had bestowed upon the military adviser in 1935 were "broad in the extreme" and difficult to alter short of voiding. In his instructions of September 18, 1935, from the Secretary of War, for instance, MacArthur had been told: "In all cases not specifically covered you will use your own judgment and are empowered to call upon the Department Commander for whatever assistance you may require. Your mission must be accomplished — ways and means are largely left to you." That same day Dern had notified the commander of the Philippine Department of MacArthur's instructions and emphasized: "It is of gravest importance to the United States that there be no failure [of MacArthur's mission], and successful accomplishment as far as your powers are concerned is hereby made the most important peacetime mission of your command." So far Holbrook had been patient and helpful in not only tolerating the attritions but also using his own men to train specialists for the Philippine Army, including Filipino officers as part of his quota to attend American service schools, and making his munitions stores available for training of the native forces. But should MacArthur decide that his staff was still overburdened and needed more of Holbrook's personnel, the annoyance already felt by the American Army commander might turn to hostility. As it was, it did not seem to MacArthur and his assistants that the Philippine Department then or ever considered the development of the Philippine Army as its "most important peacetime mission." [3]

While MacArthur pondered the problems of his training

camps, fighting suddenly broke out on July 7 between Japanese and Chinese troops near Peiping. The action spread quickly, and by August the Japanese were battering the gates of Shanghai. The Filipinos were shocked by this latest eruption of Sino-Japanese violence, which in four years would be a paramount factor in America's entry into war. The horrors of the new conflict were related in Manila by several thousand Americans, Europeans, and Filipinos who fled by ship from Shanghai in August. Many of these refugees were destitute when they arrived in the Philippines; the Red Cross, Philippine Army, and American military and naval commands worked strenuously to provide clothing, shelter, and food for them. The presence of these persons and the atrocities they described brought a sense of despair and gloom to Filipinos who had hoped for closer ties between the Philippines and Japan.

More than ever, Japanese activities in the archipelago were closely scrutinized by uneasy intelligence officers of the American and Philippine military commands. In late August the Davao provincial commander reported to Philippine Army headquarters that at a secret meeting of the Davao Japanese Association the members voted unanimously to assess the large Japanese community of Davao the following amounts as "contributions for the Imperial Japanese Army in its war against China": abaca planters to contribute 1½ per cent of profits "per hill of abaca" and six to fifteen pesos per stripping machine, depending on horsepower; coconut planters to give 1½ per cent of profits per coconut tree; merchants to contribute 1½ per cent "of their invested capitals"; and other Japanese citizens of Davao to give "any amount they can afford." Quezon and most government officials still were not excited about the potential menace of the Japanese at Davao, but the Philippine Army's war plans division was convinced that, with about 18,000 Japanese now in Davao province, the Japanese government had in mind "a quiet, silent and apparently peaceful penetration at first, but a well-planned, slowly creeping but absolutely certain territorial invasion."

Even before the new Sino-Japanese war exploded, Ord, whose main responsibility was handling the military budget, had prepared an estimate of Philippine Army expenditures for 1938 which was well above the earlier projection of $8,000,000. When MacArthur returned from his trip, he sent Ord to Washington to try again to persuade the War Department to lend or sell munitions to the Commonwealth. The final budget preparation then devolved upon Eisenhower, who finally arrived at the figure of $12,500,000 for the 1938 asking. In view of the commitment in 1935 to $8,000,000 a year for ten years, MacArthur did not relish the idea of proposing the new figure to Quezon. But military spending for 1937 had already exhausted the appropriated funds. Besides, Quezon, who still nourished the idea of independence before 1946, was now talking in terms of completing the ten-year defense program by 1941.[4] On September 1 Eisenhower wrote Ord:

It was quite a shock to hear, the other day, that the President [Quezon] is dismayed and astonished by the size of our Budget. He was recorded as being nonplussed in view of the definite promises made almost two years ago, and I gather that only the intervention of more immediate affairs has kept us from hearing about it in a big way. Naturally we will make such defense as we can on the basis of increased cost due to rising prices, emergency building, and stepping up of the whole development schedule. But we cannot dodge this fact: Our estimated expenditures for next year are ₱25,000,000 . . . The cold truth is that this sum represents more nearly than does ₱16,000,000 the necessary annual expenditures of the next 5 years, if we are to maintain the plan on its present basis. After 1938 we will, of course, cut down drastically on our construction item. It will be a long time, however, before this will come down to an inconsequential amount, due to our needs for adequate warehouses, mobilization centers and general improvements. At the same time the items for Off-Shore Patrol, Air Corps, armament, and ammunition must go up materially. Possibly you and I, two years ago, did not hold out as insistently as we should have for the ₱22,000,000 figure. In our own defense, however, we can remember that our studies and conclusions were academic ones and we had no means of demonstrating their accuracy.[5]

With war raging in China and Europe a tinderbox, Mac-Arthur was able to build a convincing argument for the increased budget. He told Quezon that the enlarged asking "was due to certain fundamental changes which have taken place during the last six months. These changes are, first, the possibility of early independence for the Philippine Islands; and, second, the greatly increased risk, due to the continuous decline of national security throughout the world, of prematurely drawing the Philippine Islands into war." A consequence, he pointed out, "of the feverish preparation of all nations for war, and the correspondingly increasing demand for war supplies and equipment, has been a very rapid rise in the unit cost of such commodities." Armed with MacArthur's arguments, Quezon went before the National Assembly and obtained the increase for 1938. He also informed the legislators boldly that the completed defense system would probably cost $130,000,000, not $80,000,000 as first planned, and would be accelerated to a five-year program. Quezon assured the National Assembly that "regardless of the aggregate authorized for the full development of our National Defense, the annual appropriations will be adjusted each year to the annual revenue, so that all other authorized government services and activities may develop in harmony with the growth of the population and the expansion of our culture." Since this statement by Quezon was from the draft prepared by Eisenhower, it must have seemed harmless to MacArthur and his staff. Perhaps it did not seem possible to them that within two years Quezon might be faced with the dilemma of "full development" of the defense system or maintenance of "all other authorized government services," but not both.[6]

Criticism of MacArthur's defense program did not abate in 1937. Indeed, disaffection among Filipinos seemed to increase when word circulated that the military schedule was to be accelerated. "Every statement they have issued shows a deplorable lack of fact," MacArthur said of his critics, "and evidences a spirit of bitter vindictiveness. Never yet have they attempted to answer the one basic question which underlies the whole problem. If the Filipinos in an emergency are not prepared to defend their country, who will defend it for them?" A persisting thorn in the side of the military adviser was General José Alejandrino, a former member of the Philippine National Defense Council who periodically wrote letters to newspaper editors belittling the equipment and efficiency of the Philippine Army. In one letter, for example, he charged that the Philippine Army's rifles (Enfields) were obsolete, its ration was inferior to American soliders', and its reserve officers were woefully untrained. In a public statement MacArthur angrily countered that Alejandrino's letter "is so full of misstatements, misrepresentations, unfounded inferences and bitter vindictive that it savours of what the Army calls 'a guardhouse lawyer.' " He then proceeded to rebut the Filipino's charges one by one with persuasive logic, though with less factual evidence than Alejandrino presented. There were, of course, many faults which could be found with the fledgling defense force.[7] Quezon summed up the most prevalent criticism in American and Philippine newspapers and periodicals in 1937 as follows:

> In good or bad faith, through ignorance or malice, allegations are being made that we are "militarizing the Philippines," that we are "sabotaging Filipino schools," that our national defense program "amounts to a covert conspiracy to keep the United States in the Islands" or is "intended to strengthen the military power of America in the Western Pacific in the event of war with Japan." On the other hand, it is also alleged that

neither the Philippines nor the United States, nor both countries combined, can ever successfully defend this country, and
we are told that we should rely upon the neutralization of the
Philippines guaranteed by international agreement for the defense of our independence.[8]

Of course, there were those who appreciated MacArthur's
plan and his efforts, the most important being Quezon and his
top Nacionalista politicians and Major General Paulino Santos,
who was chief of staff of the Philippine Army. Some Americans
saw in the building of a native army certain nonmilitary benefits to the Philippine nation. Brigadier General Creed F. Cox,
who headed the Bureau of Insular Affairs, wrote MacArthur: "I
am very sure the military system which is being built up under
your guidance will prove to be the greatest of all forces in developing a national solidarity and consciousness among the Filipino people. The value of these factors is immeasurable, aside
from the many other benefits that accrue to a nation from a wise
system of military training." [9] Frederic C. Howe, an old friend
of the Roosevelts who had recently come to the islands as special
adviser to Quezon on rural problems, wrote Secretary of Agriculture Henry A. Wallace in August, 1937:

> Before leaving Washington I had read some things in the
> New York Nation and heard some things from my pacifist
> friends to the effect that an army was in the making here of
> 200,000 men and that the school budget and other revenues
> were being depleted in the interest of a big army. Also other
> things of like nature that disturbed me. Now as a matter of
> fact the army consists of 20,000 men in training for six months
> looking in ten years to a militia of 400,000 men and trained
> almost exclusively to defense. But more important the army
> training combines just the sort of land clearance, dietary care,
> training like that of the C C Camps and preparation to do
> just the things that have to be done here and for which there
> is no other provision . . .
>   . . . I have read the programme of military training and find

it more nearly a civil programme than anything I have known. So true is this that it led me to the conviction that here was an agency that was almost a necessity to put some iron into the people and to provide it with men trained to do the things that are necessary to the civil administration of the islands and possibly an agency and the only agency that could carry through the land programme that is the first need of the Commonwealth.

It was this search for some one who could visualize the land programme that led me to General MacArthur and to the high opinion that I have of him.[10]

Liberal and pacifist journalists continued to harp on MacArthur's militaristic influence on the Philippine government and society, but his most serious opposition was still centered in the coterie of New Dealers in Washington. Larry Lehrbas, a correspondent in the national capital, told MacArthur in June, 1937: "I have it on good authority that there's a strong move on to have you recalled from Manila . . . The War Department is blocking it largely, I understand, on Gen. Craig's insistence that it would be a big mistake to pull you out of the Philippines." He added: "The dope, as I get it, is that someone doesn't agree with your defense policies and considers that your work there might antagonize the Japanese." The reporter's information must have been fairly authentic, for in early August Craig notified MacArthur that "upon completion by you of two years of absence on foreign service you are to be brought home for duty in the United States . . . There will be made available to you if practicable any command for which you may express a preference." Craig's letter was politely worded, and MacArthur's response was equally so: "I am naturally sorry to go. Particularly do I regret leaving unfinished a work which I regard as of transcendent importance . . . I look forward with anticipation to whatever duty the War Department may have decided I should now undertake in the service of my country." Quezon sent a cable to Roosevelt stating that he was "deeply disturbed" by this decision and pleaded for MacArthur's retention as his military adviser. After mulling over the alternatives, MacArthur applied for retirement on September 16, explaining to Craig that he did so because he was in poor health, felt that his work as military adviser was nearly completed, wished to make way for others to move up the promotion ladder, was anxious to retire and pursue cultural interests, and found repugnant the thought of taking a corps area command or lesser position. Some of these reasons were artificially contrived, as was obvious to Craig, who knew MacArthur well and understood that his real reason was the last-mentioned. As MacArthur admitted to him, "It would be as though Secretary Woodring were suddenly assigned to be a Bureau Chief of the War Department or as though President Roosevelt were required to go back to his former functions as Assistant Secretary of the Navy. It would not only be unsatisfactory to me but the reaction would be such as to make me an unsatisfactory subordinate commander." His application was approved, and on October 11 the War Department announced that he would retire on December 31 with the rank of general. That same day Roosevelt wrote him that he had approved his retirement "with great reluctance and deep regret" and thanked him for his "outstanding services" to the nation.[11]

MacArthur probably sensed what friends in Washington soon confirmed, that Craig was not responsible for the forcing of his retirement. In fact, Craig and Woodring were the only ones in the War Department who knew about the move until that autumn. On October 13 Brigadier General Charles Burnett, the new chief of the Bureau of Insular Affairs and a longtime friend of MacArthur, wrote him: "As Ord probably told you, I am aware of the identity of the moving spirit in this matter — I have never known a dirtier piece of politics, nor have I ever known an officer who has suffered a rawer deal than this. Should the real facts become known, there would be some unpleasant moments for certain politicians in high places."

O'Laughlin assured MacArthur that Craig "knew nothing about the orders until directed to issue them. He did not favor this action and so stated . . . This did not increase his popularity." Hurley remarked, "I am at a loss to know what caused Douglas to resign. If I knew all the facts I might change my mind but from this distance that resignation looks like a mistake." Moseley felt that, from the viewpoint of national defense, the Washington politicians had blundered and warned that "we are facing some very difficult situations, and outstanding leaders are very, very rare."

No known evidence exists which names the culprit behind the move to oust MacArthur, so speculation on the matter will go on interminably. Perhaps the most obvious nominee would be Ickes, who was interested, for unknown reasons, in getting jurisdiction over Philippine affairs. In 1939 he would succeed in obtaining the transfer of Philippine administration from the War Department to his Department of the Interior. The contempt he held for MacArthur would have probably impelled him to try to get the general out of Manila before he began interfering in the affairs of the islands. Murphy also may have been involved in the effort to recall MacArthur since the two had viewed each other antagonistically from the start, and their animosity had increased just prior to Murphy's departure from the Philippines. According to one source, Murphy had "intimated to Roosevelt that the Islands were not big enough for both MacArthur and himself. He insisted that MacArthur . . . should be directly under his own office." On the other hand, Roosevelt himself made the final decision and may have done so without undue persuasion from any of his advisers, though his motivation could be only remotely guessed.[12]

By the autumn of 1937 there was already some talk of entering MacArthur's name in the contest for the Republican presidential nomination in 1940. Ormsby McHarg, once Theodore Roosevelt's campaign manager and now head of the Citizens

National Committee, an organization of anti-Communist crusaders, told O'Laughlin: "There are people in influential positions who, like myself, have been deeply concerned over the national situation of the Republican Party . . . The General [MacArthur] would make a great candidate for the Presidency." P. W. Reeves, who had worked in the high commissioner's office in Manila, wrote MacArthur while the former was in the United States in November, 1937, that "your name was frequently mentioned in the West" for the Republican nomination. MacArthur politely rejected all political overtures, however, and also turned down several lucrative offers that fall to write his memoirs or make speaking tours in the States.[13]

By early November, MacArthur had made up his mind that he wanted to remain as Philippine military adviser after his retirement from the United States Army at the end of 1937. On the 21st of that month the National Assembly passed a resolution thanking him "for his invaluable services in organizing the Philippine Army and the national defense." But the legislators deleted a section of the resolution as originally presented by Quezon, viz.: "That the President of the Commonwealth be, and he hereby is, requested, authorized and empowered to continue the engagement of the services of General Douglas MacArthur as Military Adviser of the National Government, with the rank of Field Marshal, and to direct that his name be carried in the rolls of the Philippine Army until his death." It was reported that some members of the legislature opposed not only the relatively expensive defense program, by then constituting nearly a fourth of the Commonwealth's budget, but also the large salaried income which the military adviser enjoyed, now totalling $36,000 a year from the Philippine and American governments. MacArthur took the action in stride and issued a public statement which said, in part: "I can conceive of no greater distinction than to receive from this famous body its thanks. One of the most inspiring features of my efforts in behalf of the Philippine national defense has

been the patriotic and spontaneous support of the Assembly."
On December 31, the day of MacArthur's retirement, Quezon,
defying the wishes of some of his legislators, issued an executive
proclamation announcing that MacArthur would continue as
Philippine military adviser. As long as Quezon was in power
and supported him, MacArthur's position was secure from all
assailants.[14]

But MacArthur would now be more handicapped than ever
in completing his defense plan, as Woodring explained to
Roosevelt:

> . . . On December 31, 1937, General MacArthur ceased
> officially to represent the United States as Military Adviser to
> the Government of the Philippine Islands and accepted employ-
> ment in a private status with that Government . . .
> It is the desire of the War Department to further to the ut-
> most the establishment of an adequate native national defense
> for the Commonwealth of the Philippine Islands, and to disturb
> as little as possible the existing relations between the War
> Department and that Government. General MacArthur in his
> status as a retired officer may not exercise command, and is no
> longer a military representative of the United States with the
> Commonwealth of the Philippine Islands . . . In the future,
> since the letter of instructions to General MacArthur has lapsed
> with his retirement, requests from the Philippine Government
> for additional personnel, material, or services will be trans-
> mitted to the Commanding General, Philippine Department,
> for submission to the War Department.[15]

It had been a trying six months for MacArthur, but in the
months ahead his troubles would be compounded.

2. *Fond Dreams and Unpleasant Realities*

In early January, 1938, MacArthur conceived the idea, according to Eisenhower, that "the morale of the whole population would be enhanced if the people could see something of

their emerging army in the capital city, Manila." The military adviser put his assistants to work on his plan to bring units from the ten military districts to a camp site on the outskirts of Manila where they would stage a military show for the public, climaxed by a grand parade through the downtown area. "We told the General," said Eisenhower, "that it was impossible to do the thing within our budget." But MacArthur insisted that the planning continue. Eisenhower, who thought MacArthur had discussed the project with Quezon, was surprised one day when Quezon asked him about the preparations to move far-off cadres to Manila. "The President was horrified to think that we were ready for a costly national parade in the capital," Eisenhower stated. Quezon called MacArthur and told him to cancel the plan immediately, whereupon the military adviser, "exceedingly unhappy" and "visibly upset," chastised Eisenhower and Ord for actually setting the plan in motion. Eisenhower claimed that "General MacArthur denied that he had given us an order — which was certainly news to us." Tempers exploded in the military adviser's office, and, commented Eisenhower, "this misunderstanding caused considerable resentment — and never again were we on the same warm and cordial terms." In May, 1939, however, MacArthur was able to get Quezon's approval for a more realistic exercise, whereby 25,000 reservists trained in 1937 were suddenly given mobilization orders for a mock emergency. Though carried out only at a company level, the mobilization demonstrated the need for better organization. Once assembled, the reservists were found to be of short memory, having forgotten much of what they learned two years earlier; they were given "refresher training" before being sent back to their homes. The exercise proved to be not only more economical but also more practical in mobilization planning than the canceled project.[16]

Meanwhile, as Japanese armies seized one Chinese town after another, the reaction of the Filipino people generally and of many Commonwealth political leaders was to wallow in disillusionment and defeatism as to their own nation's defense plan. The disappointing development of the Philippine Army in 1938–40 was both a cause and an effect of this gloomy outlook, which became even darker after the European conflict began in 1939. The National Assembly continued to provide about $8,000,000 a year for military activities, but the defense establishment's share of the Commonwealth budget declined from nearly 25 per cent to 14 per cent, and the plan for accelerating the Army's growth was permanently shelved. The number of registrants under the conscription system fell steadily from 155,100 in 1936 to 90,700 in 1940. Philippine Army headquarters blamed the decreasing enrollments on "indifference on the part of local officials in many provinces," the worst records being in the Manila area and the mountain provinces of North Luzon. Likewise, the number of trainees who completed the active-duty program of five and a half months showed a discouraging trend: 36,600 in 1937, 33,200 in 1938, 29,500 in 1939, and 35,900 in 1940 — not one year's record reaching the anticipated figure of 40,000. Many registrants tore up their summons to active duty and disappeared into the jungles and mountains. By 1940 the regulars of the Philippine Army comprised only 468 officers and 3697 enlisted men. The 1st Infantry Division, intended to be the nucleus of the defense system, consisted of one regiment of less than 300 men. The rest of the regulars were scattered at various training camps, their time consumed in working with trainees of the reserve program. On paper the reserve force by 1940 consisted of about 6000 officers and 120,000–135,000 enlisted men, nominally organized into ten infantry divisions, one in each military district. But lack of equipment and deficiencies in training made realistic military leaders wonder about the readiness of the reserves to face an emergency.[17]

The training schedule had to be adjusted to the realities of geographical handicaps and munitions shortages. The schedule called for the trainees to undergo fourteen weeks of basic training, three weeks of advanced training, two weeks of rifle-range practice, two weeks of specialist training, and a week of field exercises at the end. The citizen soldiers saw few weapons during their first three and a half months in camp; for the first three years of the program, the only live ammunition fired during basic training was with 22-cal. rifles, 100 rounds per man. At the later stages of training each conscript got to fire fifty rounds with a 30-cal. Enfield rifle and 500 rounds with a 45-cal. pistol. In each company of trainees twenty-one men were chosen for training with the Browning automatic rifle, but each man got to fire it for only seventy-five rounds. Apparently much of the two weeks of rifle-range training was spent in maintenance and cleaning instructions or firing blank cartridges. Trainees in machine-gun outfits got to fire 175 30-cal. rounds per man; there was no infantry practice with 50-cal. machine guns, which were scarce even as late as December, 1940. The aggregate allowances for firing practice by field artillery units during the entire year of 1940 were 3800 37-mm. shells, 1100 75-mm. projectiles, and 875 2.95-inch howitzer shells. Field maneuvers above the company level were impracticable for reservists since the 120 camps, each with 100 to 200 trainees, were scattered through a score of islands. Besides, even when camps were on the same island, the roads were universally poor, the terrain was rugged in most locations, and the Army had only about 150 vehicles of all types and conditions, mostly antiquated.

MacArthur and the Philippine Army leaders were harassed by disciplinary problems which would have defeated less determined officers. A historian of the Commonwealth noted some of the irregularities which made headlines in Manila newspapers: "trainee strikes and demonstrations against officers; occasional terrorism by detachments in provincial areas;

individuals running amok in uniform; and botched maneuvers." As for the quality of training in the far-flung camps, Lieutenant Colonel F. G. Oboza, the Philippine adjutant general, reported frankly in June, 1940: "The individual trainee has not learned his basic duties as a soldier to a degree that upon mobilization two years later he would still know them. Officers have not acquired the mechanics of thinking and giving orders the way a commander of troops should . . . The training method prescribed has not been followed." A few months earlier a Philippine Army board which was created to evaluate the defense program seriously considered a proposal which called for drastically reducing the reserve training and using the funds instead to develop two combat-ready divisions of 6000 regulars each. The plan was dropped because of MacArthur's strenuous objections. The military adviser staunchly defended his position favoring a small professional force and a large reservoir of partially trained reserves. His argument was abetted by Finland's stubborn defense against the Soviet armies during the winter war of 1939–40. "The efficacy of the Finnish army, now being demonstrated on the battlefield, is a concrete example of this type of army, the Finnish regular army being practically negligible in strength," he pointed out to Quezon. The Philippine president did not support the plan for a larger regular force, but he may well have doubted the aptness of MacArthur's comparison.[18]

Contributing to training inefficiency and lack of discipline was a want of morale among the Philippine Army regulars, which, in turn, was related to the perennial problems of ration deficiencies and pay inequities. A study made by University of the Philippines dietary specialists in 1939 showed that the ration of the Philippine Army was "seriously deficient in animal protein, calcium content, and vitamins." In caloric content, however, it was not much less than the ration which American troops received. Pay discrepancies between Philip-

pine and American forces were wide. The monthly base pay
of a private in the United States Army was $30.00, whereas a
Philippine Army private got merely $7.00. An American mas-
ter sergeant received $126.00 in base salary each month, while
his Philippine Army counterpart was paid $22.50. At the level
of major general, the American earned $666.67, but the Fili-
pino got $325.00 a month. The Philippine Army's chief of staff
received a base salary of $354.00 per month, about the same as
an American officer in his first year of rank as a colonel. The
allowances for United States Army officers were far more
liberal, too. The low pay to Filipinos was justified, as might
be expected, on grounds of their lower cost of living and lower
earning power as civilians. Salaries in the military adviser's
office were appreciably higher than those of the Philippine Department. MacArthur, as already mentioned, received $3,000.00
a month; Eisenhower, after his promotion to lieutenant colonel in 1936, got $980.00, excluding allowances. Most other offi-
cers on MacArthur's staff earned $225.00 to $450.00 a month
in addition to their regular salaries in the United States Army.

Another persisting problem of the Philippine Army was
the low educational level of the vast majority of its reservists
and regulars. Among the trainees in the first half of 1940, for
instance, one out of five was illiterate. Out of a total of 15,537
trainees in that period, only 2829 had attained the first-year
level of high school, and but 162 had finished a year or more
of college. Much precious time therefore was still consumed
in literacy courses and primary education. The educational
level of the regulars was not much higher than that of the
Filipino reservists.

The minority of trainees and regular enlisted men with
some college experience were encouraged to apply at one of the
three reserve officers schools where they could become third
lieutenants after twenty-six weeks of concentrated work. These
schools, together with the compulsory R.O.T.C. programs in

the state-supported colleges, turned out 927 commissioned officers in 1940, while that spring the Philippine Military Academy graduated its first class, consisting of seventy-nine men. But all of these officer-training programs had been slow in getting underway, and even the output of 1940 was far from enough to satisfy the officer needs of the Philippine Army. Some Scout officers were attracted to the native defense force by the offering to them of "assimilated" ranks two or three levels above their regular ranks in the American service; this was necessary to make their salaries comparable to what they had been earning previously. But there were fewer transfers from the Scouts after 1937 since MacArthur forfeited his authority to initiate such changes when he retired.[19]

More discouraging even than the growth of the ground forces was that of the Philippine Air Corps. The first squadron, consisting of twenty-one attack and observation aircraft, was not organized until early 1939. By the end of 1940 the air arm had grown to only forty planes, 100 pilots, and about 300 ground personnel. It had five air fields, all in comparatively primitive condition; tactical training of Filipino pilots was still conducted at the American base at Clark Field. A few Filipino air officers were sent to aviation schools in America, but there they were treated as visiting foreign officers and were not allowed access to the most modern equipment, for example, the Nordin bomb sight. Because the cost of military aircraft had risen beyond the expectations or means of the Commonwealth for purchasing adequate numbers, the Philippine Bureau of Aeronautics began research toward developing a suitable training-observation plane made of kalantas and manggachapui, which were woods native to the islands. For some reason, possibly lack of funds or difficulty in getting the craft airborne, the project was dropped. Eisenhower became so interested in the flight training program that he learned to fly, gaining his license at the age of forty-nine; he was particular, however, in making sure that his instructors were American pilots and not Filipinos. Casualties in the young Philippine Air Corps were surprisingly few despite dire predictions by some veteran American flyers who witnessed the sometimes wild performances of the Filipinos. But the program cost MacArthur one of his most valuable assistants: Ord was killed in a crash in late January, 1938, while flying to Baguio in a plane piloted by one of the Filipino airmen. "From then on, more of the planning fell on my shoulders," Eisenhower lamented, "but without my friend, all the zest was gone." [20]

Besides developing a 250-plane air force by 1946, MacArthur's plan, it will be remembered, called for a fleet of fifty torpedo boats. The man MacArthur selected to head the development of the so-called "Offshore Patrol" was Lieutenant Sidney L. Huff. They had first met in the dining room of the Manila Hotel in late 1935 while Huff, a friend of Eisenhower, was on shore leave from his ship, a destroyer tender of the Asiatic Fleet. Later while playing golf with "Ike," Huff suffered a heart attack. After his recuperation in San Diego he retired from the United States Navy and accepted an invitation from MacArthur to join the military adviser's staff in late 1936. Huff described their first conference about the torpedo-boat program:

> "Sit down, Sid," he [MacArthur] commanded, motioning to a chair on one side of the big room. He lit a cigarette — this was before his pipe-smoking days — and immediately put it down on his desk and started walking back and forth across the room . . .
> "I want a Filipino navy of motor torpedo boats, Sid," he said abruptly. "If I get you the money, how many can you get built in ten years?"
> The question was about as surprising as a punch in the jaw. All I could answer was: "General, never in my life have I ever seen a torpedo boat."
> "That's all right," he snapped, a little as if I were wasting

precious time. "You will." He stopped at the desk again to line up the pencils. "Sid, I don't know anything about torpedo boats. But I want you to start work on plans for a navy. You're a Navy man and you know what to do." . . .

I went out into the hot light of Manila's December sun and began trying to pull myself together . . . If it had been any other man, I would have asked myself: Is he kidding? But I didn't, because I'd been talking to MacArthur . . . I began to think I could do it, perhaps because it was MacArthur who told me to do it.[21]

Encouraged by the Navy Department's interest in the project when MacArthur visited Washington in early 1937, Huff hoped to make a deal with the United States Navy for the construction of his torpedo boats. "This was dropped," Huff remarked, "when I realized that our Navy would use the money for experimental purposes rather than for producing well-tested boats for the Philippine Navy." Finally Huff obtained from the British Navy two of its new Thornycroft models, the craft arriving in the Philippines in 1939. Each of these so-called "Q-boats" had two torpedo tubes and two 50-cal. machine guns, its crew to consist of two officers and five enlisted men. Their cost was so great, however, that Huff negotiated a contract with a Manila shipbuilding firm for the construction of the next five vessels, but only a pilot model had been built by the time of the Japanese attack in 1941. Huff would later be commissioned as a lieutenant colonel in the United States Army and would serve on MacArthur's staff for a number of years.[22]

Relations between MacArthur's office and the headquarters of the Philippine Department were sensitive but reasonably harmonious during the period 1938–40. Holbrook was succeeded by Major General John H. Hughes as departmental commander in February, 1938. Hughes assisted the military adviser's office and the Philippine Army in a number of ways. By the end of 1938 thirty-four officers and ninety-four enlisted men of Hughes' department had been detailed to serve under

MacArthur, though the number declined markedly the next year. Portions of several United States military reservations were used by the Philippine Army for training purposes. A coastal artillery training center for the Philippine forces was established at Fort Wint, which was located on Grande Island in Subic Bay. The Philippine Army's field artillery training was concentrated on the American military reservation near Fort Stotsenburg in the Central Luzon Plain where American specialists assisted in instructing the Filipinos. As the war fever rose in the Western Pacific in 1939–40 and the Philippine Department clamored for more munitions, it became more difficult for the Philippine Army to borrow weapons for training from the American command, which considered its supply already dangerously low. The only known clash between MacArthur and Hughes was over the latter's effort to curtail aerial photography in the islands which had not been authorized by him. MacArthur told Quezon that Hughes' "responsibility for the defense of the Islands is limited in time of peace to . . . his own troops and reserves and does not imply the power in time of peace of extending his control beyond his own forces to the civil population . . . The authority that he demands . . . is greater than is exercised in the United States by any Corps Area Commander, by the War Department or even by the President himself." MacArthur, whose native air force was about to get its first planes at that time, was probably apprehensive lest Hughes would try to narrowly restrict its flying areas. Quezon finally issued an executive order on aerial navigation and photography in late 1938, which included restrictions on flights over the American installations at Corregidor, Subic Bay, and Cavite, apparently settling the matter.

When Major General George Grunert succeeded Hughes in May, 1940, MacArthur at last had in the Philippine Department's headship an old and trusted friend whom he could fully appreciate personally and professionally. Grunert, in turn, respected MacArthur as "a grand soldier" and, several months before he took the command, wrote the military adviser: "I am still imbued with the old A.E.F. spirit and hope that I may be able to exemplify it as have my associates of old, including you, Craig, Heintzelman, Simonds, Fox Conner and others." MacArthur had hoped for a commander of the Philippine Department who would press more vigorously for the enlargement of that command in personnel and matériel. Able, decisive, and impatient, Grunert was just the man. In the following months he and MacArthur would function like a double-barreled shotgun, bombarding the War Department with the defensive needs of the Philippines. The two men conferred frequently and, because of their deep mutual esteem, made the amalgamation of the American and Philippine military establishments much smoother when that action became necessary in mid-1941.[23]

A paramount reason for the slow progress of the defense program was Quezon's increasing disillusionment with the plan and with his military adviser. The first signs of trouble appeared in the summer of 1938 when Quezon and a small entourage, which did not include MacArthur, made a secret trip to Japan that June. Reporters found out about it, but they were officially told that the Philippine president was on a vacation. While in Japan, however, Quezon conferred at length with high-ranking officials of that government. Soon American newspapers were running stories which alleged that Quezon was trying to obtain a formal pledge from Japan to respect the neutrality of the Philippines when the islands gained independence, which he still anticipated achieving before 1946. Quezon emphatically denied the rumors, but MacArthur and the United States government must have been uneasy about the true nature of the trip. Also that summer the National Assembly, on Quezon's urging, passed an act reorganizing the Constabulary and divorcing it from the Philippine Army, the latter's lack of officers being accentuated thereafter. Early that fall MacArthur tried to get a reduction in the strength of the Constabulary, with the savings to go to the defense program. But Quezon flatly rejected the idea, informing MacArthur that "the creation of the Philippine Army does not justify a material reduction in the Constabulary . . . The Army has been created for purposes entirely different." Quezon was convinced that, since the frightening Sakdal rebellion of peasants in Central Luzon in 1935, problems of law and order in the islands warranted the maintenance of a full-time national police force. Meanwhile Osmeña, the Commonwealth vice president who had previously been shunted into the background in policy making, now began to move more into Quezon's confidence. Osmeña had long argued that "not only would MacArthur's program fail, but that if pursued long enough it might well create conditions of false security" which would bring disaster to the Philippines. Moreover, at the end of 1938 Chief of Staff Santos, a devoted friend of MacArthur, was replaced as head of the Philippine Army by Major General Basilio J. Valdes, who was close to Osmeña and was said to harbor grave doubts about his forces' ability to repulse a Japanese attack even when the defense program was completed.[24]

The estrangement between Quezon and MacArthur worsened in 1939. In March the Philippine president suddenly renewed his demand to the United States that the islands be freed before 1946, his hope now being to gain independence in 1940. The proposal was rejected in Washington, but a few months later Congress did pass a measure which was designed to make the islands' economic adjustment toward independence easier by establishing a fund for certain economic improvements from a special excise tax on coconut oil imports to America from the Philippines. In May the National Assembly, at Quezon's request, established the Department of National Defense, which seemed to be deliberately intended to reduce the authority of MacArthur, who had opposed Quezon's efforts to achieve independence before 1946 and was outspoken against neutralization of the archipelago. In a public statement a few weeks later MacArthur did not mention the legislature's action, but dwelled instead on the deterrent value of his defense plan when completed: "It would cost the enemy, in my opinion, at least a half million of men as casualties and upwards of five billions of dollars in money to pursue such an adventure with any hope of success." He concluded that "no rational reason exists why Japan or any other nation should covet the sovereignty of this country." Teofilo Sison, the new Secretary of Defense, countered that "the defense of the Philippines against external aggression is the full responsibility of America" until the islands were freed.

Without explicit approval from Quezon and Sison thereafter, MacArthur and the Philippine Army headquarters could not order munitions, enroll trainees, or negotiate contracts for construction of new military facilities. In succeeding months the R.O.T.C. program was cut sharply, and military-related instruction in the public schools was eliminated. Defense spending for 1940 was reduced considerably, at least 14 per cent less than for 1939; the budget for 1941 provided even fewer funds for the military establishment. In the early fall of 1939 the Philippine president told the National Assembly that "developments in the European war have convinced me of the futility of spending money to carry on our program of defending the Philippines from foreign aggression, and this objective cannot be attained with the limited resources of the country for many years to come." Casting to the wind his earlier thinking on national defense, Quezon told a large audience assembled at Rizal Stadium in Manila on the anniversary of the Commonwealth's founding: "The Philippines could not be defended even if every last Filipino were armed with modern weapons." When Francis B. Sayre, a former assistant secretary of state, arrived in October as McNutt's successor in the

office of high commissioner, Quezon talked to him about relieving the military adviser. Instead, the president thereafter required MacArthur to deal with him through Jorge Vargas,
the presidential secretary. On one occasion when Vargas told
him Quezon was too busy to talk to him, MacArthur responded,
"Jorge, some day your boss is going to want to see me more
than I want to see him." Quezon's public repudiation of the
defense plan must have been bitter for MacArthur to swallow,
but no statement by him was found which indicated any
resentment or hostility toward the president.[25]

The summer of 1940 was a frightful one for free peoples
everywhere. In June, France fell, leaving Great Britain to stand
alone against the vaunted war machine of Hitler, while Italy
entered the European conflict on the side of Nazi Germany.
In the Asian war an unexpected stalemate had developed in
the fighting in China, and Japan desperately but vainly turned
to the Netherlands East Indies for the raw materials necessary
to keep her war planes and vehicles on the move against the
Chinese. When the Dutch colonial officials courageously rejected the Nipponese overtures, Japan then penetrated the
Southeast Asian mainland, extorting military bases in northern
Indo-China from the Vichy regime. Roosevelt reacted to the
ominous developments by banning unlicensed exports of American petroleum, scrap metal, and aviation gasoline to Japan. He
also called for large increases in the ground, naval, and air
forces of the United States, which Congress granted while also
adopting the first peacetime conscription in the nation's history. In September, Japan negotiated the so-called Axis Pact
with Germany and Italy, which, in effect, stipulated that the
three powers would jointly attack the United States if it should
go to war against any one of them.

To many fearful Filipinos, the American ship of state seemed
to be no longer drifting toward war, but instead headed toward
it with full sails. In late June wild reports began to appear

in Manila newspapers, for example, *La Vanguardia* announcing that Valdes had ordered his officers "to carry their service arms at all times and be ready to answer summons from Army Headquarters." Though the report was denied by Valdes, "misgivings and alarm" spread through the populace. In July, MacArthur's office received reliable reports "of mild hysteria existing among families in the provinces who are having their children return from Manila schools because they fear that Manila is in danger of attack." Some legislators cried out that the time had come for all-out mobilization, but Quezon refused, reasoning that such action would antagonize Japan.[26]

In fact, the Philippine president was so anxious not to offend Nippon that through the first half of 1940 he continued unabatedly his campaign of delimiting the defense program. A convenient excuse was the business recession which hit the Philippines early that year. In the name of retrenchment, for example, he revoked the free franking privileges of MacArthur's office and the Philippine Army headquarters. The new budget, for 1941, provided for the number of trainees to be cut in half, sixty-one training camps to be closed, as well as all but one of the reserve officers' schools, and further military construction and armaments acquisition to be discontinued. In July, American wire services reported that Quezon "is considering giving up the national defense plan entirely." Vargas told the press that he "personally did not believe a contraction of the military activities proposed under national defense plans would mean any more than the desire to effect some savings." Yet that same week Quezon was considering a plan to create a Philippine C.C.C., financing of which would come from the savings of defense expenditures. MacArthur and other advisers were able, however, to dissuade him from such a costly venture. On August 6 the unpredictable Quezon asked the War Department for a direct subsidy of $100 per soldier to support the Philippine Army. But his plea was rejected in

Washington, Sayre having written that he "was merely looking for American funds to meet expenses that otherwise the Philippine Government would have to meet." [27]

The fast-growing war clouds in the Far East and the fear among his people finally led Quezon in the latter half of August to initiate the first steps toward civilian mobilization. A limited state of national emergency was declared on August 19, and the National Assembly authorized Quezon "to take over solely for use or operation by the government during the existence of the emergency, any public service or enterprise." Another measure empowered him to take whatever actions were necessary during the emergency to insure "the prevention of scarcity, monopolization, hoarding, injurious speculations, manipulations, private controls, and profiteering affecting supply, distribution and movement of foods, clothing, fuel, building materials, and other articles or commodities of prime necessity." A number of other legislative measures were enacted relating to control of alien immigration, "crimes against national security," and violations of United States espionage and neutrality statutes. But little was done, besides the passing of laws, to start mobilizing the nation. Deeply concerned, Grunert told Quezon in September that actual planning toward civil defense and economic and military mobilization should start at once. Belatedly that autumn the Philippine president and High Commissioner Sayre, with the advice of Grunert, MacArthur, and some of Manila's businessmen, set up a committee on mobilization planning. Its report several months later led to the creation of the Civilian Emergency Administration.[28]

In a memorandum to Quezon on Grunert's proposal and before the above action was taken, MacArthur voiced his consternation over Washington's tardiness in setting forth clear-cut policies on the Philippines and admitted forthrightly that the fate of the islands in war would depend upon American reinforcements and not upon his own defense system:

. . . The responsibility, however, for the defense of the Philippines, so long as it remains an integral part of the United States, is federal and devolves upon the American Government. The defense here is just as much a primary duty of American sovereignty as would be the defense of the State of New York or of the District of Columbia. Every resource of the Philippines, governmental or otherwise, is not only available to the United States under the terms of existing law, but is enthusiastically offered with no reservation whatsoever by the voluntary patriotism of all elements concerned. It is plainly evident, however, that the military forces maintained here by the United States are entirely inadequate for purposes of foreign defense and are little more than token symbols of the sovereignty of the United States . . . It is quite apparent that until the basic plans of defense of the American Government are known, no detailed, intelligent program for the civil or military population of these Islands can be made. A very different program would be necessary for a plan contemplating the defense of the entire archipelago than for one envisaging the defense merely of the Island of Luzon. It is not beyond the bounds of possibility that a strategic abandonment may be planned by the American Government. Until, therefore, the military concepts of Washington have been determined and communicated it would be premature to attempt civic regimentation of the populace. In this connection it is noted that General Grunert's memorandum does not in any way cover the naval aspects of the situation. This feature is quite as important as the military since the civil coordination is as intimately connected with naval plans as with Army plans. For instance, does the American Navy propose to keep open the normal maritime commerce that connects the United States with these islands? Does it intend to prevent the dispatch of an expeditionary force against these shores? Does it propose to prevent a blockade of this archipelago? All of these questions are vital to a proper consideration of the type of rigid control and centralized administration of the populace General Grunert has proposed. The more detailed matters that are brought up as to supply, transportation, hospitalization, and kindred subjects are themselves bound up and limited by the size of the army to be maintained, the number of airplanes to be operated, the types of equipment, such as heavy ordnance, to be transported, and by the extent of the terrain to be defended. It is my understanding that the Commonwealth Government would look askance at any proposition to abandon, without effort at defense, all parts of the Commonwealth except the Island of Luzon; that it would protest in the most determined way the abandonment of its shores to be ravaged without attempt at protection; that it would refuse absolutely to concur, even by indirection, in such an abject failure to render to the citizenry this primary obligation of government. Yet, in so far as is now known, such was the military plan before the Commonwealth Government broached the subject to President Roosevelt, and nothing to the contrary has yet been received locally. What good could possibly eventuate by making such civil preparations as are contemplated in General Grunert's program on the islands of Panay and Cebu, or Leyte, or Samar, or Mindanao, if they are not to be defended? What would be the psychological reaction of the citizens of those parts of the Commonwealth to contemplate regimentation without adequate attempt at defense? These are momentous questions whose answers far transcend any of the local ways and means discussed in the memorandum; yet such ways and means are entirely dependent upon the solution of the basic issues. It is hoped that the most forceful steps will be initiated with the United States, not only to determine the basic strategic plan for the defense of these Islands but also to make available adequate forces, both military and naval, to insure the safety and integrity of this part thereof.[29]

Unknown to MacArthur as he wrote this memorandum on October 12, 1940, the General Staff's war plans division in Washington was studying a proposal which would eventuate in momentous policy changes regarding the defense of the Philippines. But MacArthur's exasperation was justified if one examines the uncertain course pursued by the War Department in its previous relations with the Philippine Commonwealth.

3. *View from the Potomac*

After repeated communications from MacArthur, the War Department had hesitantly agreed in October, 1936, to supply weapons, ammunition, and other military equipment to the Philippine Army. All items except weapons were sold to the Commonwealth at cost plus charges for packing, handling, and transporting. Ammunition was sold in limited amounts and for training purposes only; it was stored on Corregidor and issued by the chief ordnance officer of the Philippine Department. Weapons were loaned at no cost to Quezon's government except for freight charges. Regulations differed according to the types of weapons as to where they were to be stored; their final disposition was left to be settled when the Philippines became independent in 1946. Only "non-standard and sub-standard" weapons were sent for the native troops' usage. The principal types of weapons loaned were models of 1917–18 vintage of 2.95-inch mountain howitzers, British 75-mm. guns, 3-inch Mark I trench mortars, 30-cal. Browning machine guns, 30-cal. Browning automatic rifles, 30-cal. Enfield rifles, and 45-cal. Colt revolvers. Though still serviceable, all of these weapons were obsolescent. Moreover, ammunition for some models was no longer manufactured and was obtainable only from dwindling stores in a few American ordnance depots. Of course, the ammunition shipped to the islands had to pass ordnance inspectors in the States, but much of it was barely acceptable at the time of shipment and deteriorated further after arrival in the Philippines, as would be discovered tragically when war came.[30]

During the visits to Washington by MacArthur and Ord in 1937 and by Eisenhower in 1938, they encountered unexpected difficulty in actually getting the allotted weapons released for shipment to the islands. One obstructionist was Murphy, who since returning to the United States had won election as governor of Michigan but had stayed in close touch with his benefactor and friend Roosevelt. A zealous pacifist, Murphy claimed that MacArthur was trying to militarize the Filipinos and argued that the field marshal should be brought home. According to Murphy's biographer, "He was instrumental in blocking arms shipments" to the Philippines for a while. Murphy himself claimed, "Thus far I haven't met an army officer in the Philippines or in Washington who shares his [MacArthur's] view that the Philippines are defensible." Though the governor exaggerated his point, there were some key persons in the War Department who were suspicious of the use to which the Filipinos would put the weapons. Brigadier General Walter Krueger, chief of the war plans division in 1936–38 and Sixth Army commander under MacArthur in 1942–45, believed that "arming the Filipinos constitutes a potential danger for the U.S." Craig told MacArthur that he had to insist on storage of the Philippine Army's munitions on Corregidor in order to "allay apprehension" in the War and State departments lest "serious disaffection" might arise among the islanders and they might seize the weapons, if stored at scattered, poorly guarded Philippine Army camps. As Cox described the War Department's attitude on the weapons loans, "Not all of the officers of the Army have a clear understanding of the present situation by any means."

Because of the slowness in getting ammunition from the United States for use in the training program, Commonwealth leaders considered the building of an ammunition factory in Manila, but the idea was dropped because of insufficient funds and staunch opposition by the War Department. In 1937 Krueger advised Craig that it was "highly desirable for the War Department to be the source of supply for as much equipment for the Philippine Army as possible, particularly weapons and ammunition, in order that we may know the quantity that is being obtained by the Philippine Army and be able to exercise control as far as possible while we are still responsible for the defense of the Philippines." The next year the War Department decided that all sales and loans of munitions would be handled through the Philippine Department, with the types and quantities to be completely at the discretion of the departmental commander. When munitions were out on loan, they were to be inspected frequently by American Army officers, and their trip expenses were to be paid by the Commonwealth. MacArthur would gradually get most of the antiquated equipment he requested, but the terms were strict and annoying.[31] By 1938, however, the War Department was satisfied that the munitions would not be used by insurrectionists. Assistant Secretary of War Louis Johnson reported to Roosevelt:

> The present policy is of practical benefit to both the United States and the Philippine Government. For the United States it assures, without additional expense, that the equipment of the Philippine Army will conform to that of the United States Army, thereby increasing the value of that force in the event it is ever needed. By retaining ownership of weapons and making them available for loan only, under proper supervision, the War Department is better able to control the number of weapons and the amount and types of ammunition in the hands of the Philippine Army. For the Philippine Government it provides suitable weapons without the expenditure of large sums of money at this time, thus permitting that Government to purchase other items of equipment which are vital to the defense of the Islands.[32]

The sending of munitions for use of the Philippine Army was not considered by the Philippine Department headquarters as augmentation of its defense reserve of weapons and ammunition. In fact, sometimes the War Department seems to have counted the Philippine Army's stores against the American allotments. The Philippine Department's problem was compounded in mid-1936 when the War Department informed Holbrook that his munitions reserves would be reduced because a recent decision of the Joint Army and Navy Board "changes the mission of the Army in the Philippines to the defense of the entrance to Manila Bay and charges the mobile ground forces of the Army with only such delaying action in the Subic Bay area and elsewhere as may be practicable without jeopardizing their timely withdrawal to the Bataan Peninsula." When the Sino-Japanese war started, Holbrook complained the ammunition reserves on Corregidor were woefully deficient for his command, and even worse for the Philippine Army. Craig responded that no ammunition could be spared from reserves in America and other overseas departments at that time. The chief of staff added a comment of little consolation: "So far as the present Sino-Japanese situation is concerned, I feel that, even though supplies and funds were available for shipment to you, Philippine stocks could not be materially augmented in time to meet an emergency growing out of the situation mentioned." The quest for adequate ammunition reserves would continue to be disappointing. As late as mid-1940 the departmental commander complained that his command had enough ammunition for "only about three or four days of fire per weapon." [33]

The concern about ammunition reserves was closely related to the provision in War Plan Orange as to the length of time the Philippine forces were expected to be self-sustaining after the start of war with Japan. In various versions of the Orange plan up to the middle 1930's it had been stipulated that the garrison would be counted upon to hold out for six months before reinforcements arrived. In view of his sparse reserves, Holbrook inquired in 1938 whether that time element was still part of the plan. The conclusion of the war plans division, as reported by Krueger to Craig, was not hopeful:

> The idea of a definite period of self-sustained defense is no longer a part of our present concept of the defense of the Philippines in an Orange war, nor is it authorized under any

approved Joint Board action now in force. Whatever form the new Joint Army and Navy Basic War Plan–Orange may take, it is highly improbable, as matters now stand, that expeditionary forces will be sent to the Philippines in the early stages of an Orange war. Even if the dispatch of such forces were contemplated, it would be impossible to predict, with any degree of accuracy, the time when they would arrive . . . The Department Commander should accomplish his mission for the maximum time possible with the personnel and reserves then available to him.[34]

Fulfilling MacArthur's munitions requirements proved easier for the War Department than meeting the Philippine Department's needs, the reason, of course, being that the former came from obsolescent stocks. By 1939 the United States had loaned the Commonwealth, among other items, 1220 3-inch trench mortars, 87,550 automatic rifles, 900 British 75-mm. guns, 3500 75-mm. guns of other models, 65,000 30-cal. machine guns, 9000 45-cal. revolvers, and about 200,000 Enfield rifles. As noted previously, however, practice with these weapons was severely limited because not enough ammunition was sent. The aggregate value of the weapons loaned by that time was about $6,000,000, though the total original cost had been nearly $16,000,000. The Commonwealth was required to purchase $6,500,000 in United States bonds as security on the loans. In addition, beginning in mid-1939, the War Department included an extra charge of 10 per cent of the current estimated value of all loaned weapons. The Philippine Department had maintained that the additional charge was necessary to cover its expenditures in facilities, personnel, and maintenance to store and issue the munitions. Vigorously but futilely MacArthur objected: "Since this property is a part of the United States Army defense reserves, subject to recall at any time, it is felt that such charge cannot be justified. Moreover, it would seriously retard the development of the defense plan to the detriment of the interests of both governments."

When MacArthur requested an increase in weapons loans in

March, 1939, the Philippine Department headquarters turned him down on the grounds that "the loan of additional weapons to the Philippine Army will not improve this Department's readiness for defense unless ammunition is available to use with the weapons," which was not then on hand. In August, however, word came from the War Department that shipments of additional weapons from American depots for loan to the Philippine Army would be made as follows: 110 3-inch mortars in fiscal 1940, 54 in 1941, and 54 in 1942; 166 automatic rifles in 1942, but none in 1940–41; 60 30-cal. machine guns in 1940, with 240 in 1941 and a like number in 1942; and 20 British 75-mm. guns in 1940, followed by 24 in 1941 and 24 in 1942. The news must have cheered MacArthur, but, of course, that schedule would be disastrously interrupted.[35]

The efficiency of staff planning, including that of the war plans division, may have been affected by the eruption in 1938–40 of the worst factionalism in the War Department in many decades. The bickering and scheming centered around a personal feud between Woodring and his assistant secretary, Louis Johnson. Members of the General Staff tended to align themselves on one side or the other, but the issues and the actual blame for the mess are difficult to delineate today. Moseley charged that Johnson "has been a disloyal skunk from the moment when he reported" in 1937 and was plotting to get Woodring's job. According to others, the Secretary of War was overly cautious in pushing preparedness, and Johnson was justified in criticizing his superior for not trying to develop the nation's defenses faster. When General George C. Marshall became chief of staff in September, 1939, he, like Craig, was caught in the Johnson-Woodring crossfire for a time. Finally in June, 1940, Roosevelt settled the matter by forcing Woodring's resignation and appointing veteran Henry Stimson in his stead, some said to the bitter disappointment of Johnson. Even with Stimson and Marshall at the helm, however, the

War Department underwent no noticeable change in attitude toward the Philippines' plight for many months. The failure to strengthen the Far Eastern outpost was due partly to the higher priority then accorded to Hawaii and Panama, but mainly to the lack of men and matériel. When Roosevelt asked Marshall if more could not be done for the Philippine defenses, the new chief of staff responded that it could be accomplished only by sending the Army's "few grains of seed corn" which were then defending the continental United States.

Within a month after he became commander of the Philippine Department in mid-1940, Grunert was bombarding the War Department with requests and warning reports — in fact, eight such communications during his first two months in the position. In September, about the time he urged Quezon to start mobilizing his nation, Grunert told Marshall that defeatism was evident among the Filipinos because of the United States' "lack of an announced policy backed by visual evidence of defense means and measures." He also voiced his opinion that America should not indulge in "appeasement and catering to Japan." His continuing requests for more troops and equipment delighted MacArthur, but brought only halting responses from the War Department at first.[36] Lieutenant Colonel William F. Marquat, an able coast artilleryman who had served two years on the military adviser's staff but had recently been transferred back to the States, wrote MacArthur that autumn:

While in Washington I tried to arouse some interest in the Chief's office in the Philippine situation but they are all so busy preparing plans for the new draft program that it is impossible to talk about anything else. There is plenty of money being spent but all types of equipment are lacking and it looks like it will be another year before the troops in the field will be benefited by the accelerated program.

There does seem to be, however, a rising apprehension about the Far Eastern situation as it relates to the United States. In

the great rush to support the defense program and give aid to
England there appear to be no definite plans for the Philippine
situation that I could locate. I hope, however, that when the
defense program acquires its full momentum it will provide support for your plans.[37]

For years General Staff planners had considered military
withdrawal from the Philippines as a possible way out of a
vulnerable situation. In late 1938 Brigadier General George V.
Strong, Krueger's successor as war plans chief, said that at a
recent meeting of the Joint Planning Committee the generals
and admirals had disagreed on that matter. Whereas the
admirals were disinclined to make an immediate decision on
the disposition of American military and naval dispositions in
the islands, the Army members argued that "we should withdraw entirely." In early 1940 at a Joint Army and Navy Board
session the admirals urged a major increase in military and
naval aviation strength in the Philippines, which prompted
a new study by the Army's war plans division as to the feasibil-
ity of trying to build an adequate defense system there. A war
plans division memorandum to the chief of staff in March indicated that a proper military defense of the islands would require
twelve times the number of Army aircraft then stationed there,
double the current strength of regulars and Scouts, and over
$22,000,000 in new construction, particularly air fields. Only
then could the Philippine Department present "a serious deterrent to any overt act" of aggression. After Grunert's barrage
of warnings and requests that summer Strong's planners set
to work anew on the Philippine defense problem. On October
10 the war plans division recommended submitting to the
President a plan to withdraw all American forces east of the
180° meridian as soon as possible, which would mean abandoning all American stations in China, the Philippines, and Guam
and Wake islands. Rather than reflecting the genuine views
of Strong and his officers, the recommendation, according to

the Army's official history of the Second World War, was probably intended "to compel a new and contrary policy decision." Increased concern over Japanese expansion, Grunert's alarming reports from Manila, and congressional approval of large increases in military manpower and munitions — all of these developments of the last half of 1940 seemed to call for a change in policy regarding defense of the Philippines.

Three weeks later Grunert wrote Washington again, this time suggesting that the Philippine Army be called into federal service as part of his command. Contrary to optimistic Manila newspaper reports, he said, the native defense force was far behind schedule in strength, training, and equipment. Grunert asked for 500 qualified American officers to be sent as instructors for the Philippine Army. But he concluded that, even then, it would be "capable of only defensive operations involving little or no maneuver, and then only in units not larger than a battalion when closely supervised by experienced officers of the U.S. Army." In December the draft of such a presidential proclamation was prepared, but Roosevelt did not believe that the time was yet propitious to mobilize the Filipino force as part of the American command. As for the 500 officers, Grunert was informed that he could expect the arrival of seventy-five.

Nevertheless, before the month of December, 1940, ended, a major change in attitude occurred in the top levels of the War Department regarding the Philippines. How the shift evolved cannot be traced with exactness, but shortly after Christmas the Philippine Department headquarters was notified that the strength of the Scouts would be doubled (to 12,000), the American infantry regiment on Luzon was to be enlarged by over 600 soldiers, additional coast artillery, field artillery, and antiaircraft batteries would be shipped, and $1,250,000 would be allotted for construction, mainly at air bases. The news must have been received with great enthusiasm at Grunert's headquarters, though he knew that these reinforcements still would not enable his command to repel a sizable invasion force. Moreover, the War Department promised more than it could deliver for many months. For example, in the case of antiaircraft guns — one of Grunert's most pressing needs — four were diverted to Manila from American ports where they were needed, and delivery of the other sixteen which were promised was postponed indefinitely. The expectation of reinforcements, of whatever quantity, raised hopes in both the American and Philippine commands, and the decision to assist the Philippines marked a changed attitude in the War Department, which until then had given higher priority to the defenses of Hawaii and the Panama Canal Zone. But as Marshall stated later, "Deficiencies in arms and equipment . . . for the immediate defense of the Western Hemisphere . . . were so serious that adequate reinforcements for the Philippines at this time would have left the United States in a position of great peril." [38]

In the autumn of 1940 MacArthur wrote his journalist-friend William Allen White, then spearheading the Committee to Defend America by Aiding the Allies. Although MacArthur's letter was in support of White's efforts to get more American aid to the beleaguered British, the military adviser's words were ironically prophetic of the fate toward which he and the Philippines were headed: "The history of failure in war can almost be summed up in two words: Too Late. Too late in comprehending the deadly purpose of a potential enemy; too late in realizing the mortal danger; too late in preparedness; too late in uniting all possible forces for resistance; too late in standing with one's friends." [39]

CHAPTER XIX

The Man and the Soldier

1. "Lonely No More"

THE MACARTHURS LIVED in an air-conditioned penthouse atop a new five-story wing of the Manila Hotel, one of the city's most luxurious buildings. The apartment had previously been General MacArthur's, but there was ample space for a family of considerable size. The tastefully decorated penthouse had an entrance hall which opened into a large reception room of Spanish-style decoration, a comfortable den or library, a formal drawing room of gold-motif design, a long hallway which led to several bedrooms and bathrooms, and, at the rear, a dining room from which could be viewed the blue expanse of Manila Bay from one exposure, the bustling waterfront from another, and the verdant hills beyond the city from a third viewpoint. The views from the two terraces were breathtakingly beautiful, with one affording a panoramic look at the city below and the other terrace overlooking the harbor. The MacArthurs enjoyed many serene moments watching the magnificent sunsets over Manila Bay, with the dark silhouette of Bataan Peninsula breaking the colorful cloud lines against the horizon. On the

terraces "the General, and sometimes Jean, would walk back
and forth for an hour or more between five o'clock and seven
each evening. We on MacArthur's staff," said Huff, "knew
that we could find him there each afternoon if something came
up." The general was so fond of the location, Huff commented,
that "eventually he conducted almost as much business while
walking up and down the terrace as he did at his office." Had
war not come, the MacArthurs might have spent the rest of
their days in peaceful, isolated splendor overlooking the "Pearl
of the Orient."

Jean MacArthur, from all accounts, was a rare and remarkable woman who became an ideal mate for the general. William
E. Beard, her uncle and an associate editor of the *Nashville
Banner,* commented: "A more generous girl — or a more completely lovable woman — I never knew. Thoughtful and kind
always, but with abundant, quiet resolution." A writer who
knew the MacArthurs well affirmed, "She was the right Mrs.
MacArthur because she understood and loved Army life, because she had great compassion for the small people, the enlisted men, but mostly because she was a lover of home." At
least in the presence of others, she addressed her husband not as
"Douglas" but "General," and he called her "Ma'am" — "a type
of traditional southern courtesy," according to one explanation.
A correspondent who was acquainted with the couple said of
their relationship: "She is vitally important to her husband's
life; he is crazy about her, and she worships him . . . [She]
maintains her role without the slightest pretension." Many
storms would swirl around the general in the years ahead, but
his home would always be the haven where he could find peace,
harmony, and love, thanks to the selfless efforts of this unusual
woman. Near his death MacArthur would write that his marriage to Jean "was perhaps the smartest thing I have ever done.
She has been my constant friend, sweetheart, and devoted supporter ever since. How she managed to put up with my eccen-

tricities and crotchets all these years is quite beyond my comprehension." [1]

MacArthur's joy was complete when Jean bore him a son on February 21, 1938. Born at Sternberg Hospital, Manila, the seven-and-one-half-pound baby was named Arthur, for his grandfather, uncle, and great grandfather. Appropriately in view of his father's strong sense of family heritage, the infant was baptized on his grandfather's birthday, June 2; the Episcopalian ceremony was witnessed by Manuel and Aurora Quezon, who served as his godparents. A Chinese amah named Loh Chiu — nicknamed "Ah Cheu" by the MacArthurs — had been employed in April, with MacArthur posting $500.00 bond as Philippine law required for alien immigrants employed on temporary visas. Loh Chiu quickly became a devoted, esteemed member of the household, and each year, as required by statute, the general renewed her permit by paying $15.91 to have her bond extended another twelve months. She and Mrs. MacArthur sometimes sided against the general on the treatment of the infant. On one occasion, for instance, the two women had been reading some literature on child psychology and concluded that Arthur was too pampered. So they decided that the next time he started crying, despite good health, a full stomach, and dry diapers, they would simply let him lie and wail. On the first such experiment, however, General MacArthur walked in unexpectedly. Seeing his wife and the amah calmly ignoring the child's wailing, he rushed over, tenderly picked him up, and walked him until he quieted. The psychology books were soon discarded, and the insatiably protective love of the father was allowed to continue in whatever form he chose, to the delight of the general and his son.

Anyone who visited in the MacArthur home very long was convinced that the imperious-looking general was a tender, sympathetic man with a heart overflowing with love for his son. The general nicknamed Arthur "Sergeant," and the name stayed with him for a number of years, to the liking of the boy. Often early in the morning the father and his son, when he had begun to walk, would march through the rooms and execute all sorts of fancy drills, many of which could never be found in a military manual. Arthur would follow him into the bathroom while the general shaved and bathed, and together they would lustily sing the few barracks songs which MacArthur knew. "The fact of the matter is," the general remarked, "that the only person who appreciates my singing in the bathroom is Arthur." The entry of Jean and Arthur into his life meant that MacArthur, in his words, "would be lonely no more." Those last years in the Manila Hotel penthouse before the onslaught of the Japanese were probably the happiest of the general's entire life.[2]

At the age of sixty MacArthur was a remarkable man physically. Very seldom ill and never seriously, his appearance was that of a man in his forties. "He carried himself," said an acquaintance, "as if he had a flagpole for a spine, and the flag of his keenness was always flying. The only sign of his age was the premonition of a paunch, but he held it in like a military secret." Each morning he performed a few calisthenics, and he took long walks late in the afternoons, although often only back and forth on his terraces. He no longer played any sports, and, except for his frequent pacing during conversations in his office, these were his only efforts toward physical fitness. He was a sound sleeper and usually got eight hours of rest, going to bed well before midnight and rising early. His breakfast and lunch were light, but at dinner he enjoyed a hearty meal. Fortunately for his weight, his tastes in foods did not include many of high caloric content. Before dinner he often had a cocktail made of orange juice and gin. On the infrequent occasions when he went to parties he usually ordered a "gimlet," which was a concoction of lime juice and gin. According to Huff, "He would hold it in his hand as he moved about the room, making a pretense of sipping it occasionally, but when he was ready to leave, the glass was almost as full as when he received it." As for his smoking habits, he resorted to cigarettes and cigars mainly, his preference for pipes being a phenomenon of the World War II years.

Unlike his earlier days in the chief of staff's office when he put in long, grueling hours, MacArthur as military adviser relied more completely on his assistants and was often away from his office. Eisenhower said that the general usually came to his office about eleven in the morning, stayed until nearly two, took an hour and a half or longer for lunch, returned to his office about three-thirty, went home about two hours later, and sometimes came back to his office a few hours in the evenings. However, MacArthur normally worked seven days a week and is never known to have enjoyed a leave or a few days' vacation during his entire period as Philippine military adviser, except for the trip to America and Mexico in early 1937. The attraction of his family, together with the reduction of the Philippine defense program in 1939–40, were factors involved in his diminished office hours, but much of the explanation lies in the variegated nature of his job, which took him frequently to the high commissioner's office, the headquarters of the Philippine Department, Malacañan Palace, and the farflung training centers of the Philippine Army.

His leisure was spent principally in playing with Arthur, reading military history, keeping up with West Point football exploits, and attending movies. His personal library, many books of which had belonged to his father, was variously estimated at 7000 to 8000 volumes, predominantly history and biography. His special interest was the Civil War, particularly biographies of Confederate generals. On the first Christmas after their marriage Mrs. MacArthur gave him Douglas S. Freeman's four-volume biography of Robert E. Lee; the next Christmas she presented him with G. F. R. Henderson's two-volume account of "Stonewall" Jackson and the following yuletide J. A. Wyeth's *Nathan Bedford Forrest*. He was a fast reader; it was said that he sometimes completed three books a day during his early morning and evening hours of reading. He also was keenly interested in international affairs and kept himself thoroughly informed on current events through extensive reading of newspapers and periodicals. A correspondent who knew him attested to the rich and varied background of learning which was evident in his conversations: "His mind crackled like lightning, and there was no telling where it might strike — he might be talking military history, and it would suddenly lick off, with a roll of thunderous rhetoric following it, across all the ologies and isms, and then come burning back again." [3]

No matter how many weighty matters he was wrestling with, MacArthur kept in close touch with Coach William H. Wood on the latest developments of his football team at West Point. In July, 1939, for example, the general, who had received a letter from Wood on the strategy for the coming season, commented on the coach's plan:

> It introduces an element of newness which will tend to break up your opponent's defensive tactics based upon any stereotyped West Point attack. It has been one of the weaknesses of the past that from year to year we did not vary our attacks sufficiently to render the enemy's defense uncertain, based upon his inability to digest anything but previous diagnosis. Too often both Notre Dame and the Navy have gone on the field against West Point knowing precisely where our attack would fall and being drilled to the last degree of minutia in defending therefrom . . . There is one factor which has potentialities of success which are rarely realized in modern teams. This is the use of an effective kicking game as an offensive weapon.[4]

MacArthur's detailed messages of advice to West Point football coaches would continue regularly through the war years ahead, regardless of whether the general was in a bomb-racked tunnel on Corregidor or a mosquito-infested jungle hut in New Guinea. He was particularly delighted when Earl "Red" Blaik, one of his former cadets and athletic stars of the early 1920's, took over the Army football squad after Wood's departure. Blaik would not disappoint his former superintendent.

For sheer relaxation nothing suited MacArthur better than a Hollywood movie. Beginning during his courtship with Jean, his fascination with movies developed into a set routine of nightly visits to Manila theaters. He preferred "Westerns" above all, but apparently could endure virtually any type or quality of movie. Huff claimed that he "never knew him to walk out on more than a couple of movies, no matter what they were, although sometimes he acknowledged that he saw some that were 'pretty bad.'" It might be that the general's escape into the make-believe world of cowboy heroes like Tom Mix and "Hopalong" Cassidy was an unconscious identification with the kind of world which he yearned for in real life — fast-moving action, dramatic moments, clearly defined issues, noble heroes, and unmistakably wicked villains. In everyday life MacArthur found it difficult to adjust to "small talk," petty administrative details and office routine, and persons who lived in gray worlds where things were never clearly black or white.

For years MacArthur had maintained no ties with any fraternal or other civilian organizations except in an honorary capacity, as his presidency of the Rainbow Division Veterans. Honorific titles continued to come to him during the late 1930's: patron of the American Military Institute, honorary officer of a Milwaukee post of the American Legion, namesake of the Milwaukee chapter of the Rainbow Division Veterans, and other similar kudos. The only fraternal group in which he exhibited an active interest during his Manila days was the Scottish Rite of Freemasonry. His father had been active in the Masons while he was in the islands at the turn of the century, and perhaps the son felt some obligation to join, especially since a few surviving members had been friends of General Arthur MacArthur. In the Scottish Rite society of Manila, Douglas rose to the 32° rank, was honored by the supreme council as "Knight Commander of the Court of Honor," and delivered the address at the dedication of the new Scottish Rite temple in Manila in late 1938. Through this association he established lifelong friendships with leading members of the city's professional and commercial community.

Likewise, he became closely associated with leading Manila businessmen through his activities with the Manila Hotel Company, of which he was a stockholder, member of the board of directors, treasurer, and vice president. The extent of his investment in this enterprise is not known, but he probably enjoyed handsome returns from the amount he put into it. President José Páez reported in 1936, for instance, that the company's profits were increasing at a rate of 15 per cent annually, the total assets then being nearly $1,000,000. Whether MacArthur also invested in the gold-mining activities around Baguio is not certain, but such speculation was common among high-ranking American officers and civilian officials. MacArthur's personal ties with certain Filipinos of large vested interests would lead to serious trouble when the civil government was restored in 1945 since some of the men reinstated had collaborated with the Nipponese, but that story will be told in the second volume of this work.[5]

2. *Friends in Manila*

Not many persons addressed General MacArthur as "Douglas." His critics might conclude from this that he enjoyed few friendships or was incapable of cultivating human relationships which would induce such familiarity. Admittedly, in public he did project a haughty image at times, and he often seemed to limit deliberately the circle of his friends. It is true, too, that he did not indulge in the barracks-type camaraderie of drinking, card playing, and joke swapping which many officers appreciated. "He doesn't enjoy meeting people merely for the sake of making new acquaintances," maintained Huff. "On the other hand, he has tremendous charm as well as a commanding, exciting personality; he can be tactful, gracious and even gallant, as the occasion demands, and he can and often does lean back in his favorite red-painted rocking chair and enjoy a real belly laugh that makes the rafters ring." But the friendships which MacArthur enjoyed on a deep, lasting basis were with peers and associates who shared the serious professional problems and responsibilities which were almost constantly on his mind. He was capable of amiability, understanding, and loyalty toward a select group of men, but they were almost inevitably those with whom he dealt daily on matters of professional concern. As one officer put it, "Who were his close friends? His key staff members, whoever they were at any given period." Normally his conversations with his colleagues were characterized by dignity and even nobility, with no indulging in belittling remarks about persons not present or in comments on trivial nonprofessional matters or personal problems. The tone of his social intercourse with his Manila staff in the late 1930's was guided, in part, by the fact that his main staff officers were men fifteen to twenty years his junior. As sprightly as he may have felt, most of his staff regarded him as one of the Army's "grand old men." As a result, although he was able to attract and fascinate and produce deep feelings of devotion in his colleagues, even his closest friends admitted that they were able to penetrate only rarely beyond the professional soldier and gentleman-aristocrat to the man himself.[6]

The most important and stormiest friendship which MacArthur had as military adviser was with Quezon. Major General Charles A. Willoughby, who came to Manila in 1939 as

a lieutenant colonel and later would serve many years as Mac-
Arthur's intelligence chief, knew Spanish well and acted as a
liaison between Grunert's office and later MacArthur's in their
dealings with the Philippine president. Willoughby said of
Quezon's personality: "If you have a picture of the typical
American politician, you simply give him a Spanish coloration
and the Philippine setting, and you have Quezon. However,
he had a personality probably superior to the average American politician, with his Spanish background and his European
culture. Volatile, excitable, sometimes overexcitable, yet always held in leash by later reconsideration. A complex personality and a patriot . . . he would alternately become enraged and depressed." Quezon's erratic temperament was at-
tributed partly to the grave condition of his health: he suffered
from tuberculosis and would die from it two years after the
war in the Pacific started. His hot and cold relations with
MacArthur were produced, in part, by the powerful personalities of the two men. But generally, despite differences over the
defense plan, Quezon and MacArthur remained "brothers," as
Mrs. Quezon once called them. "Perhaps Quezon's warmth,
his impetuous tenderness, opened up the best in MacArthur,
and called out that charming energy so much hidden in soli-
tude, in the study of history, and the service of his country,"
observed an authority of the Commonwealth's history. Near
the height of Quezon's opposition to the defense program, in
the spring of 1939, MacArthur sent him a note of birthday
greeting, whereupon the emotion-filled Filipino leader replied:
"I was so deeply touched by your note yesterday that I couldn't
even write thanks to you. Never in my life have I received a
message so rich with human sentiment and yet so short. There
I found the measure of your limitless affection for me. I cannot express my feelings as you can yours, but my love for you
is no less in any respect than yours for me." Yet a few months
later Quezon was talking to Sayre about removing MacArthur.

So ran the course of their strange but beautiful friendship until Quezon's death.[7]

MacArthur's other Filipino friends included particularly Manuel Roxas, Carlos P. Romulo, and Joaquin "Mike" Elizalde. Roxas ranked with Quezon and Osmeña as the most influential politicians in the Philippines, though he was often at odds with his two colleagues. In the 1930's Roxas was house speaker for several years and commanded a large political following, which he alternately rallied in support of and against Quezon. During the war in 1941–42 MacArthur would appoint him as a colonel on his staff, but during the Japanese occupation of the Philippines Roxas would be considered by many citizens as a leading collaborator. Nevertheless, he managed to defeat Osmeña in 1946 to become the first president of the Philippine Republic. Romulo was editor of the influential Manila *Herald* and was a staunch supporter of the defense plan and the military adviser, whom he idolized. When the war came, he, too, would gain a colonelcy on MacArthur's Corregidor staff; in the postwar years he would hold numerous political posts. "Mike" Elizalde was a member of one of the islands' wealthiest sugar-holding families. During the Commonwealth era he served as resident commissioner in Washington for a while, and after the Second World War he would become the republic's first ambassador to the United States. When the MacArthurs gave their small and infrequent dinner parties, these Filipinos, along with the Quezons, were high on the guest list. There were, as earlier stated, other Filipinos whom MacArthur knew well, and the majority of Filipino citizens held the military adviser and his wife in high esteem. Perhaps typical was the statement at the beginning of the 1938 edition of the *Philippinensian,* the University of the Philippines' yearbook which was dedicated to MacArthur as "a soldier, statesman, and devoted friend of the Filipino people." In late January, 1940, when MacArthur was troubled over defense difficulties, he must have deeply appreciated one particular note of birthday greeting he recieved: it was signed by Emilio Aguinaldo, the aging former rebel who had fought against his father four decades earlier.[8]

Among the American officers in Manila up to 1940, Eisenhower was the closest to MacArthur, although, with such contrasting personalities, the two might have antagonized each other continuously. It has been charged by several writers, indeed, that MacArthur suppressed Eisenhower's efforts to get a troop command, retarded his professional advancement, and provoked such hostility between them that Eisenhower left the Philippines in disgust. It is true that MacArthur considered him so important to the work of the military adviser's office that he turned down several requests by Eisenhower for transfer to command of troops and rather reluctantly granted it in 1939. This may have slowed "Ike's" rise in rank slightly, but since he was allowed to leave at what turned out to be the "right" time in view of his subsequent rapid advancement, it is difficult to see how his "overtime" under MacArthur was a liability to his career. Though Eisenhower would later be more closely identified with General George Marshall and the alleged anti-MacArthur faction of generals of the war and postwar years, he commented to the author with moving sincerity that he had always been "deeply grateful for the administrative experience he gained under General MacArthur," without which he did not believe that he "would have been ready for the great responsibilities of the war period." He also vehemently denied that any hostility existed between him and MacArthur when he left Manila in late 1939: "I had been with him for many years and felt that I needed other experience, especially command of troops. I had been in Manila four years, much longer than I anticipated. Hostility between us has been exaggerated. After all, there must be a strong tie for two men to work so closely for seven years."

By the time of Eisenhower's departure MacArthur was more convinced than ever of the validity of the words he had written to him a few years before: "Through all these years I have been impressed by the cheerful and efficient devotion of your best efforts to confining, difficult and often strenuous duties, in spite of the fact that your personal desires involved a return to troop command and other physically active phases of Army life, for which your characteristics so well qualify you." Quezon, as well as MacArthur, regretted seeing him leave since the Philippine president and "Ike" had enjoyed a warm, cordial relationship. On December 12, 1939, the day before the Eisenhowers sailed for America, Quezon awarded him the Philippine Distinguished Service Star, the citation lauding "his exceptional talents . . . his professional attainments, his breadth of understanding, his zeal and magnetic leadership."

Eisenhower said of his farewell conversation with MacArthur at the Manila pier, "We talked of the gloominess of world prospects, but our foreboding turned toward Europe — not Asia." The next December Eisenhower wrote him from Fort Lewis, Washington, where he was chief of staff of the 3rd Division: "So far as the U.S. is concerned, the guns, of course, are not yet roaring. But how long they can keep silent becomes more of a guess, it seems to me, with every day that passes. Once they really open up, I'll expect to see you in the thick of it." Eisenhower never had a doubt that his former superior, though retired and in his sixties, should hold a major field command when that war came.[9]

Fortunately for MacArthur, he had on his staff a most competent officer to take Eisenhower's place as chief of staff of the military mission. The man was Lieutenant Colonel Richard K. Sutherland, an infantry officer who had joined MacArthur's group as deputy chief of staff in 1938 after Ord's death. He had entered the Army in 1916 as a second lieutenant, gaining his commission by competitive examination after graduating from Yale University. He served with the A.E.F. in France and thereafter held numerous troop assignments, besides attending and graduating from the Infantry School, the Command and General Staff School, and the Army War College. He first met MacArthur while at the War College in 1932–33. When the military adviser requested his services in early 1938, Sutherland was serving with the 15th Infantry at Tientsin, China. In October of that year MacArthur wrote to an officer-friend: "Sutherland has proven himself a real find. Concise, energetic and able, he has been invaluable in helping me clarify and crystallize the situation." [10] In personality he was quite different from Eisenhower, as Willoughby's description clearly shows:

> . . . Brittle in personality, aloof, a "hard" man, Sutherland could not count on affection but found associates who were willing to work with him on the basis of devotion to the "old man." Sutherland had a difficult temper but kept it under admirable control. He inspired respect from the staff because he was an indefatigable worker . . . who demanded nothing from anyone that he was not perfectly willing to do himself. A handsome man with a Roman profile, he would sometimes break the mask of hardness with a sardonic smile and curious flashes of humor . . . He would listen to MacArthur carefully, ascertain every nuance of his views, and then present them to the other "hard" men on the staff with impeccable *sang-froid* . . . But in the end he ruffled no personal feelings, for his innate honesty and complete probity were soon recognized by his associates.[11]

Sutherland was intensely loyal to MacArthur and would continue as his chief of staff through World War II.

In September, 1939, MacArthur gained another capable officer who would serve him long and faithfully, Lieutenant Colonel Richard J. Marshall. A graduate of Virginia Military Institute, he entered the Regular Army in 1916 as a field artillery lieutenant, having previously been an officer in the Maryland National Guard. He was a battery commander with the 1st Division's field artillery brigade in World War I, but after the conflict he changed to the Quartermaster Corps. Subsequently he graduated from the Quartermaster School, the Command and General Staff School, the Army Industrial College, and the Army War College, besides holding various quartermaster assignments in construction and transportation. Marshall first met MacArthur when he came to the islands as assistant quartermaster of the Philippine Department in the winter of 1929–30. On the military adviser's staff in 1939–41 Marshall supervised procurement and storage of supplies, organized the Philippine Army's services of supply, and was instrumental in planning economic mobilization for the Commonwealth. Willoughby remarked, "As a personality, Marshall was less aggressive, less dominant than Sutherland; it was perhaps in the nature of his work that persuasion, conference methods, and compromise were more essential than the brusque decisions of execution." Major General Courtney Whitney, then a prominent Manila attorney and from 1943 onward a key officer on MacArthur's staff, commented, "General Marshall was excellent on supply problems, had unusual administrative ability, and was a very pleasant person to work with." MacArthur's personal and professional regard for Marshall was high. In 1946 he would appoint him as his chief of staff, a position which Marshall held until he returned to the States to become V.M.I. president. Recently looking back over his career and his friendship with MacArthur, Marshall remarked, "The best seven years of my professional life were spent with him."

Sutherland and Marshall would be charter members of the so-called "Bataan Gang," that small group of headquarters officers who served with MacArthur through the Philippine and Southwest Pacific campaigns, as well as the occupation of Japan. Others who were on the military adviser's staff and would work under him for many years to come were Lieutenant Colonels Hugh J. Casey and William F. Marquat, besides Huff, who in 1941 would become MacArthur's senior aide with the rank of lieutenant colonel. A high-ranking West Point graduate of 1918, Casey, by all accounts, was a brilliant engineer. He was detailed to MacArthur's staff as a captain in October, 1937, along with Captain Lucius D. Clay, another engineer, who would be the American occupation commander in Germany in the late 1940's. Both Casey and Clay were transferred elsewhere two years later, but in 1941 MacArthur, who remembered Casey's "ingenuity and speedy actions," requested his return to become his chief engineer officer. Casey would continue in that capacity under MacArthur until his retirement in 1949; in the approaching war he would prove to be one of the most valuable of MacArthur's headquarters leaders. "Pat," as he was called, was an exuberant, energetic Brooklyn native of Irish descent who was fondly regarded by MacArthur and nearly everyone with whom he worked. Marquat, who has been mentioned previously, was highly respected as a coast artillery and antiaircraft specialist and would be chief of Mac-Arthur's headquarters antiaircraft section when war came. "An irrepressible extrovert, with a flair for puns," Willoughby said of him, "his sense of humor was welcome in dark hours." Another officer called Marquat "an oasis of wit in a wilderness of stuffed shirts." This amiable, talented officer was later chosen by MacArthur to head the economic and scientific section of the administration of occupied Japan. Huff, who also has been introduced before, was looked upon by most of the staff as a pleasant, bright fellow who went about his tasks diligently first as naval adviser to MacArthur and later as his aide. He would faithfully serve the general to the end of MacArthur's career in Tokyo and was always a favorite of the general and his wife.

As noted earlier, MacArthur and Grunert were old friends and often visited each other's headquarters in Manila. In time

MacArthur became well acquainted with a number of officers serving in the Philippine Department, while, of course, there were some whom he had known from previous tours of duty. Though he might lose by transfer some of his own staff, such as Davis, Fellers, and Hutter by 1940, MacArthur was permitted, on approval by Grunert, to get a few officers detailed to his military adviser's office from the Philippine Department. Among those in Grunert's command with whom MacArthur had already established friendships by 1940 and who would be shifted to his staff in mid-1941 were Willoughby, Colonel Spencer B. Akin, Lieutenant Colonel Charles P. Stivers, and Major LeGrande A. Diller. These men would make up the second group of devotees who would soon constitute part of the "Bataan Gang." [12]

MacArthur, of course, still maintained his ties by correspondence with a few old and devoted Army companions in the States, particularly Moseley, Simonds, and Drum. But most of his longtime friends, who had included the major military leaders of the 1920's and 1930's, had retired by the beginning of the Second World War, and some had died. As the year 1941 began, MacArthur found himself the sole officer still active in a military capacity who had been a part of the Army's elite nucleus of policy makers in the drought years 1920–35. The officers who would rise meteorically to high command in World War II had been lieutenant colonels, majors, or even captains — promising, but of little influence — when MacArthur had been military head of the Army. He undoubtedly wondered if the War Department would permit him a major field command should the United States go to war in the near future. The fate of his former idol, General Leonard Wood, who had tried and failed to get a troop command in World War I, probably crossed MacArthur's mind more than once as the war clouds continued to gather over the Western Pacific in the winter of 1940–41.

3. At the Age of Sixty-One

Many of the traits which MacArthur would display during the period of World War II and after were evident in his behavior before then. The discerning student of his later career has undoubtedly detected harbingers of what would be revealed in 1941–51. But the MacArthur of later times, especially of 1951 when he was relieved of his commands, had changed in certain significant respects during the preceding decade. The comparisons and contrasts between the MacArthur of 1941 and of 1951 will be explored in detail in the second volume, but the reader is cautioned in advance not to try to find all of his later characteristics revealed in his life up to World War II. He was an immensely complex person who, unlike most adults in their sixties, was still capable of distinct changes in personality, behavior, and beliefs. The following summary of some of his traits as exhibited by early 1941 should be interpreted with the above qualification.[13]

MacArthur could inspire loyal, zealous service in his subordinates as few commanders could. Skillfully but often inexplicably, he could handle his staff members in such ways as to make them want to perform to their maximum capabilities. Most of his staff leaders of the 1930's regarded him as one of the outstanding leaders of the Army, and some saw him as a man possessed of greatness, but none yet adulated him to the point of comparing his genius of military leadership to that of Alexander the Great or Napoleon I, as some would later do. There was no "Bataan Gang" yet, though, as noted earlier, some of the charter members-to-be were already serving with him by 1940. No one talked seriously yet of MacArthur as a unique creature of destiny, nor does the evidence suggest that he thought of himself as such. The myths of his almost superhuman attributes and feats were still several years in the offing.

He was already a famous general with a long and brilliant record, but there was little to indicate from his subordinates' attitudes and his own performances that he would someday become a much-idolized, legendary figure in the eyes of millions of people. Nevertheless, the man's magnetic appeal to those working close beside him was such that none of his close subordinates before the Second World War, including Eisenhower, became his antagonist after leaving his command. Invariably, his severest critics were persons who personally knew him little or not at all.

One of his secrets in getting the most from his subordinates was his ability to convince them that their tasks were crucial to the success of the particular project, whatever it might be. The project, mission, or operation, in turn, was inevitably and convincingly portrayed by him as of utmost importance in the larger picture of national defense, whether of the United States or the Philippines. On the other hand, by the late 1930's MacArthur had begun to depend perhaps too much on his staff and tended to draw conclusions and order action on the basis of recommendations from staff members whose information, in some cases, was compiled hastily and incompletely. There was room for errors of this type in the late 1930's, whereas later such implicit trust of subordinates' advice could be dangerous to a combat operation.

There is no doubt that MacArthur possessed a quick, brilliant mind, which was undiminished as he entered his sixties. His memory, according to his colleagues, was phenomenal; he could recall easily small details from experiences and even memoranda dating back several decades. Also his ability to analyze and synthesize with careful, sound reasoning was exceptional. His mental faculties suggest that, unlike too many military men, he could have achieved success in a number of professional fields in the civilian world. Some subordinates were convinced that he possessed an uncanny prescience, though there is little in the record that substantiates this. He was surely one of the most widely read officers in the Army and could talk intelligently on a number of cultural, social, political, and technical subjects which were far afield of his formal training and experience. On the other hand, except for his reform efforts as superintendent at West Point, he never went against the current of conservatism which was dominant in American military thought between the two world wars. MacArthur would never be considered a major contributor, like Emory Upton or Alfred Thayer Mahan, to military thought and theory. His prescience did not extend, for example, to the rapidly changing scene in the Western Pacific where he was tragically amiss in his predictions on Japan's intentions and capabilities. Moreover, when in the company of men of superior knowledge on given subjects, MacArthur, unlike Roosevelt, too often learned little from them simply because he could not resist dominating the conversation.

The real MacArthur will always be elusive because, like F.D.R., the general was a master at role-taking. Depending on the occasion, he could appear flamboyant or reticent, extravagant or austere, emotionally involved or coldly objective, gracious or aloof. Nowhere was this more evident than in his public performances where he seemed always to be acutely conscious of the image which he was projecting. Whether in an informal exposition at a small dinner party or in an address before a large crowd, his command of words was masterful. If at times he engaged in hyperbole and overblown rhetoric, it was done with deliberate intent to sway his listeners to his position. Though emotion played a minor role in his behavior outside his home, he was fond of using emotionally charged words when they suited his purpose in public. It will be remembered that he early idolized colorful figures who were experts at projecting desired images — Joseph Cannon, Theodore Roosevelt, Leonard Wood, and Henri Gouraud. The unfortunate inability of his friend Hoover to project himself as a president who cared about his suffering constituents probably made MacArthur more aware than ever of the significance of role-taking, image-projecting, and commanding men's minds through commanding the right words. Some politicians, but few military men, could match his mastery of these skills.

If it were possible to discern which of his varied roles reflected his real self, it was probably that of the gentleman-aristocrat. Pictures of his parents and paternal grandparents were always kept near his desk; it was said that he considered them as reminders not only of loved ones but of his aristocratic heritage. He had been taught as a child and youth that he was of an uncommon breed of man, and in adulthood he was most comfortable in the role of the patrician. Possessed of solemn dignity and placing great stress on personal honor, MacArthur did not care to associate intimately with aristocratic society, but was sometimes vexed if his position as a peer of the patricians was not fully respected. In his personal life he was astutely proper in his ethics and etiquette, and his thinking was normally pitched on a loftier plane than ordinary men sustain except for brief periods. Rarely did he respond in anger or bitterness toward an individual who had insulted or severely criticized him, although he was prone to lash out at antagonists of general types, such as pacifists. Like the good man of nobility, his attitude toward the Filipino people was *noblesse oblige:* as a privileged aristocrat, humanitarianism was his bounden duty toward commoners, although few Filipinos below the social level of the Elizaldes were included in his circle of friends. Toward his professional associates he was cordial, but not familiar; toward others, at times, he could be aloof and condescending. A patrician in uniform was an unusual phenomenon in the democratic Army of the United States, and he could expect some ridicule, no matter how genuine the role was for him. It was unfortunate that, though possessing a fair sense of humor, MacArthur was not able to laugh at himself. For the man of serious thoughts and weighty responsibilities, the ability to view himself humorously may sometimes restrain flights into imaginative grandeur.

When MacArthur spoke, people listened, not simply because he was skilled in persuasion, but because he was one of the most experienced and best known military leaders America had produced since the Civil War. By 1941 he was a veteran of forty-two years in the military field, had been a general for twenty-three years, and had served in almost every kind of assignment possible to officers. Next to Pershing, whose faculties were declining, MacArthur was more widely known in political and military circles, American and foreign, than any other living officer of the United States Army. His reputation was firmly fixed as a courageous, able combat leader and an excellent high-level administrator. Especially in view of the discouraging progress of most officers after World War I, his professional advancement had been at a meteoric rate, which further buttressed his already strong confidence and optimism regarding any undertaking he faced. His rise to military head of the Army at an unusually early age and his subsequent prolongation of his military activity after 1937 placed him in a unique position as far as the War Department was concerned. Another former chief of staff, Wood, had been only fifty-seven when America entered the European conflict in 1917, yet the War Department had justification for refusing him a field command on grounds of physical disability. But it would be difficult and awkward to bypass the ex-chief of staff in Manila in 1941, for this man was more robust than many officers twenty years his junior.

So far MacArthur's philosophy was a curious mixture of Hoover's individualism and Moseley's nativism, and it was not clear which strand would ultimately be strongest in his thinking. For a man who had a first-rate mind and had read extensively on cultural and intellectual subjects, his philosophy was surprisingly simplistic, so much so that it defies systematizing. Christianity, democracy, and patriotism were almost synonyms to him. When he talked about war, it was often in spiritual and moral terms, rather than in the strategical and technical jargon of most officers. His value judgments were decisive and without qualification; relativity was never considered in matters of rightness or wrongness, good or evil. Whereas he tackled everyday problems of military planning with uncommonly sound, lucid reasoning, his approach to ideological issues was mystical and intuitive. Rarely did he attempt to define the terms which he used in discussing ideologies. Likewise, though known to be a deeply religious man, he never articulated his Christian beliefs in a manner whereby they could be categorized as of a certain denominational line or theological school. Like Moseley, he was convinced that America was endangered by the insidious workings of pacifists, liberals, and Communists, but he would not distinguish among these groups. It does not appear, however, that up to 1941 he believed these inner menaces were as great a danger to the United States as the external threat of totalitarian aggression.

The common thread running through his forty-two years of military service and the most predictable trait of his future was his unashamed, wholehearted dedication to duty, honor, and country. He may have had difficulty defining these principles in terms acceptable to his intellectual critics, but his fervent adherence to them was paramount in every significant decision and action of his career. In this sense, he was a veritable incarnation of the spirit of West Point; the soldierly virtues seemed to be imbedded so firmly in his being that he could not knowingly act contrary to their dictates. His unswerving devotion to the ideals of the professional soldier explains not only the measure of greatness which can be ascribed to him at this stage of his career but also the criticism which he had encountered from a growing segment of the citizenry who were re-examining the very worth of these principles and virtues.

In the late spring of 1940 when the downfall of France was imminent and the Battle of Britain was about to begin, the British government called to its helm a sixty-six-year-old gentleman named Winston Churchill. Not unlike MacArthur in certain respects, he, too, was a patrician endowed with unique abilities of leadership and more than a touch of arrogance. Churchill also had enjoyed a long and incredibly active career, which some thought had practically ended by the start of World War II. Like MacArthur, he was supremely dedicated to duty, honor, and country, would not hesitate to sacrifice his career for those principles, and spoke of them unabashedly as the factors underlying his nation's greatness. Some would say that in rhetoric and thought both men were anachronisms from the nineteenth century. But at the time when Great Britain most needed an uncommon man to lead, Churchill was called and he would serve well. The eve of America's darkest hour was approaching, and MacArthur must have wondered if the rattling of swords would bring a summons from his nation for his services. Those who knew the general well had no doubt that he would respond with vigor and brilliance.

CHAPTER XX

In the Path of the Storm

1. An Uncertain Course

"I DON'T WANT TO APPEAR PESSIMISTIC, but at this point I can hardly see how this country will be avoiding war after 60 to 90 days from now," wrote "Mike" Elizalde, the Philippine resident commissioner in Washington, to MacArthur in mid-April, 1941. Several months earlier Secretary of State Cordell Hull had begun talks with Admiral Kichisaburo Nomura, the Japanese ambassador to the United States, toward trying to negotiate the outstanding differences between their two countries. By spring, however, the discussions had progressed no further than the preliminary stage. Nomura insisted on separating the China issue from the question of Japanese-American relations, while Hull staunchly maintained that the withdrawal of Nipponese troops from China was a prerequisite to any settlements between Washington and Tokyo. Joseph Grew, the American ambassador to Japan, warned that the talks in Washington should continue by all means, for "the alternative might well be progressive deterioration of Japanese-American relations leading eventually to war." Both Hull and Nomura privately admitted to their respective advisers that the discussions had reached an impasse and war seemed a real possibility, but the two states-men did resume their talks intermittently that summer.

From January to March, 1941, British and American military staff conferences had been under way secretly in Washington and had resulted in a joint basic war plan called ABC-1. In case of war with both Germany and Japan, Great Britain and the United States would give priority to the defeat of Germany first, while maintaining a strategic defensive position in the Pacific. The American Navy, however, would cooperate with other Allied fleets in offensive operations, attacking Nipponese supply lines and possibly carrying out strikes against bases and vessels in the mandated islands. The military and naval planners of both nations accepted the plan in principle, but it did not obligate the United States to enter the war at a certain stage nor did Roosevelt ever give the plan his formal sanction. Near the close of the Anglo-American staff talks, the conferees agreed to call a meeting of their commanders in the Far East "to prepare plans for the conduct of military operations in the Far East in accordance with the provisions of ABC-1."

This conference took place at Singapore in late April, with Sir Robert Brooke-Popham, British air chief marshal in the Far East, serving as chairman. The official United States representative was Captain William R. Purnell, a member of the staff of Admiral Thomas C. Hart, who commanded the Asiatic Fleet. The meeting eventuated in the development of the so-called ADB plan, which, though couched in general terms, provided for unified commands and areas of responsibility for vigorous joint counteraction by British, Dutch, and American military and naval units in Southeast Asia in case of Japanese aggression there. Purnell was not empowered to endorse the plan officially, however, and later it was rejected by the American Army and Navy chiefs in Washington. The American chiefs claimed that it "contains political matters beyond the scope of a military agreement" and "in several major and numerous minor particulars, it is at variance" with ABC-1. In addition, the American leaders emphasized that "the United States intends to adhere to the decision not to reinforce the Philippines except in minor particulars." Nevertheless, Japanese newspapers proclaimed that the Singapore meeting had resulted in a military pact whereby the Western powers intended to close ranks to thwart Japanese plans in the Far East.[1]

A crucial difference between American and British staff leaders concerned the latter's effort to get an American commitment to contribute to the naval defense of Singapore. The British proposed that the Asiatic Fleet of the United States Navy, then based mainly in the Philippines and at Shanghai, should be heavily reinforced. Thus, in case of a Japanese thrust toward the Malay Barrier, it could operate effectively in conjunction with British and Dutch naval units to deter or delay a Nipponese advance on Singapore. American planners, on the other hand, contended that assistance in defending Singapore could result in forsaking the primary objective of ABC-1, namely, the defeat of the Nazi war machine. United States Navy leaders were agreeable to augmenting their fleets in the Atlantic and Mediterranean in order to release British surface units to move to Southeast Asia, but neither the admirals nor the generals in Washington were yet willing to contemplate a large-scale strengthening of American naval, ground, or air forces in the Far East. The latest modification of War Plan Orange, completed in April and called WPO-3, stipulated that the mission of the Philippine garrison was still the defense of the entrance of Manila Bay only, although some naval planners now estimated that it might take two years after the outbreak of war for the Navy to fight its way back to the Philippines and relieve or reinforce the garrison. The War and Navy departments no longer thought in terms of withdrawal from the Philippines, yet they had no concrete plans for augmenting or rescuing the forces situated there. In the meantime the Japanese-American "peace" talks continued in Washington, but Hull confessed confidentially in May that "everything is going hellward."

WPO-3 did not specifically state how long the Philippine garrison would have to wait for reinforcement or relief after hostilities commenced, but the war plans division still computed the Philippine Department's defense reserves in terms of six months under combat conditions. By the spring of 1941 the problem, from Grunert's point of view, was that his defense reserves — not as authorized, but as delivered — were inadequate; also the basis was only a 31,000-man garrison, and he knew he would have to meet the needs of the Philippine Army as well if war came. He pleaded with the War Department over and over to raise the basis of his ordnance and quartermaster reserves, but to no avail. It would not be until midsummer that the basis was finally computed for a war garrison of 50,000 troops, which was still far short of his need, particularly since the new reserves were not scheduled to be shipped for many months. The Philippine Department still ranked well behind the Hawaiian Department and sometimes behind the Panama Department for shipments of aircraft, munitions, and men throughout the spring of 1941. In March, for instance, Grunert emphasized to the War Department that his department was short of its authorized quotas in many categories of munitions, some of his shortages being 1,250,000 rounds of 50-cal. machine gun cartridges, 53,000 37-mm. shells, 151 37-mm. guns, and 21 3-inch antiaircraft guns. A few weeks later Grunert again pleaded for shipment of some badly needed items, especially antiaircraft guns, ammunition of all types, barrage balloons, and aircraft. Marshall, who was besieged by similar requests from all his commands, was compelled to reply: "I have looked into the matters you mentioned, but I am afraid that except for the materiel, concerning which you have already been advised, there is nothing now in the offing. We are doing everything we can for you, and I am sure you understand our limitations." To several of his later requests Grunert received the discouraging reply from Washington: "A sufficient number will be available in 1942 to meet the approved requirements of all overseas departments." [2]

If Grunert was having difficulty getting more personnel and matériel, at least he had the consolation of knowing that his soldiers were reasonably well trained, which was more than MacArthur and Valdes could be assured of their Filipino charges. With decreased funds for 1940 and 1941, the Philippine defense program, which had always been "operated on a shoestring," now existed on a severely skeletonized basis. In addition, the quality of the program still left much to be desired. Local cadres in some regions operated with virtual autonomy, creating their own training schedules and even devising their own forms of drill. In March, for example, Valdes discovered that units in certain outlying areas were learning the so-called "goose step" in close order drill, with "exaggerated movements of the body when marching to the flank, to the oblique or changing direction; raising the feet to about 10 inches from the ground at mark time and half step." When a mobilization exercise was attempted that spring, many reservists simply did not report and could not be located because they had changed residences without reporting changes of address. In some cases the trainees had moved to other islands, and by the time they returned to their former mobilization centers, the exercise had ended. Valdes in dismay issued a training memorandum calling upon company commanders to correct such matters and "all misunderstanding of duties at once."

Probably based on reports from Gunert's G-2, the War Department's opinion of the Philippine Army in June was that it "is of doubtful combat efficiency, lacking competent leadership above the company grades, important items of equipment requisite to a balanced force, and adequate supplies for an extended campaign." Grunert again proposed that the native force be federalized and placed under his more experienced officers. He suggested that such a plan could be financed from the fund of $52,000,000 which had accumulated in Philippine sugar excise taxes, much as the coconut oil excise fund was being used for economic improvements in the islands. His proposal on financing, which was endorsed by Quezon, was seriously considered in Washington, but it was not acted upon before December and invasion had come. In addition, Elizalde tried to get the Philippines included in the lend-lease program which was enacted that spring; a bill to the effect was introduced in the House, but died in committee.[3]

Civilian defense and economic mobilization preparations moved forward slowly in the spring of 1941. In April the Civilian Emergency Administration finally became active, under the headship of Secretary of Defense Teofilo Sison. The principal officials were a director of publicity and propaganda, a food administrator, an industrial production administrator, a national air raid warden, a fuel and transportation administrator, and the director of the Philippine Red Cross. At the same time the Commonwealth government began to tighten regulations on commercial and private flying areas, as well as on the purchase and use of radio transmitters, though enforcement of the latter was never effective. High Commissioner Sayre reported in June that some hoarding was already evident among the populace, who generally felt that war was near or at least a blockade of the islands. He also found that "the vicissitudes of world war, and fear of Japan's southward thrust, coupled with uncertainties as to post-independence political and economic policies served to reduce confidence. The result was curtailment of private ventures, plans for liquidation, and fairly heavy transfers of unemployed capital reserves to the United States." When the Manila *Bulletin's* forty-first anniversary edition was published on March 24, over 100 pages were devoted to the islands' ground, naval, and air defenses. The intention was obviously to boost public morale, but the wording implied that hostilities were expected soon. The civilians' anxieties were not assuaged when the Navy Department ordered the families of its personnel at Olongapo, Cavite, and other naval stations in the islands to return to the States in early 1941, which was soon followed by a similar order from the War Department regarding Army families. The old Army and Navy Club on Manila's waterfront had its busiest and saddest days that spring as parties and dances were staged there on the eve of the departures of various ships carrying servicemen's loved ones back to the United States. MacArthur, being a retired officer, was not subject to the orders recalling families; he and Mrs. MacArthur decided that they and their small son would stay together, whatever the ominous-looking future might hold.[4]

Despite the talk around Manila about impending war, MacArthur refused to believe the worst. In February he wrote Elizalde, in Washington, that a recent article in *Time* magazine "completely underestimates the fighting capacity of the Philippine Army." He added: "There has been a constant effort on the part of the Press, inspired no doubt, by imperialists to deprecate the potential ability of the Filipino along all lines, but especially in the arts of war. The purpose was undoubtedly to break down their sense of self-respect." In mid-May correspondent John Hersey visited MacArthur at his headquarters atop the old walled sector of Manila. The general was brimming with optimism and self-confidence and told Hersey, in no uncertain terms, that "if Japan entered the war, the Americans, the British and the Dutch could handle her with about half the forces they now have deployed in the Far East." The war in China, now four years old, has "eaten into the foundations of the highly complex economic and military structure of Japan," he stated. "About half the Japanese Army has been reduced in effectiveness from first-class to third-class standing," though MacArthur admitted that "the rest, which has not yet seen action, is still first-class." The military adviser told Hersey that the Japanese would not dare to push farther into Southeast Asia because the British, Dutch, and Americans there are "beginning to present a bristling united front." As for his own defense system, he remarked that "the Philippine situation looks sound; twelve Filipino divisions are already trained." A war between Japan and America was unlikely, he said, because "the Germans have told Japan not to stir up any more trouble in the Pacific. That is because Japan is helping Germany more by not fighting than she would by actually going to battle." This, he explained, was because Japan was tying down the American battleship fleet at Pearl Harbor, a large British force at Singapore, as well as Dutch and Australian military and naval units which would otherwise have been sent to the European and African theaters. Hersey commented, "The General is emphatic, analytic, precise, and seems very sure of what he says . . . You go out feeling a little brisker yourself, a little more cheery and more confident about things." [5] Such was the spell MacArthur could cast upon listeners — even when less than seven months remained before Japanese bombs would be falling on Manila.

2. *Summoned to Lead*

As early as January, 1941, the Philippine Department G-2 had recommended to Washington that an overall high command of Army forces in the Far East should be established, with Grunert as its head. Apparently, however, the War Department did not give the idea much study at the time. Sometime in April, MacArthur wrote Early, Roosevelt's secretary, asking him to approach the President with the idea of recalling him to active duty as commander of a unified Army command in the Far East. Early probably did so, but Roosevelt does not seem to have indicated his feelings on the matter to his secretary. That same month Grunert once again urged that the Philippine Army be mobilized and trained by his instructors. Joseph Stevenot, a leading Manila businessman, told Stimson in the latter's office on May 21 that there existed "a rather disturbing lack of cooperation between General Grunert commanding the Army forces there and Admiral Hart on the one side, and General MacArthur on the other." In his diary entry of that date Stimson recorded: "I then went into Marshall's office and arranged for an interview by which he could talk with Stevenot sometime this afternoon. Marshall incidentally told me that in case of trouble out there, they intended to recall General MacArthur into service again and place him in command." Available evidence does not indicate whether Roosevelt and Marshall had previously discussed the matter of MacArthur's recall, nor does it show which of them was instrumental in the selection. Meanwhile MacArthur, despairing of getting the command he had hoped for, notified Early that he would shortly close the military mission and move to San Antonio, Texas. In fact, he actually secured a reservation on the next ocean liner going to America, though, of course, he was not destined to make the trip. On May 29 he informed Marshall of his decision and stated, without revealing his source, that he knew that the Philippine Army was to be mobilized soon. It is difficult to believe that MacArthur was ready to retire; rather, he seems to have been trying to force the War Department to come to decisions on his own future and on the creation of a Far Eastern command.

On June 6 Brigadier General Leonard T. Gerow, acting head of the war plans division, recommended against the establishment of an Army command in the Far East since there was no present need for it. He suggested to Marshall that if MacArthur was recalled, it should be as Philippine Department commander.[6] Nevertheless, two weeks later Marshall wrote MacArthur:

In your letter of May 29th you state that the Philippine Army is to be absorbed by the United States Army in the near future and, consequently, you are closing out your Military Mission. At the present time the War Department plans are not so far reaching. Contingent upon the appropriation of sugar and excise tax funds, Grunert has recommended that about 75,000 troops of the Philippine Army engage in a period of training from three to nine months, in order to prepare them for the defense of the Philippines. While the decision as to the termination of the Military Mission is yours, the War Department plans do not contemplate taking over all responsibilities of your Mission in the near future.

Both the Secretary of War and I are much concerned about the situation in the Far East. During one of our discussions about three months ago it was decided that your outstanding qualifications and vast experience in the Philippines makes you the logical selection for the Army Commander in the Far East should the situation approach a crisis. The Secretary has delayed recommending your appointment as he does not feel the time has arrived for such action. However, he has authorized me to tell you that, at the proper time, he will recommend to the President that you be so appointed. It is my impression that the President will approve his recommendation.

This letter is also an acknowledgement of your letters to the President and to the Secretary of War. Please keep its contents confidential for the present.[7]

The letter to the President, to which Marshall referred, may have been MacArthur's letter to Early in late May; nothing is known of a letter to Stimson. The reference to the Stimson-Marshall conversation of about March must have been regarding a general talk, since, as noted in Stimson's diary, the Secretary learned of the definite decision about MacArthur in May.

The Second World War took a surprising and sudden turn on June 22 when German armies crossed the Russian frontier along a 2000-mile front, thereby forcing Great Britain and the Soviet Union into an awkward alliance. Hitler tried to pressure the Japanese government to make war against the U.S.S.R. also, which would have compelled Stalin to divide his forces between the European front and a Far Eastern front. But Japan had no intention of engaging her armed forces against Russia at that time. In fact, the Russo-German conflict was welcomed in Tokyo since it freed Japan of concern about the potential menace of Russia as Nipponese forces prepared to move farther into Southeast Asia. On July 2 in Tokyo a secret imperial conference of great importance was convened by Emperor Hirohito, with Prime Minister Konoye, Foreign Minister Matsuoka, War Minister Tojo, and other key leaders present. The decisions made at this meeting set in motion the final drama that led directly to war between Japan and America five months later. Plans were ratified to "advance into the Southern Regions," meaning southern China, French Indo-China, and Thailand at first: "The Imperial Government is determined to follow a policy which will result in the establishment of the Greater East Asia Co-Prosperity Sphere and world peace, no matter what international developments take place." All-out mobilization began shortly in Japan; the Army hastened its operational planning against Malaya, Singapore, Java, and the Philippines; and the Navy began preparing for its roles in the contemplated thrusts into Southeast Asia, including secret practice for the attack to be launched against Pearl Harbor. Yet Nomura was instructed to continue his conversations with Hull, just in case Japan might be able to secure by diplomacy what her troops were preparing to take by force otherwise.

On July 7 Commissioner J. M. Johnson of the Interstate Commerce Commission wrote MacArthur that a few days before at a Washington golf club he had chatted with Early, Joseph E. Davies, former ambassador to Russia, and other federal officials. Johnson suggested to the group that MacArthur ought to be appointed commander of all American forces in the Far East since he "is the best soldier that America has produced in a long time." Early responded, according to Johnson, by saying that "you had offered your services and a place was sought for you and that no suitable place had been found." [8] Not long afterward, however, War Department leaders began to undergo a change of attitude, and on July 17 Marshall approved the following recommendation of the war plans division:

> 1. That the President, by executive order, call into the service of the U.S. for the period of the emergency all organized military forces of the Commonwealth.
> 2. That General MacArthur be called to active duty in the grade of Major General and assigned as commander of Army Forces in the Far East.
> 3. That $10,000,000 of the President's Emergency Fund be allotted to cover the costs of mobilization and training of the Philippine Army for a period of three months.
> 4. That the training program of the Philippine Army for an additional six to nine months be financed from the sugar excise fund, or from other funds appropriated for this purpose.
> 5. That 425 Reserve officers be sent to the Philippines to assist in the mobilization and training of the Philippine Army.[9]

Two days later Grunert was notified by the War Department that "the level of defense reserves in the Philippine Department will be computed on the basis of 50,000 officers and men for a period of six months, less the reserves items that can be furnished by the Philippine Commonwealth for an approximate average of 30,000 officers and men of the Philippine Army." [10]

Already reports were being received in Washington that Nipponese convoys were headed toward South Indo-China, and on July 24 the news came that the Japanese occupation of South Indo-China was under way. The next day the War and Navy departments warned their commanders in the Pacific that a presidential order would be issued shortly freezing Japanese assets in the United States and that, though no immediate hostile activities were expected, "appropriate precautionary measures against possible eventualities" should be taken. That same day Stimson told Roosevelt that "due to the situation in the Far East, all practical steps should be taken to increase the defensive strength of the Philippine Islands." The Secretary of War presented the President with the draft of a proposed executive order calling the Philippine Army into active service as part of the United States Army and allocating the $10,000,000 from his emergency fund necessary for its mobilization and initial training. Stimson's communication had been preceded by reports to him that the Boeing B-17 "Flying Fortresses" in service with the Royal Air Force in Europe had achieved great successes, and, moreover, this model of bomber was being mass produced at a rate now that made large shipments of B-17's to the Philippines feasible. All at once the War Department was shifting from its view of the Philippines as an unprotected pawn to the notion that, with an adequate fleet of B-17's and other reinforcements, the islands could be held and might deter further Japanese expansion in Southeast Asia. According to some sources, MacArthur's "contagious optimism" about the progress of his defense program was also a factor in the swiftly changing position of the War Department.[11]

The 26th of July was an epochal day in Washington and Manila. Roosevelt issued executive orders closing the Panama Canal to Japanese shipping and freezing all Japanese assets in America, which meant that henceforth it would be impossible for Japan to sell or buy in the United States. The British and Dutch, furthermore, abrogated their commercial treaties with Japan. American newspapers, probably reflecting majority opinion in the nation, reacted exuberantly, the *New York Post*, for example, exclaiming, "Let there be no mistake, the United States must relentlessly apply its crushing strength." The *New York Times* praised Roosevelt for making it clear that "any action by Japan that threatens a legitimate American interest in the Far East should be met at once by efforts on our part to deal Japanese finance and industry and trade a deadly blow." But in Tokyo the reaction was hostile determination to continue the program of expansion southward. "Magic," the American code-breaking operation which had deciphered Japan's diplomatic codes, intercepted a message from the Nipponese foreign minister to his ambassador in Berlin in which he stated that the situation in the Western Pacific was "becoming so horribly strained that we cannot endure it much longer." He warned that Japan "must take immediate steps to break asunder this ever-strengthening chain of encirclement which is being woven under the guidance of and with the participation of England and the United States, acting like a cunning dragon seemingly asleep." [12]

Also on July 26 Roosevelt signed the order calling the Philippine Army into the service of the United States, the combined Army forces in the islands to be commanded by a general of the American Army designated by Stimson, though not specifically naming MacArthur. That same day the War Department established the new Far Eastern command and appointed MacArthur, with the rank of major general, as commander. The message which Marshall sent to MacArthur read:

Effective this date there is hereby constituted a command designated as the United States Army Forces in the Far East. This command will include the Philippine Department, forces of the Government of the Commonwealth of the Philippines called into the service of the armed forces of the United States for the period of the existing emergency, and such other forces as may be assigned to it. Headquarters United States Army Forces in the Far East will be established in Manila, Philippine Islands. You are hereby designated as Commanding General, United States Army Forces in the Far East. You are also designated as the General Officer United States Army referred to in a Military Order calling into the service of the armed forces of the United States the organized forces of the Government of the Commonwealth of the Philippines dated July 26, 1941. Orders calling you to active duty are being issued effective July 26, 1941. Report assumption of command by radio.[13]

MacArthur jubilantly and promptly acknowledged the orders and reported his assumption of command that day. Two days later, on the 28th, he received notice that Roosevelt had appointed him temporary lieutenant general, with date of rank from the 27th. When MacArthur first received the news of his USAFFE command, Sutherland remarked with a sense of foreboding, "You know, General, it adds up to an almost insurmountable task." MacArthur replied, "These islands must and will be defended. I can but do my best." Later he issued a press statement which said: "I am glad to be able to serve my country at this critical time. This action of the American government in establishing this new command can only mean that it intends to maintain, at any cost and effort, its full rights in the Far East. It is quite evident that its determination is immutable and that its will is indomitable. To this end both the American and Filipino soldiery can be expected to give their utmost." [14]

Congratulations poured into MacArthur's office from friends and well-wishers in the Philippines and the United States. As might be expected, Fellers, then military attaché in Cairo, was one, also Courtney Whitney, who was in Washington — both of whom would join his staff later in Australia. The file of existing letters and telegrams regarding his USAFFE appointment numbers nearly a hundred. Ruperto S. Cristobal, president of the Philippine Labor Congress, the main federation of labor groups in the islands, sent MacArthur a resolution passed by his congress which stated that since MacArthur had "proved friendly not only to the Filipino officialdom but also to the lowest member of the Philippine Army and the Filipino community," he could count on the "unswerving loyalty of the Filipino Labor" in the approaching conflict. The Katipunan, a league of opposition parties (including the sometimes violent Sakdalista) named for an old secret insurrectionist society, conveyed its congratulations to MacArthur. Miguel R. Cornejo, its president, stated that, on behalf of the Katipunan's 100,000 members, "we will demonstrate our undying faith in America and our love for Philippine freedom and democracy which she has implanted in this part of the world by offering our lives when the hour comes for the sacrifice." There was little doubt that most Filipinos had great faith in MacArthur and preferred him to any other general as their leader in defending the islands. The occasion also brought Quezon back into enthusiastic support of MacArthur and his defense efforts, the Philippine president's national role now assuming more importance in rallying his people for all-out mobilization. The USAFFE appointment also seemed to jar MacArthur into a new awareness of the Japanese menace, though he intuitively concluded that the Nipponese would surely not attack before the spring of 1942.[15]

3. An Impossible Task

MacArthur's first order of business as USAFFE commander was to appoint his staff and organize his headquarters. For his new staff he retained most of his main subordinates from the military advisory mission and obtained the rest from the headquarters staff of the Philippine Department. His chief of staff and deputy chief of staff continued to be Sutherland and Richard Marshall. As aides he kept Huff, formerly his naval adviser, and added Lieutenant Colonel LeGrande A. Diller. The staff section posts were filled by Colonel Charles P. Stivers (G-1), Colonel Willoughby (G-2), Colonel Constant L. Irwin (G-3), Colonel Lewis C. Beebe (G-4), Colonel Carl H. Seals (adjutant general), Brigadier General Edward P. King (field artillery), Colonel Marquat (antiaircraft defense), Colonel Spencer B. Akin (signal), Colonel Casey (engineers), Colonel Charles C. Drake (quartermaster), and Colonel George Hirsh (ordnance). MacArthur early asked for Major General Lewis H. Brereton, commanding the Third Air Force in the States, to serve as his air commander, but

Brereton did not arrive until the first week of November. The principal tactical commanders who were officially appointed later that autumn included Brigadier General Jonathan M. Wainwright (North Luzon Force), Brigadier General George M. Parker (South Luzon Force), Colonel William F. Sharp (Visayan-Mindanao Force), Brigadier General George F. Moore (Manila and Subic Bay defenses), and Colonel James R. N. Weaver (Provisional Tank Group). By November and early December most of the above officers had been promoted a rank higher, and some of them would be advanced again within two months. Most of the men on MacArthur's headquarters staff were in their forties, the oldest being only fifty-two. They were generally regarded by other USAFFE officers as a competent and highly efficient group. The commanders of the field forces were also able officers who would prove their mettle in the months ahead. In the higher echelons of the USAFFE command structure MacArthur was not wanting for competent officers.

The Philippine Department soon became virtually a service command, its chief function being the training and supply of the ten reserve divisions of the Philippine Army whose mobilization began on September 1. The principal American Army unit in the islands was the Philippine Division, which Wainwright commanded until he took over the North Luzon command in November. This division's fate was similar to that of the Philippine Department in general: its units were scattered, and many of its personnel, especially officers, were detailed as instructors of the Filipino forces. For some reason, possibly further friction, MacArthur recommended in October that Grunert be relieved as departmental commander: "It would be advantageous to relieve him, as I am loath, as long as he is here, to contract the functions of the Department Commander." The War Department recalled Grunert to the States and appointed MacArthur in his stead, which post he assumed on October 31 while retaining his USAFFE command.[16]

As reported by Gerow to Marshall on July 30, the strength of the forces in the Philippines (excluding naval personnel) was thus:[17]

1. *Regular Army*
   Coast Artillery Corps ————————————————— 4,400
   Air Corps ———————————————————————— 1,750
   Infantry ———————————————————————— 1,700
   Philippine Division ——————————————————— 8,500
   Supporting Units (Philippine Scouts) ————— 5,200

2. *Philippine Army*
   Regular Army (plus 616 Reserve officers on
       active duty) ———————————————————— 4,000
   Reserve Divisions (10 at approx. 7,600 each) ——— 76,000
   Grand Total ————————————————————— 101,550

The grand total looks impressive until it is remembered that the reserve divisions of the Philippine Army existed only on paper at that time.

The training and deployment of the USAFFE forces were dependent, in large measure, upon the nature of MacArthur's plan of defense. For nearly a half year he had been working on a plan which he felt was far superior to the War Department's WPO-3, at least in its provisions for the Philippines. As early as February — long before he was considered for a Far Eastern command — he proposed to Marshall that the Philippine Islands as a whole should be defended in case of war, and the enemy should be repulsed on the beaches. This, of course, was contrary to the Orange plan of defending only the entrance to Manila Bay, and the chief of staff did not indicate to him that he would propose such a revision to the Joint Board. But the War Department was agreeable to sending him some 8-inch coastal defense guns which he had requested to block the straits leading into the southern inland seas of the Philippines; the shipments, he was told, would begin in June. Perhaps MacArthur interpreted this reinforcement for the southern islands to mean that Marshall would submit his proposed expansion of the defenses to the Joint Board.

When MacArthur received the new war plan, Rainbow-5, in October, he was surprised to find that it contemplated a defense area limited to the entrances to Manila and Subic bays and by forces already in the islands, with no reinforcements to be expected and the loss of the Philippines implicitly accepted. In a heated message to the War Department, he pointed out that the new plan did not take into consideration the strength of USAFFE with its growing Filipino forces, which he expected to number nearly 200,000 by early 1942. Since, he argued, the Manila Bay area could not be adequately defended if the enemy seized the southern islands, where they could establish air bases, he urged prompt modification of the war plan to include an active defense of the entire archipelago: "The wide scope of enemy operations, especially aviation, now makes imperative the broadening of the concept of Philippine defense, and the strength and composition of the defense forces here are believed to be sufficient to accomplish such a mission." This time Marshall said he would present his plan to the Joint Board. Without waiting for further word from Washington, MacArthur organized tactical commands for North Luzon, South Luzon, and the Visayan-Mindanao region, deploying nearly half of the Philippine Army in the islands south of Luzon.

On November 21 Marshall notified him that the Joint Board had given its approval to the revision of the Rainbow plan authorizing USAFFE to defend the entire archipelago. He was also told that USAFFE would be expected, in case of war with Japan, to support the Navy in air strikes against enemy shipping and installations and cooperate with the British and Dutch forces in defense of the Malay Barrier. Recent air reinforcements to the Philippines, together with glowing reports from MacArthur about the progress of training of the Filipinos, seem to have been key considerations of Marshall and the Joint Board in revising the Rainbow plan. As it would develop in the months ahead, the main portion of personnel and munitions in the islands south of Luzon would not be involved in large-scale combat and would be practically useless in reinforcing the units on Luzon since the Japanese would quickly command the air and sea lanes from the southern islands.[18]

On August 15 MacArthur held a conference of the principal commanding officers of the Philippine Department, Philippine Army, and USAFFE headquarters sections to plan the mobilization and training of the Philippine Army. Since the trainee program of the past four years had required facilities for only 20,000 or fewer troops at a time, a rush construction program was begun to prepare housing for the 76,000 Filipinos to be inducted that fall. Mobilization was to take place in three stages, with ten infantry regiments (one from each reserve division) to be called up on September 1, the second infantry regiments of the same divisions to be mobilized in early November, and the third regiments, completing the first ten reserve divisions, to be called into service at the end of November. About forty American Army officers and approximately twenty American or Scout noncommissioned officers were to be detailed to each reserve division as instructors. Existing Philippine Army schools were to be enlarged quickly, and a number of new ones to train specialists of all kinds were to be set up.

MacArthur himself was soon working day and night and driving his headquarters officers at a grueling pace. According to a correspondent, "They all seemed to be talking on two telephones at once." One officer, and perhaps others on MacArthur's staff, collapsed from nervous exhaustion and had to be hospitalized several days. On August 30, as the first Filipino inductees were preparing to begin their training, MacArthur enthusiastically reported to Marshall that the defense preparations were "progressing by leaps and bounds" and the Filipinos' attitude had changed from "a feeling of defeatism to the highest state of morale I have ever seen." With the pending arrival of more troops, munitions, and aircraft which the War Department was sending, MacArthur declared that "the development of a completely adequate defense force will be rapid." The USAFFE commander was confident that the Philippines would be impervious to invasion — by April, 1942.[19]

The American officers who served as commanders and instructors of the Philippine Army that fall found their training problems to be staggering. The language barriers, of course, would be obvious from the first day of camp onward. Typical was the experience of Colonel Glen R. Townsend, commander of the 11th Infantry Regiment, which began its training on September 1 at Camp Holmes, near Baguio:

> . . . About 50% of the strength of the regiment was made up of Christian Filipinos, chiefly from the Ilocos provinces on the coast of the China Sea, Abra, and from the Cagayan Valley provinces of Cagayan and Isabella. The other half of the regiment was comprised of pagan Igorots from Mountain Province. There were representatives of nearly all the former head-hunting tribes, including Bontocs, Ifugaos, Kalingas, Ilongots, Beuguets and Lepantos. The units of the 1st Battalion consisted almost entirely of Christian Filipinos. The 2nd Battalion was almost exclusively Igorots. The 3rd Battalion and the Headquarters Battalion were mixed. There was no objection to this mixing of lowland Filipinos with the mountain people except that it did increase the language difficulties.
>
> With personnel drawn from so many different sources it was inevitable that lack of a common language should be one of the main difficulties encountered in training the regiment. Nearly a score of different dialects were spoken by members of the unit. Ilocano was the prevailing native dialect but it was understood by only about ½ the enlisted personnel and by about ¾ of the officers. English was understood to some extent by about 20% of the enlisted personnel; and it was spoken with more or less fluency by practically all the officers. All orders and instructions had to be translated into the several dialects in order to be understood by all; and as the translators often had but an im-

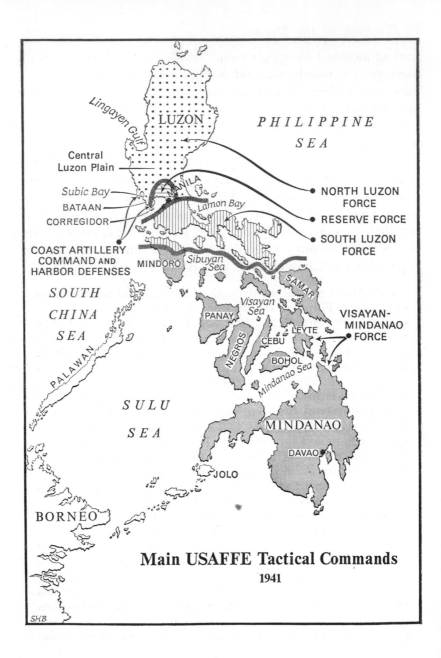

Main USAFFE Tactical Commands
1941

perfect knowledge of English the results were sometimes amusing, and often serious. On occasions when it was necessary for an American officer to address the entire regiment a minimum of five instructors had to be employed. Even then a considerable number of men could not understand what was said.[20]

Yet this regiment would be the mainstay of the 11th Division when war came, the other two regiments of that division being even less prepared as cohesive combat units.

The usual camp housing consisted of temporary barracks with thatch roofs, bamboo walls, sod floors, and bamboo-strip bunks, with little or no plumbing and sanitation facilities. Often water had to be hauled from several miles away. The camps used by the Philippine Army before 1941 were in better shape, but with three times as many men being inducted, most of the new housing was only about 80 per cent completed when the war began. The following comments by Sharp about the personal equipment of his troops were applicable to conditions throughout the Philippine Army: "There was a deplorable lack of essential supplies of all kinds . . . The clothing and equipment at the cadre camps was old and much of it not fit to use. The shoes were rubber soled of the tennis type. They had so deteriorated from age and use that most of the men were barefooted within a few days. There was a serious shortage of clothes, blankets and mosquito bars from the very beginning." There were no entrenching tools, raincoats, gas masks, or steel helmets to issue to the Filipino soldiers. "Those supplies available locally," said Sharp, "such as cleaning materials, toilet paper, target materials, lumber, nails, etc., were purchased and charged to USAFFE funds. This was necessary in order to function at all." [21]

The Philippine Scouts who served as assistant instructors and sometimes as instructors and company commanders were generally well trained and efficient. But Brigadier General Albert M. Jones, who at first commanded the 51st Division of the Philip-

pine Army and later the South Luzon Force, found that "practically no Filipino officers above the grade of captain were capable of functioning properly as staff officers and it was necessary
to replace them with young inexperienced American officers
when troops went into action." Sharp was shocked to discover
that "there were many 1st Sergeants and Company Clerks who
could neither read nor write."

As MacArthur had found in practice mobilizations in previous times, rarely did the Filipino reservists recall what they
had learned during their stints of five and a half months of active duty. Likewise, the American officers who were now rushed
in to mold combat units out of the masses of inductees learned
the same sad truth. Jones said his instructors reported that
"most of their men were quite proficient in close order drill, but
beyond that they seemed to have had no training at all." Wainwright further asserted that their pre-mobilization training "was
inadequate, particularly in rifle marksmanship and scouting and
patrolling." According to Brigadier General Clifford Bluemel,
his 31st Division enlisted men — all Filipinos who had had five
and a half months of training previously — seemed to be able
to do only two things well: "one, when an officer appeared, to
yell attention in a loud voice, jump up and salute; the other, to
demand 3 meals per day." On the other hand, Townsend said
that the inductee did possess certain assets: "Chief among these
was the eagerness of the Filipino soldier to learn. Disciplinary
problems were virtually nonexistent. And because all his life
he had been accustomed to doing with little it was not difficult
to maintain his morale. A reasonable allowance of rice; a small
amount of meat or fish each day; and fair and considerate treatment were about all that was needed." Some American officers,
however, did encounter disciplinary problems and were quite
disturbed because USAFFE and Philippine Army headquarters
would not institute courts-martial until after war was declared.[22]

Because time ran out before the three-month program of

training at the regimental level was completed, the Filipino troops had no training whatsoever in divisional exercises. Not a single division had been completely mobilized when the Japanese attack came. Furthermore, not one regiment or even company had attained its authorized strength, most being 50 to 75 per cent of full strength. No antitank units were ever organized, and most divisions went into combat without their field artillery regiments. The 11th Division's case was typical: it was scheduled to have a 1300-man field artillery regiment equipped with twenty-four 75-mm. guns, but that regiment did not go into action until late December, as the division was withdrawing into Bataan, and even then had only 60 per cent of its manpower and eighteen guns. To make matters worse, the artillerymen were poorly trained and contributed little to the support of the infantry when they did begin firing. As for practice with basic infantry weapons, Jones stated flatly that "many units went into battle without ever having fired their basic arm." As in the past, training was severely restricted by lack of weapons, even of the obsolescent models of rifles, machine guns, and mortars. Also there was a serious shortage of spare parts for the weapons on hand, and much of the ammunition proved to be "duds," including 70 per cent of the Stokes mortar projectiles.[23]

Some shortages were alleviated by shrewd improvisation and exploitation of local resources and civilian labor, as Sharp reported:

Civil Affairs Officers were appointed for each Province, coordinated through the Civil Affairs Officer at Force Headquarters, who in turn worked in close cooperation with the G-4 and the G-1. These civil affairs officers were carefully selected; prerequisites being unquestioned loyalty and ability. They were the outstanding leaders of their communities; Americans, with no political axe to grind. These officers advised the Commander and staff on matters pertaining to civil affairs within their

Philippine Military Adviser

province, and handled for the Commander in accordance with his orders, or approved policies, matters in connection with such military supervision of civil affairs as, the operation of civilian transportation, public utilities of all kinds, the distribution of foodstuffs, the rationing of motor fuels, etc.

The civilian communities and the Provincial Governments responded exceptionally well. They also were geared for peacetime and it was often necessary to reorganize, expand, and speed-up. Many prominent civilians, anxious to have a part in the war effort, volunteered their services, and were used both in the army and in civilian capacities. The Quartermaster Organization was composed almost entirely of civilians, some were commissioned as officers in the Quartermaster Corps and some served as civilian employees of the Quartermaster Corps. At the beginning of the war the Force had only a few motor vehicles, and no maintenance or operating personnel. Necessary vehicles were requisitioned. Drivers, mechanics, and operating personnel were recruited from available civilian sources. The local clergy flocked to the colors as chaplains. There were few signal supplies and no signal troops. Signal equipment was improvised locally and necessary personnel recruited to operate radio networks, lay wire, etc.

Factories were started for the manufacture of shoes, uniforms, underwear, socks, haversacks, mosquito bars, cartridge belts, hats, mess kits, cots, rifle and machine gun parts, gas masks, hand grenades, and canned emergency rations. These factories did not already exist, but necessity required that they be set in operation as soon as possible. Such materials as were available were used, and improvisation was the rule.

The Ordnance problem was by far the most difficult and serious. Soldiers must have arms and ammunition. The troops were armed with old Enfield rifles, mostly defective. New extractors had to be manufactured locally by the thousands. Many of the .30 cal. machine guns were unserviceable. The .50 cal. machine guns were obsolete in type, and without water cooling devices. The mortars were of the old Stokes 3″ type. There were no anti-tank guns. And the artillery had 8 ancient 2.95 guns, 3 of which had no sights. There were no rifle or hand grenades. Everything possible was done to remedy this situation. Machine shops were put to work making the parts necessary to make the

rifles and machine guns operate. Water cooling devices for the
.50 cal. machine guns were improvised and manufactured.
Many different types of hand grenades were made. Bolos were
made and issued to those men without other arms — the so-
called "Bolo Battalions." A few anti-tank mines were made
(and successfully used on the Digos Front). Unfortunately
there was no way to make small arms ammunition.[24]

Although units training on Luzon, especially in the vicinity
of Manila, might have been expected to be in much better shape
as to equipment and supplies than Sharp's command, the story
of shortages and improvisations was much the same throughout
the archipelago. In neither training nor equipment would the
Philippine Army be remotely prepared for the combat which it
would face in December. By the beginning of that month, however, Wainwright felt that at least "the American and Philippine Scout organizations were fit, trained in combat principles
and ready to take the field in any emergency." But these units
constituted less than one fourth of the defensive force which
MacArthur was counting on to carry out his orders "to prevent
a landing. In the event a landing was made, it was to attack and
destroy the landing force." [25]

MacArthur's order of December 3 to his field commanders
that the beaches must "be held at all costs" might have been
impossible to fulfill even if the USAFFE forces had been ten
times larger than they were. The reason, as made clear in war
plans division studies for two decades, was that the enemy
could choose his landing points along thousands of miles of
beaches of the archipelago's 7000 or more islands. Wainwright's
North Luzon Force of four infantry divisions and one cavalry
regiment, all Philippine Army and understrength, was responsible for defending the coastline of Luzon north of Manila, a
stretch of over 600 miles of shores. The South Luzon Force,
with two Philippine Army divisions, was to guard the rest of the
island south of Manila, which included 400 miles or more of

coastline, as well as the northern coast of Mindoro. Jones conservatively figured that the area "included 250 miles of possible landing beaches," excluding the Lamon Bay region since "the Navy had stated that a landing on this beach was improbable at this time of the year due to the monsoons rendering the waters unsuitable for landing operations." (In December one of the main Japanese forces would land there.) Sharp's Visayan-Mindanao Force, comprising three Philippine Army divisions, had the impossible task of defending the islands of Panay, Negros, Cebu, Bohol, Samar, Leyte, Mindanao, and southern Mindoro. The shorelines of these islands totaled several thousand miles, and most of the beaches were inaccessible by roads. Lack of inter-island shipping and the large Japanese settlement at Davao were other problems faced by Sharp. The only two areas of defense where the units assigned could reasonably hope to cover their positions were the zone of the Reserve Force, along the northeast shore of Manila Bay between Manila and San Fernando, Pampanga, where two infantry divisions were located (including most of the Philippine Division) and Moore's harbor defenses, consisting of the fortifications at the entrances to Manila and Subic bays.

When MacArthur ordered the field commands to have their beaches manned by the end of November, only the first regiments mobilized in each reserve division could go on guard duty, since the other regiments were still at training camps. Thus the number of beaches actually under guard was very limited. Moreover, there was little time left to construct beach obstacles and fortifications. Fortunately in the deployment of his meager forces, MacArthur correctly anticipated that the main Japanese invasion force would land along the shores of Lingayen Gulf, in northwestern Luzon. So most of the available troops of the North Luzon Force were concentrated there at the end of November, although in personnel and munitions the defense was inadequate even for that limited assignment.[26]

Moore, who was in charge of the coast artillery and harbor defenses of Manila and Subic bays, had his own special worries. Under him were four regiments of American and Scout troops, one of which was an antiaircraft unit and the other three assigned to the seacoast artillery batteries. Moore observed that "this personnel was insufficient to provide a complete manning detail for all the armament and no troops were available for beach defense except by dual assignment of the Coast Artillery." On Corregidor, the tadpole-shaped island which formed the heart of the defenses of the Manila Bay entrance, 800 prisoners from Bilibid Prison, Manila, were used said Moore, "for road and railway maintenance, loading and unloading cargo and for general utility labor." In addition, Moore employed several thousand civilians in last-minute activities to ready his defenses for combat. The seacoast armament at the several island forts was of pre-1914 vintage, but was adequate for its purpose of denying the bay entrance to enemy vessels. As it turned out, however, the big guns would never fire on Japanese ships because they would never attempt to force the entrance. Moore said that his seacoast batteries "were not adequately resistant to air or ground artillery high angle fire attack and, as situated and equipped with ammunition for use against naval targets, were generally incapable of efficiently contributing to the landward defense of the fortresses." Also his antiaircraft batteries were antiquated, and their ammunition was not effective at high altitudes. Moreover, Moore noted that his 3-inch guns, "due to the necessity of situating them practically on the targets to be protected and to limitations of design, were incapable of firing on attacking aircraft before the bomb release points had been reached." Fortunately the huge Malinta Tunnel and its laterals on Corregidor had been largely finished in 1940–41 and were equipped with reinforced walls, an electric car line, ventilating blowers, hospital facilities (but few medical supplies), maintenance shops, and storage areas for munitions. Moore admitted that the tunnel system was "not complete in many details as planned," but its shelters would prove indispensable in the conduct of the approaching campaign. Unfortunately overlooked, however, was provision for adequate fortifications along the tips of Bataan and Cavite provinces facing Corregidor. The Nipponese would effectively utilize these points in two months to pour artillery fire onto the island fortresses.[27]

Weaver's Provisional Tank Group had only 108 light tanks, forty-six half-tracks, and no medium or heavy tanks. His group was not even formed until seventeen days before war began, so late were the arrivals of most of the vehicles. By the first of December they were all located between Clark Field and Fort Stotsenburg, about sixty miles north of Manila and in the command area of the North Luzon Force. Weaver complained that his tanks lacked sufficient supplies of gasoline, spare parts, ammunition, and trained crews. The location assigned for tank parks was not the most desirable, commented Weaver: "It was at once obvious that an emergency move from the tank parks in darkness would be disastrous, the tank position under Watch Hill being amongst hundreds of standard drums of 100-octane gasoline and the complete bomb reserve of Clark Field — these items being irregularly scattered throughout the thick cover singly and in twos and threes, and covered with grass and palm fronds." Weaver also lamented that there was no time to conduct field exercises in which tanks worked in support of ground troops. In fact, so unfamiliar were the USAFFE soldiers with the design of Weaver's tanks that when war came, claimed Weaver, American troops fired on his vehicles and one infantry officer "at least was known to have approached a Japanese light tank to talk to the crew near Damortis, thinking it was an American tank." Weaver admitted, though, that some of his own men were not much more familiar with the tanks since about one third of them had never been inside a tank until two weeks before war was declared.[28]

Drake, who served in the dual capacity of quartermaster chief for USAFFE and the Philippine Department, faced insurmountable problems of procurement, maintenance, and distribution of supplies and equipment. He was confronted with "a complete paucity of experienced quartermaster officers," and the troops under his command constituted about one per cent of the USAFFE personnel strength, which was "ridiculously low," in his words. "Every effort was made to increase the Quartermaster Corps personnel," he said, "but very little came of it. The Quartermaster General in Washington was fully informed many times of this condition by letter and radio but his hands were tied and he could do little or nothing." Like the field commanders who turned to civilian assistance, Drake said, "We relied on civilians, both Americans and Filipinos, to meet our needs, and approximately 5,000 of them including the British, Danes, Czechs, and Norwegians, volunteered and performed heroic work in the Supply, Motor Transport, and Water Transport Services. They gave their services unstintingly without thought of any compensation." Besides lack of personnel, Drake was continuously in need of more supplies, trucks, and every kind of equipment to get his job done. His frustration was sometimes aggravated by bewildering responses of the War Department to his requisitions. For example, lacking tank trucks to supply vehicles in the field commands, Drake placed an order for 18,200 empty 55-gallon steel drums to use in distributing gasoline to field vehicles. A short time later, to his utter surprise, he received a shipment of 300,000 gallons of motor vehicle fuel in 55-gallon drums, though he had not dared to ask for the gasoline itself. Yet other more pressing needs of the quartermaster were not met by the War Department, undoubtedly because the items or the shipping spaces were not available. Of great bearing for the future was MacArthur's decision to have Drake set up advance quartermaster depots at four locations in the Central Luzon Plain, rather than concentrating the stores on Bataan. This, of course, was in accord with his plan to "fight it out on the beaches," but in late December these advance depots would be overrun by the Japanese and the USAFFE force would withdraw to Bataan without adequate provisions.[29]

The reasons for the unpreparedness of the Philippine Army when it was mobilized are manifold and largely predate 1941. The Joint Army and Navy Board had never pursued a consistent course or established a long-range policy regarding the defense of the Philippines. Indeed, the Army and Navy chiefs reversed themselves on the eve of war and yielded to MacArthur's grandiose notion of trying to defend the entire archipelago with a force which would have had difficulty holding even the Corregidor-Bataan region. Quezon and the Philippine National Assembly waxed hot and cold on the defense program, and unfortunately they had chosen to de-emphasize it during the critical two years before the coming of war. It may be that Quezon's neutrality scheme might have meant less devastation for his nation, but that decision belonged to the United States government, which halfheartedly chose to retain the islands a while longer but not to build up its defense system there. Though strapped for funds in the late 1930's, the War Department would have invested wisely if it had treated the Philippine Army like the National Guard and subsidized it on a per capita basis. In July, 1940, MacArthur had pleaded with Washington for a yearly subsidy of just $50.00 per Filipino trainee, but he was turned down; that same year the National Guard received $45,000,000 in federal funds on a strength basis of 205,000 men.[30] Furthermore, the Philippine Department headquarters, even under the vigorous leadership of Grunert, must share some of the blame for the pitiful status of the Philippine Army to 1941. That department never gave MacArthur's mission more than nominal support, though in 1935 the War Department had clearly set forth the development of the native defense program as the primary peacetime mission of the Philippine Department. In fact, the surprise of many Philippine Department officers at the woeful condition of the Filipino soldiers and facilities in September, 1941, suggests how loose the coordination had been between the two commands. Grunert and some of his staff knew the truth about the Philippine Army before its mobilization, of course, but it is hard to understand why the Filipino forces had to be federalized before receiving a larger detail of instructors from the Philippine Department.

Finally, MacArthur himself must bear a large share of the blame for the pitiful situation of the fall of 1941, which would soon lead to military disaster. He undoubtedly did his best with the men, matériel, and meager funds he was allotted from 1936 to 1941, and he was surely the most logical choice among American generals for the task of building a Filipino defense force. But his overconfidence and unjustified optimism as to the abilities of himself, his staff, and the untried Filipino soldiers unfortunately became a contagion which ultimately affected even the War Department and the Joint Army and Navy Board. As late as November 28, 1941, Marshall, in response to an enthusiastic message from MacArthur, replied with satisfaction: "The Secretary of War and I were highly pleased to receive your report that your command is ready for any eventuality." Furthermore, MacArthur's bold and successful move to get the Rainbow plan revised to comply with his own strategy came at such a late stage that confusion in deployment of troops and distribution of supplies resulted. The plan which would be followed when the Japanese invasion came would be "neither fish nor fowl," neither MacArthur's planned "last-ditch" stand on the beaches nor the Orange and Rainbow plans for immediate withdrawal of all ground forces to the Bataan-Corregidor "citadel" defense. The inadequate stockpiling of rations, medicines, munitions, and other supplies on Bataan was caused, in large part, by the effort to create a defense system for all of the archipelago. An Army historian has offered perhaps the politest comment about MacArthur's last-minute plan of defense: "Fate allowed insufficient time and matériel, manpower and training. What this impressive plan might have developed in another six months, had the Japanese attack been delayed so long, is a matter for diverting but fruitless speculation." [31]

4. *Time Runs Out*

It has been charged by some MacArthur devotees that the War Department stood by idly and did not try to reinforce the Philippines after the creation of USAFFE. Time expired before adequate reinforcements arrived in the islands, but the War Department was not negligent in its efforts to meet MacArthur's needs, though both the department and the USAFFE commander were slow to awaken to the immediacy of the menace.

Washington's endeavors to provide aircraft for the Philippines were impressive. In July, 1941, two pursuit groups of 130 fighters and four heavy bombardment groups of 272 bombers, with sixty-eight in reserve, were allocated for shipment or ferrying to the Philippines. B-17's were flown by a circuitous route from Hawaii to Midway and Wake, then down to Port Moresby and Australia, and finally northward to the Philippines. It was necessary, of course, to bypass the vicinity of the Japanese bases in the Marianas, Carolines, and Marshalls, the mandated island groups in the Central Pacific. Plans were developed and construction of runways was begun for a new air route via Christmas, Canton, Fiji, New Caledonia, and Townsville to the Philippines, but hostilities commenced before the new route could be put to use. General Brereton, who arrived in Manila in early November to organize the Far East Air Force, spent much of his time in the remaining weeks before war negotiating with Australian and Free French authorities along the southern route to try to accelerate the development of airfields for the B-17's which were scheduled to be coming in December and later. By the first week of December, in spite of the inability to get the southern route operative, Brereton had seventy-four heavy and medium bombers, 175 pursuit planes, and fifty-eight miscellaneous military aircraft in his V Bomber Command, V Interceptor Command, and Far East Service Command. Not only did his air force have seventy-six more planes than the Hawaiian Department by then, but Brereton's squadrons included thirty-five B-17's and 107 Curtiss P-40E's compared to twelve B-17's and thirty-nine P-40E's in Hawaii, these models being the most modern in production in the United States at that time. In November the air staff in Washington decided to send "all modernized B-17's" in the United States to the Philippines, and several days later it allocated all Consolidated B-24's (new heavy bombers) to the Far East Air Force. According to the official Army Air Forces history of the war, "So serious was the situation in the Far East that even the twelve B-17's of the Hawaiian Air Force were under consideration for transfer to the Philippines. The priority which the Far East Air Force now occupied not only disrupted the training activities of the Hawaiian Air Force, but it also relegated the air defense needs of Hawaii to a secondary place." But the Japanese would attack before the majority of bombers and pursuits allocated to the Philippines had arrived.

The aircraft which Brereton had when the fighting started were in quantity and quality the most formidable of any American overseas department. But there was not room for adequate dispersion of them, particularly the heavy bombers, since the number of airfields in the Philippines was small. Only one, Clark Field, near Fort Stotsenburg, could handle B-17's until Del Monte Field, in northern Mindanao, was partially completed the first week of December. On December 4 Brereton ordered two squadrons of B-17's to be moved down to Del Monte, but, for reasons to be discussed in the second volume of this work, half of the B-17's of the Far East Air Force were still concentrated at Clark Field when war erupted.

The air warning service and the antiaircraft defenses in the Philippines lagged behind the progress in obtaining modern military aircraft. Since he had only two radar sets in operation by early December, MacArthur was compelled to rely upon a primitive system of native air watchers stationed at various points in northern Luzon. An aircraft warning battalion and adequate radar equipment were being readied for shipment to the islands, but never got there. Moreover, the airfields, except for Clark, were virtually without antiaircraft protection, so scarce were the 3-inch and 37-mm. antiaircraft guns then in use. The 3-inchers, furthermore, had for ammunition only shells with powder-train fuses of low-altitude range; enemy aircraft which flew above 27,000 feet could bomb with impunity. Without sufficient facilities for dispersion of aircraft and without adequate air warning and antiaircraft weapons, the comparatively large and modern collection of bombers and pursuits based in the Philippines would become helpless ground targets for enemy attackers.[32]

Two days after his USAFFE appointment in late July, Mac-Arthur had received word from Washington that "no additional forces, except approximately 400 reserve officers to assist in training of the Philippine Army, or additional equipment over and above that now authorized will be available for your command in the near future." Within a week, however, the chief of staff had reversed this, and from then until December the War Department leaders eagerly helped MacArthur in every way possible. From August onward, MacArthur sent requisitions almost daily for supplies of all types — antitank weapons, antiaircraft guns, hospital beds, C rations, gasoline, and a host of other items. Probably correctly, MacArthur emphasized matériel rather than personnel reinforcements, though he surely could have used more specialists and trained personnel. When in September Marshall offered him a National Guard division, MacArthur said that he preferred to have the precious shipping space used for matériel reinforcements: "Equipment and supply of existing forces are the prime essential . . . I am confident if these steps are taken with sufficient speed that no further major reinforcement will be necessary for accomplishment of defense mission." In the next two months his requisitions for supplies received prompt approval and the highest priority in the War Department. By late November recent arrivals in Manila included two fifty-four-tank armored battalions, an ordnance company, twenty-five 75-mm. guns with self-propelled mounts, and an antiaircraft regiment equipped with twelve 3-inch and twenty-four 37-mm. guns. MacArthur, of course, had requested much more, including over 84,000 Garand M-1 rifles, 125,000 steel helmets, and hundreds of field artillery pieces and machine guns. In a single request, on October 1, he placed an order for 360,000 cotton sox, 240,000 cotton shirts, 240,000 flannel shirts, 240,000 cotton trousers, 120,000 pairs of service shoes, 120,000 leggins, 120,000 raincoats, 120,000 denim hats, 120,000 denim coats, and 120,000 denim trousers — all for the Philippine Army. The quartermaster general in Washington responded favorably, but noted that "at least 60 days will be required to procure the items requested."

In trying to fill MacArthur's orders, the War Department was at the same time endeavoring to meet lend-lease commitments to Great Britain, China, and the Soviet Union. There were shortages of many of the items requested since production was not yet meeting mobilization needs; a certain degree of confusion in processing requisitions existed as an inevitable attendant of the hastily expanded military establishment; and, perhaps most crucial, the War Department had difficulty finding transports and cargo vessels to ship men and matériel to the Philippines or any overseas departments. MacArthur protested to the Navy Department on one occasion when he learned of its plan to convert three transports into escort carriers, the USAFFE commander arguing that such would delay by two months the delivery of desperately needed men and supplies to him. Though Admiral Harold R. Stark, the chief of naval operations, agreeably postponed the conversions, large backlogs of personnel and equipment scheduled for the Philippines would be tied up at American ports when the war started. A last-minute concerted effort by Army, Navy, and shipping authorities resulted in a new shipping schedule to try to meet MacArthur's needs, with nine vessels to sail in November and December for the Philippines. They were scheduled to bring MacArthur two bombardment groups, one pursuit group, a reconnaissance squadron, an infantry regiment, a field artillery brigade, two light artillery battalions, and several service units. But, though some of the ships were at sea when war came, none was destined to reach the Philippines — those en route turning back and the rest never sailing. The chief authority on the first Philippine campaign states, "Had these vessels, the last of which was to leave the United States on 20 December, reached the Philippines the Japanese would have faced a far stronger force when they landed on Luzon." [33]

The defensive plight of the Philippines was not helped by the friction which developed between MacArthur and Admiral Hart, the commander of the Asiatic Fleet. The long-standing mission of his fleet in case of war had been to withdraw southward from the Philippines until the Pacific Fleet could advance westward and make coordinated offensive operations possible. In late October, however, Hart became so enthused over the increasing strength of the Far East Air Force that he recommended to Washington that his mission be changed whereby his fleet would stay and fight it out in Philippine waters. In his memoirs MacArthur sharply criticized Hart's withdrawal, apparently unaware that the admiral had tried to stay, but the Navy Department refused to permit him to make a stand in the Philippine region. MacArthur and Hart also disagreed over which service would be responsible for offshore air patrols, the former at one time thinking that the Navy was trying to get control over his air force. In late November they settled the matter by assigning the air patrols south of Luzon and as far as the Indochinese coastal waters to Hart's Patrol Wing 10, consisting of thirty-two Consolidated PBY's, while Brereton's B-17's would patrol the coastal waters off Luzon northward toward Formosa. As for the Asiatic Fleet, it was not a formidable force in early December, but Hart did have enough firepower to severely cripple enemy landing efforts if his fleet could have remained. His fleet included three cruisers, thirteen destroyers, twenty-nine submarines, and a number of gunboats, torpedo boats, and auxiliary craft. Ironically, the Navy's chief contribution in the campaign of 1941–42 would be in ground fighting: on December 1 the 4th Marine Regiment arrived at Manila from Shanghai, its experienced troops and weapons being of great value in the approaching battles.[34]

Hart, MacArthur, and Sayre met together on November 27 to discuss secret messages which each had just received. The communications from Washington announced that the Hull-Nomura talks had collapsed; MacArthur received a "final alert" from the War Department, and Hart got a "war warning" from his superiors in Washington. In later writings both Hart and Sayre agreed that at the conference on the 27th MacArthur was extremely optimistic about forthcoming events. The general paced back and forth, puffing a cigar and reassuring them that, according to Sayre, "the existing alignment and movement of Japanese troops convinced him that there would be no attack before the spring." Sayre noted that "Admiral Hart felt otherwise." The day before the Manila meeting Japanese generals and admirals had met aboard a warship off the coast of Formosa to map final plans for the invasion of the Philippines. And on the day MacArthur, Hart, and Sayre met, a large Japanese task force secretly departed from the Kurile Islands, heading eastward; its carrier planes would make the attack on Pearl Harbor ten days hence.[35]

Meanwhile the Philippine public had begun to quieten after the excitement of the national elections in November, though it had been a foregone conclusion that Quezon and Osmeña would be re-elected, as they were overwhelmingly. Clark Lee, an American correspondent in Manila during the last week before war, reported: "Life in Manila was no longer life as usual. There was an unusual number of marriages of youths called to service in the Army. As in Hong Kong and Shanghai few people could make any arrangements for the future because commercial shipping had stopped." Even as the end neared, Lee saw evidence of the ugly superior attitude of Americans. At the Manila Hotel bar an American woman slapped a Constabulary sergeant who was trying politely to get her to leave while she could still walk. "We Americans are the ruling race here," she screamed in fury, "you Filipinos are dirt." Observing some of Hart's ships at anchor in Manila Bay, Lee himself displayed a typical American attitude when he observed: "They certainly are beautiful. When the Japs come down here, they'll be playing in the Big League for the first time in their lives." At Nichols Field, just outside Manila, Lee and several other reporters chatted with some Army pilots as they watched P-40's landing and taking off in the distance. Both correspondents and pilots agreed, said Lee, that "it was undoubtedly the best pursuit ship in the world, certainly better than anything the Japs could hope to have." Though Lee believed that most Filipinos were living in quiet desperation that last week, he saw little manifestation of anxiety in their outward appearances. "ROTC cadets, with papier-mâché helmets, were going through casual bayonet drills on the green lawns surrounding the ancient walled city," Lee noticed as he drove along, adding, "They seemed to be having a lot of fun." At the University of the Philippines, he heard Quezon deliver a solemn address on war preparations. When the Philippine president warned that "bombs may be falling on this campus soon," a number of students laughed.

Nevertheless, Sayre's office and the Civilian Emergency Administration had been pushing forward civil defense preparations steadily since July. Sayre admitted, however, that there "was inescapable uncertainty and considerable confusion on the part of the general public" regarding civil defense measures. Air-raid alarm systems were set up, first-aid stations were built, and evacuation plans were laid for the populace of Manila, but practice air-raid alerts received little cooperation from most citizens. In addition, considerable administrative confusion developed in the last two weeks before war as to which office, Sayre's or Sison's, was the supreme authority on civil defense. The muddle was precipitated by Interior Department and civil defense leaders in Washington who apparently were not convinced that Sison's Civilian Emergency Administration should have ultimate responsibility. As late as November 27 Secretary of the Interior Ickes and Fiorello La Guardia, the national director of civil defense in America, considered Sayre to be the civil defense director in the Philippines.[36]

Beginning the last two days of November, American patrol planes daily spotted large numbers of Japanese transports and warships in the South China Sea, seemingly headed toward South Indo-China. A Japanese reconnaissance plane was noticed over Clark Field at dawn on December 2, but no interception was attempted. On the 4th Brereton's pursuits began nightly patrols over North Luzon's coastline; that night and the next two evenings American pilots spotted Nipponese aircraft flying about fifty miles out at sea, but they turned northward when the American fighters approached. The radar set at Iba

Field tracked several unidentified aircraft on the nights of December 5 and 6, but no contact by interceptors was made. On December 6 MacArthur ordered guards increased at all air bases, all stations manned on a twenty-four-hour basis, aircraft dispersed as well as possible, and coastal air patrols increased. He reported to Washington that a full alert was in effect, though he seems to have interpreted the last message from the War Department on the 6th as a warning against sabotage only. "There was no sense of urgency in preparing for a Japanese air attack," states an authority, "partly because our intelligence estimates had calculated that the Japanese aircraft did not have sufficient range to bomb Manila from Formosa."

Meanwhile Quezon received a cable from the Japanese Foreign Office stating that the Japanese consul to Manila, who had been visiting in Japan for a month, had contracted a cold and would not return as soon as planned. On December 5 and 6 Vice Admiral Sir Tom Phillips, the new and able British naval commander at Singapore, visited Manila to confer with Hart and MacArthur on collaboration in defense of the Malay Barrier, but no definite plans were agreed upon since the American commanders had no instructions from Washington about committing their forces in the area south of the Philippines. At the end of the meeting MacArthur and Hart held separate news conferences, and each told reporters that they thought war was imminent. But, according to Lee, "General MacArthur thought the attack would come sometime after January 1." Hart told the correspondents that he "had sent his ships to sea to scout, and he was optimistic about the striking power of his subs." Phillips apparently granted no interview, but he would be in the news four days hence when he and his flagship, H.M.S. *Prince of Wales,* would be sent to the bottom of the South China Sea by Japanese bombs.[37]

It was 2:30 A.M., Sunday, December 8, Manila time — which was 8:00 A.M., December 7, Pearl Harbor time — when a radio operator at Asiatic Fleet Headquarters in Manila received the terse message, "Air raid on Pearl Harbor. This is no drill." The message, from a Navy operator at Pearl Harbor, was quickly relayed to Hart and to his fleet commanders, the admiral hurrying to his office to begin combat preparations. Typical of the lack of coordination between Army and Navy commands in the Philippines in preceding months, neither Hart nor his staff took the trouble to inform MacArthur. At 3:40 MacArthur was awakened by the ringing of the telephone beside his bed. Sutherland, who had just heard the news from a commercial radio broadcast, told his startled commander. The report was confirmed shortly by an official communication, but, said MacArthur, "no details were given . . . My first impression was that the Japanese might well have suffered a serious setback." On Formosa, 500 miles to the north, Japanese pilots stood by nervously awaiting takeoff orders for their first attacks on Luzon, which had been scheduled for dawn but delayed by heavy fog over the Formosan airfields. Realizing that news of the Pearl Harbor attack had undoubtedly reached Manila before they took off, the Nipponese airmen feared the worst.[38] But neither the wary attackers nor the confident USAFFE commander were prepared for the surprising developments which would follow. The eighth of December would be a long, long day for General MacArthur.

ABBREVIATIONS
BIBLIOGRAPHICAL NOTE
NOTES

Abbreviations

AAG Assistant adjutant general of the Army
ABMC American Battle Monuments Commission
AEF American Expeditionary Forces
AG Adjutant general of a command; or, when followed by a number, central files of the office of the adjutant general of the Army, record groups 94 and 107, National Archives, Washington, D.C.
AGO Office of the adjutant general of the Army
AGO–CBDF Commission branch decimal files of the office of the adjutant general of the Army, record group 94, National Archives
AGO–DF Decimal files of the office of the adjutant general of the Army, record group 94, National Archives
AGO–PF Project files, 1917–25, of the office of the adjutant general of the Army, record group 407, National Archives
AM Lieutenant General Arthur MacArthur
AM Extract 201 Extracts from 201 file of Lieutenant General Arthur MacArthur, Francis G. Newlands Papers, Yale University Archives
AM Misc. 201 Miscellaneous documents from 201 file of Lieutenant General Arthur MacArthur, Office of the Chief of Military History, Washington, D.C.
ANJ *Army and Navy Journal*
ANR *Army and Navy Register*
AWC Army War College
BEF "Bonus Expeditionary Forces"
Bul. Bulletin

        CA Coast Artillery
       CCC Civilian Conservation Corps
    CF–War Confidential file — War Department, Franklin D. Roosevelt
             Papers, Franklin D. Roosevelt Library, Hyde Park, N.Y.
        CG Commanding general
      CinC Commander in chief
      CMTC Citizens Military Training Camps
        CO Commanding officer
      CofE Chief of engineers
      CofS Chief of staff of the Army (unless a specific command is
             designated)
      Cps. Corps
        DF Decimal file
        DM General Douglas MacArthur
   DM Misc. Miscellaneous documents from 201 file of General Douglas
       201 MacArthur, Office of the Chief of Military History
       DSC Distinguished Service Cross
   Eff. rpt. Efficiency report
        FA Field artillery
       FDR President Franklin D. Roosevelt
      FDRL Franklin D. Roosevelt Papers, Franklin D. Roosevelt Library
       G-1 Personnel and administration section (or chief thereof)
       G-2 Military intelligence section (or chief thereof)
       G-3 Operations and training section (or chief thereof)
       G-4 Supply section (or chief thereof)
       GHQ General headquarters
        GS General Staff of the War Department
       HHL Herbert Hoover Presidential Library, West Branch, Ia.
       Hq. Headquarters
        HR Historical records
        IG Inspector general of the Army
  Ind. serv. rpt. Individual service report
       JAG Judge advocate general of the Army
        LC Division of manuscripts, Library of Congress, Washington,
             D.C.
      MMBA MacArthur Memorial Bureau of Archives, Norfolk, Va.
        MA Military adviser to the Philippine Commonwealth
        NA National Archives, Washington, D.C.
      OCMH Office of the Chief of Military History, Department of the
             Army Headquarters, Washington, D.C.
       OCS Office of the chief of staff of the Army; or, when followed
             by a number, files of the office of the chief of staff of the
             Army, record group 165, National Archives
   Op. rpt. Operations report

PA Recs. Philippine Army records, Office of the Chief of Military History

PGGAR *Annual Report of the Philippine Governor General*

PHCAR *Annual Report of the Philippine High Commissioner*

PPAR *Annual Report of the President of the Philippine Commonwealth*

PPF President's personal files, Franklin D. Roosevelt Papers

RG Record group

SecNavy Secretary of the Navy

SecState Secretary of State

SecWar Secretary of War

TAG Adjutant general of the Army

TOA Table of allowance

USA United States Army

USAFFE United States Army Forces in the Far East

USAWW *United States Army in World War I*

USAWWII *United States Army in World War II*

USFIP United States Forces in the Philippines (March–May, 1942)

USMA United States Military Academy, West Point, N.Y. (or the archives thereof)

USN United States Navy

WCD War College division of the General Staff

WD War Department

WDAR *War Department Annual Reports* (title varies), usually Vol. I, reports of Secretary of War or chief of staff

WPD War plans division of the General Staff; or, when followed by a number, files of the war plans division of the General Staff, record group 165, National Archives

WTMA West Texas Military Academy (later Texas Military Institute), San Antonio, Tex.

YUA Yale University Archives, New Haven, Conn.

Bibliographical Note

Manuscripts

A large portion of the unpublished documents relating to MacArthur's career to December, 1941, is located in two depositories, the MacArthur Memorial Bureau of Archives, Norfolk, Virginia, and the National Archives, Washington, D.C. Because many of these documents are still classified, the researcher must first obtain security clearance from the adjutant general of the Army.

The MacArthur Memorial Bureau of Archives' holdings are much more extensive for the period of the war with Japan and after than for the pre-1942 portion of the general's life. Most helpful in the preparation of this volume were RG 1, military adviser records; RG 10, MacArthur's private correspondence; RG 17, Philippine Department records; and RG 18, chief of staff records. Also useful were the periodical files, such as those of the Rainbow Division Veterans' monthly magazine, *Rainbow Reveille*.

At the Old Military Records Division and Modern Military Records Division of the National Archives, the records on MacArthur are extensive but not always easy to locate. Most documents used herein were found in the following record groups and files: Civilian Conservation Corps records, in RG 35; AGO central files, commission branch files, decimal files, and project files (1917–25), as well as SecWar correspondence files, in RG 94 and 107; District of Washington file on the Bonus Army's eviction, as well as Army command records, in RG 98; records of the office of the Philippine high commissioner, in RG 126; records of the AEF, including GHQ AG, G-2, and G-3 files and historical and decimal files of the 1st Army, 42nd Division, and 84th Brigade, in RG 120; records of the Veracruz occupation, in RG 141; records of the General Staff, including files of the office of the chief of staff, G-1, G-2, war plans division, and War College division, in RG 165; records of the Bureau of Insular Affairs, in RG 350; and records of the III and IV Corps Area commands, in RG 394. MacArthur's 201 file to 1917 is located in AGO decimal file 487448, RG 94 (that of his father is in AGO decimal file 5551). The 201 file contains his individual service records, appointments, commissions, efficiency reports, and some medical data; the portion since 1917 is closed to researchers. Also of assistance at the National Archives was RG 59, wherein are found the despatches and miscellaneous letters of the State Department up to the early twentieth century. The USAFFE–USFIP operations report and annexes, as well as other records of Army operations in the Philippines, 1941–42, were located at the World War II Records Division, Alexandria, Virginia, when used by the author. Most of them have since been moved to the Federal Records Center, Suitland, Maryland, and the rest to the National Archives in Washington.

At the Manuscripts Division of the Library of Congress, Washington, the papers of John J. Pershing and George Van Horn Moseley have a number of letters to and from MacArthur (also his first wife). Some relevant material was also found in the papers of Elihu Root, Newton D. Baker, and Hugh L. Scott, but little or nothing of significance was uncovered in the papers of other associates of MacArthur, such as Peyton C. March, Leonard Wood, William Mitchell, Charles P. Summerall, and George B. Dern.

In the Franklin D. Roosevelt Papers of the Franklin D. Roosevelt Library, Hyde Park, New York, there is a fair amount of documentary material relating to MacArthur. It is found principally in the confidential War Department files, the President's personal files, the official files, and the presidential secretary's files. The Herbert Hoover Papers of the Herbert Hoover Presidential Library, West Branch, Iowa, has an important collection of documents on the Bonus Army episode, including some letters and reports by MacArthur or addressed to him. The Hoover-MacArthur correspondence file, however, begins in 1942.

At the Office of the Chief of Military History, Department of the Army Headquarters, Washington, there is a selected collection of material pertinent to MacArthur's commands in World War II, but not a large amount dealing with his prewar activities. There are small so-called "miscellaneous 201 files" of MacArthur and his father, containing copies of some records from the original files. The "Cater file" of sundry items and photocopied documents of General Staff activities contains some data of significance to this study. The official and unofficial reports and notes of commanders of the first Philippine campaign in some cases have information about the mobilization and training of the Philippine forces up to December 8, 1941. The important Philippine Army records, a collection which includes orders, memoranda, bulletins, and other documents of the 1936–41 period, was located at the Office of the Chief of Military History when used by the author, but these documents have since been deposited in the military history collection of the Army War College, Carlisle Barracks, Pennsylvania.

In the archives of the Yale University Library, New Haven, Connecticut, are found several collections which contain material on MacArthur or his father. They include the papers of Francis G. Newlands, Henry L. Stimson, Katherine Mayo, Edward M. House, and Frederic C. Walcott. The archives of the United States Military Academy, West Point, New York, has a MacArthur file, which contains some material about his activities there as cadet and superintendent. The historical scrapbooks were used, as well as the files of registers, regulations, board of visitors' reports, and superintendents' reports. Catalogues and other data on MacArthur's cadet days at West Texas Military Academy were found at Texas Military Institute, San Antonio, Texas. Other collections which contain letters and documents pertaining to MacArthur's career to 1941 include the Enoch H. Crowder Papers, Western Historical Manuscript Collection, University of Missouri Library, Columbia, Missouri; the Patrick J. Hurley Papers, Western History Collections, University of Oklahoma Library, Norman, Oklahoma; the Frank Murphy Papers, Michigan Historical Collections, University of Michigan, Ann Arbor, Michigan; and the William E. Brougher Papers, Mississippi State University Library, State College, Mississippi.

The most extensive of the previously mentioned record groups are several in the National Archives. Fortunately inventories have been printed: *Preliminary Inventory of the Textual Records of the American Expeditionary Forces (World War I), 1917–23 (Record Group 120)*, Part I, comp. by Aloha Broadwater and others (Washington, 1968); *Preliminary Inventory of the Textual Records of the War Department General and Special Staffs (Record Group 165)*, comp. by Harry W. John and Olive K. Liebman (Washington, 1967); and *Inventory of Certain Records of United States Army Forces in the Far East and United States Forces in the Philippines, July, 1941–May 1942*, comp. by Dennis W. Ladd (Washington, 1967). There are also two editions of a guide to the AGO central correspondence files, but that enormous collection will always baffle researchers.

Interviews and Correspondence

The number of living men who were close associates of MacArthur before the war with Japan is small. Of this group the following ones assisted me through interviews, informal conversations, correspondence, and/or preparation of brief memoirs and notes for my use: the late General of the Army Dwight D. Eisenhower, Major General Charles A. Willoughby, the late Major General Courtney Whitney, Major General Richard J. Marshall, Major General Spencer B. Akin, and Brigadier General Bonner Fellers. Others who through talks or letters contributed significantly to my understanding of MacArthur's behavior or background circumstances include General Harold K. Johnson, General J. Lawton Collins, Colonel Arnold D. Amoroso, Colonel Edgar W. Schroeder, and W. O. Spencer. On the basis of interviews already conducted and contacts made in connection with MacArthur's post-1941 career, it is expected that the oral history phase of research on this project will be considerably expanded for the second volume.

Printed Government Documents

Annual reports of the following public officials, departments, and institutions were indispensable: the War Department, especially the reports of the Secretary of War and the chief of staff; the governor general of the Philippines; the high commissioner of the Philippines; the president of the Philippine Commonwealth; the superintendent of the United States Military Academy; the board of visitors of the Military Academy. The annual registers of the officer corps of the Army and of graduates of the Military Academy were frequently consulted. The *Congressional Record* was of some value, but more important for MacArthur's relations with Congress, particularly during the years 1919–22 and 1930–35, were the hearings and reports of House and Senate committees and subcommittees on military affairs and appropriations. Special investigative hearings by congressional committees were also useful, such as those on West Point hazing (1901), Philippine affairs (1902), the War Policies Commission (1931), and the Pearl Harbor attack (1946).

The State Department's *Foreign Relations of the United States* was consulted for the period 1936–41, particularly Volume IV (Far East) of the series for 1941 and the supplementary work, *Japan, 1931–1941* (2 vols., Washington, 1943). Numerous special publications by the War Department were used, such as *Compilation of General Orders, Circulars and Bulle-*

tins of the War Department; Issued Between February 15, 1881, and December 31, 1915 (Washington, 1916); *Congressional Medal of Honor, the Distinguished Service Cross, and the Distinguished Service Medal; Issued by the War Department Since April 6, 1917, Up to and Including General Orders No. 126, War Department, November 11, 1919* (Washington, 1920); and *Final Report of War Department Special Committee on the Army Air Corps, July 18, 1934* (Washington, 1934), and others on equally wide-ranging subjects. The reader can refer to the footnotes for others, the lengthiness of public documents making it rather expensive and needless to repeat their titles.

Other Published Sources

Of course, the most important unofficial printed source is MacArthur's *Reminiscenses* (New York, 1964). His memoirs has been severely criticized by reviewers as unbelievably egotistical, full of errors, replete with near-plagiarisms of associates' writings, and ghost-written by staff members during his final illness. Most of the criticism has been directed toward the portions of the book dealing with post-1941 events. The earlier parts appear to have been written by him and are rather accurate, though I have noted some errors in my footnotes. The question of the authenticity and accuracy of his *Reminiscences* will be dealt with in detail in the bibliographical essay of the second volume of this work since nearly all criticisms concern his coverage of the 1941–51 period. For the most part, I have trusted his pre-1942 story.

MacArthur made innumerable public addresses before 1942, but he wrote surprisingly little for publication. His main printed works are his annual reports as West Point superintendent, 1919–22, and as chief of staff, 1930–35. As Philippine military adviser, he wrote the *Report on National Defense in the Philippines* (Manila, 1936), but little else except for published letters to editors occasionally. Two collections of his writings and speeches have appeared, though most of the pre-1942 items therein are from his public addresses and chief of staff reports: Frank C. Waldrop, ed., *MacArthur on War: His Military Writings* (New York, 1942); and Vorin E. Whan, ed., *A Soldier Speaks: Public Papers and Speeches of General of the Army Douglas MacArthur* (New York, 1965).

Published primary works which contain material on MacArthur to 1941 are numerous and of considerable variety in type and quality. Some of those used in preparing this volume are Robert S. Allen, *Washington Merry-Go-Round* (New York, 1931); William H. Amerine, *Alabama's Own in France [167th Infantry]* (New York, 1919); Henry H. Arnold, *Global Mission* (New York, 1949); Bernard Baruch, *Baruch: The Public*

Years (New York, 1960); Robert L. Bullard, *Personalities and Reminiscences of the War* (Garden City, 1925); R. M. Cheseldine, *Ohio in the Rainbow: Official Story of the 166th Infantry, 42nd Division, in the World War* (Columbus, 1924); Bob Considine, *It's All News to Me: A Reporter's Deposition* (New York, 1967); Joseph T. Dickman, *The Great Crusade: A Narrative of the World War* (New York, 1927); Francis P. Duffy, *Father Duffy's Story: A Tale of Humor and Heroism, of Life and Death with the Fighting Sixty-Ninth* [*165th Infantry*] . . . (New York, 1919); Dwight D. Eisenhower, *At Ease: Stories I Tell to Friends* (Garden City, 1967); James A. Farley, *Jim Farley's Story: The Roosevelt Years* (New York, 1948); Bess Furman, *Washington By-Line: The Personal History of a Newspaper Woman* (New York, 1949); William A. Ganoe, *MacArthur Close-Up: Much Then and Some Now* (New York, 1962); Joseph C. Grew, *Ten Years in Japan: A Contemporary Record* . . . (New York, 1944); James G. Harbord, *The American Army in France, 1917–1919* (Boston, 1936); Herbert Hoover, *Memoirs* (3 vols., New York, 1951–52); Sidney L. Huff, with Joe A. Morris, *My Fifteen Years with General MacArthur* (New York, 1964); Harold L. Ickes, *The Secret Diary of Harold L. Ickes* (3 vols., New York, 1953–54); Hugh S. Johnson, *The Blue Eagle from Egg to Earth* . . . (Garden City, 1935); Hunter Liggett, *Commanding an American Army: Recollections of the World War* (Boston, 1925); Marty Maher, with Nardi R. Campion, *Bringing Up the Brass: My 55 Years at West Point* (New York, 1951); Peyton C. March, *The Nation at War* (Garden City, 1932); Charles T. Menoher, "The Rainbow," *New York Times Magazine Section*, Apr. 27, 1919; Nancy H. Hooker, ed., *The Moffat Papers: Selections from the Diplomatic Journals of Jay Pierrepont Moffat, 1919–1943* (Cambridge, Mass., 1956); John J. Pershing, *My Experiences in the World War* (2 vols., New York, 1931); Manuel Quezon, *The Good Fight* (New York, 1946); Henry J. Reilly, *Americans All: The Rainbow at War: Official History of the 42nd Rainbow Division in the World War* (Columbus, 1936); Carlos P. Romulo, *I Saw the Fall of the Philippines* (Garden City, 1942); Francis B. Sayre, *Glad Adventure* (New York, 1957); Elmer W. Sherwood, *Diary of a Rainbow Veteran: Written at the Front* (Terre Haute, 1929); Henry L. Stimson, with McGeorge Bundy, *On Active Service in Peace and War* (New York, 1948); John H. Taber, *The Story of the 168th Infantry* (2 vols., Iowa City, 1925); Raymond S. Tompkins, *The Story of the Rainbow Division* (New York, 1919); Rexford G. Tugwell, *The Democratic Roosevelt* (Garden City, 1957); Jonathan M. Wainwright, with Robert Considine, *General Wainwright's Story* . . . (Garden City, 1946); Walter W. Waters, with William C. White, *B.E.F.: The Whole Story of the Bonus Army* (New York, 1933); William Allen White, *Autobiography* (New York, 1946); Walter B. Wolf, *A Brief Story of the Rainbow Division* (New York, 1919).

Relevant primary works also include the following multi-volume collections of letters and documents: Charles F. Horne, ed., *Source Records of the Great War* . . . (7 vols., Indianapolis, 1931); William S. Myers, ed., *The State Papers and Other Public Writings of Herbert Hoover* (2 vols., New York, 1934); Elliott Roosevelt, ed., *F.D.R.: His Personal Letters* (4 vols., New York, 1950); Samuel I. Rosenman, ed., *The Public Papers and Addresses of Franklin D. Roosevelt* (13 vols., New York, 1938–50); U.S. Dept. of the Army, *United States Army in the World War, 1917–1919* (17 vols., Washington, 1948).

Newspapers and Periodicals

Most heavily used were the *New York Times, Army and Navy Journal,* and *Army and Navy Register,* especially for the years 1917–41. Other newspapers and periodicals were consulted for specific events or dates. By newspapers and years, they included the *Times* (1922), *Herald* (1929, 1932, 1935), *Post* (1932, 1937), and *Star* (1932, 1964) of Washington; the *Herald Tribune* (1939), *Daily News* (1941, 1942), and *Post* (1941) of New York City; the *Tribune* (1936), *Philippine Herald* (1937), *La Vanguardia* (1940), and *Bulletin* (1940, 1941) of Manila; the *Gazette* (1880–81) of Las Vegas (New Mexico Territory); the *Post-Gazette* (1932) of Pittsburgh; the *Journal* (1898, 1937) of Milwaukee; and the *Evening Dispatch* (1934) of Columbus, Ohio.

Contemporary articles, as well as later ones which concerned MacArthur's earlier career, are found in many periodicals. They include *The Nation, New Republic, Outlook, World's Work, Time, Newsweek, Harper's, Literary Digest, Liberty, Saturday Evening Post,* and others. Of course, service-related periodicals carried stories of MacArthur's activities; some of these publications are *Army Ordnance, Infantry Journal, Reserve Officer,* and *Our Army. Rainbow Reveille,* the organ of the Rainbow Division Veterans, seldom missed a season without an article on MacArthur. A good bibliography of MacArthur items in leading newspapers and periodicals through Feb., 1942, is Florence S. Hellman, comp., *A List of References on General Douglas MacArthur* (Washington, 1942), a publication of the Library of Congress' division of bibliography.

Not many articles have appeared in so-called scholarly journals which pertain to MacArthur's pre-1942 career. Those cited in this work consist of J. Woodford Howard, "Frank Murphy and the Philippine Commonwealth," *Pacific Historical Review,* XXXIII (1964), 45–68; Louis Morton, "War Plan ORANGE: Evolution of a Strategy," *World Politics,* XI (1959), 221–50; and John W. Killigrew, "The Army and the Bonus Incident," *Military Affairs,* XXVI (1962), 59–65. Two good articles have been printed on his father's relations with Taft: Rowland T. Berthoff, "Taft and MacArthur, 1900: A Study in Civilian-Military Relations," *World Politics*, V (1953), 196–213; and Ralph E. Minger, "Taft, MacArthur, and the Establishment of Civil Government in the Philippines," *Ohio Historical Quarterly*, LXX (1961), 308–31.

MacArthur Biographies

One of the first book-length biographies of MacArthur to appear was Francis T. Miller's *General Douglas MacArthur: Fighter for Freedom*, published in early 1942 (rev. ed., 1951, entitled *General Douglas MacArthur: Soldier-Statesman*). This work set the pace for "quickie" biographies of the general from then onward; today the number of these works is at least twenty. It is unfortunate that later biographers did not follow the example of John Hersey, whose *Men on Bataan* (New York, 1943) is an artful blending of MacArthur's biography with the account of the Bataan campaign, the "flashbacks" to his previous career activities occurring in alternating chapters. Vividly written and showing evidence of some extensive research, this work would be the only biography worth mentioning for a decade. Richard H. Rovere and Arthur M. Schlesinger's partisan but perceptive work *The General and the President, and the Future of American Foreign Policy* was published in 1951 (rev. ed., 1965, entitled *The MacArthur Controversy and American Foreign Policy*), but it dealt only scantily with the general's life to 1941 and could not be considered biography.

Then in rapid succession came Clark Lee and Richard Henschel, *Douglas MacArthur* (New York, 1952); Frazier Hunt, *The Untold Story of Douglas MacArthur* (New York, 1954); Charles A. Willoughby and John Chamberlain, *MacArthur, 1941–1951* (New York, 1954); and Courtney Whitney, *MacArthur: Rendezvous with Destiny* (New York, 1955). All of these writings were precipitated by the controversy surrounding MacArthur's dismissal in 1951, and, though each makes some contribution to knowledge about MacArthur, all four are polemical and strongly pro-MacArthur. The last two works are more valuable as memoirs of two of his key officers of the years 1941–1951 and contain only passing references to the general's career before the war with Japan. The biography by Lee and Henschel is about one third pictorial, but contains some worthwhile data, particularly on MacArthur's family background and early life. Hunt, a correspondent who knew MacArthur from World War I days, had access to many of MacArthur's files, some of which have not been located since. He devotes over 220 pages to the general's career up to 1941 and surely contributed the best account of those years, though not without erring frequently on facts. If the quality of Hunt's biography had remained the same for the later period, it might be said that he had written an acceptable one-volume biography. Unfortunately he became obsessed with the alleged Communist plotting in Washington high circles against MacArthur and, in defending the general, lost all sense of objectivity and perspective. Since these four books appeared, no biographies of note have been published on MacArthur, the "quickies" continuing to spring forth periodically. (Appearing too late for use by the author in this volume was Gavin Long, *MacArthur as Military Commander* [London, 1969], a brief but perceptive study by a distinguished military historian.)

Other Secondary Works

Though more are mentioned in the citations herein, the following biographies were especially helpful: I. George Blake, *Paul V. McNutt: Portrait of a Hoosier Statesman* (Indianapolis, 1966); Edward M. Coffman, *The Hilt of the Sword: The Career of Peyton C. March* (Madison, 1966); Clarence H. Cramer, *Newton D. Baker: A Biography* (Cleveland, 1961); Burke Davis, *The Billy Mitchell Affair* (New York, 1967); Mabel E. Deutrich, *The Struggle for Supremacy: The Career of General Fred C. Ainsworth* (Washington, 1962); Kenneth S. Davis, *Soldier of Democracy: A Biography of Dwight Eisenhower* (Garden City, 1945); J. Woodford Howard, *Mr. Justice Murphy: A Political Biography* (Princeton, 1968): Isaac D. Levine, *Mitchell: Pioneer of Air Power* (New York, 1943); David A. Lockmiller, *Enoch H. Crowder: Soldier, Lawyer, and Statesman, 1859–1932* (Columbia, Mo., 1955); Don Lohbeck, *Patrick J. Hurley* (Chicago, 1956); Kevin McCann, *Man from Abilene* (Garden City, 1952); Elting E. Morison, *Turmoil and Tradition: A Study of the Life and Times of Henry L. Stimson* (Boston, 1960); Frederick Palmer, *John J. Pershing, General of the Armies: A Biography* (Harrisburg, 1948); Forrest C. Pogue, *George C. Marshall* (2 vols. to date, New York, 1963–66).

Of the numerous secondary books cited in the footnotes of this volume, the following are the ones which were most useful: Stephen E. Ambrose, *Duty, Honor, Country: A History of West Point* (Baltimore, 1966); American Battle Monuments Commission, *American Armies and Battlefields in Europe* (Washington, 1938); idem, *42d Division Summary of Operations in the World War* (Washington, 1944); Edward M. Coffman, *The War to End All Wars: The American Military Experience in World War I* (New York, 1968); Wesley F. Craven and James L. Cate, eds., *Plans and Early Operations, January 1939 to August 1942* (*The Army Air Forces in World War II*, Vol. I; Chicago, 1948); Theodore Friend,

Between Two Empires: The Ordeal of the Philippines, 1929–1946 (New Haven, 1965); Samuel P. Huntington, *The Soldier and the State: The Theory and Politics of Civil-Military Relations* (Cambridge, 1957); Morris Janowitz, *The Professional Soldier: A Social and Political Portrait* (Glencoe, 1960); Maurice Matloff and Edwin M. Snell, *Strategic Planning for Coalition Warfare, 1941–1942* (*United States Army in World War II;* Washington, 1953); Walter Millis, *Arms and Men: A Study in American Military History* (New York, 1956); Samuel E. Morison, *The Rising Sun in the Pacific, 1931–April 1942* (*History of United States Naval Operations in World War II,* Vol. III; Boston, 1948); Louis Morton, *The Fall of the Philippines* (*United States Army in World War II;* Washington, 1953); Louis Morton, *Strategy and Command: The First Two Years* (*United States Army in World War II;* Washington, 1962); Otto L. Nelson, *National Security and the General Staff* (Washington, 1946); Robert E. Quirk, *An Affair of Honor: Woodrow Wilson and the Occupation of Veracruz* (Lexington, 1962); John A. Salmon, *The Civilian Conservation Corps, 1933–1942: A New Deal Case Study* (Durham, 1967); Arthur M. Schlesinger, *The Age of Roosevelt* (3 vols. to date, Boston, 1957–   ); R. Elberton Smith, *The Army and Economic Mobilization* (*United States Army in World War II;* Washington, 1959); War Dept., *Order of Battle of the United States Land Forces in the World War* (3 vols., Washington, 1931–48); Mark S. Watson, *Chief of Staff: Prewar Plans and Preparations* (*United States Army in World War II;* Washington, 1950); Russel F. Weigley, *History of the United States Army* (*The Wars of the United States;* New York, 1967). The above-named volumes in various World War II series contain much valuable data on MacArthur and the Army before that conflict.

Two graduate theses were especially helpful: one on MacArthur's father — Henry A. Fant, "Arthur MacArthur and the Philippine Insurrection" (unpublished M.A. thesis, Mississippi State University, 1963) — and the other mainly on the War Department's relations with Congress during the period when MacArthur was chief of staff — John W. Killigrew, "The Impact of the Great Depression on the Army, 1929–1936" (unpublished Ph.D. dissertation, Indiana University, 1960). Killigrew's work represents a great amount of research and careful scholarship; his findings were relied upon heavily in Part IV of this volume. It is hoped that more such studies on subjects closely related to MacArthur's earlier career will be forthcoming soon. The valuable holdings of the MacArthur Memorial Bureau of Archives, which have been opened to historians in recent years, should prove to be a stimulus to such research.

Notes

PROLOGUE,

pages 1–4

1. DM to CofS, Sept. 16, 1937, PPF 4914, FDRL.
2. FDR to DM, Oct. 11, 1937, PPF 4914.
3. DM to CofS, Sept. 16, 1937, PPF 4914.

CHAPTER I, *"The MacArthur Heritage,"*

pages 7–47

1. Seton Gordon to DM, Feb. 12, 1951, RG 10, MMBA; Douglas Mac-Arthur, *Reminiscences* (New York, 1964), 3–4 [hereafter cited *Reminiscences*]; Clark Lee and Richard Henschel, *Douglas MacArthur* (New York, 1952), 10–12, 236–37; Robert Bain, *The Clans and Tartans of Scotland* (rev. ed., London, 1946), 174–75. Eight MacArthurs are listed in the main British biographical dictionary, six of whom won fame as 19th century leaders in Australia. None of the eight was born in Scotland, and if any of them were related to Douglas Mac-Arthur's ancestors, they were probably of distant kinship. Leslie Stephen and Sidney Lee, eds., *The Dictionary of National Biography: From Earliest Times to 1900* (22 vols., London, 1917), XII, 400–04. One genealogist contends that Sarah MacArthur remarried before her move to America, but her second husband is not named. Conklin Mann, "Some Ancestral Lines of General Douglas MacArthur," *New York Genealogical and Biographical Record*, LXXIII (July, 1942), 170. This same issue, pp. 167–69, contains an article on the "Kinship of President Roosevelt, Mr. Churchill and General MacArthur," in

which a distant relationship is traced through the colonial marriages of the Belcher family.

It is interesting to note that in legal opinions which Arthur Mac-Arthur later wrote as a judge in Milwaukee, the family name is spelled "McArthur." (The opinions are now deposited in the Milwaukee County archives.) It is not known when the family changed to "Mac-Arthur."

2. U.S. Census Bureau, *Return of the Whole Number of Persons . . . [1790]* (Philadelphia, 1791), 27; idem, *Aggregate Amount of Each Description of Persons . . . in the Year 1810* (Washington, 1811), 8–9; idem, *Census for 1820* (Washington, 1821), 6.

3. James G. Wilson and John Fiske, eds., *Appleton's Cyclopaedia of American Biography* (5 vols., New York, 1888), IV, 72; *Reminiscences,* 4. Some authorities claim that, prior to his marriage to Aurelia, he had married a girl named Zelia, who died shortly after their wedding. Mann, "Some Ancestral Lines," 172; Lee and Henschel, *MacArthur,* 11.

4. Edward M. Hunter, "Civil Life, Services and Character of William A. Barstow," in Lyman C. Draper, ed., *Collections of the State Historical Society of Wisconsin,* VI (Madison, 1872), 101–06; William F. Raney, *Wisconsin: A Story of Progress* (New York, 1940), 150–51; Milo M. Quaife, *Wisconsin: Its History and Its People* (4 vols., Chicago, 1924), I, 539.

5. *The National Cyclopaedia of American Biography,* XIII, 477; "Eighteenth Annual Report of the Executive Committee," in Draper, ed., *Collections of the State Historical Society of Wisconsin,* VI, 64; U.S. Congress, *The Statutes at Large . . .* XII (Boston, 1863), 762–65; Mann, "Some Ascestral Lines," 172. Besides compiling four volumes of major decisions of the District court, Judge MacArthur wrote *Education in Its Relation to Manual Industry* (1884), *A Biography of the English Language* (1888), *Historical Study of Mary Stuart* (1889), *Essays and Papers on Miscellaneous Topics* (1891), *History of Lady Jane Grey* (1891), and *Law as Applied in a Business Education* (1892).

6. Arthur MacArthur, *Opening Address by Judge Arthur MacArthur at the Graduating Exercises of the Law School, National University; Held in National Theatre, June 8, 1882* (Washington, 1882), 1–11; John W. Hoyt, *An Act to Incorporate a National University* (Madison, 1872); U.S. Senate, *Report of the Select Committee to Establish the University of the United States,* 52nd Cong., 2nd Sess. (1893), Senate Rpt. 1384; David Madsen, *The National University: Enduring Dream of the USA* (Detroit, 1966), 67–103. Apparently unaware of the existence of the law school, historian Madsen claims that the movement for a national university "languished" in the period 1874–

90, whereas it was during those years that the only division of the institution to become a reality was functioning.

7. *Reminiscences,* 5.
8. Bayrd Still, *Milwaukee: The History of a City* (Madison, 1948), 570–75; Raney, *Wisconsin,* 138–54.
9. James G. Flanders to Rep. Francis G. Newlands, Jan. 11, 1913, Francis G. Newlands Papers, YUA. Frank MacArthur graduated from Harvard in 1876 and became a promising patent attorney in New York, but died suddenly in Dec., 1889. Mann, "Some Ancestral Lines," 172.
10. Judge Arthur MacArthur to Pres. Abraham Lincoln, May 13, 1862, AGO–CBDF 5551, Box 231, RG 94, NA; summary of record, miscellaneous 201 file of Lt. Gen. Arthur MacArthur, OCMH [hereafter cited AM Misc. 201].
11. Summary of record, extracts from 201 file of Lt. Gen. Arthur MacArthur, Newlands Papers [hereafter cited AM Extract 201]; Robert S. Henry, *The Story of the Confederacy* (New York, 1936), 199–200; Thomas B. Van Horne, *History of the Army of the Cumberland* (2 vols., Cincinnati, 1875), I, 185–95.
12. Maj. Elisha C. Hibbard to AAG, 3rd Div., Jan. 8, 1863; op. rpt. of Lt. E. K. Holton, Jan., 1863, AM Extract 201; Bruce Catton, *This Hallowed Ground: The Story of the Union Side of the Civil War* (Garden City, 1956), 190–94.
13. Maj. Carl von Baumbach to Lt. Nieman, Nov. 27, 1863, in WD, *The War of the Rebellion: A Compilation of the Official Records of the Union and Confederate Armies* (128 vols., Washington, 1880–1901), Ser. I, Vol. XXI, Pt. 2, p. 208; Henry S. Commager, ed., *The Blue and the Gray: The Story of the Civil War as Told by Participants* (Indianapolis, 1950), 879–922; WD, *American Decorations: A List of Awards of the Congressional Medal of Honor, the Distinguished-Service Cross, and the Distinguished-Service Medal . . .* (Washington, 1927), 65; Baumbach to SecWar, n.d., AM Extract 201. In the list of his battle streamers in AM Misc. 201, MacArthur is erroneously given credit for Chickamauga and Nashville, which he missed because of typhoid fever and combat wounds, respectively.
14. Maj. Arthur MacArthur to Lt. N. P. Jackson, Sept. 12, 1864, in *Official Records,* Ser. I, Vol. XXXVIII, Pt. 1, pp. 327–30; summary of record, AM Misc. 201; Ned Bradford, ed., *Battles and Leaders of the Civil War* (New York, 1956), 491–524; MacArthur to "Buck," May 15, 1864, RG 10, MMBA. The last item, written during the march to Atlanta to an officer en route to join the 24th Wisconsin, is the only known extant letter by MacArthur during the Civil War. Probably having in mind the raids of Maj. Gen. Nathan B. Forrest, he told "Buck": "The thing is going very favorably on [the] front here," but "don't go to the rear if you can help it."

15. Capt. T. E. Balding to MacArthur, n.d., AM Extract 201; Wagner quoted in summary of record, AM Extract 201.
16. Capt. Edwin B. Parsons to Capt. R. C. Powers, Dec. 4, 1864, in *Official Records,* Ser. I, Vol. XLV, Pt. 1, p. 253; Maj. D. S. Stanley to Brig. Gen. W. D. Whippile, Feb. 25, 1865, in *ibid.,* 118; Stanley Horn, *The Army of Tennessee* (Indianapolis, 1941), 384–404; Brig. Gen. Emerson Opdycke to SecWar, Apr. 11, 1865, AM Extract 201. Stanley, who was MacArthur's corps commander at Franklin, wrote: "At the very moment all seemed to be lost, the routing of the rebels and the retaking of our batteries just as the rebels were about to turn our guns on us, was the most important crisis of that battle. In this feat of arms the regiment was gallantly and well lead by your young Colonel Arthur MacArthur, who, I hope, may always be a model of goodness and virtue for our young men, as he certainly is for bravery and manliness." Stanley to Chaplain John P. Roe, June 6, 1865, AGO–CBDF 5551.
17. Summary of record, AM Misc. 201; summary of record, AM Extract 201; *Army Register, 1912,* 457; *Reminiscences,* 11–12.
18. Summary of record, AM Misc. 201; Military Order of the Loyal Legion, Headquarters Commander of New York, *In Memoriam, Arthur MacArthur* (New York, 1912), 1.
19. Samuel P. Huntington, *The Soldier and the State: The Theory and Practice of Civil-Military Relations* (Cambridge, Mass., 1959), 226–29.
20. Summary of record, AM Misc. 201; *Army Register, 1937,* 1448; Robert W. Frazer, *Forts of the West: Military Forts and Presidios and Posts Commonly Called Forts West of the Mississippi River to 1898* (Norman, 1965), 87–88, 178, 185. Seven years after his severance from the regiment, the 7th Infantry, which included some of his former colleagues, participated in the Little Big Horn campaign, but did not suffer the disastrous fate of the 7th Cavalry.
21. MacArthur to Gen Philip H. Sheridan, July 27, 1870, AGO–CBDF 5551; summary of record, AM Misc. 201; Frazer, *Forts of the West,* 185–86; Taft A. Larson, *History of Wyoming* (Lincoln, 1965), 20–36, 63–64, 97–108. MacArthur did participate in a minor expedition against the Sioux in Feb., 1874.
22. Philippe Régis de Trobriand, *Military Life in Dakota: The Journal of Philippe Régis de Trobriand,* trans. and ed. Lucile M. Kane (St. Paul, 1951), xx–xxi, 367–68.
23. Ella Lonn, *Reconstruction in Louisiana After 1868* (New York, 1918), 73–165; E. Merton Coulter, *The South During Reconstruction, 1865–1877* (Baton Rouge, 1947), 352–53.
24. *Reminiscences,* 13–14; Frazier Hunt, *The Untold Story of Douglas MacArthur* (New York, 1954), 7–9; Francis T. Miller, *General Douglas MacArthur: Soldier-Statesman* (2nd ed., Philadelphia, 1951), 130–36. The date of birth of Arthur, III, is given as Aug. 1, 1876, in *Reminis-*

cences, 14, and as June 1, 1876, in U.S. Navy Dept., *Register of the Commissioned and Warrant Officers . . .* (1896–1923).

25. Summary of record, AM Extract 201; *WDAR, 1877,* I, xii–xiii, 86–91.

26. *Reminiscences,* 14; Lee and Henschel, *MacArthur,* 16, 240; Ira H. Larr to DM, Aug. 23, 1951, RG 10, MMBA.

27. Summary of record, AM Misc. 201; WD, *Compilation of General Orders, Circulars and Bulletins . . .* (Washington, 1916), 163–65; *WDAR, 1889,* I, 27; Frazer, *Forts of the West,* 102–03, 108–09; U.S. National Park Service, *Soldier and Brave: Indian and Military Affairs in the Trans-Mississippi West, Including a Guide to Historic Sites and Landmarks* (New York, 1963), 71–80, 200–04; Jason Betzinez, with Wilbur S. Nye, *I Fought with Geronimo* (Harrisburg, 1959), 1–17, 44–54, 122–40; Edward E. Dale, *The Indians of the Southwest: A Century of Development under the United States* (Norman, 1949), 54–55, 95, 106–15, 122–26; Gen. Ulysses S. Grant to Judge MacArthur, June 10, 1882, WD–HR, G-2, Box 128, RG 165, NA.

28. Maj. G. H. Burton to AAG, Dept. of the Missouri, Sept. 22, 1885, AGO–CBDF 5551.

29. *WDAR, 1888,* I, 6, 134–37; *idem, 1889,* I, 44–45; summary of record, AM Misc. 201; Maj. Gen. Alexander M. McCook to TAG, June 16, 1888; Judge MacArthur to SecWar, June 26, 1889; John H. Knight to Sen. William F. Vilas, Dec. 15, 1887, AGO–CBDF 5551; Elvid Hunt, *History of Fort Leavenworth, 1827–1937* (2nd ed., Ft. Leavenworth, 1937), 157–71. A pamphlet of 22 pp. of referees' letters recommending Capt. MacArthur for AAG was printed in May, 1889, probably by his father, and sent to influential military leaders in Washington. At the same time the capt. was under consideration for a post in the office of the inspector general of the Army.

30. *WDAR, 1889,* I, 44–45, 108–09; Frederick J. Turner, *The Frontier in American History* (New York, 1920), 1–6; Huntington, *The Soldier and the State,* 226–27.

31. Brig. Gen. J. C. Kelton to MacArthur, n.d., AM Extract 201. See also WD, *Compilation of General Orders,* 40–42; Von Baumbach to SecWar, June 7, 1890, AGO–CBDF 5551.

32. *WDAR, 1889,* I, 38; AWC, *Order of Battle of the United States Land Forces in the World War* (3 vols., Washington, 1931–49), III, 66–67.

33. Summary of record, AM Misc. 201; *WDAR, 1893,* I, 36–37; *idem, 1894,* I, 90–93; *idem, 1895,* I, 26–27; *Reminiscences,* 17–18.

34. Frederick L. Huidekoper, *The Military Unpreparedness of the United States* (New York, 1916), 202–19; Walter Millis, *Arms and Men: A Study in American Military History* (New York, 1956), 152–53; summary of record, AM Misc. 201; *Reminiscences,* 17–19.

35. Maj. Gen. Wesley Merritt to TAG, Aug., 1898, AM Extract 201; Edward M. Coffman, *The Hilt of the Sword: The Career of Peyton C. March* (Madison, 1966), 12–17; Leon Wolff, *Little Brown Brother:*

How the United States Purchased and Pacified the Philippine Islands at the Century's Turn (New York, 1961), 305–06; William T. Sexton, *Soldiers in the Sun: An Adventure in Imperialism* (Harrisburg, 1939), 104–15.

36. Summary of record, AM Extract 201; MacArthur's op. rpt., Mar.–May, 1899, in *WDAR, 1899*, III, 372–414; William A. Ganoe, *The History of the United States Army* (New York, 1924), 397–403; MacArthur's op. rpt., June, 1899–Apr., 1900, in *WDAR, 1900*, VI, 14–69; Edward Stratemeyer, *Under MacArthur in Luzon, or Last Battles in the Philippines* (Boston, 1901), *passim.*

37. MacArthur to Brig. Gen. Theodore Schwan [Otis' CofS], Nov. 23, 1899, in *WDAR, 1900*, VI, 59.

38. Margaret Leech, *In the Days of McKinley* (New York, 1959), 399–407; Lee and Henschel, *MacArthur*, 19.

39. *WDAR, 1901*, V, 88–131; U.S. Senate, *Hearings on Affairs in the Philippines*, 57th Cong., 1st Sess. (1902), Senate Doc. 331, II, 862–70; Henry A. Fant, "Arthur MacArthur and the Philippine Insurrection" (unpublished M.A. thesis, Miss. State University, 1963), 54–64; Coffman, *Hilt of the Sword*, 18; *Reminiscences*, 21–24; Hunt, *Untold Story*, 29, 67. Funston named his first-born son Arthur MacArthur Funston.

40. *WDAR, 1900*, VII, 142–43, 150–52, 156, 196; Philip C. Jessup, *Elihu Root* (2 vols., New York, 1938), I, 358–61; Charles B. Elliott, *The Philippines to the End of the Military Regime: America Overseas* (Indianapolis, 1917), 524–26; Dean C. Worcester and Ralston Hayden, *The Philippines, Past and Present* (2nd ed., New York, 1930), 325–31; Henry F. Pringle, *The Life and Times of William Howard Taft* (2 vols., New York, 1939), I, 167–70; Rowland T. Berthoff, "Taft and MacArthur, 1900: A Study in Civilian-Military Relations," *World Politics*, V (Jan., 1953), 196–213; Ralph E. Minger, "Taft, MacArthur, and the Establishment of Civil Government in the Philippines," *Ohio Historical Quarterly*, LXX (Dec., 1961), 308–31. When MacArthur took command of the Dept. of the Colorado, a reporter interviewed him and concluded: "He is one of the most modest and unostentatious of men." Salt Lake City *Deseret Evening News*, Mar. 10, 1902.

41. Worcester and Hayden, *Philippines*, 792–98; William H. Taft to Sec-War, Aug. 18, 1900, Elihu Root Papers, LC; U.S. Senate, *Hearings on Affairs in the Philippines*, I, 77–78; H. E. Stafford, "American Masonry in the Philippines," n.d., RG 10, MMBA; Coffman, *Hilt of the Sword*, 18. MacArthur's testimony in Apr., 1902, is found in the Senate *Hearings*, II, 849–79, 890–912, 1377–1420, 1885–1902.

42. Pres. Theodore Roosevelt to SecWar, Mar. 7, 1904, in Elting E. Morison and John M. Blum, eds., *The Letters of Theodore Roosevelt* (8 vols., Cambridge, Mass., 1951–54), IV, 744; MacArthur to TAG, July

18, 1903, AGO–DF 485098-L, RG 94, NA; Ganoe, *History of the U.S. Army*, 420, 493; George E. Mowry, *The Era of Theodore Roosevelt, 1900–1912* (New York, 1958), 125; Asceola Social Club to SecWar, Oct. 18, 1906, AGO–DF 1179431.

43. On his visits to Japan, Manchuria, China, India, and Southeast Asia, see MacArthur's extensive correspondence with the War Dept., 1904–06, especially with Maj. William D. Beach, chief of 2nd div., Gen. Staff, in WD–HR, G-2, Box 128. Neither of the main printed sources on foreign observers of the war mentions Gen. MacArthur, viz., WD, *Reports of Military Observers Attached to the Armies in Manchuria During the Russo-Japanese War* (2 vols., Washington, 1906–07); Ian Hamilton, *A Staff Officer's Scrapbook During the Russo-Japanese War* (2 vols., London, 1907).

44. Chief, WCD, to MacArthur, Dec. 28, 1907, WCD File 1322, RG 165, NA; Spec. Orders 26, WD, June 2, 1909; Capt. Charles King to TAG, Sept. 7, 1912, AGO–CBDF 5551. MacArthur's appointment as lt. gen. came on the same day, Sept. 14, 1906, as Capt. Pershing's promotion to brig. gen. William Loeb, Jr. [presidential secy.] to SecWar, Sept. 14, 1906, AGO–DF 1163706.

45. Dr. K. David Cammack to DM, May 23, 1942, RG 10, MMBA; King to TAG, Sept. 7 and 10, 1912, AGO–CBDF 5551; *Milwaukee Journal*, Sept. 6, 1912; *ANR*, Sept. 7, 14, and 28, 1912; *ANJ*, Sept. 7, 14, and 21, 1912.

46. Loyal Legion, *In Memoriam, Arthur MacArthur*, 2–3; Flanders to Newlands, Jan. 11, 1913, Newlands Papers. Reliable sketches of Gen. MacArthur's career include Allen Johnson and Dumas Malone, eds., *Dictionary of American Biography* (22 vols., New York, 1928–44), XXI, 521–22; Francis B. Heitman, comp., *Historical Register and Dictionary of the United States Army* (2 vols., Washington, 1903), I, 652. For personal insights and laudatory opinions of the general by veterans who served with him, see "Proceedings Attending the Reception and Banquet Tendered to Major General Arthur MacArthur, U.S.A., by the Commandery of Wisconsin, Milwaukee, October 3, 1901," in *War Papers Read Before the Commandery of the State of Wisconsin, Military Order of the Loyal Legion of the United States* (3 vols., Milwaukee, 1903), III, 492–524.

47. U.S. Naval Academy, *Annual Register . . .* 1893–96, 1906–07; U.S. Navy Dept., *Register of the Commissioned and Warrant Officers . . .* 1896–1923; U.S. Navy Dept., *Navy Directory . . .* 1921–23; Dudley W. Knox, *A History of the United States Navy* (rev. ed., New York, 1948), 342–73, 410–21; Marley F. Hay to DM, Jan. 13, 1951, RG 10, MMBA.

48. Mann, "Some Ancestral Lines," 170; Hay to DM, Jan. 13, 1951, RG 10, MMBA; *Reminiscences*, 17.

CHAPTER II, *"Visions of Glory,"*
pages 48–66

1. Las Vegas, N.M., *Gazette,* Nov. 10, 1880. On conditions in New Mexico in the early 1880's, see various issues of this newspaper and the Santa Fe *New Mexican.*

2. Betzinez, *I Fought with Geronimo,* 55–122; Dale, *Indians of the Southwest,* 107–08; Nat. Park Service, *Soldier and Brave,* 71–75.

3. William A. Keleher, *Violence in Lincoln County, 1869–1881: A New Mexico Item* (Albuquerque, 1957), 356–62.

4. Dane and Mary Coolidge, *The Navaho Indians* (Boston, 1930), 257–59; Las Vegas *Gazette,* Mar. 22, 1881; Chris Emmett, *Fort Union and the Winning of the Southwest* (Norman, 1965), 394–95.

5. Trobriand, *Military Life in Dakotoa,* 52–53; *Reminiscences,* 14; Eleanor P. Cushman to DM, May 10, 1944, RG 10, MMBA; USMA medical history of Cadet DM, June 3, 1899, AGO–DF 487448.

6. Trobriand, *Military Life in Dakotoa,* 52–53.

7. Frazer, *Forts of the West,* 97, 102–03; *Reminiscences,* 14–15; Nat. Park Service, *Soldier and Brave,* 38, 199–204.

8. Frazer, *Forts of the West,* 102–03; Nat. Park Service, *Soldier and Brave,* 200–01.

9. Grant to Judge MacArthur, June 10, 1882, WD–HR, G-2, Box 128; Philip M. Hamer to George Fitzpatrick, May 5, 1942, General Reference Branch, NA; Hunt, *Untold Story,* 11; *Reminiscences,* 15–16.

10. Theodore White and Annalee Jacoby, *Thunder Out of China* (2nd ed., New York, 1961), 119; James M. Burns, *Roosevelt: The Lion and the Fox* (New York, 1956), 4–6; Forrest C. Pogue, *George C. Marshall* (2 vols. to date, New York, 1963–66), I, 4, 14–15.

11. *WDAR, 1888,* I, 103–04; *idem, 1889,* I, 44–45; Nat. Park Service, *Soldier and Brave,* 125–28; *Reminiscences,* 16.

12. *WDAR, 1888,* I, 136; Lee and Henschel, *MacArthur,* 242–43; *Reminiscences,* 16. The two photographs shown in the citation from Lee and Henschel were probably made at Leavenworth about 1886.

13. Harry C. Fish to Mrs. Arthur McCalla MacArthur, Mar. 17, 1947, RG 10, MMBA; *Reminiscences,* 16.

14. Richard Hofstadter, *The Age of Reform: From Bryan to F.D.R.* (2nd ed., New York, 1960), 85–87; Harold U. Faulkner, *Politics, Reform and Expansion, 1890–1900* (2nd ed., New York, 1963), 128–36.

15. *WDAR, 1893,* I, 3, 188; *idem, 1894,* I, 90, 93; *idem, 1895,* I, 99–102; Frazer, *Forts of the West,* 67.

16. *Catalogue of the West Texas Military Academy, a Church School for Boys, San Antonio, Texas, 1893–94,* 6, 14–16.

17. *Ibid.,* 19; *idem, 1896–97,* i, 14, 22; Rev. Allen L. Burleson to TAG,

June 1, 1896, AGO–DF 38122; DM to Edward J. Condon, Oct. 2, 1936, RG 10, MMBA; *Reminiscences,* 17; John Hersey, *Men on Bataan* (New York, 1943), 56–57.

18. *WTMA Catalogue, 1893–94,* 22; *idem, 1895–96,* 34–35; *idem, 1896–97,* 10, 12, 35–37; C. A. Dravo to editor, *Sat. Evening Post,* July 30, 1949; Mercer G. Johnston to DM, Aug. 1, 1949; Charles H. Quinn to DM, Mar. 31, 1944, RG 10, MMBA; *T.M.I. Today,* VII (Spring, 1967), 6; *Texas Military Institute* (San Antonio, 1967), 15. His course of study in 1894–95 comprised commercial arithmetic, algebra, French history, Texas history, Latin, Greek, civil government, Old Testament history, composition, and declamation. *WTMA Catalogue, 1894–95,* 15.

MacArthur's courses and final grades for 1896–97, his last year at West Texas Military Academy, were:

Analytical geometry	98.75	American literature	98.56
Descriptive geometry	99.50	Greek	94.36
Latin	94.54	French	99.32
U.S.A. drill regulations	98.33	Deportment	100.00
Declamation	94.46	General average	97.53

Burleson to Lt. Col. MacArthur, June 5, 1897, AGO–DF 38122.

19. Joseph Tischer to DM, Mar. 17, 1947; John Cruger to DM, June 16, 1948; E. T. Coleman to DM, June 20, 1951; Roscoe H. Piety to DM, Apr. 2 and Oct. 28, 1942; DM to Piety, May 30, 1942, RG 10, MMBA; *T.M.I. Today,* V (Nov., 1963), 17–18.

20. T. M. Paschal to Pres. Grover Cleveland, June 5, 1896; Lt. Col. MacArthur to TAG, June 1, 1896, AGO–DF 38122. Among the better known referees for MacArthur whose letters are in this file were Senators Redfield Proctor, William F. Vilas, and John L. Mitchell; Maj. Gen. Z. R. Bliss, CG, dept. of Texas; and Brig. Gen. Samuel Breck, TAG.

21. Iola E. Millard to DM, Mar., 1947, RG 10, MMBA; *Reminiscences,* 18; Hersey, *Men on Bataan,* 58.

22. Frank C. McCutcheon to DM, May 5, 1942, RG 10, MMBA; Burke Davis, *The Billy Mitchell Affair* (New York, 1967), 11–18; Alfred F. Hurley, *Billy Mitchell: Crusader for Air Power* (New York, 1964), 3; Isaac D. Levine, *Mitchell: Pioneer of Air Power* (New York, 1943), 12–13; Lee and Henschel, *MacArthur,* 46–47. MacArthur wrote love poems to other young ladies later; several of his poetic manuscripts are in MMBA.

23. Sen. Redfield Proctor to George D. Meiklejohn, Feb. 12, 1898; Henry C. Payne to Pres. William McKinley, Jan. 4, 1898, AGO–DF 38122; *Milwaukee Journal,* June 7, 1898; *Reminiscences,* 18.

CHAPTER III, *"Monastery on the Hudson,"*
pages 67–84

1. *WDAR, 1901,* I, 401; *idem, 1900,* I, 230. MacArthur officially entered West Point on June 13, 1899, at which time he swore to be loyal to the national government and the Constitution, obey the orders and regulations of the Army, and serve in the Army for at least eight years from that date. *Regulations for the United States Military Academy at West Point, N.Y., 1900,* 12–13.

2. U.S. House, *Investigation of Hazing at the United States Military Academy,* 56th Cong., 2nd Sess. (4 pts., 1901), House Rpt. 2768, I, 1–13, IV, 1715–16; Robert E. Wood, "An Upperclassman's View," *Assembly,* XXIII (Spring, 1964), 4; Hugh S. Johnson, *The Blue Eagle from Egg to Earth* (Garden City, 1935), 24–25. *Assembly* is a periodical of the West Point Alumni Foundation.

3. U.S. House, *Hazing at the Military Academy,* I, 3, III, 917, 924, IV, 1713–14, 1717; Wood, "An Upperclassman's View," 4.

4. U.S. House, *Hazing at the Military Academy,* I, 7–13, III, 916–32, IV, 1713–17; *USMA Regulations, 1902,* 52–53; *Reminiscences,* 25–26; Hunt, *Untold Story,* 19–26. MacArthur testified before the military court on Dec. 28, 1900, and the congressional committee on Jan. 17–18, 1901. In his *Reminiscences,* his account of the hearings, based on memory six decades later, confuses the various investigations, leading the reader to believe that he never mentioned the names of the hazers to any investigating body, which is erroneous.

5. Arthur P. S. Hyde, "Douglas MacArthur," *Assembly,* I (Oct., 1942), 3; Hyde, "MacArthur — His Barracks Mate Reminisces," New York *Hudson Views,* n.d., clipping in West Point Scrapbook, XVIII, 188, USMA.

6. Morris Schaff, *The Spirit of Old West Point, 1858–1862* (Boston, 1907), 272–77; Stephen F. Ambrose, *Duty, Honor, Country: A History of West Point* (Baltimore, 1966), 206–18, 241–42; Frank E. Vandiver, *John J. Pershing and the Anatomy of Leadership* (Colorado Springs, 1963), 7–8; *WDAR,* 1901, I, 401–02.

7. *USMA Regulations, 1902,* 15–28, 40–43; Sidney Forman, *West Point: A History of the United States Military Academy* (New York, 1950), 158–61; John W. Masland and Laurence I. Radway, *Soldiers and Scholars: Military Education and National Policy* (Princeton, 1957), 198–202.

8. William E. Simons, *Liberal Education in the Service Academies* (New York, 1965), 91–92; William A. Ganoe, *MacArthur Close-up: Much Then and Some Now* (New York, 1962), 96–97.

9. Forman, *West Point,* 159–60, 165; Ambrose, *Duty, Honor, Country,*

204–06, 244–45; *Official Register of the Officers and Cadets of the U.S. Military Academy, West Point, New York, June, 1903,* 5–7; R. Ernest Dupuy, *Men of West Point: The First 150 Years of the United States Military Academy* (New York, 1951), 361–64; *Army Register, 1916,* 9; Marty Maher, with Nardi R. Campion, *Bringing Up the Brass: My 55 Years at West Point* (New York, 1951), 89–90. Michie died in 1901, his successor being Lt. Col. William B. Gordon. The other heads of depts., 1899–1903, were Cols. Charles W. Larned, drawing; Edgar S. Dudley, law and history; Gustav J. Fiebeger, civil and military engineering; and Capt. Frank E. Hobbs, ordnance and gunnery. Dr. Edward S. Holden, former president of the University of Calif., was the able librarian.

Cocheu's account of the MacArthur-Edgerton clash, related in Dupuy's book, errs in placing the incident at the end of MacArthur's last year. Since all cadets completed the program in mathematics at the end of their second year, the affair probably occurred in late spring, 1901. As for his illness, it may have been related to his poor condition at the time of the congressional hearings on hazing in Jan., 1901. Hunt, however, in his *Untold Story,* 31, says his absences were because of trouble with his eyes.

10. *USMA Register, 1900,* 17, 27; *idem, 1901,* 14, 29; *idem, 1902,* 12, 29; *idem, 1903,* 10, 26–27; Joseph M. O'Donnell to Felmore Jackson, Apr. 23, 1964; Kenneth W. Rapp to Robert C. Lapp, Mar. 24, 1967; academic record of DM, 1899–1903, DM File, USMA. Leeds was disabled in 1912, retired, and formed his own engineering firm. Fiske retired as a lt. col. in 1930 to join the New York Board of Transportation. Grant became a col. in 1934, but thereafter his main service was with civilian agencies of the federal government, not with the Regular Army. George W. Cullum, *Biographical Register of the Officers and Graduates of the U.S. Military Academy at West Point, New York, Since Its Establishment in 1802,* VII, *Supplement, 1920–1930* (Chicago, 1930), 576–78; *Army Register, 1944,* 359; *Who's Who in America,* XXV, 877.

Recent studies of the careers of generals who were graduates of West Point show little or no correlation between "academic performance and entrance into the nucleus of the military elite," MacArthur's record being "repeatedly cited as the special example." Rather, the data in one study indicates that "to have been outstanding in athletics at West Point was the best indicator that a cadet would become a general." Morris Janowitz, *The Professional Soldier: A Social and Political Portrait* (Glencoe, 1960), 134–135.

11. Record of Cadet DM's honors, DM File, USMA; George W. Cocheu, "Cadet Days, 1899–1903," *Assembly,* XXIII (Spring, 1964), 7; Wood, "An Upperclassman's View," 5.

12. *Reminiscences,* 25–27; Ambrose, *Duty, Honor, Country,* 245–46, 309–10, 313; Forman, *West Point,* 184–86; Maher, *Bringing Up the Brass,* 89–90.

13. Ambrose, *Duty, Honor, Country,* 219–22; Wood, "An Upperclassman's View," 4; *Reminiscences,* 27.

14. Lee and Henschel, *MacArthur,* 30; Hersey, *Men on Bataan,* 73; *Reminiscences,* 27; diary of Bess B. Follansbee, entries of Feb. 9–10, 1903, RG 10, MMBA; Cocheu, "Cadet Days," 6.

15. Cocheu to Col. W. J. Morton, Mar. 25, 1954; Morton to Col. James W. Riley, Apr. 1, 1954; Riley to Morton, Apr. 10, 1954, DM File, USMA; Maher, *Bringing Up the Brass,* 91.

16. Edward S. Holden, comp., *The Centennial of the United States Military Academy at West Point, New York* (2 vols., New York, 1904), I, 3–62, 113–16.

17. Maj. Gen. MacArthur to TAG, June 19, 1903, AGO–DF 1163706; Cocheu, "Cadet Days," 6; *Reminiscences,* 27–28, 423–26. A tale, repeated in several popular accounts of MacArthur's life, says that Taft presented the diploma to Douglas, who, angered because his father had not been allowed to hand it to him, took it immediately to his father and sat down at his feet. Taft, of course, was then in Manila where he was serving as Philippine governor.

CHAPTER IV, *"Travels and Tribulations of a Young Engineer,"*
pages 85–109

1. Millis, *Arms and Men,* 150–88; Elihu Root, *The Military and Colonial Policy of the United States: Addresses and Reports,* ed. Robert Bacon and James B. Scott (Cambridge, Mass., 1916), 274–94.

2. Gen. MacArthur to TAG, July 18, 1903, AGO–DF 485098-L; *Reminiscences,* 28–29; "Footnote on Los Angeles History," *Journal of the West,* III (Apr., 1964), 206.

3. Ind. serv. rpt. of DM, June 30, 1904; eff. rpts. on DM by Brig. Gens. Theodore J. Wint, Jan. 9, 1904, and Charles H. Carter, May 6, 1904, AGO–DF 487448; *Reminiscences,* 29.

4. CofE to DM, Sept. 14, 1944, RG 10, MMBA; DM to Mil. Secy. [TAG], Nov. 16, 1904; ind. serv. rpt. of DM, June 30, 1904; eff. rpt. on DM by Maj. Charles D. Townsend, Aug. 1, 1904, AGO–DF 487448; *Reminiscences,* 29–30.

5. Ind. serv. rpts. of DM, June 30, 1905, and July 9, 1906; eff. rpts. on DM by Cols. Thomas H. Handbury, July 5, 1905, and William H. Heuer, June 30, 1905, and June 30, 1906; Gen. Orders 159, WD, July 12, 1905; Maj. William W. Harts to CofE, Aug. 8, 1908, AGO–DF 487448; *WDAR, 1904,* V, 3694; *idem, 1907,* V, 809–12. Lt. William D. Leahy, USN, stationed then at Mare Island and in World War II

the presidential CofS, first became acquainted with Douglas at San Francisco in 1905. William D. Leahy, *I Was There* (New York, 1950), 64–65.

6. Capt. Paul W. West to Maj. William D. Beach, Sept. 19, 1905; Gen. MacArthur to Beach, Oct. 29 and Dec. 3, 1905, Jan. 15, 1906; DM to Beach, Oct. 31, 1905, WD–HR, G-2, Box 128; Spec. Orders 222, WD, Oct. 3, 1905, AGO–DF 487448. For a long time after the Russo-Japanese War a wild myth was perpetuated that Douglas had led a Japanese charge during the battle of Mukden. See, e.g., Helen Nicolay, *MacArthur of Bataan* (New York, 1942), 55–58; Robert B. Considine, *MacArthur the Magnificent* (Philadelphia, 1942), 41–42.

7. Gen. MacArthur to Beach, Feb. 28 and Mar. 20, 1906; Hamilton King to SecState, Apr. 10, 1906; King to Prince Krom Varprakar, Apr. 10, 1906, WD–HR, G-2, Box 128.

8. Gen. MacArthur to Beach, May 2, 1906; SecWar to SecTresy, June 2, 1906, WD–HR, G-2, Box 128; SecWar to SecState, Jan. 26, 1906; Gen. MacArthur to SecWar, Sept. 28, 1905, Misc. Letters of the State Dept., 1789–1906, RG 59, NA; *Reminiscences*, 30–32.

9. DM to Mil. Secy., Aug. 4, 1906; Spec. Orders 193, WD, Aug. 16, 1906; CofE to Mil. Secy., Aug. 3, 1906, AGO–DF 487448; Ira L. Reeves, *Military Education in the United States* (Burlington, 1914), 254–65; *WDAR, 1907*, IV, 297–301, V, 15–16, 859–60.

10. Maj. E. Eveleth Winslow to CofE, Aug. 7, 1908, AGO–DF 487448.

11. William Loeb to SecWar, Dec. 4, 1906; ind. serv. rpt. of DM, June 30, 1907; Maj. William C. Langfitt to TAG, Feb. 28, 1908; Maj. Chester Harding to CofE, Sept. 4, 1908, AGO–DF 487448; *Reminiscences*, 32–34; *WDAR, 1907*, IV, 297–98; *idem, 1908*, IV, 147.

12. Ind. serv. rpt. of DM, July 1, 1908; Maj. William V. Judson to TAG, July 17, 1908, AGO–DF 487448; Gen. MacArthur to CofS, Mar. 24, 1905, WD–HR, G-2, Box 128; *WDAR, 1908*, V, 656–60.

13. Judson to TAG, July 17, 1908, AGO–DF 487448.

14. *Ibid.;* eff. rpt. on DM by Judson, July 1, 1908; CofE to TAG, Mar. 6 and 19, 1908; Col. Hugh L. Scott to CofS, Mar. 12, 1908; TAG to CofE, Mar. 16, 1908; Spec. Orders 79, WD, Apr. 3, 1908, AGO–DF 487448.

15. See the nineteen documents, July 1–Sept. 4, 1908, relating to Judson's rpt. in AGO–DF 487448. The weakness of MacArthur's reply is evident in his response to TAG answering Judson's charge that he came to work late:

In reply to this charge I respectfully state that I frequently arrived at the office after 8:30 A.M., the opening hour, and prolonged the luncheon period beyond the time fixed for the office force; but

as soon as informed of Major Judson's wishes in the premises, I
governed myself accordingly in all particulars. I may say further in
this connection that as a large part of my time was unemployed I
fell into the view that my presence in the office was not regarded as
a matter of much practical importance.

DM to TAG, July 28, 1908, AGO–DF 487448. MacArthur ignores the
whole affair with Judson in his *Reminiscences,* just as he does most
other unpleasant occurrences of his career.
16. WD, *Compilation of General Orders,* 255–88; Reeves, *Military Education,* 203–39; *WDAR, 1910,* III, 81; Hunt, *History of Fort Leavenworth,* 33–39; Pogue, *Marshall,* I, 107; Hurley, *Mitchell,* 10–13;
Richard H. Rovere and Arthur M. Schlesinger, Jr., *The General and
the President, and the Future of American Foreign Policy* (New York,
1951), 26.
17. *Reminiscences,* 34; D. C. Buell to W. L. Park, July 27, 1909; Henry
Mikkelsen to DM, Feb. 10, 1943, RG 10, MMBA; eff. rpts. on DM
by Col. Thomas H. Rees, June 30, 1908, and Maj. Clement A. F.
Flagler, June 30, 1909, and June 30, 1910, AGO–DF 487448.
18. Brig. Gen. Thomas R. Kerr to DM, Nov. 23, 1908; Capt. George H.
Cameron to AG, Ft. Riley, Nov. 16, 1908; CofE to Flagler, June 9,
1909; ind. serv. rpts. of DM, June 30, 1909, and June 30, 1910,
AGO–DF 487448; Coffman, *Hilt of the Sword,* 33–34; John Pegram
to DM, June 13, 1942, RG 10, MMBA. Part of one of MacArthur's
lectures on demolitions at Ft. Riley's Mounted Service School, Oct.,
1908, is reprinted in Vorin E. Whan, ed., *A Soldier Speaks: Public
Papers and Speeches of General of the Army Douglas MacArthur*
(New York, 1965), 3–7. A copy of MacArthur's manual, *Military
Demolitions,* is located in MMBA.
19. Mrs. Arthur MacArthur to Edward H. Harriman, Apr. 17, 1909;
Alexander Millar to Mrs. MacArthur, Apr. 28, 1909; Millar to J.
Kruttschnitt, Apr. 28, 1909; Charles H. Bates to Kruttschnitt, May 5,
1909; Buell to Park, July 27, 1909, RG 10, MMBA. Buell did not
make a specific offer to MacArthur, but merely interviewed him as
part of the company's investigation.
20. Ind. serv. rpts. of DM, 1908–12; Flagler to Col. William T. Rossell,
June 28, 1910; Lt. Col. Joseph E. Kuhn to Rossell, July 25, 1910;
Maj. Meriwether L. Walker to Col. Daniel Coruman, Oct. 19, 1912;
eff. rpt. on DM by Coruman, Dec. 16, 1912; AGO statement of
medical history of DM, 1914, AGO–DF 487448; *WDAR, 1912,* I, 52–
59, 256–57, 433, III, 57; Pogue, *Marshall,* I, 112–14; *Reminiscences,*
34–35; Wood, "An Upperclassman's View," 5; Hunt, *Untold Story,*
42–43.
21. DM to CofE, Oct. 3, 1912; CofE to CofS, Oct. 10, 1912; SecWar to

TAG, Oct. 11, 1912; TAG to Coruman, Oct. 11, 1912; DM to Walker, Oct. 19, 1912; AGO statement of medical history of DM, 1914; eff. rpt. on DM by Maj. Gen. Leonard Wood, Dec. 31, 1912, AGO–DF 487448.

CHAPTER V, *"Important Friendships,"*
pages 110–135

1. Otto L. Nelson, Jr., *National Security and the General Staff* (Washington, 1946), 132–66; U.S. House, *Relief of the Adjutant General of the Army from the Duties of His Office*, 62nd Cong., 2nd Sess. (2 pts., 1912), House Rpt. 508; Mabel E. Deutrich, *The Struggle for Supremacy: The Career of General Fred C. Ainsworth* (Washington, 1962), 113–27; Siert F. Riepma, "Portrait of an Adjutant General: The Career of Major General Fred C. Ainsworth," *Journal of the American Military History Foundation*, II (Spring, 1938), 30–35.

2. CofS to DM, Apr. 17, 1913; eff. rpt. on DM by Wood, Jan. 29, 1914, AGO–DF 487448; Elting E. Morison, *Turmoil and Tradition: A Study of the Life and Times of Henry Stimson* (Boston, 1960), 152–63; Russell F. Weigley, *History of the United States Army* (New York, 1967), 342–43; Herman Hagedorn, *Leonard Wood: A Biography* (2 vols., New York, 1931), II, 151–53; *Reminiscences*, 39; DM to Stimson, Mar. 26, 1913, Box 97, Henry L. Stimson Papers, YUA.

3. Eff. rpts. on DM by Wood and Col. Edward Burr, Jan. 29, 1914; rpt. of physical examination of DM, No. 13, 1914, AGO–DF 487448; DM to Lt. Col. William W. Harts, Oct. 24, 1913, RG 328, NA; *WDAR, 1913*, I, 139; *Army Register, 1913*, 9; *idem, 1916*, 10; Whan, ed., *A Soldier Speaks*, 8–9; *New York Times*, Aug. 7, 1914; Clarence Thomas to DM, Apr. 23, 1951, RG 10, MMBA. Brig. Gen. Albert Mills, who was superintendent of West Point when MacArthur was a cadet, was also a member of the General Staff in 1912–17.

4. Robert F. Quirk, *An Affair of Honor: Woodrow Wilson and the Occupation of Veracruz* (Lexington, 1962), 1–25, 70–77, 85–103, 113–17; war diary of Brig. Gen. Frederick Funston, Veracruz, entries of Apr. 19–May 3, 1914, RG 94, NA.

5. Wood to TAG, Nov. 25, 1914; CofS to TAG, Apr. 23, 1914; SecWar to SecNavy, Apr. 23, 1914; Capt. Constant Cordier to Wood, May 19 and Aug. 18, 1914; Capt. William C. Ball to CofS, Jan. 23, 1915, AGO–DF 487448; war diary of Funston, entries of May 2–3, 1914.

6. DM to Wood, Sept. 30, 1914, AGO–DF 487448. This rpt. is printed in full in Hunt, *Untold Story*, 52–56, and in part in *Reminiscences*, 41–42. MacArthur refers in his rpt. of Sept. 30 to a rpt. which he sent Wood on May 9, but the latter document was not found in the NA or MMBA.

7. DM to Wood, Sept. 30, 1914; Cordier to Wood, May 19 and Aug. 18, 1914; Funston to TAG, Jan. 13, 1915, AGO–DF 487448; war diary of Funston, entries of May 8 and 12, 1914. On May 7 Funston recorded in his diary the following message to TAG, which shows his willingness, even eagerness, to move inland:

> Have just been informed foreigners and citizens in Mexico City will unite in request that U.S. Troops occupy city to prevent massacre and pillage by Zapata. If government should accede to the request recommend Brazilian Ambassador to Mexico be asked to request those in authority there to send to Vera Cruz immediately all locomotives and cars of both railways and that military commanders along these railways be directed to assist us. If consignment is refused we can go anyhow and overcome any likely opposing force taking into consideration enemy's occupation with Villa and Zapata. Would follow Interoceanic Railway carrying supplies on 175 cars drawn by horses and mules . . . If it should be desired to have this done merely give the order, inform me as to attitude of authorities referred to and leave the rest to us.

8. DM to Wood, May 7, 1914, quoted in Hagedorn, *Wood,* II, 147; *WDAR, 1915,* I, 311–12, II, 23–24; war diary of Funston, entry of May 17, 1914; "Veracruz: A Crusade," *Outlook,* CVII (July 4, 1914), 527; Quirk, *Affair of Honor,* 78–85; list of officers of 42nd Div. entitled to the Mexican Service Campaign Badge, Feb. 12, 1918, AGO–PF, Box 371, RG 407, NA.

9. CofS to TAG, Aug. 7 and 10, 1914; Wood to TAG, Nov. 25, 1914, AGO–DF 487448.

10. TAG to Funston, Dec. 7, 1914; Funston to TAG, Jan. 13, 1915, AGO–DF 487448. In his eff. rpt. of Nov. 30, 1914, Funston gave MacArthur an "excellent" on "general bearing and military appearance," but a lower rating of "very good" on "attention to duty" and "professional zeal."

11. Maj. William S. Graves to Chief, War Col. Div., Jan. 21, 1915; proceedings of a board of officers convened to report upon the awarding of a Medal of Honor to Capt. Douglas MacArthur, Feb. 9, 1915, AGO–DF 487448.

12. JAG to CofS, Feb. 17, 1915; eff. rpts. on DM by Wood, Wotherspoon, and Scott, Feb. 23, 1915; TAG to Wood, Mar. 2, 1915, AGO–DF 487448; Hunt, *Untold Story,* 59.

13. David F. Houston, *Eight Years with Wilson's Cabinet,* 1913–1920 (2 vols., Garden City, 1926), I, 120; Weigley, *History of U.S. Army,* 342–46; diary of Col. Edward M. House, entry of Dec. 15, 1915, Edward M. House Papers, YUA; Frederick Palmer, *Newton D. Baker: America at War* (2 vols., New York, 1931), I, 40–41.

14. Arthur S. Link, *Woodrow Wilson and the Progressive Era, 1910–1917* (New York, 1954), 174–96; *WDAR, 1916*, I, 49–57, 155–59, 163–70, 210–17; E. Brooke Lee, Jr., *The Politics of Our Military National Defense . . . Together with the Defense Acts of 1916 and 1920 as Studies*, 76th Cong., 3rd Sess. (1940), Sen. Doc. 274, 17–66; Weigley, *History of U.S. Army*, 346–51.

15. Brig. Gen. Montgomery M. Macomb to CofS, May 11 and July 28, 1916; TAG to DM, July 29, 1916, AGO–DF 2374240; CofS to TAG, Mar. 18, 1916; eff. rpt. on DM by Maj. Gen. Hugh L. Scott, Mar. 23, 1916, AGO–DF 487448.

16. *Army Almanac* (Washington, 1959), 353; *Reminiscences*, 43–44; Acting SecWar to TAG, Oct. 6, 1916; CofS to TAG, Feb. 6, 1915, AGO–DF 487448; *New York Times*, July 7, 1916, Mar. 18 and Apr. 6, 1917; Mrs. AM to Pershing, June 12, 1918, Box 121, John J. Pershing Papers, LC; Coffman, *Hilt of the Sword*, 39–40; Dupuy, *Men of West Point*, 131; David A. Lockmiller, *Enoch H. Crowder: Soldier, Lawyer, and Statesman, 1859–1932* (Columbia, Mo., 1955), 159–60.

17. Washington correspondents to SecWar, Apr. 4, 1917, AGO–DF 487448.

18. *WDAR, 1917*, I, 127–35; Palmer, *Baker*, I, 355–56; Gen. Scott to D. Hunter Scott, Feb. 15, 1917, Hugh L. Scott Papers, LC; John J. Pershing, *My Experiences in the World War* (2 vols., New York, 1931), I, 15–17; AWC, *Order of Battle*, III, Pt. 1, p. 52.

19. Baker quoted in Henry J. Reilly, *Americans All: The Rainbow at War: Official History of the 42nd Rainbow Division in the World War* (Columbus, 1936), 26; *Reminiscences*, 45–46; Acting CofS to TAG, Aug. 1, 1917, AGO–PF, Box 371; Palmer, *Baker*, I, 356–57; Clarence H. Cramer, *Newton D. Baker: A Biography* (Cleveland, 1961), 129. In Feb., 1918, MacArthur was again required to complete the necessary forms accepting his commission as a colonel of infantry in the National Army. The reason for the second set of forms is not known. AG, AEF, to DM, Feb. 18, 1918; DM to Pershing, Feb. 21, 1918, AEF/GHQ, AG File 8756-A-320, RG 120, NA.

CHAPTER VI, *"From Long Island to Lorraine,"*
pages 139–172

1. War diary, 42nd Div. Hq., entries of Aug. 20–Sept. 13, 1917, AEF/GHQ, G-3 Rpts., Box 3327, RG 120, NA; Acting CofS to TAG Aug. 22, 1917, AGO–PF, Box 371; Gen. Orders 2, 42nd Div. Hq., Sept. 8, 1917, 42nd Div. HR, Box 20, RG 120, NA; ABMC, *42d Division Summary of Operations in the World War* (Washington, 1944), 1, 4; *Rainbow Reveille*, XXXVI (Nov., 1956), 3, 6. A typical French division averaged about 13,000 men, a British division 12,000,

and a German division 10,600. ABMC, *A Guide to the American Battlefields in Europe* (Washington, 1927), 267.

2. Col. William Kelly to CG, 42nd Div., Sept. 11, 1917; Col. Jay W. Grissinger to Adj., 42nd Div., Sept. 22, 1917, 42nd Div. HR, Box 25; AWC, *Order of Battle,* III, Pt. 1, 753–55; war diary, 42nd Div. Hq., entries of Sept. 8–Oct. 14, 1917.

3. *Rainbow Reveille,* XV (Nov.–Dec., 1935), 11; *Reminiscences,* 52; Gen. Orders 11, 42nd Div. Hq., Oct. 6, 1917; DM to 42nd Div. COs, Oct. 6 and 12, 1917, 42nd Div. HR, Box 25; CinC, AEF, to CofS, July 28, 1917, Dept. of the Army, *United States Army in the World War, 1917–1918* (17 vols., Washington, 1948), II, 22.

4. DM to 42nd Div. COs, Sept. 25, 1917; Adj., 84th Brig., to CO, 168th Inf., Oct. 8, 1917; CO, 168th Inf., to CG, 84th Brig., Oct. 8, 1917; CO, 167th Inf., to CG, 84th Brig., Oct. 11, 1917; CG, 84th Brig., to CO, 168th Inf., Oct. 11, 1917, 42nd Div. HR, Box 25.

5. War diary, 42nd Div. Hq., entries of Oct. 18–Nov. 5, 1917; AWC, *Order of Battle,* I, 275; James Carlin to Maj. Gen. William A. Mann, Sept. 4, 1917, 42nd Div. DF 095, Box 79, RG 120, NA; *42d Div. Summary,* 4. In his *Reminiscences,* 52, MacArthur states that the cruiser *Chattanooga,* commanded by his brother, was one of the warships escorting the convoy, but the lists of escorts in the divisional hq. war diary and elsewhere in 42nd Div. documents do not include the vessel.

6. Pershing, *My Experiences,* I, 252–53; Frederick L. Paxson, *American Democracy and the World War* (2 vols., Boston, 1939), II, 311–17; *USAWW,* II, 123, 196, 208; Basil H. Liddell Hart, *The Real War, 1914–1918* (Boston, 1930), 296–366.

7. War diary, 42nd Div. Hq., entries of Nov. 6–9, 1917; Palmer, *Baker,* II, 228–29; Gen. Orders 20, 42nd Div. Hq., Dec. 18, 1917; Gen. Orders 21, 42nd Div. Hq., Dec. 19, 1918, 42nd Div. HR, Box 21; *Reminiscences,* 54.

8. War diary, 42nd Div. Hq., entries of Nov. 10–17, 1917; *Reminiscences,* 53; Hunt, *Untold Story,* 70–71; Col. Fox Conner to CinC, AEF, Nov. 20, 1917, *USAWW,* II, 77.

9. CofS, AEF, to CinC, AEF, Nov. 25, 1917, *USAWW,* III, 669–70.

10. *Reminiscences,* 53; Paxson, *American Democracy,* 315–16. Later the 32nd Div. was redesignated a combat unit, with Chaumont stripping the 33rd Div. to replenish the 32nd in men and equipment.

11. Gen. Orders 19, 42nd Div. Hq., Dec. 9, 1917, *USAWW,* III, 671; Walter B. Wolf, *A Brief Story of the Rainbow Division* (New York, 1919), 8–10; AG, AEF, to CG, 42nd Div., Dec. 16, 1917; DM to 42nd Div. COs, Dec. 18, 1917, 42nd Div. HR, Box 1; E. F. Hackett to DM, Mar. 19, 1952; Alfred Jacobson to Brig. Gen. Henry J. Reilly, Jan. 31, 1936, RG 10, MMBA; Hersey, *Men on Bataan,* 113. Pershing

visited the 42nd on Dec. 23, but, according to his diary, he was impressed only by "a well-conducted simulated attack by its training companion, Maj. Gen. Monroe's French 69th Div." Pershing, *My Experiences*, I, 264.

The 168th Inf., stricken by "contagious disease," probably measles, was quarantined at Rimaucourt until late Jan. when it was allowed to rejoin the 42nd Div., then at Rolampont. CofS, AEF, to CG, 42nd Div., Dec. 22, 1917, *USAWW*, III, 673; CofS, AEF, to CG, I Cps., Jan. 25, 1918, *ibid.,* 674.

12. Maj. T. Corbahou, suggestions for a program of combat instruction, Jan. 7, 1918; directions for instruction in hand grenade training, Jan. 14, 1918, 42nd Div. HR, Box 1; *Reminiscences*, 53–54; Frederick Palmer, *America in France* (New York, 1918), 127–37; Richard O'Connor, *Black Jack Pershing* (Garden City, 1961), 208–10; IG, AEF, to CinC, AEF, Feb. 20, 1918, 42nd Div. HR, Box 21; Gen. Orders 6, 42nd Div. Hq., Feb. 13, 1918, *USAWW*, III, 675–76. Over 1300 members of the 42nd Div. were hospitalized with various ailments at the time of Brewster's visit.

13. Lt. Col. Hugh A. Drum to Asst. G-3, AEF, Feb. 14, 1918, *USAWW*, III, 676–78; ABMC, *42d Div. Summary*, 4–5; Douglas W. Johnson, *Battlefields of the World War: Western and Southern Fronts; A Study in Military Geography* (New York, 1921), 415–29, 452–57.

14. Memo. 52, 84th Brig. Hq., Feb. 23, 1918, 84th Brig. HR, Box 418, RG 120, NA; *USAWW*, II, 189, III, 679–80, XII, 347, 354; Gen. Orders 8, 42nd Div. Hq., Feb. 23, 1918, 42nd Div. HR, Box 20; Lee and Henschel, *MacArthur*, 257–58. MacArthur reputedly wore the muffler and sweater to protect himself against tonsillitis, to which he had long been susceptible.

15. Irving S. Cobb, *The Glory of the Coming: What Mine Eyes Have Seen of Americans in Action in This Year of Grace and Allied Endeavor* (New York, 1918), 436–40; Charles T. Menoher, "The Rainbow in Lorraine," *Rainbow Reveille*, XXXI (Jan., 1952), 4; *Reminiscences*, 54–55; *New York Times*, Mar. 16, 1918.

16. Lt. Col. William N. Hughes, Jr., to Col. Fox Conner, Mar. 5, 1918, *USAWW*, III, 381; Pershing, *My Experiences*, I, 337–39; Francis P. Duffy, *Father Duffy's Story: A Tale of Humor and Heroism, of Life and Death with the Fighting Sixty-Ninth [165th Inf.]; With an Historical Appendix by Joyce Kilmer* (New York, 1919), 61–69; CG, 42nd Div., to CG, Third Army, Feb. 6, 1918, 42nd Div. HR, Box 2; Lt. Col. A. Dussuage to CG, French 164th Div., Mar. 8, 1918, 42nd Div. DF 052, Box 78; Joyce Kilmer, "The Woods Called Rouge Bouquet," *Rainbow Reveille*, XXIX (Apr., 1950), 5.

17. ABMC, *American Armies and Battlefields in Europe* (Washington, 1938), 423–24; Edward M. Coffman, *The War to End All Wars: The*

American Military Experience in World War I (New York, 1968), 150; Reilly, *Americans All*, 191; *Reminiscences*, 55–56; WD, *American Decorations*, 417; James T. Boyle to DM, May 31, 1942, RG 10, MMBA; John H. Taber, *The Story of the 168th Infantry* (2 vols., Iowa City, 1925), I, 125–31, 158.

18. Memo. 61, 84th Brig. Hq., Mar. 8, 1918, 84th Brig. HR, Box 418; *New York Times*, Mar. 26, 1918; Mrs. Arthur MacArthur to CinC, AEF, Mar. 26 and Apr. 2, 1918; AG, AEF, to CG, 42nd Div., Mar. 26, 1918; CG, 42nd Div., to CinC, AEF, Mar. 23 and 31, 1918, AEF/ GHQ, AG File 15829. For an interesting note on the wire services' competition in reporting the gassing of MacArthur, see Emmet Crozier, *American Reporters on the Western Front, 1914–18* (New York, 1959), 228.

19. Palmer, *Baker*, II, 96–103; James G. Harbord, *Leaves from a War Diary* (New York, 1925), 243–47; Ralph A. Hayes, *Secretary Baker at the Front* (New York, 1918), 87–90; *New York Times*, May 18, 1918; Curt Reiss, ed., *They Were There* (New York, 1944), 406; Drum to Asst. G-3, AEF, Mar. 27, 1918, *USAWW*, III, 683–84; Coffman, *War to End All Wars*, 150–51.

20. Liddell Hart, *Real War*, 387–88; prelim. rpt. of CinC, AEF, Jan. 16, 1919, *USAWW*, XII, 6–7; war diary, AEF/GHQ, Mar. 28, 1918, *ibid.*, II, 262; table of Allied and German strength, May, 1918, *ibid.*, II, 435; Gen. Orders 11, 42nd Div. Hq., Mar. 23, 1918, *ibid.*, III, 682–83; Spec. Orders 2741, French Eighth Army Hq., Mar. 27, 1918, *ibid.*, III, 685–86.

21. Duffy, *Father Duffy's Story*, 85; Johnson, *Battlefields*, 415–19; Menoher, "The Rainbow in Lorraine," 4–5; *idem*, "The Rainbow," *New York Times Magazine Section*, Apr. 27, 1919; *Reminiscences*, 56; war diary, 42nd Div. Hq., Mar. 26–June 20, 1918, 42nd Div. HR, Box 2; Wolf, *42nd Div.*, 16; WD cablegrams and communiques concerning op. of 42nd Div., May–June, 1918, *USAWW*, XIII, 155–205.

22. Palmer, *America in France*, 187; DM to CG, French VI Cps., June 14 and 16, 1918, 42nd Div. HR, Box 14; Raymond S. Tompkins, *The Story of the Rainbow Division* (New York, 1919), 37–39.

23. Duffy, *Father Duffy's Story*, 98–99. McCoy and Donovan, who were successive commanders of the 165th Inf., both rose to high positions in the Army in later years, with Donovan heading the OSS in World War II.

24. Menoher quoted in Tompkins, *Rainbow Div.*, v–vi; Lt. Col. R. H. Shelton to G-3, AEF, May 1, 1918, *USAWW*, III, 700–02; DM to CG, French VII Cps., Apr. 24, 1918, 42nd Div. HR, Box 14; DM to CG, French VI Cps., May 25, 1918, *ibid.*, Box 1; standing orders on defense against gas, 42nd Div. Hq., Apr. 18, 1918, *ibid.*, Box 20; Col. William P. Screws to CG, 84th Brig., Apr. 18, 1918, *ibid.*, Box

21; Col. Robert H. Tyndall to CG, 67th FA Brig., May 24, 1918, *ibid.*, Box 21; Duffy, *Father Duffy's Story*, 102–03.

25. Henry J. Reilly, "The Lorraine Mission Paid Off," *Rainbow Reveille*, XXIX (Apr., 1950), 5; Reilly, *Americans All*, 27–28; CinC, AEF, to CofS, June 14, 1918, *USAWW*, II, 464; Spec. Orders 65, French VI Cps. Hq., June 16, 1918, *ibid.*, III, 708–10; Memo., 42nd Div. Hq., June 18, 1918, 42nd Div. Hq.

26. Hunt, *Untold Story*, 74–76. The Charmes episode is not mentioned in MacArthur's *Reminiscences*.

27. *Army Register, 1921*, 10; Mrs. MacArthur to Pershing, June 12 and 29, 1918; Pershing to Mrs. MacArthur, July 12, 1918; DM to Pershing, July 11, 1918, Box 121, John J. Pershing Papers, LC; *New York Times*, June 29, 1918. MacArthur was thirty-eight at the time he became a brig. gen., but Lesley J. MacNair and Pelham D. Glassford rose to that rank on Oct. 1, 1918, both at the age of thirty-five.

CHAPTER VII, *"Turning the Tide in Champagne,"*
pages 173–195

1. *WDAR, 1919*, I, 580–81; ABMC, *42d Div. Summary*, 6–8; AWC, *Order of Battle*, I, 278–79; Shipley Thomas, *The History of the A.E.F.* (New York, 1920), 82–96; Reilly, *Americans All*, 247–48; Coffman, *War to End All Wars*, 212–13; Gen. Orders 47, 42nd Div. Hq., July 4, 1918, *USAWW*, III, 718–19; Liddell Hart, *Real War*, 420–21; *Reminiscences*, 57. Like others who have written about the operation, MacArthur erroneously credited Gouraud with originating the concept of the elastic defense in depth.

2. Johnson, *Battlefields*, 252–68; *Rainbow Reveille*, XXVI (Nov., 1946), 3; *ibid.*, XXXVI (Jan., 1957), 2; *Reminiscences*, 57; Hunt, *Untold Story*, 78–79.

3. Gouraud's order of July 7 quoted in *Rainbow Reveille*, XXIX (Oct., 1949), 4. Naulin issued the following order two days after Gouraud's:

> The attack on the Champagne front seems imminent. It is with the utmost confidence that I shall see the battle begin. Covered by a powerful artillery and reinforced by the Chasseur battalions of the French 46th Division and by the American 42nd Division, the XXI Army Corps will prove once again that, where it is, the Boche shall not pass. Let everyone fight and, if need be, die at his post, with no thought to what may happen on his flanks or in his rear, and victory is ours.

Field Order 2356–3, XXI Cps. Hq., July 5, 1918, *USAWW*, III, 719.

4. ABMC, *American Armies and Battlefields*, 330, 343; Menoher, "The Rainbow," 3; Reilly, *Americans All*, 251–54; Duffy, *Father Duffy's*

Story, 130; Taber, *Story of the 168th*, I, 280–81. Taber claims an American patrol captured the Germans who disclosed the exact time of the attack.

5. Menoher to CinC, AEF, July 15, 1918, 42nd Div. HR, Box 10; Charles MacArthur quoted in S. L. A. Marshall, *The American Heritage History of World War I* (New York, 1964), 349; *USAWW*, V, 166–74, 249; ABMC, *Guide to American Battlefields*, 189–91; Gen. Pierre Naulin to Div. CGs, XXI Cps., July 15, 1918, 42nd Div. HR, Box 1; DM to Brig. Gen. Harry J. Collins, May 31, 1943, RG 10, MMBA; rpt. on 42nd Div. relations with the French Army, Feb.–July, 1918, AEF/GHQ, G-3 Rpts., Box 3327.

6. ABMC, *American Armies and Battlefields*, 331–32, 345; *Rainbow Reveille*, XXIX (Oct., 1949), 5; Coffman, *War to End All Wars*, 223–27; *Reminiscences*, 58, 70.

7. ABMC, *42d Div. Summary*, 17–20; 42nd Div. op. rpt., July 25–Aug. 3, 1918, 42nd Div. HR, Box 14; Coffman, *War to End All Wars*, 250–53; Reilly, *Americans All*, 316–18.

8. List of 42nd Div. recipients of DSCs and Medals of Honor, 1918, AGO–PF, Box 371, RG 407, NA; ABMC, *American Armies and Battlefields*, 71; Palmer, *America in France*, 385–88; William H. Amerine, *Alabama's Own in France* [167th Inf.] (New York, 1919), 145–46.

9. Gen. Orders 51, 42nd Div. Hq., July 27, 1918; *USAWW*, V, 521; Elmer W. Sherwood, *Diary of a Rainbow Veteran: Written at the Front* (Terre Haute, 1929), 66; ABMC, *American Armies and Battlefields*, 72; 42nd Div. op. rpt., July 29, 1918, *USAWW*, V, 524; Palmer, *American in France*, 389–90; Duffy, *Father Duffy's Story*, 158–59.

10. 42nd Div. op. rpt., July 25–Aug. 3, 1918, 42nd Div. HR, Box 14; DM to AEF/GHQ, July 30, 1918, *USAWW*, XIII, 262; Francis W. Halsey, *The Literary Digest History of the World War; Compiled from Original and Contemporary Sources* (10 vols., New York, 1919), V, 269; *Reminiscences*, 59–60; George S. Viereck, ed., *As They Saw Us: Foch, Ludendorff and Other Leaders Write Our War History* (Garden City, 1929), 120.

11. Menoher to CG, I Cps., July 31, 1918, AEF/GHQ, AG File 18151-A-575; Gen. Orders 11, 84th Brig. Hq., Aug. 6, 1918, 84th Brig. HR, Box 418; *Reminiscences*, 61. On Aug. 6, MacArthur appointed Lts. William H. Wright and Wilfred J. Bazinet as his aides and Capt. Walter B. Wolf as brig. adj.

12. 42nd Div. op. rpt., July 25–Aug. 3, 1918, 42nd Div. HR, Box 14; ABMC, *42d Div. Summary*, 28–30; DM to AEF/GHQ, July 31 and Aug. 1, 1918, *USAWW*, XIII, 263–64; Gen. Orders 53, 42nd Div. Hq., Aug. 1, 1918, *ibid.*, V, 526–27.

13. Lt. Orgel to 42nd Div. Hq., July 31, 1918, 42nd Div. HR, Box 10;

W. E. Talbot to W. B. Ruggles, Oct. 21, 1937, RG 1, MMBA; *Reminiscences*, 60–61.

14. ABMC, *42d Div. Summary*, 30; Wolf, *Brief Story of Rainbow Div.*, 33–34.

15. DM to CG, 42nd Div., Aug. 2, 1918, 42nd Div. HR, Box 10.

16. ABMC, *42d Div. Summary*, 30–31; Duffy, *Father Duffy's Story*, 206; Sherwood, *Diary of a Rainbow Veteran*, 66. The 67th Field Artillery, the Rainbow's artillery brig., was attached to the 4th Div. on Aug. 3, remaining with it through the Vesle battle until Aug. 11.

17. 42nd Div. strength rpts., July 31–Aug. 15, 1918, 42nd Div. HR, Box 2; ABMC, *42d Div. Summary*, 32–33; Sherwood, *Diary of a Rainbow Veteran*, 49; Don Lawson, *The United States in World War I* (New York, 1964), 71–77.

18. Amerine, *Alabama's Own*, 164–65; Menoher to CG, I Cps., Aug. 4, 1918, 42nd Div. HR, Box 1; Tompkins, *Story of Rainbow Div.*, 94–95.

19. Coffman, *War to End All Wars*, 234–61; Menoher to AEF/GHQ, Aug. 2, 1918, *USAWW*, XIII, 270; 42nd Div. op. rpt., July 25–Aug. 3, 1918, 42nd Div. HR, Box 14.

20. *Reminiscences*, 61, 70; DM to Maj. James Shannon, Aug. 7, 1918; AG, AEF, to CG, 42nd Div., Aug. 11, 1918, AEF/GHQ, AG File 18151-A-646; Spec. Orders 227, AEF/GHQ, Aug. 15, 1918; Gen. Orders 57, 42nd Div. Hq., Aug. 18, 1918, 42nd Div. HR, Box 20; *New York Times*, Aug. 3, 1918; Hunt, *Untold Story*, 83.

CHAPTER VIII, *"The Easiest and Hardest Battles,"*
pages 196–226

1. Taber, *Story of the 168th*, II, 56–57; AWC, *Order of Battle*, I, 280–81; Drum to CG, 42nd Div., Aug. 25, 1918, 42nd Div. HR, Box 10; Gen. Orders 13, 84th Brig. Hq., Aug. 10, 1918, 84th Brig. HR, Box 418; *USAWW*, VIII, 135, 169–70, 191, 196, 245–46; Pershing, *My Experiences*, II, 259; Amerine, *Alabama's Own*, 173.

2. Coffman, *War to End All Wars*, 262–63; Marshall, *American Heritage History of World War I*, 358–59, 370–75; Weigley, *History of U.S. Army*, 385; ABMC, *Guide to American Battlefields*, 69; Liddell Hart, *Real War*, 450–51. Actually, as early as July, 1917, Pershing had talked to Foch about the St. Mihiel sector as a possible field of operations for the A.E.F.

3. Johnson, *Battlefields*, 316–31, 369–73.

4. Maj. Gen. James W. McAndrew to CofS, 1st Army, Aug. 16, 1918, *USAWW*, VIII, 129–30; order of battle, 1st Army Hq., Sept. 10, 1918, *ibid.*, 235; ABMC, *42d Div. Summary*, 35–40; Pershing, *My Experiences*, II, 226, 268; Coffman, *War to End All Wars*, 270–73.

5. ABMC, *American Armies and Battlefields,* 424; *USAWW,* VIII, 62–65, 75; *Reminiscences,* 62; William L. Langer, *Gas and Flame in World War I* (2nd ed., New York, 1965), 30–33.

6. Palmer, *America in France,* 428; Langer, *Gas and Flame,* 32–33; Col. Conrad H. Lanza's notes on American artillery action, St. Mihiel salient, Sept. 12, 1918, WD–HR, G-1, Box 79, RG 165, NA.

7. Gen. Order 17 [84th Brig.'s attack plan], 84th Brig. Hq., Sept. 10, 1918, 42nd Div. HR, Box 25; 42nd Div. op. rpt., Sept. 11–15, 1918, 42nd Div. HR, Box 14; *Reminiscences,* 62–63; Sherwood, *Diary of a Rainbow Veteran,* 121–22.

8. 42nd Div. op. rpt., Sept. 11–15, 1918, 42nd Div. HR, Box 14; *Reminiscences,* 63; Coffman, *War to End All Wars,* 282.

9. 42nd Div. op. rpt., Sept. 11–15, 1918, 42nd Div. HR, Box 14; Halsey, *Literary Digest History of the World War,* V, 376; 42nd Div. G-2 rpt., Sept. 12–13, 1918, 42nd Div. HR, Box 4; Gen. Paul von Hindenburg to Gen. Max von Gallwitz, Sept. 17, 1918, *USAWW,* VIII, 312.

10. 42nd Div. op. rpt., Sept. 11–15, 1918, 42nd Div. HR, Box 14; *Reminiscences,* 63–64; Reilly, *Americans All,* 547–48, 576–78. In his memoirs MacArthur claims that he went "into the outskirts" of Metz, but in his statement in Reilly's book, thirty years earlier, he says that he "reconnoitered in the direction of Mars-la Tour."

11. Reilly, *Americans All,* 577. Cf. *Reminiscences,* 64.

12. *Rainbow Reveille,* XI (June 15, 1932), 11; Sherwood, *Diary of a Rainbow Veteran,* 143; Thomas M. Johnson, *Without Censor: New Light on Our Greatest World War Battles* (Indianapolis, 1928), 89; Liddell Hart, *Real War,* 458–60; Pogue, *Marshall,* I, 175; Reilly, *Americans All,* 549–50; *Reminiscences,* 64.

13. Gen. Orders 18, 84th Brig. Hq., Sept. 26, 1918, 84th Brig. HR, Box 418; Reilly, *Americans All,* 578–79; Ladislas Farago, *Patton: Ordeal and Triumph* (New York, 1964), 79; DM to TAG, Sept. 24, 1918, AEF/GHQ, AG File 19718.

14. Duffy, *Father Duffy's Story,* 247; Tompkins, *Story of Rainbow Div.,* 118–20; Amerine, *Alabama's Own,* 181–83; Miller, *MacArthur,* 101; Sherwood, *Diary of a Rainbow Veteran,* 102. Menoher's headquarters was then located at Essey.

15. Reilly, *Americans All,* 579–95; *USAWW,* XIII, 330–37; Taber, *Story of the 168th,* II, 145; *Reminiscences,* 64; ABMC, *42d Div. Summary,* 49.

16. Spec. Orders 314, 1st Army Hq., Sept. 29, 1918, *USAWW,* IX, 154; Field Orders 37, 1st Army Hq., Oct. 4, 1918, *ibid.,* 213; Amerine, *Alabama's Own,* 189; R. M. Cheseldine, *Ohio in the Rainbow: Official Story of the 166th Infantry, 42nd Division, in the World War* (Columbus, 1924), 245; Duffy, *Father Duffy's Story,* 254; Sherwood, *Diary of a Rainbow Veteran,* 152; Hanson W. Baldwin, *World War I: An Outline History* (New York, 1962), 149; *Reminiscences,* 65. On

Oct. 1 the 42nd moved to Souilly, on Oct. 4 to Récicourt, and the next day to Montfaucon Woods.

17. Preliminary rpt. of CinC, AEF Jan. 16, 1919, *USAWW*, XII, 9–12; Gen. Orders 178, AEF/GHQ, Oct. 13, 1918, *ibid.*, XVI, 483; Coffman, *War to End All Wars*, 299–330; Robert L. Bullard, *Personalities and Reminiscences of the War* (Garden City, 1925), 110–14. Summerall replaced Maj. Gen. George H. Cameron, whose leadership of the V Cps. in the first phase of the offensive had greatly disappointed Pershing.

18. Gen. Orders 19, 84th Brig. Hq., Oct. 9, 1918, 84th Brig., HR, Box 418; Reilly, *Americans All*, 630–33; Taber, *Story of the 168th*, II, 160.

19. Reilly, *Americans All*, 677; Hunt, *Untold Story*, 86; *Reminiscences*, 66. Bare temporarily replaced Screws as head of the 167th Inf. when the latter was hospitalized briefly.

20. Reilly, *Americans All*, 659–60; *Reminiscences*, 66.

21. 42nd Div. op. rpt., Oct. 4–Nov. 1, 1918, 1st Army HR, Box 53, RG 120, NA; ABMC, *American Armies and Battlefields*, 242–43; Tompkins, *Story of Rainbow Div.*, 131–33; Sherwood, *Diary of a Rainbow Veteran*, 182–83; Reilly, *Americans All*, 725.

22. DM to CG, 42nd Div., Oct. 14, 1918, 2:00 P.M., 84th Brig. HR, Box 25.

23. Sherwood, *Diary of a Rainbow Veteran*, 180; 42nd Div. op. rpt., Oct. 4–Nov. 1, 1918, 1st Army HR, Box 53; Duffy, *Father Duffy's Story*, 275–77; Reilly, *Americans All*, 678–79, 725–26. Lt. Col. William Donovan of the 165th Inf. was awarded the Medal of Honor for his heroic leadership of an attack on Oct. 15 south of St. Georges, during which he was shot in the leg but continued in the assault.
   Lenihan later commanded an infantry brig. of the 77th Div.

24. ABMC, *42d Div. Summary*, 65–66; *Reminiscences*, 67; ABMC, *American Armies and Battlefields*, 243–44; Taber, *Story of the 168th*, II, 187–200; WD, *American Decorations*, 417.

25. Pershing, *My Experiences*, II, 340–41; Reilly, *Americans All*, 730, 740–41; *Reminiscences*, 67; Summerall to CG, 42nd Div., Oct. 26, 1918, 42nd Div. HR, Box 2.

26. 42nd Div. op. rpt., Oct. 4–Nov. 1, 1918, 1st Army HR, Box 53; rpt. on shortages in 42nd Div., Sept. 4–Nov. 13, 1918, 42nd Div. HR, Box 2; ABMC, *42d Div. Summary*, 66–72, 91–92; Reilly, *Americans All*, 746–48. Reilly later commented: "The Division commander occasionally ordered MacArthur and me to talk over with him the plans for the coming attack. Instead of having us come to his post of command, he always went to MacArthur's P.C., where I reported to him. There never was any doubt that MacArthur really commanded, because the Division commander, after briefly stating the situation, would listen attentively while MacArthur, walking around, would analyze it and deduce what should be done, in his typical

lucid, vivid and forceful way." Quoted in Lee and Henschel, *Mac-Arthur*, 259. Reilly exaggerated MacArthur's influence on Menoher, a forceful individual in his own right. Moreover, this statement and several in his divisional history suggest that Reilly, while respecting MacArthur's ability, may have been somewhat jealous of the attention and honors which the rival brigade commander received.

27. Order 7036, German Supreme Hq., Oct. 19, 1918, *USAWW*, IX, 561; Gallwitz to Supreme Hq., Oct. 30, 1918, *ibid.*, XI, 455; Composite Army C rpt. 3956-420, Oct. 31, 1918, *ibid.*, 459; Memo. 453, 18th Landwehr Div. Hq., Nov. 2, 1918, *ibid.*, 464; Baldwin, *World War I*, 152–53; F. Scott Fitzgerald, *Tender Is the Night* (New York, 1948), 117.

CHAPTER IX, *"The Long Road to Hoboken,"*
pages 227–256

1. Langer, *Gas and Flame*, 82–84; 1st Army op. rpt., Nov. 4–5, 1918, *USAWW*, IX, 385; Coffman, *War to End All Wars*, 343–47.
2. ABMC, *42d Div. Summary*, 72–80; Sherwood, *Diary of a Rainbow Veteran*, 210; Drum to CG, 1st Cps., Nov. 6, 1918, 42nd Div. DF, Box 82; Field Orders 91, 1st Cps. Hq., Nov. 5, 1918, 1st Army HR, G-3, Folder 120.05.
3. Tompkins, *Story of Rainbow Div.*, 242–43; ABMC, *42d Div. Summary*, 73; rpt. on shortages in 42nd Div., Sept. 4–Nov. 13, 1918, 42nd Div. HR, Box 2.
4. DM to CG, 42nd Div., Nov. 6, 1918, 42nd Div. HR, Box 11.
5. Cheseldine, *Ohio in the Rainbow*, 268; Hunter Liggett, *Commanding an American Army: Recollections of the World War* (Boston, 1925), 116–17.
6. Col. George C. Marshall, Jr., memo. on op. of First Army in the direction of Sedan, Nov. 8, 1918; Drum to Marshall, Nov. 7, 1918, 1st Army HR, G-3, Folder 120.05.
7. Drum, memo. for CGs, I and V Cps., Nov. 5, 1918, 1st Army HR, G-3, Folder 120.05. Also printed in *USAWW*, IX, 385.
8. Drum to Marshall, Nov. 7, 1918, 1st Army HR, G-3, Folder 120.05; Pershing, *My Experiences*, II, 381; *Reminiscences*, 68.
9. Summerall to CG, 1st Army, Nov. 7, 1918; Brig. Gen. Frank Parker to CG, 5th Cps., Nov. 9, 1918, 1st Army HR, G-3, Folder 120.05.
10. Maj. Gen. Joseph T. Dickman to CG, 1st Army, Nov. 8, 1918, *ibid.*; Reilly, *Americans All*, 795–96.
11. Society of the 1st Div., *History of the First Division During the World War* (Philadelphia, 1922), 229–36; ABMC, *1st Division Summary of Operations in the World War* (Washington, 1944), 84–95. Lenihan, the ex-commander of the 83rd Brig., was in command of

one of the 77th Div.'s brigs., through whose territory the 1st Div. marched.

12. DM to CG, 42nd Div., Nov. 8, 1918; Reilly, *Americans All,* 800–01, 833–34; Menoher to CofS, 1st Army, Nov. 7, 1918, 42nd Div. HR, Box 11; *New York Times,* Nov. 16, 1918; Hunter Liggett, *A.E.F.: Ten Years Ago in France* (New York, 1928), 230; Parker to CG, 1st Army, Nov. 12, 1918, 1st Army HR, G-3, Folder 120.05. In his *Reminiscences,* 68–69, MacArthur says the officer leading the patrol "recognized me at once" and did not take him in as a prisoner. The report which he gave Menoher on the day of the incident contradicts this later version.

13. Menoher to CofS, 1st Army, Nov. 7, 1918, 42nd Div. HR, Box 11; Menoher to CG, 1st Cps., Nov. 8, 1918; Gen. Maistre to CG, 1st Army, Nov. 7, 1918; Drum to Maistre, Nov. 7, 1918, 1st Army HR, G-3, Folder 120.05.

14. Liggett, *A.E.F.,* 229–30; 42nd Div. op. rpt., Nov. 1–11, 1918, AEF/GHQ, G-3 Rpts., Box 3327; Wolf, *Brief Story of Rainbow Div.,* 52; Col. J. C. Montgomery to CofS, 3rd Army, Dec. 21, 1918, 1st Army HR, Box 53. Menoher stated: "It has never been claimed or reported by this division that any of its officers or men had entered Sedan itself." Menoher to CofS, 1st Army, Nov. 10, 1918, 42nd Div. HR, Box 11.

15. Parker to Maj. Gen. James G. Harbord, Aug. 23, 1935, 1st Army HR, G-3, Folder 120.05, and various commanders' rpts. on the Sedan affair in same folder; Pershing, *My Experiences,* II, 381; Joseph T. Dickman, *The Great Crusade: A Narrative of the World War* (New York, 1927), 182–83, 189; Coffman, *War to End All Wars,* 35–53; Pogue, *Marshall,* I, 188. Harbord served in several command capacities in the AEF, but is best known as head of its Services of Supply in 1918.

16. Sherwood, *Diary of a Rainbow Veteran,* 216; Hughes to 42nd Div. COs, Nov. 11, 1918, 42nd Div. HR, Box 1. On Nov. 11 Gen. von Einem, commanding the German Third Army, defiantly told his troops: "Firing has ceased. Undefeated and tested again and again in numerous battles you are terminating the war in enemy country . . . With unbroken ranks, each one staunchly in his place, proudly as we left in 1914, so we want to return to our native soil." Order 12257, German 3rd Army Hq., Nov. 11, 1918, *USAWW,* XI, 475.

17. *ANJ,* Dec. 12, 1918; *USAWW,* XII, 355; *WDAR, 1923,* I, 163–66; *WDAR, 1926,* I, 193–240. On German opinion of the 42nd Div., see, e.g., *USAWW,* XI, 410, 412–13; Thomas, *History of A.E.F.,* 221.

18. Coffman, *Hilt of the Sword,* 113; *USAWW,* II, 644, 647–48; Hunt, *Untold Story,* 95; *Reminiscences,* 70; Col. W. H. Johnson to CG, VI Cps., Oct. 25, 1918; Davis to CG, 1st Army, Oct. 28, 1918; Davis to CG, 42nd Div., Oct. 29, 1918, AEF/GHQ, AG File 18151-C-293.

19. Menoher to CofS, 6th Cps., Nov. 10, 1918, 42nd Div. HR, Box 11; Liggett to CinC, AEF, Nov. 2, 1918; Maj. Gen. Charles D. Rhodes to CinC, AEF, Nov. 11, 1918, AEF/GHQ, AG File 18151-C-293; *Reminiscences*, 70–71; *New York Times*, Dec. 28, 1918.

20. AWC, *Order of Battle*, I, 272; Gen. Orders 70, 42nd Div. Hq., Nov. 17, 1918, 42nd Div. HR, Box 20; Davis to CG, 1st Div., Nov. 18, 1918; Davis to CG, 1st Army, Nov. 19, 1918, AEF/GHQ, AG File 20126-A-21; DM to AG, AEF, Nov. 19, 1918; Davis to CG, 42nd Div., Nov. 20, 1918, AEF/GHQ, AG File 18151-C-157.

21. Field Orders 58, 59, and 60, 42nd Div. Hq., Nov. 9–13, 1918, 42nd Div. HR, Box 8; Dickman to Chief of American Mission, Nov. 22, 1918, *USAWW*, XI, 30; *WDAR, 1919*, I, Pt. 1, 601–03; Reilly, *Americans All*, 856. The 42nd Div. was in the vicinity of Buzancy, Nov. 10–13; Landres-et-St. Georges, Nov. 14–16; and Stenay, Nov. 17–20, joining the march to the Rhine on the last date.

22. 42nd Div. op. rpt., Nov. 16, 1918–Apr. 4, 1919, 42nd Div. HR, Box 2; *USAWW*, XI, 30–62, XIII, 48–50; Wolf, *Brief Story of Rainbow Div.*, 54. On Nov. 24, during the march to the Rhine, the 42nd Div.'s actual strength was 832 officers and 22,532 enlisted men; the 84th Brig. consisted of 178 officers and 5737 men. The Rainbow had 6488 "animals" (horses and mules) on the march. Daily strength rpt., 42nd Div., Nov. 24, 1918, 42nd Div. HR, Box 2.

23. Duffy, *Father Duffy's Story*, 308–10; AEF cablegrams to WD relating to 42nd Div., Dec. 1–7, 1918, *USAWW*, XIII, 385–87; final rpt., G-3, AEF, July 2, 1919, *ibid.*, XIV, 56–57.

24. Col. Walter C. Short to CofS, 3rd Army, Nov. 21, 1918, 42nd Div. HR, Box 21; Hughes to CO, 3rd Army Mil. Police, Dec. 3, 1918; Col. George Grunert to CG, 42nd Div., Dec. 17, 1918, 42nd Div. DF, Box 82.

25. Tompkins, *Story of Rainbow Div.*, 228–30; *Reminiscences*, 71; Dickman, *Great Crusade*, 210–12, 227–28. The 83rd Brig. hq. was at Remagen, where American forces first crossed the Rhine in World War II.

26. Minutes of Interallied Conference, Lamorlaye, Dec. 20, 1918, *USAWW*, X, 357–60; 3rd Army Office of Civil Affairs, rpt. on American military government of occupied Germany, Jan. 10, 1920, *ibid.*, 1198–1203; Gregory Mason, "Occupation of the Rhineland," in Charles F. Horne, ed., *Source Records of the Great War . . .* (7 vols., Indianapolis, 1931), VII, 17–21.

27. Harry R. Rudin, *Armistice 1918* (New Haven, 1944), 385, 398; Rudolf Coper, *Failure of a Revolution: Germany in 1918–1919* (Cambridge, Mass., 1955), 236–46; Mason, "Occupation of the Rhineland," 20; 42nd Div. summary of intelligence, Jan. 2, 1919, 42nd Div. HR, Box 5.

28. Dickman, *Great Crusade*, 217–19, 221–22; O'Connor, *Pershing*, 337–39; *USAWW*, X, 223–25, 262, 1149–50.

29. Wolf, *Brief Story of Rainbow Div.*, 54–55; Hughes to COs of 167th and 168th Inf., Jan. 21, 1919; Memo. 343, 42nd Div. Hq., Dec. 26, 1918; Memo. 60, 42nd Div. Hq., Mar. 11, 1919, 42nd Div. HR, Box 21; S. L. A. Marshall, *The Officer as a Leader* (Harrisburg, 1966), 144–45; Coffman, *Hilt of the Sword*, 167.

30. Davis to CG, 42nd Div., Feb. 14, 1919; Raymond B. Fosdick, memo. on morale in the AEF, Feb. 1, 1919, 42nd Div. DF, Box 79; Gen. Orders 27, AEF/GHQ, Feb. 10, 1919, *USAWW*, XVI, 647–48; Dickman, *Great Crusade*, 239–41; Memo. 53, 42nd Div. Hq., Mar. 3, 1919, 42nd Div. HR, Box 1.

31. Amerine, *Alabama's Own*, 230–31; *Reminiscences*, 71–72; Reilly, *Americans All*, 871. On Mar. 5, 1919, a meeting was held at Sinzig to plan a divisional organization "to perpetuate in civil life the bond of wartime comradeship." Later that month at Bad Neuenahr the Rainbow Division Veterans was established, with Col. Hough elected as president. MacArthur maintained a life-long interest in the society and was elected "permanent honorary president." Proceedings of committee to form 42nd Div. veterans association, Mar. 5 and 9, 1919, 42nd Div. HR, Box 3; Reilly, *Americans All*, 883–84. See also sundry issues of *Rainbow Reveille*, the society's periodical.

32. Maj. Gen. Clement A. F. Flagler to CinC, AEF, Jan. 8, 1919; Menoher to CinC, AEF, Sept. 9 and Oct. 30, 1918, 42nd Div. DF, Box 82; Brig. Gen. Frank C. Burnett to Deputy CofS, AEF, Mar. 25, 1919, AEF/GHQ, AG File 18151-C-157; Col. Harry Coope to CG, 42nd Div., Feb. 6, 1919; Dickman to AG, AEF, Feb. 13, 1919, AEF/GHQ, AG File 18151-F-467; *Reminiscences*, 71. Brig. Gen. Malin Craig, 3rd Army CofS and future CofS of the U.S. Army, named MacArthur on a "List of Officers Considered Thoroughly Capable as General Staff Officers" requested by the WD, but by that time — May, 1919 — March had already chosen him as the next superintendent of West Point. Craig to Deputy CofS, AEF, May 6, 1919, AEF/GHQ, AG File 3358-A-93.

33. Joseph C. Chase, "Portrait of MacArthur," *World's Work*, XXXVII (Apr., 1919), 647–48. See also Chase, *Soldiers All: Portraits and Sketches of the Men of the A.E.F.* (New York, 1920), 41–45.

34. William A. White, *The Autobiography of William Allen White* (New York, 1946), 572–73. MacArthur and White would have later contacts with each other when the latter became a leader in the interventionist movement of 1940–41.

35. Pershing's speech to 42nd Div., Mar. 16, 1919, 42nd Div. HR, Box 2; *New York Times*, Mar. 18, 1919; Reilly, *Americans All*, 864–65; Dickman, *Great Crusade*, 246–47; Duffy, *Father Duffy's Story*, 324; staff

memo., 42nd Div. Hq., Apr. 12, 1919, AG 370.7, RG 94, NA.
36. Gen. Orders 23, 42nd Div. Hq., Mar. 30, 1919, 42nd Div. HR, Box
20; Gen. Orders 35, AEF/GHQ, Feb. 21, 1919, *USAWW*, XVI, 659;
AWC, *Order of Battle*, I, 287; DM to AG, AEF, Apr. 14, 1919, AEF/
GHQ, AG File 20517-F-988; Reilly, *Americans All*, 875; *Reminiscences*, 72; Coffman, *War to End All Wars*, 230, 359–60. On June 17,
1919, Allied commanders along the Rhine received word from Foch
that "the offensive of the Allied Armies is ready to start again on the
day prescribed by the Governments . . . Unless orders to the contrary
are received from the Governments, the operations will begin the
day indicated: 7 P.M., June 23." The German government agreed on
June 23 to the Versailles Treaty without reservations, and the formal
signing took place on the 28th. Memo. 3025, Supreme Allied Hq.,
June 17, 1919, *USAWW*, X, 1184.

CHAPTER X, *"Father of the New West Point,"*
pages 259-294
1. *Reminiscences*, 72. The 84th Brig. was demobilized at Camp Dodge
   on May 12, by which time the other units of the 42nd Div. had been
   demobilized at Camps Upton, Dix, and Grant. AWC, *Order of Battle*, I, 287.
2. John Blum, "Nativism, Anti-Radicalism, and the Foreign Scare, 1917–
   1920," *Midwest Journal*, III (Winter, 1950–51), 46–53; Robert K.
   Murray, *Red Scare: A Study in National Hysteria, 1919–1920* (Min-
   neapolis, 1955), *passim*.
3. *WDAR, 1919*, I, 26–27; Wood quoted in William E. Leuchtenburg,
   The Perils of Prosperity, 1914–32 (Chicago, 1958), 66. See also Hagedorn, *Wood*, II, 332–36.
4. Coffman, *Hilt of the Sword*, 186; *Reminiscences*, 77.
5. March to Acting SecWar, Oct. 1, 1918, AGO–PF, Box 25; *WDAR,
   1919*, I, 510–11; Ganoe, *MacArthur Close-up*, 13–20; *Reminiscences*,
   77–80; Jacob L. Devers, "The Mark of the Man on USMA," *Assembly*, XXIII (Spring, 1964), 17.
6. *Annual Report of Superintendent, USMA, 1920*, 1–5; Marshall, *The
   Officer as a Leader*, 144–45; Palmer, *Baker*, II, 402–05.
7. Earl Blaik, "A Cadet under MacArthur," *Assembly*, XXIII (Spring,
   1964), 8. At the time MacArthur's mother was suffering from "severe
   nose-bleed that had recurred for several years," stated the academy
   surgeon. Dr. A. G. Wilde to DM, Jan. 26, 1947, RG 10, MMBA.
8. List of USMA professors during MacArthur's superintendency, Douglas MacArthur File, USMA; *Army Register, 1924, passim*; Robert M.
   Danford, "USMA's 31st Superintendent," *Assembly*, XXIII (Spring,
   1964), 13.
9. *USMA Regulations, 1920*, 7–14; Ambrose, *Duty, Honor, Country*,

265–66; Ganoe, *MacArthur Close-up*, 35; Francis T. Miller, "General Douglas MacArthur," *Coronet*, XII (July, 1942), 176.

10. Ambrose, *Duty, Honor, Country*, 267; Davis, *Billy Mitchell Affair*, 146.

11. Ganoe, *MacArthur Close-up*, 129–42; Danford quoted in *ibid.*, 7; Hibbs quoted in Gene Schoor, *General Douglas MacArthur: A Pictorial Biography* (New York, 1951), 26; Maher, *Bringing Up the Brass*, 93.

12. Frank F. Kelley and Cornelius Ryan, *MacArthur: Man of Action* (Garden City, 1950), 80–82; Hersey, *Men on Bataan*, 129.

13. Danford, "USMA's 31st Superintendent," 13. Ganoe recalled MacArthur's words differently: "Sit down, sir. I am the Superintendent! Even if I weren't, I should be treated in a gentlemanly manner." Ganoe, *MacArthur Close-up*, 98–99.

14. *Annual Report of Superintendent, USMA, 1920*, 6, 15–33; *idem*, *1921*, 15; *idem*, *1922*, 13–18; Simons, *Liberal Education in the Service Academies*, 72–73.

15. *New York Times*, May 9 and 30, 1920.

16. Devers, "Mark of the Man on USMA," 19; *Annual Report of Superintendent, USMA, 1921*, 15–16.

17. *Annual Report of Board of Visitors, USMA, 1921*, 4–5; *Annual Report of Superintendent, USMA, 1921*, 16–17; Devers, "Mark of the Man on USMA," 19; Ganoe, *MacArthur Close-up*, 92–93.

18. DM to Maj. Gen. Enoch H. Crowder, Aug. 5, 18, and 22, 1919; Crowder to DM, Aug. 15, 16, and 20, 1919, Enoch H. Crowder Papers, Western Historical Manuscripts Collection, University of Missouri, Columbia, Mo.

19. *Annual Report of Superintendent, USMA, 1920*, 34; *idem*, *1922*, 13; Ganoe, *MacArthur Close-up*, 93. Excerpts from Superintendent MacArthur's annual rpts. of 1920 and 1922 are reprinted in Whan, ed., *A Soldier Speaks*, 10–22.

20. *New York Times*, Mar. 29, 1931; list of notable visitors at USMA, 1919–22, MacArthur File, USMA; Lee and Henschel, *MacArthur*, 264.

21. *Annual Report of Superintendent, USMA, 1920*, 9–10; *USMA Regulations, 1920*, 38–40. In 1920 the "graduating merit roll" comprised the following:

Math	375	Practical mil.		Mil. art &	
English	175	engineering	25	history	150
French	190	Philosophy	300	Economics &	
History	100	Mil. hygiene	40	government	150
Drawing	100	Ordnance &		Mil. efficiency	
Tactics	25	gunnery	150	& conduct	250
Chemistry	250	Law	150	Total merits	2720
Spanish	100				

22. *Reminiscences,* 80; Blaik, "Cadet under MacArthur," 9; Ambrose, *Duty, Honor, Country,* 278–80.
23. *USMA Regulations, 1920,* 42; *WDAR,* I, 1423–24; Ganoe, *MacArthur Close-up,* 107–07; Blaik, "Cadet under MacArthur," 9; Danford, "USMA's 31st Superintendent," 14.
24. Danford, "USMA's 31st Superintendent," 14; Blaik, "Cadet under MacArthur," 11; Ganoe, *MacArthur Close-up,* 120–21; Ambrose, *Duty, Honor, Country,* 272; *New York Times,* Aug. 19, 1920; *Reminiscences,* 81–82; DM to Ralph Cannon, Apr. 18, 1939, MacArthur File, USMA; Maher, *Bringing Up the Brass,* 82.
25. Blaik, "Cadet under MacArthur," 9; DM to Pershing, Nov. 19, 1919, Pershing Papers, Box 121.
26. Marshall to DM, Mar. 13, 1922; Marshall to Pershing, Mar. 11, 1922, Pershing Papers, Box 121.
27. MacArthur's correspondence with alumni was always cordial and appreciative. See, e.g., DM to Col. James J. Hoyt, Nov. 17, 1920, Katherine Mayo Papers, YUA.
28. *Reminiscences,* 77–78; Ganoe, *MacArthur Close-up,* 142.
29. *The National Defense Act, Approved June 3, 1916, as Amended to March 4, 1929* (Washington, 1929), 1–22; Nelson, *National Security and the General Staff,* 295–99; Huntington, *The Soldier and the State,* 282–85. On West Point's budgets and finances, 1919–22, see AGO–PF, Box 19.
30. *Reminiscences,* 78; *Annual Report of Superintendent, USMA, 1920,* 13–14; *idem, 1921,* 10–13; Danford, "USMA's 31st Superintendent," 14.
31. Forman, *West Point,* 194–95.
32. Mrs. MacArthur to Pershing, June 12, 1918, Pershing Papers, Box 121; Peyton C. March, *The Nation at War* (Garden City, 1932), 259.
33. DM to Pershing, May 14, 1921; Pershing to DM, May 17, 1921, Pershing Papers, Box 121. Pershing indirectly complimented MacArthur when in June, 1920, he included him on a select list of thirteen A.E.F. generals whose opinions he asked on the report of the A.E.F. Superior Board on Organization and Tactics. Pershing to DM, June 16, 1920, AEF/GHQ, AG File 21960-W.
34. Mark S. Watson, *Chief of Staff: Prewar Plans and Preparations* (*USAWWII;* Washington, 1950), 15–19; Pogue, *Marshall,* I, 217–27; John W. Killigrew, "The Impact of the Great Depression on the Army, 1929–1936" (unpublished Ph.D. dissertation, Indiana University, 1960), iv-vi.
35. Pershing to DM, Nov. 22, 1921, Pershing Papers, Box 121; *New York Times,* Feb. 5, 1922.
36. *New York Times,* Jan. 31, 1922; *Army Register, 1925,* 551; Ganoe, *MacArthur Close-up,* 157; Ambrose, *Duty, Honor, Country,* 282–83.

37. Pershing to DM, Jan. 30, 1922; DM to Pershing, Feb. 2, 1922, Pershing Papers, Box 121.
38. On the perpetuation of the exile myth, see, e.g., Kelley and Ryan, *MacArthur*, 43–45; Lee and Henschel, *MacArthur*, 48–50; John Gunther, *The Riddle of MacArthur: Japan, Korea and the Far East* (New York, 1950), 44–45; Jack Lait and Lee Mortimer, *Washington Confidential* (New York, 1951), 143–44. The wedding ceremony was performed by Chaplain Wheat of West Point, with James R. Cromwell, Louise's brother, serving as MacArthur's best man. *New York Times,* Feb. 15, 1922. According to correspondent Bob Considine, whose source is not known, on the morning after her wedding Louise told her brother, who accompanied them on the honeymoon, that MacArthur "may be a general in the Army, but he's a buck private in the boudoir." Robert Considine, *It's All News to Me: A Reporter's Deposition* (New York, 1967), 342.
39. *New York Times,* Feb. 10, 1922; *Reminiscences,* 83.
40. Mrs. Douglas MacArthur to Pershing, June 7, 1922, Pershing Papers, Box 121; Washington *Times,* Jan. 13, 1922; O'Connor, *Pershing,* 357–58.
41. *New York Times,* Feb. 10, 1922; *Reminiscences,* 84; summary of record, DM Misc. 201, OCMH.
42. Ambrose, *Duty, Honor, Country,* 283; Ganoe, *MacArthur Close-up,* 167. Four cadets during MacArthur's superintendency served later as chiefs of staff: Gens. Maxwell D. Taylor and Lyman L. Lemnitzer both held the positions of Army chief of staff and chairman of the Joint Chiefs of Staff. Gens. Hoyt S. Vandenberg and Thomas D. White became chief of staff of the Air Force. Lemnitzer became NATO commander in 1963 and continues to hold that post.
List of distinguished USMA graduates, 1919–22, MacArthur File, USMA.

CHAPTER XI, *"The Discouraging Years,"*
pages 295–324

1. *WDAR, 1920,* III, 3–6, 19; *idem, 1927,* III, 2–6; Maj. O. S. Albright to WPD, Nov. 26, 1924; JAG to TAG, Mar. 2, 1925; Brig. Gen. Harry A. Smith to CofS, Aug. 3, 1925; CofS to SecNavy, Aug. 6, 1925, WPD 1949, RG 165, NA; *PGGAR, 1922,* 109; *Reminiscences,* 84.
2. Denby and Weeks quoted in Col. B. H. Wells to Deputy CofS, Oct. 20, 1922, WPD 532-3; Brig. Gen. LeRoy Eltinge to CofS, Feb. 24, 1925, WPD 2058. In 1923 the War Dept. permitted a Japanese military mission to inspect all Army stations in the Philippines, except Corregidor. Col. W. K. Naylor to CofS, May 28, 1923, AGO-PF, Box 301.
3. Weeks to Wood, Nov. 4, 1922, WPD 532-4.

4. Wells to Deputy CofS, Oct. 20, 1922, WPD 532-3; Brig. Gen. Stuart Heintzelman to Col. Guy V. Henry, June 17, 1924, WPD 532-17; Maj. Gen. George W. Read to TAG, July 30, 1923, AGO–PF, Box 300.
5. Col. E. R. Stone to Asst. CofS, G-4, June 9, 1925, WPD 2189.
6. Maj. Gen. William M. Wright to Deputy CofS, May 10, 1922, AGO–PF, Box 299; Maj. Peter Bowditch to Brig. Gen. George V. H. Moseley, Apr. 28, 1922, George Van Horn Moseley Papers, LC; Wright to TAG, Aug. 24, 1922; Read to TAG, July 30, 1923, and July 30, 1924; Maj. Gen. James H. McRae to TAG, July 30, 1925, AGO–PF, Boxes 300–01; Coffman, *War to End All Wars,* 276, 286.
7. IG to CofS, Oct. 22, 1925, AGO–PF, Box 301; Read to TAG, July 30, 1923, AGO–PF, Box 300; *USMA Register, 1967,* 283; Hunt, *Untold Story.* The only other unit of American foot soldiers then in the Philippines was a battalion of the 15th Inf., its other battalions being in China.
8. Maj. Gen. Francis J. Kernan to TAG, Sept. 7, 1921; Wright to TAG, Aug. 24, 1922, AGO–PF, Box 300; *Reminiscences,* 84; Coffman, *War to End All Wars,* 216–17, 269–70.
9. Read to TAG, July 30, 1923, and July 30, 1924, AGO–PF, Boxes 300–01; *Reminiscences,* 84; Lt. Col. Henry C. Jevett to CofE, Apr. 30, 1925, AGO–PF, Box 162.
10. Henry to Asst. CofS, WPD, Oct. 1, 1924, WPD 1031-9; McRae to TAG, July 30, 1925, AGO–PF, Box 301; *PGGAR, 1924,* 3; Eltinge to CofS, Feb. 24, 1925, WPD 2058; Read to TAG, Sept. 6 and Oct. 21, 1924; Henry to Asst. CofS, WPD, Oct. 31, 1924, WPD 532-18; Whan, ed., *A Soldier Speaks,* xxiii. In his *Reminiscences,* 84, MacArthur states erroneously that he succeeded Bundy as CG, 23rd Brig., in Jan., 1925.
11. Maj. H. W. T. Eglin to Asst. CofS, G-2, Sept. 28 and Nov. 14, 1923, GS G-2 Files 2610-72 and 2610-H-20, RG 165, NA. In the fall of 1924 Maj. Gen. Robert C. Davis, TAG, named MacArthur on his list of the seven best public speakers of the general officers. The others were Maj. Gen. Edward M. Lewis and Brig. Gens. Fox Conner, John M. Palmer, Edward L. King, Frank R. McCoy, and Samuel D. Rockenbach. TAG to Asst. CofS, G-2, Nov. 14, 1924, GS G-2 File 1026-71.

In Sept., 1926, G-2 recommended MacArthur as "eminently qualified" for the post of military attaché at Paris, but again he was not appointed. Col. James H. Reeves to CofS, Sept. 7, 1926, GS G-2 File 2482-55.
12. Mrs. MacArthur to Pershing, n.d. [c. Aug., 1924], Pershing Papers.
13. *New York Times,* Sept. 23, 1924.
14. DM to TAG, July 20, 1925, AGO–PF, Box 240; *Reminiscences,* 84–85. The IV Corps Area had an inexplicably large turnover of com-

manding generals during this period, MacArthur being the seventh in ten months.

15. Davis, *Mitchell Affair*, 89–91, 142–43, 164–65, 240–43, 267; O'Connor, *Pershing*, 256–57; Wesley F. Craven and James L. Cate, eds., *Plans and Early Operations, January 1939 to August 1942 (The Army Air Forces in World War II*, Vol. I; Chicago, 1948), 21–28. Menoher was convinced that Mitchell exploited air tragedies "to advance his pet ideas for personal gain," and, in 1921, tried to get Weeks to oust Mitchell as asst. chief of the air service. When Weeks would not do it, Menoher himself resigned.

16. Davis, *Mitchell Affair*, 295. Davis' work is not a definitive study of Mitchell, but his account of the court-martial is the most authentic yet.

17. *Ibid.*, 242–43, 267, 295, 327; Levine, *Mitchell*, chs. 12–13; Hurley, *Mitchell*, 103–05; *Reminiscences*, 84–95; Rovere and Schlesinger, *The General and the President*, 28–30. After his court-martial, Mitchell commented, "My greatest pride in life is to be . . . according to the principles laid down by our forefathers . . . a free American citizen." In one of his speeches after his dismissal in 1951, MacArthur similarly stated: "I shall stand . . . for those sacred and immutable ideals and concepts which guided our forefathers . . . I still proudly possess, that to me, the greatest of all honors and distinctions — I am an American." Lee and Henschel, *MacArthur*, 269.

   Capt. Eddie Rickenbacker, a witness for Mitchell, said that during the court martial he and MacArthur "had disagreed vigorously and had said some unpleasant things to each other." Edward V. Rickenbacker, *Rickenbacker* (Englewood Cliffs, 1967), 332.

18. Arthur M. Schlesinger, Jr., *The Crisis of the Old Order, 1919–1933 (The Age of Roosevelt*, Vol. I; Boston, 1957), 71–76; John E. Wiltz, *From Isolation to War, 1931–1941* (New York, 1968), 6–14; *WDAR, 1926*, I, 57; Weigley, *History of U.S. Army*, 402–03.

19. DM to TAG, Oct. 22 and Nov. 9, 1925, AGO–PF, Box 240; Col. Isaac C. Jenks to TAG, Aug. 20, 1918, III Cps. Area DF 1928 300–20, Box 468, RG 394, NA.

20. Jenks to TAG, Aug. 20, 1928, III Cps. Area DF 1928 300–20, Box 468; *WDAR, 1924*, I, 161; *idem, 1926*, I, 179; *idem, 1927*, I, 194.

21. DM to TAG, Aug. 21, 1925, AGO–PF, Box 240; *WDAR, 1926*, I, 183; *idem, 1927*, I, 198; DM to TAG, July 22, 1927, AGO-PF, Box 239.

22. DM to TAG, Aug. 21, 1925, AGO–PF, Box 240.

23. John D. Hicks, *Republican Ascendancy, 1921–1933* (New York, 1960), 146–63; *Congressional Record*, 70th Cong., 2nd Sess., 1929, 1728.

24. *New York Times*, Apr. 7, 1927.

25. *Ibid.*, Jan. 15 and Feb. 15, 1922; *New York Daily News*, Feb. 1, 1942; *Washington Post*, June 1, 1965; *USMA Register, 1967*, 309.

26. Mrs. Douglas MacArthur to Pershing, n.d. [c. Mar. 1, 1926], Pershing
    Papers, Box 121. In his answer to Louise, Pershing said of Queke-
    meyer's death: "I have never had anything outside of my own family
    that gave me such a severe blow . . . I hope some of these days to
    have the pleasure of seeing you again and of having an opportunity
    to talk about our dear mutual friend." Pershing to Mrs. Douglas
    MacArthur, Mar. 17, 1926, *ibid.*
       In 1929, just before her divorce, Louise arranged through Pershing
    to have "Mr. Quekemeyer," possibly the colonel's brother Frederick,
    admitted to Walter Reed Hospital. Mrs. MacArthur to Pershing,
    May 6, 1929; Capt. G. E. Adamson [Pershing's aide] to Mrs. Mac-
    Arthur, May 6 and 7, 1929, *ibid.*
27. Mrs. Katharine C. Gamble to DM, Feb. 12, 1951; C. A. Dravo to
    editor, *Sat. Evening Post,* July 30, 1949, RG 10, MMBA; *Washington
    Post,* June 1, 1965; Gunther, *Riddle of MacArthur,* 44–45; *New York
    Times,* June 28, 1924; Lee and Henschel, *MacArthur,* 49–51; *New
    York Daily News,* Feb. 1, 1942.
28. Interviews, author with Gen. of the Army Dwight D. Eisenhower and
    Maj. Gens. Charles A. Willoughby and Courtney Whitney, all of
    whom first knew MacArthur in the years 1925–32.
29. Anton Myrer, *Once an Eagle* (New York, 1968), 343–44.
30. *New York Times,* Aug. 9, 1927, Mar. 28, 1928, June 18, 1929; *Wash-
    ington Sunday Star,* Apr. 19, 1964; *Washington Herald,* June 18,
    1929; Mrs. Douglas MacArthur to Pershing, Feb. 20, 1928, Pershing
    Papers, Box 121; Lee and Henschel, *MacArthur,* 51–52; *Reminis-
    cences,* 83.
31. Frederick L. Allen, *Only Yesterday* (New York, 1959), 86.

CHAPTER XII, *"Olympus and Beyond,"*

pages 325–347
1. *New York Times,* Sept. 18 and Nov. 26, 1927, Mar. 28 and July 11,
   1928.
2. *Ibid.,* various issues of July 29–Aug. 12, 1928; interview, author with
   W. O. Spencer; Considine, *MacArthur,* 58. The American flag-
   bearer in the opening parade and a gold-medal winner in swimming
   was John Weissmuller, later the "Tarzan" of movie fame.
3. *Report of the American Olympic Committee: Ninth Olympic Games,
   Amsterdam, 1928; Second Olympic Winter Sports, St. Moritz, 1928*
   (New York, 1928), 1–3; *New York Times,* Aug. 13, 1928.
4. Saurer quoted in Hersey, *Men on Bataan,* 141; Summerall quoted in
   Reminiscences, 87; Avery Brundage to Russell L. Durgin, Apr. 25,
   1947; Gustavus T. Kirby to DM, Jan. 4, 1950, RG 10, MMBA; Arthur
   G. Lentz (exec. director, U.S. Olympic Committee) to author, May 3,

1968. In *The Olympic Games* (rev. ed., New York, 1967), 3, a booklet of the U.S. Olympic Committee, the last paragraph in the quoted portion of MacArthur's report is prominently featured.

In 1950 MacArthur wrote Gustavus T. Kirby, a past president of the U.S. Olympic Association: "Rarely have I enjoyed any period as much as my short Olympic experience. The friendships and ties which I formed then will last me to the end of my days." DM to Kirby, Jan. 13, 1950, RG 10, MMBA.

5. *Report of the American Olympic Committee, 1928*, 1, 4–6.
6. Considine, *MacArthur*, 59. In Rovere and Schlesinger, *The General and the President*, 30, the assertion is made that "as head of the Olympic Games Committee, he constructed a fantasy world in which his role was that of a man rescuing the American people from grossness and degeneracy through athletics." Except for his report to Coolidge, however, MacArthur did not seem to be absorbed excessively with the efficacy of athletics — at least no more so than critic Schlesinger's former employer, President John F. Kennedy.
7. *WDAR, 1929*, I, 13; *PGGAR, 1928*, 1–2; *idem, 1929*, 1; *Reminiscences*, 87–88; Robert S. Allen, *Washington Merry-Go-Round* (New York, 1931), 105–07; DM to Stimson, Dec. 22, 1928, Jan. 29 and Feb. 7, 1929, Stimson Papers, Boxes 277–79.
8. *Reminiscences*, 88; Theodore Friend, *Between Two Empires: The Ordeal of the Philippines, 1929–1946* (New Haven, 1965), 78; Hunt, *Untold Story*, 123–24. In Jan., 1929, Sen. Villaneuva delivered a highly laudatory speech before the Philippine Senate praising MacArthur's sincere interest in the Filipino people. Referring to a recent address by MacArthur, Villaneuva exclaimed, "These words uttered from lips which interpret the feelings of a noble heart, constitute for us a hope which we should look forward to and we feel proud of having the good will of such men as General MacArthur and his father." Address of Sen. Villaneuva, enclosed with DM to TAG, Jan. 12, 1929, AG 014.12 Phil. Is. (1-12-29).
9. *New York Times*, Apr. 21, 1929.
10. Brig. Gen. George S. Simonds to CofS, June 25, 1928, WPD 3022–8; Friend, *Between Two Empires*, 77; *Reminiscences*, 88; W. Cameron Forbes to CofS, Oct. 17, 1927, WPD 3022-2. See also Col. Stanley D. Embick to Joint Planning Committee, Sept. 7, 1927; Col. Jackson Morris to CofS, Sept. 14, 1927; Simonds to CofS, Oct. 21, 1927, WPD 3022.
11. CofS to cps. area CGs and chiefs of branches and bureaus, Aug. 29, 1929; DM to TAG, Aug. 23, 1929, AG 333; GS rpt. of survey of military establishment, Nov. 1, 1929, WPD 3345; *PGGAR, 1930*, 1.
12. Diary of Henry L. Stimson, entry of Jan. 6, 1929, YUA; *PGGAR, 1930*, 1; Theodore Friend, "The Philippine Sugar Industry and thr

Politics of Independence, 1929–1935," *Journal of Asian Studies,* XXII (Feb., 1963), 179–92.

13. Manuel L. Quezon to N. Inouye, Aug. 14, 1930, in Grant K. Goodman, *Davao: A Case Study in Japanese-Philippine Relations* (Lawrence, Kan., 1967), 14; Col. J. T. Conrad to TAG, Aug. 7, 1926, AG 049.21 Phil. Is. (7-1-26); *WDAR, 1930,* I, 25. See also Goodman, *Davao,* 6–25.

14. *PGGAR, 1930,* 15, 48; *Reminiscences,* 88; *The Government Employee,* I (Sept., 1930), 4. *The Government Employee* was a periodical of the association of civil-service workers in the Philippines; it was published in Manila and carried many news items which had first appeared in local newspapers.

15. DM to TAG, Sept. 27, 1928; Simonds to TAG, Nov. 19, 1928, WPD 3255; DM to TAG, Aug. 30, 1929, WPD 1361–2; DM to Gov. Dwight F. Davis, Sept. 9, 1929, WPD 3022; program of Phil. Dept. athletic meet, Dec. 16–19, 1929, RG 17, MMBA; *PGGAR, 1928,* 15–16, 45–46; Stimson to DM, Dec. 22, 1928, AG 014.2 Phil. Is. (12–22–28).

16. *Reminiscences,* 88–89; Hunt, *Untold Story,* 125. Gen. Willoughby, later G-2 under MacArthur, did not view MacArthur's decision against the engineer headship as a judgment of shrewd calculation, but, instead, insisted that it "truly reflected MacArthur's basic personal character — a character whose nobility and modesty have at times been so wantonly misrepresented." Charles A. Willoughby and John Chamberlain, *MacArthur, 1941–1951* (New York, 1954), 263.

17. SecWar to Sen. Hiram Bingham, May 22, 1930, quoted in Hunt, *Untold Story,* 126–27. During this period Gen. Moseley and Maj. Eisenhower ("my brainy assistant," as Moseley called him) composed many of Hurley's speeches, letters, and other communications. Moseley to SecWar, June 7, 1930, Moseley Papers, Box 5.

18. DM to TAG, July 7, 1930, and TAG to DM, July 8, 1930, quoted in Hunt, *Untold Story,* 126. These two documents, as well as the letter to Hurley, were not located in any archives; MacArthur apparently lent them to Hunt from his personal files. The general's post-1917 201 File is closed to researchers.

19. *Army Register, 1930,* 1–2; *USMA Register, 1967, passim;* Lee and Henschel, *MacArthur,* 52; Hunt, *Untold Story,* 127–28; Coffman, *Hilt of the Sword,* 242; Allen, *Washington Merry-Go-Round,* 167; Herbert Hoover, *The Memoirs of Herbert Hoover* (3 vols., New York, 1951–52), II, 339; *New York Times,* Aug. 7, 1930. The maj. gens. ranking ahead of MacArthur in 1930 were, in order, Charles P. Summerall, John L. Hines, William Lassiter, Hanson E. Ely, Fred W. Sladen, and William R. Smith. The ten below him with at least four years of active duty left were Dennis E. Nolan, Johnson Hagood, William D. Connor, Fox Conner, Preston Brown, Malin Craig, Briant H. Wells,

Paul B. Malone, Frank Parker, and Frank R. McCoy. All of these officers retired before the Second World War; three returned to active duty in 1941–45, but only MacArthur held a major assignment.

20. WD news release, Aug. 6, 1930, DM File, RG 350, NA; *New York Times,* Aug. 7, 10, and 17, 1930; Washington *National Tribune,* Nov. 27, 1930.

21. MacArthur's address, Sept. 18, 1930, quoted in *The Government Employee,* I, 4.

22. *Reminiscences,* 89–90; Washington *National Tribune,* Nov. 27, 1930; Katherine T. Marshall, *Together: Annals of an Army Wife* (Atlanta, 1946), 57. Maj. Gen. Edward A. Kreger, JAG, administered the oath of office to MacArthur on Nov. 21, with Hurley present as witness. For some reason, the order detailing him as CofS and gen. was not issued for nearly three weeks thereafter, though it made the appointments retroactive to Nov. 21. Gen. Orders 13, WD, Dec. 8, 1930, DM File, RG 350, NA.

CHAPTER XIII, *"A Matter of Survival,"*
pages 351–381

1. Schlesinger, *Crisis of the Old Order,* 166–72; Arthur S. Link and William B. Catton, *American Epoch: A History of the United States Since the 1890's* (3rd ed., 3 vols., New York, 1967), II, 367–79; Stimson diary, entry of Nov. 1, 1930.

2. Sundry letters, 1942–64, Hoover–DM Correspondence File, Herbert Hoover Papers, HHL; Herbert Hoover, *American Individualism* (New York, 1922), 8–48; Harris G. Warren, *Herbert Hoover and the Great Depression* (New York, 1967), 32–36; Robert S. Allen and Drew Pearson, *More Merry-Go-Round* (New York, 1932), 156–57, 166–78; David A. Shannon, *Between the Wars, 1919–1941* (Boston, 1965), 126–28; *Reminiscences,* 418.

3. *WDAR, 1930,* I, 137–40; Killigrew, "Impact of the Great Depression on the Army," Ch. III, 1–7. See also Benjamin G. Franklin, "The Military Policy of the United States, 1918–33: A Study in the Influence of World War I on Army Organization and Control" (unpublished Ph.D. dissertation, University of California, 1943).

4. *WDAR, 1930,* I, 139.

5. Killigrew, "Impact of the Great Depression on the Army," Ch. III, 20–24; U.S. House, Committee on Appropriations, *Hearings on War Department Appropriations Bill for 1932* . . . 71st Cong., 3rd Sess. (1930), Pt. I, 979–92.

6. *Congressional Record,* 72nd Cong., 1st Sess. (1932), Pt. LXXV, 9932–35; Memphis *Commercial Appeal,* July 14, 1967; *WDAR, 1932,* I, 56–64; *ANJ,* Jan. 30, 1932.

7. WDAR, *1931*, I, 3; *ANJ*, May 16, 1931; Killigrew, "Impact of the Great Depression on the Army," Ch. IV, 9–17, 20–21; Mildred H. Gillie, *Forging the Thunderbolt: A History of the Development of the Armored Force* (Harrisburg, 1947), Chs. II–III. Chaffee was the ex-CofS's son.

8. SecWar to Rep. Joseph W. Byrns, Feb. 26, 1932, Moseley Papers, Box 5; U.S. House, Committee on Appropriations, *Hearings on War Department Appropriations Bill for 1933* . . . 72nd Cong., 1st Sess. (1932), Pt. I, *passim,* especially MacArthur's testimony, 1–30; ANJ, Jan. 30 and May 7, 1932.

9. DM to Rep. Bertrand D. Snell, May 9, 1932, AG 111. See also *New York Times,* May 10, 1932. In his annual rpt. as CofS for 1932 MacArthur included a quotation from the Snell letter and went into further detail in defense of the officer corps. "No other attack aimed exclusively at the Army during the year," he stated therein, "was so surely calculated to accomplish the disastrous emasculation of our defensive system as was this one." Collins' supporters included "a small section of the press" which, said MacArthur, "invariably misstated the General Staff's motives in combating the project, constantly assuming that the department was actuated solely by a desire to protect individual officers from a diminution of income." *WDAR, 1932,* I, 60–62.

10. Killigrew, "Impact of the Great Depression on the Army," 18–20; DM to Frederick H. Payne, July 12, 1932, AG 111; *ANJ,* July 16, 1932; *WDAR, 1932,* I, 94–102.

11. *WDAR, 1932,* I, 9–27, 107–78; SecWar to Byrns, Feb. 26, 1932, Moseley Papers, Box 5; SecWar to Pres., Oct. 27, 1933, CF–War, Roosevelt Papers, FDRL; *New York Times,* May 15, 1931; *WDAR, 1931,* I, 1–2; Allen and Pearson, *More Merry-Go-Round,* 187–88.

12. *WDAR, 1930,* I, 157–65; Ray S. Cline, *Washington Command Post: The Operations Division (USAWWII;* Washington, 1951), 6–7; Weigley, *History of U.S. Army,* 429.

13. DM to SecWar, Jan. 3, 1931, and SecWar to TAG, Jan. 3, 1931, in *WDAR, 1931,* I, 70–73; interview, author with Gen. Eisenhower. The asst. chiefs of staff in 1931 were Gens. Albert J. Bowley (G-1), Alfred T. Smith (G-2), Edward L. King (G-3), Robert E. Callan (G-4), and George S. Simonds (WPD). Drum, who was IG in 1931, succeeded Moseley as Deputy CofS in Feb., 1933. Simonds left WPD to serve as military adviser to the American disarmament delegation at Geneva; in Feb., 1935, he succeeded Drum as Deputy CofS.

14. *WDAR, 1933,* I, 11–15; DM to Cps. Area CGs, Aug 9, 1932; DM to CGs of 1st, 2nd, 3rd, and 4th Armies, Oct. 22, 1932, AG 320.2 (8–6–32) Sec. 1A; Hersey, *Men on Bataan,* 250; Kent R. Greenfield, Robert R. Palmer, and Bell I. Wiley, *The Organization of Ground Combat*

Troops (*USAWWII;* Washington, 1947), 3–6. After World War II the four-army plan was dropped in favor of a three-army organization, but in recent years the Dept. of the Army has been considering a return to a modified form of MacArthur's plan. Interview, author with Col. Edgar W. Schroeder.

15. *WDAR, 1931,* I, 38; *New York Times,* Jan. 10 and 12, 1931.
16. Jay Pierrepont Moffat, *The Moffat Papers: Selections from the Diplomatic Journals of Jay Pierrepont Moffat, 1919–1943,* ed. by Nancy H. Hooker (Cambridge, Mass., 1956), 62; Craven and Cate, eds., *Plans and Early Operations,* 30, 61–69.
17. William L. Shirer, *The Rise and Fall of the Third Reich: A History of Nazi Germany* (New York, 1960), 135–204; *New York Times,* Aug. 9, Sept. 6, 11, 12, 15, 17, and 22, 1931; Brig. Gen. Stanley H. Ford to G-2, Sept. 18, 1931, GS G-2 File 2015–1095. His voyages to and from Europe in 1931 were on the S. S. *Leviathan,* the liner on which he had returned to the States in 1919.
18. *New York Times,* Sept. 17, 26, and 28, and Oct. 4, 1931, Aug. 31, Sept. 13, 16, 22, and 24, and Oct. 8, 1932; Hersey, *Men on Bataan,* 148–51; *Reminiscences,* 97–99; Brig. Gen. Alfred T. Smith to G-2, June 3, 1933, GS G-2 File 2257-ZZ-164; Capt. James C. Crockett to G-2, Aug. 28, 1933, GS G-2 File 2450-B-203. For most official Army documents concerning MacArthur's European trip of 1931, see GS G-2 File 2257-ZZ-158; for his trip of 1932, see GS G-2 File 2257-ZZ-164. Blomberg visited Washington in 1931 and later wrote of MacArthur: "We did not see him. He did not like us Germans. On the contrary, he was bitterly hostile towards us. During a European tour, which he took later on, he carefully avoided crossing Germany's borders. I was unable to determine why MacArthur was so anti-German. To have known why would have been enlightening since the General was an outstanding figure. He was an aggressive Anglo-American and therefore, of course, unsympathetic to our national traits." Blomberg, "Erinnerungen bis 1933," p. 3 (EAP 21-a-14/30c, NA microfilm), quoted from copy in possession of Philip P. Brower, MMBA director.
19. Armin Rappaport, *Henry L. Stimson and Japan, 1931–33* (Chicago, 1963), 154–55, 179–80, 213–15; *New York Times,* Feb. 1, 4, and 5, 1932; Whan, ed., *A Soldier Speaks,* 41; Thomas A. Bailey, *A Diplomatic History of the American People* (7th ed., New York, 1964), 699. On Feb. 23, 1932, Stimson sent a public letter to Sen. William E. Borah declaring that the United States would insist on its treaty rights in East Asia and expected other nations to endorse the nonrecognition doctrine. Upon reading the Borah letter, MacArthur wrote Stimson a note praising it as "a master stroke." Stimson diary, entry of Feb. 25, 1932; Stimson to DM, Feb. 25, 1932, Stimson Papers.
20. *The World Tomorrow,* May 16, 1931.

21. *Ibid.,* June 2, 1931. MacArthur's letter was widely reprinted, among other places, in *New York Times,* June 3, 1931, and Whan, ed., *A Soldier Speaks,* 36–40.
22. *New York Times,* June 14, 18, 20, and 21, 1931; Col. Alfred T. Smith to J. Edgar Hoover, Aug. 18, 1931; Hoover to Smith, Sept. 4, 1931, GS G-2 File 10312–2781.
23. Moffat, *Moffat Papers,* 56–57; Lt. Col. Charles L. Sampson to Asst. Chiefs of Staff, Chief of Air Corps, and Chief of Chemical Warfare Service, Aug. 12, 1932; Simonds to DM, Aug. 2, 1932, WPD 599–149; Simonds to Moseley, May 24, 1933, Moseley Papers, Box 5.
24. Moffat, *Moffat Papers,* 63–64.
25. *Ibid.,* 69–70.
26. *Ibid.,* 91–92.

CHAPTER XIV, *"Prophet Without Honor,"*
pages 382–414

1. Irving Bernstein, *The Lean Years: A History of the American Worker, 1920–1933* (Boston, 1960), 425–36; Charles J. Tull, *Father Coughlin and the New Deal* (Syracuse, 1965), 3–4.
2. Moseley to Payne, Oct. 9, 1930, Moseley Papers, Box 5.
3. Hurley to Rep. W. Frank James, Jan. 31, 1931; DM to Sen. Charles L. McNary, June 16, 1932, AG 400.38; DM to SecWar, Aug. 15, 1932, Hoover Papers, File OF/95-C, Box 1-E/300.
4. William S. Myers and Walter H. Newton, *The Hoover Administration: A Documented Narrative* (New York, 1936), 68–69; Ray L. Wilbur and Arthur M. Hyde, *The Hoover Policies* (New York, 1937), 198–202.
5. Mauritz A. Hallgren, "The Bonus Army Scares Mr. Hoover," *Nation,* CXXXV (July 27, 1932), 71–72; Schlesinger, *Crisis of the Old Order,* 256–57.
6. John Dos Passos, "Red Day on Capitol Hill," *New Republic,* LXIX (Dec. 23, 1931), 153–55; *New York Times,* Jan. 8, 1932; Maurice Sugar, "Bullets — Not Food — for Ford Workers," *Nation,* CXXXIV (Mar. 23, 1932), 333–35; *Reminiscences,* 92–93.
7. John Dos Passos, "Washington and Chicago," *New Republic,* LXXI (June 29, 1932), 178–79.
8. Walter W. Waters, with William C. White, *B.E.F.: The Whole Story of the Bonus Army* (New York, 1933), 65–134; Schlesinger, *Crisis of the Old Order,* 256–57; Bernstein, *Lean Years,* 438–41.
9. Fleta C. Springer, "Glassford and the Siege of Washington," *Harper's,* CLXV (Nov., 1932), 641–43; Constance M. Green, *Washington* (2 vols., Princeton, 1962–63), II, 365–66, 368–72; "The Human Side of the Bonus Army," *Literary Digest,* CXIII (June 25, 1932), 28–30.

10. *Reminiscences,* 93; Payne to Rep. John J. McSwain, June 25, 1932, AG 240; H. W. Blakeley, "When the Army Was Smeared," *Combat Forces Journal,* II (Feb., 1952), 28; John W. Killigrew, "The Army and the Bonus Incident," *Military Affairs,* XXV (Summer, 1962), 59.

11. Pittsburgh *Post-Gazette,* June 9, 1932; *New York Times,* June 9, 1932; *Reminiscences,* 90; DM to SecWar, Aug. 15, 1932, Hoover Papers, File OF/95-C, Box 1-E/300.

12. Brig. Gen. Alfred T. Smith to TAG, June 10, 1932; rpts. on bonus marchers by cps. area CGs to CofS, June 11–July 9, 1932; TAG to DM, June 12, 1932, AG 240; Brig. Gen. Perry L. Miles to DM, June 4, 1932, Mil. District of Washington File on Operations against Bonus Marchers, 1932, Box 1, RG 98 [hereafter cited as District File].

13. *New York Times,* June 16 and 18, 1932; *Washington Star,* June 19, 1932; Waters, *B.E.F.,* 145–64; *Congressional Record,* 72nd Cong., 1st Sess. (1932), Pt. LXXV, 1375–77. Overriding Roosevelt's veto, Congress approved a measure in Jan., 1936, which provided for payment of the bonus in full. John M. Blum, *From the Morgenthau Diaries,* Vol. I, *Years of Crisis, 1928–1938* (Boston, 1959), 258–59.

14. Miles to DM, June 4, 1932; Maj. Alexander D. Surles to Miles, Aug. 5, 1932, District File. In 1942 Moseley wrote MacArthur:

> . . . Well do I recall that day when I suggested the preparation that you should make to control the city of Washington in the event of emergency due to the Bonus March. You disagreed with me entirely, but the next day you walked into my office when you arrived at the War Department, saying, in effect, "George, you were right yesterday. Go ahead with the preparations that you suggested."

Moseley to DM, Nov. 3, 1942, RG 10, MMBA.

15. Waters, *B.E.F.,* 164–206; Green, *Washington,* II, 369–71; Schlesinger, *Crisis of the Old Order,* 258–61.

16. DM to SecWar, Aug. 15, 1932, Hoover Papers, File OF/95-C, Box 1-E/300; Bernstein, *Lean Years,* 449–50; Green, *Washington,* II, 372–73.

17. Bennett M. Rich, *Presidents and Civil Disorders* (Washington, 1941), 150–63; Warren, *Hoover and the Great Depression,* 232; T. G. Joslin, *Hoover Off the Record* (New York, 1934), 267–69; *New York Times,* July 26, 1932.

18. *Washington Herald,* July 29, 1932; Miles to DM, Aug. 4 and Sept. 23, 1932, District File; Paul Y. Anderson, "Tear-Gas, Bayonets, and Votes," *Nation,* CXXXV (Aug. 17, 1932), 139–40; *idem,* "Republican Handsprings," *ibid.* (Aug. 31, 1932), 188–89; L. H. Reichelderfer to Pres., July 28, 1932; DM to Attorney Gen. William D. Mitchell, Aug. 2, 1932, Hoover Papers, File OF/95-C, Box 1-E/300.

19. *Washington Post,* July 29, 1932; DM to SecWar, Aug. 15, 1932, Hoover Papers, File OF/95-C, Box 1-E/300. In the rpt. to Hurley just cited, MacArthur stated, "Several policemen were hurt, one most seriously, while another, in defending himself, was forced to shoot and kill one of the Bonus Marchers," his account differing considerably from those of reporters and other witnesses.

20. Hurley to DM, July 28, 1932, Bonus Riot File, Patrick J. Hurley Papers, University of Oklahoma Library, Norman, Okla.

21. WD Message Center log, July 28–29, 1932; Lt. Col. Louis A. Kunzig to Miles, July 30, 1932; Miles to DM, Aug. 4, 1932, District File. Previous printed accounts state that six tanks were used on July 28, but the commanders' op. rpts. list only five.

22. Miles to DM, Aug. 4, 1932, District File; DM to SecWar, Aug. 15, 1932, Hoover Papers, File OF/95-C, Box 1-E/300; *Reminiscences,* 95; Dwight D. Eisenhower, *At Ease: Stories I Tell to Friends* (Garden City, 1967), 216. As expected, critical comments on MacArthur's attire can be found in such biased works as Rovere and Schlesinger, *The General and the President,* 32, and Allen and Pearson, *More Merry-Go-Round,* 49. But it is surprising that many reputedly "objective" authorities on the era feel compelled to mention MacArthur's "dress uniform," no matter how brief the description of the bonus incident. See, e.g., Dexter Perkins, *The New Age of Franklin Roosevelt, 1932–45* (Chicago, 1957), 4; Frank Freidel, *Franklin D. Roosevelt* (3 vols. to date, 1952–56), III, 327.

23. Miles to DM, Sept. 23, 1932; *idem* to Moseley, Sept. 23, 1932, District File; *New York Times,* July 29, 1932; John Forell, "The Bonus Crusade," *Virginia Quarterly Review,* IX (Jan., 1933), 47–49.

24. Kunzig to Miles, Aug. 6, 1932; Capt. Raymond Dailey to Miles, Aug. 1, 1932, District File.

25. Eisenhower, *At Ease,* 217; Lt. Col. Clement H. Wright to DM, July 28, 1932, District File; DM to Mitchell, Aug. 6, 1932, Bonus Riot File, Hurley Papers.

26. Surles to Miles, Aug. 5, 1932; Miles to DM, Aug. 4, 1932, District File; *New York Times,* July 29, 1932; Eisenhower, *At Ease,* 217; Waters, *B.E.F.,* 207–38.

27. Eisenhower, *At Ease,* 217–18.

28. *New York Times,* July 29, 1932; DM's press interview, July 28, 1932, Alphabetical Misc. File, Box 1-Q/150, HHL. The previous riot experiences to which MacArthur referred are not known, but may have been public disorders in the Philippines during his tours there in the 1920's. The Scout mutiny at Fort McKinley, however, seems to have been nonviolent.

29. *New York Times,* July 29, 1932; Eisenhower, *At Ease,* 218.

30. Surles to Miles, July 30 and Aug. 5, 1932; WD Message Center log,

July 28–29, 1932, District File; Warren, *Hoover and the Great Depression*, 234–35.

31. Lt. Col. James M. Lockett to Kunzig, Aug. 4, 1932; Kunzig to Miles, Aug. 8, 1932; Miles to DM, Sept. 23, 1932; Lt. Col. A. T. Cooper to Miles, Aug. 2, 1932; Kunzig to Miles, Aug. 5, 1932; Capt. H. B. Smith to Miles, Sept. 8, 1932; Gen. Orders 6, 12th Inf. Hq., Aug. 5, 1932 (quotes DM's commendation); Gen. Orders 4, 16th Brig. Hq., Aug. 3, 1932, District File.

32. Hoover to Reichelderfer, July 29, 1932; press statement by Hurley, July 29, 1932, Hoover Papers, File OF/95-C, Box 1-E/300; Frederick L. Allen, *Since Yesterday* (New York, 1940), 83–86; Warren, *Hoover and the Great Depression*, 235; Green, *Washington*, II, 375–76.

33. Bess Furman, *Washington By-Line: The Personal History of a Newspaper Woman* (New York, 1949), 125–26; Thomas L. Stokes, *Chip Off My Shoulder* (Princeton, 1940), 303–04; Hicks, *Republican Ascendancy*, 275–76.

34. *New York Times,* July 31, 1932; *Congressional Record,* 81st Cong., 1st Sess. (1949), Pt. XCV, 12529–31; Benjamin Gitlow, *The Whole of Their Lives* (New York, 1948), 228–30; Hoover, *Memoirs,* III, 231; William D. Leuchtenburg, *Franklin D. Roosevelt and the New Deal, 1932–1940* (New York, 1963), 15–16; Jacob Spolansky, *The Communist Trail in America* (New York, 1951), 51–52; Col. William H. Wilson to G-2, 6th Cps. Area, Aug. 13, 1932, GS G-2 File 10110–2685(1).

35. DM to SecWar, Aug. 15, 1932, Hoover Papers, File OF/95-C, Box 1-E/300; DM to Lawrence Richey [Hoover's secy.], Aug. 12, 1932, AG 240; Killigrew, "The Army and the Bonus Incident," 65. In 1949 Hurley wrote MacArthur: "You and President Hoover have been smeared unmercifully in political campaigns by falsehoods pertaining to that event. Distorted and false statements concerning the Bonus March have also been used against me politically, with telling effect." Hurley to DM, Aug. 19, 1949, Bonus Riot File, Hurley Papers.

36. Rexford G. Tugwell, *The Democratic Roosevelt: A Biography of Franklin D. Roosevelt* (Garden City, 1957), 348–51.

37. *New York Times,* May 17, 1934; Drew Pearson, "My Life in the White House Doghouse," *Saturday Evening Post,* CCXXIX (Nov. 10, 1956), 38, 72; *Columbus [Ohio] Evening Dispatch,* Nov. 12, 1934; Rep. A. P. Lamneck to FDR, Nov. 17, 1934, WD File 25-T, FDRL; Josephus Daniels to FDR, Oct. 8, 1934, PPF, FDRL; interview, author with Gen. Eisenhower. Recently Pearson said that when MacArthur brought the suit Ross Collins informed him, "You know, MacArthur's been keeping a girl in the Chastleton Apartments on 16th Street." Pearson claimed that he checked out the story and learned from the girl, a Chinese, that she was the general's "girl friend" and had been brought by him from Manila when he became chief of staff. "She'd

been keeping a diary, with all these entries [about MacArthur],"
Pearson maintained, "so we just got in touch with MacArthur's attorney. That was all there was to it [terminating the suit]." Robert G.
Sherrill, "Drew Pearson: An Interview," *Nation*, CCIX (July 7,
1969), 15; *Parade*, Aug. 24, 1969.

38. *Reminiscences*, 96–97; Pinchot quoted in Bernstein, *Lean Years*, 455.
On Aug. 30, 1932, MacArthur sailed for Europe. Though the trip was
undoubtedly a welcome relief from the B.E.F. controversy, his itinerary
was scheduled long before the eviction occurred.

CHAPTER XV, *"Those Strange New Dealers,"*
pages 415–447

1. Franklin D. Roosevelt, *The Public Papers and Addresses of Franklin
D. Roosevelt*, ed. by Samuel I. Rosenman (13 vols., New York, 1938–
50), I, 810–11; Walter Lippmann, *Interpretations, 1931–1932*, ed. by
Allan Nevins (New York, 1932), 257–59; Pershing to DM, Feb. 26,
1933, Pershing Papers, Box 121; *New York Times*, Mar. 1, 1933; Green,
Washington, II, 387–88.

2. *Reminiscences*, 99–101; Gunther, *Riddle of MacArthur*, 9–11; Tugwell, *Democratic Roosevelt*, 12–13; Raymond Moley, *After Seven
Years* (New York, 1939), 10; James M. Burns, *Roosevelt: The Lion
and the Fox* (New York, 1956), 486–87.

3. John A. Salmon, *The Civilian Conservation Corps, 1933–1942: A New
Deal Case Study* (Durham, 1967), 9, 16–23; Killigrew, "Impact of the
Great Depression on the Army," Ch. XII, 1–12; Alfred B. Rollins, Jr.,
Roosevelt and Howe (New York, 1962), 402–06. In Jan., 1933, Sen.
James Couzens of Mich. introduced a bill authorizing the Army to
clothe, feed, and house unemployed youths. The bill was shelved
because of intense military opposition; a modified version of it became
an amendment to the Army appropriations bill, but the amendment
also was dropped. Such agitation in Congress, however, did prompt
MacArthur to initiate a study by the Gen. Staff of the cost of and the
Army's capacity to handle an indigent force. Salmon, *Civilian Conservation Corps*, 9.

4. *Ibid.*, 40–43; Killigrew, "Impact of the Great Depression on the Army,"
Ch. XII, 6–20.

5. Col. Duncan K. Major, Jr., to Robert Fechner, June 30, 1933, OF 268,
FDRL.

6. DM to cps. area CGs, May 13, 1933, AG 324.5 CCC (3–25–33); Killigrew, "Impact of the Great Depression on the Army," Ch. XIII, 18.

7. Major to Fechner, June 30, 1933, OF 268, FDRL.

8. *WDAR, 1933*, I, 8.

9. DM to cps. area CGs, June 30, 1933, AG 324.5 CCC (3–25–33); DM to Stephen Early, Aug. 15, 1933; Early to DM, Aug. 15, 1933, OF 268, FDRL.

10. Salmon, *Civilian Conservation Corps,* 47–53, 188–90; Killigrew, "Impact of the Great Depression on the Army," Ch. XIII, 1–12.

11. Harry H. Woodring, "The Army Stands Ready," *Liberty,* Jan. 6, 1934; Early to Woodring, Jan. 5, 1934; Charles A. Beard to FDR, Jan. 20, 1934; Woodring to Howe, Feb. 24, 1934, OF 25, FDRL; *New York Times,* Feb. 20, 1935; Salmon, *Civilian Conservation Corps,* 118–19. As expected, Moseley, then commanding the IV Corps Area, vociferously supported the idea of military training in the CCC. Later he proposed "Youth Conservation Camps" for the CCC applicants who were rejected as physically unfit. At these camps, or convalescent centers, the readily curable youth would be treated by the Army Medical Corps. The War Department rejected the idea, however, on the grounds that it would be too costly and would commit the Army to a public health program tangential to its basic mission. Moseley to TAG, Oct. 21, 1936; Col. E. R. Gentry to TAG, Nov. 18, 1936, Moseley Papers, Box 5.

12. Fechner to DM, Sept. 26, 1935, CofS Correspondence, Box 1, RG 18, MMBA.

13. DM to Fechner, Sept. 27, 1935, *ibid.*

14. Killigrew, "Impact of the Great Depression on the Army," Ch. IX; *New York Times,* Jan. 15, 1933; *WDAR, 1933,* I, 15–18.

15. Pershing to DM, Feb. 27, 1933, Pershing Papers, Box 121; Craig to DM, Mar. 13, 1933, OF 25-T, FDRL; Hunt, *Untold Story,* 147–52; Hersey, *Men on Bataan,* 156–63; *New York Times,* Apr. 21, 1933; *ANJ,* Feb. 4 and 11, Apr. 29, May 6, 1933; U.S. House, *Hearings on War Department Appropriations Bill for 1934* . . . 72nd Cong., 2nd Sess. (1933), Pt. I, 1–33. In 1942 Early, at the President's request, informed an editor of the *New York Times* that "at no time was the retirement of 3,000 to 4,000 officers a part of the President's economy move." (But, as conceived by the congressmen pushing the measure, furloughing would have been practically tantamount to retirement.) FDR to Early, June 23, 1942; Early to Samuel T. Williamson, June 25, 1942; Williamson to Early, July 6, 1942, PPF 675, FDRL.

16. *Reminiscences,* 101. See also Hunt, *Untold Story,* 151–52.

17. *ANJ,* July 8 and 29, 1933; Killigrew, "Impact of the Great Depression on the Army," Ch. X, 22–25.

18. DM to FDR, July 26, 1933; Harold L. Ickes to FDR, Aug. 5, 1933, OF 25-T, FDRL; *ANJ,* Aug. 19, 1933; *New York Times,* Sept. 14, 1933; Killigrew, "Impact of the Great Depression on the Army," Ch. X, 25–30, Ch. XI, 1–31.

19. Harold L. Ickes, *The Secret Diary of Harold L. Ickes* (3 vols., New

York, 1953–54), I, 71. On July 21, while discussing a public statement by Dern criticizing the Public Works Board, Roosevelt told Ickes that "Dern had allowed himself to be put in an unfortunate position by the Chief of Staff, General MacArthur." Ickes wrote in his diary: "The President went on to tell me how he had had to sit down on General MacArthur pretty hard himself on one occasion, and he expressed the opinion that MacArthur is running the War Department." *Ibid.*, 68–69.

20. Daniel W. Bell to Howe, May 1, 1935, OF 25, FDRL; *WDAR, 1935,* I, 53–54.

21. *WDAR, 1933,* I, 49. In Sept., 1933, Pershing wrote MacArthur: "The world situation is now such that it does not seem possible that Congress would have the temerity to do anything but strengthen the Army and Navy, and I believe we can look forward with considerable confidence that the full pay bill will be restored and that no further attempts will be made to please the unthinking pacifist by measures that reduce efficiency." Pershing to DM, Sept. 14, 1933, Pershing Papers, Box 121.

22. Huntington, *The Soldier and the State,* 414; Elias Huzar, *The Purse and the Sword: Control of the Army by Congress through Military Appropriations, 1933–1950* (Ithaca, 1950), 128, 147.

23. Typescript of minutes of meeting of Senate subcommittee on War Dept. appropriations bill for 1935, Mar. 12, 1934, OF 25, FDRL.

24. *New York Times,* Mar. 6 and Apr. 22, 1934; *WDAR, 1934,* I, 34.

25. Killigrew, "Impact of the Great Depression on the Army," Appendix I; *Reminiscences,* 101. All budget and appropriations totals, unless otherwise stated, are based on Killigrew's Appendix I, which was derived from the Cater File, OCMH.

26. *ANJ,* Sept. 2, 1933; Pogue, *Marshall,* I, 281–82, 294–96; Robert Payne, *The Marshall Story: A Biography of General George C. Marshall* (New York, 1951), 108–09; Marshall, *Together,* 17–18; Coffman, *Hilt of the Sword,* 236–40; John C. O'Laughlin to Pershing, Sept. 16, 1935; Pershing to Marshall, Oct. 4, 1935, Pershing Papers, Box 121.

27. Arthur M. Schlesinger, Jr., *The Coming of the New Deal (The Age of Roosevelt,* Vol. II; Boston, 1959), 446–55; *New York Times,* Feb. 10 and Mar. 13, 1933; Henry H. Arnold, *Global Mission* (New York, 1949), 109–11; James A. Farley, *Jim Farley's Story* (New York, 1948), 47. Maj. Henry H. Arnold, who would head the Army Air Forces in World War II, was in charge of air mail operations on the Pacific coast in the spring of 1934.

28. Typescript of minutes of meeting of Senate subcommittee on War Dept. appropriations bill for 1935, Mar. 12, 1934, OF 25, FDRL. This subcommittee delved into the air mail decision when one senator, while consideration of the Air Corps' budgetary needs was

underway, suggested that more funds would have provided adequate equipment, which, in turn, would have reduced the accident rate when the Air Corps was carrying the mails.

29. *New York Times*, Mar. 13, May 17, June 20 and 24, 1934; Hersey, *Men on Bataan*, 230–35; press statement by Woodring, Mar. 3, 1934, OF 25, FDRL. Friends of Pearson in the Cabinet told him that the President was "so irked" by some of his published remarks that he encouraged MacArthur to instigate libel proceedings to put the "Washington Merry-Go-Round" out of business. Pearson, "My Life in the White House Doghouse." 38, 72.

30. Stephen Raushenbush to DM, Sept. 4, 1934; DM to Raushenbush, Sept. 6, 1934, GS G-2 File 2724-70 (37); U.S. Senate, *Munitions Industry: Hearings before the Special Committee Investigating the Munitions Industry* . . . 73d and 74th Cong. (40 pts., 1934–43), IV, 829, 983, V, 1073–74, 1080–81, 1125, 1190–91; FDR to Col. Edward M. House, Sept. 17, 1935, in Elliott Roosevelt, ed., *F. D. R.: His Personal Letters, 1928–1945* (2 vols., New York, 1950), I, 506–07. On Sept. 13, 1934, MacArthur wrote Nye: "I never discussed American military equipment with the Turkish General Staff or with any other Turkish authorities. Neither directly nor indirectly did I have anything whatsoever to do with any attempt to influence American sales in Turkey." U.S. Senate, *Munitions Industry*, V, 1081.

31. Blum, *From the Morgenthau Diaries*, I, 61–62; Tugwell, *Democratic Roosevelt*, 202; Tull, *Father Coughlin*, 139, 230–33. Maj. Gen. Courtney Whitney, MacArthur's closest friend after 1943 and sometimes called his "alter ego," dedicated his work, *MacArthur: Rendezvous with History* (New York, 1956), "to James H. Rand, industrial pioneer, who had the vision to guide MacArthur's brilliant mind toward new horizons after a willful president foreclosed the old."

32. Interview, author with Gen. Eisenhower; Considine, *MacArthur*, 12, 14. Eisenhower was working in the office of Payne, the asst. secy. of war for procurement, when he was transferred to MacArthur's office at the request of the chief of staff. In talking with the author, Gen. Eisenhower did not indicate any knowledge of the affair which MacArthur, according to Pearson's allegation, had with a Chinese girl. Perhaps the relationship, if it existed, had been terminated before Eisenhower joined MacArthur's staff.

33. Daniels to FDR, Mar. 14 and Oct. 8, 1934; Rep. Kenneth McKellar to FDR, Oct. 2, 1934; E. S. J. Greble to FDR, Oct. 16, 1934; and other letters in opposition to MacArthur's reappointment, OF 25-T, FDRL.

34. *New York Times*, Sept. 9, 1934; Mrs. J. C. Wood, to FDR, Apr. 10, 1934, OF 25-T, FDRL. In Mar., 1933, Roosevelt had asked for a detailed report on Simonds' record, for what purpose is not known.

35. Sen. Morris Sheppard to FDR, June 26, 1934; and other letters in support of MacArthur's retention, OF 25-T, FDRL.
36. Rep. Joseph W. Byrns to Howe, July 6, 1934, *ibid.*
37. Presidential press conferences, Oct. 17–Nov. 14, 1934, Vol. IV, PPF 1-P, FDRL; *New York Times*, Nov. 15 and 16, 1934; *ANR*, Nov. 24, 1934.
38. Presidential press conference, Dec. 12, 1934, Vol. IV, PPF 1-P, FDRL. See also Special Orders 296, WD, Dec. 14, 1934, OF 25-T, FDRL.
39. *New York Times*, Dec. 13, 1934; *ANJ*, Dec. 15, 1934.

CHAPTER XVI, *"A Few Steps Forward,"*
pages 448–476

1. U.S. House, *Hearings on War Department Appropriations Bill for 1936 . . .* 74th Cong., 1st Sess. (1935), Pt. I, 1–48; U.S. Senate, *Hearings on War Department Appropriations Bill for 1936 . . .* 74th Cong., 1st Sess. (1935), 4–32, 52–66; Killigrew, "Impact of the Great Depression on the Army," Ch. XIV, 27–40.
2. *Literary Digest*, CXIX (Feb. 19, 1935), 17; *New York Times*, Mar. 30, 1935; *WDAR, 1936,* I, 31.
3. *WDAR, 1935,* I, 41.
4. *Ibid.,* 44; Killigrew, "Impact of the Great Depression on the Army," Ch. XIV, 34–35; Weigley, *History of U.S. Army,* 568–69.
5. *WDAR, 1935,* I, 47–49; Ambrose, *Duty, Honor, Country,* 290–91; Whan, ed., *A Soldier Speaks,* 42–44.
6. *WDAR, 1935,* I, 45–47, 49–51; *ANJ,* Jan. 27 and Aug. 18, 1934, Aug. 3, 1935; U.S. House, *To Promote the Efficiency of National Defense: Report to Accompany S. 1404,* 74th Cong., 1st Sess. (1935), House Doc. 1323, 2–3; Dern to FDR, Jan. 2, 1935; FDR to Dern, Jan. 17, 1935, OF 25, FDRL. Moseley and Simonds, among other top generals, felt that the Army should end promotion by seniority. Moseley to Simonds, June 14, 1934; Simonds to Moseley, July 2, 1934, Moseley Papers, Box 5.
7. Washington *Herald,* Aug. 2, 1935.
8. *ANR,* Nov. 15, 1930; *ANJ,* Jan. 14, 1933; *WDAR, 1934,* I, 64–65; *idem, 1935,* I, 47.
9. *WDAR, 1935,* I, 51–54; Weigley, *History of U.S. Army,* 414–15; Millis, *Arms and Men,* 235–36; Constance M. Green, Harry C. Thompson, and Peter C. Roots, *The Ordnance Department: Planning Munitions for War (USAWWII;* Washington, 1955), 189–94, 199–203.
10. Green, *et al., Ordnance Department,* 193–94.
11. *WDAR, 1935,* I, 72–73; Whan, ed., *A Soldier Speaks,* 63–64.
12. *WDAR, 1934,* I, 45–51; *idem, 1935,* I, 53, 61–63; Craven and Cate, eds., *Plans and Early Operations,* 30–33; WD, *Final Report of War Department Special Committee on Army Air Corps, July 18, 1934*

(Washington, 1934), 29. Army officers on the eleven-man Bakei Board were Drum, Simonds, Foulois, Brig. Gen. John W. Gulick, and Maj. Albert E. Brown.

Arnold commanded the western wing of the G.H.Q. Air Force at March Field, Calif.; Lt. Col. H. Conger Pratt, the eastern wing at Langley Field; and Lt. Col. Harold C. Brant, the central wing at Barksdale Field, La.

13. Killigrew, "Impact of the Great Depression on the Army," Appendix I; *WDAR, 1935,* I, 65–71; Weigley, *History of U.S. Army,* 414.

14. Interview, author with Gen. Eisenhower; Civilian Production Administration, *Industrial Mobilization for War: History of the War Production Board and Predecessor Agencies, 1940–1945,* Vol. I, *Program and Administration* (Washington, 1947), 3–4; R. Elberton Smith, *The Army and Economic Mobilization (USAWWII;* Washington, 1959), 73–75; *WDAR, 1931,* I, 25. In Dec., 1930, MacArthur was appointed "Military Intelligence representative" on the National Industrial Conference Board. Maj. O. H. Saunders to G-2, Dec. 19, 1930, GS G-2 File 5-443 (177).

15. Harold J. Tobin and Percy W. Bidwell, *Mobilizing Civilian America* (New York, 1940), 177–79; George C. Reinhardt and William R. Kintner, *The Haphazard Years: How America Has Gone to War* (Garden City, 1960), 149–51; Bernard Baruch, *Baruch: The Public Years* (New York, 1960), 265–66; U.S. House, *Documents by War Policies Commission . . .* 72nd Cong., 1st Sess. (1932), House Doc. 271; U.S. House, *War Policies Commission Report to the President,* 72nd Cong., 1st Sess. (1932), House Doc. 163; *WDAR, 1932,* I, 303–05. MacArthur's statement before the War Policies Commission in 1931 appears in *WDAR, 1931,* I, 47–69. Eisenhower served as asst. executive secy. of the commission.

16. Tobin and Bidwell, *Mobilizing Civilian America,* 44–54, 82–84, 93–94, 107–09, 134–39; Byron Fairchild and Jonathan Grossman, *The Army and Industrial Manpower (USAWWII;* Washington, 1959), 11–20; *WDAR, 1935,* I, 33–40.

17. Watson, *Chief of Staff,* 26, 29–30; *WDAR, 1933,* I, 11–15; *idem, 1938,* I, 1–2; Marvin A. Kreidberg and Merton G. Henry, *History of Military Mobilization in the United States Army, 1775–1945* (Washington, 1955), 437–38.

18. *WDAR, 1939,* I, 23.

19. Millis, *Arms and Men,* 236.

20. Stimson to Bingham, Feb. 15, 1932, Stimson Papers, Box 305; George E. Taylor, *The Struggle for North China* (New York, 1940), 119; 48 *U.S. Statutes at Large* 456; *PGGAR, 1934,* 1.

21. Parker to TAG, Aug. 1, 1934, AG 093.5 Phil. Is. (8-1-34); Manila newspapers quoted in preceding.

22. Parker to TAG, Aug. 1, 1934.

23. Louis Morton, "American and Allied Strategy in the Far East," *Military Affairs,* XXIX (Dec., 1949), 22–39; Morton, "War Plan ORANGE: Evolution of a Strategy," *World Politics,* II (1959), 221–50; Watson, *Chief of Staff,* 412–17; *WDAR,* 1930–35, strength tables.

24. Brig. Gen. Stanley D. Embick to Maj. Gen. Ewing E. Booth, Apr. 19, 1933, WPD 3251-15.

25. Brig. Gen. Charles E. Kilbourne to DM, Mar. 26, 1934, WPD 3646-1; Kilbourne to DM, Apr. 5, 1934; DM to Parker, July 6, 1934, WPD 3251-17.

26. Kilbourne to DM, Sept. 12, 1934; TAG to Parker, Sept. 14, 1934, WPD 3489-5.

27. Kilbourne to DM, Nov. 22, 1934, WPD 3251-22.

CHAPTER XVII, *"A Year of Changes,"*

pages 479–509

1. Quezon to FDR, Nov. 17, 1934; FDR to Quezon, Nov. 29, 1934, PPF 1984, FDRL; Quezon to Dern, Nov. 19, 1934, RG 18, MMBA.

2. Quezon to Dern, Nov. 19, 1934; Hull to Dern, Nov. 28, 1934; Dern to Rep. John McDuffie, Nov. 19, 1934; Quezon to Sen. Millard E. Tydings, Nov. 19, 1934; DM to Quezon, Dec. 4, 1934, RG 18, MMBA; WD Bulletin 4, July 10, 1926, AG 210.68 (5-19-26).

3. Manuel L. Quezon, *The Good Fight* (New York, 1946), 153–55; John Gunther, "Manuel Quezon," *Atlantic Monthly,* CLXIII (Jan., 1939), 61; *Reminiscences,* 102.

4. Dern to McDuffie, Nov. 19, 1934, SecWar Recs., RG 107, NA.

5. DM to Quezon, Dec. 27, 1934, RG 18, MMBA. Quezon responded: "I am counting upon our understanding for success of our national undertaking. My colleagues have been confidentially appraised of your plan and are enthusiastic over it." Quezon to DM, Dec. 28, 1934, *ibid.*

6. DM to McSwain, Feb. 12, 1935, RG 18, MMBA.

7. *The First Report of the United States High Commissioner to the Philippine Islands, Covering the Period from November 15, 1935, to December 31, 1936* (Washington, 1937), 13; memo. of terms of agreement for Philippine military adviser, 1935, RG 1, MMBA.

8. Spec. Orders 220, WD, Sept. 18, 1935, RG 18, MMBA.

9. *First Report of U.S. High Commissioner,* 13; Eisenhower, *At Ease,* 219–21.

10. Brig. Gen. C. E. Nathorst to DM, Feb. 21, 1935, AG 230.64 Phil. Is. (2-21-35); Brig. Gen. D. C. McDonald to DM, Nov. 12, 1934; Quezon to DM, May 21, 1935, RG 18, MMBA.

11. DM to Quezon, June 1, 1935, RG 18, MMBA.

12. FDR to DM, Aug. 31, 1935; Early to DM, Sept. 1, 1935; DM to FDR, Sept. 2, 1935, PPF 4914, FDRL; DM to FDR, Sept. 9, 1935, RG 18, MMBA; *New York Times,* Sept. 4, 1935. Nine months later Drum, then commanding the Hawaiian Dept., wrote MacArthur urging him to accept the post of high commissioner if it was offered to him when Murphy resigned, as was soon expected: "It seems to me that you could really do both; that is, the High Commissioner's job and that of the Military Adviser." He added: "The combination would have many advantages. Then again, I have not changed my views as given to you in Washington one afternoon relative to 1940. Such a possibility is in the offing through the backyard you have created." Drum to DM, June 29, 1936, RG 10, MMBA.

13. FDR to DM, Sept. 19, 1935, in Elliott Roosevelt, ed., *F.D.R.: His Personal Letters* (4 vols., New York, 1950), III, 507–08.

14. George A. Malcolm to DM, Aug. 14, 1935, RG 18, MMBA; DM to FDR, Sept. 26, 1935, and Murphy to FDR, Dec. 16, 1935, quoted in J. Woodford Howard, "Frank Murphy and the Philippine Commonwealth," *Pacific Historical Review,* XXXIII (1964), 61–62; Blum, *From the Morgenthau Diaries,* I, 257.

15. Dern to FDR, July 17, 1935, CF–War, FDRL.

16. FDR to Dern, July 18, 1935, *ibid.;* Presidential press conferences, 1935, VI, 55–56, 131, PPF 1-P, FDRL.

17. *New York Times,* June 11, July 15, and Sept. 6, 1935; Whan, ed., *A Soldier Speaks,* 67–75; Frank C. Waldrop, ed., *MacArthur on War: His Military Writings* (New York, 1942), 31–37; *Reminiscences,* 103; Gen. Orders 7, WD, Sept. 12, 1935; Woodring to DM, Sept. 30, 1935; DM to Quezon, Sept. 18, 1935; Quezon to DM, Sept. 20, 1935, RG 18, MMBA; *ANJ,* Oct. 5, 1935; DM to Pershing, Sept. 19, 1935, Pershing Papers, Box 121.

18. FDR to Woodring, Oct. 2, 1935, CF–War, FDRL; Eisenhower, *At Ease,* 223; DM to Woodring, Oct. 2, 1935; DM to FDR, Oct. 2, 1935; DM to Craig, Oct. 2, 1935, RG 1, MMBA.

19. Farley, *Farley's Story,* 55. On the other hand, in CF–War, FDRL, there is a MS list of CofS prospects, Oct., 1935, in Roosevelt's handwriting, which has a note beside Simond's name: "Second choice of Dern & MacArthur." When interviewed by the author in 1967, Gen. Eisenhower said, "I was not aware of the Simonds situation. I thought the President kept MacArthur in order to allow him to finish some program in the War Department and also, perhaps, because Roosevelt had not made up his mind on a successor for the chief of staff position."

20. *Reminiscences,* 103; *New York Times,* Oct. 25, 1935; DM to Murphy, Oct. 23, 1935, Frank Murphy Papers, Mich. Historical Collections, University of Mich., Ann Arbor, Mich.; Eisenhower, *At Ease,* 224;

Jorge B. Vargas to Admin. Asst. to High Commissioner, Jan. 9, 1935, Bureau of Insular Affairs Recs., RG 350, NA.

21. *Reminiscences,* 107; Lee and Henschel, *MacArthur,* 282–83; Hersey, *Men on Bataan,* 275–76.

22. DM to TAG, July 2, 1935, RG 18, MMBA; Quezon to DM, Oct. 15, 1935; DM to Quezon, Oct. 15, 1935, RG 1, MMBA; Murphy to McDonald, Nov. 13, 1935, AG 093.5 Phil. Is. (11-13-35); DM to Murphy, Nov. 28, 1935, Murphy Papers; *First Report of U.S. High Commissioner,* 1–5; Hull to Early, Nov. 16, 1935, PPF 4914, FDRL.

23. *First Report of U.S. High Commissioner,* 4; DM to Dern, Aug. 20, 1935, SecWar Recs., RG 107, NA.

24. DM to Dern, Aug. 20, 1935, SecWar Recs., RG 107, NA.

25. Brig. Gen. Creed F. Cox to DM, Sept. 14, 1935, RG 18, MMBA; Maj. Gen. Edgar T. Conley to Parker, Oct. 15, 1935; Dern to FDR, Nov. 9, 1935, AG 093.5 Phil. Is. (10-15-35).

26. Friend, *Between Two Empires,* 185; FDR to Dern, Nov. 9, 1935; Dern to FDR, Nov. 12, 1935; FDR to Dern, Nov. 12, 1935, AG 093.5 Phil. Is. (10-15-35).

27. DM to TAG, Jan. 13, 1936; Maj. Gen. Lucius R. Holbrook to TAG, Jan. 16, 1936; Maj. Gen. A. W. Brown to G-1, Jan. 28, 1936; Dern to Hull, Feb. 28, 1936; Maj. Gen. Frank C. Burnett to Holbrook, Apr. 20, 1936, AG 093.5 Phil. Is. (1-16-36).

28. Phil. Commonwealth Act No. 1, "An Act to Provide for the National Defense of the Philippines," approved Dec. 21, 1935, AG 093.5 Phil. Is. (1-13-36).

29. Embick to CofS, Dec. 2, 1935, WPD 3389-29. The maj. gens. who concurred in Embick's rpt. were Simonds, Nolan, Malone, Conner, Brown, and Moseley.

30. DM, *Report on National Defense in the Philippines* (Manila, 1936), *passim;* interview, author with Gen. Eisenhower; Bul. 20, PA Hq., Apr. 30, 1936; Bul. 63, PA Hq., June 1, 1940, PA Recs., OCMH; *Newsweek,* VIII (Sept. 5, 1936), 8–9. MacArthur's 52-page rpt. was submitted to Quezon on Apr. 27, 1936, and approved by the National Assembly in mid-June; it was printed as a public document of the Philippine government. The rpt. is reprinted, with significant omissions and incorrect ellipses, in Whan, ed., *A Soldier Speaks,* 79–99.

31. DM to Murphy, Jan. 17, 1936, RG 1, MMBA; *PPAR, 1936,* 2–5; Adm. O. G. Murfin to DM, Aug. 7, 1936; Drum to DM, Sept. 4, 1936; Foulois to DM, June 20, 1936, RG 10, MMBA; Lt. Col. J. H. Cunningham to Col. Walter Krueger, July 14, 1936, WPD 3646-1.

32. Manila *Tribune,* Aug. 30, 1936; Vargas to DM, July 30, 1936; J. Weldon Jones to DM, Aug. 25, 1936; Capt. Bonner F. Fellers to DM, Aug. 29, 1936; Moseley to DM, Sept. 4, 1936, RG 10, MMBA; interview, author with Gen. Eisenhower. Gen. Miles, of B.E.F. eviction

fame, wrote MacArthur: "It is a great pleasure to know that you will now carry the baton. I remember how you felt about carrying the saber. There is no one in our service who has the qualities and experience necessary for such a high military rank to compare with yourself. I congratulate not you but the Philippines." Miles to DM, Sept. 14, 1936, RG 10, MMBA.

33. Harold E. Fey, "Militarizing the Philippines," *Nation,* CXLII (June 10, 1936), 736–37; Hersey, *Men on Bataan,* 264–65; Hunt, *Untold Story,* 182–83.

34. DM, *Report on National Defense in the Philippines,* 21–22.

35. Whan, ed., *A Soldier Speaks,* 100–10; *Reminiscences,* 104–06; interview, author with Gen. Eisenhower.

CHAPTER XVIII, *"Unexpected Problems,"*
pages 510–552

1. McDonald to CofS, Jan. 25, 1937; Capt. H. T. Perrin to TAG, Feb. 2, 1937; TAG to Drum, Feb. 8, 1937; Simonds to TAG, Feb. 13, 1937; TAG to McCoy, Feb. 16, 1937; McCoy to TAG, Feb. 19, 1937, AG 093.5 Phil. Is.; *PHCAR, 1937,* 1–2, 12; Joseph C. Grew, *Ten Years in Japan* (New York, 1944), 204–05; J. Weldon Jones to SecWar, Jan. 25, 1937, Bureau of Insular Affairs Recs., RG 350, NA; Early to Ross McIntyre, Feb. 19, 1937, PPF 4471, FDRL; Friend, *Between Two Empires,* 185; *Reminiscences,* 106. On Feb. 27, 1937, Quezon and MacArthur attended the ceremony in Woodring's office when McNutt was sworn in as high commissioner. MacArthur and McNutt enjoyed friendly relations with each other throughout the latter's stay in Manila. I. George Blake, *Paul V. McNutt: Portrait of a Hoosier Statesman* (Indianapolis, 1966), 185–86, 230.

2. Col. F. H. Lincoln to TAG, Apr. 2, 1937; Francis B. Sayre to SecWar, Apr. 5, 1937, AG 093.5 Phil. Is.; Lt. Col. H. E. Marshburn to G-2, GS G-2 File 2257-Z-5(9); DM to Pershing, Apr. 23, 1937, Pershing Papers, Box 121; *Reminiscences,* 106–07; Washington *Post,* Apr. 30, 1937; *New York Times,* May 1, 1937.

3. DM's statement to Vicente A. Pacis, July, 1937; Eisenhower to Ord, July 8 and 29, 1937, RG 1, MMBA; Bul. 63, PA Hq., May 4, 1937; Gen. Orders 74, PA Hq., May 14, 1937, PA Recs.; Brig. Gen. H. E. Knight to CofS, June 22, 1936; TAG to CofS, Apr. 20, 1937; Eisenhower to TAG, Apr. 30, 1937; Brig. Gen. George P. Tyner to CofS, Apr. 30, 1937; TAG to CofS, Aug. 3, 1937, AG 093.5 Phil. Is. At Army schools in the United States in 1937, Philippine Army officer-students were denied instruction in 50-cal. machine guns. MacArthur wrote a heated protest to the WD against the practice of denying Filipino officers access to "certain types of instruction on the ground

that military secrets of the United States might otherwise fall into foreign hands." The restriction was ultimately revised. DM to TAG, Oct. 21, 1937, GS G-2 File 2257-7-3(6).

4. *PHCAR, 1937,* 5–7; *WDAR, 1938,* I, 14; Brig. Gen. Vincente Lim to CofS, PA, Apr. 29, 1937; Maj. S. de Jesus to AG, PA, Aug. 25, 1937; Ord to DM, Oct. 30, 1937, RG 1, MMBA. On June 21, 1937, Mac-Arthur was dined and entertained aboard Vice Adm. Mineichi Koga's flagship *Iwate,* which headed a visiting Japanese naval squadron in Manila Bay. The musical program by the Japanese band included, besides Japanese numbers, some "Southern Plantation Songs." See program cards, June 21–22, 1937, RG 1, MMBA.

5. Eisenhower to Ord, Sept. 1, 1937, RG 1, MMBA.

6. Eisenhower to DM, Oct. 13, 1937; DM to Quezon, Oct. 14, 1937, RG 1, MMBA. Eisenhower drafted Quezon's message to the National Assembly in late 1937, as well as other messages for him and some for MacArthur.

   Hunt maintains that Ord went to Quezon with the enlarged budget estimate without first consulting MacArthur, who became angry with Ord and also with Eisenhower, who came to Ord's defense. The documents, however, do not support Hunt's story nor his assertion that both Ord and Eisenhower "coveted" MacArthur's job. Hunt, *Untold Story,* 192–93.

7. Gregorio Aglipay to DM, Jan. 26, 1937; statements by DM to reporters, 1937, RG 1, MMBA; Manila *Philippine Herald,* Jan. 19, 1937.

8. Quezon's address to the R.O.T.C. of the University of the Philippines, Jan. 18, 1937, SecWar Recs., RG 107, NA.

9. Brig. Gen. Creed F. Cox to DM, May 22, 1937, RG 1, MMBA.

10. Frederick C. Howe to Henry A. Wallace, Aug. 28, 1937, RG 1, MMBA. In the same file is a similarly worded letter from Howe to Mrs. F. D. Roosevelt, dated Sept. 7, 1937; this letter is reprinted, in part, in Hunt, *Untold Story,* 188–89.

11. Larry Lehrbas to DM, June 14, 1937, RG 1, MMBA; Hunt, *Untold Story,* 186–88; DM to CofS, Sept. 16, 1937; Woodring to FDR, Oct. 11, 1937; FDR to DM, Oct. 11, 1937, PPF 4914, FDRL; Spec. Orders 238, WD, Oct. 11, 1937; Craig to DM, Jan. 3, 1938, DM Misc. 201, OCMH.

12. Brig. Gen. Charles Burnett to DM, Oct. 13, 1937; Moseley to DM, Jan. 26, 1938; O'Laughlin to DM, Mar. 25, 1942, RG 1, MMBA; Whitney, *MacArthur,* 5. In his *Reminiscences,* 107, MacArthur said of his recall: "Roosevelt had become concerned about Hawaii, and wished me to return and take command of both the island and the West Coast." The Hawaiian Dept. and the IX Corps Area (Pacific coast) were separate commands; no WD plans to consolidate them were uncovered.

13. Ormsby McHarg to O'Laughlin, June 16, 1938; P. W. Reeves to DM,

Nov. 25, 1937; Harold R. Peet to DM, Oct. 12, 1937; John N. Wheeler to DM, Oct. 14, 1937; Frank C. Waldrop to DM, Oct. 14, 1937; Theodore Roosevelt to DM, Nov. 11, 1937, RG 1, MMBA.

14. "Resolution of the Philippine National Assembly Thanking General Douglas MacArthur for His Meritorious Services to the Commonwealth of the Philippines," Nov. 21, 1937; DM's statement acknowledging the resolution, Nov. 21, 1937, enclosed with Vargas to DM, Nov. 24, 1937, RG 10, MMBA. On Mar. 29, 1938, the University of the Philippines conferred a doctor of laws degree upon MacArthur.

15. Woodring to FDR, Jan. 21, 1938, PPF 4771, FDRL.

16. Eisenhower, *At Ease*, 225–26; *PPAR, 1939,* 12.

17. Gen. Orders 49, PA Hq., Apr. 4, 1938; Bul. 206, PA Hq., Dec. 9, 1938; Bul. 74, PA Hq., June 13, 1939; Bul. 130, PA Hq., Oct. 18, 1939; Bul. 63, PA Hq., June 1, 1940, PA Recs.; *PPAR, 1938,* 10; *idem, 1940,* 4.

18. Trng. Dir. 75, PA Hq., Aug. 16, 1940; Bul. 47, PA Hq., Apr. 11, 1940; Trng. Memo. 46, PA Hq., June 20, 1940; TOA for inf. cadres, PA Hq., Oct. 17, 1938; Gen. Orders 167, PA Hq., Oct. 5, 1939, PA Recs.; DM to Quezon, Dec. 9, 1939, RG 1, MMBA; Friend, *Between Two Empires,* 167.

19. Bul. 90, PA Hq., July 17, 1939; Gen. Orders 178, PA Hq., Nov. 12, 1938; Bul. 84, PA Hq., July 5, 1940; Bul. 164, PA Hq., Oct. 28, 1940; master schedule for schools for reserve commission, PA Hq., Dec. 10, 1938, PA Recs.; Hughes to TAG, July 14, 1938; Brig. Gen. L. D. Gasser to CofS, Aug. 6, 1938; Hughes to TAG, Aug. 25, 1938, AG 093.5 Phil. Is. Though Tagalog was the main dialect in the Philippine Army, a candidate for the Philippine Military Academy had to pass entrance examinations in English grammar, composition, and literature, as well as history, algebra, plane geometry, and plane trigonometry. Bul. 153, PA Hq., Dec. 7, 1939, PA Recs.

20. Gasser to TAG, Apr. 9, 1939; Lt. Col. E. B. Colladay to CofS, Aug. 23, 1938; Maj. T. J. Davis to TAG, Oct. 12, 1939, AG 350.2 Phil. Is.; *PPAR, 1938,* 10, 16; *idem, 1939,* 13; *idem, 1940,* 5; Eisenhower, *At Ease,* 226–28.

21. Sidney L. Huff, with Joe A. Morris, *My Fifteen Years with General MacArthur* (New York, 1964), 27–28.

22. *Ibid.,* 29; *PPAR, 1938,* 10; *idem, 1939,* 13; *idem, 1940,* 5; Maj Gen. William C. Rivers to editor, New York *Herald Tribune,* Aug. 6, 1939, RG 10, MMBA.

23. *PPAR, 1938,* 22; *PHCAR, 1939,* 22–23; *idem, 1941,* 3; Bul. 167, PA Hq., Oct. 4, 1938, PA Recs.; DM to Quezon, Oct. 18, 1938; Maj. Gen. George Grunert to DM, Sept. 9, 1939, RG 1, MMBA; Louis Morton, *The Fall of the Philippines (USAWWII;* Washington, 1953), 15, 23; interview, author with Gen. Willoughby.

24. *PPAR, 1938,* 32; *PHCAR, 1939,* 34; Friend, *Between Two Empires,* 160–68, 192–93; James K. Eyre, *The Roosevelt-MacArthur Conflict* (Chambersburg, 1950), 28–32; DM to Quezon, Sept. 26, 1938; Quezon to DM, Oct. 4, 1938; Maj. Gen. Paulino Santos to DM, Jan. 22, 1939, RG 1, MMBA.

25. DM's statement, June 27, 1939, RG 1, MMBA; Friend, *Between Two Empires,* 190–94; Eyre, *Roosevelt-MacArthur Conflict,* 33; *PPAR, 1939,* 38. McNutt left the high commissionership in 1939 to become head of the Federal Security Administration. "All you needed," MacArthur wrote him, "was such a chance to sell yourself to the people at large. It will prove perhaps the most vital decision of your life." MacArthur himself was recommended for the post by Rep. Martin Kennedy. DM to McNutt, July 12, 1939, quoted in Blake, *McNutt,* 230; Early to Rep. Martin Kennedy, July 13, 1939, PPF 4471, FDRL. In his memoirs MacArthur did not mention Quezon's disaffection.

26. Manila *La Vanguardia,* June 27, 1940; journal of the military adviser's office, June–Aug., 1940, entry of July 5, 1940, RG 1, MMBA. The preceding journal was probably kept by Lt. Col. Richard J. Marshall, who was MacArthur's deputy CofS at that time.

27. *PHCAR, 1941,* 26; MA journal, entries of June 5, July 8, Aug. 9 and 12, 1940; Manila *Bulletin,* July 26, 1940; Quezon to FDR, Aug. 6, 1940, WPD 3389-34; Watson, *Chief of Staff,* 419–20.

28. *PPAR, 1940,* 25–27; Bul. 98, PA Hq., July 24, 1940, PA Recs.; Vargas to Grunert, Sept. 21, 1940, RG 1, MMBA; *PHCAR, 1941,* 4.

29. DM to Quezon, Oct. 12, 1940, RG 1, MMBA.

30. DM to CofS, July 9 and Sept. 10, 1936; Craig to DM, Aug. 5, 1936; Louis Johnson to FDR, May 13, 1938; DM to TAG, July 6, 1939; Lt. Col. H. C. Minton to TAG, Nov. 10, 1939, AG 093.5 Phil. Is.

31. Craig to DM, Aug. 5 and Sept. 25, 1936; Craig to SecWar, Dec. 17, 1936; Krueger to CofS, Dec. 24, 1936, and July 21, 1937; Holbrook to TAG, Jan. 22, 1938, AG 093.5 Phil. Is.; Ord to Eisenhower, July 27 and Aug. 10, 1937; Cox to DM, May 22, 1937, RG 1, MMBA; J. Woodford Howard, Jr., *Mr. Justice Murphy: A Political Biography* (Princeton, 1968), 104–09. Murphy is best remembered as one of the Supreme Court's most liberal justices; he served on that bench from 1940 to 1949.

32. Johnson to FDR, May 13, 1938, AG 093.5 Phil. Is. (5-13-38).

33. Holbrook to CofS, Sept. 9, 1937, AG 093.5 Phil. Is. (9-9-37); Krueger to CofS, Oct. 19, 1937, WPD 3602-13; Craig to Holbrook, Oct. 20, 1937, OCS 18812-39; Krueger to CofS, Aug. 15, 1936, OCS 20061-19; Brig. Gen. George V. Strong to CofS, July 30, 1940, AG 471 Phil. Dept. (7-5-40).

34. Krueger to CofS, Feb. 16, 1938, AG 660.2 Phil. Dept. (1-13-38).

35. Brig. Gen. George R. Spalding to CofS, Sept. 29, 1937; Tyner to CofS, Jan. 20, 1939; DM to TAG, Feb. 3, 1939; Capt. Ralph Pulsifer to TAG, Mar. 13 and July 15, 1939; DM to TAG, July 6, 1939; Davis to Grunert, Aug. 12, 1939; Minton to TAG, Nov. 10, 1939, AG 093.5 Phil. Is.

36. Moseley to DM, Sept. 26, 1938, and Oct. 21, 1939, Moseley Papers; Baruch, *Public Years,* 276–77; Tugwell, *Democratic Roosevelt,* 526; Pogue, *Marshall,* I, 318–19; Watson, *Chief of Staff,* 412–22. When Moseley retired in 1938, he issued a press statement criticizing the War Dept. and FDR, which Woodring charged contained "flagrantly disloyal" allegations. Press releases by Moseley, Sept. 30, 1938, and Woodring, Oct. 1, 1938, Moseley Papers, Box 5.

37. Lt. Col. William F. Marquat to DM, Dec. 8, 1940, RG 1, MMBA. Quezon awarded Marquat the Philippine Distinguished Service Star in July, 1940, mainly for his leadership in organizing the Philippine Army's coast artillery training center at Ft. Wint. Gen. Orders 134, PA Hq., July 23, 1940, PA Recs.

38. Strong to CofS, Dec. 29, 1938, WPD 3389-28; Strong to CofS, Mar. 2, 1940, WPD 4191-3; Strong to CofS, Oct. 10, 1940, WPD 3251-37; Grunert to CofS, Sept. 1, 1940, AG 093.5 Phil. Is. (7-2-40); Grunert to CofS, Nov. 2, 1940; Brig. Gen. Leonard T. Gerow to CofS, Dec. 26, 1940, and Jan. 21, 1941, WPD 3251-39; *WDAR, 1940,* I, 1–2; Watson, *Chief of Staff,* 415–25; Pogue, *Marshall,* II, 176–79. In Sept., 1940, Robert J. Dillon, of Baltimore, urged FDR to appoint MacArthur as selective service director, but the post went to Brig. Gen. Lewis B. Hershey. Early to Robert J. Dillon, Oct. 1, 1940, PPF 4771, FDRL.

39. White to DM, Sept 14, 1940; DM to White, n.d. [c. Sept. 15, 1940], RG 1, MMBA. Contrary to a popular notion that MacArthur opposed aiding the European allies, he endorsed White's committee and also De Gaulle's Free French organization in late 1940. Some of Mac-Arthur's friends, however, were against any American assistance to Great Britain. Moseley, for example, commented to him, "Personally, I do not believe in going to war to save the prestige of the British." Moseley to DM, Oct. 21, 1939, RG 1, MMBA.

CHAPTER XIX, *"The Man and the Soldier,"*
pages 553–576
1. Hersey, *Men on Bataan,* 276–78; Huff, *My Fifteen Years,* 23–24; Gunther, *Riddle of MacArthur,* 45–46; Miller, *MacArthur,* 143; New York *Daily News,* Feb. 1, 1942; *Reminiscences,* 106.
2. WD release, Feb. 21, 1938, Bureau of Insular Affairs Recs., RG 350, NA; Lee and Henschel, *MacArthur,* 286; Kelley and Ryan, *Mac-*

Arthur, 55; Huff, *My Fifteen Years,* 25; DM to Engracio Fabre, Nov. 9, 1939, RG 10, MMBA; *Reminiscences,* 107.

3. Hersey, *Men on Bataan,* 279–80; Huff, *My Fifteen Years,* 16; Miller, *MacArthur,* 142–44; interviews, author with Gens. Eisenhower and Whitney.

4. DM to Capt. William H. Wood, July 27, 1939, RG 1, MMBA.

5. Huff, *My Fifteen Years,* 16–17; George D. Haupt to DM, Jan. 4, 1938; James F. Burns to DM, Oct. 28, 1939; DM to Burns, Dec. 1, 1939; Frederic H. Stevens to DM, Nov. 21, 1938; Vice Adm. William L. Rodgers to DM, July 13, 1939; DM to Rodgers, Aug. 19, 1939, RG 1, MMBA; F. A. Delgado to DM, Nov. 6, 1937; announcement of Ancient and Accepted Scottish Rite of Freemasonry, Valley of Manila, Mar., 1938; Francisco Mendoza to DM, Apr. 29, 1936; Manila Hotel Co. stockholders' rpt., Apr. 20, 1936, RG 10, MMBA.

6. Huff, *My Fifteen Years,* 12; interviews, author with Gens. Eisenhower and Whitney; Maj. Gen. Spencer B. Akin to author, May 6, 1968.

7. Interview, author with Gen. Willoughby; Friend, *Between Two Empires,* 164–65; Quezon to DM, May 16, 1939, RG 1, MMBA.

8. Friend, *Between Two Empires,* 117, 166, 249–63; Carlos P. Romulo. *I Saw the Fall of the Philippines* (New York, 1942), 14–89; interview, author with Gen. Whitney; Delfin L. Gonzales to DM, Mar. 27, 1938; Emilio Aguinaldo to DM, Jan. 26, 1940, RG 1, MMBA.

9. Interview, author with Gen. Eisenhower; Eisenhower, *At Ease,* 230–32; Eisenhower, *Crusade in Europe* (Garden City, 1952), 19–20. Some of the allegations regarding the MacArthur-Eisenhower affinity are related in the following popular works: Kenneth S. Davis, *Soldier of Democracy: A Biography of Dwight Eisenhower* (Garden City, 1945), 246–56; John Gunther, *Eisenhower: The Man and the Symbol* (New York, 1951), 65–66; Kevin McCann, *Man from Abilene* (Garden City, 1952), 24–29, 93–103; Marquis W. Childs, *Eisenhower, Captive Hero: A Critical Study of the General and the President* (New York, 1958), 43–49. On Eisenhower's views on the defense program, see Louis Morton, "The Philippine Army 1935–1939; Eisenhower's Memorandum to Quezon [June 22, 1942]," *Military Affairs,* XII (Summer, 1948), 103–07.

10. Interviews, author with Gens. Willoughby and Whitney; Maj. Gen. Richard J. Marshall, notes on MacArthur and his staff, 1939–41, MS in possession of author; George C. Kenney, *General Kenney Reports* (New York, 1949), 26.

11. Willoughby and Chamberlain, *MacArthur,* 35.

12. Interviews, author with Gens. Willoughby and Whitney; Marshall notes, 1939–41; Marshall to author, May 4, 1968; Willoughby and Chamberlain, *MacArthur,* 35–36; Marquat to DM, Dec. 8, 1940; Willoughby to DM, May 5, 1940; DM to Willoughby, June 8, 1940,

RG 1, MMBA. Fellers would rejoin MacArthur's staff in Australia after the fall of the Philippines.

Two future chiefs of staff of the Army were serving in the Philippine Dept. while MacArthur was military adviser and met him for the first time then: Maj. J. Lawton Collins, who would be chief when MacArthur was relieved in 1951; and Lt. Harold K. Johnson, who would fight in the first Philippine campaign, spend over three years as a prisoner of war, and serve as chief of staff in 1964–68. Interviews, author with Gens. J. Lawton Collins and Harold K. Johnson.

13. The following section is based on the author's conclusions from the documentary and oral evidence gathered in his research. Some statements are reworded views expressed to the author by former associates of MacArthur — several of whom preferred not to be named — but most of the judgments are the author's and do not reflect the views of any one of MacArthur's colleagues or even a particular group of the general's associates.

Two Ph.D. dissertations on MacArthur's oratory have been written: Stephen Robb, "Fifty Years of Farewell: Douglas MacArthur's Commemorative and Deliberative Speaking" (Indiana University, 1967); Armel Dyer, "The Oratory of Douglas MacArthur" (University of Oregon, 1968).

CHAPTER XX, *"In the Path of the Storm,"*
pages 577–619

1. Joaquin M. Elizalde to DM, Apr. 16, 1941, RG 1, MMBA; Herbert Feis, *The Road to Pearl Harbor: The Coming of the War Between the United States and Japan* (New York, 1965), 153–201; Joseph C. Grew to SecState, May 27, 1941, in U.S. State Dept., *Foreign Relations of the United States: Diplomatic Papers, 1941,* Vol. IV (Washington, 1956), 232; Watson, *Chief of Staff,* 367–99; William L. Langer and S. Everett Gleason, *The Undeclared War, 1940–1941* (New York, 1953), 485–87; Col. J. W. Anderson to CofS, Apr. 1, 1941; Cdr. L. R. McDowell to Secy., British Military Mission, June 7, 1941, WPD 4402-18. On the development of American and Japanese strategic planning to 1941, see Louis Morton, *Strategy and Command: The First Two Years* (USAWWII; Washington, 1962), 21–91.

2. Richard M. Leighton and Robert W. Coakley, *Global Logistics and Strategy, 1940–1943* (USAWWII; Washington, 1955), 52–57; Watson, *Chief of Staff,* 397–99; Feis, *Road to Pearl Harbor,* 201; Marshall to Grunert, Feb. 8, 1941, WPD 4477-1; Brig. Gen. Joseph T. McNarney to TAG, Apr. 24, 1941, WPD 3602-21; McNarney to CofS, Apr. 24, 1941, WPD 3489-16; Brig. Gen. Leonard T. Gerow to CofS, June 16, 1941, WPD 3602-21; Gerow to TAG, June 18, 1941, WPD 3489-11;

Gerow to CofS, June 26, 1941, WPD 4471-1; Marshall to Grunert, July 3, 1941, OCS 18812-58.

3. Trng. Memo. 51, PA Hq., Jan. 2, 1941; Bul. 2, PA Hq., Jan. 7, 1941; Bul. 31, PA Hq., Feb. 28, 1941; Trng. Memo. 52, PA Hq., Mar. 1, 1941; Trng. Memo. 54, PA Hq., May 2, 1941, PA Recs.; Gerow to CofS, June 16, 1941, WPD 3602-21; Elizalde to Quezon, Feb. 10, 1941, RG 1, MMBA.

4. *PHCAR, 1941,* 1–5, 87–124; *idem, 1942,* 104; Bul. 83, PA Hq., June 21, 1941; Bul. 96, PA Hq., July 10, 1941; Bul. 102, July 21, 1941, PA Recs.; Manila *Bulletin,* Mar. 24, 1941; Brig. Gen. William E. Brougher, "The Final Despedida" (MS poem and note on Manila farewell party, May, 1941), William E. Brougher Collection, Mitchell Memorial Library, Miss. State University, State College, Miss.; Hunt, *Untold Story,* 204.

5. DM to Elizalde, Feb. 25, 1941, RG 1, MMBA; Hersey, *Men on Bataan,* 287–91.

6. Hunt, *Untold Story,* 204–05; Stimson diary, entry of May 21, 1941; Morton, *Fall of the Philippines,* 15–16; Watson, *Chief of Staff,* 434–35; Gerow to CofS, June 6, 1941, WPD 3251-50. Also on May 21, Grunert recommended to Marshall that MacArthur and other Commonwealth officials be invited to conferences at his headquarters to plan expansion of the islands' defenses, funds for which were expected to be available from sugar excise taxes. Marshall approved the invitations, but the funds were never approved by Congress. Watson, *Chief of Staff,* 434–35.

7. Marshall to DM, June 20, 1941, OCS 20850-15.

8. Feis, *Road to Pearl Harbor,* 202–18; "An Outline of the Policy of the Imperial Government in View of Present Developments," in U.S. Senate, *Pearl Harbor Attack: Hearings before the Joint Committee on the Investigation of the Pearl Harbor Attack,* 79th Cong., 1st Sess. (39 pts., 1946), XX, 4018–19; J. M. Johnson to DM, July 7, 1941, RG 10, MMBA.

9. Gerow to CofS, July 17, 1941, WPD 3251-52. This memo. had been first submitted by Gerow on June 16. See also Gerow to CofS, June 16, 1941, WPD 3602-21; Gerow to CofS, July 14, 1941, WPD 3251-52.

10. Gerow to TAG, July 19, 1941; TAG to Grunert, July 19, 1941, WPD 3602-21.

11. Pogue, *Marshall,* II, 182–83, 186; Stimson to FDR, July 25, 1941, OCS 18136-34; Watson, *Chief of Staff,* 438–40.

12. Feis, *Road to Pearl Harbor,* 236–50; *New York Post,* July 26, 1941; *New York Times,* July 24, 1941; Blum, *From the Morgenthau Diaries,* II, 378–80.

13. Marshall to DM, July 26, 1941, OCS 18136-35. The message (in the same file and of the same date) which Marshall sent to Grunert read:

> The President has issued a military order this date calling into the service of the armed forces of the United States for the period of the existing emergency all of the organized military forces of the Government of the Commonwealth of the Philippines.

Apparently Grunert was notified in a later message of USAFFE and MacArthur's appointment, but that communication was not found.

14. DM to TAG, July 27, 1941; TAG to DM, July 29, 1941, DM Misc. 201; Whitney, *MacArthur*, 8; Lee and Henschel, *MacArthur*, 288; *ANR*, Aug. 2, 1941; *ANJ*, Aug. 23, 1941.

15. Fellers to DM, Aug. 7, 1941; Whitney to DM, July 29, 1941; Ruperto S. Cristobal to DM, Aug. 4, 1941; Miguel R. Cornejo to DM, July 31, 1941, RG 10, MMBA; Francis B. Sayre, *Glad Adventure* (New York, 1957), 216–17; *Reminiscences*, 109; Jonathan M. Wainwright, with Robert Considine, *General Wainwright's Story: The Account of Four Years of Humiliating Defeat, Surrender, and Captivity* (Garden City, 1946), 12–13.

16. USAFFE–USFIP op. rpt., annex 1, Federal Records Center, Suitland, Md.; Morton, *Fall of the Philippines,* 19, 23, 25; DM to TAG, Oct. 31, 1941, AG 323.24 Phil. Dept. (10-31-41); Fellers to author, June 17, 1969. The principal existing rpts. of the first Philippine campaign are in USAFFE–USFIP op. rpt. They consist of a basic rpt. by Wainwright (prepared in 1946) and eighteen annexes, which are actually op. rpts. of various Philippine commands. Hereafter Wainwright's rpt. will be cited as USAFFE–USFIP op. rpt., and the annexes will be listed by their titles and numbers.

Shortly after MacArthur's USAFFE appointment, Murphy proposed to Roosevelt that a "National Defense Commission for the Far East" be created, its membership to consist of the Philippine high commissioner, the governors of Guam and Hawaii, "an admiral of the Navy," and "a general of the Army." Murphy wanted its formation "at once," though not specifying its purpose. Since he urged that its first meeting take place in Singapore, it is presumed that the commission would coordinate American defense efforts with those of the British and Dutch. Nothing came of Murphy's proposal, however. Brig. Gen. Edwin M. Watson to FDR, July 30, 1941, PPF 4471, FDRL.

17. Gerow to CofS, July 30, 1941, WPD 4561-1. In Morton, *Fall of the Philippines,* 22, 24, the strength of the Phil. Div. is given as 10,473 officers and men, and the aggregate strength of American Army forces in the islands on July 31 is given as 22,532, including 11,963 Scouts.

18. Watson, *Chief of Staff,* 425–33; Morton, *Fall of the Philippines,* 61–69; DM to CofS, Feb. 1, 1941, OCS 10891-88; DM to TAG, Oct. 1, 1941, WPD 4178-18; Marshall to DM, Nov. 21, 1941, WPD 4402-112.

19. USAFFE–USFIP op. rpt., 2–8; Morton, *Fall of the Philippines,* 25–26;

Hersey, *Men on Bataan,* 14–16; DM to CofS, Aug. 30, 1941, quoted in Marshall to FDR, Sept. 9, 1941, OCS 18136-48; Visayan-Mindanao Force op. rpt., 9–10, USAFFE–USFIP annex 9.

20. 11th Inf. (PA) op. rpt., 2, OCMH.
21. *Ibid.,* 5–8; Visayan-Mindanao Force op. rpt., 18–19. Gas masks were distributed in "Government offices, bureaus, and agencies" in Manila. Bul. 153, PA Hq., Nov. 19, 1941, PA Recs.
22. Morton, *Fall of the Philippines,* 28; Visayan-Mindanao Force op. rpt., 18–19; North Luzon Force and I Phil. Cps. op. rpt., 6, USAFFE–USFIP annex 4; South Luzon Force, Bataan Defense Force, and II Phil. Cps. op. rpt., 3, USAFFE–USFIP annex 5; 11th Inf. (PA) op. rpt., 8.
23. 11th Inf. (PA) op. rpt., 12, 22; South Luzon Force, Bataan Defense Force, and II Phil. Cps. op. rpt., 6–7; Col. Clyde A. Selleck, notes on 71st Div. (PA), 5–8, OCMH.
24. Visayan-Mindanao Force op. rpt., 24–26. The Philippine Army had only 194 motor vehicles when mobilization started. Gen. Orders 140, PA Hq., Aug. 12, 1941, PA Recs.
25. USAFFE–USFIP op. rpt., 26; North Luzon Force and I Phil. Cps. op. rpt., 2.
26. North Luzon Force and I Phil. Cps. op. rpt., 2–3; South Luzon Force, Bataan Defense Force, and II Phil. Cps. op. rpt., 8–9; Visayan-Mindanao op. rpt., 22; USAFFE–USFIP op. rpt., 9–10.
27. Phil. CA Command and Harbor Defenses of Manila and Subic Bays op. rpt., 5–10, USAFFE–USFIP annex 8; James H. and ·William M. Belote, *Corregidor: The Saga of a Fortress* (New York, 1967), 1–29.
28. Provisional Tank Group op. rpt., 2–4, USAFFE–USFIP annex 10.
29. Quartermaster Cps. op. rpt., 2–5, 9–10, USAFFE–USFIP annex 13.
30. MA journal entry of July 26, 1940.
31. Watson, *Chief of Staff,* 432.
32. Craven and Cate, eds., *Plans and Early Operations,* 175–93; Morton, *Fall of the Philippines,* 37–45; Walter D. Edmonds, *They Fought with What They Had* (Boston, 1951), 1–56; Lewis H. Brereton, *The Brereton Diaries, 3 October 1941–8 May 1945* (New York, 1946), 14–39.
33. Gerow to TAG, July 28, 1941, OCS 18136-39; Brig. Gen. Raymond A. Wheeler to Gerow, Oct. 7, 1941, GS G-4 File 23833-119; Maurice Matloff and Edwin M. Snell, *Strategic Planning for Coalition Warfare, 1941–1942 (USAWWII;* Washington, 1953), 66–69, 72–73; Pogue, *Marshall,* II, 174–89; Morton, *Fall of the Philippines,* 32–37.
34. Samuel E. Morison, *The Rising Sun in the Pacific, 1931–April 1942 (History of United States Naval Operations in World War II,* Vol. III; Boston, 1948), 151–60; Watson, *Chief of Staff,* 450–52.
35. Morison, *Rising Sun in the Pacific,* 155–56; Sayre, *Glad Adventure,*

221; U.S. Senate, *Report of the Joint Committee on the Investigation of the Pearl Harbor Attack,* 79th Cong., 2nd Sess. (1946), Sen. Doc. 244, p. 102.

36. Romulo, *I Saw the Fall of the Philippines,* 12, 26–28; Clark Lee, *They Call It Pacific: An Eye-Witness Story of Our War Against Japan from Bataan to the Solomons* (New York, 1943), 22–31; *PHCAR, 1942,* 20–21; *Reminiscences,* 110–11.

37. Craven and Cate, eds., *Plan and Early Operations,* 191; Charles A. Willoughby and others, eds., *Reports of General MacArthur* (4 vols., Washington, 1966), I, 6; Roberta Wohlstetter, *Pearl Harbor: Warning and Decision* (Stanford, 1962), 396; Friend, *Between Two Empires,* 207; Morison, *Rising Sun in the Pacific,* 156; Lee, *They Call It Pacific,* 31–32; Matloff and Snell, *Strategic Planning,* 77–78.

38. Morton, *Fall of the Philippines,* 79–81, 84; Hunt, *Untold Story,* 223; Wainwright, *General Wainwright's Story,* 18; *Reminiscences,* 117. In his memoirs MacArthur stated that he received the news at 3:40 by "a long-distance telephone call from Washington," but he probably had reference to a later confirmation of the Pearl Harbor attack.

After the war Willoughby and his intelligence officers interrogated a number of high-ranking Japanese Army officers, several of whom said that the rapid American reinforcement in the Philippines was "an important factor" in the Japanese decision to attack in early Dec. Willoughby and others, eds., *Reports of MacArthur,* I, 2n.

INDEX

Index